# THE BROADVIEW
## *Introduction to*
## Literature
## *Drama*

D0768012

# THE BROADVIEW
# *Introduction to*
# Literature

## *Drama*

***General Editors***
Lisa Chalykoff
Neta Gordon
Paul Lumsden

broadview press

**Library and Archives Canada Cataloguing in Publication**

The Broadview introduction to literature, drama / general editors, Lisa Chalykoff, Neta Gordon, Paul Lumsden.

Includes index.
ISBN 978-1-55481-178-6 (pbk.)

1. English drama. 2. American drama. 3. Canadian drama (English). 4. Drama—Translations into English. I. Chalykoff, Lisa, editor of compilation II. Gordon, Neta, 1971-, editor of compilation III. Lumsden, Paul, 1961-, editor of compilation IV. Title: Introduction to literature, drama.

PN6112.B78 2013          808.82          C2013-903878-7

Broadview Press is an independent, international publishing house, incorporated in 1985. We welcome comments and suggestions regarding any aspect of our publications—please feel free to contact us at the addresses below or at broadview@broadviewpress.com.

| | |
|---|---|
| North America | PO Box 1243, Peterborough, Ontario, Canada K9J 7H5<br>2215 Kenmore Ave., Buffalo, New York, USA 14207<br>Tel: (705) 743-8990; Fax: (705) 743-8353<br>email: customerservice@broadviewpress.com |
| UK, Europe, Central Asia,<br>Middle East, Africa, India,<br>and Southeast Asia | Eurospan Group,<br>3 Henrietta St., London WC2E 8LU, United Kingdom<br>Tel: 44 (0) 1767 604972; Fax: 44 (0) 1767 601640<br>email: eurospan@turpin-distribution.com |
| Australia and<br>New Zealand | NewSouth Books c/o TL Distribution,<br>15-23 Helles Ave., Moorebank, NSW, Australia 2170<br>Tel: (02) 8778 9999; Fax: (02) 8778 9944<br>email: orders@tldistribution.com.au |

www.broadviewpress.com

Broadview Press acknowledges the financial support of the Government of Canada through the Canada Book Fund for our publishing activities.

This book is printed on paper containing 50% postconsumer fibre.

PRINTED IN CANADA

# Contributors to *The Broadview Introduction to Literature*

| | |
|---|---|
| MANAGING EDITORS | Don LePan<br>Marjorie Mather |
| DEVELOPMENTAL AND TEXTUAL EDITOR | Laura Buzzard |
| EDITORIAL COORDINATORS | Tara Bodie<br>Bryanne Miller |
| CONTRIBUTING EDITORS AND TRANSLATORS | Lisa Chalykoff<br>Neta Gordon<br>Ian Johnston<br>David Swain |
| CONTRIBUTING WRITERS | Laura Buzzard<br>Paul Johnston Byrne<br>Tara Bodie |

EDITORIAL ASSISTANTS

| | |
|---|---|
| Tara Bodie | Amanda Mullen |
| Alicia Christianson | Virginia Philipson |
| Joel DeShaye | Anja Pujic |
| Victoria Duncan | Andrew Reszitnyk |
| Rose Eckert-Jantzie | David Ross |
| Emily Farrell | Nora Ruddock |
| Travis Grant | Kate Sinclair |
| Karim Lalani | Jack Skeffington |
| Phil Laven | Kaitlyn Till |
| Kellen Loewen | Morgan Tunzelmann |

PRODUCTION COORDINATOR        Tara Lowes
PRODUCTION ASSISTANT          Allison LaSorda
COPY EDITOR                   Colleen Franklin
PROOFREADERS                  Joe Davies
                              Judith Earnshaw
DESIGN AND TYPESETTING        Eileen Eckert
PERMISSIONS COORDINATOR       Merilee Atos
COVER DESIGN                  Michel Vrana

# Contents

PREFACE — ix
ACKNOWLEDGEMENTS — xi
THE STUDY OF LITERATURE: INTRODUCTION — xiii

## DRAMA

DRAMA: INTRODUCTION — 1
WILLIAM SHAKESPEARE (1564–1616) — 11
    *Twelfth Night, or What You Will* — 12
RICHARD BRINSLEY SHERIDAN (1751–1816) — 105
    *The School for Scandal* — 106
HENRIK IBSEN (1828–1906) — 182
    *A Doll's House* — 183
SAMUEL BECKETT (1906–1989) — 243
    *Krapp's Last Tape* — 243
TENNESSEE WILLIAMS (1911–1983) — 252
    *Cat on a Hot Tin Roof* — 252
SHARON POLLOCK (B. 1936) — 337
    *Blood Relations* — 338
TOM STOPPARD (B. 1937) — 386
    *Arcadia* — 387
HANNAH MOSCOVITCH (B. 1978) — 478
    *Essay* — 479

GLOSSARY — 509
PERMISSION ACKNOWLEDGEMENTS — 525
INDEX OF AUTHORS AND TITLES — 527

# Preface

On hearing that Broadview was planning a new anthology designed to provide an overview of literature at the first-year level, more than a few people have expressed surprise. What could a new anthology have to offer that really is different—that gives something new and valuable to academics and students alike? We hope that you will find your own answers to that question once you have looked through this volume. Certainly our intent has been to offer something that is in many ways different. We have brought fresh eyes to the process of choosing a table of contents; in the drama component, as with the other genres, you'll find material that has not been widely anthologized elsewhere. You'll also find more visual material than in competing anthologies—including images from the first productions of *The School for Scandal* and *A Doll's House*.

Many of the selections in *The Broadview Introduction to Literature: Drama* will, we hope, be familiar to instructors; as to which of the "old chestnuts" continue to work well in a teaching context we have in large part been guided by the advice provided to us by academics at a variety of institutions across Canada. But even where familiar authors and selections are concerned, we think you'll find quite a bit here that is different. We have worked hard to pitch both the author introductions and the explanatory notes at a consistent level throughout—and, in both introductions and notes, to give students more by way of background.

Finally, you'll find fresh material posted on the companion website associated with the anthology. The site <http://sites.broadviewpress.com/BIL/> features additional material on many literary sub-genres and movements; material on reading poetry (including exercises that will help those unfamiliar with the patterns of accentual-syllabic metre in English); material on writing essays about literature—and on referencing and citation; a much fuller glossary of literary terms than it is possible to include in these pages; a self-test quiz on the information provided in the introduction to the genre; and several additional selections that we were unable to find space for in the bound book. All are introduced and annotated according to the same principles and presented in the same format as the selections in the bound-book anthology. Those wishing to go beyond these choices may assign any one of the more than 300 volumes in the acclaimed Broadview Editions series, and we can arrange to have that volume bundled together with the bound book anthology in a shrink-wrapped package, at little or no additional charge to the student.

Any of the genre volumes of the anthology may also be bundled together in special-price shrink-wrapped packages; whatever genres your course covers, and whatever works you would like to cover within those genres, we will do our best to put together a package that will suit your needs. (Instructors should note that, in addition to the main companion website of materials that may be of interest both to students and to instructors, we have posted instructor-related materials on a separate website.)

I do hope you will like what you see—and I hope as well that you will be in touch with any questions or suggestions; we will always be on the lookout for good ideas as to what we should add to the anthology's companion web-site—and/or for what we should look to include in the next edition of *The Broadview Introduction to Literature*.

[D.L.]

# Acknowledgements

The general editors, managing editors, and all of us at Broadview owe a debt of gratitude to the academics who have offered assistance and feedback at various stages of the project:

Rhonda Anderson
Trevor Arkell
Veronica Austen
John Ball
David Bentley
Shashi Bhat
Nicholas Bradley
Jocelyn Coates
Richard Cole
Alison Conway
Heidi J. Tiedemann Darroch
Celeste Daphne Derksen
Lorraine DiCicco
Kerry Doyle
Monique Dumontet
Michelle Faubert
Rebecca Gagan
Jay Gamble
Dana Hansen
Alexander Hart
Linda Harwood
Chandra Hodgson
Kathryn Holland
Ashton Howley
Renee Hulan
Kathleen James-Cavan
Karl Jirgens
Diana Frances Lobb

Kathyrn MacLennan
Shelley Mahoney
Joanna Mansbridge
Mark McDayter
Lindsey McMaster
Susan McNeill-Bindon
Craig Melhoff
Bob Mills
Stephanie Morley
Andrew Murray
Russell Perkin
Allan Pero
Mike Perschon
John Pope
Phyllis Rozendal
Cory Rushton
Laura Schechter
Stephen Schryer
Peter Slade
Marjorie Stone
Daniel Tysdal
Linda Van Netten Blimke
Molly Wallace
David Watt
Nanci White
David Wilson
Dorothy Woodman
Gena Zuroski-Jenkins

# The Study of Literature

The Nobel prize-winning physicist Paul Dirac reportedly said, "The aim of science is to make difficult things understandable in a simple way; the aim of poetry is to state simple things in an incomprehensible way." More recently, noted Language poet Charles Bernstein—whose work typically challenges the limits of simple comprehension—published the poem "Thank you for saying thank you," in which he explicitly takes up the issue of how poetry "states" things:

> This is a totally
> accessible poem.
> There is nothing
> in this poem
> that is in any
> way difficult.
> All the words
> are simple &
> to the point.

Though Bernstein's work is undoubtedly meant to register as ironic, both his poem and Dirac's comment draw attention to the idea that literature uses language in a peculiar way, and that one of the most fundamental questions readers of literature must ask themselves is: "How is this said?" Or—with apologies to Dirac—the question might be: "How do the language choices in this text make a seemingly simple thing—for example, a statement about love, or family, or justice, or grief—not incomprehensible, but rather more than just something simple?"

Another way of approaching the question of how literature works is to consider the way this anthology of literature is organized around the idea of genre, with texts chosen and categorized according to the way they fit into the classifications of poetry, short fiction, drama, and literary non-fiction. One way of organizing an introductory anthology of literature is the historical, in which selections are sorted from oldest to most recent, usually grouped together according to what have become acknowledged as distinctive historical periods of literary output. Another is the topical or thematic, in which historically and generically diverse selections are grouped together according to subject matter, so that students may compare differing attitudes toward, for example, gender relations, personal loss, particular historical events, or the process of growing up. The decision by an editor of an anthology—or the instructor of a course—to select one organizing principle over another is not arbitrary, but reflects a choice in terms of teaching students how to approach the reading of literature. In very simple terms, one might regard the three options thus: the historical configuration emphasizes discovering the "what" and "when" of literature—what is the body of written work that has come to be considered "literature" (especially in terms of tracing the outlines of a national literature), and when were examples from this distinguished corpus written? The thematic configuration emphasizes sorting through the "why" of literature—why do writers turn to literature to work through complex ideas, and what can we make of our complex responses to differing, often competing, stances on various topics? The generic configuration, finally, emphasizes the "how" of literature—how is the text put together? What are its working parts? How does an attention to the formal attributes of a literary piece help the reader understand the way it achieves its intellectual and emotional—its more than just simple—effects?

What do literary critics mean when they refer to genre? The word was introduced into the English language sometime in the late eighteenth century, borrowed from the French word *genre*, which meant "kind" or "style" of art, as when the British agricultural reformer Arthur Young refers in his travel narratives to the "genre" of Dutch painting, which he finds wanting in comparison to the work of the Italian masters. We can look back further to the Latin root *genus*, or even the Greek γένος (*génos*), a term which also refers to the idea of a distinct family or clan; thus, the notion of "kind" might helpfully be thought of as a way of thinking about resemblances, relationships, and keys to recognition among the literary genres. Another helpful analogy is the way biologists have taken up the term *genus* as part of the taxonomy of organisms. The term *genus felis*, for example, refers to a particular order of small cats, including such species as the domestic cat (*felis catus*) and the wildcat (*felis silvestris*); both species share common generic attributes, such as a similar size and a preferred diet of small rodents. For biologists and literary critics alike, the concept of genus or genre, respectively, is used to group things together according to a system of shared, identifiable features, with both terms allowing for the idea that larger groupings can be further broken down into even more specific ones (thus we can refer to the various breeds of domestic cats, or the distinctions among the Petrarchan, Shakespearian, and Spenserian sonnets).

Biologists tend to use the word "characteristics" to designate the features of a genus; literary critics, on the other hand, make use of the word "convention," a somewhat more complicated term. Like *characteristics*, the term *conventions* refers to distinguishing elements of a genre, which is why the study of literature requires a thorough understanding of the specialized descriptive vocabulary used to discuss such elements as a text's metre, its narrative point of view, its use of figurative language, etc. The introductions to each section of this anthology will draw attention to this specialized vocabulary, and students will also want to refer to the extensive glossary of literary terms located at the end of the anthology. The idea of convention, though, has additional conceptual importance relating to the way texts are built to be read. While a domestic cat is simply born with retractable claws and a taste for mice, a literary text is constructed, written in a particular way, often with the aim of eliciting a particular response from a reader. The word convention, in this sense, harks back to the legal concept of agreement, so that when writers make use of conventions associated with a genre, they set up a kind of contract with the reader whereby the reader has a sense of what to expect from the text. For example: when the first five minutes of a film include a long shot of the Pentagon, along with a few quickly edited shots of grim-looking military personnel moving quickly through underground hallways, and perhaps a shot of someone in a dark suit yelling into a cellphone, "Operation Silvestris has been aborted!" the audience understands that they are in for some sort of political thriller. They need not know anything about the details of Operation Silvestris to make this interpretive leap, as the presence of a few conventions of the political thriller (the shot of the Pentagon, the phrase "Operation [blank] has been aborted!") are enough to provide the general outline of a contract entered into between film and audience. Likewise, recognizing that a poem has 14 lines and makes use of a rhyming couplet at the end will provide knowledgeable readers of literature with an inkling as to what they should expect, as these readers will be familiar with the structural conventions of the Shakespearean sonnet.

Whereas a legal contract is a fairly straightforward affair—it outlines the terms of agreement for both sides and more or less explicitly refers to the penalties for undermining those terms—the contract between text and reader is multifaceted. One of the most fascinating things about the way writers make use of literary convention is that the terms of agreement are constantly subject to further consideration, thoughtful challenge, or outright derision. Thus, when the speaker of Shakespeare's sonnet 130 refers to his lady's "dun" breasts and "reek[ing]" breath, the point is not to insult his mistress, or even to admire her in a new, more realistic way; rather, the point is to ridicule the way other poets slavishly adhere to the convention that sonnets glorify a woman's beauty, comparing her eyes to the sun and her breath to the smell of roses. This reading is available for the reader who knows that by the time Shakespeare decided to try his hand at the genre, translations and imitations of the Petrarchan sonnet had been circulating at the Elizabethan court for many decades. Like organisms, or even laws, conventions of literature evolve over time as writers seek to rethink the rules of the form they wish to explore. In the prologue to her recent collection *XEclogue*, Lisa Robertson declares, "I needed a genre to gloss my ancestress' complicity with a socially expedient code"; she explains how, in turning to the conventions of the eclogue—a collection of pastoral poems, often satiric—she has found a suitable formal framework for her exploration of the way social insiders and outsiders are marked by class and gender.

Is it somehow problematic to inquire too tenaciously into the working parts of a literary text? Does one risk undermining the emotional force of a poem, the sharp wit of a play, or the exciting plot of an adventure tale if one pays too much attention to seemingly mundane issues of plot structure or metre? To paraphrase a common grievance of the distressed student: by examining the way literature works, are we, somehow, just wrecking it? These questions might, paradoxically, recall Dirac's complaint that literature makes simple things incomprehensible: while we know that literature can manage to communicate difficult notions, making what is mysterious more comprehensible, it is often difficult to articulate or make a viable argument about how it does so. By paying attention to the way a text is built and to the way an author constructs his or her end of the contract, the reader can begin to understand and respond explicitly to the question of how literature produces its particular effects.

Consider the following two textual excerpts:

> Come live with me and be my love,
> And we shall all the pleasures prove.
> (Christopher Marlowe, 1590)

> Boom, boom, boom, let's go back to my room,
> And we can do it all night, and I can make you feel right.
> (Paul Lekakis, 1987)

Based on a quick reading: which excerpt is more appropriate for inclusion in a Valentine's Day card? A poll of employees at Hallmark, not to mention the millions of folks invested in the idea that Valentine's Day is a celebration of romance, would likely make an overwhelming case for the Marlowe excerpt. But why? Answering that question might involve a methodological inquiry into how each excerpt produces a particular response, one which might be broken down into five stages:

**Level One: Evaluation—Do I like this text? What is my gut reaction to it?** No doubt, most students of literature have heard an instructor proclaim, with more or less vitriol, "It doesn't matter if you like the poem/story/play! This is a literature class, not a book club!" And, while it is true that the evaluative response does not constitute an adequate final critical response to a text, it's important to acknowledge one's first reaction. After all, the point of literature is to produce an effect, sometimes an extreme response. When a text seems confusing, or hilarious, or provocative, or thrilling, it prompts questions: How are such effects produced using mere words in particular combinations? Why would an author want to generate feelings of confusion, hilarity, provocation, etc.? How am I—the reader—being positioned on the other end of such effects?

**Level Two: Interpretation—What is the text about?** This is a trickier level of reading than it might seem. Students sometimes think, mistakenly, that all literature—and especially poetry—is "open to interpretation," and that all interpretations are therefore correct. This line of thinking leads to snap, top-down interpretations, in which the general "mood" of the text is felt at a gut level (see above), and the ensuing reading of the poem is wrangled into shape to match that feeling. It is sometimes helpful to think about interpretation as a kind of translation, as in the way those who work at the United Nations translating talking points from Arabic to Russian are called "interpreters." Though no translation is flawless, the goal of simultaneous translation is to get as close as possible to the meaning of the original. Thus, an interpretation should be thought of as a carefully paraphrased summary or, for particularly dense works, a line by line explication of the literary text, both of which may require several rereadings and some meticulous use of a dictionary. As with reading for evaluation, reading for interpretation can help generate useful critical questions, such as: How does the way this text is written affect my attitude toward the subject matter? What is the point of all the fancy language, which makes this text more or less difficult to interpret? Now that I've figured out what this text is about—at least in terms of its subject matter—can I begin to determine what sorts of themes are being tackled?

A note about the distinction between subject matter and **theme**: while these terms are sometimes used interchangeably, the notion of theme differs from subject matter in that it implies an idea about or attitude toward the subject matter. A good rule of thumb to remember is that theme can never be summed up in just one word (so, there is no such thing as the theme of "Love" or "Family" or "Women"). Whereas the subject matter of Shakespeare's sonnet "Shall I compare thee to a summer's day" is admiration or the nature of beauty, one theme of the poem, arguably, is that the beloved's good qualities are best made apparent in poetry, and that art is superior to nature. Another theme of the poem, arguably, is that the admiration of youth is best accomplished by someone older. Thus, identifying a text's subject matter via interpretation aims to pinpoint a general topic, while the process of contemplating a text's theme is open to elaboration and argumentation.

**Level Three: Description—What does the text look like, at least at first glance? Can you give a quick account of its basic formal features?** At this level of reading, one starts to think about how a text is built, especially in terms of basic generic features. For example, are we dealing with poetry? Short fiction? Drama? If poetry, can we identify a sub-genre the text fits into—for instance, the sonnet, the ode, or the elegy—and can we begin to assess whether the author is following or challenging conventions associated with that genre? Of course, answering these questions requires prior knowledge of what, for example, a conventional ode is supposed to look like, which is why the student of literature must have a thorough understanding of the specific terminology associated with the discipline. At this level of reading, one might also begin to think about and do some preliminary research on when and where the text was written, so that the issues of literary history and cultural context are broached; likewise, one might begin to think about who is writing the poem, as the matter of the author's societal position might prove a fruitful avenue for further investigation. Thus, a consequent objective at this level of reading is to map the terrain of inquiry, establishing some general facts about the text as building blocks that underpin critical analysis.

**Level Four: Analysis—How are particular formal features working, especially as they interact with content?** The word analysis comes from the Greek terms ἀνά- (ana-), meaning "throughout," and λύειν (lysis), meaning "to loose." Thus, the procedure for analysis involves taking a text and shaking it apart in order to see more clearly all its particular bits and pieces. This level of reading is akin to putting a text under a microscope. First, one has to identify individual formal features of the text. Then one needs to consider how all the parts fit together. It is at this level that one's knowledge of generic conventions and particular literary techniques—the way figurative language works, the ways in which rhythm and rhyme affect our response to language, the way plotting and point of view can be handled, and so on—is crucial. It may be the case that not everything one notices will find its way into an essay. But the goal at this level of reading should be to notice as much as possible (and it is usually when working at this level that an instructor will be accused of "reading too much into a text," as if that image of a moth beating its wings against a window means nothing more than that the moth is trapped, and that it just happens to have been included in a work). Careful analysis shows that nothing in a text "just happens" to be there. A text is constructed out of special uses of language that beg to be "read into." Reading at this level takes time and a certain amount of expertise so as to tease out how the work is built and begin to understand the connections between form and content.

**Level Five: Critical Analysis—How do the formal elements of a literary work connect with what the work has to say to the reader?** It is at this level of reading that one begins to make an argument, to develop a thesis. In order to construct a viable thesis, one needs to answer a question, perhaps one of the questions that arose at an earlier level of reading. For example, why does this poem, which seems on the surface to be about love, make use of so many images that have to do with science? What is up with this narrator, who seems to be addressing another character without in any way identifying who he is speaking to? What is significant about the fact that the climax of this play hangs on the matter of whether a guy is willing to sell a portrait? It is at this level of reading, rather than at the level of interpretation, that the literary critic is able to flex his or her creative muscles, as a text poses any number of viable questions and suggests any number of viable arguments. Note, however, that the key word here is "viable." In order to make an argument—in order to convincingly answer a question posed—one must have the textual evidence to make the case, evidence that has been gleaned through careful, meticulous, and thoughtful reading.

Returning now to the two texts, let's see if we can come up with one viable argument as to why Marlowe's text seems more likely to show up in a Valentine's Day card, going through each level of reading to build the foundation—the case—for making that argument.

**Level One: Evaluation.** At first glance, the Marlowe text just seems more romantic than the Lekakis text: it uses flowery words and has a nice flow to it, while the phrase "do it all night" is kind of blunt and unromantic. On a gut level, one might feel that a Valentine's Day card should avoid such blunt language (although this gut reaction might suggest a first useful research question: why should romance be associated with flowery language rather than blunt expressions?).

Moving on to **Level Two: Interpretation.** Well, the Lekakis text is certainly the more straightforward one when it comes to interpretation, though one has to know that the phrase "do it" refers to having sex as opposed to some other activity (and it is interesting to note that even in the more straightforward text, the author has used a common euphemism). The phrase "Boom boom boom" seems to be untranslatable, which begs the question of why the author used it. Is the phrase still meaningful, even if it's just a series of sounds?

As for the Marlowe text, a careful paraphrase would go something like this: "Move in with me and be my lover, and we can enjoy all kinds of pleasures together." Hmmm—wait a minute: what does the author mean by "pleasures"? Eating good food? Playing card games? Though the word is arguably vague, the references in the first line to moving in together and love make it pretty clear that "pleasures" is another euphemism for having sex (though perhaps a more elegant one than "doing it").

If both texts can be interpreted similarly—both are the words of a would-be lover trying to convince the object of his/her affection to have sex—why does it matter which phrase ends up in a Valentine's Day card? What are the significant differences between each text that cause them to generate distinct gut responses?

**Level Three: Description.** The Marlowe text, at least this piece of it, is a **couplet**, written in iambic **tetrameter** (or eight syllables in each line that follow the rhythmic pattern of unstressed/stressed). The language is flowery, or, to use a slightly more technical phrase, the **diction** is elevated, which means that this is not the way people normally talk in everyday life. In fact, there seems to have been a lot of attention paid to making the words sound pleasing to the ear, through patterns of rhythm and rhyme, and also through patterns of alliteration in the consonants (of the soft "l" sound in the first line, and then of powerful plosives at the end of the second).

The Lekakis text also makes use of rhyme, but in a different way: each line includes an **internal rhyme**, so that "boom" rhymes with "room" and "night" rhymes with "right." The rhythmic pattern is harder to make sense of, as there are a different number of syllables in each line and a lot of short, sharp words that undermine a sing-song effect. The sound effects of the text are comparatively harsher than in the Marlowe text, with many "b" and "k" and "t" sounds.

The Marlowe text was written in the 1590s, while the Lekakis text is a popular dance song from the 1980s; it might be interesting to follow up on the distinct cultural contexts out of which each work emerges. It might also be interesting to examine how each text thematizes the subject of having sex: whereas the Marlowe text seems to promote the attitude that the "pleasures" of sex should be tried out (to "prove" in sixteenth-century English meant to test or to try out) within the context of "living with" someone, or that love and sex go hand-in-hand, the Lekakis text seems to suggest that even sex on one "night" in someone's "room" can make one feel "right." Or, good sex has nothing at all to do with love.

Because these texts are so short and are fairly simple, much of the work of **Level Four: Analysis** has already been touched on. A closer inspection of the use of rhyme and **alliteration** in the Marlowe text demonstrates the way the poem insists on the idea that love can be "proved" by sex, while the internal rhyming of the words "me," "be," and "we" further indicates a strong emphasis on how the joining of two people represents a significant change. The use of elevated diction is consistent, suggesting that discussions of love and sex are worthy of serious consideration.

As for the Lekakis text, a major point to analyze is the phrase "boom boom boom." Is this **onomatopoeia**? If so, what "sense" is the sound trying to express? The sound of sex? If so, what kind of sex are we talking about here? Or is it the sound of something else, perhaps dancing (as is suggested by the cultural context of which the text emerges)? Maybe the phrase is simply meant to express excitement? What do we make of the plain speech the text employs? Does the use of such diction debase notions of sex, or is it simply more candid about the way sex and love might be separated?

As you can see, the level of **Critical Analysis**, or argument, is quickly and organically developing. If the research question one decides on is, What is interesting about the distinct way each text thematizes the relationship between love and sex?, a viable argument, based on evidence gleaned from close reading, might be: "Whereas Marlowe's text suggests that the pleasures of sex are best discovered within the context of a stable, long-term relationship, the text by Lekakis asserts that sex can be enjoyed in and of itself, undermining the importance of the long-term relationship." One might take this argument further. Why is what you have noted significant or particularly interesting? A possible answer to that question—and an even more sophisticated thesis—might be: "Thus, while the Lekakis text is, on the surface, less romantic, its attitude toward sex is much less confining than the attitude presented in Marlowe's text." Or, one might pursue an entirely different argument: "Whereas Marlowe's text indicates that sex is to be enjoyed mutually by two people, the Lekakis text implies that sex is something one 'does' to another person. Further, it implies that sex is a fairly meaningless and potentially aggressive activity."

The above description of the steps taken toward critical analysis shows how students of literature are meant to approach the works they read. What the description does not convey is why one would bother to make the effort at all, or why the process of critical literary analysis is thought to be a meaningful activity. In order to answer that question, it is helpful to consider how the discipline of literary studies came to be considered a worthwhile course of study for university and college students.

The history of literary studies is both very old and, in terms of the study of English literature, very fresh. In the fifth century, Martianus Capella wrote the allegory *De nuptiis Philologiae et Mercurii* ("The Marriage of Philology and Mercury"), in which he described the seven pillars of learning: grammar, dialectic, rhetoric, geometry, arithmetic, astronomy, and musical harmony. Collectively, such subjects came to be referred to as the liberal arts; as such, they were taken up by many of the high medieval universities as constituting the core curriculum. During the Early Modern period, the study of the so-called *trivium* (grammar, dialectic, rhetoric) was transformed to include the critical analysis of classical texts, i.e., the study of literature. As universities throughout Europe, and later in North America, proliferated and flourished between the sixteenth and nineteenth centuries, the focus remained on classical texts. As Gerald Graff explains, "In theory, the study of Greek and Latin was supposed to inspire the student with the nobility of his cultural heritage." (Somewhat paradoxically, classical texts were studied primarily in terms of their language use as opposed to their literary quality, perhaps because no one read or spoke Greek or Latin outside the classroom.) Until the late nineteenth century, the university system did not consider literary works written in English (or French or German or Italian) to be worthy of rigorous study, but only of *appreciation*. As Terry Eagleton notes in *Literary Theory: An Introduction*, the reading of works of English Literature was thought best left to working-class men, who might attend book clubs or public lectures, and to women; it was "a convenient sort of non-subject to palm off on the ladies, who were in any case excluded from science and the professions." It was only in the early twentieth century—hundreds of years after the founding of the great European universities—that literature came to be taken seriously as a university or college subject.

Over the past century and more, the discipline of literary studies has undergone a number of shifts. In the very early twentieth century, literature was studied largely for the way in which it embodied cultural tradition; one would learn something about being American or British by reading so-called great works of literature. (As British subjects, Canadians were also taught what it was to be a part of the British tradition.) By mid-century the focus had shifted to the aesthetic properties of the work itself. This fresh approach was known as Formalism and/or the New Criticism. Its proponents advocated paying close attention to literary form—in some cases, for an almost scientific approach to close reading. They tended to de-emphasize authorial biography and literary history. The influence of this approach continues to be felt in university and college classrooms (giving rise to such things as, for example, courses organized around the concept of literary genre). But it is important to keep in mind here that the emphasis on form—on generic conventions, on literary terminology, on the aesthetic as opposed to the cultural, philosophical, or moral qualities of literature—is not the only way to approach the study of literature, but was, rather, institutionalized as the best, most scholarly way. The work of close reading and producing literary criticism is not in any way "natural," but is how the study of literature has been "disciplined"; thus the student in a literature classroom should not feel discouraged if the initial steps of learning what it is he or she is supposed to be doing are challenging or seem strange.

The most recent important shift to have occurred in the "disciplining" of literary studies was the rise in the 1960s and 1970s of what became known as "literary theory." There is not room enough here to adequately elucidate the range of theories that have been introduced into literary studies, but a crude comparison between how emerging methods were set in opposition to New Criticism (which is itself a type of literary theory) may be useful. John Crowe Ransom's *The World's Body*—a sort of manifesto for New Criticism—argues that the work of the literary critic must strenuously avoid, among other things, "Any other special studies which deal with some abstract or prose content taken out of the work … [such as] Chaucer's command of medieval sciences … [or] Shakespeare's understanding of the law." In other words, the New Critic should focus solely on the text itself. In contrast, those today who make use of such theoretical frameworks as New Historicism, Gender Studies, or Postcolonial Studies will strenuously *embrace* all manner of "special studies" in order to consider how the text interacts with context. As Graff puts it, "Theory is what is generated when some aspect of literature, its nature, its history, its place in society, its conditions for production and reception, its meaning in general … ceases to be a given and becomes a question to be argued." What this means for the student of literature trying to work out what to do with a text is that the question "Why is what I have noticed in the text significant?" can be approached from an almost limitless set of knowledge contexts. How might a particular poem illuminate historical notions of class divisions? How might a particular play tell us something about how technological advances have changed the way humans think about identity? And, though it might seem that the focus on form that so defines the New Critical approach becomes irrelevant once Literary Theory arrives on the disciplinary scene, the fact is that most field practitioners (i.e., writers of literary criticism) still depend heavily on the tools of close reading; formal analysis becomes the foundation on which a more theoretical analysis is built.

Thus, we might consider a sixth level of reading: advanced critical analysis. At this level the stakes are raised as arguments about why a text's formal construction is meaningful are set within a larger conceptual framework. The work of advanced critical analysis requires that the literary critic think about and research whatever conceptual framework is being pursued. For example, after noticing that the Marlowe text and the Lekakis text are written about 400 years apart, one might further research cultural attitudes toward sex in the two time periods to come up with another, even more sophisticated, layer of argumentation, one which would not only provide insight into two literary texts, but show how the comparative analysis of such texts tells us something about how viewpoints on sex have shifted. Or, after noticing that both texts are written by male authors, one might further research and consider what they reveal about masculine approaches to sex and seduction. Or, after discovering that Marlowe's poem follows the conventions of **pastoral** poetry, or that "Boom boom boom (let's go back to my room)" became popular within the LGBT community, one might contemplate and develop an argument about the implications of the way sex is idealized and/or becomes part of a complex cultural fantasy. Or, after discovering that Marlowe presented homoerotic material frequently in his other writing (in his poem "Hero and Leander," for example, he writes of one of the male protagonists that "in his looks were all that men desire"), one might inquire into the ways in which the author's or narrator's sexual orientation may or may not be relevant to a discussion of a love poem. To put it bluntly (and anachronistically), does it matter if Marlowe was gay?

Because the reading of literature entails a painstaking, thoughtful interaction with some of the most multifaceted, evocative, and provocative uses of language humans have produced, thinking about such work critically may tell us something about what it means to be human.

[N.G.]

# Drama

In Tom Stoppard's *Rosencrantz and Guildenstern Are Dead*, the character of The Player contemplates the peculiarity of what it means to be a stage actor: "There we are—demented children mincing about in clothes that no one ever wore, speaking as no man ever spoke, swearing love in wigs and rhymed couplets, killing each other with wooden swords ... Don't you see?! We're actors—we're the opposite of people!" While it is true that texts belonging to other generic categories might more or less explicitly refer to their own status as fictions, dramatic texts must foreground the matter of the conventions that go along with fictionality, at least in terms of form. (In referring to "fiction" here, the issue is not genre or "drama" versus "fiction" versus "poetry," but rather that the dramatic text tells a fictitious story, that it is a product of the imagination.) Consider the act of going to see a play: you and several or several hundred other people gather together in a specific place and, at a specific time, quiet down and focus your attention at a specific location. In that location, for a certain length of time, other people say and do things, all the while pretending to be other people and pretending that they have no idea they are being watched by several or several hundred others. For your part, you pretend that the people pretending to be other people are in fact those other people, and that you, and several or several hundred others, are completely invisible. In what other context would such bizarre conduct seem not only reasonable, but absolutely necessary? Daniel MacIvor's play *House Humans* describes an instance when this strange balancing act of reciprocal pretending is threatened: "Harold is an old man who goes to the theatre ... He always sits at the front and claps in all the wrong places and yells out Marxist slogans during the tender moments and calls the actors by their real names. (Once he went to see a play where at one point a watermelon would roll out and surprise the audience, and he went back several times so that just before the watermelon would roll out he could yell: 'Here comes the watermelon!')" No other literary genre is at risk for this type of sabotage. In considering some of the basic conventions of drama, then, it is helpful to think about how they flow from both its central principle and its central constraint: the drama is built around the potentially fragile concept of the willing suspension of disbelief.

# The Drama and the Performance

The expression "willing suspension of disbelief" was coined by the poet Samuel Taylor Coleridge in his 1817 autobiography, *Biographia Literaria*. Coleridge explained that, in order for readers to appreciate some of his more fantastical narratives—for example, his ballad *The Rime of the Ancient Mariner*, with its ghostly figures and supernatural events—they would have to temporarily set aside—or suspend—any inclination towards skepticism about the truthfulness of such a tale. Willing suspension of disbelief is a crucial component of what makes the dramatic performance work. In the eighteenth century, Denis Diderot asserted that actors should perform as if the spectator did not exist, as if a "large wall" separated the stage from the audience, and as if "the curtain did not rise."

Diderot's treatise on acting technique followed the development of the **proscenium stage**, as his mention of a "curtain" makes clear; proscenium stages, introduced in Europe during the seventeenth century, make use of an archway or large frame to separate the stage area from the audience area and thus provide for the possibility of hanging a curtain and marking more easily, for example, the beginnings and endings of acts. Before the advent of the proscenium stage, dramatists often wrote plays meant to be performed on a **thrust stage**, a raised platform encircled by the audience on three sides; thus, a play such as Shakespeare's *Twelfth Night* was written before it was possible to use a curtain, and one might consider the different techniques employed to indicate the breaks between scenes and acts. Other popular stage formats are the **arena** or **theatre-in-the-round stage**, in which the audience, sitting in sloped seating, completely (or almost completely) encircles the stage area, or the **found space**, in which the stage area and audience area might be configured in any number of ways. In the contemporary era, directors and stage designers have the opportunity to stage plays along various designs, though unless a found space or a specially built space is being used, they must take into account an existing physical structure, be it an arena, proscenium stage, or otherwise.

What becomes interesting to consider is the way dramatists sometimes make explicit reference to the idea of the willing suspension of disbelief, not only in terms of a clear addressing of the audience—as in Viola's asides in *Twelfth Night*, but also in terms of a thematic concern with the operation of illusion that is so easily observable in drama. Though the **realism** of Henrik Ibsen and Tennessee Williams, whereby everything on stage is meant to register as a potential, everyday activity, has not been entirely abandoned in recent years (witness Hannah Moscovitch's *Essay*), interest in **metafictional** theatre, or plays that call attention to their own fictionality in their content, has also exploded. From an absurdist play such as Samuel Beckett's *Krapp's Last Tape* to Sharon Pollock's incorporation of the figure of the Actress in *Blood Relations*, dramatists have made use of the inherent strangeness at the heart of playgoing to raise such questions as how we believe what we believe, why humans are so engrossed by illusion-making and art, and how our perceptions can be produced and undermined by mere words.

This notion of a reader or audience member's temporary willingness to simply believe things that are patently untrue is a crucial factor in the success of the drama, especially the success of the drama's performance. For the critical analysis of this genre, it is important to distinguish between the notion of the drama or play, that is, the written version of the work, and theatre, which is the live enactment of mutual pretending described above. In his critical work *The Semiotics of Performance*, Marco De Marinis helpfully refines this distinction, referring to the **dramatic text** vs. the **performance text**. The dramatic text—the written play—consists of dialogue and **stage directions**, which are the instructions contained in the written play that specify how characters are supposed to move on, off, and about the stage, and sometimes how they are meant to behave. While the stage directions in some plays, especially older ones, are basically limited to such instructions as "*Enter*" and "*Exit*," they may also provide detailed, evocative information on the mood of the play, as in Tennessee Williams's stage directions for *Cat on a Hot Tin Roof*, or about the arrangement of stage décor, as in those for Stoppard's *Arcadia*. The performance text, on the other hand, consists of the intended or implicit acting out of the written play. Thus, the performance text is not quite the same thing as a specific theatrical production of a given play on a given evening; rather, it is the *potential* of theatrical production that is embedded in the written play, a potential that readers of the dramatic text must somehow imagine in their mind's eye, and that to a large extent limits the type of action that can be portrayed. While it is true that some authors—for example, Mary Sidney and Percy Shelley—have written what are called **closet dramas**, or plays not meant to be performed, most plays are predicated on the idea of being acted out and of requiring a temporary agreement between actors and audience to accept all manner of imitation, impersonation, and active use of the imagination.

## Constructing the Drama: Plot, Character, Space, and Speech

In the earliest surviving work of dramatic theory, *The Poetics*, Aristotle compares tragic drama to epic poetry, asserting that, while both genres should be concerned with heroic action, the events portrayed in a tragic drama must "fall within a single revolution of the sun, or slightly exceed this," while the epic is "unlimited in point of time." Later in the work, Aristotle adds that tragic drama should present "an action that is heroic and complete and of a certain magnitude." During the sixteenth and seventeenth centuries, Italian, French, and English neoclassicists expanded upon and refined these remarks, claiming that, ideally, all dramas should adhere to what were termed the three classical unities. Italian critic Lodovico Castelvetro explained that a play must have a **unity of action** (a focus on a single incident or two interrelated incidents), a **unity of time**, and a **unity of space**, with the dramatized events taking place within a 24-hour time frame and in a single locale. Later critics noted that exceptions might be made; for example, Pierre Corneille argued that the restricted timeframe of Aeschylus's *Agamemnon* was absurd and that the periods of time represented in a play should not strain verisimilitude (except in the final act, when the audience is more interested in finding out what happens than they are in the likelihood that it might all happen very quickly). In *Of Dramatic Poesy: An Essay*, John Dryden noted that while Ben Jonson "has given us the most correct plays," in which the adherence to the three unities provide "profitable rules for perfecting the stage," Shakespeare's ignorance of such rules might be forgiven because of his great wit.

By the beginning of the nineteenth century, most drama critics and theorists had abandoned the notion of the three unities, at least as a prescriptive set of rules. That said, these foundational conventions are still worth keeping in mind for the student of literature attuned to how the drama is built. It may be helpful to consider how the notion of unity of action is associated with the **plotting** of drama. The terms associated with **Freytag's pyramid**, such as **exposition, rising action, climax, falling action**, and **dénouement/resolution**, are often used to discuss prose narratives, though Gustav Freytag himself was concerned only with the five-act plot structure of classical and Renaissance plays. While few contemporary plays retain the five-act structure, the student of literature should consider how the plotting of dramas tends to retain a sense of tightness, chronological simplicity, and forward momentum, likely because the implied audience of the performance text will experience the performance in real time. For example, though Williams's *Cat on a Hot Tin Roof* is broken down into four acts, the limited timeframe and strict chronology of the action are controlled by the simple fact that the action takes place over the course of a single evening, as the family celebrates Big Daddy's birthday. What, then, might one say about the relationship between this formal choice in structuring the plot of the play and its thematic concern with domestic space, family relationships, and the way humans confront death? Other important plotting techniques associated with drama include suspense—or the anticipation about how things will turn out—and suspense's customary partner, **foreshadowing**—or how anticipation is created via hints. In thinking about suspense, one might consider whether the play leaves the audience in the dark as to what might occur in the end, thus leading up to a feeling of surprise, or whether foreshadowing makes it seem as if the resolution to the plot is inevitable.

Moreover, it is often important to think about how the dramatist negotiates breaking the action down into chunks that can be performed, i.e., into **acts** and scenes. Whereas a prose narrative can suggest a change in action or space or time using mere words, the convention of the embedded performance text necessitates that the dramatist consider how each unit of action will be made evident, whether by the closing and opening of a curtain, by the dimming of lights, or by some other means. In Pollock's *Blood Relations*, the stage directions indicate that units of action should not be marked, with the exception of a blackout at the end of Act I, despite the fact that various moments in time and space are represented. One might ask how this formal directive is related to the play's emphasis on questioning authority, or on changing attitudes toward women over time. The implicit performance text within a drama also complicates the way one thinks of **characterization**: while all fictional narrative texts might contain characters—that is, represented individuals who have particular personality traits—in a drama the process of defining and indicating those traits cannot be achieved through direct authorial exposition, whereby the author simply tells the reader what the character is like via narration. In a drama, the character reveals his- or herself through speech and action, though it is sometimes the case that dramatists "cheat," as in moments where characters describe one another or when a character describes—sometimes at length—his- or herself. Some characters will go so far as to articulate their **motivations**, the reasons for particular actions or desires, though it is often left to the student of literature to glean a character's motivations based on what that character says and does. And, just as with first-person narrators, it is sometimes the case that the motivations characters give to us, or the way a character might describe his- or herself, is inaccurate; it is the task of the audience member to evaluate the information that is given. Usually, if a character's motivations can be assessed and analyzed, one is dealing with what is called a **round character**, one that is fully developed and whose actions are credible. At the other end of the spectrum is the **flat character**, one defined by a small number of traits, or that functions as a **stock character**, which is a familiar stereotype—for example, the young, naïve female lover, the scheming revenge-seeker, or the bumbling father figure. A character may be thought of as a **foil** if his or her main function is to reflect something important about a main character. For example, Gooper from *Cat on a Hot Tin Roof* is portrayed as conventionally masculine so as to further emphasize his brother Brick's more complex struggle with his gender identity and sexuality. Though it is often the case that a foil is also a flat character, it is certainly possible for such a figure—like Gooper—to be fully and complexly developed.

Castelvetro made his case for the unity of space by drawing attention to "the limitation of the space in which [the play] is acted"; in other words, the theoretical concept and literary convention derive from a practical concern: how many places can one reasonably include in a drama, given the implicit performance text embedded in every play and the necessity of representing those places, live? And what, then, is the significance of the place or places a dramatist chooses to include, especially given that the selections must be limited? Ibsen's *A Doll's House* is set entirely in one room, the living room of the Helmers' apartment, though various other rooms are gestured toward as characters move off stage. Why does Ibsen choose this space—which is both domestic, and yet somehow public—for his exploration of the Helmers' marriage?

The term dramatists and literary critics use to refer to the location of represented action is **setting**, a term also associated with prose narratives, but used in a very specific way for discussions of dramas. The French term **mise en scène** is perhaps a more helpful way to refer to a drama's setting, as it encompasses the scenery, the properties or moveable set pieces, the way everything on stage is arranged, and even the way lighting and sound effects are to be used throughout a performance. The issue of properties (usually called props) is especially interesting, as it is often the case that such items take on **symbolic** meaning, which is not surprising given—again—that there are only so many items a dramatist can reasonably have cluttering up the performance area. Any item that is important enough to be lugged onto a stage thus has the potential to transcend its function as décor—even in a play such as *A Doll's House*, the setting of which is meant to register as a real living room. For example, in Act III, the stage directions inform the reader that, while preparing to open his letter-box, "*Helmer takes his bunch of keys from his pocket and goes into the hall.*" It is perfectly realistic that a man wishing to unlock his letter-box would fish keys out of his pocket. Yet Ibsen's choice to represent this action on the stage—which requires that a fake set of keys be made up and carried by the actor playing Torvald Helmer—leads one to ask whether the keys might have any additional or symbolic significance. Might they indicate, for example, the sort of control Helmer holds over his wife? Similarly, the portrait of Sir

Oliver Surface in Richard Brinsley Sheridan's *The School for Scandal* operates as a complex prop—especially if one considers that for every new production of the play, a portrait of the *actor* playing Sir Oliver Surface must be fabricated. The Surface portrait may thus be seen as a symbolic anchor for the play's exploration of true and false identities.

Another distinguishing convention of the drama is that, unlike a prose or poetry narrative, in which an omniscient narrator or speaker might describe what is happening, in a drama the action must be expressed through what can be physically represented on stage and what the characters in a play say to one another, or to themselves. The term **dialogue**, which comes from the Greek words meaning "through" (dia) and "to speak" (legein), refers to the way conversations between two or more persons on stage work to reveal character and to advance the plot. The drama's formal dependence on dialogue—as opposed to expository or descriptive or figurative writing, such as is used regularly and to great effect in other genres—is often accompanied by explorations within the drama of the power of language. Consider, for example, Moscovitch's play *Essay*, in which the characters deal with the way a footnote in a history textbook becomes the source of a complex power struggle, or how Beckett's *Krapp's Last Tape* explores the way certain words define our identities and memories. It is sometimes the case in a drama that only one person is speaking, either in a **monologue** or in a **soliloquy**. Monologues occur when one person is speaking aloud, for an extended length of time, to one or more listeners, while soliloquies are meant to represent a circumstance in which a character talks to him- or herself. In a prose narrative, such internal musing is common and, arguably, most lyric poems represent this same contemplative activity. In a drama, however, the audience must accept the convention that people do their internal musing aloud, as when, in Act II of *Twelfth Night*, Viola meditates (out loud, in iambic pentameter) on the frailty of women. Another convention of speech used in drama, one that seems to oppose so many of the genre's other conventions, is the **aside**. This is a moment when the spell of mutual pretending is broken and a character directly addresses the audience, with the implicit understanding that the character's words to the audience cannot be heard by anyone else on stage. After Viola swears to Orsino that she—in the guise of Cesario—will help him court Olivia, for example, she then makes an aside to the audience asserting that she wishes Orsino would have her as a wife.

The aside is an example of what is known as "breaking the fourth wall," an expression that references Diderot's assertion about "the large wall." Asides draw attention to the idea that, when an audience is watching a play, they are peeking into a room—a room with one invisible wall—where people are simply going about their business. Other examples of breaking the fourth wall in dramas include the use of prologues or epilogues, the use of a **chorus**, when a group of characters offer commentary on the action, and the inclusion of a song, or even a dance in the middle of the play. In much historical drama, for example Renaissance and Restoration drama, the aside is meant to register as "truth," whereby the character looks through the invisible wall and confesses something genuine to the audience. Contemporary playwrights have often experimented with the convention of character-audience interaction, as when, in *Blood Relations*, Pollock's use of language associated with a courtroom case implicitly asks the audience to "judge" the truth of Lizzie Borden's case. A kind of opposition to the aside is the notion of **dramatic irony**, a type of irony in which the audience knows more about a particular situation than the characters themselves (an archetypal instance occurs in Shakespeare's *Romeo and Juliet*, when the audience knows that Juliet is not really dead but only drugged, but can only watch helplessly as Romeo poisons himself out of grief).

## Drama and Mode

Another important effect of the dramatic text being linked with its implicit performance text is that clues about the play's **mode**—whether the play fits into the subgenre of tragedy, comedy, or something else—can be given very efficiently. As with a film, the drama can make use of both words and aspects of the mise en scène, lighting, and music to set up expectations about the treatment of the subject matter. The idea of mode as a defining trait of a subgenre such as the tragic or comedic play derives out of the notion that the same subject can be handled in a variety of ways, and that choices made in the handling will produce different expectations. If, in the first five minutes of a film set in a high school, the audience is faced with grainy images of unhappy teens loitering about the back door and exhausted teachers trying to bring order to unruly classrooms, the audience may reasonably expect a gritty and possibly tragic film about youth. On the other hand, if the opening shots of the high school reveal brightly dressed, laughing teens engaging in back-to-school chatter and hijinks, the audience may reasonably expect a lighthearted and comedic film about youth. The drama has often been crudely considered as being an either/or affair when it comes to mode. Lord Byron summarized it this way: "All tragedies are finished by death, / All comedies are ended by marriage." Aristotle, for his part, saw tragedies as intended to inspire "pity and fear," and comedies as intended to entertain via wit and humour.

Such simplistic divisions do not always make sense. Even the exemplary tragic hero Oedipus doesn't die at the end of Sophocles' play, and some of Shakespeare's romantic comedies, in particular *Measure for Measure* and *The Merchant of Venice*, are not exactly lighthearted (though they do both end with a focus on marriage). Playwrights often make use of the expectations associated with the modes of tragedy or comedy to explore the grey area between the two. For example, in seventeenth- and eighteenth-century France, the idea of tragedy was associated with plays about history or public matters. Such material was considered important enough to warrant serious treatment; the issue of death was not mandatory. In some contemporary tragedies the conventional focus on a hero is set aside, or explicitly challenged. In Arthur Miller's *Death of a Salesman*, Willy Loman is just an ordinary businessman who has a fraught relationship with his sons, and ends up committing suicide. A play such as Ibsen's *A Doll's House* also fits into the mode of tragedy, though it is unclear if the audience is meant to fear or be inspired by Nora's escape from her marriage. Likewise, the comedic mode is made use of in many plays that have nothing to do with marriage. Throughout the Elizabethan and Jacobean periods, both the comedy of humours and the city comedy were popular alternatives to the romantic comedy; both of these subgenres take a satiric view of human behaviour, showing how ordinary humans let the faults in their own nature get the better of them. (Ben Jonson's city comedy *Volpone*, for example, focuses on the greed of various men and the foolish behaviour that greed generates.) In the Restoration period and through the eighteenth century the **comedy of manners** (exemplified by Sheridan's *The School for Scandal*) was likewise focused on human folly, especially in terms of the way particular characteristics were associated with social class. The **farce** may be defined as a comedy that depicts broadly humourous situations, in which plot devices such as mistaken identities, plans gone awry, and surprise endings take precedent over the subtleties of characterization or thematic development. The farce has a very long history, from the Roman comedies of Plautus, which featured all manner of clever servants, braggart warriors, and disguised lovers, to Michael Frayn's 1982 play *Noises Off*, a somewhat metafictional farce about a theatre company's rehearsals and performance of *Nothing On*, a fictional play chiefly about people trying to get in and out of each others' bedrooms.

One of the most interesting grey areas between tragedy and comedy is the subgenre of the **tragicomedy**. In the classical period, the term was used by Plautus to describe the mixing of low- and high-born characters in a single play. Many of Shakespeare's so-called problem plays might also be thought to fit into the idea of tragicomedy as a catch-all category, whereby the marriages at the end of *A Winter's Tale* don't quite make up for the cruelty of Leontes and the suffering of Hermione. In the more contemporary period, playwrights such as Ibsen, Anton Chekhov, and Sean O'Casey experimented with the idea that everyday existence could be both funny and unhappy, often because a character—for example Chekhov's Uncle Vanya—mistakenly perceives him- or herself to be living a noble life. Many plays associated with the Theatre of the Absurd might be considered tragicomedies. In Beckett's *Krapp's Last Tape*, the audience is presented with a man who takes outlandish pleasure in eating bananas and repeating the word "Spool," but who is also faced with the emptiness of his life in old age. The metafictional plays of Pollock and Stoppard are similarly mixed in terms of the expectations they seem to raise, as both playwrights use wit to explore dark or complex themes.

[N.G.]

# William Shakespeare
## 1564–1616

The plays of Shakespeare have influenced literary culture more broadly and more deeply than almost any other group of texts in the English-speaking world. The imagery and poetic facility of his plays; their ways of telling stories; the variety and depth of their characterizations; their innovative dramatic qualities; their complex exploration of ideas—for all these qualities his work has been widely regarded as the highest achievement in English literature.

The son of a glove-maker and alderman, Shakespeare was born in Stratford-upon-Avon in 1564. He was probably educated at the local grammar school, but he did not go on to university; at the time, university attendance would have been highly unusual for a person from the middle class. When Shakespeare was 18, he married Anne Hathaway, with whom he had three children.

Probably in the late 1580s, Shakespeare moved to London and joined the professional theatre. At this time four permanent theatres had recently been established in the London area (all just beyond the city limits, so as to be outside the regulatory authority of the city). Their presence created a steady and ongoing demand for new plays, and helped to shape a new approach to theatre; whereas the travelling troupes of the early Elizabethan era had focused on plays that imitated Roman models (featuring long set-piece speeches, and keeping comedy and tragedy as entirely separate spheres), the new plays were filled with rapid movement and rapid dialogue. Comic characters and scenes were introduced into serious dramatic works, and plays began to depict characters of all sorts—commoners as well as nobles, women as well as men (though the women's roles were played by adolescent males—it was considered unseemly for women to appear on the stage). With remarkable speed the Elizabethan stage became the site of unprecedented vitality, sophistication, and theatrical agility; the list of accomplished playwrights who flourished in the 1590s and the early seventeenth century includes not only Shakespeare but also Christopher Marlowe, Ben Jonson, and dozens of others.

Unlike most other playwrights of the age, Shakespeare wrote in every major dramatic genre: history plays, including *Richard II*; comedies, such as *Much Ado About Nothing*; tragedies, notably *Hamlet* and *King Lear*; a series of tragicomical "romances," such as *The Tempest*; and the "problem plays" or "dark comedies," among them *All's Well That Ends Well*, that ambivalently mingle levity and bitterness.

Shakespeare's work appears to have been extremely well regarded in his own time—when he died Jonson lauded him as "soul of the age" and "the wonder of our stage." Before long a consensus had developed that his work was unrivalled in English literature. Although he often borrowed the basic elements of his stories from other sources, his characters were much more psychologically realistic than any that had previously been represented in English literature. He was also an innovator in his use of the English language, revealing its largely unexplored potential for subtle expression and even expanding its vocabulary—an estimated 1700 English words have their first known usage in Shakespeare's writing.

Twelfth Night has always remained among the most popular of Shakespeare's comedies. Its title alludes to the irreverence, reversals, and general misrule that obtained on the Feast of Epiphany, the culminating twelfth night of traditional Christmas revels. Infused with this festive spirit, Twelfth Night satirizes puritanical self-righteousness while playing in a variety of ways with the comedy of sexual identity. But like all of Shakespeare's finest comedies, it is not without serious undercurrents.

# Twelfth Night, or What You Will[1]

## DRAMATIS PERSONAE

Orsino, *Duke (or Count) of Illyria*[2]
Valentine, *gentleman attending on the Duke*
Curio, *gentleman attending on the Duke*

Viola, *later disguised as Cesario*
Sea Captain, *friend of Viola*
Sebastian, *twin brother of Viola*
Antonio, *a sea captain, friend of Sebastian*

---

1   *Twelfth Night ... Will* The present text has been edited for Broadview Press by David Swain, and is copyright © Broadview Press. *Twelfth Night* appeared in print for the first time in the First Folio of Shakespeare's works (1623). The 1623 text is remarkably clean and free of errors. There is evidence, however, that either the scribe of the copy-text or the compositor himself made some corrections. For instance, Orsino is called a duke four times in Act 1 but a count 13 times throughout, and in scene directions he is always *Duke*. Editors continue to debate inconsistencies in the plot such as that between Viola's stated intention to feign being a eunuch who sings and her actual disguise as a page, or the temporal problem of reconciling Viola and Orsino's three-day acquaintance with Sebastian and Antonio's three-month sojourn, with some arguing that Shakespeare or a printer must have revised the text and others (including the present editor) holding that these contradictions serve the play's deliberate indeterminacy. This edition restores readings from the First Folio that have traditionally been corrected for the sake of consistency. Spelling and punctuation have been modernized except where rhythm and character are better served by contractions and old spelling. Stage directions in square brackets have been inserted by the current editor; those appearing in parentheses derive from the First Folio.

2   *Illyria* Ancient, mysterious region on the Balkan peninsula bordering the Adriatic, although the play occupies an imagined geography and time.

Olivia, *a countess*
Maria, *Olivia's lady-in-waiting*
Sir Toby Belch, *uncle of Olivia*
Sir Andrew Aguecheek, *companion of Sir Toby*
Malvolio, *steward to Olivia*
Fabian, *servant to Olivia*
Feste, *a clown, servant to Olivia*

A Priest
First Officer
Second Officer
Lords, Musicians, Sailors, and other Attendants

## ACT 1, SCENE 1

([*Music.*] *Enter Orsino, Duke of Illyria, Curio, and other Lords.*)

| | |
|---|---|
| ORSINO.  If music be the food of love, play on, | |
| Give me excess of it that,° surfeiting, | *so that* |
| The appetite may sicken[1] and so die. | |
| That strain again, it had a dying fall.[2] | |
| O, it came o'er my ear like the sweet sound° | *spring breeze*  5 |
| That breathes upon a bank of violets,[3] | |
| Stealing and giving odour. Enough, no more, | |
| 'Tis not so sweet now as it was before. | |
| O spirit of love, how quick and fresh° art thou! | *lively and eager* |
| That, notwithstanding thy capacity | 10 |
| Receiveth as the sea, nought enters there, | |
| Of what validity° and pitch° so e'er, | *value / intensity* |
| But falls into abatement° and low price[4] | *depreciation* |
| Even in a minute. So full of shapes is fancy,° | *imagination* |
| That it alone is high fantastical.[5] | 15 |
| CURIO.  Will you go hunt, my lord? | |
| ORSINO.                              What, Curio? | |

---

1    *surfeiting ... sicken* I.e., exceeding its need (for music), my desire might grow sick of it.
2    *That strain ... fall* He orders the musicians to repeat a melancholy falling cadence.
3    *violets* Considered an antidote for melancholy.
4    *notwithstanding ... low price* I.e., capacious like the sea, love receives all sensations, but no matter their excellence, love quickly devalues and tires of them.
5    *So full of ... high fantastical* I.e., imagination is so full of envisioned forms (of love) that it alone is supremely creative (compared with the other mental faculties of reason and memory).

CURIO.                                             The hart.

ORSINO.  Why, so I do, the noblest that I have.[1]
    O, when mine eyes did see Olivia first,
    Methought she purged the air of pestilence.[2]
20    That instant was I turned into a hart,
    And my desires, like fell° and cruel hounds,          *fierce*
    E'er since pursue me.[3]

    (*Enter Valentine.*)

                      How now, what news from her?
VALENTINE.  So please my lord, I might not be admitted,[4]
25    But from her handmaid do return this answer:
    The element° itself, till seven years' heat,°       *sky / summers*
    Shall not behold her face at ample° view,           *full*
    But like a cloistress° she will veilèd walk,    *cloistered nun*
    And water once a day her chamber round
30    With eye-offending brine°—all this to season°  *tears / preserve*
    A brother's dead love, which she would keep fresh
    And lasting in her sad remembrance.
ORSINO.  O, she that hath a heart of that fine frame°  *exquisite form*
    To pay this debt of love but to a brother,
35    How will she love when the rich golden shaft°   *Cupid's arrow*
    Hath killed the flock of all affections else[5]
    That live in her—when liver, brain, and heart,
    These sovereign thrones,[6] are all supplied and filled,
    Her sweet perfections, with one selfsame king![7]
40    Away before me to sweet beds of flowers:
    Love-thoughts lie rich when canopied with bowers.

    (*Exeunt.*)

---

1    *hart ... I have* Punning on "hart" and "heart" (his noblest part).
2    *she purged ... pestilence* I.e., cleansed the air of plague (Renaissance medicine held that disease was propagated by noxious vapours).
3    *was I turned ... pursue me* In Ovid's *Metamorphoses*, after the hunter Actaeon sees Diana bathing, she turns him into a deer pursued by his own hounds.
4    *might not be admitted* I.e., was not allowed in (to see her).
5    *How will ... affections else* I.e., how much more might she love (me) when Cupid's arrow kills all other feelings.
6    *liver ... thrones* In Renaissance psychology, these organs were the respective seats ("thrones") of the faculties of passion, reason, and feeling.
7    *one selfsame king* I.e., myself as king (playing on "thrones"); in the First Folio, "one self king."

# ACT 1, SCENE 2

(*Enter Viola, a Captain, and Sailors.*)

VIOLA. What country, friends, is this?

CAPTAIN.                                              This is Illyria, lady.

VIOLA. And what should I do in Illyria?
My brother he is in Elysium.[1]
Perchance° he is not drowned. What think you, sailors?                     *Perhaps*

CAPTAIN. It is perchance° that you yourself were saved.                      *by chance*     5

VIOLA. O my poor brother! And so perchance may he be.

CAPTAIN. True, madam, and to comfort you with chance,°                    *possibility*
Assure yourself, after our ship did split,
When you, and those poor number saved with you,
Hung on our driving° boat, I saw your brother,                               *drifting*   10
Most provident° in peril, bind himself—                                     *far-thinking*
Courage and hope both teaching him the practice—
To a strong mast that lived° upon the sea,                                   *floated*
Where, like Arion on the dolphin's back,
I saw him hold acquaintance with the waves[2]                                                15
So long as I could see.

VIOLA.                        For saying so, there's gold. [*Gives him money.*]
Mine own escape unfoldeth to° my hope,                                      *encourages*
Whereto thy speech serves for authority,
The like of him.[3] Know'st thou this country?

CAPTAIN. Ay, madam, well, for I was bred and born                                           20
Not three hours' travel from this very place.

VIOLA. Who governs here?

CAPTAIN. A noble duke, in nature as in name.

VIOLA. What is his name?

CAPTAIN.                        Orsino.

VIOLA. Orsino! I have heard my father name him.                                             25
He was a bachelor then.

CAPTAIN. And so is now, or was so very late,°                               *recently*
For but a month ago I went from hence,
And then 'twas fresh in murmur°—as, you know,                               *newly rumoured*
What great ones° do, the less° will prattle of—                 *nobility / commoners*   30
That he did seek the love of fair Olivia.

---

1    *Elysium* In Greek mythology, the state or place of happiness after death.

2    *Arion … waves* In Ovid's *Fasti*, the poet Arion escapes murder at sea by jumping over-
     board and playing his lyre for the dolphins, who bear him ashore.

3    *The like of him* I.e., that he also escaped alive.

VIOLA. What's she?[1]

CAPTAIN.  A virtuous maid, the daughter of a count
　　That died some twelvemonth since, then leaving her
35　In the protection of his son, her brother,
　　Who shortly also died, for whose dear love,
　　They say, she hath abjured° the sight　　　　　　　　　　　*renounced*
　　And company of men.[2]

VIOLA.　　　　　　　　　O that I served that lady,
　　And might not be delivered° to the world　　　　　　　　*revealed*
40　Till I had made mine own occasion mellow°　　　　　　　*ripen*
　　What my estate is.[3]

CAPTAIN.　　　　　　　That were hard to compass,°　　　*bring about*
　　Because she will admit no kind of suit,
　　No, not° the Duke's.　　　　　　　　　　　　　　　*not even*

VIOLA. There is a fair behaviour° in thee, Captain,　　　　*conduct*
45　And though that nature with a beauteous wall
　　Doth oft close in pollution,[4] yet of thee
　　I will believe thou hast a mind that suits
　　With this thy fair and outward character.°　　　　　　　*appearance*
　　I prithee°—and I'll pay thee bounteously—　　　　　　*pray thee*
50　Conceal me what I am,[5] and be my aid
　　For such disguise as haply shall become°　　　　　　　*suit*
　　The form of my intent.[6] I'll serve this duke.
　　Thou shalt present me as an eunuch[7] to him.
　　It may be worth thy pains, for I can sing,
55　And speak to him in many sorts of music
　　That will allow° me very worth his service.　　　　　　*prove*
　　What else may hap,° to time I will commit,　　　　　　*happen*
　　Only shape thou thy silence to my wit.[8]

---

1　*What's she?* I.e., what is her rank and situation?

2　*the sight / And company of men* Some editors alter the First Folio text to read "the com-
　pany / And sight of men."

3　*Till I … estate is* I.e., until I determined the time was right to reveal my rank.

4　*a beauteous wall … pollution* I.e., a wall of beauty often encloses a corrupt nature.

5　*Conceal me what I am* I.e., do not reveal that I am a woman.

6　*form of my intent* I.e., shape of my strategy (and her male appearance).

7　*eunuch* Castrato, a castrated male soprano, which explains "I can sing." But Viola never
　sings and is disguised as a page, leading some editors to argue that the text was revised but
　retains unresolved inconsistencies.

8　*shape thou … my wit* I.e., be prepared to keep quiet where my ingenuity requires
　it; *wit* Mental agility (associated with verbal skill and improvisation).

CAPTAIN.  Be you his eunuch, and your mute[1] I'll be.

When my tongue blabs, then let mine eyes not see.[2]    60

VIOLA.  I thank thee. Lead me on.

(*Exeunt.*)

## ACT 1, SCENE 3

(*Enter Sir Toby [Belch] and Maria.*)

SIR TOBY.  What a plague[3] means my niece to take the death of her brother thus? I am sure care's an enemy to life.[4]

MARIA.  By my troth,[5] Sir Toby, you must come in earlier a-nights. Your cousin, my lady, takes great exceptions to your ill[6] hours.

SIR TOBY.  Why, let her except, before excepted.[7]    5

MARIA.  Ay, but you must confine yourself within the modest limits of order.

SIR TOBY.  Confine? I'll confine myself no finer than I am.[8] These clothes are good enough to drink in, and so be these boots too; an[9] they be not, let them hang themselves in their own straps.

MARIA.  That quaffing and drinking will undo you. I heard my lady talk of    10
it yesterday, and of a foolish knight that you brought in one night here to be her wooer.

SIR TOBY.  Who, Sir Andrew Aguecheek?[10]

MARIA.  Ay, he.

SIR TOBY.  He's as tall[11] a man as any's in Illyria.    15

MARIA.  What's that to the purpose?

SIR TOBY.  Why, he has three thousand ducats a year.

MARIA.  Ay, but he'll have but a year in all these ducats.[12] He's a very fool and a prodigal.[13]

---

1    *your mute* Tongueless servant (mutes attended eunuchs who guarded Turkish harems).

2    *When my ... not see* I.e., if I betray you, blind me.

3    *What a plague* Equivalent to "what the devil."

4    *care's an enemy to life* I.e., excessive mourning will drive her to an early grave.

5    *By my troth* I.e., by my faith (a mild oath).

6    *ill* Late.

7    *except ... excepted* I.e., make whatever exceptions (playing on Latin legal jargon, *exceptis excipiendis*, "except for the previously mentioned exceptions").

8    *I'll confine ... I am* I.e., not restrain myself with any more social refinement than is natural to me (literally, bind my figure no thinner).

9    *an* If.

10   *Aguecheek* Suggesting a pale, lean complexion from an ague (fever).

11   *tall* Worthy, but taken literally.

12   *he'll have ... ducats* I.e., he'll soon be broke.

13   *prodigal* Spendthrift.

20   SIR TOBY.  Fie that you'll say so! He plays o' the viol-de-gamboys,[1] and speaks three or four languages word for word without book,[2] and hath all the good gifts[3] of nature.

      MARIA.  He hath indeed, almost natural,[4] for besides that he's a fool, he's a great quarreller, and but that he hath the gift of a coward to allay the gust[5]

25   he hath in quarrelling, 'tis thought among the prudent he would quickly have the gift of a grave.[6]

      SIR TOBY.  By this hand, they are scoundrels and substractors[7] that say so of him. Who are they?

      MARIA.  They that add,[8] moreover, he's drunk nightly in your company.

30   SIR TOBY.  With drinking healths to my niece; I'll drink to her as long as there is a passage in my throat and drink in Illyria. He's a coward and a coystrill[9] that will not drink to my niece till his brains turn o' the toe like a parish-top.[10] What wench, *Castiliano vulgo*![11] for here comes Sir Andrew Agueface.

      *(Enter Sir Andrew [Aguecheek].)*

      SIR ANDREW.  Sir Toby Belch! How now, Sir Toby Belch!

35   SIR TOBY.  Sweet Sir Andrew.

      SIR ANDREW.  Bless you, fair shrew.[12]

      MARIA.  And you too, sir.

      SIR TOBY.  Accost, Sir Andrew, accost.[13]

      SIR ANDREW.  What's[14] that?

40   SIR TOBY.  My niece's chambermaid.[15]

---

1   *viol-de-gamboys* Viola da gamba, a bass viol held between the legs (with an innuendo on "gamboys").

2   *without book* By memory.

3   *gifts* Talents.

4   *almost natural* I.e., nearly a born simpleton.

5   *gust* Appetite.

6   *but that he … a grave* I.e., if he were not such a coward his habit of picking fights would earn him a quick death.

7   *substractors* Detractors, slanderers (a tipsy malapropism). "Substract" is an archaic form of "subtract."

8   *add* Playing on "substract."

9   *coystrill* Low fellow (literally, a horse groom).

10   *parish-top* Large top spun with a whip, provided by parishes for exercise and entertainment.

11   *Castiliano vulgo* Equivalent to "speak of the devil" (although the derivation is uncertain, the phrase perhaps means "base Castilian" and draws upon popular stereotypes of evil Spaniards).

12   *shrew* Woman, a generic use intended as a compliment (otherwise meaning "scold").

13   *accost* Address courteously or woo; originally, a naval term for "go alongside."

14   *What's* Who is.

15   *chambermaid* Lady-in-waiting.

SIR ANDREW.  Good Mistress Accost, I desire better acquaintance.

MARIA.  My name is Mary, sir.

SIR ANDREW.  Good Mistress Mary Accost—

SIR TOBY.  You mistake, knight. "Accost" is front her, board her, woo her, assail her.[1]                                                                                    45

SIR ANDREW.  By my troth, I would not undertake her[2] in this company. Is that the meaning of "accost?"

MARIA.  Fare you well, gentlemen. [*leaving*]

SIR TOBY.  An thou let part so,[3] Sir Andrew, would thou mightst never draw sword[4] again.                                                                               50

SIR ANDREW.  An you part so, mistress, I would I might never draw sword again. Fair lady, do you think you have fools in hand?[5]

MARIA.  Sir, I have not you by the hand.

SIR ANDREW.  Marry, but you shall have, and here's my hand.

MARIA.  [*taking his hand*] Now, sir, thought is free.[6] I pray you, bring your  55
hand to th' buttery-bar[7] and let it drink.

SIR ANDREW.  Wherefore, sweetheart? What's your metaphor?[8]

MARIA.  It's dry,[9] sir.

SIR ANDREW.  Why, I think so. I am not such an ass but I can keep my hand dry.[10] But what's your jest?                                                           60

MARIA.  A dry jest,[11] sir.

SIR ANDREW.  Are you full of them?

MARIA.  Ay, sir, I have them at my fingers' ends;[12] marry, now I let go your hand, I am barren.[13]

(*Exit Maria.*)

---

1    *front her … assail her*  Naval terms of battle (each with innuendo).

2    *undertake her*  I.e., take her on (with innuendo).

3    *An thou let part so*  I.e., if you let her part like this (without "accosting" her).

4    *draw sword*  I.e., be gentlemanly.

5    *fools in hand*  I.e., are dealing with fools.

6    *thought is free*  Proverbial answer to "do you think I'm a fool?"

7    *buttery-bar*  Shelf formed by the open hatch to a butter (or bottle) room (in performance, she would bring his hand to her breasts).

8    *What's your metaphor*  I.e., what does a drinking hand signify?

9    *dry*  Thirsty (but also weak or impotent).

10    *an ass … hand dry*  A proverbial response, as in "any fool can keep his head dry."

11    *dry jest*  I.e., foolish joke (a joke for a fool).

12    *at my fingers' ends*  I.e., always ready (literally, "by the hand").

13    *barren*  I.e., empty of jokes (playing on "full," also meaning "pregnant").

65   SIR TOBY. O knight, thou lack'st a cup of canary![1] When did I see thee so put
      down?[2]

SIR ANDREW. Never in your life, I think, unless you see canary put me down.[3]
      Methinks sometimes I have no more wit than a Christian[4] or an ordinary man
      has, but I am a great eater of beef, and I believe that does harm to my wit.[5]

70   SIR TOBY. No question.

SIR ANDREW. An I thought that, I'd forswear it.[6] I'll ride home tomorrow,
      Sir Toby.

SIR TOBY. *Pourquoi*,[7] my dear knight?

SIR ANDREW. What is "pourquoi?" Do, or not do? I would I had bestowed
75    that time in the tongues[8] that I have in fencing, dancing, and bear-baiting.
      Oh, had I but followed the arts![9]

SIR TOBY. Then hadst thou had an excellent head of hair.[10]

SIR ANDREW. Why, would that have mended my hair?

SIR TOBY. Past question,[11] for thou seest it will not curl by nature.[12]

80   SIR ANDREW. But it becomes me well enough, does't not?

SIR TOBY. Excellent. It hangs like flax on a distaff,[13] and I hope to see a house-
      wife take thee between her legs and spin it off.[14]

SIR ANDREW. Faith, I'll home to-morrow, Sir Toby. Your niece will not be
      seen, or if she be, it's four to one she'll none of me. The Count[15] himself
85    here hard by[16] woos her.

---

1    *canary* Sweet wine from the Canary Islands.
2    *so put down* Dejected.
3    *put me down* I.e., make me pass out.
4    *Christian* Common.
5    *great eater … to my wit* Renaissance dietary manuals cautioned that beef made the intel-
      lect sluggish.
6    *An I … forswear it* I.e., if I really believed that, I'd swear off beef.
7    *Pourquoi* French: why.
8    *tongues* Languages.
9    *the arts* Liberal arts.
10   *excellent head of hair* Punning on "tongues" (pronounced "tongs") and "curling-tongs."
11   *Past question* Without a doubt.
12   *nature* Playing off *the arts*.
13   *flax on a distaff* Straw-coloured fibre spun (usually by a housewife) on a cleft pole held
      between the knees; *flax* Flaxen hair was thought to indicate cowardice and anger; *dis-
      taff* Woman's work, a wife's duties.
14   *housewife … spin it off* In the First Folio "huswife," suggesting "hussy" or "prosti-
      tute"; *spin it off* Make you lose your hair (thought to be a symptom of venereal disease).
15   *Count* Orsino is consistently called a duke in stage directions and speech headings, but
      in the text he is called a duke only in the first two scenes and in 1.4.1, after which he is
      always called a count. This inconsistency might be due to scribal errors, but may also re-
      flect Shakespeare's habit of making counts young lovers and dukes older men of authority
      (Orsino combines both).
16   *hard by* Nearby.

SIR TOBY. She'll none o' the Count. She'll not match above her degree, neither in estate, years, nor wit,[1] I have heard her swear't. Tut, there's life in't,[2]
man.

SIR ANDREW. I'll stay a month longer. I am a fellow o' th' strangest mind in
the world. I delight in masques and revels sometimes altogether.[3]          90

SIR TOBY. Art thou good at these kickshawses,[4] knight?

SIR ANDREW. As any man in Illyria, whatsoever he be, under the degree of
my betters; and yet I will not compare with an old man.[5]

SIR TOBY. What is thy excellence in a galliard,[6] knight?

SIR ANDREW. Faith, I can cut a caper.[7]          95

SIR TOBY. And I can cut the mutton[8] to't.

SIR ANDREW. And I think I have the back-trick[9] simply as strong as any man
in Illyria.

SIR TOBY. Wherefore are these things hid? Wherefore have these gifts a curtain before 'em? Are they like to take dust, like Mistress Mall's[10] picture?   100
Why dost thou not go to church in a galliard and come home in a coranto?[11]
My very walk should be a jig. I would not so much as make water[12] but
in a sink-a-pace.[13] What dost thou mean? Is it a world to hide virtues in? I

1   *She'll not match ... wit* She won't marry above her rank, age, or education (Olivia is a countess, so Orsino's actual rank must be higher).

2   *there's life in't* Proverbial: "While there is life, there is hope."

3   *masques and revels* Courtly entertainments featuring dancing; *altogether* In all respects.

4   *kickshawses* Dainty dishes (referring to dances), trifles; a corruption of the French *quelque
chose*, "something."

5   *any man ... old man* I.e., any man who is not above me in rank; but I don't compare to
an expert (suggesting Toby's experience, but also his age).

6   *galliard* Lively five-step dance in triple time.

7   *caper* Leap before the fifth step in a *galliard*, but also a delicacy used in a sauce for mutton.

8   *mutton* Slang for prostitute.

9   *back-trick* Back-step in the *galliard*.

10  *Mistress Mall's* Like *Moll*, *Mall* was a nickname for Mary, and here is probably used
generically as an example of a woman's portrait. At this time, *Moll* is also beginning to
signify a disgraced woman, especially a prostitute, and many candidates have been proposed for this allusion, ranging from Olivia's lady-in-waiting, Maria, to Mary Frith (also
known as Moll Cutpurse), a cross-dressing purse thief first arrested in 1600 and sensa-
tionalized in Thomas Dekker and Thomas Middleton's play *The Roaring Girl* (1611). In
combination with *go to church in a galliard*, this may also be a mocking reference to the
Puritan disapproval of idolatrous images (such as the Virgin Mary) as well as dancing
and plays.

11  *coranto* Running dance.

12  *make water* Urinate.

13  *sink-a-pace* Cinque pace, a "five-step" dance equivalent to a *galliard* (punning on *sink*,
sewer).

did think, by the excellent constitution of thy leg, it was formed under the
105    star[1] of a galliard.

SIR ANDREW. Ay, 'tis strong, and it does indifferent[2] well in dun-coloured
stock.[3] Shall we set about some revels?

SIR TOBY. What shall we do else? Were we not born under Taurus?

SIR ANDREW. Taurus? That's sides and heart.

110    SIR TOBY. No, sir; it is legs and thighs.[4] Let me see the caper. Ha, higher! Ha,
ha, excellent.

(*Exeunt.*)


## ACT 1, SCENE 4

(*Enter Valentine, and Viola in man's attire.*)

VALENTINE. If the Duke continue these favours towards you, Cesario,[5] you
are like to be much advanced.[6] He hath known you but three days,[7] and
already you are no stranger.

VIOLA. You either fear his humour[8] or my negligence, that you call in ques-
5    tion the continuance of his love. Is he inconstant, sir, in his favours?

VALENTINE. No, believe me.

(*Enter [Orsino], Curio, and Attendants.*)

VIOLA. I thank you. Here comes the Count.

ORSINO. Who saw Cesario, ho?

VIOLA. On your attendance,° my lord, here.                           *at your service*

10    ORSINO. [*to Curio and Attendants*] Stand you awhile aloof. Cesario,
Thou know'st no less but all.° I have unclasped                      *than everything*
To thee[9] the book even of my secret soul.°                         *private feelings*
Therefore, good youth, address thy gait[10] unto her.

---

1    *star* Astrological sign.
2    *does indifferent* Does tolerably.
3    *dun-coloured stock* Beige stockings. In the First Folio "dam'd coloured"; some editors substitute "flame-" or "divers-coloured."
4    *born under Taurus … and thighs* Renaissance anatomy charts assigned the zodiac to parts
of the body; Taurus the bull governed the throat (i.e., a sign for drinkers).
5    *Cesario* Viola's adopted name.
6    *advanced* Promoted.
7    *but three days* This line introduces a double-time problem, for in 5.1.88 three months are
said to have elapsed in the same time-frame as Viola's service to Orsino.
8    *fear his humour* Doubt his character (implying he is "inconstant").
9    *Thou know'st … To thee* Orsino uses the familiar forms *thou* and *thee*.
10   *address thy gait* Direct your steps.

Be not denied access, stand at her doors,
And tell them there thy fixèd foot shall grow°                                    *take root*    15
Till thou have audience.

VIOLA.                              Sure,° my noble lord,                              *But*
If she be so abandoned° to her sorrow                                              *given up*
As it is spoke, she never will admit me.

ORSINO.  Be clamorous and leap all civil bounds,[1]
Rather than make unprofited° return.                                              *unsuccessful*    20

VIOLA.  Say I do speak with her, my lord, what then?

ORSINO.  O, then unfold° the passion of my love,                                  *display*
Surprise[2] her with discourse of my dear faith.
It shall become thee well[3] to act my woes,
She will attend it better in thy youth                                                                    25
Than in a nuncio's° of more grave aspect.°          *messenger's / appearance*

VIOLA.  I think not so, my lord.

ORSINO.                              Dear lad, believe it,
For they shall yet° belie thy happy years°                                *as yet / youth*
That say thou art a man: Diana's lip
Is not more smooth and rubious;° thy small pipe°          *ruby red / voice*    30
Is as the maiden's organ, shrill° and sound,°              *high / unbroken*
And all is semblative a woman's part.[4]
I know thy constellation[5] is right apt
For this affair. [*to Curio and Attendants*] Some four or five attend him—
All, if you will, for I myself am best                                                                    35
When least in company. Prosper well° in this,                              *succeed*
And thou shalt live as freely° as thy lord,                          *independently*
To call his fortunes thine.

VIOLA.                              I'll do my best
To woo your lady. [*aside*] Yet, a barful strife[6]—
Whoe'er I woo, myself would be his wife.                                                                    40

---

1    *leap all civil bounds* I.e., disregard all constraints of politeness.
2    *Surprise* Capture unawares (a military term).
3    *become thee well* I.e., suit your strategy best.
4    *semblative a woman's part* Resembling a woman's voice (or acting role).
5    *constellation* Character and ability (thought to be predetermined by astrology).
6    *barful strife* Conflict full of obstacles ("bars").

## ACT 1, Scene 5

*(Enter Maria and [Feste,[1] a] clown.)*

MARIA.  Nay, either tell me where thou hast been, or I will not open my lips so wide as a bristle may enter in way[2] of thy excuse. My lady will hang thee for thy absence.

FESTE.  Let her hang me. He that is well hanged in this world needs to fear
5    no colours.[3]

MARIA.  Make that good.[4]

FESTE.  He shall see none to fear.

MARIA.  A good lenten[5] answer. I can tell thee where that saying was born, of "I fear no colours."

10  FESTE.  Where, good Mistress Mary?

MARIA.  In the wars, and that[6] may you be bold to say in your foolery.

FESTE.  Well, God give them wisdom that have it, and those that are fools, let them use their talents.[7]

MARIA.  Yet you will be hanged for being so long absent, or to be turned
15    away[8]—is not that as good as a hanging to you?

FESTE.  Many a good hanging prevents a bad marriage;[9] and for turning away, let summer bear it out.[10]

MARIA.  You are resolute, then?

FESTE.  Not so, neither; but I am resolved on two points.[11]

20  MARIA.  That if one break, the other will hold; or if both break, your gaskins[12] fall.

FESTE.  Apt, in good faith, very apt. Well, go thy way. If Sir Toby would leave drinking, thou wert as witty a piece of Eve's flesh[13] as any in Illyria.

---

1    *Feste* Pronounced "fest-ay," from the Latin or Italian *festa,* "festival."

2    *in way* By way.

3    *He that ... fear no colours* Proverbial: "only the dead have no one to fear"; *colours* Military flags (punning on "collars," hangman's nooses).

4    *Make that good* Explain that.

5    *lenten* Meagre (Lent is a time of fasting).

6    *that* Referring to either "in the wars" or "fear no colours" (i.e., he should be clearer and braver).

7    *God give ... their talents* I.e., let the wise make the most of their wisdom, and fools the most of their comic talents (paraphrasing the parable of the talents in Matthew 25.29).

8    *turned away* Dismissed.

9    *Many a good ... bad marriage* Proverbial: "better to be half hanged than badly married" (with innuendo on "good hanging").

10   *bear it out* Make it endurable; masterless men were considered vagabonds by law and were either imprisoned or forced into homeless wandering.

11   *points* Matters, but also laces that tied breeches to a doublet.

12   *gaskins* Wide breeches.

13   *If Sir Toby ... Eve's flesh* I.e., if Toby were sober, he'd appreciate what a clever woman you are.

MARIA. Peace, you rogue, no more o' that. Here comes my lady. Make your excuse wisely, you were best.[1]                                                  25

[*Exit.*]

(*Enter Lady Olivia, with Malvolio*[2] [*and Attendants.*])

FESTE. Wit, an't be thy will,[3] put me into good fooling![4] Those wits that think they have[5] thee do very oft prove fools, and I that am sure I lack[6] thee may pass for a wise man. For what says Quinapalus?[7] "Better a witty fool than a foolish wit." God bless thee, lady.

OLIVIA. Take the fool away.                                                  30

FESTE. Do you not hear, fellows? Take away the lady.

OLIVIA. Go to,[8] y'are a dry[9] fool. I'll no more of you. Besides, you grow dishonest.[10]

FESTE. Two faults, madonna,[11] that drink and good counsel will amend, for give the dry fool drink, then is the fool not dry.[12] Bid the dishonest man   35 mend[13] himself: if he mend, he is no longer dishonest; if he cannot, let the botcher[14] mend him. Anything that's mended is but patched,[15] virtue that transgresses is but patched with sin, and sin that amends is but patched with virtue. If that this simple syllogism[16] will serve, so. If it will not, what remedy? As there is no true cuckold but calamity, so beauty's   40 a flower.[17] The lady bade take away the fool, therefore I say again, take her away.

OLIVIA. Sir, I bade them take away you.

---

1   *you were best* I.e., if you know what's best.
2   *Malvolio* "Ill-will," from Italian *mal* (bad) and *voglia* (desire).
3   *will* Desire.
4   *Wit, an't be ... good fooling* Mock invocation of his muse, the spirit of ingenuity, to inspire his performance.
5   *have* Outwit.
6   *lack* Fall short of.
7   *Quinapalus* Nonsense classical authority.
8   *Go to* Enough.
9   *dry* Empty.
10  *dishonest* Unfaithful.
11  *madonna* My lady.
12  *dry* Thirsty.
13  *mend* Reform.
14  *botcher* Clothes mender.
15  *patched* Imperfect, but alluding to fools' costumes, which were sewn from mismatched cloth.
16  *syllogism* Logical argument from two claims (here, regarding "virtue" and "sin").
17  *no true ... a flower* I.e., nothing less faithful than calamity (if you are wedded to it), so beauty will fade (by the time Olivia is done mourning).

FESTE. Misprision[1] in the highest degree! Lady, "*Cucullus non facit monach-*
45   *um*";[2] that's as much to say as I wear not motley[3] in my brain. Good madonna, give me leave to prove you a fool.

OLIVIA. Can you do it?

FESTE. Dexteriously,[4] good madonna.

OLIVIA. Make your proof.

50   FESTE. I must catechize[5] you for it, madonna. Good my mouse[6] of virtue,
answer me.

OLIVIA. Well, sir, for want of other idleness, I'll bide[7] your proof.

FESTE. Good madonna, why mourn'st thou?

OLIVIA. Good fool, for my brother's death.

55   FESTE. I think his soul is in hell, madonna.

OLIVIA. I know his soul is in heaven, fool.

FESTE. The more fool, madonna, to mourn for your brother's soul, being in
heaven. Take away the fool, gentlemen.

OLIVIA. What think you of this fool, Malvolio? Doth he not mend?[8]

60   MALVOLIO. Yes, and shall do, till the pangs of death shake him. Infirmity,[9]
that decays the wise, doth ever make the better fool.

FESTE. God send you, sir, a speedy infirmity,[10] for the better increasing your
folly. Sir Toby will be sworn that I am no fox, but he will not pass[11] his word
for twopence that you are no fool.[12]

65   OLIVIA. How say you to that, Malvolio?

MALVOLIO. I marvel your ladyship takes delight in such a barren rascal. I
saw him put down the other day with an ordinary fool[13] that has no more
brain than a stone. Look you now, he's out of his guard[14] already. Unless
you laugh and minister[15] occasion to him, he is gagged. I protest I take

---

1   *Misprision* Misunderstanding, wrongful arrest.

2   *Cucullus non facit monachum* Latin: the cowl does not make the monk.

3   *motley* Many-coloured ("patched") costume worn by fools.

4   *Dexteriously* Dextrously.

5   *catechize you* Question you; the Catechism tested the orthodoxy of one's faith through a
series of formal questions and answers.

6   *Good my mouse* My good mouse (a term of endearment).

7   *idleness* Pastime; *bide* Endure.

8   *mend* I.e., improve his fooling.

9   *Infirmity* Senility.

10   *speedy infirmity* Playing on "speedy recovery."

11   *pass* Give.

12   *no fox ... no fool* I.e., not cunning, but he won't swear you aren't sly.

13   *ordinary fool* Common fool, but also a fool who frequents an ordinary, a commoners'
tavern (alluding to a popular tavern-fool named Stone).

14   *out of his guard* Off guard.

15   *minister* Provide.

these wise men that crow so at these set[1] kind of fools no better than the    70
fools' zanies.[2]

OLIVIA.  O, you are sick of[3] self-love, Malvolio, and taste with a distempered[4]
appetite. To be generous, guiltless, and of free disposition, is to take those
things for bird-bolts that you deem cannon bullets.[5] There is no slander in
an allowed fool, though he do nothing but rail, nor no railing in known    75
discreet man, though he do nothing but reprove.[6]

FESTE.  Now Mercury endue thee with leasing,[7] for thou speak'st well of fools.

([*Re-*]*enter Maria.*)

MARIA.  Madam, there is at the gate a young gentleman much[8] desires to
speak with you.

OLIVIA.  From the Count Orsino, is it?    80

MARIA.  I know not, madam. 'Tis a fair young man, and well attended.

OLIVIA.  Who of my people hold him in delay?

MARIA.  Sir Toby, madam, your kinsman.

OLIVIA.  Fetch him off, I pray you, he speaks nothing but madman.[9] Fie on
him. [*Exit Maria.*] Go you, Malvolio; if it be a suit from the Count, I am    85
sick, or not at home—what you will[10] to dismiss it. (*Exit Malvolio.*) Now
you see, sir, how your fooling grows old, and people dislike it.

FESTE.  Thou hast spoke for us, madonna, as if thy eldest son should be a
fool,[11] whose skull Jove cram with brains, for—here he comes—

(*Enter Sir Toby.*)

one of thy kin has a most weak *pia mater*.[12]    90

OLIVIA.  By mine honour, half drunk. What is he[13] at the gate, cousin?

SIR TOBY.  A gentleman.

---

1    *set* Rehearsed.

2    *zanies* Buffoons, from Italian *zanni*: comic sidekicks in *commedia dell'arte*.

3    *of* From.

4    *distempered* Unhealthy.

5    *to take those things ... cannon bullets* I.e., to be optimistic where you are pessimistic; *bird-bolts* Blunt crossbow arrows for birding.

6    *no slander ... nothing but reprove* Fools traditionally had licence to reprove their masters while stewards were trusted to regulate a household by maintaining decorum among its members.

7    *leasing* Lying (Mercury was the god of deception).

8    *much* Who much.

9    *nothing but madman* Madman's talk.

10    *what you will* Do whatever you like.

11    *thy eldest ... a fool* Playing on the parable "a wise man has a foolish son."

12    *pia mater* Latin: brain (literally "tender mother").

13    *What is he* I.e., what is his rank and situation.

OLIVIA. A gentleman? What gentleman?

SIR TOBY. 'Tis a gentleman here. [*Belches.*] A plague o' these pickle-herring!
95   How now, sot!¹

FESTE. Good Sir Toby.

OLIVIA. Cousin, cousin, how have you come so early by this lethargy?²

SIR TOBY. Lechery? I defy lechery. There's one at the gate.³

OLIVIA. Ay, marry,⁴ what is he?

100  SIR TOBY. Let him be the devil an he will, I care not. Give me faith, say I.
Well, it's all one.⁵ (*Exit.*)

OLIVIA. What's a drunken man like, fool?

FESTE. Like a drowned man, a fool, and a madman: one draught above heat⁶
makes him a fool; the second mads him; and a third drowns him.

105  OLIVIA. Go thou and seek the crowner, and let him sit o' my coz⁷ for he's in
the third degree of drink, he's drowned. Go look after him.

FESTE. He is but mad yet, madonna, and the fool shall look to the madman.
[*Exit.*]

(*Enter Malvolio.*)

MALVOLIO. Madam, yond young fellow swears he will speak with you. I told
him you were sick. He takes on him⁸ to understand so much, and therefore
110  comes to speak with you. I told him you were asleep, he seems to have a
foreknowledge of that too, and therefore comes to speak with you. What is
to be said to him, lady? He's fortified against any denial.

OLIVIA. Tell him he shall not speak with me.

MALVOLIO. H'as⁹ been told so, and he says he'll stand at your door like a
115  sheriff's post,¹⁰ and be the supporter¹¹ to a bench, but he'll speak with you.

OLIVIA. What kind o' man is he?

MALVOLIO. Why, of mankind.¹²

---

1   *sot* Fool.
2   *lethargy* Drunken stupor.
3   *There's one at the gate* He resumes announcing the visitor.
4   *marry* Indeed.
5   *Give me faith … it's all one* Toby winks at two controversies of Reformation faith, the Protestant doctrine of salvation by faith (not works), and the theory that some theological debates were indifferent (or "all one") and thus inessential to salvation.
6   *above heat* I.e., beyond normal body temperature; wine was thought to alter personality by heating the body beyond its temperate state.
7   *crowner … my coz* Coroner, and let him hold an inquest for my cousin.
8   *takes on him* Claims.
9   *H'as* He has.
10  *sheriff's post* Decorative post placed before the houses of mayors and sheriffs.
11  *supporter* Support.
12  *of mankind* I.e., an ordinary man.

OLIVIA.  What manner of man?

MALVOLIO.  Of very ill manner—he'll speak with you, will you or no.

OLIVIA.  Of what personage and years is he?                                    120

MALVOLIO.  Not yet old enough for a man, nor young enough for a boy, as
a squash is before 'tis a peascod, or a codling[1] when 'tis almost an apple.
'Tis with him in standing water,[2] between boy and man. He is very well-
favoured,[3] and he speaks very shrewishly.[4] One would think his mother's
milk were scarce out of him.[5]                                               125

OLIVIA.  Let him approach. Call in my gentlewoman.

MALVOLIO.  Gentlewoman, my lady calls.

   (*Exit.*)

   (*Enter Maria.*)

OLIVIA.  Give me my veil; come, throw it o'er my face.
We'll once more hear Orsino's embassy.[6]

   (*Enter [Viola as Cesario.]*)

VIOLA.  The honourable lady of the house, which is she?                       130

OLIVIA.  Speak to me, I shall answer for her. Your will?

VIOLA.  Most radiant, exquisite, and unmatchable beauty—[*to Maria*] I pray
you tell me if this be the lady of the house, for I never saw her. I would be
loath to cast away my speech, for besides that it is excellently well penned,
I have taken great pains to con[7] it. Good beauties, let me sustain no scorn; 135
I am very comptible, even to the least sinister usage.[8]

OLIVIA.  Whence came you, sir?

VIOLA.  I can say little more than I have studied,[9] and that question's out of
my part. Good gentle one, give me modest assurance if you be the lady of
the house, that I may proceed in my speech.                                   140

OLIVIA.  Are you a comedian?[10]

---

1   *squash* Undeveloped peapod ("peascod"); *codling* Unripe apple.
2   *in standing water* I.e., like the turning tide, midway.
3   *well-favoured* Attractive.
4   *shrewishly* I.e., in a squeaky voice (like a shrew).
5   *mother's milk ... him* Barely weaned (proverbial).
6   *embassy* Message.
7   *con* Memorize.
8   *let me sustain ... sinister usage* I.e., do not scorn me; I am sensitive, even to the slightest
    rudeness (addressing Maria and attendants).
9   *than I have studied* I.e., other than what I have rehearsed ("my part").
10  *comedian* Actor.

VIOLA.   No, my profound heart;[1] and yet—by the very fangs of malice[2] I
swear—I am not that[3] I play. Are you the lady of the house?

OLIVIA.   If I do not usurp[4] myself, I am.

145 VIOLA.   Most certain, if you are she, you do usurp yourself, for what is yours
to bestow is not yours to reserve. But this is from[5] my commission. I will
on with my speech in your praise, and then show you the heart of my
message.

OLIVIA.   Come to what is important in't. I forgive you[6] the praise.

150 VIOLA.   Alas, I took great pains to study it, and 'tis poetical.

OLIVIA.   It is[7] the more like to be feigned,[8] I pray you keep it in.[9] I heard
you were saucy[10] at my gates, and allowed your approach rather to wonder
at you than to hear you. If you be mad,[11] be gone. If you have reason, be
brief. 'Tis not that time of moon with me to make one in so skipping a
155 dialogue.[12]

MARIA.   Will you hoist sail, sir? Here lies your way.

VIOLA.   No, good swabber, I am to hull[13] here a little longer. [to Olivia] Some
mollification for your giant,[14] sweet lady.

OLIVIA.   Tell me your mind.[15]

160 VIOLA.   I am a messenger.

OLIVIA.   Sure, you have some hideous matter to deliver, when the courtesy[16]
of it is so fearful. Speak your office.

---

1    *my profound heart* By my soul.
2    *very fangs of malice* Equivalent to "all that is evil" (a strong oath).
3    *that* The character.
4    *usurp* Misrepresent.
5    *from* Not in.
6    *forgive you* Excuse.
7    *It is* As it is.
8    *and 'tis poetical … feigned* Lyrical and dramatic poetry were considered fiction (unlike
     history or philosophy), and Renaissance critics of imaginative literature suspected that
     eloquent ("poetical") language misrepresented ("feigned") truth.
9    *in* To yourself.
10   *saucy* Insolent.
11   *be mad* In the First Folio, "be not mad" (likely a scribal error).
12   *time of moon … skipping a dialogue* I.e., phase of the moon (thought to create lunacy)
     that I would indulge you in aimless conversation.
13   *hoist sail* Nautical term meaning "leave port"; *swabber* Seaman who cleans the deck; *to*
     *hull* To remain at anchor.
14   *Some mollification … giant* I.e., please pacify your protector; *giant* Alluding to legen-
     dary giants who protected ladies (and to Maria's small size).
15   *mind* Message.
16   *courtesy* Polite preamble.

VIOLA.  It alone concerns your ear. I bring no overture of war, no taxation of
homage.[1] I hold the olive[2] in my hand. My words are as full of peace as
matter.                                                                                                165

OLIVIA.  Yet you began rudely. What are you? What would you?

VIOLA.  The rudeness that hath appeared in me have I learned from my entertainment.[3] What I am and what I would are as secret as maidenhead[4]—to
your ears, divinity;[5] to any other's, profanation.

OLIVIA.  Give us the place alone. We will hear this divinity.                      170

[*Exit Maria and Attendants.*]

Now, sir, what is your text?

VIOLA.  Most sweet lady—

OLIVIA.  A comfortable[6] doctrine, and much may be said of it. Where lies
your text?

VIOLA.  In Orsino's bosom.                                                                       175

OLIVIA.  In his bosom? In what chapter of his bosom?

VIOLA.  To answer by the method,[7] in the first of his heart.

OLIVIA.  O, I have read it. It is heresy. Have you no more to say?

VIOLA.  Good madam, let me see your face.

OLIVIA.  Have you any commission from your lord to negotiate with my face?  180
You are now out of[8] your text, but we will draw the curtain and show you
the picture.[9] [*unveiling*] Look you, sir, such a one I was this present.[10] Is't
not well done?

VIOLA.  Excellently done, if God did all.[11]

OLIVIA.  'Tis in grain, sir, 'twill endure wind and weather.                          185

VIOLA.  'Tis beauty truly blent, whose red and white
Nature's own sweet and cunning hand laid on.[12]
Lady, you are the cruell'st she° alive,                                          *woman*

---

1    *overture ... homage* Declaration of war, demand for tribute.
2    *olive* Olive branch (of peace).
3    *entertainment* Reception.
4    *maidenhead* Virginity.
5    *your ears, divinity* I.e., heaven to your ears; love as a secular religion is played upon in
     religious terminology in the lines that follow: "text" (a biblical theme for a sermon), "doc-
     trine" (established belief), and "heresy" (belief against doctrine).
6    *comfortable* Comforting.
7    *by the method* In the same style.
8    *out of* Digressing from.
9    *picture* Portrait; the theme of portraiture is taken up in painting terms in the lines that
     follow: "in grain" (indelible), "blent" (blended), "laid on," and "copy."
10   *this present* Just now.
11   *if God did all* I.e., if your beauty is yours by nature (not painted by art).
12   *'Tis beauty ... laid on* See Shakespeare's Sonnet 20, lines 1–2.

If you will lead these graces to the grave,
190       And leave the world no copy.[1]
OLIVIA.  O, sir, I will not be so hard-hearted. I will give out divers schedules[2]
      of my beauty. It shall be inventoried, and every particle and utensil labelled
      to my will: as, *item*,[3] two lips indifferent[4] red; *item*, two grey eyes with lids
      to them; *item*, one neck, one chin, and so forth. Were you sent hither to
195       praise me?
VIOLA.  I see you what you are. You are too proud;
      But, if° you were the devil, you are fair.                                    *even if*
      My lord and master loves you. O, such love
      Could be but recompensed, though[5] you were crowned
      The nonpareil[6] of beauty!
200  OLIVIA.                        How does he love me?
VIOLA.  With adorations, fertile° tears,                                          *abundant*
      With groans that thunder love, with sighs of fire.
OLIVIA.  Your lord does know my mind—I cannot love him.
      Yet I suppose him virtuous, know him noble,
205       Of great estate, of fresh and stainless° youth,                          *uncorrupted*
      In voices well divulged, free,[7] learned, and valiant,
      And in dimension and the shape of nature[8]
      A gracious person. But yet I cannot love him.
      He might have took his answer long ago.
VIOLA.  If I did love you in my master's flame,°                                 *passion*
210       With such a suffering, such a deadly° life,                             *death-like*
      In your denial I would find no sense,
      I would not understand it.
OLIVIA.                        Why, what would you?[9]
VIOLA.  Make me a willow cabin[10] at your gate,
215       And call upon my soul[11] within the house.

---

1   *Lady, you are … no copy* You are the cruellest woman alive if you plan to die childless,
    i.e., without making copies of your beauty; *graces* The three graces—Charm, Grace, and
    Beauty—were goddesses led to Hell by the deceitful god Mercury.
2   *schedules* Various inventories.
3   *item* Latin: likewise (used to indicate articles in a formal list such as a will).
4   *indifferent* Tolerably.
5   *but recompensed, though* Merely repaid, even if.
6   *nonpareil* French: one without equal.
7   *In voices well divulged, free* In the general opinion (he is praised as) generous.
8   *dimension … shape of nature* Synonymous terms for "physical form."
9   *what would you* I.e., what would you do to show me your master's passion.
10  *willow cabin* Small shelter of willow boughs (a willow was an emblem of unrequited
    love).
11  *my soul* I.e., Olivia.

Write loyal cantons of contemned love[1]
And sing them loud even in the dead of night.
Halloo° your name to the reverberate° hills,                          *Shout / echoing*
And make the babbling gossip[2] of the air
Cry out "Olivia!" O, you should not rest                              220
Between the elements of air and earth[3]
But you should pity me.
OLIVIA.  You might do much.[4]
  What is your parentage?
VIOLA.  Above my fortunes, yet my state is well.[5]                   225
  I am a gentleman.
OLIVIA.                  Get you to your lord.
  I cannot love him. Let him send no more—
  Unless, perchance, you come to me again
  To tell me how he takes it. Fare you well.
  I thank you for your pains—spend this for me. [*Offers a purse.*]   230
VIOLA.  I am no fee'd post,° lady. Keep your purse.                   *paid messenger*
  My master, not myself, lacks recompense.
  Love make his heart of flint that you shall love,[6]
  And let your fervour like my master's be,[7]
  Placed in contempt! Farewell, fair cruelty. (*Exit.*)             235
OLIVIA.  "What is your parentage?"
  "Above my fortunes, yet my state is well.
  I am a gentleman." I'll be sworn thou art.
  Thy tongue, thy face, thy limbs, actions, and spirit,
  Do give thee five-fold blazon.[8] Not too fast. Soft, soft—        240
  Unless the master were the man.[9] How now?°                       *What then*
  Even so quickly may one catch the plague?[10]
  Methinks I feel this youth's perfections°                           *beauties*
  With an invisible and subtle stealth

1   *loyal cantons ... love* Faithful songs of unrequited love; *cantons* From Italian *canto*: verse.
2   *babbling gossip* Echo, a nymph who wasted away for love of Narcissus until only her voice
    remained to echo other lovers' complaints.
3   *rest / Between ... and earth* I.e., find peace anywhere.
4   *do much* I.e., persuade me to pity you.
5   *fortunes ... state is well* Present situation (as a servant), but my social standing is high.
6   *Love make ... shall love* May Love (Cupid) harden the heart of the man whom you choose
    to love.
7   *like my master's be* I.e., be treated like (you treat) my master's (with contempt).
8   *blazon* Listing of multiple (i.e., five-fold) physical virtues, a popular device in sonnets
    (literally, a heraldic description of a coat of arms).
9   *Unless ... the man* I.e., but what if the messenger were the one wooing me.
10  *catch the plague* I.e., fall in love.

245　To creep in at mine eyes.[1] Well, let it be.
　　　What ho, Malvolio!

　　　(*Enter Malvolio.*)

MALVOLIO.　　　Here, madam, at your service.
OLIVIA.　Run after that same peevish° messenger,　　　　　*obstinate*
　　　The County's° man. He left this ring behind him,　　　*Count's*
　　　Would I or not.[2] Tell him I'll none of it.
250　Desire him not to flatter with his lord,
　　　Nor hold him up[3] with hopes. I am not for him.
　　　If that the youth will come this way tomorrow,
　　　I'll give him reasons for't. Hie thee,° Malvolio.　　　*Hurry*
MALVOLIO.　Madam, I will. (*Exit.*)
255　OLIVIA.　I do I know not what, and fear to find
　　　Mine eye too great a flatterer for my mind.[4]
　　　Fate, show thy force. Ourselves we do not owe.°　　　*own*
　　　What is decreed must be, and be this so.[5]

　　　[*Exit.*]

## ACT 2, SCENE 1

(*Enter Antonio and Sebastian.*)

ANTONIO.　Will you stay no longer, nor will you not[6] that I go with you?
SEBASTIAN.　By your patience, no. My stars shine darkly over me; the malignancy of my fate might perhaps distemper yours.[7] Therefore I shall crave of you your leave that I may bear my evils[8] alone. It were a bad recompense
5　　for your love to lay any of them on you.
ANTONIO.　Let me know of you whither you are bound.
SEBASTIAN.　No, sooth, sir; my determinate[9] voyage is mere extravagancy.[10] But I perceive in you so excellent a touch of modesty[11] that you will not extort

---

1　*at mine eyes* Love was traditionally thought to enter at the eyes (as in "love at first sight").
2　*Would I or not* Whether I wanted it or not.
3　*flatter with … hold him up* Lead him on or encourage him (synonymous phrases).
4　*Mine eye … mind* I.e., that my eye has misled my judgment.
5　*Fate … be this so* This and line 240 above restate the proverb, "what must be must be," and also echo contemporary religious debates about the doctrine of predestination.
6　*will you not* Do you not wish?
7　*stars shine darkly … distemper yours* Astrological terms for the evil influence of fate, which he fears will infect ("distemper") Antonio's fortunes.
8　*evils* Misfortunes.
9　*determinate* Intended.
10　*extravagancy* Aimless wandering.
11　*modesty* Politeness.

from me what I am willing to keep in. Therefore it charges me in manners
the rather to express[1] myself. You must know of me then, Antonio, my     10
name is Sebastian, which I called Roderigo. My father was that Sebastian
of Messaline[2] whom I know you have heard of. He left behind him myself
and a sister, both born in an hour. If the heavens had been pleased, would
we had so ended. But you, sir, altered that, for some[3] hour before you took
me from the breach of the sea[4] was my sister drowned.                     15

ANTONIO.  Alas the day!

SEBASTIAN.  A lady, sir, though it was said she much resembled me, was yet
of many accounted beautiful. But though I could not with such estimable
wonder overfar[5] believe that, yet thus far I will boldly publish[6] her—she
bore a mind that envy could not but call fair. She is drowned already, sir,  20
with salt water, though I seem to drown her remembrance again with more.

ANTONIO.  Pardon me, sir, your bad entertainment.[7]

SEBASTIAN.  O good Antonio, forgive me your trouble.[8]

ANTONIO.  If you will not murder me for my love,[9] let me be your servant.

SEBASTIAN.  If you will not undo what you have done—that is, kill him whom  25
you have recovered—desire it not. Fare ye well at once. My bosom is full
of kindness,[10] and I am yet so near the manners of my mother that, upon
the least occasion more, mine eyes will tell tales of me.[11] I am bound to the
Count Orsino's court. Farewell.

    (*Exit.*)

ANTONIO.  The gentleness° of all the gods go with thee         *favour*   30
    I have many enemies in Orsino's court,
    Else° would I very shortly see thee there.        *Otherwise*
    But come what may, I do adore thee so
    That danger shall seem sport, and I will go.

    (*Exit.*)

---

1  *express* Reveal.
2  *Messaline* A Shakespearean invention, but perhaps derived from Massila (now Marseilles);
   Massilians and Illyrians are mentioned together in Plautus's *Menaechmi* in a passage describing one twin's search for his sibling.
3  *some* About an.
4  *breach of the sea* Breakers.
5  *estimable wonder overfar* Exceeding esteem and wonder.
6  *publish* Proclaim.
7  *your bad entertainment* I.e., my poor hospitality.
8  *your trouble* I.e., the trouble I have caused you.
9  *murder ... love* I.e., punish me for my act of human kindness (that altered your fate).
10 *kindness* Feeling.
11 *yet so near ... tales of me* I.e., still so liable to cry like a woman that, at the least emotion,
   my tears will betray my feelings.

# ACT 2, SCENE 2

(*Enter Viola and Malvolio at several*[1] *doors.*)

MALVOLIO.  Were you not ev'n now with the Countess Olivia?

VIOLA.  Even now, sir, on a moderate pace I have since arrived but hither.[2]

MALVOLIO.  She returns this ring to you, sir. You might have saved me my
pains, to have taken it away yourself. She adds, moreover, that you should
5     put your lord into a desperate assurance[3] she will none of him. And one
thing more—that you be never so hardy[4] to come again in his affairs, unless it be to report your lord's taking of this. Receive it so.[5]

VIOLA.  She took the ring of[6] me. I'll none of it.

MALVOLIO.  Come, sir, you peevishly threw it to her, and her will is it should
10    be so returned. If it be worth stooping for, there it lies in your eye.[7] If not,
be it his that finds it.

(*Exit.*)

VIOLA.  I left no ring with her. What means this lady?
Fortune forbid my outside° have not charmed her!                    *appearance*
She made good view of me,[8] indeed, so much
15    That methought[9] her eyes had lost her tongue,
For she did speak in starts distractedly.[10]
She loves me, sure. The cunning° of her passion                      *craftiness*
Invites me in° this churlish messenger.                               *by means of*
None of° my lord's ring! Why, he sent her none.                      *Refuse*
20    I am the man.[11] If it be so—as 'tis—
Poor lady, she were better love a dream.
Disguise, I see thou art a wickedness
Wherein the pregnant enemy does much.[12]
How easy is it for the proper false

---

1     *several* Different (suggesting simultaneous arrival at both stage entrances).
2     *hither* This far.
3     *desperate assurance* Hopeless certainty.
4     *hardy* Eager.
5     *Receive it so* I.e., take the ring on these terms.
6     *of* From.
7     *eye* Sight.
8     *made good view of me* Looked me over carefully.
9     *That methought* Some editors mend the rough metre here with "That sure methought."
10    *eyes had … distractedly* She was so perplexed that she became tongue-tied, for she spoke
      in disjointed "fits and starts."
11    *the man* I.e., man she desires.
12    *pregnant … much* Resourceful enemy (Cupid or the devil) can take advantage.

In women's waxen hearts to set their forms!¹                                      25
Alas, our frailty is the cause, not we
For such as we are made of, such² we be.
How will this fadge?° My master loves her dearly,                    *turn out*
And I, poor monster,³ fond° as much on him,                             *dote*
And she, mistaken, seems to dote on me.                                       30
What will become of this? As I am man,
My state is desperate for my master's love.⁴
As I am woman, now, alas the day,
What thriftless° sighs shall poor Olivia breathe.                    *fruitless*
O Time, thou must untangle this, not I.                                          35
It is too hard a knot for me t'untie!

    [*Exit.*]


## ACT 2, SCENE 3

(*Enter Sir Toby and Sir Andrew.*)

SIR TOBY.  Approach, Sir Andrew. Not to be abed after midnight is to be up
betimes,⁵ and *diluculo surgere*⁶ thou know'st—
SIR ANDREW.  Nay, by my troth, I know not, but I know to be up late is to
be up late.
SIR TOBY.  A false conclusion! I hate it as an unfilled can.⁷ To be up after       5
midnight and to go to bed then is early, so that to go to bed after midnight
is to go to bed betimes. Does not our lives consist of the four elements?⁸
SIR ANDREW.  Faith, so they say, but I think it rather consists of eating and
drinking.

---

1    *for the ... their forms* For handsome deceitful (men) to leave impressions on women's
    hearts (as wax takes the impression of a seal).
2    *our frailty ... such* Traditionally, women were considered the "weaker vessel," and suscep-
    tibility to passion was thought to derive from physical weakness.
3    *monster* I.e., being both man and woman; Renaissance medical manuals used "monster"
    for unusual births of all types, particularly those of uncertain or dual gender.
4    *As I am ... master's love* I.e., since I am now considered a man, my love for my master is
    hopeless.
5    *betimes* Early.
6    *diluculo surgere* Latin. From the proverb, *Diluculo surgere saluberrimum est* ("to rise at
    dawn is most healthy"), found in popular school texts and medical advice books, which
    urged moderation in food, drink, exercise, and rest to avoid unhealthy imbalances of bod-
    ily humours.
7    *can* Tankard.
8    *four elements* Air, earth, fire, and water; the elements were thought to compose all things
    and corresponded to the four humours of the body (blood, phlegm, choler, and melan-
    choly), which were thought to govern behaviour and health.

10 SIR TOBY. Th'art a scholar, let us therefore eat and drink. Marian,[1] I say, a stoup[2] of wine.

(*Enter [Feste.]*)

SIR ANDREW. Here comes the fool, i' faith.

FESTE. How now, my hearts! Did you never see the picture of "we three?"[3]

SIR TOBY. Welcome, ass. Now let's have a catch.[4]

15 SIR ANDREW. By my troth, the fool has an excellent breast.[5] I had rather than forty shillings I had such a leg,[6] and so sweet a breath to sing, as the fool has. In sooth, thou wast in very gracious fooling last night, when thou spok'st of Pigrogromitus, of the Vapians passing the equinoctial of Queubus.[7] 'Twas very good, i' faith. I sent thee sixpence for thy leman.[8] Hadst it?

20 FESTE. I did impeticos thy gratility, for Malvolio's nose is no whipstock. My lady has a white hand, and the Myrmidons are no bottle-ale houses.[9]

SIR ANDREW. Excellent! Why, this is the best fooling, when all is done. Now, a song.

SIR TOBY. Come on, there is sixpence for you. Let's have a song.

25 SIR ANDREW. There's a testril[10] of me too. If one knight give a—[11]

FESTE. Would you have a love-song, or a song of good life?[12]

SIR TOBY. A love-song, a love-song.

SIR ANDREW. Ay, ay, I care not for good life.

---

1    *Marian* Diminutive of Mary.

2    *stoup* Two-pint tankard.

3    *we three* This caption accompanied illustrations on inn signs depicting two fools or asses; the third ass was the viewer.

4    *catch* Song sung in a three-part round.

5    *breast* Voice.

6    *leg* Dancing skill.

7    *Pigrogromitus ... Queubus* Sir Andrew is repeating (or perhaps mangling) Feste's exotic nonsense names, which seem to imitate popular travel literature or the pseudo-classical names in Rabelais's *Gargantua and Pantagruel* (c. 1532); *equinoctial* Equator.

8    *leman* Mistress.

9    *I did ... bottle-ale houses* Feste's speech mingles near sense with "fooling" illogic; *impeticos thy gratility* Mock Latin for "pocketed your gratuity"; *whipstock* Handle of a whip (i.e., Malvolio can look down his nose at me, but he can't punish me); *My lady ... hand* I.e., Olivia is of noble birth and manners; *Myrmidons ... bottle-ale* Myrmidons were followers of Achilles, but this is likely a joke on the Mermaid Inn, whose literary clientele presumably drank no common "bottle-ale."

10   *testril* Diminutive of "tester," a sixpence piece (fools entertained for money).

11   *give a—* In the First Folio this line ends at the margin without punctuation, and perhaps the next line was dropped from the text; in performance, this provides Feste an opportunity to interrupt Sir Andrew.

12   *love-song ... good life* I.e., a song of courtly love or a drinking song (although Sir Andrew takes "good" to mean "righteous").

We Three Loggerheads, *early seventeenth century. It is likely that Feste—who refers to this type of "we three" image in Act 2, Scene 3 of* Twelfth Night—*wore jester's clothes in the play's first production. If he did, his costume would have been similar to those worn by the characters in this painting: multicoloured clothes decorated with bells and accompanied by a fool's cap. There were several varieties of fool's cap, but many such caps, like the two shown here, had the ears of an ass or the head of a cock attached. One of the figures in the painting also bears a common fool's accessory called a "marotte," a carved fool's head on a stick with which the possessor could conduct pretend conversations.*

FESTE. (*Sings.*)
    O mistress mine,[1] where are you roaming?
30    O, stay and hear, your true love's coming,
        That can sing both high and low.
    Trip° no further, pretty sweeting.°                    *Go / darling*
    Journeys end in lovers meeting,
        Every wise man's son doth know.[2]
35 SIR ANDREW. Excellent good, i' faith.
SIR TOBY. Good, good!
FESTE. [*Sings.*]
    What is love? 'Tis not hereafter,
    Present mirth hath present laughter.
        What's to come is still° unsure.                   *always*
40    In delay there lies no plenty,°                      *gain*
    Then come kiss me, sweet and twenty.[3]
        Youth's a stuff will not endure.[4]
SIR ANDREW. A mellifluous voice, as I am true knight.
SIR TOBY. A contagious breath.[5]
45 SIR ANDREW. Very sweet and contagious, i' faith.
SIR TOBY. To hear by the nose, it is dulcet in contagion.[6] But shall we make
    the welkin[7] dance indeed? Shall we rouse the night-owl in a catch that will
    draw three souls out of one weaver?[8] Shall we do that?
SIR ANDREW. An you love me, let's do't. I am dog at[9] a catch.
50 FESTE. By'r lady,[10] sir, and some dogs will catch well.
SIR ANDREW. Most certain. Let our catch be "Thou knave."

---

1    *O mistress mine* While the words to this song might be Shakespeare's, what tune was
    played in performance is uncertain; one likely accompaniment is a tune in Thomas Mor-
    ley's *First Book of Consort Lessons* (1599).

2    *wise man's son* Proverbial: "a wise man has a foolish son."

3    *sweet and twenty* I.e., twenty times as sweetly.

4    *Youth's ... endure* I.e., our youth will not last (so let's seize the day).

5    *contagious breath* I.e., infectious voice, playing on "catch" in two senses: it is a "catchy"
    tune easily remembered, and they will "catch" the plague from Feste's foul breath (al-
    though Andrew mistakes "contagious" as a compliment).

6    *To hear ... contagion* I.e., if you could hear through your nose, it would be sweetly con-
    tagious (winking at Andrew's confusion, but also alluding to the plague-time practice of
    breathing through perfumed handkerchiefs).

7    *welkin* Heavens.

8    *draw three ... weaver* Many weavers in London were Calvinist refugees who would have
    sung only Psalms; *three souls* Both a joke on the three-part "catch" and an allusion to the
    three faculties of the soul—reason, feeling, and passion.

9    *dog at* Good at.

10    *By'r lady* By our Lady, the Virgin Mary (a mild oath).

FESTE.  "Hold thy peace, thou knave"[1] knight? I shall be constrained[2] in't to call thee knave, knight.

SIR ANDREW.  'Tis not the first time I have constrained one to call me knave.[3] Begin, fool. It begins "Hold thy peace."                                                    55

FESTE.  I shall never begin if I hold my peace.[4]

SIR ANDREW.  Good, i' faith. Come, begin. (*Catch sung.*)

(*Enter Maria.*)

MARIA.  What a caterwauling[5] do you keep here! If my lady have not called up her steward Malvolio, and bid him turn you out of doors, never trust me.

SIR TOBY.  My lady's a Cathayan, we are politicians, Malvolio's a Peg-a-Ramsey,[6]  60 and (*He sings.*) "Three merry men be we."[7] Am not I consanguineous?[8] Am I not of her blood? Tilly-vally. "Lady!"[9] [*Sings.*] "There dwelt a man in Babylon, lady, lady."[10]

FESTE.  Beshrew me,[11] the knight's in admirable fooling.

SIR ANDREW.  Ay, he does well enough if he be disposed, and so do I too. He  65 does it with a better grace, but I do it more natural.[12]

SIR TOBY.  [*Sings.*] "O' the twelfth day of December—"[13]

MARIA.  For the love o' God, peace.

(*Enter Malvolio.*)

---

1    *Hold thy peace, thou knave* In this round each singer in turn is told to be silent and called a knave.

2    *constrained* Compelled.

3    *'Tis not ... me knave* Sir Andrew may be recalling how Maria treated him in 1.3, or simply admitting he is more knave than knight.

4    *peace* Punning on "piece," slang for "penis."

5    *caterwauling* Crying of cats in heat.

6    *Cathayan, we are ... Peg-a-Ramsey* This sequence mimics Feste's nonsense statements earlier in this scene; *Cathayan* Literally, an inhabitant of Cathay (China, and perhaps an insult), but Toby more likely means Catharan (from *cathari*, Latin for "the pure"), a term often used for Puritans (implying she is morally inflexible); *politicians* I.e., shrewd self-servers; *Peg-a-Ramsey* Title of a lewd popular song and dance.

7    *Three merry ... be we* Fragment of a song that appeared in George Peele's *The Old Wives Tale* (1595); other versions of this song contrast "merry men" with "wise men."

8    *consanguineous* Of the same blood (as Olivia).

9    *Tilly-vally. "Lady!"* Nonsense expression of impatience at Maria's "my lady" above.

10   *There dwelt ... lady* Opening line and refrain from the popular ballad, *Constant Susanna* (c. 1562), about Susanna and the Elders in Daniel 13.

11   *Beshrew me* Curse me.

12   *better grace ... natural* More artfully, but I do it like a natural (a born fool).

13   *O' ... December* Possibly the opening line of a popular war ballad, *Musselburgh Field* (tune unknown), but it is plausible that Toby is drunkenly misquoting "On the twelfth day of Christmas."

MALVOLIO. My masters,[1] are you mad? Or what are you? Have you no wit,
70    manners, nor honesty,[2] but to gabble like tinkers at this time of night? Do
ye make an ale-house of my lady's house, that ye squeak out your coziers'
catches[3] without any mitigation or remorse[4] of voice? Is there no respect of
place, persons, nor time,[5] in you?

SIR TOBY.    We did keep time, sir, in our catches. Sneck up.[6]

75    MALVOLIO.    Sir Toby, I must be round[7] with you. My lady bade me tell you
that, though she harbours you as her kinsman, she's nothing allied to your
disorders.[8] If you can separate yourself and[9] your misdemeanours, you are
welcome to the house. If not, and it would please you to take leave of her,
she is very willing to bid you farewell.

80    SIR TOBY.    [Sings.] "Farewell, dear heart, since I must needs be gone."[10]

MARIA.    Nay, good Sir Toby.[11]

FESTE.    [Sings.] "His eyes do show his days are almost done."

MALVOLIO.    Is't even so?

SIR TOBY.    [Sings.] "But I will never die."

85    FESTE.    [Sings.] "Sir Toby, there you lie."[12]

MALVOLIO.    This is much credit to you.

SIR TOBY.    [Sings.] "Shall I bid him go?"

FESTE.    [Sings.] "What and if you do?"

SIR TOBY.    [Sings.] "Shall I bid him go, and spare not?"

90    FESTE.    [Sings.] "O, no, no, no, no, you dare not."

---

1    *masters* Sir Toby and Sir Andrew are Malvolio's social superiors.

2    *wit* Sense; *honesty* Decency.

3    *gabble like tinkers ... catches* Insulting comparisons to vagrant salesmen (with a reputation for drinking and foul language), and to cobblers (who presumably sung as they
worked).

4    *mitigation or remorse* Moderation or consideration.

5    *place, persons, nor time* I.e., "don't you know your place, who I am, and what time it is"
(alluding to Aristotle's dramatic unities, which required consistency in setting, characterization, and chronology).

6    *Sneck up* Shut up.

7    *round* Direct.

8    *nothing allied to your disorders* I.e., disowns your misconduct.

9    *and* From.

10    *Farewell ... be gone* Toby sings a shortened version of the ballad *Corydon's Farewell to
Phyllis*, from Robert Jones's *First Book of Songs and Ayres* (1600), sharing lines with Feste.

11    *Nay, good Sir Toby* In performance, Toby may try to embrace Maria after *dear heart*.

12    *will never die ... you lie* Here, Toby might parody a melodramatic death, but "die" also
means to experience sexual pleasure, a pun Feste trades with "there you lie"; Feste's line in
the ballad reads "so long as I can spy."

SIR TOBY. [*rising*] Out o' tune,[1] sir? Ye lie. Art any more than a steward? Dost thou think, because thou art virtuous, there shall be no more cakes and ale?[2]

FESTE. Yes, by Saint Anne,[3] and ginger[4] shall be hot i' th' mouth too.[5]

SIR TOBY. Th' art i' th' right. Go, sir, rub your chain with crumbs.[6] A stoup      95
of wine, Maria!

MALVOLIO. Mistress Mary, if you prized my lady's favour at anything more than contempt, you would not give means[7] for this uncivil rule.[8] She shall know of it, by this hand.

(*Exit.*)

MARIA. Go shake your ears.[9]                                                          100

SIR ANDREW. 'Twere as good a deed as to drink when a man's a-hungry,[10] to challenge him the field,[11] and then to break promise with him and make a fool of him.[12]

SIR TOBY. Do't, knight. I'll write thee a challenge, or I'll deliver thy indignation to him by word of mouth.                                                          105

MARIA. Sweet Sir Toby, be patient for to-night. Since the youth of the Count's was to-day with my lady, she is much out of quiet.[13] For Monsieur Malvo-lio, let me alone with him.[14] If I do not gull him into a nayword,[15] and make

---

1   *Out o' tune* I.e., in disorder (recalling Malovolio's comments before the song). Many edi-
    tors emend the First Folio to read "out o' time" to recall his earlier punning response to
    Malvolio, "we did keep time."

2   *thou art virtuous … cakes and ale* A common complaint against Puritan reformers who
    agitated for the suppression of traditional parish celebrations of holy-days, among them
    "church-ales," which raised funds for the local parish by selling ale and baked goods.

3   *Saint Anne* Mother of the Virgin Mary (a mild oath).

4   *ginger* Used for spicing Christmas ales and considered an aphrodisiac.

5   *too* Feste has no lines after this point, and most editions have him exit here; however, in
    some modern performances Feste remains on stage in silent detachment.

6   *rub … crumbs* I.e., exercise your authority on insignificant matters; *chain* Stewards
    wore a ceremonial chain signalling their office.

7   *give means* Provide drink.

8   *uncivil rule* Disorderly conduct.

9   *shake your ears* I.e., like the ass that you are.

10  *'Twere as good … a-hungry* The first phrase is proverbial ("it's good to drink when you are
    thirsty") but rendered nonsense by the second.

11  *the field* To a duel.

12  *a fool of him* In fact, the code of honour that governed duelling would make a fool of Sir
    Andrew if he then refused to duel.

13  *out of quiet* Troubled.

14  *let me alone with him* Leave him to me.

15  *gull him … nayword* I.e., trick him into being a byword (for gullibility).

him a common recreation,[1] do not think I have wit enough to lie straight
110    in my bed. I know I can do it.

SIR TOBY. Possess[2] us, possess us, tell us something of him.

MARIA. Marry, sir, sometimes he is a kind of puritan.[3]

SIR ANDREW. O, if I thought that, I'd beat him like a dog.

SIR TOBY. What, for being a puritan? Thy exquisite[4] reason, dear knight?

115    SIR ANDREW. I have no exquisite reason for't, but I have reason good enough.

MARIA. The devil a puritan that he is,[5] or anything constantly but a time-
pleaser;[6] an affectioned[7] ass that cons state without book and utters it by
great swarths;[8] the best persuaded[9] of himself, so crammed, as he thinks,
with excellencies that it is his grounds of faith that all that look on him love
120    him; and on that vice[10] in him will my revenge find notable cause to work.

SIR TOBY. What wilt thou do?

MARIA. I will drop in his way some obscure epistles[11] of love, wherein, by the
colour of his beard, the shape of his leg, the manner of his gait, the expressure[12] of his eye, forehead, and complexion, he shall find himself most feel-
125    ingly personated.[13] I can write very like my lady, your niece. On forgotten
matter[14] we can hardly make distinction of our hands.

SIR TOBY. Excellent! I smell a device.[15]

SIR ANDREW. I have't in my nose too.

SIR TOBY. He shall think, by the letters that thou wilt drop, that they come
130    from my niece, and that she's in love with him.

---

1    *common recreation* Laughingstock.

2    *Possess* Acquaint.

3    *kind of a puritan* I.e., morally rigid, highly scrupled person; the term does not necessarily refer (as Andrew thinks) to Puritans, the radical reformers of the English Protestant
church.

4    *exquisite* Carefully considered.

5    *The devil … he is* I.e., he is no more a Puritan than the devil.

6    *constantly … time-pleaser* Consistently except for a time-server (i.e., he serves only his
own interests).

7    *affectioned* Affected.

8    *cons state … great swarths* Memorizes the rules of decorum and proclaims them at great
length; *swarths* Swaths, amounts of hay or corn that could be cut with one sweep of a
scythe.

9    *best persuaded* Highest opinion.

10    *that vice* I.e., pride, one of the seven deadly sins.

11    *obscure epistles* Ambiguous letters.

12    *expressure* Expression.

13    *feelingly personated* Sensitively portrayed.

14    *forgotten matter* I.e., routine matters either of us could have recorded in a household
book.

15    *device* Stratagem.

MARIA.  My purpose is, indeed, a horse of that colour.[1]
SIR ANDREW.  And your horse now would make him an ass.
MARIA.  Ass,[2] I doubt not.
SIR ANDREW.  O, 'twill be admirable!
MARIA.  Sport royal,[3] I warrant you. I know my physic[4] will work with him.    135
   I will plant you two—and let the fool make a third[5]—where he shall find
   the letter. Observe his construction[6] of it. For this night, to bed, and dream
   on the event. Farewell.

   (*Exit.*)

SIR TOBY.  Good night, Penthesilea.[7]
SIR ANDREW.  Before me,[8] she's a good wench.                                    140
SIR TOBY.  She's a beagle[9] true-bred, and one that adores me. What o' that?
SIR ANDREW.  I was adored once too.
SIR TOBY.  Let's to bed, knight. Thou hadst need send for more money.[10]
SIR ANDREW.  If I cannot recover your niece, I am a foul way out.[11]
SIR TOBY.  Send for money, knight. If thou hast her not i' th' end, call me cut.[12]   145
SIR ANDREW.  If I do not, never trust me, take it how you will.
SIR TOBY.  Come, come, I'll go burn some sack.[13] 'Tis too late to go to bed
   now. Come, knight, come, knight.

   (*Exeunt.*)

---

1   *horse of that colour* I.e., precisely that (a proverbial expression Andrew doesn't recognize).
2   *Ass* Punning on "as" and "ass," but also suggesting Andrew is an ass.
3   *Sport royal* Entertainment worthy of royalty.
4   *physic* Medicine.
5   *fool make a third* This is usually cited as evidence that Feste has left the scene after his last
    line above, and that Shakespeare originally planned for him to be the third observer (in
    fact, Fabian replaces Feste in 2.5). In performance, Maria may add this as a nod to the
    silent Fool, who replies with a dismissive gesture.
6   *construction* Interpretation.
7   *Penthesilea* Queen of the Amazons.
8   *Before me* On my soul.
9   *beagle* Small hunting dog noted for its tenacity and intelligence.
10  *more money* Of Andrew's annual income of three thousand ducats, Toby has by 3.2 re-
    ceived "some two thousand strong, or so."
11  *foul way out* I.e., I will be in a difficult situation; *out* In debt.
12  *cut* A cart horse (either with a cropped tail or gelded).
13  *burn some sack* I.e., heat up some sherry with spices.

# ACT 2, SCENE 4

(*Enter Orsino, Viola, Curio, and others.*)

ORSINO.  Give me some music. Now, good morrow, friends. (*Musicians enter.*)
    Now, good Cesario, but° that piece of song,                    *sing just*
    That old and antic° song we heard last night.        *rustic and antique*
    Methought it did relieve my passion much,
5    More than light airs[1] and recollected terms[2]
    Of these most brisk and giddy-pacèd° times.             *dizzying*
    Come, but one verse.
CURIO.  He is not here, so please your lordship, that should sing it.
ORSINO.  Who was it?
10 CURIO.  Feste, the jester, my lord, a fool that the Lady Olivia's father took much
    delight in. He is about the house.
ORSINO.  Seek him out, and play the tune the while.

    [*Exit Curio.*]

    (*Music plays.*)

    Come hither, boy. If ever thou shalt love,
    In the sweet pangs of it remember me,
15    For such as I am all true lovers are,
    Unstaid° and skittish in all motions° else       *Unsteady / emotions*
    Save in° the constant° image of the creature       *Except for / true*
    That is beloved. How dost thou like this tune?
VIOLA.  It gives a very echo to the seat
20    Where Love is thronèd.[3]
ORSINO.                  Thou dost speak masterly.
    My life upon't, young though thou art, thine eye
    Hath stayed° upon some favour° that it loves,         *fixed / face*
    Hath it not, boy?
VIOLA.           A little, by your favour.[4]
ORSINO.  What kind of woman is't?
VIOLA.                  Of your complexion.°         *temperament*

---

1    *airs* Fashionable courtly songs popularized by John Dowland's *First Book of Songs or Airs*
    (1597).
2    *recollected terms* Rehearsed, artificial language.
3    *It gives … Love is thronèd* It perfectly echoes the feelings of the heart (where love was
    thought to have its seat).
4    *by your favour* By your leave, but also punning on "some favour that it loves."

ORSINO.  She is not worth thee, then. What years, i' faith?                         25
VIOLA.  About your years, my lord.
ORSINO.  Too old, by heaven! Let still° the woman take                    *always*
    An elder than herself. So wears° she to him;                      *conforms*
    So sways she level[1] in her husband's heart.
    For, boy, however we do praise ourselves,                                   30
    Our fancies° are more giddy and unfirm,                           *affections*
    More longing, wavering, sooner lost and won,
    Than women's are.
VIOLA.           I think it well, my lord.
ORSINO.  Then let thy love be younger than thyself,
    Or thy affection cannot hold the bent.[2]                                       35
    For women are as roses, whose fair flower
    Being once displayed, doth fall[3] that very hour.
VIOLA.  And so they are. Alas, that they are so,
    To die, even when they to perfection grow.

    (*Enter Curio and Feste.*)

ORSINO.  O, fellow, come, the song we had last night.                    40
    Mark it, Cesario, it is old and plain.
    The spinsters[4] and the knitters in the sun,
    And the free° maids that weave their thread with bones,[5]         *care-free*
    Do use to chant it. It is silly sooth,°                               *simple truth*
    And dallies with° the innocence of love,                          *dwells on*   45
    Like the old age.[6]
FESTE.  Are you ready, sir?
ORSINO.  Ay, prithee, sing.

    (*Music.*)

---

1   *So wears she ... sways she level* Thus she conforms herself to him; thus she maintains a balanced influence.

2   *hold the bent* I.e., remain strong and true (a term from archery for a bow's strength under tension).

3   *displayed, doth fall* In full bloom, wilts.

4   *spinsters* Women spinning (but hinting at the modern meaning, unmarried women).

5   *weave their ... bones* Make their lace with bone bobbins (often fish bones instead of metal pins). The aristocratic taste for fine lace supported a labour-intensive cottage industry in which girls and young women contributed to their dowries by lace-making.

6   *old age* Mythic golden age of pastoral simplicity.

FESTE.  [*Sings.*]

    Come away,° come away, death,[1]               *Come quickly*

50        And in sad cypress[2] let me be laid.

    Fie away,° fie away, breath,                      *Begone*

        I am slain by a fair cruel maid.

    My shroud of white, stuck all with yew,[3]

        O, prepare it.

55    My part of death no one so true

        Did share it.[4]


    Not a flower, not a flower sweet,

        On my black coffin let there be strown.

    Not a friend, not a friend greet°                  *to greet*

60        My poor corpse where my bones shall be thrown.

    A thousand thousand to save,

        Lay me, O, where

    True[5] lover never° find my grave,              *may never*

        To weep there.

65 ORSINO.  There's for thy pains. [*Gives him money.*]

FESTE.  No pains, sir. I take pleasure in singing, sir.

ORSINO.  I'll pay thy pleasure, then.

FESTE.  Truly, sir, and pleasure will be paid one time or another.

ORSINO.  Give me now leave to leave thee.[6]

70 FESTE.  Now the melancholy god[7] protect thee, and the tailor make thy doublet of changeable taffeta,[8] for thy mind is a very opal.[9] I would have men of such constancy put to sea,[10] that their business might be everything, and their intent everywhere,[11] for that's it that always makes a good voyage of nothing.[12] Farewell.

---

1    *Come away ... death* This song may or may not be Shakespeare's; no contemporary musical setting survives.

2    *sad cypress* A black coffin of cypress.

3    *yew* Sprigs of yew; like the cypress, the yew was associated with death.

4    *My part ... Did share it* No one so true (to love) as I has ever shared my portion of death (i.e., died of love).

5    *True* Many editions read "Sad true" to correct the metre in this line.

6    *Give me ... leave thee* Allow me to dismiss you.

7    *melancholy god* Saturn (thought to govern moodiness).

8    *changeable taffeta* Shot silk, woven with contrasting thread colours to iridesce in changing light (associated with changes of mind).

9    *opal* Iridescent gemstone (i.e., your mood is changeable).

10    *sea* Traditional image of changeability.

11    *their business ... intent everywhere* Proverbial: "he that is everywhere is nowhere."

12    *that's it ... of nothing* I.e., that changeable attitude makes something out of nothing.

(*Exit* [*Feste*].)

ORSINO.  Let all the rest give place.°                                                      *leave*    75

[*Exit Curio and others.*]

Once more, Cesario,
Get thee to yond same sovereign cruelty.°                                          *cruel lady*
Tell her my love, more noble than the world,°                                    *material things*
Prizes not quantity of dirty lands.
The parts° that fortune hath bestowed upon her,                          *wealth and rank*    80
Tell her I hold as giddily° as Fortune.                                                    *lightly*
But 'tis that miracle and queen of gems[1]
That Nature pranks° her in attracts my soul.                                      *adorns*
VIOLA.  But if she cannot love you, sir?
ORSINO.  I cannot be so answered.                                                                  85
VIOLA.  Sooth,° but you must.                                                                  *In truth*
Say that some lady, as perhaps there is,
Hath for your love as great a pang of heart
As you have for Olivia. You cannot love her.
You tell her so. Must she not then be answered?                                    90
ORSINO.  There is no woman's sides
Can bide° the beating of so strong a passion                                      *withstand*
As love doth give my heart; no woman's heart
So big to hold so much. They lack retention.[2]
Alas, their love may be called appetite,                                                        95
No motion of the liver, but the palate,
That suffer surfeit, cloyment, and revolt;[3]
But mine is all as hungry as the sea,
And can digest as much. Make no compare
Between that love a woman can bear me                                                100
And that I owe° Olivia.                                                                            *have for*
VIOLA.  Ay, but I know—
ORSINO.  What dost thou know?
VIOLA.  Too well what love women to men may owe.
In faith, they are as true of heart as we.                                                105
My father had a daughter loved a man,
As it might be perhaps, were I a woman,
I should your lordship.

---

1    *that miracle ... gems* A diamond (i.e., her rare and matchless beauty).
2    *retention* In Renaissance medicine, the power to retain the contents of one's body.
3    *No motion ... revolt* A mere hunger, not a deep passion, easily satisfied, but quickly sickened; *cloyment* Satiety; *revolt* Revulsion.

ORSINO.                    And what's her history?

110  VIOLA.  A blank, my lord. She never told her love,
         But let concealment, like a worm i' th' bud,°              *rosebud*
         Feed on her damask° cheek. She pined in thought,          *pink and white*
         And with a green and yellow melancholy[1]
         She sat like Patience on a monument,[2]
115      Smiling at grief. Was not this love indeed?
         We men may say more, swear more, but indeed
         Our shows are more than will.[3] For still we prove
         Much in our vows, but little in our love.

ORSINO.  But died thy sister of her love, my boy?

120  VIOLA.  I am all the daughters of my father's house,
         And all the brothers too, and yet I know not.
         Sir, shall I to this lady?

ORSINO.                    Ay, that's the theme.
         To her in haste. Give her this jewel. Say
         My love can give no place, bide no denay.[4]

         (*Exeunt [separately.]*)


## ACT 2, SCENE 5

(*Enter Sir Toby, Sir Andrew, and Fabian.*[5])

SIR TOBY.  Come thy ways, Signior Fabian.

FABIAN.  Nay, I'll come. If I lose a scruple[6] of this sport let me be boiled to
         death with melancholy.[7]

SIR TOBY.  Wouldst thou not be glad to have the niggardly[8] rascally sheep-biter[9]
5        come by some notable shame?

FABIAN.  I would exult, man. You know he brought me out o' favour with my
         lady about a bear-baiting[10] here.

---

1   *green ... melancholy* Pale and yellow sadness, referring to "green-sickness" (chlorosis), an
    anemia thought to afflict virgins.
2   *Patience on a monument* Minerva, the goddess of patience, was often portrayed on tombs.
3   *Our shows ... will* I.e., our displays of love suggest more than our actual passion.
4   *give no place ... denay* I.e., not hold back, endure no denial.
5   *Fabian* Fabian is introduced to replace Feste as the third observer (see 2.3.136).
6   *a scruple* A bit.
7   *boiled to death with melancholy* Melancholy was in fact a cold humour.
8   *niggardly* Grudging.
9   *sheep-biter* Literally, a guard dog that bites sheep, but figuratively a whore-monger (punning
    on "mutton," meaning "whore") and associated with Puritans by the satirist Thomas Nashe.
10  *bear-baiting* A popular entertainment condemned by Puritans (Shakespeare's Globe
    theatre was located next to a bear-baiting arena).

SIR TOBY.  To anger him we'll have the bear again, and we will fool him black
and blue, shall we not, Sir Andrew?

SIR ANDREW.  An we do not, it is pity of our lives.                    10

(*Enter Maria.*)

SIR TOBY.  Here comes the little villain. How now, my metal of India![1]

MARIA.  Get ye all three into the box-tree.[2] Malvolio's coming down this walk.
He has been yonder i' the sun practicing behaviour[3] to his own shadow
this half hour. Observe him, for the love of mockery, for I know this letter
will make a contemplative[4] idiot of him. Close,[5] in the name of jesting.   15
[*They hide and she drops a letter.*] Lie thou there, for here comes the trout
that must be caught with tickling.[6] (*Exit.*)

(*Enter Malvolio.*)

MALVOLIO.  'Tis but fortune, all is fortune.[7] Maria once told me she did affect[8] me, and I have heard herself come thus near, that should she fancy, it
should be one of my complexion.[9] Besides, she uses[10] me with a more ex-   20
alted respect than anyone else that follows[11] her. What should I think on't?

SIR TOBY.  Here's an overweening rogue.

FABIAN.  O, peace! Contemplation makes a rare turkeycock of him, how he
jets under his advanced[12] plumes!

SIR ANDREW.  'Slight,[13] I could so beat the rogue.                   25

SIR TOBY.  Peace, I say.

MALVOLIO.  To be Count Malvolio!

SIR TOBY.  Ah, rogue.

SIR ANDREW.  Pistol[14] him, pistol him.

SIR TOBY.  Peace, peace.                                                30

---

1   *metal of India*  Gold (i.e., my treasure);  *India*  The West Indies.
2   *box-tree*  Boxwood bush, an evergreen (a common stage property).
3   *behaviour*  Courtly gestures.
4   *contemplative*  Thoughtless.
5   *Close*  Keep close.
6   *trout ... with tickling*  Proverbial: to be duped by flattery (literally, a technique for catching trout without tackle).
7   *all is fortune*  Everything is subject to changeable fortune.
8   *she did affect*  Olivia was fond of.
9   *complexion*  Character.
10   *uses*  Treats.
11   *follows*  Serves, woos.
12   *turkeycock*;  Peacock;  *jets*  Struts;  *advanced*  Displayed.
13   *'Slight*  By God's light.
14   *Pistol*  Pistol-whip.

MALVOLIO.    There is example[1] for't: the Lady of the Strachy married the yeoman of the wardrobe.[2]

SIR ANDREW.    Fie on him, Jezebel.[3]

FABIAN.    O, peace, now he's deeply in. Look how imagination blows him.[4]

35    MALVOLIO.    Having been three months married to her, sitting in my state[5]—

SIR TOBY.    O, for a stone-bow[6] to hit him in the eye!

MALVOLIO.    Calling my officers[7] about me, in my branched[8] velvet gown, having come from a day-bed[9] where I have left Olivia sleeping—

SIR TOBY.    Fire and brimstone!

40    FABIAN.    O, peace, peace.

MALVOLIO.    And then to have the humour of state,[10] and after a demure travel of regard,[11] telling them I know my place as I would they should do theirs, to ask for my kinsman Toby[12]—

SIR TOBY.    Bolts and shackles![13]

45    FABIAN.    O, peace, peace, peace, now, now.

MALVOLIO.    Seven of my people, with an obedient start, make out for him. I frown the while, and perchance wind up my watch, or play with my[14]— some rich jewel. Toby approaches, curtsies[15] there to me—

SIR TOBY.    Shall this fellow live?

50    FABIAN.    Though our silence be drawn from us with cars,[16] yet peace.

MALVOLIO.    I extend my hand to him thus, quenching my familiar smile with an austere regard of control[17]—

---

1    *example* Precedent.

2    *Lady of the Strachy ... wardrobe* Like "Mistress Mall's picture" in 1.3.100, this may be a fictional example; however, records indicate that in 1606 a gentleman named William Strachey was a part-owner of the rival Blackfriar's Theatre, whose wardrobe master was David Yeomans, a tailor; *married* Likely a euphemism.

3    *Jezebel* Proverbial: "as proud as Jezebel," the infamous widow of King Ahab in 2 Kings 9.30–37.

4    *blows him* Puffs him up.

5    *state* Chair of state.

6    *stone-bow* Crossbow that fired stones to kill birds.

7    *officers* Attendants.

8    *branched* Embroidered with a pattern of branches.

9    *day-bed* Couch.

10    *state* Stately demeanour.

11    *demure travel of regard* I.e., grave survey of those present.

12    *kinsman Toby* Dropping the "Sir."

13    *Bolts and shackles* Fetters for prisoners.

14    *play with my* Here, he reaches for his steward's chain.

15    *curtsies* Bows.

16    *cars* Horse-drawn carts; prisoners might be tied between carts and "drawn" until they confessed.

17    *regard of control* Gaze of authority.

SIR TOBY.  And does not Toby take[1] you a blow o' the lips then?

MALVOLIO.  Saying "Cousin Toby, my fortunes, having cast me on your niece, give me this prerogative of speech"— 55

SIR TOBY.  What, what!

MALVOLIO.  "You must amend your drunkenness."

SIR TOBY.  Out, scab![2]

FABIAN.  Nay, patience, or we break the sinews of[3] our plot.

MALVOLIO.  "Besides, you waste the treasure of your time with a foolish 60 knight"—

SIR ANDREW.  That's me, I warrant you.

MALVOLIO.  "One Sir Andrew."

SIR ANDREW.  I knew 'twas I, for many do call me fool.

MALVOLIO.  What employment have we here? 65

[*Picks up the letter.*]

FABIAN.  Now is the woodcock near the gin.[4]

SIR TOBY.  O, peace! And the spirit of humours intimate reading aloud to him![5]

MALVOLIO.  By my life, this is my lady's hand. These be her very c's, her u's, and her t's,[6] and thus makes she her great P's. It is, in contempt of[7] ques- 70 tion, her hand.

SIR ANDREW.  Her c's, her u's, and her t's. Why that?

MALVOLIO.  [*Reads.*] "To the unknown beloved, this, and my good wishes." Her very phrases. By your leave, wax.[8] Soft[9]—and the impressure her Lu- crece[10] with which she uses to seal—'tis my lady. To whom should this be? 75

FABIAN.  This wins him, liver[11] and all.

MALVOLIO.  [*Reads.*]

"Jove knows I love,
    But who?

---

1   *take* Give.

2   *scab* Scoundrel.

3   *break the sinews of* I.e., disable.

4   *woodcock near the gin* Woodcocks were proverbially foolish birds; *gin* Engine, a snare.

5   *And the spirit … to him* I.e., may his eccentric disposition inspire him to read it aloud.

6   *c's, her u's, and her t's* I.e., cut, slang for female genitals (making an obscene joke with "great P's").

7   *in contempt of* Beyond.

8   *By your leave, wax* He breaks the wax seal.

9   *Soft* Wait.

10   *her Lucrece* Olivia's seal is the emblematic figure of chastity, stabbing herself after being raped (and the subject of Shakespeare's narrative poem, *Lucrece*).

11   *liver* I.e., his passions.

Lips, do not move,
80        No man must know."
    "No man must know." What follows? The numbers¹ altered. "No man
    must know." If this should be thee, Malvolio?
SIR TOBY.  Marry, hang thee, brock!²
MALVOLIO.  [Reads.]
85    "I may command where I adore,
        But silence, like a Lucrece knife,
    With bloodless stroke my heart doth gore.
        M. O. A. I. doth sway my life."
FABIAN.  A fustian³ riddle.
90  SIR TOBY.  Excellent wench, say I.
MALVOLIO.  "M. O. A. I. doth sway my life." Nay, but first let me see, let me
    see, let me see.
FABIAN.  What dish o' poison has she dressed⁴ him!
SIR TOBY.  And with what wing the staniel checks at⁵ it!
95  MALVOLIO.  "I may command where I adore." Why, she may command me. I
    serve her, she is my lady. Why, this is evident to any formal capacity,⁶ there
    is no obstruction in this. And the end—what should that alphabetical
    position⁷ portend? If I could make that resemble something in me. Softly,⁸
    M. O. A. I.—
100  SIR TOBY.  O, ay,⁹ make up that! He is now at a cold scent.¹⁰
FABIAN.  Sowter will cry upon't for all this, though it be as rank as a fox.¹¹
MALVOLIO.  "M." Malvolio. "M," why, that begins my name.
FABIAN.  Did not I say he would work it out? The cur is excellent at faults.¹²
MALVOLIO.  "M." But then there is no consonancy in the sequel; that suffers
105    under probation.¹³ "A" should follow, but "O" does.

---

1   *numbers* Metre.
2   *brock* Badger, perhaps alluding to his black-and-white attire.
3   *fustian* Pompous.
4   *dressed* Prepared for.
5   *wing ... checks at* I.e., how quickly the kestrel (a bird of prey) veers to pursue.
6   *capacity* Common sense.
7   *position* Arrangement.
8   *Softly* Slowly.
9   *O, ay* Punning on "O. A."
10  *at a cold scent* I.e., like a hound who has lost its quarry's scent.
11  *Sowter will cry ... as a fox* I.e., he will pick up the trail even though it's been crossed by
    the strong scent of a fox; *Sowter* Cobbler, but here the traditional name of a hound past
    his prime.
12  *faults* Lost scents.
13  *consonancy ... under probation* I.e., agreement in what follows; that ("the sequel," conclu-
    sion) breaks down when tested. In the First Folio, these phrases are run together without
    punctuation.

FABIAN.  And "O" shall end,[1] I hope.

SIR TOBY.  Ay, or I'll cudgel him, and make him cry "O!"

MALVOLIO.  And then "I" comes behind.

FABIAN.  Ay, an you had any eye behind you, you might see more detraction[2] at your heels than fortunes before you.    110

MALVOLIO.  M. O. A. I. This simulation is not as the former,[3] and yet, to crush this a little, it would bow[4] to me, for every one of these letters are in my name. Soft, here follows prose: [*Reads.*] "If this fall into thy hand, revolve.[5] In my stars I am above thee, but be not afraid of greatness. Some are become great,[6] some achieve greatness, and some have    115 greatness thrust upon 'em. Thy Fates open their hands, let thy blood and spirit embrace them, and to inure[7] thyself to what thou art like to be, cast thy humble slough and appear fresh.[8] Be opposite[9] with a kinsman, surly with servants. Let thy tongue tang[10] arguments of state; put thyself into the trick of singularity.[11] She thus advises thee that sighs for thee. Remem-    120 ber who commended thy yellow stockings, and wished to see thee ever cross-gartered.[12] I say, remember, go to, thou art made,[13] if thou desir'st to be so. If not, let me see thee a steward still, the fellow of servants, and not worthy to touch Fortune's fingers. Farewell. She that would alter services[14] with thee,    125

The Fortunate-Unhappy."

---

1    *"O" shall end*  I.e., he'll end in the circle of the hangman's noose.

2    *detraction*  Misfortune.

3    *This simulation … the former*  I.e., this riddle is not as easy as the former ("I may command where I adore").

4    *crush*  Force; *bow*  Yield.

5    *revolve*  Carefully consider; in performance, Malvolio sometimes takes this literally and spins slowly.

6    *become great*  Beginning with Nicolas Rowe's 1714 edition, this famous phrase in the First Folio has traditionally been corrected to "born great" because Malvolio recalls it that way in 3.4.34 and Feste quotes that wording in 5.1.349.

7    *inure*  Accustom.

8    *cast thy humble slough*  I.e., abandon your humble manner (like a snake "sloughs" its old skin); *fresh*  Bold.

9    *opposite*  Contrary.

10    *tang*  Ring out.

11    *trick of singularity*  Habit of eccentricity.

12    *cross-gartered*  Wearing stocking garters wrapped above and below the knee so as to cross behind it.

13    *go to … art made*  I.e., be sure, you are a made man.

14    *alter services*  I.e., exchange places (by marrying below her rank, and making him her lord).

Daylight and champain discovers[1] not more. This is open.[2] I will be proud,
I will read politic authors, I will baffle Sir Toby, I will wash off gross[3] acquaintance, I will be point-device[4] the very man. I do not now fool myself
to let imagination jade[5] me, for every reason excites to[6] this, that my lady
loves me. She did commend my yellow stockings of late, she did praise my
leg being cross-gartered, and in this she manifests herself to my love, and
with a kind of injunction drives me to these habits[7] of her liking. I thank
my stars, I am happy. I will be strange, stout,[8] in yellow stockings, and
cross-gartered, even with the swiftness of putting on. Jove[9] and my stars
be praised. Here is yet a postscript: [*Reads.*] "Thou canst not choose but
know who I am. If thou entertain'st[10] my love, let it appear in thy smiling,
thy smiles become thee well. Therefore in my presence still[11] smile, dear my
sweet, I prithee." Jove, I thank thee. I will smile, I will do everything that
thou wilt have me.

(*Exit.*)

FABIAN.  I will not give my part of this sport for a pension of thousands to be
paid from the Sophy.[12]
SIR TOBY.  I could marry this wench for this device.
SIR ANDREW.  So could I too.
SIR TOBY.  And ask no other dowry with her but such another jest.

(*Enter Maria.*)

SIR ANDREW.  Nor I neither.
FABIAN.  Here comes my noble gull-catcher.[13]
SIR TOBY.  Wilt thou set thy foot o' my neck?
SIR ANDREW.  Or o' mine either?

---

1    *champain discovers* Open countryside reveals.
2    *open* Obvious.
3    *politic* Political; *baffle* Disgrace; *gross* Common.
4    *point-device* I.e., to the point of perfection.
5    *jade* Trick.
6    *excites to* Urges.
7    *habits* Idiosyncrasies.
8    *strange, stout* Aloof, firm.
9    *Jove* Jupiter, the Roman god of justice.
10   *entertain'st* Accept.
11   *still* Always.
12   *the Sophy* Shah of Persia; in 1598, Sir Anthony Shirley and his brothers travelled to the
     Shah's court and in 1600 reported his munificence in a popular travel narrative.
13   *gull-catcher* Fool-catcher.

SIR TOBY.  Shall I play[1] my freedom at tray-trip,[2] and become thy bond-slave?   150
SIR ANDREW.  I' faith, or I either?
SIR TOBY.  Why, thou hast put him in such a dream that when the image of
   it leaves him he must run mad.
MARIA.  Nay, but say true. Does it work upon him?
SIR TOBY.  Like aqua-vita with a midwife.[3]   155
MARIA.  If you will then see the fruits of the sport, mark his first approach be-
   fore my lady. He will come to her in yellow stockings, and 'tis a colour she
   abhors, and cross-gartered, a fashion she detests, and he will smile upon
   her, which will now be so unsuitable to her disposition, being addicted to a
   melancholy as she is, that it cannot but turn him into a notable contempt.[4]   160
   If you will see it, follow me.
SIR TOBY.  To the gates of Tartar,[5] thou most excellent devil of wit.
SIR ANDREW.  I'll make one[6] too.

   (*Exeunt.*)


## ACT 3, SCENE 1

(*Enter Viola, and [Feste playing on a pipe and tabor.*[7]])

VIOLA.  Save[8] thee, friend, and thy music. Dost thou live by[9] thy tabor?
FESTE.  No, sir, I live by the church.
VIOLA.  Art thou a churchman?
FESTE.  No such matter, sir. I do live by the church, for I do live at my house,
   and my house doth stand by the church.   5
VIOLA.  So thou mayst say the king lies by a beggar, if a beggar dwell near
   him, or the church stands[10] by thy tabor, if thy tabor stand by the church.
FESTE.  You have said, sir. To see this[11] age! A sentence[12] is but a chev'rel[13] glove
   to a good wit. How quickly the wrong side may be turned outward.

---

1   *play* Gamble away.
2   *tray-trip* Dice game in which rolling a three (Old French *treis*) wins.
3   *aqua-vita with a midwife* Likely a stereotype associating distilled spirits with midwives
    and nurses; in *Romeo and Juliet*, for instance, the nurse twice asks for some to calm her.
4   *notable contempt* Object of contempt.
5   *Tartar* Tartarus, a region of hell.
6   *make one* Come along.
7   *tabor* Small drum typically played by jesters while piping.
8   *Save* God save.
9   *live by* I.e., make your living by playing.
10  *stands* I.e., is maintained by.
11  *To see this* Bear witness to this.
12  *sentence* Saying.
13  *chev'rel* Kid leather.

10 VIOLA. Nay, that's certain. They that dally nicely[1] with words may quickly
    make them wanton.[2]

FESTE. I would, therefore, my sister had had[3] no name, sir.

VIOLA. Why, man?

FESTE. Why, sir, her name's a word, and to dally with that word might make
15    my sister wanton. But indeed words are very rascals since bonds disgraced
    them.[4]

VIOLA. Thy reason, man?

FESTE. Troth, sir, I can yield you none without words, and words are grown
    so false I am loath to prove reason with them.

20 VIOLA. I warrant thou art a merry fellow and car'st for nothing.

FESTE. Not so, sir, I do care for something. But in my conscience, sir, I do
    not care for you. If that be to care for nothing, sir, I would it would make
    you invisible.

VIOLA. Art not thou the Lady Olivia's fool?

25 FESTE. No, indeed, sir. The Lady Olivia has no folly. She will keep no fool,
    sir, till she be married, and fools are as like husbands as pilchards are to
    herrings—the husband's the bigger.[5] I am indeed not her fool, but her cor-
    rupter of words.

VIOLA. I saw thee late[6] at the Count Orsino's.

30 FESTE. Foolery, sir, does walk about the orb like the sun[7]—it shines every-
    where. I would be sorry, sir, but the fool should be[8] as oft with your master
    as with my mistress. I think I saw your wisdom there.[9]

VIOLA. Nay, an thou pass upon me, I'll no more[10] with thee. Hold, there's
    expenses for thee. [*She gives coins.*]

35 FESTE. Now Jove in his next commodity[11] of hair send thee a beard.

VIOLA. By my troth, I'll tell thee, I am almost sick for one, [*aside*] though I
    would not have it grow on my chin. Is thy lady within?

---

1   *dally nicely* I.e., play subtly.

2   *wanton* I.e., equivocal (but taken to mean "unchaste").

3   *had* Been given.

4   *words are ... disgraced them* I.e., words are suspect when they require a legal contract to
    enforce them (playing on the adage "a man's word is his bond").

5   *fools are as like ... the bigger* A double comparison, since pilchards and herrings are simi-
    lar, yet husbands are greater fools.

6   *late* Recently.

7   *walk about ... the sun* The sun was still believed to circle the earth (the "orb").

8   *but the fool should be* I.e., if the fool were not allowed to be.

9   *I think ... wisdom there* I.e., I think you are also serving two masters; *there* I.e., at Orsi-
    no's.

10  *an thou pass ... no more* I.e., if you pass judgment on me, I'll deal no more.

11  *commodity* Shipment.

FESTE.  Would not a pair of these have bred,[1] sir?

VIOLA.  Yes, being kept together and put to use.[2]

FESTE.  I would play Lord Pandarus of Phrygia, sir, to bring a Cressida to this   40
Troilus.[3]

VIOLA.  I understand you, sir, 'tis well begged. [*Giving more coins.*]

FESTE.  The matter[4] I hope is not great, sir, begging but a beggar:[5] Cressida
was a beggar.[6] My lady is within, sir. I will conster[7] to them whence you
come. Who you are and what you would are out of my welkin—I might   45
say "element" but the word is overworn.[8]

(*Exit [Feste.]*)

VIOLA.  This fellow is wise enough to play the fool,[9]
And to do that well craves a kind of wit.
He must observe their mood on whom he jests,
The quality of persons, and the time,   50
And like the haggard, check at every feather
That comes before his eye.[10] This is a practice°   *skill*
As full of labour as a wise man's art,
For folly that he wisely shows is fit,[11]
But wise men, folly-fall'n, quite taint° their wit.   *discredit*  55

(*Enter Sir Toby and Sir Andrew.*)

SIR TOBY.  Save you, gentleman.

VIOLA.  And you, sir.

SIR ANDREW.  *Dieu vous garde, monsieur.*

---

1   *pair of these ... bred* Coins have accrued interest.

2   *put to use* I.e., invested.

3   *Lord Pandarus ... to this Troilus* Cressida's uncle acted as their go-between ("pander"),
a story familiar from Chaucer's narrative poem, *Troilus and Criseyde* (c. 1380s); Shakespeare's *Troilus and Cressida* was written soon after *Twelfth Night.*

4   *matter* Amount.

5   *begging but a beggar* Here "beggar" means both servant (i.e., a servant begging from a
servant) and orphan, and may allude to the practice of "begging" the Queen for guardian-
ship of rich wards of the state.

6   *Cressida was a beggar* Pandarus was Cressida's guardian.

7   *conster* Explain.

8   *out of my ... overworn* "Out of my element" was by this time indeed a cliché, and "welkin" was a showy substitute.

9   *wise enough ... fool* Proverbial: "no man can play the fool so well as the wise man."

10  *the haggard ... before his eye* Wild hawks ("haggards") were trained not to shy away from
("check at") the falconer's hand by first touching them with feathers.

11  *For folly ... is fit* I.e., playing the fool with discretion is appropriate.

VIOLA. *Et vous aussi; votre serviteur.*[1]

60 SIR ANDREW. I hope, sir, you are, and I am yours.

SIR TOBY. Will you encounter the house?[2] My niece is desirous you should enter, if your trade[3] be to her.

VIOLA. I am bound to your niece, sir. I mean, she is the list[4] of my voyage.

SIR TOBY. Taste your legs, sir, put them to motion.[5]

65 VIOLA. My legs do better understand me, sir, than[6] I understand what you mean by bidding me taste my legs.

SIR TOBY. I mean, to go, sir, to enter.

VIOLA. I will answer you with gait and entrance.[7] But we are prevented.

(*Enter Olivia and [Maria].*)

Most excellent accomplished lady, the heavens rain odours on you.

70 SIR ANDREW. That youth's a rare courtier—"Rain odours"—well.[8]

VIOLA. My matter hath no voice, lady, but to your own most pregnant and vouchsafed[9] ear.

SIR ANDREW. "Odours," "pregnant," and "vouchsafed"—I'll get 'em all three all ready.[10]

75 OLIVIA. Let the garden door be shut,[11] and leave me to my hearing. [*Exeunt all but Olivia and Viola.*] Give me your hand, sir.

VIOLA. My duty, madam, and most humble service.

OLIVIA. What is your name?

VIOLA. Cesario is your servant's name, fair Princess.

80 OLIVIA. My servant, sir? 'Twas never merry world
   Since lowly feigning° was called compliment.          *pretended humility*
   Y'are servant to the Count Orsino, youth.

VIOLA. And he is yours, and his must needs be yours.
   Your servant's servant is your servant, madam.

---

1   *Dieu vous garde ... votre serviteur* French: God save you, sir. And you also; (I am) your servant.

2   *encounter the house* I.e., go to meet Olivia (a mock-courtly phrase).

3   *trade* Business.

4   *list* Destination.

5   *Taste your legs ... to motion* I.e., test your seafaring legs on land (continuing the nautical metaphors in the previous lines).

6   *than* Better than.

7   *gait and entrance* Her nouns answer Toby's verbs, "go" and "enter."

8   *well* Well said.

9   *pregnant and vouchsafed* I.e., receptive and kindly disposed.

10  *all ready* I.e., ready to use in courtly conversation.

11  *garden door be shut* She is receiving Cesario in a walled, private garden.

OLIVIA.  For him, I think not on him. For his thoughts,                              85
  Would they were blanks[1] rather than filled with me.

VIOLA.  Madam, I come to whet° your gentle thoughts                    *encourage*
  On his behalf.

OLIVIA.                    O, by your leave, I pray you.
  I bade you never speak again of him,
  But would you undertake another suit,                                      90
  I had rather hear you to solicit that
  Than music from the spheres.[2]

VIOLA.                              Dear lady—

OLIVIA.  Give me leave, beseech you. I did send,
  After the last enchantment you did here,
  A ring in chase of you. So did I abuse°                        *wrong*  95
  Myself, my servant, and I fear me, you.
  Under your hard construction° must I sit,                     *judgment*
  To force that on you in a shameful cunning
  Which you knew none of yours. What might you think?
  Have you not set mine honour at the stake,                              100
  And baited it with all th' unmuzzled thoughts[3]
  That tyrannous heart can think? To one of your receiving°      *perception*
  Enough is shown: a cypress,[4] not a bosom,
  Hides my heart. So, let me hear you speak.

VIOLA.  I pity you.                                                                    105

OLIVIA.                That's a degree to love.

VIOLA.  No, not a grise,[5] for 'tis a vulgar proof°          *common experience*
  That very oft we pity enemies.

OLIVIA.  Why, then, methinks 'tis time to smile again.
  O world, how apt the poor are to be proud.
  If one should be a prey, how much the better                            110
  To fall before the lion than the wolf.[6] (*Clock strikes.*)
  The clock upbraids me with the waste of time.[7]
  Be not afraid, good youth, I will not have you,
  And yet, when wit and youth is come to harvest,°                    *maturity*

---

1   *blanks* Empty sheets of paper.

2   *music … spheres* I.e., heavenly music said to be produced by the movement of crystalline
    spheres containing the planets, stars, and heavenly firmament.

3   *at the stake … unmuzzled thoughts* Olivia compares her distress to a chained bear attacked
    by dogs.

4   *cypress* Transparent veil, often black to signal mourning.

5   *grise* Synonym for "step," as is "degree."

6   *To fall … the wolf* I.e., to be defeated by a noble creature (Cesario) than an ignoble one
    (Orsino).

7   *the waste of time* I.e., my fruitless efforts to win your love.

115   Your wife is like to reap a proper man.
       There lies your way, due west.
VIOLA.                              Then westward-ho![1]
       Grace and good disposition attend your ladyship.
       You'll nothing,° madam, to my lord by me?                    *say nothing*
OLIVIA. Stay—
120   I prithee tell me what thou[2] think'st of me.
VIOLA. That you do think you are not what you are.[3]
OLIVIA. If I think so, I think the same of you.[4]
VIOLA. Then think you right, I am not what I am.
OLIVIA. I would you were as I would have you be.[5]
125 VIOLA. Would it be better, madam, than I am?
       I wish it might, for now I am your fool.[6]
OLIVIA. O, what a deal of scorn looks beautiful
       In the contempt and anger of his lip![7]
       A murd'rous guilt shows not itself more soon
130   Than love that would seem hid. Love's night is noon.[8]
       Cesario, by the roses of the spring,
       By maidhood, honour, truth, and everything,
       I love thee so that, maugre° all thy pride,                   *despite*
       Nor wit nor reason can my passion hide.
135   Do not extort thy reasons from this clause:
       For that I woo, thou therefore hast no cause.[9]
       But rather reason thus with reason fetter:[10]
       Love sought is good, but given unsought is better.

---

1    *due west ... westward-ho* In Renaissance humoural theory, west was associated with Ve-
     nus or the Moon and with water, all synonymous with women (i.e., your destiny is to
     find a wife); *westward ho* The cry of Thames watermen taking passengers to Westminster
     from London.
2    *thou* Olivia switches from the formal "you" to the familiar form.
3    *you do think ... what you are* There are several possible readings: you don't see yourself as
     people see you; you won't admit you love beneath your rank; or, you won't admit you love
     a woman.
4    *the same of you* I.e., you are something other than what you seem.
5    *I would you ... have you be* I.e., I wish you could return my love; or, I wish you were the
     right rank (or sex) to be my lover.
6    *I am your fool* I.e., I am performing for you like your fool; or, you are forcing me to
     equivocate with words like your fool.
7    *deal of scorn ... of his lip* The signs of anger only intensify his beauty.
8    *more soon ... night is noon* I.e., love reveals itself in trying to hide.
9    *Do not extort ... hast no cause* Do not draw false conclusions from this premise: that since
     I woo you, you need not woo me.
10   *reason ... reason fetter* Overrule that argument with this one.

VIOLA.  By innocence I swear, and by my youth,
  I have one heart, one bosom, and one truth,                    140
  And that no woman has, nor never none[1]
  Shall mistress be of it, save I alone.
  And so adieu, good madam. Never more
  Will I my master's tears to you deplore.[2]
OLIVIA.  Yet come again, for thou perhaps mayst move             145
  That heart which now abhors, to like his love.

  (*Exeunt.*)


## ACT 3, SCENE 2

(*Enter Sir Toby, Sir Andrew and Fabian.*)

SIR ANDREW.  No, faith, I'll not stay a jot longer.
SIR TOBY.  Thy reason, dear venom,[3] give thy reason.
FABIAN.  You[4] must needs yield your reason, Sir Andrew.
SIR ANDREW.  Marry, I saw your niece do more favours[5] to the Count's serv-
  ingman than ever she bestowed upon me. I saw't i' th' orchard.[6]          5
SIR TOBY.  Did she see thee the while, old boy? Tell me that.
SIR ANDREW.  As plain as I see you now.
FABIAN.  This was a great argument[7] of love in her toward you.
SIR ANDREW.  'Slight, will you make an ass o' me?
FABIAN.  I will prove it legitimate,[8] sir, upon the oaths of judgment and rea-    10
  son.
SIR TOBY.  And they have been grand-jurymen since before Noah was a sailor.[9]
FABIAN.  She did show favour to the youth in your sight only to exasperate
  you, to awake your dormouse[10] valour, to put fire in your heart and brim-

---

1  *nor never none* Each term of this triple negative corresponds to her three possessions,
   "heart," "bosom," and "truth."
2  *deplore* I.e., tell with grief.
3  *Thy reason, dear venom* Andrew enters with "venom" (violent intentions) regarding Olivia's attention to Cesario.
4  *You* Fabian's polite "you" contrasts with Toby's familiar "thy."
5  *I saw ... more favours* As he left the stage in 3.1, he evidently saw Olivia give Cesario her
   hand.
6  *orchard* Garden.
7  *argument* Proof.
8  *prove it legitimate* I.e., make good my claim (that she does love you).
9  *grand-jurymen ... was a sailor* Grand juries decided whether the evidence (i.e., "oaths of
   judgment and reason") merited a trial; *before Noah was a sailor* I.e., since time immemorial.
10  *dormouse* Dormant, timid.

15    stone in your liver.[1] You should then have accosted her, and with some
excellent jests, fire-new from the mint,[2] you should have banged the youth
into dumbness. This was looked for at your hand, and this was baulked.
The double gilt[3] of this opportunity you let time wash off, and you are
now sailed into the north of my lady's opinion, where you will hang like an
20    icicle on a Dutchman's beard,[4] unless you do redeem it by some laudable
attempt either of valour or policy.[5]

SIR ANDREW.  An't be any way, it must be with valour, for policy I hate. I had
as lief[6] be a Brownist[7] as a politician.

SIR TOBY.  Why, then, build me[8] thy fortunes upon the basis of valour. Chal-
25    lenge me the Count's youth to fight with him. Hurt him in eleven places.[9]
My niece shall take note of it, and assure thyself there is no love-broker
in the world can more prevail in man's commendation with woman than
report of valour.

FABIAN.  There is no way but this, Sir Andrew.

30    SIR ANDREW.  Will either of you bear me a challenge to him?

SIR TOBY.  Go, write it in a martial hand,[10] be curst[11] and brief. It is no matter
how witty, so it be eloquent and full of invention.[12] Taunt him with the
license of ink.[13] If thou thou'st him[14] some thrice, it shall not be amiss. And
as many lies as will lie in thy sheet of paper, although the sheet were big
35    enough for the bed of Ware[15] in England, set 'em down. Go about it. Let
there be gall enough in thy ink, though thou write with a goose-pen,[16] no
matter. About it.

---

1    *put fire ... your liver* I.e., give you courage and passion.
2    *fire-new ... mint* I.e., newly forged (blank coins were hammered or "banged" onto a die).
3    *gilt* I.e., high value (higher currency coins were gilded rather than being minted of solid
     gold).
4    *sailed into the ... Dutchman's beard* You will now suffer her cold indifference (alluding to
     the Arctic voyage in 1596–97 of the Dutchman, William Barentz).
5    *policy* I.e., cleverness (but taken to mean political position).
6    *lief* Rather.
7    *Brownist* Member of a radical Puritan sect founded by Robert Browne, an advocate for
     separation of church and state.
8    *build me* Build for me.
9    *eleven places* In addition to the deadly point thrust to the abdomen, Italian fencing man-
     uals described ten potential sabre cuts.
10   *martial hand* Military style.
11   *curst* Forceful.
12   *eloquent and full of invention* Clear and full of substance. Unlike Toby's advice, duelling
     manuals advised against using insulting language or repeating charges of lying.
13   *license of ink* I.e., freedom of writing (rather than confronting him face to face).
14   *thou thou'st him* Using the familiar form with a stranger was insulting.
15   *bed of Ware* A famous bedstead in Ware nearly eleven feet square.
16   *gall enough ... goose-pen* I.e., write with enough bitterness in your words to hide your
     cowardice (ink was made from oak galls, pens from goose-feathers).

SIR ANDREW. Where shall I find you?

SIR TOBY. We'll call thee at the cubiculo.[1] Go.

(*Exit Sir Andrew.*)

FABIAN. This is a dear manikin[2] to you, Sir Toby.                                                    35

SIR TOBY. I have been dear[3] to him, lad, some two thousand strong, or so.

FABIAN. We shall have a rare letter from him, but you'll not deliver't?

SIR TOBY. Never trust me then, and by all means stir on the youth to an
answer. I think oxen and wainropes[4] cannot hale them together.[5] For Andrew, if he were opened and you find so much blood in his liver as will clog    40
the foot of a flea, I'll eat the rest of th' anatomy.[6]

FABIAN. And his opposite, the youth, bears in his visage no great presage[7] of
cruelty.

(*Enter Maria.*)

SIR TOBY. Look where the youngest wren of nine[8] comes.

MARIA. If you desire the spleen,[9] and will laugh yourselves into stitches, fol-    45
low me. Yond gull Malvolio is turned heathen, a very renegado,[10] for there
is no Christian that means to be saved by believing rightly can ever believe
such impossible passages of grossness.[11] He's in yellow stockings.

SIR TOBY. And cross-gartered?

MARIA. Most villainously,[12] like a pedant that keeps a school i' th' church.[13] I    50
have dogged[14] him like his murderer. He does obey every point of the letter
that I dropped to betray him. He does smile his face into more lines than

---

1    *cubiculo* Italian: bedchamber.

2    *manikin* Puppet.

3    *dear* Costly.

4    *wainropes* Wagon ropes.

5    *hale them together* I.e., get them to fight.

6    *opened ... anatomy* An anatomist opened the body to demonstrate the organs; before
William Harvey's *On the Circulation of Blood* (1628), blood was thought to be produced
by the liver; *so much blood ... a flea* I.e., so little courage; *th' anatomy* Skeleton (implying Andrew is just "skin and bones").

7    *presage* Sign.

8    *youngest wren of nine* I.e., the littlest of the brood.

9    *spleen* The spleen was believed to be the seat of laughter.

10   *renegado* Spanish: deserter of his faith.

11   *passages of grossness* I.e., stupid statements (in the letter, and implying that Malvolio is a
credulous literalist).

12   *villainously* Abominably.

13   *pedant ... i' th' church* Maria alludes to the obsolescent practice of rural schools meeting
in churches; *pedant* Overly formal, dogmatic teacher.

14   *dogged* Followed.

is in the new map with the augmentation of the Indies.[1] You have not seen
such a thing as 'tis. I can hardly forbear hurling things at him. I know my
55    lady will strike him. If she do, he'll smile and take't for a great favour.

SIR TOBY.  Come, bring us, bring us where he is.

(*Exeunt omnes.*)

## ACT 3, SCENE 3

(*Enter Sebastian and Antonio.*)

SEBASTIAN.  I would not by my will have troubled you,
      But since you make your pleasure of your pains,
      I will no further chide you.
ANTONIO.  I could not stay behind you. My desire,
5      More sharp than filèd° steel, did spur me forth,                     sharpened
      And not all° love to see you—though so much                          only for
      As might have drawn one to a longer voyage—
      But jealousy° what might befall your travel,                          concern
      Being skilless in° these parts, which to a stranger,        unacquainted with
10    Unguided and unfriended, often prove
      Rough and unhospitable. My willing love,
      The rather° by these arguments of fear,                                urged
      Set forth in your pursuit.
SEBASTIAN.                        My kind Antonio,
      I can no other answer make but thanks,
15    And thanks, and ever thanks; and oft° good turns                   too often
      Are shuffled off° with such uncurrent° pay.         dismissed / worthless
      But were my worth as is my conscience firm,[2]
      You should find better dealing. What's to do?
      Shall we go see the relics° of this town?                         antiquities
20  ANTONIO.  Tomorrow, sir, best first go see your lodging.
SEBASTIAN.  I am not weary, and 'tis long to night.
      I pray you, let us satisfy our eyes
      With the memorials and the things of fame
      That do renown this city.
ANTONIO.                        Would you'd pardon me.
25    I do not without danger walk these streets:

---

1    *new map ... the Indies* Edward Wright's world map, produced in 1599, showed the East
     Indies in detail and featured longitudinal rhumb lines to aid navigation.
2    *worth ... firm* I.e., wealth as great as my sense of indebtedness.

Once in a sea-fight 'gainst the Count his° galleys          *Count's*
I did some service, of such note indeed
That were I ta'en here it would scarce be answered.[1]
SEBASTIAN.  Belike° you slew great number of his people.          *Perhaps*
ANTONIO.  Th' offence is not of such a bloody nature,          30
  Albeit the quality° of the time and quarrel          *circumstances*
  Might well have given us bloody argument.[2]
  It might have since been answered in repaying
  What we took from them, which for traffic's° sake          *trade's*
  Most of our city did. Only myself stood out,          35
  For which if I be lapsed° in this place,          *caught*
  I shall pay dear.
SEBASTIAN.          Do not then walk too open.
ANTONIO.  It doth not fit me.[3] Hold, sir, here's my purse.
  In the south suburbs, at the Elephant,[4]
  Is best to lodge. I will bespeak our diet[5]          40
  Whiles you beguile° the time and feed your knowledge          *pass*
  With viewing of the town. There shall you have me.
SEBASTIAN.  Why I your purse?
ANTONIO.  Haply your eye shall light upon some toy°          *trifle*
  You have desire to purchase, and your store          45
  I think is not for idle markets,[6] sir.
SEBASTIAN.  I'll be your purse-bearer, and leave you for
  An hour.
ANTONIO.    To th' Elephant.
SEBASTIAN.                    I do remember.

  (*Exeunt.*)

---

1    *scarce be answered*  No reparation I could make would suffice.
2    *bloody argument*  Justification for violence.
3    *It doth not fit me*  I.e., it's not in my nature to be secretive.
4    *the Elephant*  An Elephant Inn existed in Southwark near the Globe theatre around 1599
     (it may have doubled as a brothel).
5    *bespeak our diet*  Order our food (parallel to "feed your knowledge").
6    *your store … idle markets*  I.e., you don't have enough money for luxuries.

## ACT 3, SCENE 4

(*Enter Olivia and Maria.*)

OLIVIA. [*aside*] I have sent after him, he says[1] he'll come.
How shall I feast him? What bestow of him?
For youth is bought more oft than begged or borrowed.[2]
I speak too loud. [*to Maria*] Where's Malvolio? He is sad and civil,[3]
5    And suits well for a servant with my fortunes.
Where is Malvolio?

MARIA. He's coming, madam, but in very strange manner.
He is sure possessed,[4] madam.

OLIVIA. Why, what's the matter? Does he rave?

10    MARIA. No, madam, he does nothing but smile. Your ladyship were best
to have some guard about you if he come, for sure the man is tainted in's
wits.

OLIVIA. Go call him hither.

([*Maria leaving,*] *enter Malvolio.*)[5]

I am as mad as he,
If sad and merry madness equal be.
15    How now, Malvolio!

MALVOLIO. Sweet lady, ho, ho.

OLIVIA. Smil'st thou?
I sent for thee upon a sad[6] occasion.

MALVOLIO. Sad, lady? I could be sad. This does make some obstruction in the
20    blood, this cross-gartering, but what of that? If it please the eye of one, it is
with me as the very true sonnet is, "Please one and please all."[7]

OLIVIA. Why, how dost thou, man? What is the matter with thee?

---

1    *he says* I.e., what if he says.
2    *bought ... borrowed* Proverbial: "Better to buy than to borrow" (or "to beg").
3    *sad and civil* Serious and shows restraint.
4    *possessed* By the devil, insane.
5    *Maria leaving, enter Malvolio* Most editors have Maria exit here, leaving Olivia to speak
     her couplet alone, and immediately return with Malvolio; comic timing is better served
     with his entrance while Olivia speaks her lines, thinking she is alone.
6    *sad* Serious (as in "sad and civil" above), but Malvolio takes it to mean melancholy caused
     by poor circulation, an "obstruction in the blood" caused by his crossed garters.
7    *Please one and please all* A line from a bawdy ballad about wilful women.

*A cross-gartered German cavalier, from* Omnium pene Europae, Asiae, Aphricae atque Americae gentium habitus, *1581. To wear stockings "cross-gartered" is to hold up each stocking with a ribbon crossed behind the knee and tied with a bow at the front or side. It may be that, by the time* Twelfth Night *was written, cross-gartering was perceived as an out-of-date affectation of pretenders to high class. It is also possible that cross-gartering was still very much in style—but only among fashionable young people. In either case, the fashion would have been wholly inappropriate for Malvolio.*

MALVOLIO. Not black in my mind, though yellow[1] in my legs. It did come to
his hands, and commands shall be executed. I think we do know the sweet
25   Roman hand.[2]
OLIVIA. Wilt thou go to bed,[3] Malvolio?
MALVOLIO. To bed? Ay, sweetheart, and I'll come to thee.
OLIVIA. God comfort thee! Why dost thou smile so, and kiss thy hand so oft?
MARIA. How do you, Malvolio?
30   MALVOLIO. At your request? Yes, nightingales answer daws.[4]
MARIA. Why appear you with this ridiculous boldness before my lady?
MALVOLIO. "Be not afraid of greatness." 'Twas well writ.
OLIVIA. What mean'st thou by that, Malvolio?
MALVOLIO. "Some are born great,"—
35   OLIVIA. Ha?
MALVOLIO. "Some achieve greatness,"—
OLIVIA. What say'st thou?
MALVOLIO. "And some have greatness thrust upon them."
OLIVIA. Heaven restore thee!
40   MALVOLIO. "Remember who commended thy yellow stockings,"—
OLIVIA. "Thy yellow stockings?"
MALVOLIO. "And wished to see thee cross-gartered."
OLIVIA. "Cross-gartered?"
MALVOLIO. "Go to, thou art made, if thou desir'st to be so."
45   OLIVIA. Am I made?
MALVOLIO. "If not, let me see thee a servant still."
OLIVIA. Why, this is very midsummer madness.[5]

(*Enter Servant.*)

SERVANT. Madam, the young gentleman of the Count Orsino's is returned. I
could hardly[6] entreat him back. He attends your ladyship's pleasure.
50   OLIVIA. I'll come to him.

(*Exit [Servant.]*)

---

1   *black ... yellow*  Black and yellow bile corresponded with melancholy and choler, and yellow
stockings were thought to indicate jealousy. "Black and Yellow" was also a popular song.
2   *Roman hand*  Fashionable italic lettering (rather than common English cursive).
3   *to bed*  I.e., to rest and recover from his madness.
4   *nightingales answer daws*  I.e., even a nightingale sings at the crowing of a jackdaw.
5   *midsummer madness*  Proverbial: "it is midsummer moon with you."
6   *hardly*  Only with difficulty (persuade him to return).

Good Maria, let this fellow be looked to. Where's my cousin Toby? Let some of my people have a special care of him. I would not have him miscarry[1] for the half of my dowry.

(*Exit [Olivia and Maria].*)

MALVOLIO.  O, ho, do you come near me[2] now? No worse man than Sir Toby to look to me. This concurs directly with the letter; she sends him on   55
purpose, that I may appear stubborn to him, for she incites me to that in the letter. "Cast thy humble slough," says she. "Be opposite with kinsman, surly with servants. Let thy tongue tang with[3] arguments of state, put thyself into the trick of singularity," and consequently[4] sets down the manner how, as a sad face, a reverend carriage, a slow tongue, in the habit of some   60
sir of note,[5] and so forth. I have limed[6] her, but it is Jove's doing, and Jove make me thankful. And when she went away now—"Let this fellow be looked to"—"fellow," not "Malvolio" nor after my degree,[7] but "fellow." Why, everything adheres together, that no dram of a scruple, no scruple of a scruple,[8] no obstacle, no incredulous[9] or unsafe circumstance—what can   65
be said?—nothing that can be can come between me and the full prospect of my hopes. Well, Jove, not I, is the doer of this, and he is to be thanked.

(*Enter Sir Toby, Fabian, and Maria.*)

SIR TOBY.  Which way is he, in the name of sanctity?[10] If all the devils of hell be drawn in little,[11] and Legion[12] himself possessed him, yet I'll speak to him.
FABIAN.  Here he is, here he is. How is't with you, sir?   70
SIR TOBY.  How is't with you, man?
MALVOLIO.  Go off, I discard you. Let me enjoy my private.[13] Go off.

---

1  *miscarry* Come to harm.
2  *come near me* I.e., begin to appreciate my value.
3  *tang with* The First Folio reads "langer with," a printer's error, while the letter in the First Folio reads "tang arguments."
4  *consequently* Subsequently.
5  *sir of note* I.e., distinguished gentleman.
6  *limed* I.e., caught; bird lime is a sticky paste smeared on branches to trap birds.
7  *my degree* I.e., my position as steward.
8  *no dram ... scruple* I.e., without a doubt, even the smallest doubt; drams and scruples were tiny measures used by apothecaries, with a scruple being one third of a dram.
9  *incredulous* Incredible.
10  *in the ... of sanctity* I.e., by God.
11  *drawn in little* Contracted into a space, drawn in miniature.
12  *Legion* Toby mistakenly names a spirit who possessed a man in Mark 5.9 saying, "my name is legion, for we are many."
13  *private* Privacy.

MARIA. Lo, how hollow[1] the fiend speaks within him. Did not I tell you? Sir Toby, my lady prays you to have a care of him.

75 MALVOLIO. Ah ha, does she so?

SIR TOBY. Go to, go to. Peace, peace, we must deal gently with him. Let me alone.[2] How do you, Malvolio? How is't with you? What, man, defy the devil. Consider, he's an enemy to mankind.

MALVOLIO. Do you know what you say?[3]

80 MARIA. La[4] you, an you speak ill of the devil, how he takes it at heart. Pray God he be not bewitched.

FABIAN. Carry his water to th' wise woman.[5]

MARIA. Marry, and it shall be done tomorrow morning,[6] if I live. My lady would not lose him for more than I'll say.

85 MALVOLIO. How now, mistress?

MARIA. O Lord!

SIR TOBY. Prithee hold thy peace, this is not the way. Do you not see you move[7] him? Let me alone with him.

FABIAN. No way but gentleness—gently, gently. The fiend is rough,[8] and will
90 not be roughly used.

SIR TOBY. Why, how now, my bawcock.[9] How dost thou, chuck?[10]

MALVOLIO. Sir!

SIR TOBY. Ay, biddy,[11] come with me. What, man, 'tis not for gravity[12] to play at cherrypit[13] with Satan. Hang him, foul collier.[14]

95 MARIA. Get him to say his prayers, good Sir Toby, get him to pray.

MALVOLIO. My prayers, minx![15]

MARIA. No, I warrant you, he will not hear of godliness.

---

1    *hollow* Insincerely.
2    *alone* Alone with him.
3    *Do you ... say* I.e., how dare you (a drunk) moralize.
4    *La* Look.
5    *Carry his water ... woman* Have his urine examined (for signs of disease); *wise woman* A medical practitioner with knowledge of basic medicine and herbal remedies, but often associated with witchcraft.
6    *tomorrow morning* I.e., after the chamber pot is emptied.
7    *move* Anger.
8    *rough* Violent.
9    *bawcock* Fine bird.
10   *chuck* Chicken.
11   *biddy* Hen (with "bawcock" and "chuck," a term of affection).
12   *gravity* A man of gravity or dignity.
13   *cherrypit* Children's game in which cherry stones are tossed into a hole.
14   *collier* Coalman (i.e., Satan).
15   *minx* Impudent woman.

MALVOLIO.  Go, hang yourselves all! You are idle shallow things, I am not of your element.[1] You shall know more hereafter.

(*Exit.*)

SIR TOBY.  Is't possible?                                                                100
FABIAN.  If this were played upon a stage now, I could condemn it as an improbable fiction.[2]
SIR TOBY.  His very genius[3] hath taken the infection of the device,[4] man.
MARIA.  Nay, pursue him now, lest the device take air and taint.[5]
FABIAN.  Why, we shall make him mad indeed.                                               105
MARIA.  The house will be the quieter.
SIR TOBY.  Come, we'll have him in a dark room and bound.[6] My niece is already in the belief that he's mad. We may carry it thus, for our pleasure and his penance till our very pastime, tired out of breath, prompt us to have mercy on him. At which time we will bring the device to the bar and   110 crown thee for a finder of madmen.[7] But see, but see.

(*Enter Sir Andrew.*)

FABIAN.  More matter[8] for a May morning.
SIR ANDREW.  Here's the challenge, read it. I warrant there's vinegar and pepper in't.
FABIAN.  Is't so saucy?[9]                                                                115
SIR ANDREW.  Ay, is't, I warrant him. Do but read.
SIR TOBY.  Give me. [*Reads.*] "Youth, whatsoever thou art, thou art but a scurvy fellow."
FABIAN.  Good, and valiant.
SIR TOBY.  [*Reads.*] "Wonder not, nor admire not in thy mind, why I do call   120 thee so, for I will show thee no reason for't."
FABIAN.  A good note, that keeps you from the blow of the law.[10]

---

1    *I am ... your element* I.e., I am made of better stuff than you.
2    *improbable fiction* Along with immorality, stage plays were condemned for their lack of realism.
3    *genius* Soul.
4    *the device* I.e., the letter trick.
5    *take air and taint* Spoil, grow stale (playing on "taken the infection").
6    *dark room and bound* The customary sixteenth-century treatment of the mad.
7    *to the bar ... finder of madmen* Alluding to jury trials where a "finder" demonstrated the defendant's madness.
8    *matter* Entertainment.
9    *saucy* Spicy.
10   *blow of the law* Legal punishment for breaking the peace (the usual punishment for duelling).

SIR TOBY. [*Reads.*] "Thou com'st to the Lady Olivia, and in my sight she uses thee kindly; but thou liest in thy throat, that is not the matter[1] I challenge thee for."

125

FABIAN. Very brief, and to exceeding good sense [*aside*] –less.

SIR TOBY. [*Reads.*] "I will waylay thee going home, where if it be thy chance to kill me"—

FABIAN. Good.

130  SIR TOBY. "Thou kill'st me like a rogue and a villain."[2]

FABIAN. Still you keep o' th' windy side[3] of the law—good.

SIR TOBY. [*Reads.*] "Fare thee well, and God have mercy upon one of our souls. He may have mercy upon mine, but my hope is better, and so look to thyself. Thy friend, as thou usest[4] him, and thy sworn enemy,

135
                                                Andrew Aguecheek."

If this letter move him not, his legs cannot. I'll give't him.

MARIA. You may have very fit occasion for't. He is now in some commerce[5] with my lady, and will by and by depart.

SIR TOBY. Go, Sir Andrew. Scout me[6] for him at the corner of the orchard,

140  like a bum-baily.[7] So soon as ever thou seest him, draw, and as thou draw'st, swear horrible, for it comes to pass oft that a terrible oath, with a swaggering accent sharply twanged off, gives manhood more approbation than ever proof[8] itself would have earned him. Away.

SIR ANDREW. Nay, let me alone for swearing.[9]

(*Exit.*)

145  SIR TOBY. Now will not I[10] deliver his letter, for the behaviour of the young gentleman gives him out to be of good capacity and breeding.[11] His employment between his lord and my niece confirms no less. Therefore this letter, being so excellently ignorant, will breed no terror in the youth. He will find it comes from a clodpole.[12] But, sir, I will deliver his challenge by

150  word of mouth, set upon Aguecheek a notable report of valour, and drive

---

1    *thou liest ... not the matter* Andrew's accusation of a deep lie would have meant an automatic challenge, but "not the matter" (like "no reason" above) cancels the accusation.

2    *kill'st me ... villain* Ambiguous, as "rogue and a villain" follows either "thou" or "me."

3    *windy side* Windward (i.e., the safe side).

4    *as thou usest* I.e., to the extent that you consider him a friend.

5    *commerce* Conversation.

6    *Scout me* Look out.

7    *bum-baily* A bailiff (Sheriff's officer) who snuck up behind debtors to arrest them.

8    *horrible* Horribly; *approbation* Credit; *proof* A duel.

9    *let me alone for swearing* Leave the swearing to me.

10   *Now will not I* I will not.

11   *of good ... and breeding* Intelligent and well-bred.

12   *clodpole* Blockhead.

the gentleman—as I know his youth will aptly receive it[1]—into a most hideous opinion of his rage, skill, fury, and impetuosity. This will so fright them both that they will kill one another by the look, like cockatrices.[2]

(*Enter Olivia and Viola.*)

FABIAN.  Here he comes with your niece. Give them way[3] till he take leave, and presently after him.                                                                                                      155

SIR TOBY.  I will meditate the while upon some horrid[4] message for a challenge.

[*Exeunt Sir Toby, Fabian, and Maria.*]

OLIVIA.  I have said too much unto a heart of stone,
   And laid mine honour too unchary on't.[5]
   There's something in me that reproves my fault,                                                        160
   But such a headstrong potent fault it is
   That it but mocks reproof.

VIOLA.  With the same 'haviour° that your passion bears                                  *behaviour*
   Goes on my master's griefs.[6]

OLIVIA.  Here, wear this jewel[7] for me, 'tis my picture.                                             165
   Refuse it not, it hath no tongue to vex you.
   And I beseech you come again tomorrow.
   What shall you ask of me that I'll deny,
   That honour saved may upon asking give?[8]

VIOLA.  Nothing but this: your true love for my master.                                        170

OLIVIA.  How with mine honour may I give him that
   Which I have given to you?

VIOLA.  I will acquit you.[9]

OLIVIA.  Well, come again tomorrow. Fare thee well.
   A fiend like thee might bear my soul to hell.                                                              175

   [*Exit Olivia.*]

   (*Enter Sir Toby and Sir Fabian.*)

---

1   *his youth ... receive it*  Because of his inexperience, he will readily believe the report.
2   *cockatrices*  Basilisks, legendary serpents that could kill on sight.
3   *way*  Room.
4   *horrid*  Terrifying.
5   *laid mine ... on't*  Staked my honour too rashly on it ("a heart of stone"); *on't*  In the First Folio, but often emended to "out."
6   *your passion ... master's griefs*  Passion and grief were said to be both indications of lovesickness.
7   *jewel*  Miniature painting set in a jewelled pendant.
8   *honour saved ... asking give*  Honour may grant without yielding (her chastity).
9   *acquit you*  I.e., release you (from the love you have given me).

SIR TOBY. Gentleman, God save thee.

VIOLA. And you, sir.

SIR TOBY. That defence thou hast, betake thee to't.[1] Of what nature the wrongs are thou hast done him, I know not, but thy interceptor, full of despite,[2] bloody as the hunter, attends[3] thee at the orchard end.[4] Dismount thy tuck, be yare[5] in thy preparation, for thy assailant is quick, skilful, and deadly.

VIOLA. You mistake, sir. I am sure no man hath any quarrel to me.[6] My remembrance is very free and clear from any image of offence done to any man.

SIR TOBY. You'll find it otherwise, I assure you. Therefore, if you hold your life at any price, betake you to[7] your guard, for your opposite hath in him what youth, strength, skill, and wrath, can furnish man withal.

VIOLA. I pray you, sir, what is he?

SIR TOBY. He is knight, dubbed with unhatched[8] rapier and on carpet consideration,[9] but he is a devil in private brawl. Souls and bodies hath he divorced three, and his incensement[10] at this moment is so implacable that satisfaction can be none but by pangs of death and sepulchre. "Hob-nob" is his word—give't or take't.[11]

VIOLA. I will return again into the house and desire some conduct[12] of the lady. I am no fighter. I have heard of some kind of men that put quarrels purposely on others to taste[13] their valour. Belike[14] this is a man of that quirk.[15]

SIR TOBY. Sir, no. His indignation derives itself out of a very competent[16]

---

1   *That defence ... thee to't* Prepare to use what means of defence you possess.

2   *despite* Defiance.

3   *attends* Awaits.

4   *the orchard end* I.e., at the end of the garden; Sir Andrew awaits Cesario at the corner of the orchard, so the duel may take place outside Olivia's private garden.

5   *Dismount thy tuck ... yare* Draw your rapier ("dismount" usually indicates setting a cannon in place for firing); *yare* Quick.

6   *quarrel to me* I.e., reason to challenge me to a duel.

7   *betake you to* Be on.

8   *unhatched* Unhacked (i.e., ceremonial).

9   *carpet consideration* Courtly merit, not military valour; Andrew is a "carpet knight."

10  *incensement* Wrath.

11  *"Hob-nob" ... take't* "Have or have not" is his motto—kill or be killed; *Hob-nob* From the Middle English *habbe he, nabbe he.*

12  *some conduct* I.e., someone to escort me (or serve as a second).

13  *taste* Test.

14  *Belike* Perhaps.

15  *quirk* Peculiar behaviour, alluding to a fashion among gentlemen for duelling on superficial grounds.

16  *competent* Legally sufficient (and therefore requiring satisfaction).

injury. Therefore, get you on and give him his desire. Back you shall not to    200
the house, unless you undertake that with me which with as much safety
you might answer him.[1] Therefore on, or strip your sword stark naked.[2]
For meddle[3] you must, that's certain, or forswear to wear iron[4] about you.

VIOLA.    This is as uncivil as strange. I beseech you do me this courteous office
as to know of[5] the knight what my offence to him is. It is something of my    205
negligence, nothing of my purpose.

SIR TOBY.    I will do so. Signior Fabian, stay you by this gentleman till my
return.

(*Exit Toby.*)

VIOLA.    Pray you, sir, do you know of this matter?

FABIAN.    I know the knight is incensed against you, even to a mortal    210
arbitrement,[6] but nothing of the circumstance more.

VIOLA.    I beseech you, what manner of man is he?

FABIAN.    Nothing of that wonderful promise, to read him by his form,[7] as
you are like to find him in the proof of his valour. He is indeed, sir, the
most skilful, bloody, and fatal opposite that you could possibly have found    215
in any part of Illyria. Will you[8] walk towards him, I will make your peace
with him if I can.

VIOLA.    I shall be much bound to you for't. I am one that would rather go
with Sir Priest than Sir Knight.[9] I care not who knows so much of my
mettle.[10]    220

(*Exeunt.*)

(*Enter Sir Toby and Sir Andrew.*)

SIR TOBY.    Why, man, he's a very devil. I have not seen such a firago.[11] I had a
pass with him, rapier, scabbard, and all, and he gives me the stuck in with

---

1    *undertake that ... answer him* I.e., fight a duel with me, who am no less dangerous than
     he.
2    *strip ... naked* I.e., be publicly shamed for cowardice.
3    *meddle* Engage him.
4    *iron* A sword.
5    *know of* Learn from.
6    *mortal arbitrement* Fight to the death.
7    *Nothing of ... his form* Not promising, judging by his appearance.
8    *Will you* If you will.
9    *I am one ... Sir Knight* I.e., I'd rather make peace than fight (priests were called "sir,"
     either by courtesy or to indicate a college degree).
10   *mettle* Disposition.
11   *firago* Virago, a woman warrior (implying Cesario's ferocity is at odds with his feminine
     appearance).

such a mortal motion[1] that it is inevitable. And on the answer, he pays[2] you as surely as your feet hit the ground they step on. They say he has been
225    fencer to the Sophy.

SIR ANDREW.  Pox on't. I'll not meddle with him.

SIR TOBY.  Ay, but he will not now be pacified. Fabian can scarce hold him yonder.

SIR ANDREW.  Plague on't an I thought he had been valiant, and so cunning
230    in fence, I'd have seen him damned ere I'd have challenged him. Let him let the matter slip, and I'll give him my horse, grey Capilet.[3]

SIR TOBY.  I'll make the motion.[4] Stand here, make a good show on't, this shall end without the perdition of souls.[5] [aside] Marry, I'll ride your horse as well as I ride[6] you.

(Enter Fabian and Viola.)

235    [aside to Fabian] I have his horse to take up the quarrel. I have persuaded him the youth's a devil.

FABIAN.  [aside to Sir Toby] He is as horribly conceited[7] of him, and pants and looks pale, as if a bear were at his heels.

SIR TOBY.  [to Viola] There's no remedy, sir. He will fight with you for's oath[8]
240    sake. Marry, he hath better bethought him of his quarrel,[9] and he finds that now scarce to be worth talking of.[10] Therefore draw for the supportance of his vow. He protests he will not hurt you.

VIOLA.  [aside] Pray God defend me. A little thing would make me tell them how much I lack of a man.[11]

245  FABIAN.  [to Sir Andrew] Give ground if you see him furious.

SIR TOBY.  Come, Sir Andrew, there's no remedy. The gentleman will, for his honour's sake, have one bout with you. He cannot by the duello avoid it,

---

1    *stuck in … mortal motion* Thrust with such a practiced movement (that it would have inevitable deadly consequences); *stuck* From Italian, *stoccata.*

2    *on the answer, he pays* As you attempt to parry his thrust, he kills.

3    *Capilet* Spelling in the First Folio, although spelled "Capulet" in *Romeo and Juliet,* both variants on the obsolete word "caple," meaning "horse."

4    *motion* Offer.

5    *perdition of souls* I.e., deaths (but alluding to the damnation of murderers).

6    *ride* Make a fool of.

7    *is as horribly conceited* I.e., has as terrifying an image.

8    *for's oath* His oath's.

9    *bethought … quarrel* Reconsidered the reasons for his challenge.

10    *scarce … talking of* Duelling code (the duello) required an oath to be upheld even if its motives no longer existed; as Toby explains below, "he cannot by the duello avoid it."

11    *A little thing … lack of a man* It would not take much (of a threat from Andrew) to expose my fear, or to reveal that I am a woman (with innuendo on "a little thing").

but he has promised me, as he is a gentleman and a soldier, he will not hurt
   you. Come on, to't.
SIR ANDREW.  Pray God he keep his oath.                                        250

   (*Enter Antonio.*)[1]

VIOLA.  I do assure you 'tis against my will. [*Sir Andrew and Viola draw.*]
ANTONIO.  Put up your sword. If this young gentleman
   Have done offence, I take the fault on me.
   If you offend him, I for him defy you.[2]
SIR TOBY.  You, sir? Why, what are you?                                        255
ANTONIO.  One, sir, that for his love[3] dares yet do more
   Than you have heard him brag to you he will.
SIR TOBY.  Nay, if you be an undertaker, I am for you. [*Draws his sword.*]

   (*Enter Officers.*)

FABIAN.  O good Sir Toby, hold. Here come the officers.
SIR TOBY.  [*to Antonio*] I'll be with you anon.                               260
VIOLA.  Pray, sir, put your sword up, if you please.
SIR ANDREW.  Marry, will I, sir. And for that I promised[4] you, I'll be as good
   as my word. He will bear you easily and reins well.
FIRST OFFICER.  This is the man, do thy office.
SECOND OFFICER.  Antonio, I arrest thee at the suit[5] of Count Orsino.        265
ANTONIO.  You do mistake me, sir.
FIRST OFFICER.  No, sir, no jot. I know your favour[6] well,
   Though now you have no sea-cap on your head.[7]
   Take him away; he knows I know him well.
ANTONIO.  I must obey. [*to Viola*] This comes with seeking you.               270
   But there's no remedy, I shall answer it.[8]
   What will you do, now my necessity
   Makes me to ask you for my purse? It grieves me

---

1   *Enter Antonio* Antonio's sudden entrance, and the arrival of officers below, indicates that
    the duel occurs in a public place, and not in Olivia's garden.
2   *take the fault ... defy you* Antonio offers to act as proxy for Cesario (whom he mistakes
    for Sebastian throughout this scene, since the siblings look alike), a practice that helped
    prevent unevenly matched opponents.
3   *his love* I.e., love of him (Sebastian, but indicating Cesario).
4   *that I promised* His horse, Capilet (Toby has kept Andrew's offer to himself).
5   *suit* Petition.
6   *favour* Face.
7   *Though now ... on your head* This line condenses and confirms Antonio's account in 3.3
    of a sea-battle and piracy.
8   *answer it* I.e., accept the consequences of my former actions.

Much more for what I cannot do for you
275 Than what befalls myself. You stand amazed,°                    *bewildered*
But be of comfort.
SECOND OFFICER. Come, sir, away.
ANTONIO. [*to Viola*] I must entreat of you some of that money.
VIOLA. What money, sir?
280 For the fair kindness you have showed me here,
And part being prompted by your present trouble,
Out of my lean and low ability°                                *meagre resources*
I'll lend you something. My having is not much.
I'll make division of my present[1] with you.
285 Hold, [*offering money*] there's half my coffer.
ANTONIO. [*refuses money*] Will you deny me now?
Is't possible that my deserts to you
Can lack persuasion?[2] Do not tempt my misery,
Lest that it make me so unsound[3] a man
290 As to upbraid you with those kindnesses
That I have done for you.
VIOLA.                          I know of none,
Nor know I you by voice or any feature.
I hate ingratitude more in a man
Than lying, vainness, babbling drunkenness,
295 Or any taint of vice whose strong corruption
Inhabits our frail blood.
ANTONIO.                          O heavens themselves!
SECOND OFFICER. Come, sir, I pray you go.
ANTONIO. Let me speak a little. This youth that you see here
I snatched one half out of the jaws of death,[4]
300 Relieved him with such sanctity[5] of love,
And to his image, which methought did promise
Most venerable worth,[6] did I devotion.
FIRST OFFICER. What's that to us? The time goes by away.
ANTONIO. But O, how vile an idol proves this god!
305 Thou hast, Sebastian, done good feature° shame.            *physical perfection*

---

1   *My having* What I own; *my present* My ready money.
2   *deserts … lack persuasion* I.e., services that merit reward do not move you.
3   *unsound* Morally weak (because kindness should expect no reward).
4   *snatched one … jaws of death* Pulled half-dead from the sea.
5   *sanctity* Devotion; this is the first in a series of religious terms: *image, venerable, devotion, idol, god.*
6   *venerable worth* Worthy of devotion.

In nature there's no blemish but the mind.
None can be called deformed but the unkind.[1]
Virtue is beauty, but the beauteous evil
Are empty trunks, o'er-flourished by the devil.[2]
FIRST OFFICER. The man grows mad. Away with him.
    Come, come, sir.                                                          310
ANTONIO. Lead me on.

    (*Exit [with Officers.*])

VIOLA. Methinks his words do from such passion fly
    That he believes himself. So do not I.[3]
    Prove true, imagination, O, prove true,
    That I, dear brother, be now ta'en for you!                               315
SIR TOBY. Come hither, knight. Come hither, Fabian. We'll whisper o'er a
    couplet or two of most sage saws.[4]
VIOLA. He named Sebastian. I my brother know
    Yet living in my glass.[5] Even such and so
    In favour was my brother. And he went                                     320
    Still° in this fashion, colour, ornament,                  *Always*
    For him I imitate. O, if it prove,°                     *proves true*
    Tempests are kind, and salt waves fresh in love!

    [*Exit Viola.*]

SIR TOBY. A very dishonest paltry[6] boy, and more a coward than a hare.[7] His
    dishonesty appears in leaving his friend here in necessity and denying him.  325
    And for his cowardship, ask Fabian.
FABIAN. A coward, a most devout coward, religious in it.
SIR ANDREW. 'Slid,[8] I'll after him again and beat him.
SIR TOBY. Do, cuff him soundly, but never draw thy sword.
SIR ANDREW. An I do not—[9] [*Exit.*]                                         330

---

1    *unkind* Cruel, unnatural (i.e., morally deformed).
2    *the beauteous evil ... the devil* Those who are beautiful yet evil are like empty chests lav-
    ishly decorated (to tempt desire).
3    *So do not I* I.e., I dare not believe the hope (that Sebastian is alive).
4    *sage saws* Wise sayings; Sir Toby invites Fabian to contemplate the unexpected outcome
    of the duel (but possibly also mocking Viola's preceding couplets).
5    *I my brother ... my glass* I know my brother is mirrored in my disguise.
6    *dishonest paltry* Dishonourable, weak.
7    *more a coward than a hare* Proverbial: "as fearful as a hare."
8    *'Slid* By God's eyelid.
9    *An I do not* I.e., if I don't ("cuff him soundly").

FABIAN. Come, let's see the event.[1]

SIR TOBY. I dare lay any money 'twill be nothing yet.[2]

(*Exit.*)

## ACT 4, SCENE 1

(*Enter Sebastian and Feste.*)

FESTE. Will you[3] make me believe that I am not sent for you?

SEBASTIAN. Go to, go to, thou art a foolish fellow. Let me be clear of[4] thee.

FESTE. Well held out,[5] i' faith! No, I do not know you, nor I am not[6] sent
to you by my lady, to bid you come speak with her, nor your name is not
5   Master Cesario, nor this is not my nose[7] neither. Nothing that is so is so.

SEBASTIAN. I prithee vent thy folly somewhere else. Thou know'st not me.

FESTE. Vent my folly! He has heard that word of some great man, and now
applies it to a fool. Vent my folly—I am afraid this great lubber,[8] the world,
will prove a cockney.[9] I prithee now, ungird thy strangeness,[10] and tell me
10   what I shall "vent" to my lady. Shall I "vent" to her that thou art coming?

SEBASTIAN. I prithee, foolish Greek,[11] depart from me.
There's money for thee. If you tarry longer I shall give worse payment.[12]

FESTE. By my troth, thou hast an open hand.[13] These wise men that give fools
money get themselves a good report after fourteen years' purchase.[14]

(*Enter [Sir] Andrew, [Sir] Toby, and Fabian.*)

15   SIR ANDREW. Now, sir, have I met you again? [*striking Sebastian*] There's for
you.

---

1    *event* Outcome.
2    *yet* After all.
3    *Will you* I.e., are you trying to.
4    *clear of* Free from.
5    *held out* Insisted (the scene begins mid-conversation).
6    *I am not* Am I not (establishing a series of double negatives).
7    *not my nose* Proverbial: "as plain as the nose on my face."
8    *lubber* Clumsy, lazy fellow.
9    *cockney* Spoiled child.
10   *ungird thy strangeness* Drop your aloof formality.
11   *Greek* I.e., buffoon.
12   *worse payment* On stage, Sebastian may threaten Feste here by raising his hand.
13   *thou hast an open hand* You are generous (perhaps ironic, but Cesario gave him money in
     3.1).
14   *good report ... purchase* I.e., good reputation provided they pay well enough (the typical
     price of a plot of land was equal to twelve years' rent).

SEBASTIAN. Why, [*beating Sir Andrew*] there's for thee, and there, and there.
(*Beats Sir Andrew.*) Are all the people mad?

SIR TOBY. [*holding Sebastian*] Hold, sir, or I'll throw your dagger o'er the
house.  20

FESTE. This will I tell my lady straight. I would not be in some of your coats
for two-pence.[1] [*Exit.*]

SIR TOBY. Come on, sir, hold.

SIR ANDREW. Nay, let him alone. I'll go another way to work[2] with him. I'll
have an action of battery[3] against him if there be any law in Illyria. Though  25
I struck him first, yet it's no matter for that.

SEBASTIAN. Let go thy hand.

SIR TOBY. Come, sir, I will not let you go. Come, my young soldier, put up
your iron. You are well fleshed.[4] Come on.

SEBASTIAN. I will be free from thee. What wouldst thou now?  30
If thou dar'st tempt me further, draw thy sword. [*Draws.*]

SIR TOBY. What, what? Nay, then I must have an ounce or two of this malapert[5] blood from you. [*Draws.*]

(*Enter Olivia.*)

OLIVIA. Hold, Toby. On thy life, I charge thee hold.

SIR TOBY. Madam.  35

OLIVIA. Will it be ever thus? Ungracious wretch,
Fit for the mountains and the barbarous caves,
Where manners ne'er were preached. Out of my sight!
Be not offended, dear Cesario—
Rudesby,° be gone!  *Ruffian*  40

[*Exeunt Sir Toby, Sir Andrew, and Fabian.*]

I prithee, gentle friend,
Let thy fair wisdom, not thy passion, sway
In this uncivil and unjust extent[6]
Against thy peace. Go with me to my house,
And hear thou there how many fruitless pranks  45

---

1  *two-pence* Either Feste is being ironic or this small sum is significant to him.

2  *go another way to work* Find other means to revenge myself.

3  *action of battery* Lawsuit for armed assault (although "I struck him first" undercuts his
claim).

4  *young soldier … well fleshed* Thinking Sebastian is the once-timid Cesario, Toby compares
him to a soldier who is used to bloodshed; a young hawk or hound was "fleshed" by feeding on its kill.

5  *malapert* Impudent.

6  *extent* Attack (from the legal term *extendi facias*, to seize goods for the king).

This ruffian hath botched up,° that thou thereby        *clumsily contrived*
Mayst smile at this. Thou shalt not choose but go.
Do not deny. Beshrew° his soul for me.                *Curse*
He started one poor heart of mine in thee.[1]
50 SEBASTIAN. What relish is in this? How runs the stream?[2]
Or° I am mad, or else this is a dream.              *Either*
Let fancy still my sense in Lethe steep.[3]
If it be thus to dream, still let me sleep.
OLIVIA. Nay, come, I prithee. Would thou'dst be ruled by me.
55 SEBASTIAN. Madam, I will.
OLIVIA.                 O, say so, and so be!

    (*Exeunt.*)

## ACT 4, SCENE 2

(*Enter Maria and Feste.*)

MARIA. Nay, I prithee, put on this gown and this beard. Make him believe
thou art Sir Topaz[4] the curate.[5] Do it quickly. I'll call Sir Toby the whilst.
[*Exit.*]
FESTE. Well, I'll put it on, and I will dissemble myself in't; and I would I
were the first that ever dissembled[6] in such a gown. I am not tall enough to
5 become the function well nor lean enough to be thought a good student.[7]
But to be said "an honest man and a good housekeeper" goes as fairly as to
say "a careful man and a great scholar." The competitors[8] enter.

    (*Enter [Sir] Toby [and Maria].*)

SIR TOBY. Jove bless thee, Master Parson.[9]

---

1   *started ... in thee* Made my heart leap in fear for you (punning on "start"—to rouse a
    resting animal—and "hart," a deer).
2   *What relish ... runs the stream* Both phrases mean, figuratively, "what does this
    mean?"; *relish* Flavour.
3   *Let fancy ... Lethe steep* May imagination drown my (confused) senses in oblivi-
    on; *Lethe* Mythological river of forgetfulness; *steep* Flowing quickly.
4   *Sir Topaz* "Topas" in the First Folio; *Topaz* Precious stone thought to cure madness (but
    associated with changeability like opal in 2.4.71).
5   *curate* Parish priest.
6   *dissembled* Put on false appearances, acted hypocritically.
7   *not tall enough ... good student* Feste alludes to two clerical stereotypes, that tall priests
    had more authority, and that scholars of divinity spent more money on books than
    food; *function* Priestly office.
8   *competitors* Partners.
9   *Master Parson* This generic title suggests Topaz has earned his "Sir" with a Master of
    Divinity degree.

FESTE. *Bonos dies*,[1] Sir Toby, for as the old hermit of Prague,[2] that never saw
   pen and ink, very wittily said to a niece of King Gorboduc[3] "that that is,    10
   is."[4] So I, being Master Parson, am Master Parson, for what is "that" but
   that, and "is" but is?
SIR TOBY. To him,[5] Sir Topaz.
FESTE. What ho, I say, peace in this prison.[6]
SIR TOBY. The knave counterfeits well—a good knave.    15

   (*Malvolio within.*)[7]

MALVOLIO. Who calls there?
FESTE. Sir Topaz the curate, who comes to visit Malvolio the lunatic.
MALVOLIO. Sir Topaz, Sir Topaz, good Sir Topaz, go to my lady.
FESTE. Out, hyperbolical fiend,[8] how vexest thou this man! Talkest thou
   nothing but of ladies?    20
SIR TOBY. Well said, Master Parson.
MALVOLIO. Sir Topaz, never was man thus wronged. Good Sir Topaz, do not
   think I am mad. They have laid me here in hideous darkness.
FESTE. Fie, thou dishonest Satan! I call thee by the most modest[9] terms, for I
   am one of those gentle ones[10] that will use the devil himself with courtesy.    25
   Say'st thou that house is dark?
MALVOLIO. As hell, Sir Topaz.
FESTE. Why, it hath bay windows transparent as barricadoes, and the clere-
   stories toward the south north are as lustrous as ebony,[11] and yet complain-
   est thou of obstruction?    30

---

1   *Bonos dies* Good day; Feste makes mock Latin out of the Spanish greeting, *Buenos dias*.
2   *hermit of Prague* Mock authority like "Quinapalus" in 1.5.28.
3   *King Gorboduc* Legendary English king.
4   *that that is, is* Feste is spoofing logical tautologies, things self-evidently evident.
5   *To him* Go to him.
6   *peace in this prison* An allusion to the "Order for the Visitation of the Sick" in the *Book of Common Prayer* (1559), instructing priests to say "peace be in this house" as they enter.
7   *Malvolio within* This stage direction in the First Folio suggests that Malvolio is heard from his dark cell, but not seen; some productions place him off-stage, while some place him in an imaginary cell upstage.
8   *Out, hyperbolical fiend* Feste paraphrases Mark 5.8, "Come out of the man, thou unclean spirit"; *hyperbolical* Outrageous, extreme.
9   *modest* Mildest.
10   *those gentle ones* Methods of exorcism ranged from using physical force to expel the demon to debating the demon on theological matters, hoping to trap it in contradictions, as Feste does below.
11   *transparent as ... as ebony* Oxymorons (along with "south north"), both equivalent to "clear as mud"; *barricadoes* From Spanish: barricades, thick earthen barriers; *clerestories* Upper windows in halls and churches.

MALVOLIO. I am not mad, Sir Topaz. I say to you this house is dark.

FESTE. Madman, thou errest.[1] I say there is no darkness but ignorance, in which thou art more puzzled than the Egyptians in their fog.[2]

MALVOLIO. I say this house is as dark as ignorance, though ignorance were as
35      dark as hell, and I say there was never man thus abused. I am no more mad than you are. Make the trial of it in any constant question.[3]

FESTE. What is the opinion of Pythagoras concerning wild fowl?[4]

MALVOLIO. That the soul of our grandam might haply[5] inhabit a bird.

FESTE. What think'st thou of his opinion?

40   MALVOLIO. I think nobly of the soul,[6] and no way approve his opinion.

FESTE. Fare thee well. Remain thou still in darkness. Thou shalt hold th' opinion of Pythagoras ere I will allow of thy wits,[7] and fear to kill a woodcock, lest thou dispossess the soul of thy grandam. Fare thee well.

MALVOLIO. Sir Topaz, Sir Topaz!

45   SIR TOBY. My most exquisite[8] Sir Topaz!

FESTE. Nay, I am for all waters.[9]

MARIA. Thou mightst have done this without thy beard and gown. He sees thee not.

SIR TOBY. To[10] him in thine own voice, and bring me word how thou find'st
50      him. I would we were well rid of this knavery. If he may be conveniently delivered,[11] I would he were, for I am now so far in offence with my niece that I cannot pursue with any safety this sport to the upshot.[12] Come by and by to my chamber.[13]

(*Exit [with Maria].*)

---

1    *say to you ... thou errest* Malvolio uses the polite "you," Feste the condescending "thou."

2    *Egyptians in their fog* One of the ten plagues on Egypt was described in Exodus 10.21 as a "darkness that may be felt."

3    *Make the trial ... constant question* Test my sanity with any logical problem.

4    *Pythagoras concerning wild fowl* This ancient Greek philosopher held that after death a soul could transmigrate to either a newborn child or an animal; one follower of Pythagoras, Empedocles, claimed "before now, I too have been a boy, a girl, a bush, a bird, and a scaly fish in the sea."

5    *haply* Perhaps.

6    *nobly of the soul* Christian philosophers rejected transmigration by asserting the nobility of the soul, arguing that it was indivisible and unique to God's highest creation.

7    *ere ... thy wits* Before I accept that you are sane.

8    *exquisite* Perfect.

9    *for all waters* Proverbial: "to have a cloak for all waters" (i.e., prepared for anything).

10   *To* Go to.

11   *delivered* Released.

12   *to the upshot* To its outcome (the "upshot" was the winning shot in an archery contest).

13   *come by ... my chamber* This line is addressed to Feste (following on "bring me word") and not Maria, as some editors argue.

FESTE. [*Sings.*] "Hey, Robin, jolly Robin,[1]
            Tell me how thy lady does."                                                        55
MALVOLIO. Fool!
FESTE.        "My lady is unkind, perdie."[2]
MALVOLIO. Fool!
FESTE.        "Alas, why is she so?"
MALVOLIO. Fool, I say!                                                                                          60
FESTE.        "She loves another."
   Who calls, ha?
MALVOLIO. Good fool, as ever thou wilt deserve well at my hand, help me
   to a candle, and pen, ink, and paper. As I am a gentleman, I will live to be
   thankful to thee for't.                                                                                       65
FESTE. Master[3] Malvolio?
MALVOLIO. Ay, good fool.
FESTE. Alas, sir, how fell you besides[4] your five wits?[5]
MALVOLIO. Fool, there was never man so notoriously[6] abused. I am as well in
   my wits, fool, as thou art.                                                                                70
FESTE. But as well? Then you are mad indeed, if you be no better in your
   wits than a fool.
MALVOLIO. They have here propertied me,[7] keep me in darkness, send minis-
   ters to me, asses, and do all they can to face[8] me out of my wits.
FESTE. Advise you[9] what you say, the minister is here. [*speaking as Sir To-*    75
   *paz*] Malvolio, Malvolio, thy wits the heavens restore. Endeavour thyself
   to sleep, and leave thy vain bibble-babble.[10]
MALVOLIO. Sir Topaz!
FESTE. [*as Sir Topaz*] Maintain no words with him, good fellow. [*as himself*]
   Who, I, sir? Not I, sir. God buy you,[11] good Sir Topaz. [*as Sir Topaz*] Marry,    80
   amen.[12] [*as himself*] I will sir, I will.

---

1    *Hey, Robin, jolly Robin* This song is probably traditional, but it may be based on the ver-
     sion by Sir Thomas Wyatt (1503–42) and music by William Cornish (1465–1523), both
     contemporaries of King Henry VIII.
2    *perdie* By God, from French: *par dieu.*
3    *Master* The First Folio reads "M. Malvolio"; Maria earlier refers to him as "Monsieur,"
     but "master" equally suggests Malvolio's social pretension (and winks at "Master Parson").
4    *besides* Out of.
5    *five wits* Medical texts variously named three principal wits—judgment, memory, and
     imagination—while some added fantasy and common sense.
6    *notoriously* Outrageously.
7    *propertied me* Treated me as stage property (i.e., like furniture).
8    *face* Bully.
9    *Advise you* Be careful.
10   *bibble-babble* Common expression for empty talk.
11   *God buy you* God be with you.
12   *Marry, amen* Indeed, so be it (as if closing a prayer).

MALVOLIO. Fool, fool, fool, I say!

FESTE. Alas, sir, be patient. What say you, sir? I am shent[1] for speaking to you.

85 MALVOLIO. Good fool, help me to some light and some paper. I tell thee I am as well in my wits as any man in Illyria.

FESTE. Well-a-day[2] that you were, sir.

MALVOLIO. By this hand, I am. Good fool, some ink, paper, and light, and convey what I will set down to my lady. It shall advantage thee more than
90   ever the bearing of letter did.

FESTE. I will help you to't. But tell me true, are you not mad indeed, or do you but counterfeit?

MALVOLIO. Believe me, I am not. I tell thee true.

FESTE. Nay, I'll ne'er believe a madman till I see his brains.[3] I will fetch you
95   light and paper and ink.

MALVOLIO. Fool, I'll requite[4] it in the highest degree. I prithee be gone.

FESTE. [*Sings.*]

   I am gone, sir,[5]

   And anon,° sir,                                 *right away*

   I'll be with you again,

100   In a trice,

   Like to the old Vice[6]

   Your need to sustain,

   Who with dagger of lath,°                         *wood*

   In his rage and his wrath,

105   Cries, "aha" to the devil,

   Like a mad lad,

   Pare thy nails, dad.

   Adieu, goodman devil.[7]

    (*Exit.*)

---

1   *shent* Rebuked.

2   *Well-a-day* Alas.

3   *till I see his brains* In fact, anatomists by this time knew there was no visible difference in the brains of criminals or the insane.

4   *requite* Repay.

5   *I am gone, sir* It is uncertain whether this song is by Shakespeare; no contemporary music survives.

6   *the old Vice* A comic character from the morality plays, typically associated with human foibles and often cast as the son of the devil; the Vice typically wore a wooden stage-dagger ("dagger of lath").

7   *goodman devil* Either the Vice's farewell to his father, the devil, or Feste's parting shot at Malvolio; *goodman* Usually a title of respect, but here used ironically (in most performances, Feste delivers it with a sneer).

# ACT 4, SCENE 3

(*Enter Sebastian.*)

SEBASTIAN.  This is the air, that is the glorious sun,
This pearl she gave me, I do feel't and see't,
And though 'tis wonder that enwraps me thus,
Yet 'tis not madness. Where's Antonio, then?
I could not find him at the Elephant,                                                   5
Yet there he was,° and there I found this credit,°          *had been / report*
That he did range° the town to seek me out.                          *roam*
His counsel now might do me golden° service.                      *valuable*
For though my soul disputes well with my sense[1]
That this may be some error, but no madness,                                          10
Yet doth this accident and flood of fortune
So far exceed all instance, all discourse,
That I am ready to distrust mine eyes
And wrangle° with my reason, that persuades me                    *argue*
To any other trust° but that I am mad,                        *conclusion*  15
Or else the lady's mad. Yet if 'twere so,
She could not sway° her house, command her followers,          *rule*
Take and give back affairs and their dispatch[2]
With such a smooth, discreet, and stable° bearing,              *poised*
As I perceive she does.[3] There's something in't                                     20
That is deceivable.° But here the lady comes.                  *deceptive*

(*Enter Olivia and Priest.*)

OLIVIA.  Blame not this haste of mine. If you mean well,
Now go with me and with this holy man
Into the chantry by.[4] There, before him
And underneath that consecrated roof,                                                 25
Plight° me the full assurance of your faith,                      *Pledge*
That my most jealous° and too doubtful soul                      *anxious*
May live at peace. He shall conceal it

---

1    *disputes ... my sense* Agrees with the evidence of my senses, although "disputes" typically
      means "argue against," as in "wrangle with my reason" below.
2    *Take and give ... their dispatch* Ensure that her business affairs are carried out.
3    *I perceive she does* Sebastian has no knowledge of the misrule in her household during
      Acts 1–3.
4    *chantry by* Nearby chapel; ruling families endowed chapels where priests sang daily mass
      for the souls of its founders and their families (presumably, Olivia's chantry sang for her
      father and brother).

Whiles° you are willing it shall come to note,[1]          *Until*
30   What° time we will our celebration keep                    *At which*
According to my birth.° What do you say?                      *rank*
SEBASTIAN.  I'll follow this good man, and go with you,
And having sworn truth, ever will be true.
OLIVIA.  Then lead the way, good father, and heavens so shine
35   That they may fairly note this act of mine.

(*Exeunt.*)

## ACT 5, SCENE 1

(*Enter Feste and Fabian.*)

FABIAN.  Now, as thou lov'st me, let me see his[2] letter.
FESTE.  Good Master Fabian, grant me another request.
FABIAN.  Anything.
FESTE.  Do not desire to see this letter.
5   FABIAN.  This is to give a dog, and in recompense desire my dog again.[3]

(*Enter [Orsino], Viola, Curio, and Lords.*)

ORSINO.  Belong you to the Lady Olivia, friends?
FESTE.  Ay, sir, we are some of her trappings.[4]
ORSINO.  I know thee well. How dost thou, my good fellow?[5]
FESTE.  Truly, sir, the better for my foes and the worse for my friends.
10   ORSINO.  Just the contrary: the better for thy friends.
FESTE.  No, sir, the worse.
ORSINO.  How can that be?
FESTE.  Marry, sir, they praise me and make an ass of me. Now my foes tell
me plainly I am an ass, so that by my foes, sir, I profit in the knowledge
15   of myself,[6] and by my friends I am abused.[7] So that, conclusions to be as

---

1   *conceal it ... come to note* A betrothal was as binding as marriage, but it could remain private until the publication of the marriage banns, the public declaration of an intention to marry.
2   *his* Malvolio's.
3   *give a dog ... my dog again* Fabian recalls an anecdote in which the Queen and her kinsman Dr. Boleyn discuss his beloved dog: asking that he grant her one request, she demands the dog, to which he replies, asking her for one request, and demands the dog back.
4   *trappings* Ornamental fittings on a horse's harness.
5   *I know thee ... good fellow* Orsino replies in verse, and uses the condescending "thee" and "thou."
6   *knowledge of myself* Feste plays on the fashionable Socratic dictum, *nosce teipsum,* "know thyself."
7   *abused* Deceived (by false praise).

kisses, if your four negatives make your two affirmatives,[1] why then, the worse for my friends, and the better for my foes.

ORSINO. Why, this is excellent.

FESTE. By my troth, sir, no, though it please you to be one of my friends.

ORSINO. Thou shalt not be the worse for me. There's gold. [*Gives a coin.*]    20

FESTE. But that it would be double-dealing,[2] sir, I would you could make it another.

ORSINO. O, you give me ill counsel.

FESTE. Put your grace in your pocket, sir, for this once, and let your flesh and blood obey it.[3]    25

ORSINO. Well, I will be so much a sinner to be a double-dealer. There's another.

FESTE. *Primo, secundo, tertio*[4] is a good play; and the old saying is "the third pays for all."[5] The triplex,[6] sir, is a good tripping measure, or the bells of Saint Bennet,[7] sir, may put you in mind—one, two, three.    30

ORSINO. You can fool no more money out of me at this throw.[8] If you will let your lady know I am here to speak with her, and bring her along with you, it may awake my bounty[9] further.

FESTE. Marry, sir, lullaby[10] to your bounty till I come again. I go, sir, but I would not have you to think that my desire of having is the sin of covet-    35
ousness.[11] But, as you say, sir, let your bounty take a nap. I will awake it anon.[12] (*Exit.*)

(*Enter Antonio and Officers.*)

VIOLA. Here comes the man, sir, that did rescue me.

---

1    *conclusions to be ... two affirmatives* I.e., assuming that (as in grammar) a double-negative is an affirmative, then logical conclusions are like kisses in that a woman who refuses a kiss four times must be requesting one twice.

2    *But that ... double-dealing* Except for the fact that it would be double-tipping.

3    *Put your grace ... blood obey it* Set your sense of propriety (*grace*) aside and let your hand obey your instinct (*ill counsel*).

4    *Primo, secundo, tertio* Latin: first, second, third; an allusion to a mathematical game for children called *Primus secundus* in which, for example, 3 could be captured by 1 and 2.

5    *third pays for all* Proverbial, equivalent to the modern "three's a charm" or "third time lucky."

6    *triplex* Triple time in music.

7    *Saint Bennet* Probably Saint Bennet (Benedict) Hithe, a church across the Thames from the Globe theatre.

8    *at this throw* On this dice throw (i.e., on this occasion).

9    *bounty* Generosity.

10    *lullaby* Sing a lullaby (so it will "take a nap," below).

11    *sin of covetousness* Among the seven deadly sins, greed was considered the deadliest.

12    *anon* Soon.

ORSINO. That face of his I do remember well,
40    Yet when I saw it last it was besmeared°                    *dirtied*
      As black as Vulcan[1] in the smoke of war.
      A baubling° vessel was he captain of,                      *toy-like*
      For shallow draught and bulk unprizable,[2]
      With which such scathful grapple° did he make              *harmful attack*
45    With the most noble bottom[3] of our fleet
      That very envy and the tongue of loss
      Cried fame and honour on him.[4] What's the matter?
FIRST OFFICER. Orsino,[5] this is that Antonio
      That took the Phoenix and her fraught° from Candy.         *freight*
50    And this is he that did the Tiger board[6]
      When your young nephew Titus lost his leg.
      Here in the streets, desperate of shame and state,[7]
      In private brabble° did we apprehend° him.                 *brawl / arrest*
VIOLA. He did me kindness, sir, drew on my side,[8]
55    But in conclusion put strange speech upon[9] me.
      I know not what 'twas but distraction.[10]
ORSINO. Notable° pirate, thou salt-water thief,                 *Notorious*
      What foolish boldness brought thee to their mercies[11]
      Whom thou, in terms so bloody and so dear,[12]
60    Hast made thine enemies?
ANTONIO.                      Orsino, noble sir,
      Be pleased that I shake off[13] these names you give me:
      Antonio never yet was thief or pirate,
      Though I confess, on base and ground enough,[14]

---

1    *Vulcan* Roman god of fire and metal-working.
2    *For shallow ... unprizeable* Of such small displacement and size (that it was not worth
     capturing).
3    *bottom* Hull (i.e., ship).
4    *very envy ... honour on him* Even envy and those he defeated declared his fame and hon-
     our.
5    *Orsino* The officer drops his title (perhaps to appear impartial and plainspoken).
6    *took the Phoenix ... Tiger board* The *Phoenix* and *Tiger* are ships in Orsino's navy;
     *Candy* Candia, a port town on the island of Crete.
7    *desperate of shame and state* Disregarding his guilt and the public order (contrasting with
     *private brabble*).
8    *drew on my side* Defended me with his sword.
9    *put strange speech upon* Spoke strangely to.
10   *but distraction* If not madness.
11   *their mercies* Put yourself at the mercy of those.
12   *terms so ... dear* Circumstances so violent and so grievous.
13   *Be pleased that I shake off* Please allow me to repudiate.
14   *base and ground enough* Sufficient grounds; *base* Foundation.

Orsino's enemy. A witchcraft° drew me hither:                       *spell*   65
That most ingrateful boy there by your side
From the rude° sea's enraged and foamy mouth                        *rough*
Did I redeem. A wreck° past hope he was.                            *shipwreck*
His life I gave him, and did thereto add
My love without retention° or restraint,                            *reservation*   70
All his in dedication.[1] For his sake,
Did I expose myself, pure° for his love,                            *solely*
Into the danger of this adverse° town,                             *hostile*
Drew to defend him when he was beset,
Where being apprehended, his false cunning,                                         75
Not meaning to partake° with me in danger,                          *share*
Taught him to face me out of his acquaintance,[2]
And grew a twenty years removèd thing
While one would wink,[3] denied me mine own purse,
Which I had recommended° to his use                                 *committed*   80
Not half an hour before.

VIOLA.                    How can this be?
ORSINO.  When came he to this town?
ANTONIO.  Today, my lord, and for three months before,
    No int'rim,° not a minute's vacancy,°              *interim / interval*
    Both day and night did we keep company.[4]                                    85

(*Enter Olivia and Attendants.*)

ORSINO.  Here comes the Countess; now heaven walks on earth.
    But for thee, fellow—fellow, thy words are madness.
    Three months this youth hath tended upon me.
    But more of that anon. Take him aside.
OLIVIA.  What would my lord, but that he may not have,[5]                          90
    Wherein Olivia may seem serviceable?°              *be of service*
    Cesario, you do not keep promise[6] with me.
VIOLA.  Madam—

---

1   *All his in dedication* I.e., dedicated myself entirely to him.
2   *face me ... acquaintance* Deny he knew me.
3   *grew a twenty ... would wink* Became, in the blink of an eye, like someone who had not
    seen me in twenty years.
4   *for three months ... we keep company* This account establishes the play's dual-time scheme;
    in l. 88 below, Orsino now claims the same time has elapsed since he has known Cesario,
    while in 1.4.2 it was "but three days."
5   *but that he may not have* Except for that (i.e., my love) which I will not give.
6   *keep promise* Uphold your vow; Cesario's appearance in service to Orsino would seem to
    bring into question Sebastian's betrothal.

ORSINO. Gracious Olivia—

95  OLIVIA. What do you say, Cesario? Good my lord—

VIOLA. My lord would speak, my duty hushes me.

OLIVIA. If it be aught to the old tune,[1] my lord,
 It is as fat° and fulsome° to mine ear                                   *gross / revolting*
 As howling[2] after music.

100  ORSINO. Still so cruel?

OLIVIA. Still so constant,° lord.                                         *consistent*

ORSINO. What, to perverseness?° You uncivil lady,                         *obstinacy*
 To whose ingrate and unauspicious[3] altars
 My soul the faithfull'st off'rings[4] hath breathed out

105  That e'er devotion tendered.° What shall I do?                        *offered*

OLIVIA. Even what it please my lord that shall become him.[5]

ORSINO. Why should I not, had I the heart to do it,
 Like to the Egyptian thief at point of death,
 Kill what I love[6]—a savage jealousy

110  That sometime savours nobly.[7] But hear me this:
 Since you to non-regardance° cast my faith,                              *disregard*
 And that I partly know the instrument
 That screws[8] me from my true place in your favour,
 Live you the marble-breasted tyrant[9] still;

115  But this your minion,[10] whom I know you love,
 And whom, by heaven I swear, I tender° dearly,                           *care for*
 Him will I tear out of that cruel eye[11]
 Where he sits crowned in his master's spite.[12]

---

1    *aught to the old tune* I.e., any of your usual romantic rhetoric.

2    *howling* Like a dog.

3    *ingrate and unauspicious* Ungrateful and unpromising.

4    *faithfull'st off'rings* Pledges of absolute fidelity.

5    *Even what ... become him* I.e., whatever suits you (equivalent to "what you will").

6    *the Egyptian thief ... what I love* Orsino compares himself to Thyamis, an Egyptian robber-chief in the Greek romance *Ethiopica* by Heliodorus (translated into English in 1569), who tries to kill his beloved Chariclea when his own life is threatened by rival robbers; critics debate the degree to which this is an implicit threat to Olivia or a melodramatic scenario that unwittingly reveals his love for Viola.

7    *savours nobly* I.e., tastes or smells of nobility.

8    *instrument that screws* Instrument of torture (i.e., Cesario) that wrenches.

9    *marble-breasted tyrant* I.e., the stereotypically cold, aloof object of unrequited courtly love.

10   *minion* Sexual favourite, as in Shakespeare's Sonnet 126.11–12: "Yet fear her, O thou minion of her pleasure: / She may detain, but not still keep, her treasure!"

11   *tear out of that cruel eye* I.e., forcibly remove him from your sight.

12   *in his master's spite* To spite his master (Orsino).

Come, boy, with me, my thoughts are ripe in mischief.[1]
I'll sacrifice the lamb that I do love[2]                                                   120
To spite a raven's heart within a dove.[3]

VIOLA.  And I, most jocund,° apt, and willingly,                        *cheerfully*
To do° you rest, a thousand deaths would die.                          *give*

OLIVIA.  Where goes Cesario?

VIOLA.                           After him I love
More than I love these eyes, more than my life,                       125
More, by all mores,[4] than e'er I shall love wife.
If I do feign, you witnesses above,°                                  *in heaven*
Punish my life for tainting of my love.

OLIVIA.  Ay me, detested,° how am I beguiled!                          *rejected*

VIOLA.  Who does beguile you? Who does do you wrong?                   130

OLIVIA.  Hast thou forgot thyself? Is it so long?
Call forth the holy father. [*Exit an Attendant.*]

ORSINO.                           Come, away!

OLIVIA.  Whither, my lord? Cesario, husband, stay.

ORSINO.  Husband?

OLIVIA.                  Ay, husband. Can he that deny?

ORSINO.  Her husband, sirrah?                                         135

VIOLA.                           No, my lord, not I.

OLIVIA.  Alas, it is the baseness of thy fear
That makes thee strangle thy propriety.[5]
Fear not, Cesario, take thy fortunes up,[6]
Be that thou know'st thou art, and then thou art
As great as that thou fear'st.[7]                                     140

(*Enter Priest* [*and Attendant*].)

                           O, welcome, father!
Father, I charge thee, by thy reverence
Here to unfold—though lately we intended

---

1    *ripe in mischief* Prepared to do harm.
2    *sacrifice … I do love* This probable allusion to Abraham's near-sacrifice of Isaac in Genesis
     22 recasts the story of Thyamis and Chariclea in Judeo-Christian terms.
3    *raven's heart within a dove* I.e., a raven (Olivia) that pretends to be a dove; "raven" may
     also be a slighting reference to Olivia's mourning (in some performances she is still wear-
     ing black at this point).
4    *mores* I.e., such comparisons.
5    *strangle thy propriety* I.e., deny your identity (as my betrothed).
6    *take thy fortunes up* I.e., accept your good fortune (in marrying a countess).
7    *As great as that thou fear'st* I.e., equal to whom you fear (Orsino); not technically true, as
     marriage to Olivia would bring Cesario into the nobility, but not elevate him to count.

To keep in darkness what occasion° now                                 *circumstance*
    Reveals before 'tis ripe—what thou dost know
145  Hath newly passed between this youth and me.
  PRIEST.  A contract of eternal bond of love,
    Confirmed by mutual joinder° of your hands,[1]               *joining*
    Attested by the holy close° of lips,                              *union*
    Strengthened by interchangement° of your rings,              *exchange*
150  And all the ceremony of this compact°                         *agreement*
    Sealed in my function,[2] by my testimony;
    Since when, my watch hath told me, toward my grave,
    I have travelled but two hours.
  ORSINO.  (*to Viola*) O thou dissembling cub![3] What wilt thou be,
155  When time hath sowed a grizzle° on thy case?°          *grey hair / skin*
    Or will not else thy craft° so quickly grow                    *craftiness*
    That thine own trip[4] shall be thine overthrow?
    Farewell, and take her, but direct thy feet
    Where thou and I henceforth may never meet.
160 VIOLA.  My lord, I do protest.
  OLIVIA.                                      O, do not swear!
    Hold little° faith, though thou has too much fear.              *a little*

  (*Enter Sir Andrew.*)

  SIR ANDREW.  For the love of God, a surgeon—send one presently to Sir
    Toby.
  OLIVIA.  What's the matter?
165 SIR ANDREW.  Has broke[5] my head across, and has given Sir Toby a bloody
    coxcomb[6] too. For the love of God, your help! I had rather than forty
    pound I were at home.
  OLIVIA.  Who has done this, Sir Andrew?
  SIR ANDREW.  The Count's gentleman, one Cesario. We took him for a cow-
170  ard, but he's the very devil incardinate.[7]
  ORSINO.  My gentleman, Cesario?

---

1   *contract ... your hands* Betrothal was a pre-marital contract, in this case followed by the
    ceremony of hand fasting.
2   *Sealed in my function* Attested by my priestly authority.
3   *dissembling cub* Alluding to the proverb "as wily as a fox."
4   *trip* Leg movement used in wrestling to "overthrow" an opponent.
5   *Has broke* He has cut.
6   *bloody coxcomb* Synonymous with "head," deriving from a fool's cap shaped like a cock's
    comb.
7   *incardinate* To appoint as a cardinal; Andrew means "incarnate," in human form.

SIR ANDREW. 'Od's lifelings,[1] here he is! You broke my head for nothing, and
that that I did, I was set on to do't by Sir Toby.

VIOLA.  Why do you speak to me? I never hurt you.
You drew your sword upon me without cause,                                    175
But I bespake you fair[2] and hurt you not.

(*Enter [Sir] Toby and Feste.*)

SIR ANDREW.  If a bloody coxcomb be a hurt, you have hurt me. I think you
set nothing by[3] a bloody coxcomb. Here comes Sir Toby halting.[4] You shall
hear more, but if he had not been in drink, he would have tickled you
othergates[5] than he did.                                                     180

ORSINO.  How now, gentleman? How is't with you?

SIR TOBY.  That's all one,[6] h'as hurt me, and there's th' end on't. Sot,[7] didst see
Dick Surgeon,[8] sot?

FESTE.  O, he's drunk, Sir Toby, an hour agone. His eyes were set at eight i'
th' morning.[9]                                                                185

SIR TOBY.  Then he's a rogue and a passy measures pavin.[10] I hate a drunken
rogue.[11]

OLIVIA.  Away with him! Who hath made this havoc with them?

SIR ANDREW.  I'll help you, Sir Toby, because we'll be dressed[12] together.

SIR TOBY.  Will *you* help—an ass-head and a coxcomb and a knave, a thin-    190
faced knave, a gull?[13]

OLIVIA.  Get him to bed, and let his hurt be looked to.

[*Exeunt Sir Toby, Sir Andrew, Fabian, and Feste.*]

(*Enter Sebastian.*)

---

1    *'Od's lifelings* By God's little lives (a mild oath).
2    *bespake you fair* Addressed you courteously.
3    *set nothing by* Think nothing of.
4    *halting* Limping.
5    *tickled you othergates* Beat you otherwise.
6    *all one* No matter.
7    *Sot* Fool.
8    *Dick Surgeon* I.e., Dick the surgeon (a generic name).
9    *set at … morning* I.e., fixed and unfocused like hands on a clock (not "closed by eight").
10   *passy measures pavin* Toby's tipsy attempt at "passing measures pavan," from Italian: *pas-samezzo pavana*, a slow dance in double time.
11   *I hate a drunken rogue* Toby is perhaps self-consciously comparing the movements of the dance to a swaying drunkard.
12   *dressed* Bandaged.
13   *Will you help … a gull* In performance, Toby's sudden turn on Andrew usually registers in his complete shock; *you* Editor's emphasis; *gull* Dupe (of Toby).

SEBASTIAN. I am sorry, madam, I have hurt your kinsman,
    But had it been the brother of my blood,[1]
195 I must have done no less with wit and safety.[2]
    You throw a strange regard° upon me, and by that          *look*
    I do perceive it hath offended you.
    Pardon me, sweet one, even for[3] the vows
    We made each other but so late ago.°                        *recently*
200 ORSINO. One face, one voice, one habit,° and two persons!   *costume*
    A natural perspective,[4] that is and is not.
    SEBASTIAN. Antonio! O my dear Antonio,
    How have the hours racked and tortured me
    Since I have lost thee!
205 ANTONIO. Sebastian are you?
    SEBASTIAN.                    Fear'st thou[5] that, Antonio?
    ANTONIO. How have you made division of[6] yourself?
    An apple cleft in two is not more twin
    Than these two creatures.[7] Which is Sebastian?
    OLIVIA. Most wonderful!
210 SEBASTIAN. [*seeing Viola*] Do I stand there? I never had a brother,
    Nor can there be that deity in my nature
    Of here and everywhere.[8] I had a sister
    Whom the blind waves and surges° have devoured.           *swells*
    [*to Viola*] Of charity,[9] what kin are you to me?
215 What countryman, what name, what parentage?
    VIOLA. Of Messaline. Sebastian was my father.
    Such a Sebastian was my brother too.
    So went he suited[10] to his watery tomb;
    If spirits can assume both form and suit,°                 *body and clothing*
220 You come to fright us.

---

1   *brother of my blood* My own brother.
2   *wit and safety* Sensible concern and self-protection.
3   *even for* Especially considering.
4   *natural perspective* I.e., an optical illusion produced by nature (not magic).
5   *Fear'st thou* Do you doubt.
6   *made division of* Split.
7   *An apple cleft ... two creatures* In Plato's *Symposium*, Aristophanes gives a theory of love:
    humans are female and male halves split (like an apple) by Zeus from an androgynous
    original; love draws every person to seek their "lost" half in lovers that are like or unlike
    themselves.
8   *that deity ... here and everywhere* I.e., divine power of omnipresence.
9   *Of charity* I.e., out of kindness (please tell me).
10  *suited* Dressed (as you are).

SEBASTIAN.                  A spirit I am indeed,
   But am in that dimension grossly clad[1]
   Which from the womb I did participate.[2]
   Were you a woman, as the rest goes even,[3]
   I should my tears let fall upon your cheek,
   And say "thrice welcome, drownèd Viola!"
VIOLA.  My father had a mole upon his brow.                    225
SEBASTIAN.  And so had mine.
VIOLA.  And died that day when Viola from her birth
   Had numbered thirteen years.[4]
SEBASTIAN.  O, that record is lively[5] in my soul!
   He finishèd indeed his mortal act                          230
   That day that made my sister thirteen years.
VIOLA.  If nothing lets° to make us happy both          *hinders*
   But this my masculine usurped attire,
   Do not embrace me[6] till each circumstance
   Of place, time, fortune, do cohere and jump[7]             235
   That I am Viola, which to confirm,
   I'll bring you to a captain in this town
   Where[8] lie my maiden weeds,° by whose gentle help    *clothes*
   I was preserved to serve this noble Count.
   All the occurrence of my fortune since                      240
   Hath been between this lady and this lord.
SEBASTIAN.  [*to Olivia*] So comes it, lady, you have been mistook,°   *mistaken*
   But nature to her bias drew in that.[9]
   You would have been contracted° to a maid;             *married*

---

1   *A spirit … grossly clad* I have a soul, but it is dressed in common flesh (echoing the
    Platonic and Christian idea of the immortal soul housed in an imperfect body); *dimen-*
    *sion* Physical (not spiritual).
2   *participate* Share with other humans.
3   *the rest goes even* Everything else suggests.
4   *numbered thirteen years* Placing herself in the third person, Viola offers her birthday as
    corroborating evidence that Sebastian can confirm (below), but without external confir-
    mation either can still be seen as impersonating the other.
5   *record is lively* Memory is vivid; *record* Pronounced "recòrd."
6   *Do not embrace me* Viola defers the celebration of their reunion until she has resumed her
    feminine identity.
7   *cohere and jump* Come together and agree.
8   *Where* I.e., at whose house.
9   *nature … drew in that* I.e., nature drew you to me through your love for one disguised as
    me; *bias* The curve of a weighted ball in the game of bowls.

245     Nor are you therein, by my life, deceived:
      You are betrothed both to a maid and man.[1]
   ORSINO. *[to Olivia]* Be not amazed. Right noble is his blood.
      If this be so, as yet the glass seems true,[2]
      I shall have share in this most happy wreck.°       *shipwreck*
250    *[to Viola]* Boy, thou hast said to me a thousand times
      Thou never shouldst love woman like to me.[3]
   VIOLA. And all those sayings will I overswear,°     *swear again*
      And all those swearings° keep as true in soul     *oaths*
      As doth that orbèd continent[4] the fire
255    That severs day from night.
   ORSINO.               Give me thy hand,
      And let me see thee in thy woman's weeds.
   VIOLA. The captain that did bring me first on shore
      Hath my maid's garments. He upon some action°   *legal charge*
      Is now in durance,° at Malvolio's suit,[5]     *imprisoned*
260    A gentleman and follower of my lady's.
   OLIVIA. He shall enlarge° him. Fetch Malvolio hither.   *free*
      And yet, alas, now I remember me,
      They say, poor gentleman, he's much distract.°   *distraught*

     (*Enter [Feste] with a letter, and Fabian.*)

      A most extracting° frenzy of mine own     *distracting*
265    From my remembrance clearly banished his.
      How does he, sirrah?
   FESTE. Truly, madam, he holds Beelzebub at the stave's end[6] as well as a man
      in his case may do. H'as here writ a letter to you. I should have given you
      today morning, but as a madman's epistles are no gospels,[7] so it skills[8] not
270    much when they are delivered.

---

1   *both to a maid and man* I.e., to one (Sebastian) who is both a virgin and a man; "maid" or "maiden" was frequently used to indicate an innocent or virginal youth.
2   *the glass seems true* The "natural perspective" still appears to reflect truth (and not appearances).
3   *like to me* I.e., as well as (you love) me.
4   *orbèd continent* The sun; *orbèd* The planets and stars were thought to be fixed in crystalline spheres (orbs); *continent* Container (of fire).
5   *at Malvolio's suit* The unexplained lawsuit serves to justify the captain's absence and to defer retrieving Viola's "woman's weeds" (and emphasizes Malvolio's arbitrary legalism).
6   *holds Beelzebub ... end* Proverbial: "keeps the devil at a distance"; *stave* Quarterstaff (used in fighting).
7   *epistles are no gospels* I.e., words convey no truth (playing on the New Testament Epistles and the first four Gospels).
8   *skills* Matters.

OLIVIA. Open't, and read it.

FESTE. Look then to be well edified when the fool delivers[1] the madman. [*Reads madly.*] "By the Lord, madam"—

OLIVIA. How now, art thou mad?

FESTE. No, madam, I do but read madness. An your ladyship will have it as  275
it ought to be, you must allow *vox*.[2]

OLIVIA. Prithee read i'thy right wits.

FESTE. So I do, Madonna, but to read his right wits[3] is to read thus. Therefore perpend,[4] my Princess, and give ear.

OLIVIA. [*to Fabian*] Read it you, sirrah.  280

FABIAN. (*Reads.*) "By the Lord, madam, you wrong me, and the world shall know it. Though you have put me into darkness and given your drunken cousin rule over me, yet have I the benefit of my senses as well as your ladyship. I have your own letter that induced me to the semblance I put on, with the which I doubt not but to do myself much right[5] or you much  285
shame. Think of me as you please. I leave my duty a little unthought of,[6] and speak out of my injury.[7]

The madly-used Malvolio."

OLIVIA. Did he write this?

FESTE. Ay, Madam.  290

ORSINO. This savours not much of distraction.

OLIVIA. See him delivered,[8] Fabian; bring him hither. [*Exit Fabian.*]
My lord, so please you, these things further thought on,
To think me as well a sister as a wife,[9]
One day shall crown th' alliance on't,[10] so please you,  295
Here at my house, and at my proper° cost.                                         *own*

ORSINO. Madam, I am most apt° t'embrace your offer.                          *ready*
[*to Viola*] Your master quits° you, and for your service done him      *releases*
So much against the mettle° of your sex,                                 *temperament*
So far beneath your soft and tender breeding,  300
And since you called me master for so long,

---

1    *delivers* Speaks the words of.

2    *vox* Latin: voice (i.e., the appropriate voice).

3    *right wits* Mental state.

4    *perpend* Consider, attend.

5    *I doubt not ... much right* I intend to vindicate myself.

6    *unthought of* Neglected.

7    *injury* Sense of wrong.

8    *Delivered* Freed, the third sense of this word in this scene (see ll. 270 and 272).

9    *think me ... a wife* Think as well of me as a sister-in-law as you would have as a wife.

10    *crown th' alliance on't* I.e., celebrate our relationship with a double wedding.

Here is my hand. You shall from this time be
Your master's mistress.[1]

OLIVIA.  [*to Viola*] A sister—you are she.

(*Enter Malvolio [with a letter, and Fabian]*.)

305 ORSINO.  Is this the madman?

OLIVIA.                              Ay, my lord, this same.
How now, Malvolio!

MALVOLIO.                    Madam, you have done me wrong,
Notorious° wrong.                                                                      *Egregious*

OLIVIA.                Have I, Malvolio? No.

MALVOLIO. [*Shows the letter.*] Lady, you have, pray you peruse that letter.
You must not now deny it is your hand.

310 Write from it° if you can, in hand or phrase,                              *differently*
Or say 'tis not your seal, not your invention.°                              *composition*
You can say none of this. Well, grant it then,
And tell me, in the modesty of honour,[2]
Why you have given me such clear lights° of favour,                        *signs*

315 Bade me come smiling and cross-gartered to you,
To put on yellow stockings, and to frown
Upon Sir Toby and the lighter° people,                                            *lesser*
And, acting° this in an obedient hope,                                            *doing*
Why have you suffered me to be imprisoned,

320 Kept in a dark house, visited by the priest,
And made the most notorious geck° and gull                                    *fool*
That e'er invention° played on? Tell me why.                                  *trickery*

OLIVIA.  Alas, Malvolio, this is not my writing,
Though, I confess, much like the character,°                                    *style*

325 But out of question 'tis Maria's hand.
And now I do bethink me, it was she
First told me thou wast mad; then cam'st° in smiling,                      *you came*
And in such forms which here were presupposed
Upon[3] thee in the letter. Prithee, be content;

330 This practice hath most shrewdly° passed upon thee,                    *maliciously*
But, when we know the grounds° and authors of it,                          *reasons*

---

1    *master's mistress* Compare with Shakespeare's Sonnet 20, l. 2, "the master-mistress of my
     passion."

2    *modesty of honour* Propriety of (your) honour.

3    *presupposed / Upon* Previously suggested.

Thou shalt be both the plaintiff and the judge
Of thine own cause.[1]

FABIAN.  Good madam, hear me speak,
    And let no quarrel nor no brawl to come                                                335
    Taint the condition° of this present hour,                      *Spoil the mood*
    Which I have wondered° at. In hope it shall not,                    *marvelled*
    Most freely I confess myself and Toby
    Set this device° against Malvolio here,                                      *trick*
    Upon° some stubborn and uncourteous parts°    *Because of / behaviour*  340
    We had conceived against° him. Maria writ                        *attributed to*
    The letter, at Sir Toby's great importance,°                           *insistence*
    In recompense whereof he hath married her.
    How with a sportful malice it was followed°                       *carried out*
    May rather pluck on° laughter than revenge,                       *induce*  345
    If that the injuries° be justly weighed                                      *wrongs*
    That have on both sides passed.

OLIVIA.  [*to Malvolio*] Alas, poor fool, how have they baffled° thee!   *disgraced*

FESTE.  Why, "some are born great, some achieve greatness, and some have
    greatness thrown upon them." I was one, sir, in this interlude,[2] one Sir To-   350
    paz, sir; but that's all one. "By the Lord, fool, I am not mad"—but do you
    remember, "madam, why laugh you at such a barren rascal, an you smile
    not, he's gagged"—and thus the whirligig of time brings in his revenges.[3]

MALVOLIO.  I'll be revenged on the whole pack[4] of you. [*Exit.*]

OLIVIA.  He hath been most notoriously abused.                                             355

ORSINO.  Pursue him, and entreat him to a peace.
    He hath not told us of the captain yet. [*Exit Fabian.*]
    When that[5] is known, and golden time[6] convents,°               *comes about*
    A solemn combination shall be made
    Of our dear° souls. Meantime, sweet sister,                              *loving*  360

---

1   *the plaintiff ... own cause* This reverses the proverbial saying: "no man ought to be judge
    in his own cause."

2   *interlude* Play.

3   *whirligig of time ... revenges* Feste combines the images of a *whirligig*, a child's spinning-
    top, and the wheel of fortune (suggesting that Malvolio's treatment was less personal
    revenge than fate).

4   *pack* Of dogs (for hounding him).

5   *that* I.e., the motivation for Malvolio's lawsuit against the captain.

6   *golden time* A standard Renaissance allusion to the mythical, ideal world of the classical
    "Golden Age," typically a time of youth and hope such as in Shakespeare's Sonnet 3, "in
    this thy golden time" (but in the context of the imprisoned captain and Viola's missing
    *weeds*, this nostalgic image functions as another deferral of marriage).

We will not part from hence.[1] Cesario, come—
For so you shall be while you are a man;
But when in other habits you are seen,
Orsino's mistress, and his fancy's queen.[2]

(*Exeunt [all but Feste].*)

FESTE.  (*Sings.*)
365    When that I was and a little tiny boy,[3]
        With hey, ho, the wind and the rain,
    A foolish thing was but a toy,
        For the rain it raineth every day.

    But when I came to man's estate,[4]
370        With hey, ho, the wind and the rain,
    'Gainst knaves and thieves men shut their gate,
        For the rain it raineth every day.

    But when I came, alas, to wive,°               *take a wife*
        With hey, ho, the wind and the rain,
375    By swaggering° could I never thrive,        *bullying*
        For the rain it raineth every day.

    But when I came unto my beds,[5]
        With hey, ho, the wind and the rain,
    With toss-pots° still had drunken heads,        *drunkards*
380        For the rain it raineth every day.

    A great while ago the world begun,
        With hey, ho, the wind and the rain,
    But that's all one, our play is done,
        And we'll strive to please you every day.

    [*Exit.*]

—c. 1601

---

1   *hence* I.e., Olivia's house.
2   *his fancy's queen* Ruler of his desire.
3   *When that ... tiny boy* It is unknown if Shakespeare wrote this song, but a variation on stanza 1 is sung in *King Lear* 3.2.73–77.
4   *when I ... man's estate* I.e., when I became a man.
5   *beds* I.e., the speaker sleeps where he can.

# Richard Brinsley Sheridan
## 1751–1816

The Irish writer and politician Richard Brinsley Sheridan was one of the leading playwrights of the late eighteenth century. Writing in a style that had been pioneered a century before by Restoration playwrights (though without the overt sexual innuendo that permeates many of the plays of the earlier period), Sheridan created light yet pointed comedies of social and sexual politics. His plays were wildly popular with audiences of his time, and two of them—*The Rivals* (1775) and *The School for Scandal* (1777)—have remained popular ever since as the period's most successful exemplars of the comedy of manners.

As a playwright who also owned and managed London's Drury Lane Theatre for over 30 years, Sheridan took a pragmatic view of the stage as a means of supporting himself and financing his political ambitions; his desire to profit from his work ensured that he attended closely to the prevailing appetites of his audiences. His aptitude as a dramatist consisted not only of a talent for witty dialogue and intricate comic plots, but also in an ability to at once indulge and exceed popular expectations by infusing stock types and familiar devices with new vitality. As the critic William Hazlitt observed, Sheridan "could imitate with the spirit of an inventor," and "whatever he touched, he adorned with all the ease, grace, and brilliancy of his style."

Despite his talents, Sheridan died in poverty. He devoted the latter part of his life to the management of Drury Lane—which proved to be a financial sinkhole—and to a career as a member of the Whig opposition in Parliament, where he developed a reputation as a fine orator and a radical liberal. He was an incidental player on the political stage, but Sheridan's generation recognized his importance as a key figure in the history of English theatre, and he was buried with great pomp in Poet's Corner in Westminster Abbey.

# The School for Scandal

## PROLOGUE

*Spoken by Mr. King*[1]
*Written by D. Garrick,*[2]
*Esq.*

A School for Scandal! tell me, I beseech you,
Needs there a school this modish° art to teach you?                    *fashionable*
No need of lessons now, the knowing think—
We might as well be taught to eat and drink.
5   Caused by a dearth of scandal, should the vapours[3]
Distress our fair ones—let 'em read the papers;
Their pow'rful mixtures such disorders hit;
Crave what they will, there's *quantum sufficit.*[4]
      "Lord!" cries my Lady Wormwood (who loves tattle,
10  And puts much salt and pepper in her prattle),
Just ris'n at noon, all night at cards when threshing
Strong tea and scandal—"Bless me, how refreshing!
Give me the papers, Lisp—how bold and free! (*sips*)
*Last night Lord L—— (sips) was caught with Lady D——*
15  For aching heads what charming sal volatile![5] (*sips*)
*If Mrs. B.—— will still continue flirting,*
*We hope she'll* DRAW, *or we'll* UNDRAW *the curtain.*
Fine satire, poz°—in public all abuse it,                              *positively*
But, by ourselves (*sips*), our praise we can't refuse it.
20  Now, Lisp, *read you*—there, at that dash and star."[6]
      "Yes, ma'am.—A *certain Lord had best beware,*
*Who lives not twenty miles from Grosv'nor Square;*[7]
*For should he Lady W—— find willing,*
WORMWOOD *is bitter*"—"Oh! that's me! the villain!

---

1   *Mr. King* Actor Thomas King (1730–1805), who appeared in the play's original cast as
      Peter Teazle.
2   *D. Garrick* Famous actor and theatre manager David Garrick (1717–79).
3   *the vapours* State of depression or ill health.
4   *quantum sufficit* Latin: sufficient quantity (i.e., enough to satisfy the readers).
5   *sal volatile* Substance used in smelling salts.
6   *dash and star* In eighteenth-century print media, dashes and asterisks marked places
      where a name or other identifying detail had been withheld.
7   *Grosv'nor Square* Grosvenor Square, site of aristocratic residences in London's West End.

Throw it behind the fire, and never more 25
Let that vile paper come within my door."—
    Thus at our friends we laugh, who feel the dart;
    To reach our feelings, we ourselves must smart.
    Is our young bard so young, to think that he
    Can stop the full spring-tide of calumny? 30
    Knows he the world so little, and its trade?
    Alas! the devil is sooner raised than laid.
    So strong, so swift, the monster there's no gagging:
    Cut Scandal's head off—still the tongue is wagging.
    Proud of your smiles once lavishly bestowed, 35
    Again your young Don Quixote[1] takes the road:
    To show his gratitude, he draws his pen,
    And seeks this hydra,[2] Scandal, in his den.
For your applause all perils he would through—
He'll fight—that's *write*—a cavalliero[3] true, 40
Till every drop of blood—that's *ink*—is spilt for you.

## DRAMATIS PERSONAE

| [MEN] | [WOMEN] |
|---|---|
| Sir Peter Teazle | Lady Teazle |
| Sir Oliver Surface | Lady Sneerwell |
| Joseph Surface | Mrs. Candour |
| Charles Surface | Maria |
| Snake | |
| Rowley | |
| Moses | |
| Careless | |
| Sir Toby Bumper[4] | |
| Trip | |
| Sir Benjamin Backbite | |
| Crabtree | |
| [Servants] | |

---

1   *Don Quixote* Title character of a Spanish comic romance (1605, 1615) by Miguel de
    Cervantes. The idealistic Quixote reads too many romances and believes himself to be a
    chivalric hero.
2   *hydra* Greek mythological monster that has multiple heads and grows two more when-
    ever one is cut off.
3   *cavalliero* Spanish: knight or gentleman.
4   *Bumper* Full glass of alcohol used for a toast.

## ACT 1, SCENE 1. [LADY SNEERWELL'S HOUSE.]¹

*(Lady Sneerwell at the dressing table; Mr. Snake drinking chocolate.)*

LADY SNEERWELL. The paragraphs you say, Mr. Snake, were all inserted?

SNAKE. They were, madam, and as I copied them myself in a feigned hand, there can be no suspicion whence they came.

LADY SNEERWELL. Did you circulate the report of Lady Brittle's intrigue with Captain Boastall?

SNAKE. That is in as fine a train as your ladyship could wish; in the common course of things, I think it must reach Mrs. Clackit's ears within four-and-twenty hours, and then you know the business is as good as done.

LADY SNEERWELL. Why truly, Mrs. Clackit has a very pretty talent and a great deal of industry.

SNAKE. True, madam, and has been tolerably successful in her day. To my knowledge she has been the cause of six matches being broken off and three sons being disinherited, of four forced elopements, as many close confinements,² nine separate maintenances,³ and two divorces. Nay, I have more than once traced her causing a tête-à-tête in the *Town and Country Magazine*⁴ when the parties perhaps had never seen each others' faces before in the course of their lives.

LADY SNEERWELL. She certainly has talents, but her manner is gross.⁵

SNAKE. 'Tis very true: she generally designs well, has a free tongue and a bold invention, but her colouring is too dark and her outline often extravagant. She wants⁶ that delicacy of hint and mellowness of sneer which distinguishes your ladyship's scandal.

LADY SNEERWELL. Ah! You are partial, Snake.

SNAKE. Not in the least: everybody allows that Lady Sneerwell can do more with a word or a look than many can with the most laboured detail, even when they happen to have a little truth on their side to support it.

LADY SNEERWELL. Yes, my dear Snake, and I am no hypocrite to deny the satisfaction I reap from the success of my efforts. Wounded myself in the early part of my life by the envenomed tongue of slander, I confess I have since known no pleasure equal to the reducing others to the level of my own reputation.

---

1   *[LADY SNEERWELL'S HOUSE.]* Stage directions not appearing in the original play have been added in square brackets.

2   *close confinements* Secret childbirths.

3   *separate maintenances* Living allowance given by one member of a separated couple to the other; in the eighteenth century, a maintenance was provided by the husband.

4   *Town and Country Magazine* Gossip periodical publicizing high-society scandals.

5   *gross* Unrefined.

6   *wants* Lacks.

SNAKE. Nothing can be more natural.. But Lady Sneerwell, there is one affair in which you have lately employed me wherein I confess I am at a loss to guess your motives.

LADY SNEERWELL. I conceive you mean with respect to my neighbour, Sir 35 Peter Teazle, and his family?

SNAKE. I do. Here are two young men to whom Sir Peter has acted as a kind of guardian since their father's death: the eldest possessing the most amiable character and universally well spoken of; the youngest the most dissipated and extravagant young fellow in the kingdom, without friends 40 or character. The former an avowed admirer of your ladyship's and apparently your favourite; the latter attached to Maria, Sir Peter's ward, and confessedly beloved by her. Now on the face of these circumstances, it is utterly unaccountable to me why you, the widow of a City knight[1] with a good jointure,[2] should not close with the passion of a man of such char- 45 acter and expectation as Mr. Surface, and more so, why you should be so uncommonly earnest to destroy the mutual attachment between his brother Charles and Maria.

LADY SNEERWELL. Then at once to unravel this mystery, I must inform you that love has no share whatever in the intercourse between Mr. Surface 50 and me.

SNAKE. No!

LADY SNEERWELL. His real attachment is to Maria or her fortune, but finding in his brother a favoured rival, he has been obliged to mask his pretensions and profit by my assistance. 55

SNAKE. Yet still I am more puzzled why you should interest yourself in his success.

LADY SNEERWELL. Heavens, how dull you are! Cannot you surmise the weakness which I hitherto through shame have concealed even from you? Must I confess that Charles, that libertine, that extravagant, that bankrupt in 60 fortune and reputation, that he it is for whom I am thus anxious and malicious and to gain whom I would sacrifice everything?

SNAKE. Now, indeed your conduct appears consistent, but how came you and Mr.[3] Surface so confidential?

LADY SNEERWELL. For our mutual interest. I have found him out a long time 65 since. I know him to be artful, selfish, and malicious—in short, a sentimental knave[4]—while with Sir Peter, and indeed with all his acquaintance, he passes for a miracle of prudence, good sense, and benevolence.

---

1    *City knight* I.e., knighted London merchant; *City* City of London, the oldest area of London and the location of its business centres.

2    *jointure* Estate left to a widow by her husband to provide for her until the end of her life.

3    *Mr.* I.e., the older of the two Surface brothers.

4    *sentimental knave* I.e., a hypocrite who expresses respectably moral sentiments.

SNAKE. Nay, Sir Peter vows he has not his equal in England, and above all he
70    praises him as a Man of Sentiment.[1]

LADY SNEERWELL. True, and with the assistance of sentiments and hypocrisy,
he has brought him entirely into his interest with regard to Maria, while
poor Charles has no friend in the house, though I fear he has a powerful
one in Maria's heart, against whom we must direct our schemes.

(*Enter servant.*)

75 SERVANT. Mr. Surface.

LADY SNEERWELL. Show him up.

(*Exit servant.*)

He generally calls about this time; I don't wonder at people's giving him to
me for a lover.

(*Enter Joseph Surface.*)

JOSEPH SURFACE. My dear Lady Sneerwell, how do you do today? Mr. Snake,
80    your most obedient.

LADY SNEERWELL. Snake has just been arraigning me on our mutual attachment, but I have informed him of our real views. You know how useful he
has been to us, and believe me, the confidence is not ill placed.

JOSEPH SURFACE. Madam, it is impossible for me to suspect a man of Mr.
85    Snake's sensibility and discernment.

LADY SNEERWELL. Well, well, no compliments now, but tell me when you
saw your mistress, Maria, or what is more material to me, your brother.

JOSEPH SURFACE. I have not seen either since I left you, but I can inform
you that they never meet. Some of your stories have taken a good effect
90    on Maria.

LADY SNEERWELL. Ah my dear Snake, the merit of this belongs to you.—But
do your brother's distresses increase?

JOSEPH SURFACE. Every hour. I am told he has had another execution[2] in his
house yesterday; in short, his dissipation and extravagance exceed every-
95    thing I ever heard of.

LADY SNEERWELL. Poor Charles!

JOSEPH SURFACE. True, madam, notwithstanding his vices, one cannot help
feeling for him. Aye, poor Charles indeed. I am sure I wish it was in my
power to be of any essential service to him. For the man who does not

---

1    *Man of Sentiment* Phrase with a double meaning; it could mean that Joseph Surface is
     "sentimental" in the sense used above, or that he is virtuously sympathetic.

2    *execution* Legal acquisition of a debtor's possessions in lieu of an unpaid debt.

share in the distresses of a brother, even though merited by his own mis- 100
conduct, deserves—

LADY SNEERWELL.   Oh Lud![1] You are going to be moral and forget that you
are among friends.

JOSEPH SURFACE.   Egad that's true. I'll keep that sentiment till I see Sir Peter.
However, it is certainly a charity to rescue Maria from such a libertine, 105
who, if he is to be reclaimed, can be so only by one of your ladyship's superior accomplishments and understanding.

SNAKE.   I believe, Lady Sneerwell, here's company coming; I'll go and copy
the letter I mentioned to you.—Mr. Surface, your most obedient. (*Exit.*)

JOSEPH SURFACE.   Sir, your very devoted—Lady Sneerwell, I am very sorry 110
you have put any further confidence in that fellow.

LADY SNEERWELL.   Why so?

JOSEPH SURFACE.   I have lately detected him in frequent conference with old
Rowley, who was formerly my father's steward and has never, you know,
been a friend of mine.                                                      115

LADY SNEERWELL.   And do you think he would betray us?

JOSEPH SURFACE.   Nothing more likely, take my word for it, Lady Sneerwell,
that fellow has not virtue enough to be faithful or constant even to his own
villainy.—Hah, Maria!

(*Enter Maria.*)

LADY SNEERWELL.   Maria, my dear, how do you do? What's the matter?       120

MARIA.   Oh, there's that disagreeable lover of mine, Sir Benjamin Backbite,
has just called at my guardian's with his odious uncle Crabtree, so I slipped
out and ran hither to avoid them.

LADY SNEERWELL.   Is that all?

JOSEPH SURFACE.   If my brother Charles had been of the party, madam, per- 125
haps you would not have been so much alarmed.

LADY SNEERWELL.   Nay now, you are severe, for I dare swear the truth of the
matter is, Maria heard you were here.—But my dear, what has Sir Benjamin done that you should avoid him so?

MARIA.   Oh, he has done nothing, but 'tis for what he has said. His conversa- 130
tion is a perpetual libel on all his acquaintance.

JOSEPH SURFACE.   Aye, and the worst of it is, there is no advantage in not
knowing him, for he'll abuse a stranger just as soon as his best friend, and
his uncle is as bad.

LADY SNEERWELL.   Nay, but we should make allowance: Sir Benjamin is a wit 135
and a poet.

---

1   *Lud* Swear word meaning "Lord."

MARIA. For my part I own, madam, wit loses its respect with me when I see it in company with malice.—What do you think, Mr. Surface?

JOSEPH SURFACE. Certainly, madam, to smile at the jest which plants a thorn
140    in another's breast is to become a principal in the mischief.

LADY SNEERWELL. Pshaw! There's no possibility of being witty without a little ill nature; malice of a good thing is the barb which makes it stick.—What's your opinion, Mr. Surface?

JOSEPH SURFACE. To be sure, madam, that conversation where the spirit of
145    raillery¹ is suppressed will ever appear tedious and insipid.

MARIA. Well, I'll not debate how far scandal may be allowable, but in a man I am sure it is always contemptible. We have pride, envy, rivalship, and a thousand little motives to depreciate each other, but the male slanderer must have the cowardice of a woman before he can traduce one.

*(Enter servant.)*

150  SERVANT. Madam, Mrs. Candour is below and, if your ladyship's at leisure, will leave her carriage.

LADY SNEERWELL. Beg her to walk in.

*(Exit servant.)*

Now Maria, however, here is a character to your taste, for though Mrs. Candour is a little talkative, everybody allows her to be the best natured
155    and best sort of woman.

MARIA. Yet with a very gross affectation of good nature and benevolence, she does more mischief than the direct malice of old Crabtree.

JOSEPH SURFACE. I'faith, 'tis very true, Lady Sneerwell. Whenever I hear the current running against the characters of my friends, I never think them in
160    such danger as when Candour undertakes their defence.

LADY SNEERWELL. Hush! Here she is.

*(Enter Mrs. Candour.)*

MRS. CANDOUR. My dear Lady Sneerwell, how have you been this century? Mr. Surface, what news do you hear, though indeed it is no matter, for I think one hears nothing else but scandal.

165  JOSEPH SURFACE. Just so indeed, madam.

MRS. CANDOUR. Ah! Maria, child, is the whole affair off between you and Charles? His extravagance, I presume; the Town² talks of nothing else.

MARIA. I am very sorry, ma'am, the Town have so little to do.

---

1    *raillery* Teasing.
2    *the Town* I.e., London high society.

MRS. CANDOUR. True, true, child, but there is no stopping people's tongues. I own I was hurt to hear it, as indeed I was to learn from the same quarter 170 that your guardian, Sir Peter, and Lady Teazle have not agreed lately so well as could be wished.

MARIA. 'Tis strangely impertinent for people to busy themselves so. I'm sure such reports are—

MRS. CANDOUR. Very true, child, but what's to be done? People will talk, 175 there's no preventing it. Why it was but yesterday I was told that Miss Gadabout had eloped with Sir Filagree Flirt—but Lord, there is no minding what one hears—though to be sure I had this from very good authority.

MARIA. Such reports are highly scandalous.

MRS. CANDOUR. So they are, child—shameful! shameful! But the world is 180 so censorious no character escapes. Lord now! Who would have suspected your friend Miss Prim of an indiscretion? Yet such is the ill nature of people that they say her uncle stopped her last week just as she was stepping into the York diligence[1] with her dancing master.

MARIA. I'll answer for it, there are no grounds for the report. 185

MRS. CANDOUR. Oh, no foundation in the world, I dare swear, no more probably than for the story circulated last month of Mrs. Festino's affair with Colonel Cassino,[2] though to be sure that matter was never rightly cleared up.

JOSEPH SURFACE. The license of invention some people take is monstrous 190 indeed!

MARIA. 'Tis so, but in my opinion those who report such things are equally culpable.

MRS. CANDOUR. To be sure they are: tale bearers are as bad as tale makers; 'tis an old observation and a very true one. But what's to be done, as I said 195 before? How will you prevent people from talking? Today Mrs. Clackit assured me Mr. and Mrs. Honeymoon were at last become mere man and wife like the rest of her acquaintance. She likewise hinted that a certain widow in the next street had got rid of her dropsy[3] and recovered her shape in a most surprising manner, and the same time Miss Tattle, who 200 was by, affirmed that Lord Buffalo had discovered his lady at a house of no extraordinary fame and that Sir Harry Bouquet and Tom Saunter were to measure swords on a similar provocation. But Lord, do you think I would report these things? No, no, tale-bearers, as I said before, are just as bad as tale-makers. 205

---

1   *York diligence* Public horse-drawn coach to York.

2   *Festino* Italian: party; *Cassino* Italian: dance hall; also the name of a card game.

3   *dropsy* Swelling caused by accumulation of fluid (here used as a cover for pregnancy).

JOSEPH SURFACE. Oh Mrs. Candour, if everybody had your forbearance and good nature!

MRS. CANDOUR. I confess, Mr. Surface, I cannot bear to hear people attacked behind their backs, and when ugly circumstances come out against one's
210    acquaintances, I own I always love to think the best. By the bye, I hope 'tis not true that your brother is absolutely ruined.

JOSEPH SURFACE. I am afraid his circumstances are very bad indeed, madam.

MRS. CANDOUR. Ah, I heard so, but you must tell him to keep up his spirits: Sir Thomas Splint, Captain Quinzes, and Mr. Nickit, all up,[1] I hear, within
215    this week, so if Charles is undone, he will find half his acquaintances ruined too, and that, you know, is a consolation.

JOSEPH SURFACE. Doubtless, ma'am, a very great one.

(*Enter servant.*)

SERVANT. Mr. Crabtree and Sir Benjamin Backbite. (*Exit.*)

LADY SNEERWELL. So Maria, you see your lover pursues you. Positively you
220    shan't escape.

(*Enter Crabtree and Sir Benjamin Backbite.*)

CRABTREE. Lady Sneerwell, I kiss your hands.—Mrs. Candour, I don't believe you are acquainted with my nephew, Sir Benjamin Backbite. Egad ma'am, he has a pretty wit and is a pretty poet too.—Isn't he, Lady Sneerwell?

SIR BENJAMIN. Oh fie, Uncle!

225    CRABTREE. Nay, egad 'tis true: I'll back him at a rebus or a charade[2] against the best rhymer in the kingdom. Has your ladyship heard the epigram he wrote last week on Lady Frizzle's feather catching fire! Do, Benjamin, repeat it, or the charade you made last night extempore at Mrs. Drowzy's conversazione.[3] Come now, your first is the name of a fish, your second a
230    great naval commander—and—

SIR BENJAMIN. Uncle—now—prithee!

CRABTREE. I'faith, madam, 'twould surprise you to hear how ready he is at these things.

LADY SNEERWELL. I wonder, Sir Benjamin, you never publish anything.

235    SIR BENJAMIN. To say truth, ma'am, 'tis very vulgar to print, and as my little productions are mostly satires and lampoons on particular people, I find they circulate more by giving copies in confidence to the friends of the

---

1    *Quinzes* French card game; *all up* Completely broke.

2    *rebus* Puzzle in which players must decode a message made up of pictures and letters; *charade* Riddle involving wordplay.

3    *conversazione* Small party intended for refined intellectual conversation.

parties; however, I have some love elegies which, when favoured with this lady's smiles, I mean to give to the public.

CRABTREE.  'Fore Heaven, ma'am, they'll immortalize you; you'll be handed    240
down to posterity like Petrarch's Laura or Waller's Sacharissa.[1]

SIR BENJAMIN.  Yes madam, I think you will like them when you shall see them on a beautiful quarto page,[2] where a neat rivulet of text shall murmur through a meadow of margin. 'Fore gad, they will be the most elegant things of their kind—    245

CRABTREE.  But ladies, that's true. Have you heard the news?

MRS. CANDOUR.  What, sir, do you mean the report of—

CRABTREE.  No ma'am, that's not it. Miss Nicely is going to be married to her own footman.

MRS. CANDOUR.  Impossible!    250

CRABTREE.  Ask Sir Benjamin.

SIR BENJAMIN.  'Tis very true, ma'am: everything is fixed and the wedding livery bespoke.

CRABTREE.  Yes, and they do say there were pressing reasons for it.

LADY SNEERWELL.  Why, I have heard something of this before.    255

MRS. CANDOUR.  It can't be, and I wonder anyone should believe such a story of so prudent a lady as Miss Nicely.

SIR BENJAMIN.  Oh Lud ma'am, that's the very reason 'twas believed at once. She has always been so cautious and so reserved that everybody was sure there was some reason for it at bottom.    260

MRS. CANDOUR.  Why, to be sure a tale of scandal is as fatal to the credit of a prudent lady of her stamp as a fever is generally to those of the strongest constitutions. But there is a sort of puny, sickly reputation that is always ailing yet will outlive the robuster character of a hundred prudes.

SIR BENJAMIN.  True madam, there are valetudinarians[3] in reputation as well    265
as constitution, who, being conscious of their weak part, avoid the least breath of air and supply their want of stamina by care and circumspection.

MRS. CANDOUR.  Well, but this may be all a mistake. You know, Sir Benjamin, very trifling circumstances often give rise to the most injurious tales.

---

1    *Laura* Subject of the love sonnets of Francesco Petrarch (1304–74); *Waller's Sacharissa* In the 1630s Edmund Waller wrote a series of poems to Lady Dorothy Sidney (referred to in the poems as "Sacharissa"), which were extremely popular in the seventeenth and eighteenth centuries.

2    *on a ... quarto page* I.e., in print; quarto books are produced using large sheets of paper folded to produce four pages each.

3    *valetudinarians* Unhealthy people, or people who go to great lengths to preserve their health.

270    CRABTREE.  That they do, I'll be sworn, ma'am. Did you ever hear how Miss
       Piper came to lose her lover and her character last summer at Tunbridge?[1]
       Sir Benjamin, you remember it?

       SIR BENJAMIN.  Oh, to be sure! The most whimsical circumstance—

       LADY SNEERWELL.  How was it pray?

275    CRABTREE.  Why, one evening at Mrs. Ponto's assembly[2] the conversation
       happened to turn on the difficulty of breeding Nova Scotia sheep in this
       country; says a lady in company, "I have known instances of it, for Miss
       Laetitia Piper, a first cousin of mine, had a Nova Scotia sheep that pro-
       duced her twins." "What!" cries the Dowager Lady Dundizzy (who you
280    know is as deaf as a post) "has Miss Laetitia Piper had twins?" This mis-
       take, as you may imagine, threw the whole company into a fit of laughter;
       however, 'twas the next day reported, and in a few days believed by the
       whole Town, that Miss Laetitia Piper had actually been brought to bed
       of a fine boy and a girl, and in less than a week there were people who
285    could name the father and the farmhouse where the babies were put out
       to nurse.[3]

       LADY SNEERWELL.  Strange indeed.

       CRABTREE.  Matter of fact, I assure you.—Oh Lud, Mr. Surface, pray is it true
       that your Uncle Sir Oliver is coming home?

290    JOSEPH SURFACE.  Not that I know of, indeed sir.

       CRABTREE.  He has been in the East Indies a long time; you can scarcely re-
       member him, I believe. Sad comfort whenever he returns to hear how your
       brother has gone on.

       JOSEPH SURFACE.  Charles has been imprudent, sir, to be sure, but I hope
295    no busy people have already prejudiced Sir Oliver against him; he may
       reform.

       SIR BENJAMIN.  To be sure he may. For my part I never believed him so utterly
       void of principle as people say, and though he has lost all his friends, I am
       told nobody is better spoken of by the Jews.[4]

300    CRABTREE.  That's true, egad Nephew. If the old Jewry was a ward,[5] I believe
       Charles would be an alderman. No man more popular there. 'Fore gad, I

---

1    *Tunbridge* Tunbridge Wells, a fashionable resort town.

2    *assembly* I.e., party.

3    *put out to nurse* Sent to live in the country with a wet nurse.

4    *nobody … Jews* Refers to the stereotypical association between Jews and moneylending.
     Moneylending was a common profession for Jewish people, as social and legal discrimina-
     tion prevented them from working in most professions, while religious doctrine forbade
     Christians from making loans for profit (a prohibition not always obeyed in practice).

5    *old Jewry* Street in the City where many moneylenders' offices were located; *ward* Re-
     gion of a city that elects an alderman as its representative in the city government.

hear he pays as many annuities as the Irish tontine[1] and that whenever he's sick they have prayers for the recovery of his health in the synagogue.

SIR BENJAMIN. Yet no man lives in greater splendour. They tell me when he entertains his friends, he can sit down to dinner with a dozen of his own securities, have a score of tradesman in the anti-chamber and an officer behind every guest's chair. 305

JOSEPH SURFACE. This may be entertainment to you, gentlemen, but you pay very little regard to the feelings of a brother.

MARIA. [*aside*] Their malice is intolerable.—Lady Sneerwell, I must wish you a good morning—I'm not very well. (*Exit.*) 310

MRS. CANDOUR. Oh dear, she changes colour very much.

LADY SNEERWELL. Do Mrs. Candour follow her, she may want assistance.

MRS. CANDOUR. That I will with all my soul, ma'am. Poor dear creature, who knows what her situation may be? (*Exit.*) 315

LADY SNEERWELL. 'Twas nothing but that she could not bear to hear Charles reflected on, notwithstanding their difference.

SIR BENJAMIN. The young lady's penchant is obvious.

CRABTREE. But Benjamin, you mustn't give up the pursuit for that. Follow her and put her into good humour, repeat her some of your verses. Come, I'll assist you. 320

SIR BENJAMIN. Mr. Surface, I did not mean to hurt you, but depend on't, your brother is utterly undone.[2]

CRABTREE. Oh Lud! Aye! undone as ever man was, can't raise a guinea.[3]

SIR BENJAMIN. Everything sold, I am told, that was moveable.[4] 325

CRABTREE. I have seen one that was at his house: not a thing left but some empty bottles that were overlooked and the family pictures, which I believe are framed in the wainscot.[5]

SIR BENJAMIN. And I am very sorry to hear also some bad stories against him. (*going*) 330

CRABTREE. Oh, he has done many mean[6] things, that's certain.

SIR BENJAMIN. But however, as he's your brother—(*going*)

CRABTREE. We'll tell you all another opportunity.

---

1   *tontine* Money-raising method in which a large group of participants contribute funds, for which they receive annuities (periodic payments) that increase as the other participants die. The Irish Parliament undertook several tontines in the latter half of the eighteenth century.

2   *utterly undone* Financially ruined.

3   *guinea* Coin worth slightly more than a pound.

4   *moveable* I.e., not land or buildings.

5   *framed in the wainscot* I.e., embedded in the wall panelling.

6   *mean* Base, contemptible.

(*Exeunt Sir Benjamin and Crabtree.*)

335    LADY SNEERWELL.  Ha, ha, ha! 'tis very hard for them to leave a subject they
have not quite run down.

JOSEPH SURFACE.  And I believe their abuse was no more acceptable to your
ladyship than Maria.

LADY SNEERWELL.  I doubt[1] her affections are further engaged than we imag-
340    ined. But the family are to be here this evening, so you may as well dine
where you are, and we shall have an opportunity of observing further; in
the meantime, I'll go and plot mischief, and you shall study sentiments.

(*Exeunt.*)

## ACT 1, SCENE 2. SIR PETER TEAZLE'S HOUSE.

(*Enter Sir Peter.*)

SIR PETER.  When an old bachelor takes a young wife, what is he to expect?
'Tis now six months since Lady Teazle made me the happiest of men, and I
have been the miserablest dog ever since. We tiffed a little going to church
and came to a quarrel before the bells were done ringing. I was more than
5    once nearly choked with gall during the honeymoon and had lost all comfort in life before my friends had done wishing me joy. Yet I chose with
caution: a girl bred wholly in the country, who never knew luxury beyond
one silk gown nor dissipation above the annual gala of a race ball. Yet now
she plays her part in all the extravagant fopperies of the fashion and the
10    Town with as ready a grace as if she had never seen a bush nor a grass plot
out of Grosvenor Square. I am sneered at by my old acquaintance, para-
graphed in the newspapers; she dissipates my fortune and contradicts all
humours. Yet the worst of it is, I doubt I love her, or I should never bear
all this; however, I'll never be weak enough to own it.

(*Enter Rowley.*)

15    ROWLEY.  Oh Sir Peter, your servant. How is it with you, sir?

SIR PETER.  Very bad, Master Rowley, very bad. I meet with nothing but
crosses and vexations.

ROWLEY.  What can have happened to trouble you since yesterday?

SIR PETER.  A good question to a married man.

20    ROWLEY.  Nay, I'm sure Sir Peter, your lady can't be the cause of your uneasiness.

SIR PETER.  Why, has anyone told you she was dead?

---

1    *doubt* Fear or suspect.

ROWLEY.  Come, come, Sir Peter, you love her, notwithstanding your tempers don't exactly agree.

SIR PETER.  But the fault is entirely hers, Master Rowley. I am myself the    25
sweetest tempered man alive and hate a teasing temper, and so I tell her an hundred times a day.

ROWLEY.  Indeed!

SIR PETER.  Aye, and what is very extraordinary, in all our disputes she is always in the wrong. But Lady Sneerwell and the set she meets at her house    30
encourage the perverseness of her disposition. Then to complete my vexations, Maria, my ward, whom I ought to have the power of a father over, is determined to turn rebel too and absolutely refuses the man whom I have long resolved on for her husband, meaning, I suppose, to bestow herself on his profligate brother.    35

ROWLEY.  You know, Sir Peter, I have always taken the liberty to differ with you on the subject of these two young gentlemen. I only wish you may not be deceived in your opinion of the elder; for Charles, my life on't, he will retrieve his errors yet. Their worthy father, once my honoured master, was at his years nearly as wild a spark, but when he died, he did not leave    40
a more benevolent heart to lament his loss.

SIR PETER.  You are wrong, Master Rowley. On their father's death you know I acted as a kind of guardian to them both 'till their uncle Sir Oliver's eastern liberality[1] gave them an early independence. Of course, no person could have more opportunities of judging of their hearts, and I was never    45
mistaken in my life. Joseph is indeed a model for the young men of the age: he is a man of sentiment and acts up to the sentiments he professes. But for the other, take my word for't, if he had any grains of virtue by descent, he has dissipated them with the rest of his inheritance. Ah, my old friend Sir Oliver will be deeply mortified when he finds how part of his    50
bounty has been misapplied.

ROWLEY.  I am sorry to find you so violent against the young man because this may be the most critical period of his fortune; I came hither with news that will surprise you.

SIR PETER.  What? let me hear.    55

ROWLEY.  Sir Oliver is arrived and at this moment in Town.

SIR PETER.  How! You astonish me! I thought you did not expect him this month.

ROWLEY.  I did not, but his passage has been remarkably quick.

SIR PETER.  Egad, I shall rejoice to see my old friend; 'tis sixteen years since we met. We have had many a day together. But does he still enjoin us not    60
to inform his nephews of his arrival?

---

1    *eastern liberality*  I.e., generosity; Sir Oliver acquired his wealth in Southeast Asia.

ROWLEY.  Most strictly. He means before it is known to make some trial of their dispositions.

SIR PETER.  Ah, there needs no art to discover their merits; however, he shall
65    have his way. But pray, does he know I am married?

ROWLEY.  Yes, and will soon wish you joy.

SIR PETER.  What, as we drink health to a friend in a consumption?[1] Ah! Oliver will laugh at me. We used to rail at[2] matrimony together, but he has been steady to his text. Well, he must be at my house though. I'll instantly
70    give orders for his reception. But Master Rowley, don't drop a word that Lady Teazle and I disagree.

ROWLEY.  By no means—

SIR PETER.  For I should never be able to stand Noll's[3] jokes, so I'd have him think, Lord forgive me, that we are a very happy couple.

75 ROWLEY.  I understand you. But then you must be very careful not to differ while he's in the house with you.

SIR PETER.  Egad, and so we must—and that's impossible. Ah Master Rowley, when an old bachelor marries a young wife, he deserves—no, the crime carries the punishment along with it.

(*Exeunt.*)

## ACT 2, SCENE 1. SIR PETER TEAZLE'S HOUSE.

(*Enter Sir Peter and Lady Teazle.*)

SIR PETER.  Lady Teazle, Lady Teazle, I'll not bear it.

LADY TEAZLE.  Sir Peter, Sir Peter, you may bear it or not, as you please, but I ought to have my own way in everything, and what's more, I will too. What, though I was educated in the country, I know very well that women
5    of fashion in London are accountable to nobody after they are married.

SIR PETER.  Very well, ma'am, very well, so a husband is to have no influence, no authority?

LADY TEAZLE.  Authority! No, to be sure. If you wanted authority over me, you should have adopted me and not married me; I am sure you were old
10    enough.

SIR PETER.  Old enough! Aye, there it is, well, well, Lady Teazle, though my life may be made unhappy by your temper, I'll not be ruined by your extravagance.

---

1    *in a consumption* With a wasting disease such as tuberculosis.
2    *rail at* Make fun of.
3    *Noll* Contracted form of "Oliver."

LADY TEAZLE.  My extravagance? I'm sure I'm not more extravagant than a
woman of fashion ought to be.                                                    15

SIR PETER.  No, no, madam, you shall throw away no more sums on such
unmeaning luxury. 'Slife,[1] to spend as much to furnish your dressing room
with flowers in winter, as would suffice to turn the Pantheon into a green-
house and give a fête champêtre[2] at Christmas.

LADY TEAZLE.  Lord, Sir Peter, am I to blame because flowers are dear[3] in cold    20
weather; you should find fault with the climate and not with me. For my
part I am sure I wish it were spring all the year round and that roses grew
under our feet.

SIR PETER.  'Oons[4] madam! If you had been born to this, I should not wonder
at your talking thus, but you forget what your situation was when I mar-    25
ried you.

LADY TEAZLE.  No, no, I don't: 'twas a very disagreeable one, or I should never
have married you.

SIR PETER.  Yes, yes, madam, you were then somewhat in an humbler style:
the daughter of a plain country squire. Recollect, Lady Teazle, when I first    30
saw you sitting at your tambour in a pretty figured[5] linen gown, with a
bunch of keys by your side, your hair combed smoothly over a roll, and
your apartment hung round with fruits in worsted of your own working.

LADY TEAZLE.  Oh yes, I remember it very well, and a curious life I led! My
daily occupation: to inspect the dairy, superintend the poultry, make ex-    35
tracts from the family receipt[6] book, and comb my aunt Deborah's lapdog.

SIR PETER.  Yes, yes, madam, 'twas so indeed.

LADY TEAZLE.  And then you know my evening amusements: to draw patterns
for ruffles which I had not the materials to make, to play Pope Joan with
the curate, read a sermon to my aunt, or be stuck down to an old spinet[7]    40
to strum my father to sleep after a fox chase.

SIR PETER.  I am glad you have so good a memory. Yes madam, these were the
recreations I took you from. But now you must have your coach, vis-à-vis,
and three powdered footmen before your chair[8]—and in summer a pair

---

1    *'Slife* Swear word meaning "God's life."
2    *Pantheon* Neoclassical building of impressive size, constructed in London in the late
     eighteenth century as a site for fashionable entertainment; *fête champêtre* French: garden
     party.
3    *dear* Costly.
4    *'Oons* Contraction of "Zounds," a swear word meaning "God's wounds."
5    *tambour* Round frame used for embroidery; *pretty figured* With pretty designs.
6    *receipt* Recipe.
7    *Pope Joan* Card game for three players; *spinet* Small harpsichord.
8    *vis-à vis* Two-person carriage in which the passengers sit facing each other; *chair* Sedan
     chair, carried on poles by servants as a mode of transport.

45 of white cats to draw you to Kensington Gardens.[1] No recollection I suppose when you were content to ride double behind the butler on a docked coach horse?[2]

LADY TEAZLE. No, I swear I never did that, I deny the butler and the coach horse.

50 SIR PETER. This, madam, was your situation, and what have I not done for you? I have made you a woman of fashion, of fortune, of rank; in short, I have made you *my wife*.

LADY TEAZLE. Well then, and there is but one thing more you can make me to add to the obligation—and that is—

55 SIR PETER. My widow, I suppose?

LADY TEAZLE. Hem, hem!

SIR PETER. Thank you, madam, but don't flatter yourself, for though your ill conduct may disturb my peace, it shall never break my heart, I promise you; however, I am equally obliged to you for the hint.

60 LADY TEAZLE. Then why will you endeavour to make yourself so disagreeable to me and thwart me in every little elegant expense?

SIR PETER. 'Slife madam, I say, had you any of these elegant expenses when you married me?

LADY TEAZLE. Lord, Sir Peter, would you have me be out of fashion?

65 SIR PETER. The fashion indeed! What had you to do with the fashion when you married me?

LADY TEAZLE. For my part I should think you would like to have your wife thought a woman of taste.

SIR PETER. Aye, there again—taste—Zounds, Madam! You had no taste
70 when you married me.

LADY TEAZLE. That's very true indeed, Sir Peter, and after having married you, I should never pretend to taste again, I allow. But now Sir Peter, if we have finished our daily jangle, I presume I may go to my engagement at Lady Sneerwell's?

75 SIR PETER. Aye, there's another precious circumstance, a charming set of acquaintance you have made there.

LADY TEAZLE. Nay Sir Peter, they are people of rank and fortune, and remarkably tenacious of reputation.

---

1   *cats* Presumably a slang term meaning "horses" or "ponies"; *Kensington Gardens* Fashionable London park. Members of high society travelled "the Ring," a path between Kensington Gardens and nearby Hyde Park, in order to display themselves and their carriages.

2   *docked coach horse* Large horse intended for heavy labour; working horses' tails were "docked" (cropped short) to keep them from getting caught in equipment.

SIR PETER. Yes, egad, they are tenacious of reputation with a vengeance! For they don't choose anybody should have a character but themselves. Such a crew! Ah! Many a wretch has rid on a hurdle[1] who has done less mischief than these utterers of forged tales, coiners of scandal, and clippers[2] of reputation. 80

LADY TEAZLE. What, would you restrain the freedom of speech?

SIR PETER. Oh, they have made you just as bad as any one of the society. 85

LADY TEAZLE. Why I believe I do bear a part with a tolerable grace, but I vow I have no malice against the people I abuse. When I say an ill-natured thing, 'tis out of pure good humour, and I take for granted they'll deal exactly in the same manner with me. But Sir Peter, you know you promised to come to Lady Sneerwell's too. 90

SIR PETER. Well, well, I'll call in just to look after my own character.

LADY TEAZLE. Then, indeed, you must make haste after me or you'll be too late. So goodbye to you. (*Exit.*)

SIR PETER. So! I have gained much by my intended expostulations. Yet with what a charming air she contradicts everything I say and how pleasingly 95 she shows her contempt of my authority. Well, though I can't make her love me, there is great satisfaction in quarrelling with her, and I think she never appears to such advantage as when she's doing everything in her power to plague me.

(*Exit.*)

## ACT 2, SCENE 2. LADY SNEERWELL'S HOUSE.

(*Lady Sneerwell, Mrs. Candour, Crabtree, Sir Benjamin Backbite, and Joseph Surface discovered;[3] servants attending with tea.*)

LADY SNEERWELL. Nay, positively we will have it.

JOSEPH SURFACE. Yes, yes, the epigram, by all means.

SIR BENJAMIN. Oh plague on't, Uncle, 'tis mere nonsense.

CRABTREE. No, no, 'fore gad, very clever for an extempore.

SIR BENJAMIN. But ladies, you should be acquainted with the circumstance. 5 You must know that one day last week, as Lady Betty Curricle[4] was taking

---

1    *hurdle* Frame to which criminals were tied before being pulled by horse to their execution.

2    *clippers* Refers to the criminal practice of "clipping," devaluing a coin by shaving small amounts of precious metal from its edges. Like forgery, clipping was punishable by execution.

3    *discovered* Revealed.

4    *Curricle* Small carriage.

the dust in Hyde Park in a sort of duodecimo phaeton,[1] she desired me to write some verses on her ponies, upon which I took out my pocket book and in one moment produced the following:

10      Sure never were seen two such beautiful ponies,
        Other horses are clowns, and these macaronies;[2]
        Nay, to give them this title I'm sure is not wrong,
        Their legs are so slim, and their tails are so long.

CRABTREE.   There ladies, done in the smack of a whip and on horseback too.

15  JOSEPH SURFACE.  A very Phoebus[3] mounted indeed, Sir Benjamin.

SIR BENJAMIN.  Oh dear sir, trifles, trifles!

(*Enter Lady Teazle and Maria.*)

MRS. CANDOUR.  I must have a copy.

LADY SNEERWELL.  Lady Teazle, I hope we shall see Sir Peter.

LADY TEAZLE.  I believe he'll wait on your ladyship presently.

20  LADY SNEERWELL.  Maria my dear, you look grave. Come, you shall sit down to piquet[4] with Mr. Surface.

MARIA.  I take very little pleasure in cards; however, I'll do as your ladyship pleases.

LADY TEAZLE.  [*aside*] I am surprised Mr. Surface should sit down with her.
25      I thought he would have embraced this opportunity of speaking to me before Sir Peter came.

MRS. CANDOUR.  Now, I'll die but you are so scandalous, I'll foreswear your society.

LADY TEAZLE.  What's the matter, Mrs. Candour?

30  MRS. CANDOUR.  They'll not allow our friend, Miss Vermillion, to be handsome.

LADY SNEERWELL.  Oh surely, she's a pretty woman.

CRABTREE.  I'm very glad you think so, madam.

MRS. CANDOUR.  She has a charming, fresh colour.

35  LADY TEAZLE.  Yes, when it is fresh put on.

MRS. CANDOUR.  Oh fie! I'll swear her colour is natural. I have seen it come and go.

LADY TEAZLE.  I dare swear you have, ma'am; it goes off at night and comes again in the morning.

40  MRS. CANDOUR.  Ha, ha, ha! How I hate to hear you talk so. But surely now, her sister *is* or *was* very handsome.

---

1   *duodecimo phaeton* Very small open carriage pulled by two horses.
2   *macaronies* Flamboyantly fashionable men.
3   *Phoebus* Name applied to the Greek god Apollo in his role as sun god. He rides his chariot across the sky to bring sunlight to the earth.
4   *piquet* Two-player card game.

CRABTREE.  Who, Mrs. Evergreen? Oh Lord! She's six-and-fifty if she's an hour.

MRS. CANDOUR.  Now positively you wrong her, fifty-two or fifty-three is the utmost, and I don't think she looks more.                                              45

SIR BENJAMIN.  Oh there's no judging by her looks, unless one could see her face.

LADY SNEERWELL.  Well, well, if Mrs. Evergreen does take some pains to repair the ravages of time, you must allow she effects it with great ingenuity, and surely that's better than the careless manner in which the Widow   50 Ochre caulks her wrinkles.

SIR BENJAMIN.  Nay now Lady Sneerwell, you are severe upon the widow. Come, come, it is not that the widow paints so ill, but when she has finished her face, she joins it on so badly to her neck that she looks like a mended statue in which the connoisseur discovers at once that the head is   55 modern though the trunk's antique.

CRABTREE.  Ha, ha, ha! Well said, Nephew.

MRS. CANDOUR.  Well, you make me laugh, but I vow I hate you for't. What do you think of Miss Simper?

SIR BENJAMIN.  Why, she has very pretty teeth.                                     60

LADY TEAZLE.  Yes, and on that account when she is neither speaking nor laughing, which very seldom happens, she never absolutely shuts her mouth but leaves it always on ajar as it were.

MRS. CANDOUR.  How can you be so ill-natured?

LADY TEAZLE.  I'll allow that's better than the pains Mrs. Prim takes to con-   65 ceal her losses in front. She draws her mouth till it positively resembles the aperture of a poor box,[1] and all her words appear to slide out edgeways.

LADY SNEERWELL.  Very well, Lady Teazle, I see you can be a little severe.

LADY TEAZLE.  In defence of a friend it is but justice.—But here comes Sir Peter to spoil our pleasantry.                                                   70

(*Enter Sir Peter.*)

SIR PETER.  Ladies, your most obedient—Mercy on me, here is the whole set: a character dead at every word, I suppose.

MRS. CANDOUR.  I am rejoiced you are come, Sir Peter; they have been so censorious, they'll allow good qualities to nobody, not even good nature to our friend, Mrs. Pursey.                                                      75

LADY TEAZLE.  What, the fat dowager who was at Mrs. Codille's[2] last night?

MRS. CANDOUR.  Nay, her bulk is her misfortune, and when she takes such pains to get rid of it, you ought not to reflect on her.

---

1    *aperture of a poor box*  Narrow slit in the top of a box used for charity collection.
2    *Codille*  Term used in Ombre, a popular card game.

LADY SNEERWELL. That's very true, indeed.

80  LADY TEAZLE. Yes, I know she almost lives upon acids and small whey, laces herself by pulleys, and often in the hottest noon in summer you may see her on a little, squat pony with her hair plaited up behind like a drummer and puffing around the Ring in a full trot.

MRS. CANDOUR. I thank you, Lady Teazle, for defending her.

85  SIR PETER. Yes, a good defence, truly.

MRS. CANDOUR. But Sir Benjamin is as censorious as Miss Sallow.

CRABTREE. Yes, and she is a curious being to pretend to be censorious, an awkward gawky without any one good point under heaven.

MRS. CANDOUR. Positively you shall not be so severe. Miss Sallow is a rela-
90  tion of mine by marriage, and as for her person, great allowance is to be made, for let me tell you, a woman labours under many disadvantages who tries to pass for a girl at six-and-thirty.

LADY SNEERWELL. Though surely she *is* handsome still, and for the weakness in her eyes, considering how much she reads by candlelight, it is not to be
95  wondered at.

MRS. CANDOUR. True, and then as to her manner, upon my word I think it is particularly graceful, considering she never had the least education, for you know her mother was a Welsh milliner[1] and her father a sugar baker at Bristol.

100  SIR BENJAMIN. Ah, you are both of you too good-natured.

SIR PETER. Yes, damned good-natured—this is their own relation, mercy on me!

SIR BENJAMIN. And Mrs. Candour is of so moral a turn.

MRS. CANDOUR. Well, I will never join in ridiculing a friend. And so I con-
105  stantly tell my cousin Ogle, and you well know what pretensions she has to be critical in beauty.

CRABTREE. Oh, to be sure, she has herself the oddest countenance that ever was seen; 'tis a collection of features from all the different countries of the globe.

110  SIR BENJAMIN. She has indeed an Irish front.

CRABTREE. Caledonian[2] locks.

SIR BENJAMIN. Dutch nose.

CRABTREE. Austrian lip.[3]

SIR BENJAMIN. Complexion of a Spaniard.

---

1    *milliner* Hat-maker.

2    *Caledonian* Scottish.

3    *Austrian lip* Lip deformity also known as "Hapsburg lip" because of its prevalence among the Hapsburgs, an Austrian royal family that held power in several European nations.

CRABTREE.  And teeth *à la chinoise*.[1]  115

SIR BENJAMIN.  In short, her face resembles a table d'hôte at Spa,[2] where no two guests are of a nation.

CRABTREE.  Or a congress at the close of a general war, where all the members, even to her eyes, appear to have a different interest, and her nose and chin are the only parties likely to join issue.  120

MRS. CANDOUR.  Ha, ha, ha!

SIR PETER.  Mercy on my life! A person they dine with twice a week.

MRS. CANDOUR.  Nay, but I vow you shall not carry the laugh off so, for give me leave to say that Mrs. Ogle—

SIR PETER.  Madam, madam, I beg your pardon, there is no stopping these  125 good gentlemen's tongues, but when I tell you, Mrs. Candour, that the lady they are abusing is a particular friend of mine, I hope you'll not take her part.

LADY SNEERWELL.  Well said, Sir Peter, but you are a cruel creature: too phleg-matic[3] yourself for a jest and too peevish to allow it in others.  130

SIR PETER.  Ah madam, true wit is more nearly allied to good nature than your ladyship is aware of.

LADY TEAZLE.  True, Sir Peter, I believe they are so near of kin they can never be united.

SIR BENJAMIN.  Oh! Rather, ma'am, suppose them man and wife, because one  135 so seldom sees them together.

LADY TEAZLE.  But Sir Peter is such an enemy to scandal, I believe he would have it put down[4] by Parliament.

SIR PETER.  'Fore Heaven, madam, if they were to consider the sporting with reputation of as much importance as the poaching on manors[5] and pass  140 an Act for the Preservation of Fame, I believe many would thank them for the bill.

LADY SNEERWELL.  Oh Lud! Sir Peter, would you deprive us of our privileges?

SIR PETER.  Aye madam, and then no person should be permitted to kill char-acters or run down reputations but qualified old maids and disappointed  145 widows.

LADY SNEERWELL.  Go, you monster!

---

1    *à la chinoise* French: in Chinese style. A tradition of coating teeth with black enamel was practiced in Japan and Vietnam, but not in China.

2    *table d'hôte at Spa* Table shared by tourists in the Belgian resort town of Spa.

3    *phlegmatic* Sluggish and apathetic.

4    *put down* I.e., made illegal.

5    *poaching on manors* Game preservation laws were severe, forbidding all but the most wealthy and propertied individuals to hunt.

MRS. CANDOUR.  But sure you would not be quite so severe on those who only report what they hear?

150 SIR PETER.  Yes madam, I would have law-merchant[1] for them too, and in all cases of slander currency, whenever the drawer of the lie was not to be found, the injured party should have a right to come on any of the endorsers.

CRABTREE.  Well, for my part, I believe there never was a scandalous tale without some foundation.

155 LADY SNEERWELL.  Come ladies, shall we sit down to cards in the next room?

(*Enter servant, who whispers to Sir Peter.*)

SIR PETER.  I'll be with them directly.

[*Exit servant.*]

[*aside*] I'll get away unperceived. (*going*)

LADY SNEERWELL.  Sir Peter, you are not leaving us?

SIR PETER.  Your ladyship must excuse me; I'm called away by particular busi-

160 ness—but I'll leave my character behind me. (*Exit.*)

SIR BENJAMIN.  Well certainly, Lady Teazle, that lord of yours is a strange being. I would tell you some stories of him that would make you laugh heartily, if he wasn't your husband.

LADY TEAZLE.  Oh pray don't mind that, come, do, let's hear them.

(*They retire. Joseph Surface and Maria come forward.*)

165 JOSEPH SURFACE.  Maria, I see you have no satisfaction in this society.

MARIA.  How is it possible I should? If to raise malicious smiles at the infirmi-ties and misfortunes of those who have never injured us be the province of wit or humour, Heaven grant me a double portion of dullness.

JOSEPH SURFACE.  Yet they appear more ill-natured than they are; they have

170 no malice at heart.

MARIA.  Then is their conduct more inexcusable, for in my opinion, nothing but a depravity of heart could tempt them to such practices.

JOSEPH SURFACE.  But can you, Maria, feel thus for others and be unkind to me alone; is hope to be denied the tenderest passion?

175 MARIA.  Why will you distress me by renewing the subject?

JOSEPH SURFACE.  Ah Maria! You would not treat me thus and oppose your guardian's, Sir Peter's, will but that I see that profligate Charles is still a favoured rival.

MARIA.  Ungenerously urged! But whatever my sentiments of that unfortu-

180 nate young man are, assured I shall not feel more bound to give him up because his distresses have lost him the regard even of a brother.

---

1    *law-merchant* Assemblage of laws and customs governing mercantile transactions.

(*Lady Teazle returns.*)

JOSEPH SURFACE. [*kneeling*] Nay, but Maria, do not leave me with a frown. By all that's honest, I swear—(*aside*) Gad's life, here is Lady Teazle.—You must not, no, you shall not, for though I have the greatest regard for Lady Teazle—                                                                                     185
MARIA. Lady Teazle!
JOSEPH SURFACE. Yet were Sir Peter once to suspect—
LADY TEAZLE. [*aside*] What's this, pray? Does he take her for me?—Child, you are wanted in the next room.

(*Exit Maria.*)

What's all this, pray?                                                                                     190
JOSEPH SURFACE. Oh, the most unlucky circumstance in nature. Maria has somehow suspected the tender concern which I have for your happiness and threatened to acquaint Sir Peter with her suspicions, and I was just endeavouring to reason with her when you came.
LADY TEAZLE. Indeed! But you seemed to adopt a very tender method of   195
reasoning: Do you usually argue on your knees?
JOSEPH SURFACE. Oh, she's a child, and I thought a little bombast—But Lady Teazle, when are you to give me your judgment on my library[1] as you promised?
LADY TEAZLE. No, no, I begin to think it would be imprudent, and you know   200
I admit you as a lover no further than fashion requires.
JOSEPH SURFACE. True, a mere platonic cicisbeo,[2] what every wife is entitled to.
LADY TEAZLE. Certainly, one must not be out of the fashion; however, I have so many of my country prejudices left that though Sir Peter's ill humour   205
may vex me ever so, it shall never provoke me to—
JOSEPH SURFACE. The only revenge in your power. Well, I applaud your moderation.
LADY TEAZLE. Go, you are an insinuating wretch. But we shall be missed; let us join the company.                                                                                     210
JOSEPH SURFACE. But we had best not return together.
LADY TEAZLE. Well, don't stay, for Maria shan't come to hear any more of your reasoning, I promise you. (*Exit.*)
JOSEPH SURFACE. A curious dilemma, truly, my politics have run me into: I wanted at first only to ingratiate myself with Lady Teazle that she might   215
not be my enemy with Maria, and I have, I don't know how, become her

---

1    *give me ... my library* Literally, "examine the books in my library"; also a sexual innuendo.
2    *cicisbeo* Italian term for a married woman's male companion or escort.

serious lover! Sincerely, I begin to wish I had never made such a point of gaining so very good a character, for it has led me into so many rogueries that I doubt I shall be exposed at last.

(*Exit.*)

## ACT 2, SCENE 3. SIR PETER TEAZLE'S HOUSE.

(*Enter Rowley and Sir Oliver.*)

SIR OLIVER.  Ha, ha, ha! and so my old friend is married, hey! A young wife out of the country, ha, ha, ha! That he should have stood bluff[1] to old bachelor so long, and sink into husband at last.

ROWLEY.  But you must not rally him on the subject, Sir Oliver; 'tis a tender
5    point I assure you, though he has been married only seven months.

SIR OLIVER.  Then he has been just half a year on the stool of repentance. Poor Peter! But you say he has entirely given up Charles? Never sees him, hey?

ROWLEY.  His prejudice against him is astonishing and, I'm sure, greatly increased by a jealousy of him with Lady Teazle, which he has been industri-
10    ously led into by a scandalous society in the neighbourhood, who have contributed not a little to Charles's ill name, whereas the truth is, I believe, if the lady is partial to either of them, his brother is the favourite.

SIR OLIVER.  Aye, I know there is a set of malicious, prating, prudent gossips, both male and female, who murder characters to kill time and will rob a
15    young fellow of his good name before he has years to know the value of it. But I am not to be prejudiced against my nephew by such, I promise you; no, no, if Charles has done nothing false or mean, I shall compound for his extravagance.

ROWLEY.  Then my life on't, you will reclaim him. Ah sir, it gives me new life
20    to find that your heart is not turned against him and that the son of my good old master has one friend, however, left.

SIR OLIVER.  What, shall I forget, Master Rowley, when I was at his years myself? Egad, my brother and I were neither very prudent youths, and yet I believe you have not seen many better men than your old master was.

25  ROWLEY.  Sir, 'tis this reflection gives me assurance that Charles may yet be a credit to his family.—But here comes Sir Peter.

SIR OLIVER.  Egad, so he does. Mercy on me! he's greatly altered and seems to have a settled, married look! One may read husband in his face at this distance.

(*Enter Sir Peter.*)

---

1    *bluff* Unfalteringly.

Sir Peter. Hah! Sir Oliver, my old friend, welcome to England a thousand    30
times.

Sir Oliver. Thank you, thank you, Sir Peter. And i'faith, I'm as glad to find
you well, believe me.

Sir Peter. Ah! 'Tis a long time since we met: sixteen years, I doubt, Sir Oliver, and many a cross accident in the time.    35

Sir Oliver. Aye, I have had my share. But what, I find you are married, hey,
my old boy! Well, well, it can't be helped, and so I wish you joy with all
my heart.

Sir Peter. Thank you, thank you, Sir Oliver. Yes, I have entered into the
happy state—but we'll not talk of that now.    40

Sir Oliver. True, true, Sir Peter, old friends should not begin on grievances
at first meeting, no, no, no.

Rowley. (*to Sir Oliver*) Take care, pray sir.

Sir Oliver. So, one of my nephews I find is a wild, extravagant young rogue,
hey!    45

Sir Peter. Wild! Ah my old friend, I grieve for your disappointment there:
he's a lost young man indeed. However, his brother will make you amends;
Joseph is indeed what a youth should be. Everybody in the world speaks
well of him.

Sir Oliver. I am sorry to hear it: he has too good a character to be an honest    50
fellow. Everybody speaks well of him! Pshaw! Then he has bowed as low to
knaves and fools as to the honest dignity of genius or virtue.

Sir Peter. What, Sir Oliver, do you blame him for not making enemies?

Sir Oliver. Yes, if he has merit enough to deserve them.

Sir Peter. Well, well, you'll be convinced when you know him. 'Tis edifica-    55
tion to hear him converse. He possesses the noblest sentiments.

Sir Oliver. Oh plague of his sentiments! If he salutes[1] me with a scrap of
morality in his mouth, I shall be sick directly. But, however, don't mistake
me, Sir Peter, I don't mean to defend Charles's errors, but before I form my
judgment of either of them, I intend to make a trial of their hearts, and my    60
friend Rowley and I have planned something for the purpose.

Rowley. And Sir Peter shall own he has been for once mistaken.

Sir Peter. Oh, my life on Joseph's honour.

Sir Oliver. Well, come, give us a bottle of good wine, and we'll drink your
lady's good health and tell you all our scheme.    65

Sir Peter. Allons[2] then.

---

1    *salutes* Kisses in greeting.
2    *Allons* French: we shall go.

SIR OLIVER. And don't, Sir Peter, be so severe against your old friend's son. 'Odd's[1] my life! I'm not sorry that he has run out of the course a little. For my part, I hate to see prudence clinging to the green suckers of youth. 'Tis
70 like ivy round a sapling and spoils the growth of the tree.

(*Exeunt.*)

### ACT 3, SCENE 1. SIR PETER TEAZLE'S HOUSE.

(*Enter Sir Peter, Sir Oliver, and Rowley.*)

SIR PETER. Well then, we will see this fellow first and have our wine afterwards. But how is this, Master Rowley? I don't see the gist of your scheme.
ROWLEY. Why sir, this Mr. Stanley, whom I was speaking of, is nearly related to them by their mother. He was once a merchant in Dublin but has been
5 ruined by a series of undeserved misfortunes. He has applied by letter since his confinement both to Mr. Surface and Charles. From the former he has received nothing but evasive promises of future service, while Charles has done all that his extravagance has left him power to do, and he is at this time endeavouring to raise a sum of money, part of which in the midst of
10 his own distresses, I know, he intends for the service of poor Stanley.
SIR OLIVER. Ah! He is my brother's son.
SIR PETER. Well, but how is Sir Oliver personally to—
ROWLEY. Why sir, I will inform Charles and his brother that Stanley has obtained permission to apply in person to his friends, and as they have
15 neither of them ever seen him, let Sir Oliver assume the character, and he will have a fair opportunity of judging at least of the benevolence of their dispositions. And believe me, sir, you will find in the youngest brother one, who in the midst of folly and dissipation, has still, as our immortal bard expresses it,
20         A tear for pity and a hand
        Open as day for melting charity.[2]
SIR PETER. Pshaw! What signifies his having an open hand or a purse either when he has nothing left to give? Well, well, make the trial if you please, but where is the fellow whom you brought for Sir Oliver to examine rela-
25 tive to Charles's affairs?
ROWLEY. Below, waiting his commands, and no one can give him better intelligence.—This, Sir Oliver, is a friendly Jew, who to do him justice, has done everything in his power to bring your nephew to a proper sense of his extravagance.

---

1    *'Odds* Swear word meaning "God's."
2    *A tear … charity* From Shakespeare, *2 Henry IV* 4.4.31–32.

SIR PETER.  Pray, let us have him in.                                      30

ROWLEY.  Desire Mr. Moses to walk upstairs.

SIR PETER.  But pray, why should you suppose he will speak the truth?

ROWLEY.  Oh, I have convinced him he has no chance of recovering certain
sums advanced to Charles but through the bounty of Sir Oliver, who he
knows is arrived, so that you may depend on his fidelity to his own interest.   35
I have also another evidence[1] in my power, one Snake, whom I have detected
in a matter little short of forgery, and shall shortly produce him to remove
some of *your* prejudices, Sir Peter, relative to Charles and Lady Teazle.

SIR PETER.  I have heard too much on that subject.

ROWLEY.  Here comes the honest Israelite.                                  40

(*Enter Moses.*)

ROWLEY.  This is Sir Oliver.

SIR OLIVER.  Sir, I understand you have lately had great dealings with my
nephew, Charles?

MOSES.  Yes, Sir Oliver. I done all my power for him, but he was ruined before he came to me for assistance.                                         45

SIR OLIVER.  That was unlucky, truly, for you have had no opportunity of
showing your talents.

MOSES.  None at all. I had not the pleasure of knowing his distresses till he
was some thousands worse than nothing.

SIR OLIVER.  Unfortunate indeed! But I suppose you have done all in your   50
power for him, honest Moses?

MOSES.  Yes, he knows that. This very evening I was to have brought him
a gentleman from the City, who does not know him and will, I believe,
advance him some money.

SIR PETER.  What, one Charles never had money from before?               55

MOSES.  Yes, Mr. Premium, of Crutched Friars,[2] formerly a broker.

SIR PETER.  Egad, Sir Oliver, a thought strikes me.—Charles, you say, doesn't
know Mr. Premium?

MOSES.  Not at all.

SIR PETER.  Now then, Sir Oliver, you may have an opportunity of satisfying  60
yourself better than by an old romancing tale of a poor relation.—Go with
my friend, Moses, and present Mr. Premium.—And then I'll answer for't,
you will see your nephew in all his glory.

SIR OLIVER.  Egad, I like this idea better than the other, and I may visit Joseph
afterwards as old Stanley.                                                 65

SIR PETER.  True, so you may.

1   *evidence* I.e., giver of evidence.
2   *Crutched Friars* Street in London.

ROWLEY. Well, this is taking Charles at a disadvantage to be sure; however, Moses, you understand Sir Peter and will be faithful.

MOSES. You may depend upon me. This is near the time I was to have gone.

70 SIR OLIVER. I'll accompany you as soon as you please, Moses, but hold, I forgot one thing: How the plague shall I be able to pass for a Jew?

MOSES. There is no need: the principal[1] is Christian.

SIR OLIVER. Is he? I am sorry to hear it. But then again, an't I too smartly dressed to look like a moneylender?

75 SIR PETER. Not at all. 'Twould not be out of character if you went in your own carriage, would it, Moses?

MOSES. Not in the least.

SIR OLIVER. Well, but how must I talk? There's certainly some cant of usury and mode of treating that I ought to know.

80 SIR PETER. Oh, there's not much to learn. The great point, as I take it, is to be exorbitant enough in your demands, hey Moses?

MOSES. Yes, that's a very great point.

SIR OLIVER. I'll answer for't; I'll not be wanting in that. I'll ask him eight, or ten percent, upon the loan, at least.

85 MOSES. If you ask him no more than that, you'll be discovered immediately.

SIR OLIVER. Hey, what a plague! How much then?

MOSES. That depends upon circumstances; if he appears not very anxious for the supply, you should require only forty or fifty percent, but if you find him in great distress and want the monies very bad, you may ask him

90 double.

SIR PETER. A good, honest trade you are learning, Sir Oliver.

SIR OLIVER. Truly, I think so, and not unprofitable.

MOSES. Then, you know, you haven't the monies yourself but are forced to borrow them for him of a friend.

95 SIR OLIVER. Oh! I borrow it of a friend, do I?

MOSES. Yes, and your friend is an unconscionable dog, but you can't help it.

SIR OLIVER. My friend is an unconscionable dog, is he?

MOSES. Yes, and he himself has not the monies by him but is forced to sell stock at a great loss.

100 SIR OLIVER. He's forced to sell stock at a great loss, is he? Well, that's very kind of him.

SIR PETER. I'faith, Sir Oliver, Mr. Premium I mean, you'll soon be master of the trade.

SIR OLIVER. Right, right! Well, Moses shall give me further instructions as

105 we go together.

---

1   *principal* I.e., the broker for whom Moses is acting as an agent.

SIR PETER.  You will not have much time, for your nephew lives hard by.

SIR OLIVER.  Oh, never fear, my tutor appears so able that, though Charles lived in the next street, it must be my own fault if I'm not a complete rogue before I turn the corner.

(*Exeunt Sir Oliver and Moses.*)

SIR PETER.  So now I think Sir Oliver will be convinced you are partial, Row- 110
ley, and would have prepared Charles for the other plot.

ROWLEY.  No, upon my word, Sir Peter.

SIR PETER.  Well, go bring me this Snake, and I'll hear what he has to say presently.—I see Maria and want to speak with her.

(*Exit Rowley.*)

I should be glad to be convinced my suspicions of Lady Teazle and Charles 115
were unjust. I have never yet opened my mind on this subject to my friend Joseph; I am determined I will do it: he will give me his opinion sincerely.

(*Enter Maria.*)

SIR PETER.  So child, has Mr. Surface returned with you?

MARIA.  No sir, he was engaged.

SIR PETER.  Well Maria, do you not reflect the more you converse with that 120
amiable young man what return his partiality for you deserves?

MARIA.  Indeed, Sir Peter, your frequent importunity on this subject distresses me extremely; you compel me to declare that I know no man who has ever paid me a particular attention whom I would not prefer to Mr. Surface.

SIR PETER.  So, here's perverseness! No, no, Maria, 'tis Charles only whom 125
you would prefer; 'tis evident his vices and follies have won your heart.

MARIA.  This is unkind, sir. You know I have obeyed you in neither seeing nor corresponding with him. I have heard enough to convince me that he is unworthy my regard, yet I cannot think it culpable if, while my under-standing severely condemns his vices, my heart suggests some pity for his 130
distresses.

SIR PETER.  Well, well, pity him as much as you please, but give your heart and hand to a worthier object.

MARIA.  Never to his brother.

SIR PETER.  Go, perverse and obstinate! But take care, madam, you have 135
never yet known what the authority of a guardian is; do not compel me to inform you of it.

MARIA.  I can only say you shall not have just reason. 'Tis true, by my father's will I am for a short period bound to regard you as his substitute but must cease to think you so when you would compel me to be miserable. (*Exit.*) 140

SIR PETER.  Was there ever man so crossed[1] as I am! Everything conspiring to fret me. I had not been involved in matrimony a fortnight[2] before her father, a hale and hearty man, died, on purpose, I believe, for the pleasure of plaguing me with the care of his daughter. But here comes my helpmate.
145   She appears in great good humour. How happy I should be if I could tease her into loving me, though but a little.

(*Enter Lady Teazle.*)

LADY TEAZLE.  Lud! Sir Peter, I hope you haven't been quarrelling with Maria? It isn't using me well to be ill-humoured when I'm not by.
SIR PETER.  Ah! Lady Teazle, you might have the power to make me good-
150   humoured at all times.
LADY TEAZLE.  I am sure I wish I had, for I want you to be in a charming, sweet temper at this moment. Do be good-humoured now and let me have two hundred pounds, will you?
SIR PETER.  Two hundred pounds! What, an't I to be in a good humour with-
155   out paying for it? But speak to me thus, and i'faith, there's nothing I would refuse you. You shall have it but seal me a bond[3] for the repayment.
LADY TEAZLE.  Oh no! There's my note of hand[4] will do as well.
SIR PETER.  And you shall no longer reproach me with not giving you an independent settlement—I mean shortly to surprise you—but shall we
160   always live thus, hey?
LADY TEAZLE.  If you please. I'm sure I do not care how soon we leave off quarrelling, provided you'll own you were tired first.
SIR PETER.  Well then, let our future contest be who shall be most obliging.
LADY TEAZLE.  I assure you, Sir Peter, good nature becomes you; you look
165   now as you did before we were married! When you used to walk with me under the elms and tell me stories of what a gallant you were in your youth, and chuck me under the chin, you would, and ask me if I thought I could love an old fellow who would deny me nothing, didn't you?
SIR PETER.  Yes, yes, and you were as kind and attentive—
170  LADY TEAZLE.  Aye, so I was and would always take your part when my acquaintance used to abuse you and turn you into ridicule.
SIR PETER.  Indeed!
LADY TEAZLE.  Aye, and when my cousin Sophy called you a stiff, peevish old bachelor and laughed at me for thinking of marrying one who might be

1    *crossed* Unlucky in fate.
2    *a fortnight* Two weeks.
3    *bond* Formal promise of repayment on a loan; Sir Peter is playfully requesting a kiss.
4    *note of hand* Literally, a signed note; in performance, Lady Teazle would hold out her hand for Sir Peter to kiss.

my father, I have always defended you and said I didn't think you so ugly    175
by any means.

SIR PETER.  Thank you!

LADY TEAZLE.  And that I dared say you would make a very good sort of a
husband.

SIR PETER.  And you prophesied right, and we shall certainly now be the    180
happiest couple—

LADY TEAZLE.  And never differ again.

SIR PETER.  No, never—though at the same time indeed, my dear Lady Teazle, you must watch your temper very narrowly, for in all our little quarrels,
my dear—if you recollect, my love, you always began first.    185

LADY TEAZLE.  I beg pardon, my dear Sir Peter, indeed you always gave the
provocation.

SIR PETER.  Now see my angel, contradicting isn't the way to keep friends.

LADY TEAZLE.  Then don't you begin it, my love.

SIR PETER.  There now—you—you are going on, you don't perceive, my life,    190
that you are just doing the very thing which you know always makes me
angry.

LADY TEAZLE.  Nay, you know if you will be angry without any reason—

SIR PETER.  There now, you want to quarrel again.

LADY TEAZLE.  No, I'm sure I don't, but if you will be so peevish—    195

SIR PETER.  There, *now* who begins first?

LADY TEAZLE.  Why, you, to be sure. I said nothing, but there's no bearing
your temper.

SIR PETER.  No, no, madam, the fault is in your own temper.

LADY TEAZLE.  Aye, you are just what my cousin Sophy said you would be—    200

SIR PETER.  Your cousin Sophy is a forward, impertinent Gypsy.

LADY TEAZLE.  And you a great bear to abuse my relations.

SIR PETER.  Now may all the plagues of marriage be doubled on me if ever I
try to be friends with you any more.

LADY TEAZLE.  So much the better.    205

SIR PETER.  No, no, madam, 'tis evident you never cared a pin for me, and I
was a madman to marry you: a pert, rural coquette[1] that had refused half
the honest squires in the neighbourhood.

LADY TEAZLE.  And I am sure I was a fool to marry you: an old, dangling
bachelor, who was single at fifty only because he never could meet with    210
anyone who would have him.

SIR PETER.  Aye, aye, madam, but you were pleased enough to listen to me:
you never had such an offer before.

---

1    *coquette* Flirt.

LADY TEAZLE.  No! Didn't I refuse Sir Tivy Terrier, who everybody said would
215   have been a better match? For his estate is just as good as yours, and he has
broke his neck since we have been married.

SIR PETER.  Oh, oh, oh! I have done with you, madam. You are unfeeling,
ungrateful—but there is an end of everything. I believe you capable of
anything that's bad. Yes madam, I now believe the report relative to you
220   and Charles, madam. Madam—yes, madam, you and Charles, not without grounds.

LADY TEAZLE.  Take care, Sir Peter. You had better not insinuate any such
thing. I'll not be suspected without a cause, I promise you.

SIR PETER.  Very well, madam, very well, a separate maintenance as soon as
225   you please—yes madam, or a divorce. I'll make an example of myself for
the benefit of all old bachelors. Let us separate, madam.

LADY TEAZLE.  Agreed, agreed. And now my dear Sir Peter, we are of a mind
once more; we may be the happiest couple and never differ again, you
know, ha, ha! Well, you are going to be in a passion, I see, and I shall only
230   interrupt you, so bye bye. (*Exit.*)

SIR PETER.  Plagues and tortures! Can't I make her angry either? Oh, I am the
miserablest fellow! But I'll not bear her presuming to keep her temper. No,
she may break my heart, but she shall not keep her temper.

(*Exit.*)

### ACT 3, SCENE 2. A CHAMBER IN CHARLES'S HOUSE.

(*Enter Trip, Moses, and Sir Oliver.*)

TRIP.  Here master, master, if you will stay a moment, I'll try whether—what's
the gentleman's name?

SIR OLIVER.  [*aside*] Mr. Moses, what is my name?

MOSES.  Mr. Premium.

5   TRIP.  Premium—very well. (*Exit taking snuff.*)

SIR OLIVER.  To judge by the servants, one would believe the master was ruined. But what! Sure this was my brother's house!

MOSES.  Yes sir, Mr. Charles bought it of Mr. Joseph, with the furniture, pictures, etcetera, just as the old gentleman left it. Sir Peter thought it a great
10   piece of extravagance in him.

SIR OLIVER.  In my mind the other's economy in selling it him was more
reprehensible by half.

(*Enter Trip.*)

TRIP.  My master says you must wait, gentleman, he has company and can't
speak with you yet.

SIR OLIVER. If he knew who it was wanted to see him, perhaps he wouldn't  15
have sent such a message.

TRIP. Yes, yes, sir, he knows you are here; I didn't forget little Premium, no,
no, no.

SIR OLIVER. Very well, and I pray sir, what may be your name?

TRIP. Trip, sir, my name is Trip, at your service.  20

SIR OLIVER. Well then Mr. Trip, you have a pleasant sort of place here I guess?

TRIP. Why yes, here are three or four of us pass our time agreeably enough,
but then our wages are sometimes a little in arrear, and not very good either, but fifty pounds a year and find our own bags[1] and bouquets.

SIR OLIVER. Bags and bouquets! Halters and bastinadoes.[2]  25

TRIP. But apropos, Moses! Have you been able to get me that little bill
discounted?[3]

SIR OLIVER. [*aside*] Wants to raise money too—mercy on me—has his distresses, I warrant, like a lord, and affects creditors and duns.[4]

MOSES. 'Twas not to be done indeed, Mr. Trip.  30

TRIP. Good lack! You surprise me. My friend Brush has endorsed it, and I
thought, when he puts his mark to the back of the bill, 'twas as good as
cash.

MOSES. No, 'twouldn't do.

TRIP. A small sum—but twenty pounds. Harkee, Moses, do you think you  35
could get it me by way of annuity?[5]

SIR OLIVER. [*aside*] An annuity! Ha, ha, ha! A footman raise money by annuity! Well done, luxury, egad!

MOSES. But you must insure your place.

TRIP. Oh, with all my heart I'll insure my place—and my life too if you  40
please.

SIR OLIVER. [*aside*] It's more than I would your neck.

MOSES. But is there nothing you could deposit?

TRIP. Why nothing capital of my master's wardrobe has dropped lately,[6] but
I could give you a mortgage on some of his winter clothes, with equity  45

---

1  *bags* Wigs.
2  *Halters* Hangings; *bastinadoes* Canings of the feet.
3  *bill* I.e., bill of exchange, a document similar to a cheque in which one party promises to
   pay the holder at a specified date, usually some months in the future; *discounted* Sold for
   a reduced amount of immediate cash.
4  *duns* Debt collectors. Sir Oliver is suggesting that Trip is too low-class to have debt of this
   kind.
5  *annuity* Annual payment, usually obtained by way of an investment or insurance agreement.
6  *my master's ... dropped lately* As a senior servant, Trip would sometimes receive hand-me-
   down clothing from Charles Surface.

and redemption before November, or you shall have the reversion of the French velvet or a post-obit[1] on the blue and silver—these, I should think, Moses, with a few pair of point[2] ruffles, as a collateral security, hey my little fellow?

50  MOSES.  Well, well—

(*Bell rings.*)

TRIP.  Egad, I heard the bell. I believe, gentlemen, I can now introduce you.—Don't forget the annuity, little Moses.—This way, gentlemen.—Insure my place, you know!

SIR OLIVER.  [*aside*] If the man be the shadow of the master, this is the temple

55  of dissipation indeed!

(*Exeunt.*)

## ACT 3, SCENE 3.

5

(*Charles, Careless, Sir Toby Bumper, etc. discovered at a table drinking wine.*)

CHARLES.  'Fore Heaven 'tis true, there's the great degeneracy of the age: many of our acquaintance have taste, spirit, and politeness, but plague on't, they won't drink.

CARELESS.  It is so indeed, Charles; they give into all the substantial luxuries of the table and abstain from nothing but wine and wit.

CHARLES.  Oh certainly, society suffers by it intolerably, for now instead of the social spirit of raillery that used to mantle over a glass of bright burgundy, their conversation is become just like the spa-water[3] they drink, which has all the pertness and flatulence of champagne without its spirit or flavour.

10  FIRST GENTLEMAN.  But what are they to do, who love play better than wine?

CARELESS.  True, there's Harry diets himself for gaming and is now under a hazard[4] regimen.

CHARLES.  Then he'll have the worst of it. What! You wouldn't train a horse for the course by keeping him from corn?[5] For my part, egad, I am now

15  never so successful as when I am a little merry; let me throw on a bottle of

---

1    *reversion* I.e., ownership rights after the current owner's death; *post-obit* Loan agreement in which repayment is postponed until the death of a person from whom the borrower expects to inherit.

2    *point* I.e., lace.

3    *spa-water* Water from a mineral spring.

4    *hazard* Complicated dice game.

5    *corn* Food grain, such as oats.

champagne, and I never lose, at least I never feel my losses, which is exactly
the same thing.

SECOND GENTLEMAN.  Aye, that I believe.

CHARLES.  And then, what man can pretend to be a believer in love who is an
abjurer of wine? 'Tis the test by which the lover knows his own heart. Fill     20
a dozen bumpers to a dozen beauties, and she that floats at top is the maid
that has bewitched you.

CARELESS.  Now then, Charles, be honest and give us your real favourite.

CHARLES.  Why, I have withheld her only in compassion to you; if I toast her,
you must give a round of her peers, which is impossible on earth.               25

CARELESS.  Oh, then we'll find some canonized vestals[1] or heathen goddesses
that will do, I warrant.

CHARLES.  Here then, bumpers, you rogues, bumpers. Maria, Maria!

FIRST GENTLEMAN.  Maria who?

CHARLES.  Oh damn the surname, 'tis too formal to be registered in love's       30
calendar.—But now, Sir Toby, beware, we must have beauty's superlative.

CARELESS.  Nay, never study, Sir Toby; we'll stand to the toast though your
mistress should want an eye, and you know you have a song will excuse
you.

SIR TOBY.  Egad, so I have, and I'll give him the song instead of the lady.     35

[Song and Chorus.]
Here's to the maiden of bashful fifteen;
  Here's to the widow of fifty;
Here's to the flaunting, extravagant quean,°             *whore*
  And here's to the housewife that's thrifty.
[Chorus.]
    Let the toast pass,                40
    Drink to the lass,
I'll warrant she'll prove an excuse for the glass.

Here's to the charmer whose dimples we prize;
  Now to the maid who has none, sir;
Here's to the girl with a pair of blue eyes,            45
  And here's to the nymph° with but one, sir.    *young woman*
    Let the toast pass, etc.

Here's to the maid with a bosom of snow;
  Now to her that's as brown as a berry;

---

1   *vestals* I.e., virgins.

50—    Here's to the wife with her face full of woe,
          And now for the damsel that's merry.
                Let the toast pass, etc.


          For let them be clumsy or let them be slim,
              Young or ancient I care not a feather;
55        So fill a pint bumper quite up to the brim,
              And let us e'en toast them together.
                Let the toast pass, etc.

ALL.  Bravo, Bravo!

    (*Enter Trip, who whispers to Charles.*)

CHARLES.  Gentlemen, you must excuse me a little.—Careless, take the chair,
60    will you?
CARELESS.  Nay prithee Charles, what now? This is one of your peerless beau-
    ties, I suppose, has dropped in by chance.
CHARLES.  No, faith, to tell you the truth, 'tis a Jew and a broker who are
    come by appointment.
65  CARELESS.  Oh damn it, let's have the Jew in.
FIRST GENTLEMAN.  Aye, and the broker too, by all means.
SECOND GENTLEMAN.  Yes, yes, the Jew and the broker.
CHARLES.  Egad, with all my heart.—Trip, bid the gentlemen walk in, (*Exit
    Trip.*) though there's one of them a stranger, I can assure you.
70  CARELESS.  Charles, let us give them some generous burgundy, and perhaps
    they'll grow conscientious.
CHARLES.  Oh hang 'em, no, wine does but draw forth the natural qualities
    of a man, and to make them drink would only be to whet their knavery.

    (*Enter Trip, Sir Oliver, and Moses.*)

75  CHARLES.  So, honest Moses, walk in, walk in pray, Mr. Premium. That's the
    gentleman's name, isn't it, Moses?
MOSES.  Yes sir.
CHARLES.  Set chairs, Trip.—Sit down, Mr. Premium.—Glasses, Trip.—Sit
    down, Moses.—Come, Mr. Premium, I'll give you a sentiment: here's suc-
80    cess to usury.—Moses, fill the gentleman a bumper.
MOSES.  Success to usury.
CARELESS.  Right, Moses, usury is prudence and industry and deserves to
    succeed.
SIR OLIVER.  Then here's all the success it deserves.
85  CARELESS.  No, no, that won't do, Mr. Premium. You have demurred to the
    toast and must drink it in a pint-bumper.

FIRST GENTLEMAN.  A pint bumper at least.

MOSES.  Oh pray sir, consider Mr. Premium's a gentleman.

CARELESS.  And therefore loves good wine.

SECOND GENTLEMAN.  Give Moses a quart-glass; this is mutiny and a high     90
contempt of the chair.

CARELESS.  Here now for't. I'll see justice done to the last drop of my bottle.

SIR OLIVER.  Nay, pray gentlemen, I did not expect this usage.

CHARLES.  No, hang it, Careless, you shan't. Mr. Premium's a stranger.

SIR OLIVER.  [*aside*] 'Odd, I wish I was well out of their company.     95

CARELESS.  Plague on them, then. If they won't drink, we'll not sit down with
them. Come Harry, the dice are in the next room. Charles, you'll join us
when you've finished your business with these gentlemen.

(*Exeunt Sir Toby and gentlemen.*)

CHARLES.  I will, I will. Careless!

CARELESS.  Well.     100

CHARLES.  Perhaps I may want you.

CARELESS.  Oh, you know I am always ready; word, note, or bond, 'tis all the
same to me. (*Exit.*)

MOSES.  Sir, this is Mr. Premium, a gentleman of the strictest honour and
secrecy and always performs what he undertakes. Mr. Premium, this is—     105

CHARLES.  Pshaw! Have done.—Sir, my friend Moses is a very honest fellow
but a little slow at expression; he'll be an hour giving us our titles. Mr.
Premium, the plain state of the matter is this: I am an extravagant young
fellow who wants money to borrow; you I take to be a prudent old fellow
who has got money to lend. I am blockhead enough to give fifty per cent[1]     110
sooner than not have it, and *you*, I presume, are rogue enough to take an
hundred if you can get it. Now sir, you see we are acquainted at once and
may proceed to business without any further ceremony.

SIR OLIVER.  [*aside*] Exceeding frank, upon my word.—I see, sir, you are not
a man of many compliments.     115

CHARLES.  Oh no, sir, plain dealing in business I always think best.

SIR OLIVER.  Sir, I like you the better for't. However, you are mistaken in one
thing: I have no money to lend. But I believe I could procure some of a
friend, but then he's an unconscionable dog, isn't he, Moses? and must sell
stock to accommodate you, mustn't he, Moses?     120

MOSES.  Yes indeed. You know I always speak the truth and scorn to tell a lie.

CHARLES.  Right! People that speak the truth generally do.—But these are
trifles, Mr. Premium. What, I know money isn't to be bought without
paying for't.

---

1    *give fifty per cent*  I.e., pay 50 per cent interest on the borrowed money.

125 SIR OLIVER. Well, but what security could you give? You have no land, I
suppose?

CHARLES. Not a mole-hill nor a twig but what's in beau-pots[1] out at the
window.

SIR OLIVER. Nor any stock, I presume?

130 CHARLES. Nothing but livestock, and that's only a few pointers and ponies.
But pray, Mr. Premium, are you acquainted at all with any of my connections?

SIR OLIVER. Why to say truth, I am.

CHARLES. Then you must know that I have a devilish rich uncle in the East
135 Indies, Sir Oliver Surface, from whom I have the greatest expectations.

SIR OLIVER. That you have a wealthy uncle, I have heard, but how your expectations will turn out is more, I believe, than you can tell.

CHARLES. Oh no! There can be no doubt; they tell me I'm a prodigious favourite and that he talks of leaving me everything.

140 SIR OLIVER. Indeed! This is the first I have heard of it.

CHARLES. Yes, yes, 'tis just so. Moses knows 'tis true, don't you, Moses?

MOSES. Oh yes, I'll swear to it.

SIR OLIVER. [aside] Egad, they'll persuade me presently I'm at Bengal.

CHARLES. Now I propose, Mr. Premium, if it is agreeable to you, to grant
145 you a post-obit on Sir Oliver's life, though at the same time the old fellow
has been so liberal to me that I give you my word I should be very sorry to
hear anything had happened to him.

SIR OLIVER. Not more than I should, I assure you. But the bond you mention happens to be just the worst security you could offer me, for I might
150 live to an hundred and never recover the principal.

CHARLES. Oh, yes you would, the moment Sir Oliver dies you know you
would come on me for the money.

SIR OLIVER. Then I believe I should be the most unwelcome dun you ever
had in your life.

155 CHARLES. What, I suppose you are afraid Sir Oliver is too good a life?

SIR OLIVER. No indeed, I am not though I have heard he is as hale and
healthy as any man of his years in Christendom.

CHARLES. There again you are misinformed; no, no, the climate has hurt him
considerably. Poor Uncle Oliver! Yes, he breaks apace, I am told, and so
160 much altered lately that his nearest relations would not know him.

SIR OLIVER. No? Ha, ha, ha! So much altered lately that his relations would
not know him, ha, ha, ha! That's droll, egad, ha, ha, ha!

CHARLES. Ha, ha, ha! You're glad to hear that, little Premium?

---

1   *beau-pots* Containers of flowers.

SIR OLIVER.  No, no, I am not.

CHARLES.  Yes, yes, you are, ha, ha, ha! You know that mends your chance.   165

SIR OLIVER.  But I'm told Sir Oliver is coming over; nay, some say he is actually arrived.

CHARLES.  Pshaw! Sure I must know better than you whether he's coming or not; no, no, rely on't, he is at this moment at Calcutta, isn't he, Moses?

MOSES.  Yes, certainly.   170

SIR OLIVER.  Very true, as you say, you must know better than I, though I have it from pretty good authority, haven't I, Moses?

MOSES.  Yes, most undoubted.

SIR OLIVER.  But sir, as I understand you want a few hundreds immediately, is there nothing you would dispose of?   175

CHARLES.  How do you mean?

SIR OLIVER.  For instance, now, I have heard that your father left behind him a great quantity of massy old plate.[1]

CHARLES.  Oh, Lud! That's gone long ago; Moses can tell you how better than I.   180

SIR OLIVER.  [*aside*] Good lack! All the family race-cups and corporation bowls![2]—Then it was also supposed his library was one of the most valuable and complete.

CHARLES.  Yes, yes, so it was, vastly too much so for a private gentleman; for my part I was always of a communicative disposition, so I thought it was a   185 shame to keep so much knowledge to myself.

SIR OLIVER.  [*aside*] Mercy on me! Learning that had run in the family like an heirloom.—Pray, what are become of the books?

CHARLES.  You must inquire of the auctioneer, Master Premium, for I don't believe even Moses can direct you there.   190

MOSES.  I know nothing of books.

SIR OLIVER.  So, so, nothing of the family property left, I suppose?

CHARLES.  Not much indeed, unless you have a mind to the family pictures. I have got a room full of ancestors above, and if you have taste for old paintings, egad, you shall have them a bargain.   195

SIR OLIVER.  Hey, the devil! Sure you won't sell your forefathers, would you?

CHARLES.  Every man of them to the best bidder.

SIR OLIVER.  What, your great uncles and aunts?

CHARLES.  Yes, and my grandfathers and grandmothers too.

---

1   *plate*  Silver plate.

2   *race-cups*  Trophies for horse racing; *corporation bowls*  Bowls given by the city in recognition of service.

SIR OLIVER. [*aside*] Now I give him up.—What the plague, have you no bowels for your kindred? 'Odd's life! Do you take me for Shylock[1] in the play, that you would raise money of me on your own flesh and blood?

CHARLES. Nay, my little broker, don't be angry. What need you care, if you have your money's worth?

SIR OLIVER. Well, I'll be the purchaser; I think I can dispose of the family canvas. [*aside*] Oh! I'll never forgive him this—never.

(*Enter Careless.*)

CARELESS. Come Charles, what keeps you?

CHARLES. I can't come yet, i'faith; we are going to have a sale above. Here's little Premium will buy all my ancestors.

CARELESS. Oh, burn your ancestors!

CHARLES. No, he may do that afterwards, if he pleases. Stay, Careless, we want you; egad, you shall be auctioneer, so come along with us.

CARELESS. Oh, have with you, if that's the case; I can handle a hammer as well as a dice-box. A-going, a-going,[2] etcetera.

SIR OLIVER. [*aside*] Oh the profligates!

CHARLES. Come, Moses. You shall be appraiser, if we want one.—Gad's life, little Premium, you don't seem to like the business?

SIR OLIVER. Oh, yes, I do vastly, ha, ha! Yes, yes, I think it a rare joke to sell one's family by auction, ha, ha! (*aside*) Oh the prodigal!

CHARLES. To be sure! When a man wants money, where the plague should he get assistance if he can't make free with his own relations?

SIR OLIVER. [*aside*] I'll never forgive him! Never, never!

(*Exeunt.*)

## ACT 4, SCENE 1. PICTURE ROOM AT CHARLES'S HOUSE.

(*Enter Charles, Sir Oliver, Moses, and Careless.*)

CHARLES. Walk in, gentlemen, walk in pray. Here they are, the family of the Surfaces up to the Conquest.[3]

SIR OLIVER. And in my opinion, a goodly collection.

---

1    *Shylock* Moneylender in Shakespeare's *The Merchant of Venice*. In Shakespeare's play, Shylock gives a loan on the condition that, if he is not repaid by a specified time, he is entitled to a pound of flesh from the person who guaranteed the loan.

2    *A-going, a-going* Auctioneer's call.

3    *up to the Conquest* I.e., as far back as the eleventh century; the Norman Conquest was in 1066.

CHARLES.  Aye, aye, they are done in the true spirit of portrait painting, no
volunteer grace or expression, not like the works of your modern Raphael,[1]
who gives you the strongest resemblance yet contrives to make your own
portrait independent of you, so that you may sink the original and not
hurt the pictures. No, no, the merit of these is the inveterate likeness:
all stiff and awkward as the originals and like nothing in human nature
beside.

SIR OLIVER.  Ah! We shall never see such figures of men again.

CHARLES.  I hope not. Well, you see, Master Premium, what a domestic character I am; here I sit of an evening surrounded by my family. But come, go
to your pulpit, Mr. Auctioneer. Here's an old gouty chair[2] of my grandfather's will answer the purpose.

CARELESS.  Aye, aye, this will do, but Charles, I have ne'er a hammer, and
what's an auctioneer without his hammer?

CHARLES.  Egad, that's true. What parchment do we have here? Richard, heir
to Thomas[3]—Oh, our genealogy in full.—Here Careless, you shall have no
common bit of mahogany; here's the family tree for you, you rogue. This
shall be your hammer, and now you may knock down my ancestors with
their own pedigree.

SIR OLIVER.  [*aside*] What an unnatural rogue! An *ex post facto*[4] parricide!

CARELESS.  Yes, yes, here's a list of your generation, indeed. 'Faith, Charles,
this is the most convenient thing you could have found for the business,
for 'twill serve not only as a hammer but a catalogue into the bargain. But
come, begin, a-going, a-going, a-going—

CHARLES.  Bravo, Careless! Well, here's my great uncle, Sir Richard Raveline,[5]
a marvellous good general in his day, I assure you; he served in all the
Duke of Marlborough's wars and got that cut over his eye at the Battle of
Malplaquet.[6] What say you, Mr. Premium, look at him, there's a hero: not
cut out of his feathers as your modern clipped captains are but enveloped in
wig and regimentals as a general should be. What do you bid?

SIR OLIVER.  (*aside to Moses*) Bid him speak.

MOSES.  Mr. Premium would have you speak.

---

1    *modern Raphael*  Phrase Sheridan used elsewhere to refer to his friend Sir Joshua Reynolds
(1723–92), an influential portrait painter. Raphael (1483–1520) was a major painter of
the Italian Renaissance.

2    *gouty chair*  Chair made for someone with gout.

3    *Richard, heir to Thomas*  Reference to the playwright's own family tree—Richard Brinsley
Sheridan's father was named Thomas.

4    *ex post facto*  Latin: after the fact.

5    *Raveline*  Suggestive of "ravelin," a form of fortification.

6    *Battle of Malplaquet*  High-casualty battle (1709) in the War of the Spanish Succession
(1701–14).

CHARLES. Why, then he shall have him for ten pounds, and I'm sure that's not dear for a staff officer.

SIR OLIVER. [*aside*] Heaven deliver me! His famous uncle Richard for ten pounds!—Very well, sir, I take him at that.

40 CHARLES. Careless, knock down my Uncle Richard. Here now is a maiden sister of his, my great aunt Deborah, done by Kneller[1] in his best manner and esteemed a very formidable likeness; there she is, you see, a shepherdess feeding her flock. You shall have her at five pounds ten; the sheep are worth the money.

45 SIR OLIVER. [*aside*] Ah, poor Deborah! A woman who set such a value on herself.—Five pounds ten, she is mine.

CHARLES. Knock down my Aunt Deborah. This now is a grandfather of my mother's, a learned judge, well-known on the western circuit. What do you rate him at, Moses?

50 MOSES. Four guineas.

CHARLES. Four guineas! Gad's life, you don't bid me the price of his wig.— Mr. Premium, you have more respect for the woolsack.[2] Do let us knock his lordship down at fifteen.

SIR OLIVER. By all means.

55 CARELESS. Gone.

CHARLES. And there are two brothers of his, William and Walter Blunt, Esquires, both members of Parliament and noted speakers, and what's very extraordinary, I believe this is the first time they were ever bought and sold.

60 SIR OLIVER. That is very extraordinary indeed! I'll take them at your own price for the honour of Parliament.

CARELESS. Well said, little Premium; I'll knock them down at forty.

CHARLES. Here's a jolly fellow. I don't know what relation, but he was Mayor of Norwich. Take him at eight pounds.

65 SIR OLIVER. No, no, six will do for the mayor.

CHARLES. Come, make it guineas, and I'll throw you the two aldermen into the bargain.

SIR OLIVER. They are mine.

CHARLES. Careless, knock down the mayor and aldermen. But plague on't, 70 we shall be all day retailing in this manner. Do let us deal wholesale. What say you, Premium, give me three hundred pounds, and take all that remains on each side in the lump.

---

1 *Kneller* Sir Godfrey Kneller (1646–1723), a painter famous for his portraits of English nobility and prominent intellectuals.

2 *woolsack* I.e., the office of the Lord Chancellor in the House of Lords; his seat was made of a large sack of wool.

SIR OLIVER. Well, well, anything to accommodate you; they are mine. But there is one portrait which you have always passed over.

CARELESS. What! That little ill-looking fellow over the settee?                    75

SIR OLIVER. Yes sir, I mean that, though I don't think him so ill-looking a little fellow by any means.

CHARLES. What, that! Oh, that's my Uncle Oliver; 'twas done before he went to India.

CARELESS. Your Uncle Oliver! Gad, then you'll never be friends, Charles.    80 That now to me is as stern a looking rogue as ever I saw: an unforgiving eye and a damned disinheriting countenance. An inveterate knave, depend on't. Don't you think so, little Premium?

SIR OLIVER. Upon my soul, sir, I do not. I think it as honest a looking face as any in the room, dead or alive.—But I suppose your Uncle Oliver goes    85 with the rest of the lumber.[1]

CHARLES. No, hang it, I'll not part with poor Noll; the old fellow has been very good to me, and egad, I'll keep his picture while I've a room to put it in.

SIR OLIVER. [*aside*] The rogue's my nephew after all!—But sir, I have somehow taken a fancy to that picture.                    90

CHARLES. I'm sorry for't, for you certainly will not have it. 'Oons! Haven't you got enough of 'em?

SIR OLIVER. [*aside*] I forgive him everything!—But sir, when I take a whim in my head, I don't value money. I'll give you as much for that as for all the rest.                    95

CHARLES. Don't tease me, Master Broker, I tell you I'll not part with it, and there's an end on't.

SIR OLIVER. [*aside*] How like his father the dog is. Well, well, I have done. I did perceive it before, but I never saw such a resemblance.—Well sir, here's a draft for the sum.                    100

CHARLES. Why, 'tis for eight hundred pounds.

SIR OLIVER. You will not let Oliver go?

CHARLES. Zounds! No, I tell you once more.

SIR OLIVER. Then never mind the difference; we'll balance another time. But give me your hand on the bargain. You are an honest fellow, Charles. I beg    105 pardon for being so free.—Come, Moses.

CHARLES. [*aside*] Egad, this is a whimsical old fellow!—But harkee, Premium, you'll prepare lodgings for these gentlemen?

SIR OLIVER. Yes, yes, I'll send for them in a day or two.

CHARLES. But hold, do now send a genteel conveyance for them, for I assure    110 you they were most of them used to ride in their own carriages.

---

1    *lumber*    Household clutter filling up storage space.

SIR OLIVER. I will, I will, for all but—Oliver.

CHARLES. Aye, all but the little nabob.[1]

SIR OLIVER. You're fixed!

115 CHARLES. Peremptorily.

SIR OLIVER. [*aside*] A dear extravagant rogue.—Good day. Come, Moses, let me hear now who dares call him profligate.

(*Exeunt Sir Oliver and Moses.*)

CARELESS. Why this is the oddest genius of the sort I ever saw.

CHARLES. Egad, he's the prince of brokers, I think. I wonder how the devil
120 Moses got acquainted with so honest a fellow? But hark! Here's Rowley. Do, Careless, say that I'll join the company in a moment.

CARELESS. I will. But don't now let that old blockhead persuade you to squander any of that money on old musty debts or any such nonsense, for tradesmen, Charles, are the most exorbitant fellows.

125 CHARLES. Very true, and paying them is only encouraging them.

CARELESS. Nothing else.

CHARLES. Aye, aye, never fear.

(*Exit Careless.*)

So, this was an odd fellow indeed—let me see—two thirds of this, five hundred and thirty odd pounds are mine by right. Fore Heaven, I find
130 one's ancestors are more valuable relations than I took them for! Ladies and gentlemen, your most obedient and very grateful humble servant.

(*Enter Rowley.*)

Hah! Old Rowley, egad, you are just come in time to take leave of your old acquaintance.

ROWLEY. Yes, I heard they were going, but I wonder you can have such spirits
135 under so many distresses.

CHARLES. Why, there's the point: my distresses are so many that I can't afford to part with my spirits. But I shall be rich and splenetic[2] all in good time; however, I suppose that you are surprised that I am not more sorrowful at parting with so many near relations. To be sure, 'tis very affecting, but rot
140 'em, you see they never move a muscle, so why should I?

ROWLEY. There's no making you serious a moment.

---

1    *nabob* British person who became rich working for the East India Company, a powerful British trading company that dominated the government of India during the late eighteenth and early nineteenth centuries.

2    *splenetic* Ill-humoured.

CHARLES. Yes, faith I am so now. Here, my honest Rowley, here, get me this changed directly and take a hundred pounds of it immediately to old Stanley.

ROWLEY. A hundred pounds! Consider only—                                    145

CHARLES. Gad's life, don't talk about. Poor Stanley's wants are pressing, and if you don't make haste, we shall have someone call that has a better right to the money.

ROWLEY. Ah! there's the point. I never will cease dunning you with the old proverb—                                                              150

CHARLES. "Be just before you're generous." Hey! Why, so I would if I could, but justice is an old, lame, hobbling beldam,[1] and I can't get her to keep pace with generosity for the soul of me.

ROWLEY. Yet Charles, believe me, one hour's reflection—

CHARLES. Aye, aye, it is very true, but harkee, Rowley, while I have, by    155
heaven I will give. So damn your economy and now for hazard.

(*Exeunt.*)

## ACT 4, SCENE 2. THE PARLOUR.

(*Enter Sir Oliver and Moses.*)

MOSES. Well sir, I think, as Sir Peter said, you have seen Mr. Charles in high glory; 'tis great pity he's so extravagant.

SIR OLIVER. True, but he wouldn't sell my picture.

MOSES. And loves wine and women so much.

SIR OLIVER. But he wouldn't sell my picture.                                5

MOSES. And game so deep.

SIR OLIVER. But he wouldn't sell my picture.—Oh, here's Rowley.

(*Enter Rowley.*)

ROWLEY. Oh Sir Oliver, I find you have made a purchase.

SIR OLIVER. Yes, yes, our young rake has parted with his ancestors like old tapestry.                                                              10

ROWLEY. And here has he commissioned me to redeliver you a part of the purchase money, I mean, though, in your necessitous character of Old Stanley.

MOSES. Ah! There is the pity of all, he's so damned charitable.

ROWLEY. And I left a hosier and two tailors in the hall, who I'm sure won't be   15
paid, and this hundred would satisfy them.

---

1   *beldam* Elderly woman.

SIR OLIVER. Well, well, I'll pay his debts and his benevolence too. But now I'm no more a broker, and you shall introduce me to the brother as Old Stanley.

20   ROWLEY. Not yet a while. Sir Peter, I know, means to call there about this time.

(*Enter Trip.*)

TRIP. Oh gentlemen, I beg pardon for not showing you out. This way, gentlemen.—Moses, a word—

(*Exeunt Trip and Moses.*)

SIR OLIVER. There's a fellow for you. Would you believe it, that puppy inter-
25   cepted the Jew on our coming and wanted to raise money before he got to his master.

ROWLEY. Indeed!

SIR OLIVER. Yes, they are now planning an annuity business. Ah Master Rowley, in my days servants were content with the follies of their masters
30   when they were worn a little threadbare, but now they have their vices like their birthday clothes,[1] with the gloss on.

(*Exeunt.*)

## ACT 4, SCENE 3. A LIBRARY.

(*Enter Joseph Surface and servant.*)

JOSEPH SURFACE. No letter from Lady Teazle?

SERVANT. No sir.

JOSEPH SURFACE. I am surprised she has not sent if she is prevented from coming. Sir Peter certainly does not suspect me, yet I wish I may not lose
5   the heiress through the scrape I have drawn myself in with the wife. However, Charles's imprudence and bad character are great points in my favour.

[*Knock within.*]

SERVANT. Sir, I believe that must be Lady Teazle.

JOSEPH SURFACE. Hold! See whether it is or not before you go to the door; I have a particular message for you if it should be my brother.

10   SERVANT. 'Tis her ladyship, sir, she always leaves her chair at the milliner's in the next street.

---

1   *birthday clothes* New, ornate clothing worn by those attending the king's birthday celebrations.

JOSEPH SURFACE.  Stay, stay, draw that screen before the window; that will do. My opposite neighbour is a maiden lady of a curious temper.

(*Servant draws the screen, and exit.*)

I have a difficult hand to play in this affair. Lady Teazle has lately suspected my views on Maria, but she must by no means be let into that secret, at    15 least till I have her more in my power.

(*Enter Lady Teazle.*)

LADY TEAZLE.  What, sentiment in soliloquy! Have you been very impatient now? O Lud, don't pretend to look grave. I vow I couldn't come before.

JOSEPH SURFACE.  Oh madam! Punctuality is a species of constancy—very unfashionable quality in a lady.    20

LADY TEAZLE.  Upon my word, you ought to pity me. Do you know that Sir Peter is grown so ill-natured of late and so jealous of Charles too? That's the best of the story, isn't it?

JOSEPH SURFACE.  (*aside*) I am glad my scandalous friends keep that up.

LADY TEAZLE.  I'm sure I wish he would let Maria marry him, and then per-    25 haps he would be convinced. Don't you, Mr. Surface?

JOSEPH SURFACE.  (*aside*) Indeed I do not.—Oh, certainly I do, for then my dear Lady Teazle would also be convinced how wrong her suspicions were of my having any design on the silly girl.

LADY TEAZLE.  Well, well, I'm inclined to believe you, but isn't it provoking    30 to have the most ill-natured things said to one. There is my friend Lady Sneerwell has circulated I don't how many scandalous tales of me—and all without any foundation too. That's what vexes me.

JOSEPH SURFACE.  Aye madam, that is the provoking circumstance—without foundation; yes, yes, there's the mortification indeed. For when a scandal-    35 ous story is believed against one, there certainly is no comfort like the consciousness of having deserved it.

LADY TEAZLE.  No, to be sure. Then I'd forgive their malice. But to attack *me*, who am really so innocent and who never says an ill-natured thing of any-body, that is, of my friends—and then Sir Peter too to have him so peevish    40 and so suspicious—when I know the integrity of my own heart—indeed 'tis monstrous.

JOSEPH SURFACE.  But my dear Lady Teazle, 'tis your own fault if you suffer it. When a husband entertains a groundless suspicion of his wife and with-draws his confidence from her, the original compact is broke, and she owes    45 it to the honour of her sex to endeavour to outwit him.

LADY TEAZLE.  Indeed! So that if he suspects me without cause, it follows that the best way of curing his jealousy is to give him reason for't?

JOSEPH SURFACE. Undoubtedly, for your husband should never be deceived
50    in you, and in that case it becomes *you* to become frail in compliment to
his discernment.

LADY TEAZLE. To be sure what you say is very reasonable, and when the
consciousness of my own innocence—

JOSEPH SURFACE. Ah, my dear madam, there is the great mistake; 'tis this
55    very conscious innocence that is of the greatest prejudice to you. What
is it makes you negligent of forms and careless of the world's opinion?
Why, the consciousness of your innocence. What makes you thoughtless
in your conduct and apt to run into a thousand little imprudences? Why,
the consciousness of your innocence. What makes you impatient of Sir
60    Peter's temper, and outrageous at his suspicions? Why, the consciousness
of your own innocence.

LADY TEAZLE. 'Tis very true.

JOSEPH SURFACE. Now my dear Lady Teazle, if you would but once make
a trifling faux-pas, you can't conceive how cautious you would grow and
65    how ready to humour and agree with your husband.

LADY TEAZLE. Do you think so?

JOSEPH SURFACE. Oh, I'm sure on't. And then you'd find all scandal would
cease at once, for in short, your character at present is like a person in a
plethora:[1] absolutely dying of too much health.

70  LADY TEAZLE. Why, if my understanding were once convinced—

JOSEPH SURFACE. Oh certainly, madam. Your understanding *should* be convinced—yes, yes. Heaven forbid I should persuade you to do anything you
thought wrong—no, no. I have too much honour to desire it.

LADY TEAZLE. Don't you think we may as well leave honour out of the argu-
75    ment.

JOSEPH SURFACE. Ah! The ill effects of your country education I see still remain with you.

LADY TEAZLE. I doubt they do, indeed, and I will fairly own to you that, if
I could be persuaded to do wrong, it would be Sir Peter's ill usage sooner
80    than your honourable logic after all.

JOSEPH SURFACE. Then by this hand which he is unworthy of—

(*Enter Servant.*)

'Sdeath,[2] you blockhead, what do you want?

SERVANT. I beg pardon, sir, but I thought you wouldn't choose Sir Peter's
coming upstairs without announcing him.

---

1    *plethora* Sickness thought to be caused by an overabundance of blood.

2    *'Sdeath* Swear word meaning "God's death."

JOSEPH SURFACE.  Sir Peter, 'oons, and the devil!   85
LADY TEAZLE.  Sir Peter! Oh Lud, I'm ruined! I'm ruined!
SERVANT.  Sir, 'twasn't I let him in.
LADY TEAZLE.  Oh! I'm undone. What will become of me now, Mr. Logic? Oh mercy, he's on the stairs! I'll get behind here, and if ever I'm so imprudent again! (*Goes behind the screen.*)   90
JOSEPH SURFACE.  Give me a book.

(*Enter Sir Peter.*)

SIR PETER.  Aye, ever improving himself.—Mr. Surface! Mr. Surface!
JOSEPH SURFACE.  Oh my dear Sir Peter, I beg your pardon, (*gaping and throwing away the book*) I have been dozing over a stupid book. Well, I am much obliged to you for this call. You have not been here, I believe,   95
since I fitted up this room. Books, you know, are the only things I am a coxcomb[1] in.
SIR PETER.  'Tis very neat indeed. Well, well, that's proper, and you make even your screen a source of knowledge: hung, I perceive, with maps.
JOSEPH SURFACE.  Oh yes, I find great use in that screen.   100
SIR PETER.  I dare say you must, certainly, when you want to find anything in a hurry.
JOSEPH SURFACE.  (*aside*) Aye, or to hide anything in a hurry either.
SIR PETER.  Well, I have a little private business.
JOSEPH SURFACE.  You needn't stay.   105
SERVANT.  No sir. (*Exit.*)
JOSEPH SURFACE.  Here's a chair, Sir Peter. I beg—
SIR PETER.  Well now we are alone, there is a subject, my dear friend, on which I wish to unburden my mind to you, a point of greatest moment to my peace—in short, my good friend, Lady Teazle's conduct of late has   110
made me very unhappy.
JOSEPH SURFACE.  Indeed, I am sorry to hear it.
SIR PETER.  Yes, 'tis but too plain she has not the least regard for me, but what's worse, I have pretty good authority to suppose that she must have formed an attachment to another.   115
JOSEPH SURFACE.  Indeed! You astonish me!
SIR PETER.  Yes, and between ourselves, I think I have discovered the person.
JOSEPH SURFACE.  How! You alarm me exceedingly!
SIR PETER.  Ah my dear friend, I knew you would sympathize with me!
JOSEPH SURFACE.  Yes, believe me, Sir Peter, such a discovery would distress me   120
just as much as it would you.

---

1   *coxcomb* Dandy; excessively showy man.

SIR PETER. I am convinced of it. Ah, it is a happiness to have a friend whom one can trust even with one's family secrets. But have you no guess who I mean?

125 JOSEPH SURFACE. I haven't the most distant idea. It can't be Sir Benjamin Backbite?

SIR PETER. Oh, no. What say you to Charles?

JOSEPH SURFACE. My brother! Impossible!

SIR PETER. It's very true.

130 JOSEPH SURFACE. Oh no, Sir Peter, you must not credit the scandalous insinuation you hear. No, no, Charles, to be sure, has been charged many things of this kind, but I can never think he could meditate[1] so gross an injury.

SIR PETER. Ah, my dear friend! The goodness of your own heart misleads you; you judge of others by yourself.

135 JOSEPH SURFACE. Certainly, Sir Peter, the heart that is conscious of its own integrity is ever slow to credit another's baseness.

SIR PETER. True, but your brother has no sentiment; you never hear him talk so.

JOSEPH SURFACE. Yet I can't but think that Lady Teazle herself has too much

140 principle.

SIR PETER. Aye, but what's her principle against the flattery of a handsome, lively, young fellow.

JOSEPH SURFACE. That's very true.

SIR PETER. And then you know the difference of our ages makes it highly

145 improbable that she should have any violent affection for me, and if she were to be frail, and I were to make it public, why the Town would only laugh at me, the foolish old bachelor who had married a girl.

JOSEPH SURFACE. That's true. To be sure, they would laugh.

SIR PETER. Laugh, aye, and make ballads and paragraphs and the devil knows

150 what of me.

JOSEPH SURFACE. No, you must never make it public.

SIR PETER. But then again, that the nephew of my old friend, Sir Oliver, should be the person to do such a wrong hurts one more nearly.

JOSEPH SURFACE. Aye, there's the point: When ingratitude barbs the dart of

155 injury, the wound has double danger in it.

SIR PETER. Aye, I that was in a manner left his guardian, in whose house he has been so often entertained, who never in my life denied him my advice.

JOSEPH SURFACE. Oh 'tis not to be credited. There may be a man capable of such baseness to be sure, but for my part, till you can give me positive

160 proofs, I cannot but doubt it; however, if this should be proved on him, he

---

1   *meditate* Consider.

is no longer a brother of mine. I disclaim kindred with him. For the man who can break through the laws of hospitality and attempt the wife of his friend deserves to be branded as the pest of society.

SIR PETER. What a difference there is between you! What noble sentiments!

JOSEPH SURFACE. Yet I cannot suspect Lady Teazle's honour.   165

SIR PETER. I am sure I wish to think well of her and to remove all ground of quarrel between us. She has lately reproached me more than once with having made no settlement on her, and in our last quarrel she almost hinted that she would not break her heart if I was dead. Now as we seem to differ in our ideas of expense, I have resolved she shall be her own mistress   170 in that respect for the future, and if I were to die, she shall find that I have not been inattentive to her interests while living. Here, my friend, are the drafts of two deeds which I wish to have your opinion on: by one, she will enjoy eight hundred a year, independent, while I live, and by the other, the bulk of my fortune after my death.   175

JOSEPH SURFACE. This conduct, Sir Peter, is indeed truly generous! (*aside*) I wish it may not corrupt my pupil.

SIR PETER. Yes, I am determined she shall have no cause to complain, though I would not have her acquainted with the latter instance of my affection yet awhile.   180

JOSEPH SURFACE. [*aside*] Nor I, if I could help it.

SIR PETER. And now, my dear friend, if you please, we will talk over the situation of your hopes with Maria.

JOSEPH SURFACE. [*softly*] No, no, Sir Peter, another time if you please.

SIR PETER. I am sensibly chagrined at the little progress you seem to make in   185 her affections—

JOSEPH SURFACE. (*softly*) I beg you will not mention it, sir. What are my disappointments when your happiness is in debate. [*aside*] 'Sdeath, I shall be ruined every way.

SIR PETER. And though you are so averse to my acquainting Lady Teazle with   190 your passion, I am sure she is not your enemy in the affair.

JOSEPH SURFACE. Pray Sir Peter, oblige me—I am really too much affected by the subject we have been talking to bestow a thought on my own concerns. The man who is entrusted with his friend's distresses—can never—Well, sir—   195

(*Enter Servant.*)

SERVANT. Your brother, sir, is speaking to a gentleman in the street and says he knows you are within.

JOSEPH SURFACE. 'Sdeath! Blockhead, I am not within; I am out for the day.

SIR PETER. Stay, hold, a thought has struck me: you shall be at home.

200 JOSEPH SURFACE.  Well, well, let him up. (*Exit Servant.*)

(*aside*) He'll interrupt Sir Peter, however.

SIR PETER.  Now my good friend, oblige me, I entreat you: before Charles comes, let me conceal myself some-where; then do you tax him on the point we have been talking on, and his answers may satisfy me at once.

205 JOSEPH SURFACE.  Oh fie, Sir Peter! Would you have me join in so mean a trick—to trepan[1] my brother too—

SIR PETER.  Nay, you tell me you are sure he's innocent; if so, you do him the greatest service in giving him an opportunity to clear himself, and you will set my heart at rest. Come, you shall not refuse me. Here behind

210 this screen will be—Hey! What the devil! There seems to be one listener already. I'll swear I saw a petticoat.

JOSEPH SURFACE.  Ha, ha, ha! Well, this is ridiculous enough. I'll tell you, Sir Peter, though I hold a man of intrigue to be a most despicable character, yet you know it does not follow that one is to be an absolute Joseph[2] either.

215 Harkee, 'tis a little French milliner, a silly[3] rogue that plagues me, and having some character, on your coming in she ran behind the screen.

SIR PETER.  Ah, you rogue. But egad, she has overheard all I have been saying of my wife.

JOSEPH SURFACE.  Oh, 'twill never go any farther, you may depend on't.

220 SIR PETER.  No! Then i'faith, let her hear it out. Here's a closet will do as well.

JOSEPH SURFACE.  Well, go in then.

SIR PETER.  Sly rogue, sly rogue! (*Goes into the closet.*)

JOSEPH SURFACE.  A narrow escape indeed, and a curious situation I am in, to part man and wife in this manner.

225 LADY TEAZLE.  (*peeping out*) Couldn't I steal off?

JOSEPH SURFACE.  Keep close, my angel.

SIR PETER.  (*peeping out*) Joseph, tax him home.

JOSEPH SURFACE.  Back, my dear friend.

LADY TEAZLE.  Couldn't you lock Sir Peter in?

230 JOSEPH SURFACE.  Lie still, my life.

SIR PETER.  You are sure the little milliner won't blab?

JOSEPH SURFACE.  In, in, my dear Sir Peter. Foregad, I wish I had a key to the door.

(*Enter Charles.*)

---

1    *trepan* I.e., trick into confessing his behaviour.

2    *Joseph* Biblical figure who is propositioned by his master's wife and refuses her.

3    *silly* Simple, insignificant.

CHARLES. Holla, brother! What has been the matter? Your fellow wouldn't let me up at first. What, have you had a Jew or a wench with you?   235

JOSEPH SURFACE. Neither brother, I assure you.

CHARLES. And what has made Sir Peter steal off? I thought he had been with you.

JOSEPH SURFACE. He was, brother, but hearing you were coming, he did not choose to stay.   240

CHARLES. What! Was the old gentleman afraid I wanted to borrow money of him?

JOSEPH SURFACE. No, sir. But I am sorry to find, Charles, that you have lately given that worthy man grounds for great uneasiness.

CHARLES. Yes, yes, they tell me I do that to a great many worthy men, but   245 how so pray?

JOSEPH SURFACE. To be plain with you, brother, he thinks you are endeavouring to gain Lady Teazle's affections from him.

CHARLES. Who I? Oh Lud! Not I, upon my word. Ha, ha, ha! So the old fellow has found out that he has got a young wife, has he?   250

JOSEPH SURFACE. This is no subject to jest upon, brother. He who can laugh—

CHARLES. True, true, as you were going to say—then seriously, I never had the least idea of what you charge me with, upon my honour.

JOSEPH SURFACE. Well, well, it will give Sir Peter great satisfaction to hear it.

CHARLES. To be sure, I once thought the lady seemed to have taken a fancy   255 to me, but upon my soul, I never gave the least encouragement; besides, you know my attachment to Maria.

JOSEPH SURFACE. But sure brother, if Lady Teazle had betrayed the fondest partiality for you—

CHARLES. Why, look ye Joseph, I hope I shall never deliberately do a dishon-   260 ourable action—but if a pretty woman were purposely to throw herself in my way—and that pretty woman married to a man old enough to be her father—

JOSEPH SURFACE. Well!

CHARLES. Why, I believe I should be obliged to borrow a little of your moral-   265 ity, that's all. But brother, do you know now that you surprise me exceedingly by naming me with Lady Teazle, for 'faith, I always understood *you* were her favourite.

JOSEPH SURFACE. For shame, Charles, this retort is foolish.

CHARLES. Nay, I swear I have seen you exchange such significant glances.   270

JOSEPH SURFACE. Nay, nay sir, this is no jest.

CHARLES. Egad, I'm serious, don't you remember one day when I called here—

JOSEPH SURFACE. Nay prithee Charles—

275  CHARLES.  And found you together—

JOSEPH SURFACE.  Zounds sir! I insist—

CHARLES.  And another time when your servant—

JOSEPH SURFACE.  Brother, brother, a word with you. (*aside*) Gad I must stop him.

280  CHARLES.  Informed me, I say, that—

JOSEPH SURFACE.  Hush! I beg your pardon, but Sir Peter has overheard all we have been saying; I knew you would clear yourself, or I should not have consented.

CHARLES.  How! Sir Peter! Where is he?

285  JOSEPH SURFACE.  Softly—there. (*Points to the closet.*)

CHARLES.  Oh! 'Fore Heaven, I'll have him out.—Sir Peter, come forth.

JOSEPH SURFACE.  No, no.

CHARLES.  I say, Sir Peter, come into court. (*Pulls in Sir Peter.*) What, my old guardian! What! Turned inquisitor, and taking evidence incog?[1]

290  SIR PETER.  Give me your hand, Charles, I believe I have suspected you wrongfully. But you mustn't be angry with Joseph—'twas my plan.

CHARLES.  Indeed!

SIR PETER.  But I acquit you. I promise you, I don't think near so ill of you as I did. What I have heard has given me great satisfaction.

295  CHARLES.  Egad then! 'twas lucky you didn't hear any more.—Wasn't it, Joseph?

SIR PETER.  Ah! You would have retorted on him.

CHARLES.  Aye, aye, that was a joke.

SIR PETER.  Yes, yes, I know his honour too well.

300  CHARLES.  But you might as well have suspected *him* as me in this matter for all that.—Mightn't he, Joseph?

SIR PETER.  Well, well, I believe you.

JOSEPH SURFACE.  (*aside*) I wish they were both well out of the room.

SIR PETER.  And in future perhaps we may not be such strangers.

(*Enter servant who speaks to Joseph Surface.*)

305  SERVANT.  Sir, Lady Sneerwell is below and says she will come up.

JOSEPH SURFACE.  (*to the servant*) Lady Sneerwell—Gad's life! She mustn't come here.—Gentlemen, I beg pardon—I must wait on you downstairs— here is a person come on particular business.

CHARLES.  Well, well, you can see him in another room; Sir Peter and I have
310      not met for a long time, and I have something to say to him.

---

1    *incog* Incognito.

JOSEPH SURFACE. [*aside*] They must not be left together. I'll send Lady Sneer-
    well away directly.—Sir Peter, not a word of the French milliner.

SIR PETER. Oh not for the world!

    (*Exit Joseph Surface [and servant].*)

Ah Charles, if you associated more with your brother, one might indeed
    hope for your reformation. He is a man of sentiment. Well, there's nothing  315
    so noble as a man of sentiment.

CHARLES. Pshaw, he is too moral by half and so apprehensive of his good
    name, as he calls it, that I suppose he would as soon let a priest into his
    house as a wench.

SIR PETER. No, no, come, come, you wrong him. No, no, Joseph is no rake,  320
    but he is no such saint in that respect either. (*aside*) I have a great mind to
    tell him; we should have such a laugh.

CHARLES. Oh, hang him! He's a very anchorite—a young hermit!

SIR PETER. Hark ye, you must not abuse him; he may chance to hear of it
    again, I promise.  325

CHARLES. Why, you won't tell him?

SIR PETER. No—but—this way—[*aside*] Egad, I'll tell him.—Hark ye, have
    you a mind to have a good laugh against Joseph?

CHARLES. I should like it of all things.

SIR PETER. Then, faith, we will. [*aside*] I'll be quit with him for discovering[1]  330
    me. (*whispers*) He had a girl with him when I called.

CHARLES. What, Joseph! You jest.

SIR PETER. Hush! A little French milliner—and the best of the jest is—she's
    in the room now.

CHARLES. The devil she is! (*looking at the closet*)  335

SIR PETER. Hush I tell you! (*Points to the screen.*)

CHARLES. Behind the screen? 'Odd's life! Let us unveil her.

SIR PETER. No, no, he's coming, you shan't indeed.

CHARLES. Oh egad, we'll have a peep at the little milliner!

SIR PETER. No, not for the world—Joseph will never forgive me.  350

CHARLES. I'll stand by you.

SIR PETER. 'Odd's life! Here he is.

    (*Joseph enters as Charles throws down the screen.*)

CHARLES. Lady Teazle, by all that's wonderful!

SIR PETER. Lady Teazle, by all that's damnable!

---

1   *discovering* Revealing.

355  CHARLES.  Sir Peter, this is one of the smartest French milliners I ever saw.
     Egad, you seem all to have been diverting yourselves at hide and seek. And
     I don't see who is out of the secret.—Shall I beg your ladyship to inform
     me? Not a word!—Brother, will you please to explain this matter? What, is
     morality dumb too?—Sir Peter, though I found you in the dark, perhaps
360  you are not so now. All mute! Well, though I can make nothing of this af-
     fair, I suppose you perfectly understand one another, so I shall leave you to
     yourselves. (*going*) Brother, I am sorry to find you have given that worthy
     man grounds for so much uneasiness.—Sir Peter, there's nothing in the
     world so noble as a man of sentiment! (*Exit.*)
365  JOSEPH SURFACE.  Sir Peter, notwithstanding I confess that appearances are
     against me, if you will afford me your patience, I make no doubt but I shall
     explain everything to your satisfaction.
     SIR PETER.  If you please, sir.
     JOSEPH SURFACE.  The fact is, sir—that Lady Teazle, knowing my pretensions
370  to your ward, Maria—I say, sir, Lady Teazle being apprehensive of the

*James Roberts, Act 4, Scene 3 of* The School for Scandal, *1777. This painting shows the
actors who appeared in the first production of* The School for Scandal, *staged at Drury
Lane Theatre in 1777. The subject is a well-known portion of the play that is often referred to as the "screen scene"; in front of Lady Teazle is the fallen screen, which Charles
has thrown down to reveal her.*

jealousy of your temper and knowing my friendship to the family—she, sir, I say, called here, in order that I might explain those pretensions—but on your coming, being apprehensive as I said of your jealousy—she withdrew—and this, you may depend on't, is the whole truth of the matter.

SIR PETER. A very clear account upon my word, and I dare swear the lady will 375 vouch for every article of it.

LADY TEAZLE. For not one word of it, Sir Peter.

SIR PETER. How! Don't you think it worthwhile to agree in the lie?

LADY TEAZLE. There is not one syllable of truth in what that gentleman has told you. 380

SIR PETER. I believe you, upon my soul, madam.

JOSEPH SURFACE. 'Sdeath, madam, will you betray me?

LADY TEAZLE. Good Mr. Hypocrite, by your leave, I will speak for myself.

SIR PETER. Aye, let her alone, sir; you'll find she'll make a better story than you without prompting. 385

LADY TEAZLE. Hear me, Sir Peter, I came hither on no matter relating to your ward and even ignorant of this gentleman's pretensions to her. But I came here seduced by his insidious arguments, at least to listen to his pretended passion, if not to sacrifice your honour to his baseness.

SIR PETER. Now I believe the truth is coming indeed. 390

JOSEPH SURFACE. The woman's mad.

LADY TEAZLE. No sir, she has recovered her senses, and your own arts have furnished her with the means.—Sir Peter, I do not expect you to credit me, but the tenderness you expressed for me, when I'm sure you could not think I was a witness to it, has penetrated so to my heart that, had I 395 left the place without the shame of the discovery, my future life should have spoken the sincerity of my gratitude. As for that smoothed-tongue hypocrite, who would have seduced the wife of his too credulous friend while he affected honourable addresses to his ward, I behold him now in a light so truly despicable that I never again shall respect myself for having 400 listened to him. (*Exit.*)

JOSEPH SURFACE. Notwithstanding all this, Sir Peter, Heaven knows—

SIR PETER. That you are a villain, and so I leave you to your conscience.

JOSEPH SURFACE. You are too rash, Sir Peter—you shall hear me—the man who shuts out conviction by refusing to— 405

SIR PETER. Oh, damn your sentiment!

(*Exeunt.*)

## ACT 5, SCENE 1. A LIBRARY.

*(Enter Joseph Surface and servant.)*

JOSEPH SURFACE. Mr. Stanley! and why should you think I would see him? You must know he comes to ask something.

SERVANT. Sir, I should not have let him in, but that Mr. Rowley came to the door with him.

5 JOSEPH SURFACE. Pshaw! Blockhead! To suppose that I should now be in a temper to receive visits from poor relations! Well, why don't you show the fellow up?

SERVANT. I will, sir. Why sir, it wasn't my fault that Sir Peter discovered my lady. *(Exit.)*

10 JOSEPH SURFACE. Go, fool. Sure, Fortune never played a man of my policy such a trick before. My character with Sir Peter, my hopes with Maria, destroyed in a moment! I am in a rare humour to listen to other people's distresses! I shan't be able to bestow even a benevolent sentiment on Stanley.—Oh, here he comes, and Rowley with him. I must try to recover

15 myself and put a little charity into my face, however. *(Exit.)*

*(Enter Sir Oliver and Rowley.)*

SIR OLIVER. What, does he avoid us? That was he, was it not?

ROWLEY. It was, sir, but I doubt you are come a little too abruptly. His nerves are so weak that the sight of a poor relation may be too much for him. I should have gone first to break you to him.

20 SIR OLIVER. A plague of his nerves! Yet this is he whom Sir Peter extols as a man of the most benevolent way of thinking.

ROWLEY. As to his way of thinking, I cannot pretend to decide, for to do him justice, he appears to have as much speculative benevolence as any private gentleman in the kingdom, though he is seldom so sensual as to indulge

25 himself in the exercise of it.

SIR OLIVER. Yet has a string of charitable sentiments, I suppose, at his fingers' ends.

ROWLEY. Or rather at his tongue's end, Sir Oliver, for I believe there is no sentiment he has more faith in than that "Charity begins at home."

30 SIR OLIVER. And his, I presume, is of that domestic sort, it never stirs abroad at all.

ROWLEY. I doubt you'll find it so. But he's coming. I must not seem to interrupt you, and you know, immediately as you leave him, I come in to announce your arrival in your real character.

35 SIR OLIVER. True, and afterwards you'll meet me at Sir Peter's.

ROWLEY. Without losing a moment. *(Exit.)*

SIR OLIVER. So! I don't like the complaisance of his features.

(*Enter Joseph Surface.*)

JOSEPH SURFACE. Sir, I beg you ten thousand pardons for keeping you a moment waiting. Mr. Stanley, I presume?

SIR OLIVER. At your service, sir.                                                40

JOSEPH SURFACE. Sir, I beg you will do me the honour to sit down. I entreat you, sir.

SIR OLIVER. Dear sir, there's no occasion. (*aside*) Too civil by half.

JOSEPH SURFACE. I have not the pleasure of knowing you, Mr. Stanley, but I am extremely happy to see you look so well. You were nearly related to my   45 mother, Mr. Stanley, I think?

SIR OLIVER. I was, sir, so nearly that my present poverty, I fear, may do discredit to her wealthy children, else I should not have presumed to trouble you.

JOSEPH SURFACE. Dear sir, there needs no apology. He that is in distress,   50 though a stranger, has a right to claim kindred with the wealthy. I'm sure I wish I was of that class and had it in my power to offer you even a small relief.

SIR OLIVER. If your uncle Sir Oliver was here, I should have a friend.

JOSEPH SURFACE. I wish he was, sir, with all my heart. You should not want   55 an advocate with him, believe me Sir.

SIR OLIVER. I should not need one; my distresses would recommend me. But I imagined his bounty had enabled you to become the agent of his charity.

JOSEPH SURFACE. My dear sir, you are strangely misinformed. Sir Oliver is a worthy man, a very worthy sort of a man, but avarice, Mr. Stanley, is the   60 vice of the age. I will tell you, my good sir, in confidence, what he has done for me has been a mere nothing, though people, I know, have thought otherwise, and for my part, I never chose to contradict the report.

SIR OLIVER. What! Has he never transmitted you bullion, rupees, pagodas?[1]

JOSEPH SURFACE. Oh dear sir! Nothing of the kind. No, no, a few presents   65 now and then, china, shawls, congou tea, avadavats, and India crackers,[2] little more, believe me.

SIR OLIVER. [*aside*] Here's gratitude for twelve thousand pounds! Avadavats and India crackers!

JOSEPH SURFACE. Then, my dear sir, you have heard, I doubt not, of the ex-   70 travagance of my brother; there are very few would credit what I have done for that unfortunate young man.

---

1    *bullion* Unminted gold or silver; *rupees, pagodas* Indian money.
2    *congou tea* Chinese black tea; *avadavats* South Asian birds often kept as pets; *India crackers* I.e., firecrackers.

Sir Oliver. (*aside*) Not I, for one.

Joseph Surface. The sums I have lent him—Indeed I have been exceedingly
75      to blame. It was an amiable weakness; however, I don't pretend to defend
it, and now I feel it doubly culpable since it has deprived me of the power
of serving you, Mr. Stanley, as my heart directs.

Sir Oliver. [*aside*] Dissembler!—Then, sir, you cannot assist me.

Joseph Surface. At present it grieves me to say I cannot, but whenever I
80      have the ability, you may depend upon hearing from me.

Sir Oliver. I am extremely sorry—

Joseph Surface. Not more than I am, believe me; to pity without the power
to relieve is still more painful than to ask and be denied.

Sir Oliver. Kind sir, your most obedient humble servant.

85  Joseph Surface. You leave me deeply affected, Mr. Stanley—William, be
ready to open the door.

Sir Oliver. Oh dear sir, no ceremony!

Joseph Surface. Your very obedient.

Sir Oliver. Sir, your most obsequious.

90  Joseph Surface. You may depend upon hearing from me, whenever I can
be of service.

Sir Oliver. Sweet sir, you are too good.

Joseph Surface. In the meantime, I wish you health and spirits.

Sir Oliver. Your ever grateful and perpetual humble servant.

95  Joseph Surface. Sir, yours as sincerely.

Sir Oliver. Now I'm satisfied. (*Exit.*)

Joseph Surface. This is one of the bad effects of a good character. It invites
application from the unfortunate, and there needs no small degree of address to gain the reputation of benevolence without incurring the expense.
100     The silver ore of pure charity is an expensive article in the catalogue of a
man's good qualities, whereas the sentimental French plate I use instead of
it makes just as good a show and pays no tax.

(*Enter Rowley.*)

Rowley. Mr. Surface, your servant. I was apprehensive of interrupting you,
though my business demands immediate action, as this note will inform
105     you.

Joseph Surface. Always happy to see Mr. Rowley. (*aside*) A rascal!—How!
Sir Oliver Surface, my uncle, arrived!

Rowley. He is indeed—we have just parted—quite well after a speedy voyage, and impatient to embrace his worthy nephew.

110  Joseph Surface. I am astonished!—William, stop Mr. Stanley if he's not
gone.

ROWLEY.  Oh he's out of reach, I believe.

JOSEPH SURFACE.  Why didn't you let me know this when you came in together?

ROWLEY.  I thought you had particular business, but I must be gone to inform    115
your brother and appoint him here to meet his uncle. He will be with you
in a quarter of an hour.

JOSEPH SURFACE.  So he says. Well, I'm strangely overjoyed at his coming.
(*aside*) Never was anything, to be sure, so damned unlucky.

ROWLEY.  You will be delighted to see how well he looks.    120

JOSEPH SURFACE.  Oh, I am rejoiced to hear it. (*aside*) Just at this time.

ROWLEY.  I will tell him how impatient you expect him. (*Exit.*)

JOSEPH SURFACE.  Do, do, pray give my best duty and affection.—Indeed, I
cannot express the sensations I feel at the thought of seeing him. Certainly
his coming just at this time is the cruellest piece of ill fortune.    125

(*Exit.*)

## ACT 5, SCENE 2. SIR PETER TEAZLE'S HOUSE.

(*Enter Mrs. Candour and maid.*)

MAID.  Indeed, ma'am, my lady will see nobody at present.

MRS. CANDOUR.  Did you tell her it was her friend, Mrs. Candour?

MAID.  Yes ma'am, but she begs you will excuse her.

MRS. CANDOUR.  Do go again. I shall be glad to see her only for a moment,
for I'm sure she must be in great distress. (*Exit maid.*) Dear heart, how pro-    5
voking! I'm not mistress of half the circumstances. We shall have the whole
affair in the newspapers with the names of the parties at full length before
I have dropped the story at a dozen houses. (*Enter Sir Benjamin Backbite.*)
Oh dear, Sir Benjamin! You have heard I suppose—

SIR BENJAMIN.  Of Lady Teazle and Mr. Surface.    10

MRS. CANDOUR.  And Sir Peter's discovery.

SIR BENJAMIN.  Oh, the strangest piece of business, to be sure!

MRS. CANDOUR.  Well, I never was so surprised in my life. I am sorry for all
parties indeed!

SIR BENJAMIN.  Now, I don't pity Sir Peter at all; he was so extravagantly    15
partial to Mr. Surface.

MRS. CANDOUR.  Mr. Surface! Why, 'twas with Charles Lady Teazle was detected.

SIR BENJAMIN.  No such thing. Mr. Surface is the gallant.

MRS. CANDOUR.  No, no, Charles is the man. 'Twas Mr. Surface brought Sir    20
Peter on purpose to discover them.

SIR BENJAMIN.  I tell you I have it from one—

MRS. CANDOUR.  And I have it from one—

SIR BENJAMIN.  Who had it from one—who had it—

25  MRS. CANDOUR.  From one immediately—but here's Lady Sneerwell; perhaps she knows the whole affair.

(*Enter Lady Sneerwell.*)

LADY SNEERWELL.  So my dear Mrs. Candour, here's a sad affair of our friend Teazle.

MRS. CANDOUR.  Aye, my dear friend, who could have thought it.

30  LADY SNEERWELL.  Well, there's no trusting to appearances, though indeed she was always too lively for me.

MRS. CANDOUR.  To be sure, her manners were a little too free, but she was very young.

LADY SNEERWELL.  And had indeed some good qualities.

35  MRS. CANDOUR.  She had indeed—but have you heard the particulars?

LADY SNEERWELL.  No, but everybody says that Mr. Surface—

SIR BENJAMIN.  Aye, there I told you, Mr. Surface was the man.

MRS. CANDOUR.  No, no indeed, the assignation was with Charles.

LADY SNEERWELL.  With Charles! You alarm me, Mrs. Candour.

40  MRS. CANDOUR.  Yes, yes, he was the lover; Mr. Surface, to do him justice, was only the informer.

SIR BENJAMIN.  Well, I'll not dispute with you, Mrs. Candour. Be it which it may, I hope that Sir Peter's wound will not—

MRS. CANDOUR.  Sir Peter's wound! Oh mercy, I did not hear a word of their
45    fighting.

LADY SNEERWELL.  Nor I a syllable.

SIR BENJAMIN.  No! What, no mention of the duel!

MRS. CANDOUR.  Not a word.

SIR BENJAMIN.  Oh Lord! Yes, yes, they fought before they left the room.

50  LADY SNEERWELL.  Pray, let us hear.

MRS. CANDOUR.  Aye, do oblige us with the duel.

SIR BENJAMIN.  "Sir," says Sir Peter, immediately after the discovery, "you are a most ungrateful fellow"—

MRS. CANDOUR.  Aye, to Charles.

55  SIR BENJAMIN.  No, no, to Mr. Surface—"a most ungrateful fellow, and old as I am, sir," says he, "I insist on immediate satisfaction."

MRS. CANDOUR.  Aye, that must have been to Charles, for 'tis very unlikely Mr. Surface should go fight in his own house.

SIR BENJAMIN.  Gad's life, madam, not at all—"giving me immediate satis-
60    faction"—on this, madam, Lady Teazle, seeing Sir Peter in such danger,

ran out of the room in strong hysterics and Charles after her, calling for hartshorn[1] and water; then madam, they began to fight with swords—

(*Enter Crabtree.*)

CRABTREE. With pistols, Nephew, I have it from undoubted authority.

MRS. CANDOUR. Oh Mr. Crabtree, then it's all true.

CRABTREE. Too true indeed, ma'am, and Sir Peter is dangerously wounded.   65

SIR BENJAMIN. By a thrust in segoon,[2] quite through his left side.

CRABTREE. By a bullet lodged in the thorax.

MRS. CANDOUR. Mercy on me, poor Sir Peter!

CRABTREE. Yes ma'am, though Charles would have avoided the matter if he could.   70

MRS. CANDOUR. I knew Charles was the person.

SIR BENJAMIN. My uncle, I see, knows nothing of the matter.

CRABTREE. But Sir Peter taxed him with the basest ingratitude.

SIR BENJAMIN. That I told you, you know.

CRABTREE. Do, Nephew, let me speak—and insisted on immediate satisfac-   75
tion.

SIR BENJAMIN. Just as I said.

CRABTREE. 'Odd's life! Nephew, allow others to know something too—a pair of pistols lay on the bureau (for Mr. Surface, it seems, had come the night before late from Salt Hill where he had been to see the Montem[3] with a   80 friend who has a son at Eton), so unluckily the pistols were left charged.

SIR BENJAMIN. I heard nothing of this.

CRABTREE. Sir Peter forced Charles to take one, and they fired, it seems, pretty nearly together; Charles's shot took place as I tell you, and Sir Peter's missed. But what is very extraordinary, the ball struck against a little   85 bronze Shakespeare that stood over the chimneypiece, grazed out of the window at a right angle, and wounded the postman, who was just coming to the door with a double letter[4] from Northamptonshire.

SIR BENJAMIN. My uncle's account is more circumstantial,[5] I must confess— but I believe mine is the true one for all that.   90

LADY SNEERWELL. [*aside*] I am more interested in this affair than they imagine and must have better information. (*Exit.*)

SIR BENJAMIN. Ah! Lady Sneerwell's alarm is very easily accounted for.

---

1   *hartshorn* Smelling salt made from a deer's (hart's) horn.
2   *segoon* Seconde, a position in fencing.
3   *Montem* Customary trek in which the students at Eton boys' school walked to Salt Hill, two miles away, requesting money from the people they passed.
4   *double letter* Two-page letter.
5   *circumstantial* Detailed.

CRABTREE.  Yes, yes, they certainly *do* say—but that's neither here nor there.

95  MRS. CANDOUR.  But pray, where is Sir Peter at present?

CRABTREE.  Oh, they brought him home, and he is now in the house, though the servants are ordered to deny it.

MRS. CANDOUR.  I believe so, and Lady Teazle, I suppose, attending him.

CRABTREE.  Yes, yes, I saw one of the Faculty[1] enter just before me.

100  SIR BENJAMIN.  Hey! Who comes here?

CRABTREE.  Oh this is he! Physician, depend on't.

MRS. CANDOUR.  Oh certainly, it must be the physician—and now we shall know.

*(Enter Sir Oliver.)*

CRABTREE.  Well, Doctor, what hopes?

MRS. CANDOUR.  Aye Doctor, how's your patient?

105  SIR BENJAMIN.  Now Doctor, isn't it a wound with a small sword?

CRABTREE.  A bullet lodged in the thorax, for a hundred.

SIR OLIVER.  Doctor! A wound with a small sword and a bullet in the thorax! What, are you mad, good people?

SIR BENJAMIN.  Perhaps, sir, you are not a doctor?

110  SIR OLIVER.  Truly, I am to thank you for my degrees if I am.

CRABTREE.  Only a friend of Sir Peter's then, I presume. But sir, you must have heard of his accident?

SIR OLIVER.  Not a word.

CRABTREE.  Not of his being dangerously wounded?

115  SIR OLIVER.  The devil he is!

SIR BENJAMIN.  Run through the body!

CRABTREE.  Shot in the breast.

SIR BENJAMIN.  By one Mr. Surface.

CRABTREE.  Aye, by the younger.

120  SIR OLIVER.  Hey! What the plague! You seem to differ strangely in your accounts. However, you agree that Sir Peter is dangerously wounded?

SIR BENJAMIN.  Oh yes, we agree in that.

CRABTREE.  Yes, yes, I believe there can be no doubt of that.

SIR OLIVER.  Then upon my word, for a person in that situation, he is the
125  most imprudent man alive, for here he comes walking as if nothing at all was the matter.

*(Enter Sir Peter.)*

'Odd's heart! Sir Peter, you are come in good time, I promise you, for we had just given you over.

---

1    *one of the Faculty*  I.e., a medical doctor.

SIR BENJAMIN. Egad Uncle, this is the most sudden recovery—

SIR OLIVER. Why man, what do you do out of your bed, with a small sword   130
through your body and a bullet lodged in your thorax?

SIR PETER. A small sword and a bullet?

SIR OLIVER. Aye, these gentlemen would have killed you without law or
physic and wanted to dub me a doctor to make me an accomplice.

SIR PETER. Why, what is all this?   135

SIR BENJAMIN. We rejoice, Sir Peter, that the story of the duel is not true and
are sincerely sorry for your other misfortunes.

SIR PETER. [*aside*] So, it's all over the Town already.

CRABTREE. Though, Sir Peter, you were certainly vastly to blame to marry at
all at your years.   140

SIR PETER. What business is that of yours, sir?

MRS. CANDOUR. Though indeed, as Sir Peter made so good a husband, he's
very much to be pitied.

SIR PETER. Plague on your pity, ma'am, I desire none of it.

SIR BENJAMIN. However, Sir Peter, you mustn't mind the laughing and jests   145
you will meet with on the occasion.

SIR PETER. Sir, I desire to be master of my own house.

CRABTREE. 'Tis no uncommon case—that's one comfort.

SIR PETER. I insist on being left to myself; without ceremony, I insist on your
leaving my house directly.   150

MRS. CANDOUR. Well, well, we are going—and depend on't, we'll make the
best report of you we can.

SIR PETER. Leave my house.

CRABTREE. And tell how hard you have been treated.

SIR PETER. Leave my house.   155

SIR BENJAMIN. And how patiently you bear it.

SIR PETER. Leave my house—

(*Exeunt Mrs. Candour, Sir Benjamin, and Crabtree.*)

Fiends! Vipers! Furies! Oh that their own venom would choke them.

SIR OLIVER. They are very provoking indeed, Sir Peter.

(*Enter Rowley.*)

ROWLEY. I heard high words. What has ruffled you, Sir Peter?   160

SIR PETER. Pshaw! What signifies asking? Do I ever pass a day without my
vexations?

SIR OLIVER. Well, I'm not inquisitive. I come only to tell you that I have seen
both my nephews in the manner we proposed.

SIR PETER. A precious couple they are!   165

ROWLEY. Yes, and Sir Oliver is convinced that your judgement was right, Sir Peter.

SIR OLIVER. Yes, I find Joseph is indeed the man after all.

ROWLEY. Aye, as Sir Peter says, he's a man of sentiment.

170  SIR OLIVER. And acts up to the sentiments he professes.

ROWLEY. It's certainly edification to hear him talk!

SIR OLIVER. Oh, he's a model for the young men of the age! But how's this, Sir Peter? You don't join in your friend Joseph's praise, as I expected.

SIR PETER. Sir Oliver, we live in a damned, wicked world, and the fewer we

175  praise, the better.

ROWLEY. What, do you say so, Sir Peter, who never were mistaken in your life?

SIR PETER. Pshaw! Plague on you both. I see by your sneering you have heard the whole affair. I shall go mad among you.

180  ROWLEY. Then, to fret you no longer, Sir Peter, we are indeed acquainted with it all. I met Lady Teazle coming from Mr. Surface's so humbled that she deigned to request me to be her advocate with you.

SIR PETER. And does Sir Oliver know all too?

SIR OLIVER. Every circumstance.

185  SIR PETER. What, of the closet—and the screen, hey?

SIR OLIVER. Yes, yes, and the little French milliner! Oh, I have been vastly diverted with the story—ha, ha!

SIR PETER. 'Twas very pleasant.

SIR OLIVER. I never laughed more in my life, I assure you, ha, ha, ha!

190  SIR PETER. Oh, vastly diverting, ha, ha, ha!

ROWLEY. To be sure, Joseph with his sentiments—ha, ha, ha!

SIR PETER. Yes, yes, his sentiments—ha, ha, ha! A hypocritical villain!

SIR OLIVER. Aye, and that rogue Charles to pull Sir Peter out of the closet—ha, ha, ha!

195  SIR PETER. Ha, ha!—'twas devilish entertaining, to be sure.

SIR OLIVER. Ha, ha! Egad, Sir Peter, I should like to have seen your face when the screen was thrown down—ha, ha, ha!

SIR PETER. Yes, yes, my face when the screen was thrown down—ha, ha! Oh, I must never show my head again.

200  SIR OLIVER. But come, come, it isn't fair to laugh at you neither, my old friend, though upon my soul I can't help it.

SIR PETER. Oh pray, don't restrain your mirth on my account; it doesn't hurt me at all. I laugh at the whole affair myself. Yes, yes, I think being a standing jest for all one's acquaintances a very happy situation. Oh yes,

205  and then of a morning to read the paragraphs about Lady T. and Sir P. will

be so entertaining. I shall certainly leave town tomorrow and never look mankind in the face again.

ROWLEY. Without affectation, Sir Peter, you may despise the ridicule of fools. But I see Lady Teazle going towards the next room; I am sure you must desire a reconciliation as much as she does.                                    210

SIR OLIVER. Perhaps my being here prevents her coming to you. Well, I'll leave honest Rowley to mediate between you—but he must bring you all presently to Mr. Surface's, where I am now returning, if not to reclaim a libertine, at least to expose hypocrisy. (*Exit.*)

SIR PETER. Ah! I'll be present at your discovering yourself there with all my    215 heart, though 'tis a vile, unlucky place for discoveries.

ROWLEY. We'll follow.

SIR PETER. She's not coming here, you see, Rowley.

ROWLEY. No. But she has left the door of that room open, you perceive. She's in tears.                                                                          220

SIR PETER. Certainly a little mortification appears very becoming in a wife. Don't you think 'twill do her good to let her pine a little?

ROWLEY. Oh! This is ungenerous in you.

SIR PETER. Well, I know not what to think. You remember, Rowley, the letter I found of hers evidently intended for Charles.                             225

ROWLEY. Oh mere forgery, Sir Peter, laid in your way on purpose; this is one of the points I intend Snake shall give you conviction on.

SIR PETER. I wish I was once satisfied of that.—She looks this way. What a remarkably elegant turn of the head she has.—Rowley, I'll go to her.

ROWLEY. Certainly.                                                            230

SIR PETER. Though when 'tis known we are reconciled, people will laugh at me ten times more.

ROWLEY. Let them laugh, and retort their malice only by showing you are happy in spite of it.

SIR PETER. I'faith, so I will, and if I am not mistaken we may be the happiest    235 couple in the country.

ROWLEY. Nay Sir Peter, he who once lays aside suspicion—

SIR PETER. Hold, Master Rowley! If you have any regard for me, never let me hear you utter anything like a sentiment. I have had enough of *them* to serve me the rest of my life.                                                    240

(*Exeunt.*)

## ACT 5, SCENE 3. THE LIBRARY.

*(Enter Joseph Surface and Lady Sneerwell.)*

LADY SNEERWELL.  Impossible! Will not Sir Peter immediately be reconciled to Charles and of consequence no longer oppose his union with Maria? The thought is distraction to me.

JOSEPH SURFACE.  Can passion furnish a remedy?

5 LADY SNEERWELL.  No, nor cunning either. Oh, I was a fool! an idiot! to league with such a blunderer.

JOSEPH SURFACE.  Sure Lady Sneerwell, I am the greatest sufferer, yet you see I bear the accident with calmness.

LADY SNEERWELL.  Because the disappointment doesn't reach your heart; your
10   interest only attached you to Maria. Had you felt for her what I have felt for that ungrateful libertine, neither your temper nor hypocrisy could prevent your showing the sharpness of your vexation.

JOSEPH SURFACE.  But why should your reproaches fall on me for this disappointment?

15 LADY SNEERWELL.  Are you not the cause of it? What had you to do to bate in your pursuit of Maria, to pervert Lady Teazle by the way? Had you not a sufficient field for your roguery in blinding Sir Peter and supplanting your brother? I hate such an avarice of crimes; 'tis an unfair monopoly and never prospers.

20 JOSEPH SURFACE.  Well, I admit I have been to blame. I confess I have deviated from the direct road of wrong, but I don't think we are so totally defeated either.

LADY SNEERWELL.  No?

JOSEPH SURFACE.  You tell me you have made a trial of Snake since we met
25   and that you still believe him faithful to us?

LADY SNEERWELL.  I do believe so.

JOSEPH SURFACE.  And that he has undertaken, should it be necessary, to swear and prove that Charles is at this time contracted by vows and honour to your ladyship, which some of his former letters to you will serve to
30   support.

LADY SNEERWELL.  This indeed might have assisted.

JOSEPH SURFACE.  Come, come, it is not too late yet.

*(Knocking.)*

But hark! This is probably my uncle, Sir Oliver. Retire to that room and we'll consult farther when he's gone.

35 LADY SNEERWELL.  I have no diffidence of your abilities, only to be constant to one roguery at a time. (*Exit.*)

JOSEPH SURFACE.  I will, I will—So, 'tis confounded hard after such bad fortune to be baited by one's confederate in evil. Well, at all events my character is so much better than Charles's that I certainly—Hey! What! This is
not Sir Oliver but old Stanley again. Plague on't that he should return to     40
tease me just now. We shall have Sir Oliver come and find him here and—

  (*Enter Sir Oliver.*)

Gad's life, Mr. Stanley, you have come back to plague me at this time? You
must not stay, upon my word.

SIR OLIVER.  Sir, I hear your uncle Sir Oliver is expected here, and though he
has been so penurious to you, I'll try what he will do for me.                 45

JOSEPH SURFACE.  Sir, 'tis impossible for you to stay now. So I must beg you,
come any other time, and I promise you, you shall be assisted.

SIR OLIVER.  No. Sir Oliver and I must be acquainted.

JOSEPH SURFACE.  Zounds sir, then I insist on your quitting the room directly.

SIR OLIVER.  Nay sir—                                                          50

JOSEPH SURFACE.  Sir, I insist on't.—Here William, show this gentleman out.—
Since you compel me, sir—not one moment—this is such insolence—

  (*Enter Charles.*)

CHARLES.  Heyday! What's the matter? What the devil, have you got hold of
my little broker here? Zounds, don't hurt little Premium! What's the matter, my little fellow?                                                         55

JOSEPH SURFACE.  So he has been with you too, has he?

CHARLES.  To be sure he has. Why, 'tis as honest a little—But sure, Joseph,
you have not been borrowing money too, have you?

JOSEPH SURFACE.  Borrowing! No. But Brother, you know here we expect Sir
Oliver every—                                                                  60

CHARLES.  Oh gad! That's true. Noll mustn't find the little broker here, to be
sure.

JOSEPH SURFACE.  Yet Mr. Stanley insists—

CHARLES.  Stanley! Why, his name is Premium.

JOSEPH SURFACE.  No, no, Stanley.                                              65

CHARLES.  No, no, Premium.

JOSEPH SURFACE.  Well, no matter which—but—

CHARLES.  Aye, aye, Stanley or Premium, 'tis the same thing, as you say, for I
suppose he goes by half an hundred names, besides A and B at the coffee
house.[1]                                                                      70

  (*Knocking.*)

---

1    *A and ... coffee house* Anonymous newspaper advertisements sometimes gave the adver-
     tiser's initials as "A.B." and directed readers to a coffee house where they could respond to
     the posting.

JOSEPH SURFACE. 'Sdeath! Here's Sir Oliver at the door. Now I beg, Mr. Stanley—

CHARLES. Aye, aye, and I beg, Mr. Premium—

SIR OLIVER. Gentlemen—

75 JOSEPH SURFACE. Sir, by Heaven you shall go.

CHARLES. Aye, out with him certainly.

SIR OLIVER. This violence—

JOSEPH SURFACE. 'Tis your own fault.

CHARLES. Out with him to be sure.

(*Both forcing Sir Oliver out. Enter Sir Peter, Lady Teazle, Maria and Rowley.*)

80 SIR PETER. My old friend, Sir Oliver, hey! What in the name of wonder! Here are dutiful nephews! assault their uncle at the first visit.

LADY TEAZLE. Indeed, Sir Oliver, 'twas well we came in to rescue you.

ROWLEY. Truly it was, for I perceive, Sir Oliver, the character of Old Stanley was not a protection to you.

85 SIR OLIVER. No, nor of Premium either: the necessities of the former couldn't extort a shilling from that benevolent gentleman, and with the other I stood a chance of faring worse than my ancestors and being knocked down without being bid for.

JOSEPH SURFACE. Charles!

90 CHARLES. Joseph!

JOSEPH SURFACE. 'Tis now complete.

CHARLES. Very.

SIR OLIVER. Sir Peter, my friend, and Rowley too, look on that elder nephew of mine. You know what he has already received from my bounty, and

95 you know also how gladly I would have regarded half my fortune as held in trust for him. Judge then my disappointment in discovering him to be destitute of truth, charity, and gratitude.

SIR PETER. Sir Oliver, I should be more surprised at this declaration if I had not myself found him to be selfish, treacherous, and hypocritical.

100 LADY TEAZLE. And if the gentleman pleads not guilty to these, pray let him call me to his character.

SIR PETER. Then I believe we need add no more. If he knows himself, he will consider it as the most perfect punishment that he is known by the world.

CHARLES. [*aside*] If they talk this way to honesty, what will they say to me

105 by and by?

SIR OLIVER. As for that prodigal his brother there—

CHARLES. [*aside*] Aye, now comes my turn—the damned family pictures will ruin me.

JOSEPH SURFACE.  Sir Oliver! Uncle! If you will honour me with a hearing.

SIR OLIVER.  (*Turns from him with contempt.*) Pshaw! 110

CHARLES.  (*aside*) Now if Joseph would make one of his long speeches, I might recollect myself a little.

SIR OLIVER.  I suppose you would undertake to justify yourself entirely.

JOSEPH SURFACE.  I trust I could.

SIR OLIVER.  Pshaw. Nay, if you desert your roguery in its distress and try 115 to be justified, you have even less principle than I thought you had. (*to Charles*) Well sir, and you could justify yourself too, I suppose.

CHARLES.  Not that I know of, Sir.

SIR OLIVER.  What, little Premium has been let too much into the secret, I presume. 120

CHARLES.  True, sir, but they were family secrets and should never be mentioned again, you know.

ROWLEY.  Come, Sir Oliver, I know you cannot speak of Charles's follies with anger.

SIR OLIVER.  'Odd's heart! No more I can, nor with gravity either.—Sir Pe- 125 ter, do you know the rogue bargained with me for all his ancestors: sold me judges and generals by the foot, and maiden aunts as cheap as broken china.

CHARLES.  To be sure, Sir Oliver, I did make free with the family canvas, that's the truth on't; my ancestors may certainly rise in evidence against 130 me, there's no denying. But believe me sincere when I tell you, and upon my soul I would not say it if it was not, that, if I do not appear mortified at the exposure of my follies, it is because I feel at this moment the warmest satisfaction in seeing *you*, my liberal benefactor.

SIR OLIVER.  Charles, I believe you, give me your hand: the ill-looking little 135 fellow over the settee has made your peace.

CHARLES.  Then sir, my gratitude to the original is still increased.

LADY TEAZLE.  Yet I believe, Sir Oliver, there is one whom Charles is still more anxious to be reconciled to.

SIR OLIVER.  Oh, I have heard of his attachment there, and with the young 140 lady's pardon, if I construe right that blush—

SIR PETER.  Well, child, speak your sentiments.

MARIA.  Sir, I have little to say but that I shall rejoice to hear that he is happy; for me, whatever claim I had to his attention, I willingly resign it to one who has a better title. 145

CHARLES.  How Maria!

SIR PETER.  Heyday! What's the mystery now? While he appeared an incorrigible rake, you would give your hand to no one else, and now that he's likely to reform, I warrant you won't have him.

150 MARIA. His own heart and Lady Sneerwell's knows the cause.

CHARLES. Lady Sneerwell!

JOSEPH SURFACE. Brother, it is with great concern I am obliged to speak on this point, but my regard to justice obliges me, and Lady Sneerwell's injuries can no longer be concealed. (*Goes to the door.*)

(*Enter Lady Sneerwell.*)

155 ALL. Lady Sneerwell!!!

SIR PETER. So! Another French milliner. Egad, he has one in every room in the house, I suppose.

LADY SNEERWELL. Ungrateful Charles! Well may you be surprised and feel for the indelicate situation which your perfidy has forced me into.

160 CHARLES. Pray, Uncle, is this another plot of yours, for as I have life, I don't understand it.

JOSEPH SURFACE. I believe, sir, there is but the evidence of one person more necessary to make it extremely clear.

SIR PETER. And that person, I imagine, is Mr. Snake.—Rowley, you were
165 perfectly right to bring him with us, and pray let him appear.

ROWLEY. Walk in, Mr. Snake.

(*Enter Snake.*)

I thought his testimony might be wanted; however, it happens unluckily that he comes to confront Lady Sneerwell and not to support her.

LADY SNEERWELL. A villain! treacherous to me at last. Speak fellow, have you
170 conspired against me?

SNAKE. I beg your ladyship ten thousand pardons: You paid me extremely liberally for the lie in question, but I have unfortunately been offered double the sum to speak the truth.

SIR PETER. Plot and counterplot.

175 LADY SNEERWELL. The torments of shame and disappointment on you all.

LADY TEAZLE. Hold, Lady Sneerwell, before you go, let me thank you for the trouble you and that gentleman have taken in writing letters to me from Charles and answering them yourself. And let me also request you to make my respects to the Scandalous College, of which you are president, and
180 inform them that Lady Teazle, licentiate, begs leave to return the diploma they granted her—as she leaves off practice and kills characters no longer.

LADY SNEERWELL. You too, madam—provoking—insolent—may your husband live these fifty years. (*Exit.*)

LADY TEAZLE. What a malicious creature it is!

185 SIR PETER. Hey! What, not for her last wish?

LADY TEAZLE. Oh, no.

SIR OLIVER.  Well sir, what have you to say now?

JOSEPH SURFACE.   Sir, I am so confounded that Lady Sneerwell could be guilty of suborning Mr. Snake in this manner to impose on us all that I know not what to say; however, lest her revengeful spirit should prompt 190 her to injure my brother, I had certainly better follow her directly. (*Exit.*)

SIR PETER.  Moral to the last drop.

SIR OLIVER.  Aye, and marry her, Joseph, if you can, oil and vinegar, egad you'll do very well together.

ROWLEY.  I believe we have no more occasion for Mr. Snake at present.         195

SNAKE.  Before I go, I beg pardon once for all for whatever uneasiness I have been the humble instrument of causing to the parties present.

SIR PETER.  Well, well, you have made atonement by a good deed at last.

SNAKE.  But I must request of the company that it shall never be known.

SIR PETER.  Hey! What the plague, are you ashamed of having done a right 200 thing once in your life.

SNAKE.  Ah sir, consider I live by the badness of my character. I have nothing but my infamy to depend on, and if it were once known that I had been betrayed into an honest action, I should lose every friend I have in the world. (*Exit.*)                                205

SIR PETER.  Here's a precious rogue.

SIR OLIVER.  Well, well, we'll not traduce you by saying any thing to your praise, never fear.

LADY TEAZLE.  See, Sir Oliver, there needs no persuasion now to reconcile your nephew and Maria.                            210

SIR OLIVER.  Aye, aye, that's as it should be, and egad, we'll have the wedding tomorrow morning.

CHARLES.  Thank you, my dear uncle.

SIR PETER.  What, you rogue! Don't you ask the girl's consent first?

CHARLES.  I have done that a long time—a minute—ago, and she looked— 215 yes.

MARIA.  For shame, Charles.—I protest, Sir Peter, there has not been a word.

SIR OLIVER.  Well then, the fewer the better. May your love for each other never know abatement.

SIR PETER.  And may you live as happily together as Lady Teazle and I—in- 220 tend to do.

CHARLES.  Rowley, my old friend, I am sure you congratulate me, and I suspect that I owe you much.

SIR OLIVER.  You do indeed, Charles.

ROWLEY.  If my efforts to serve you had not succeeded, you would have been 225 in my debt for the attempt, but deserve to be happy, and you overpay me.

SIR PETER.  Aye! Honest Rowley always said you would reform.

CHARLES. Why as to reforming, Sir Peter, I'll make no promises—and that I
take to be a proof that I intend to set about it. But here shall be my moni-
230 tor, my gentle guide. Ah! can I leave the virtuous path those eyes illumine?
(*to the audience*)
For thou, dear maid, shouldst waive thy beauty's sway.
Thou still must rule because I will obey.
An humbled fugitive from folly view—
No sanctuary near but love and you.
235 You can indeed each anxious fear remove,
For even scandal dies if you approve.

[*Exeunt.*]

## THE END.

## EPILOGUE
*Written by G. Colman,*[1] *Esq.*
*Spoken by Mrs. Abington*[2]

I, who was late so volatile and gay,
Like a trade-wind must now blow all one way,
Bend all my cares, my studies, and my vows,
To one old rusty weathercock—my spouse!
5 So wills our virtuous bard—the motley Bayes[3]
Of crying epilogues and laughing plays!
Old bachelors, who marry smart young wives,
Learn from our play to regulate your lives:
Each bring his dear to town, all faults upon her—
10 London will prove the very source of honour.
Plunged fairly in, like a cold bath it serves,
When principles relax, to brace the nerves.
Such is my case—and yet I might deplore
That the gay dream of dissipation's o'er;
15 And say, ye fair, was ever lively wife,
Born with a genius for the highest life,
Like me untimely blasted in her bloom,
Like me condemned to such a dismal doom?

---

1    *G. Colman* George Colman the Elder (1732–99), English theatre manager and playwright.
2    *Mrs. Abington* Actress Frances Abington (1737–1815), who appeared in the play's ori-
     ginal cast as Lady Teazle.
3    *Bayes* Playwright. "Bayes" is the name of the playwright character mocked in the Duke
     of Buckingham's *The Rehearsal* (1671).

Save money—when I just knew how to waste it!
Leave London—just as I began to taste it!                                        20
Must I then watch the early crowing cock,
The melancholy ticking of a clock;
In the lone rustic hall for ever pounded,
With dogs, cats, rats, and squalling brats surrounded?
With humble curates can I now retire,                                            25
(While good Sir Peter boozes with the squire)
And at backgammon mortify my soul,
That pants for loo,[1] or flutters at a vole?[2]
Seven's the main![3] Dear sound!—that must expire,
Lost at hot cockles,[4] round a Christmas fire!                                  30
The transient hour of fashion too soon spent,
Farewell the tranquil mind, farewell content!
Farewell the plumèd head, the cushioned tête,[5]
That takes the cushion from its proper seat!
That spirit-stirring drum!—card drums° I mean,                   *parties*   35
Spadille—odd trick—pam—basto—king and queen![6]
And you, ye knockers, that, with brazen throat,
The welcome visitors' approach denote;
Farewell! all quality of high renown,
Pride, pomp, and circumstance of glorious town!                                 40
Farewell! your revels I partake no more,
And Lady Teazle's occupation's o'er!
All this I told our bard°—he smiled, and said 'twas clear,    *playwright*
I ought to play deep tragedy next year.
Meanwhile he drew wise morals from his play,                                    45
And in these solemn periods stalked away:—
"Blest were the fair like you; her faults who stopped,
And closed her follies when the curtain dropped!
No more in vice or error to engage,
Or play the fool at large on life's great stage."                              50

—1777

---

1    *loo* Gambling card game.
2    *vole* Round of cards in which the same player wins every trick.
3    *Seven's the main* Phrase that might be spoken by a player of hazard; the choice of main
     affects what dice rolls win and lose during the caster's turn.
4    *hot cockles* Unsophisticated game, often played by families at Christmas, in which a play-
     er is blindfolded and hit from behind, and must then guess who did it.
5    *cushioned tête* Padded head; padding was used to add volume to elaborate hairstyles.
6    *Spadille ... king and queen* Terms from popular card games.

# Henrik Ibsen
1828–1906

Henrik Ibsen's plays, which sought to be true to life and tackled serious moral issues, shocked audiences far more used to the light, diverting works of drama that were common during his era. His influence reached far beyond his native Norway, helping to shape such major English-language playwrights as Bernard Shaw and Arthur Miller.

Ibsen was born to prosperous parents, but the dissolution of his father's business led to the family's exile from the bourgeois circles they had comfortably moved within. After some time working as a director and theatre manager in Norway, Ibsen exiled himself in 1864; thereafter he lived in Italy and then in Germany, where he composed many of his most famous plays. These plays—among them *A Doll's House* (1879), *Ghosts* (1881), and *Hedda Gabler* (1890)—present unflattering portraits of the hypocrisies and expectations of late nineteenth-century society. Ibsen's work from this period often concerns a central character placed under pressure by societal forces such as religion, marriage, or middle-class norms; moreover, we frequently see these characters brought to a moment of crisis by the burden of their own dark secrets or moral failings. Toward the end of his career, Ibsen's emphasis gradually shifted from the examination of social problems to the exploration of psychological complexity in his characters.

Ibsen returned to Norway in 1891, by which time his international reputation as an important, if controversial, playwright was firmly established; Shaw would publish an essay expounding the concept of "Ibsenism" that same year. Writing in 1905, the British theatre critic William Archer observed that "Ibsen sees one side of a case intensely at one moment, and the other side at another moment, with no less intensity." That intensity, whether focused on social or on psychological forces, continues to engage audiences more than a century after Ibsen's death.

# A Doll's House[1]

## CHARACTERS

Torvald Helmer
Nora, his wife
Dr. Rank
Mrs. Linden[2]
Nils Krogstad
Anna[3] } Servants
Ellen }
Ivar }
Emmy } *The Helmers' children*
Bob }
A porter.

*Scene: Sitting-room in Helmer's house (a flat) in Christiania.[4]*
*Time: The present day;[5] Christmastime.*
*The action takes place on three consecutive days.*

## ACT 1

*A room furnished comfortably and tastefully, but not expensively. In the background, on the right, a door leads to the hall; to the left another door leads to Helmer's study. Between the two doors a piano. In the middle of the left wall, a door, and nearer the front a window. Near the window a round table with armchairs and a small sofa. In the right wall, somewhat to the back, a door; and against the same wall, further forward, a porcelain stove; in front of it a couple of armchairs and a rocking chair. Between the stove and the side door a small table. Engravings on the walls. A display cabinet with china and small decorative items. A small bookcase filled with showily bound books. Carpet. A fire in the stove. A winter day.*

---

1   *A Doll's House* Translated by William Archer, from the Walter H. Baker edition prepared by Edmund Gosse. The translation has been lightly modernized for this anthology by Broadview Press.
2   *Mrs. Linden* Called Linde in Ibsen's original.
3   *Anna* Called Anne-Marie in Ibsen's original.
4   *Christiania* Freetown Christiania, a small, partially autonomous neighbourhood in Copenhagen, Denmark.
5   *present day* I.e., around 1879.

*A bell rings in the hall outside. Presently the outer door is heard to open. Then Nora enters, humming contentedly. She is wearing outdoor clothes, and carries several parcels, which she lays on the right-hand table. She leaves the door into the hall open behind her, and a porter is seen outside, carrying a Christmas tree and a basket, which he gives to the maidservant who has opened the door.*

NORA.  Hide the Christmas tree carefully, Ellen; the children mustn't see it before this evening, when it's lit up. (*To the porter, taking out her purse.*) How much?

PORTER.  Fifty øre.[1]

5  NORA.  There's a crown. No, keep the change.

(*The porter thanks her and goes. Nora shuts the door. She continues smiling in quiet glee as she takes off her cloak and hat. Then she takes from her pocket a bag of macaroons, and eats one or two. As she does so, she goes on tip-toe to her husband's door and listens.*)

10  NORA.  Yes; he is at home. (*She begins humming again, going to the table on the right.*)

HELMER.  (*In his room.*) Is that my lark twittering there?

NORA.  (*Busy opening some of her parcels.*) Yes, it is.

HELMER.  Is it the squirrel skipping about?

NORA.  Yes!

15  HELMER.  When did the squirrel get home?

NORA.  Just this minute. (*Hides the bag of macaroons in her pocket and wipes her mouth.*) Come here, Torvald, and see what I've bought.

HELMER.  Don't disturb me. (*A little later he opens the door and looks in, pen in hand.*) "Bought," did you say? What! All that? Has my little spendthrift
20  been making the money fly again?

NORA.  Why, Torvald, surely we can afford to launch out a little now! It's the first Christmas we haven't had to pinch.

HELMER.  Come, come; we can't afford to squander money.

NORA.  Oh yes, Torvald, do let us squander a little—just the least little bit,
25  won't you? You know you'll soon be earning heaps of money.

HELMER.  Yes, from New Year's Day. But there's a whole quarter before my first salary is due.

NORA.  Never mind; we can borrow in the meantime.

HELMER.  Nora! (*He goes up to her and takes her playfully by the ear.*) Thought-
30  less as ever! Supposing I borrowed a thousand crowns today, and you spent

---

1    *øre* Danish currency; one hundred *øre* equals one *krone* (crown).

it during Christmas week, and that on New Year's Eve a tile blew off the
roof and knocked my brains out—

NORA. (*Laying her hand on his mouth.*) Hush! How can you talk so horridly?

HELMER. But supposing it were to happen—what then?

NORA. If anything so dreadful happened, I shouldn't care whether I was in    35
debt or not.

HELMER. But what about the creditors?

NORA. They! Who cares for them? They're only strangers.

HELMER. Nora, Nora! What a woman you are! But seriously, Nora, you know
my ideas on these points. No debts! No credit! Home life ceases to be free    40
and beautiful as soon as it is founded on borrowing and debt. We two have
held out bravely till now, and we won't give in at the last.

NORA. (*Going to the fireplace.*) Very well—as you like, Torvald.

HELMER. (*Following her.*) Come come; my little lark mustn't let her wings
droop like that. What? Is the squirrel pouting there? (*Takes out his purse.*)    45
Nora, what do you think I've got here?

NORA. (*Turning round quickly.*) Money!

HELMER. There! (*Gives her some notes.*) Of course I know all sorts of things
are wanted at Christmas.

NORA. (*Counting.*) Ten, twenty, thirty, forty. Oh! Thank you, thank you,    50
Torvald. This will go a long way.

HELMER. I should hope so.

NORA. Yes, indeed, a long way! But come here, and see all I've been buying.
And so cheap! Look, here is a new suit for Ivar, and a little sword. Here are
a horse and a trumpet for Bob. And here are a doll and a cradle for Emmy.    55
They're only simple; but she'll soon pull them all to pieces. And dresses
and neckties for the servants; only I should have got something better for
dear old Anna.

HELMER. And what's in that other parcel?

NORA. (*Crying out.*) No, Torvald, you're not to see that until this evening.    60

HELMER. Oh! Ah! But now tell me, you little rogue, what have you got for
yourself?

NORA. For myself? Oh, I don't want anything.

HELMER. Nonsense. Just tell me something sensible you would like to have.

NORA. No. Really I want nothing … Well, listen, Torvald—    65

HELMER. Well?

NORA. (*Playing with his coat buttons, without looking him in the face.*) If you
really want to give me something, you might, you know, you might—

HELMER. Well, well? Out with it!

NORA. (*Quickly.*) You might give me money, Torvald. Only just what you    70
think you can spare; then I can buy something with it later.

HELMER. But, Nora—

NORA. Oh, please do, dear Torvald, please do! Then I would hang the money in lovely gilt paper on the Christmas tree. Wouldn't that be fun?

75 HELMER. What do they call the birds that are always making the money fly?

NORA. Yes, I know—spendthrifts, of course. But please do as I say, Torvald. Then I shall have time to think what I want most. Isn't that very sensible, now?

HELMER. (*Smiling.*) Certainly; that is to say, if you really kept the money

80 I gave you, and really bought yourself something with it. But it all goes toward housekeeping, and for all sorts of useless things, and then I have to find more.

NORA. But, Torvald—

HELMER. Can you deny it, Nora dear? (*He puts his arm round her.*) It's a sweet

85 little lark; but it gets through a lot of money. No one would believe how much it costs a man to keep such a little bird as you.

NORA. For shame! How can you say so? Why, I really save as much as I can.

HELMER. (*Laughing.*) Very true—as much as you can—but you can't.

NORA. (*Hums and smiles in quiet satisfaction.*) H'm! You should just know,

90 Torvald, what expenses we larks and squirrels have.

HELMER. You're a strange little being! Just like your father—always eager to get hold of money; but the moment you have it, it seems to slip through your fingers; you never know what becomes of it. Well, one must take you as you are. It's in the blood. Yes, Nora, that sort of thing

95 is inherited.

NORA. I wish I had inherited many of my father's qualities.

HELMER. And I don't wish you to be anything but just what you are—my own, sweet little songbird. But I say—it strikes me you look so—so—what can I call it? So suspicious today—

100 NORA. Do I?

HELMER. You do, indeed. Look me full in the face.

NORA. (*Looking at him.*) Well?

HELMER. (*Threatening with his finger.*) Hasn't the little sweet-tooth been breaking the rules today?

105 NORA. No! How can you think of such a thing!

HELMER. Didn't she just look in at the confectioner's?

NORA. No, Torvald, really—

HELMER. Not to sip a little jelly?

NORA. No, certainly not.

110 HELMER. Hasn't she even nibbled a macaroon or two?

NORA. No, Torvald, indeed, indeed!

HELMER. Well, well, well; of course I'm only joking.

NORA. (*Goes to the table on the right.*) I shouldn't think of doing what you disapprove of.

HELMER. No, I'm sure of that; and, besides, you've given me your word. (*Going towards her.*) Well, keep your little Christmas secrets to yourself, Nora darling. The Christmas tree will bring them all to light, I daresay.

NORA. Have you remembered to ask Doctor Rank?

HELMER. No. But it's not necessary; he'll come as a matter of course. Besides, I shall invite him when he looks in today. I've ordered some fine wine. Nora, you can't think how I look forward to this evening.

NORA. And I too. How the children will enjoy themselves, Torvald!

HELMER. Ah! It's glorious to feel that one has an assured position and ample means. Isn't it delightful to think of?

NORA. Oh, it's wonderful!

HELMER. Do you remember last Christmas? For three whole weeks beforehand you shut yourself up every evening till long past midnight to make flowers for the Christmas tree, and all sorts of other marvels that were to have astonished us. I was never so bored in my life.

NORA. I did not bore myself at all.

HELMER. (*Smiling.*) And it came to so little after all, Nora.

NORA. Oh! Are you going to tease me about that again? How could I help the cat getting in and spoiling it all?

HELMER. To be sure you couldn't, my poor little Nora. You did your best to amuse us all, and that's the main thing. But, all the same, it's a good thing the hard times are over.

NORA. Oh, isn't it wonderful?

HELMER. Now I needn't sit here boring myself all alone; and you needn't tire your dear eyes and your delicate little fingers—

NORA. (*Clapping her hands.*) No, I needn't, need I, Torvald? Oh! It's wonderful to think of! (*Takes his arm.*) And now I'll tell you how I think we ought to manage, Torvald. As soon as Christmas is over—(*The hall doorbell rings.*) Oh, there's a ring! (*Arranging the room.*) That's somebody come to call. How vexing!

HELMER. I am not at home to callers; remember that.

ELLEN. (*In the doorway.*) A lady to see you, ma'am.

NORA. Show her in.

ELLEN. (*To Helmer.*) And the doctor is just come, sir.

HELMER. Has he gone into my study?

ELLEN. Yes, sir.

(*Helmer goes into his study. Ellen ushers in Mrs. Linden, in travelling clothes, and shuts the door behind her.*)

MRS. LINDEN. (*Timidly and with hesitation.*) How do you do, Nora?

NORA. (*Doubtfully.*) How do you do?

MRS. LINDEN. I daresay you don't recognize me?

NORA. No, I don't think—oh yes!—I believe—(*Effusively.*) What! Christina!
155   Is it really you?

MRS. LINDEN. Yes, really I!

NORA. Christina! And to think I didn't know you! But how could I—(*More softly.*) How changed you are, Christina!

MRS. LINDEN. Yes, no doubt. In nine or ten years—

160   NORA. Is it really so long since we met? Yes, so it is. Oh! The last eight years have been a happy time, I can tell you. And now you have come to town? All that long journey in midwinter! How brave of you!

MRS. LINDEN. I arrived by this morning's steamer.

NORA. To keep Christmas, of course. Oh, how delightful! What fun we shall
165   have! Take your things off. Aren't you frozen? (*Helping her.*) There, now we'll sit down here cosily by the fire. No, you take the armchair; I'll sit in this rocking chair. (*Seizes her hand.*) Yes, now I can see your dear old face again. It was only at first glance—But you're a little paler, Christina, and perhaps a little thinner.

170   MRS. LINDEN. And much, much older, Nora.

NORA. Yes, perhaps a little older—not much—ever so little. (*She suddenly stops; seriously.*) Oh! What a thoughtless wretch I am! Here I sit chattering on, and—Dear, dear Christina, can you forgive me!

MRS. LINDEN. What do you mean, Nora?

175   NORA. (*Softly.*) Poor Christina! I forgot, you are a widow?

MRS. LINDEN. Yes, my husband died three years ago.

NORA. I know, I know, I saw it in the papers. Oh! Believe me, Christina, I did mean to write to you; but I kept putting it off, and something always came in the way.

180   MRS. LINDEN. I can quite understand that, Nora dear.

NORA. No, Christina; it was horrid of me. Oh, you poor darling! How much you must have gone through! And he left you nothing?

MRS. LINDEN. Nothing.

NORA. And no children?

185   MRS. LINDEN. None.

NORA. Nothing, nothing at all?

MRS. LINDEN. Not even a sorrow or a longing to dwell upon.

NORA. (*Looking at her incredulously.*) My dear Christina, how is that possible?

MRS. LINDEN. (*Smiling sadly and stroking her hair.*) Oh, it happens so some-
190   times, Nora.

NORA. So utterly alone. How dreadful that must be! I have three of the loveliest children. I can't show them to you just now; they're out with their nurse. But now you must tell me everything.

MRS. LINDEN. No, no, I want you to tell me—

NORA. No, you must begin; I won't be egotistical today. Today, I will think of you only. Oh! I must tell you one thing; but perhaps you've heard of our great stroke of fortune? 195

MRS. LINDEN. No. What is it?

NORA. Only think! My husband has been made manager of the Joint Stock Bank. 200

MRS. LINDEN. Your husband! Oh, how fortunate!

NORA. Yes, isn't it? A lawyer's position is so uncertain, you see, especially when he won't touch any business that's the least bit ... shady, as of course Torvald won't; and in that I quite agree with him. Oh! You can imagine how glad we are. He is to enter on his new position at the New Year, and 205 then he will have a large salary, and percentages. In future we shall be able to live quite differently—just as we please, in fact. Oh, Christina, I feel so light and happy! It's splendid to have lots of money, and no need to worry about things, isn't it?

MRS. LINDEN. Yes, it must be delightful to have what you need. 210

NORA. No, not only what you need, but heaps of money—heaps!

MRS. LINDEN. (*Smiling.*) Nora, Nora, haven't you learnt reason yet? In our school days you were a shocking little spendthrift!

NORA. (*Quietly smiling.*) Yes, Torvald says I am still. (*Threatens with her finger.*) But "Nora, Nora," is not so silly as you all think. Oh! I haven't had the 215 chance to be much of a spendthrift. We have both had to work.

MRS. LINDEN. You too?

NORA. Yes, light needlework—crochet, and embroidery, and things of that sort, (*significantly*) and other work too. You know, of course, that Torvald left the Government service when we were married. He had little chance of 220 promotion, and of course he needed to make more money. But in the first year of our marriage he overworked himself terribly. He had to undertake all sorts of odd jobs, you know, and to work early and late. He couldn't stand it, and fell dangerously ill. Then the doctors declared he must go to the South. 225

MRS. LINDEN. Yes, you spent a whole year in Italy, didn't you?

NORA. We did. It wasn't easy to manage, I can tell you. It was just after Ivar's birth. But of course we had to go. Oh, it was a delicious journey! And it saved Torvald's life. But it cost a frightful lot of money, Christina.

MRS. LINDEN. So I should think. 230

NORA. Twelve hundred dollars! Four thousand eight hundred crowns! Isn't that a lot of money?

MRS. LINDEN. How lucky you had the money to spend!

NORA. I must tell you we got it from father.

235 MRS. LINDEN. Ah, I see. He died just about that time, didn't he?

NORA. Yes, Christina, just then. And only think! I couldn't go and nurse him! I was expecting little Ivar's birth daily. And then I had my Torvald to attend to. Dear, kind old father! I never saw him again, Christina. Oh! That's the hardest thing I have had to bear since my marriage.

240 MRS. LINDEN. I know how fond you were of him. And then you went to Italy?

NORA. Yes; we had the money, and the doctors insisted. We started a month later.

MRS. LINDEN. And your husband returned completely cured?

245 NORA. Sound as a bell.

MRS. LINDEN. But—the doctor?

NORA. What about him?

MRS. LINDEN. I thought as I came in your servant announced the doctor—

NORA. Oh, yes, Doctor Rank. But he doesn't come as a doctor. He's our best
250 friend, and never lets a day pass without looking in. No, Torvald hasn't had an hour's illness since that time. And the children are so healthy and well, and so am I. (*Jumps up and claps her hands.*) Oh, Christina, Christina, it's so lovely to live and to be happy! Oh! But it's really too horrid of me! Here am I talking about nothing but my own concerns. (*Sits down upon*
255 *a footstool close to her and lays her arms on Christina's lap.*) Oh! Don't be angry with me! Now just tell me, is it really true that you didn't love your husband? What made you take him?

MRS. LINDEN. My mother was alive then, bedridden and helpless; and I had my two younger brothers to think of. I thought it my duty to accept him.

260 NORA. Perhaps it was. I suppose he was rich then?

MRS. LINDEN. Very well off, I believe. But his business was uncertain. It fell to pieces at his death, and there was nothing left.

NORA. And then—?

MRS. LINDEN. Then I had to fight my way by keeping a shop, a little school,
265 anything I could turn my hand to. The last three years have been one long struggle for me. But now it's over, Nora. My poor mother no longer needs me; she is at rest. And the boys are in business, and can look after themselves.

NORA. How free your life must feel!

270 MRS. LINDEN. No, Nora, only inexpressibly empty. No one to live for. (*Stands up restlessly.*) That is why I couldn't bear to stay any longer in that out-of-

the-way corner. Here it must be easier to find something really worth doing—something to occupy one's thoughts. If I could only get some settled
employment—some office work.

NORA. But, Christina, that's so tiring, and you look worn out already. You 275
should rather go to some health resort and rest.

MRS. LINDEN. (*Going to the window.*) I have no father to give me the money,
Nora.

NORA. (*Rising.*) Oh! Don't be angry with me.

MRS. LINDEN. (*Going toward her.*) My dear Nora, don't you be angry with 280
me. The worst of a position like mine is that it makes one bitter. You have
no one to work for, yet you have to strain yourself constantly. You must
live; and so you become selfish. When I heard of the happy change in your
circumstances—can you believe it?—I rejoiced more on my own account
than on yours. 285

NORA. How do you mean? Ah! I see. You mean Torvald could perhaps do
something for you.

MRS. LINDEN. Yes, I thought so.

NORA. And so he shall, Christina. Just you leave it all to me. I shall lead up
to it beautifully, and think of something pleasant to put him in a good 290
humour! Oh! I should so love to do something for you.

MRS. LINDEN. How good of you, Nora! And doubly good in you, who know
so little of the troubles of life.

NORA. I? I know so little of—?

MRS. LINDEN. (*Smiling.*) Ah, well! A little needlework, and so forth. You're 295
a mere child, Nora.

NORA. (*Tosses her head and paces the room.*) Oh, come, you mustn't be so
patronizing!

MRS. LINDEN. No?

NORA. You're like the rest. You all think I'm fit for nothing really serious— 300

MRS. LINDEN. Well—

NORA. You think I've had no troubles in this weary world.

MRS. LINDEN. My dear Nora, you've just told me all your troubles.

NORA. Pooh—these trifles! (*Softly.*) I haven't told you the great thing.

MRS. LINDEN. The great thing? What do you mean? 305

NORA. I know you look down upon me, Christina; but you've no right to.
You are proud of having worked so hard and so long for your mother?

MRS. LINDEN. I'm sure I don't look down upon anyone, but it's true I'm both
proud and glad when I remember that I was able to make my mother's last
days free from care. 310

NORA. And you're proud to think of what you have done for your brothers,
too.

MRS. LINDEN. Don't I have the right to be?

NORA. Yes, surely. But now let me tell you, Christina—I, too, have some-
315    thing to be proud and glad of.

MRS. LINDEN. I don't doubt it. But what do you mean?

NORA. Hush! Not so loud. Only think, if Torvald were to hear! He mustn't—
not for anything in the world! No one must know about it, Christina—no
one but you.

320 MRS. LINDEN. What can it be?

NORA. Come over here. (*Draws her beside her on the sofa.*) Yes—I, too, have
something to be proud and glad of. *I* saved Torvald's life.

MRS. LINDEN. Saved his life? How?

NORA. I told you about our going to Italy. Torvald would have died but for that.

325 MRS. LINDEN. Yes—and your father gave you the money.

NORA. (*Smiling.*) Yes, so Torvald and everyone believes, but—

MRS. LINDEN. But—?

NORA. Father didn't give us one penny. *I* found the money.

MRS. LINDEN. You? All that money?

330 NORA. Twelve hundred dollars. Four thousand eight hundred crowns. What
do you say to that?

MRS. LINDEN. My dear Nora, how did you manage it? Did you win it in the
lottery?

NORA. (*Contemptuously.*) In the lottery? Pooh! Any fool could have done
335    that!

MRS. LINDEN. Then wherever did you get it from?

NORA. (*Hums and smiles mysteriously.*) H'm; tra-la-la-la!

MRS. LINDEN. Of course you couldn't borrow it.

NORA. No? Why not?

340 MRS. LINDEN. Why, a wife can't borrow without her husband's consent.

NORA. (*Tossing her head.*) Oh! When the wife knows a little of business, and
how to set about things, then—

MRS. LINDEN. But, Nora, I don't understand—

NORA. Well you needn't. I never said I borrowed the money. Perhaps I got it
345    another way. (*Throws herself back on the sofa.*) I may have got it from some
admirer. When one is so—attractive as I am—

MRS. LINDEN. You're too silly, Nora.

NORA. Now I'm sure you're dying of curiosity, Christina—

MRS. LINDEN. Listen to me, Nora dear. Haven't you been a little rash?

350 NORA. (*Sitting upright again.*) Is it rash to save one's husband's life?

MRS. LINDEN. I think it was rash of you, without his knowledge—

NORA. But it would have been fatal for him to know! Can't you understand
that? He was never to suspect how ill he was. The doctors came to me

privately and told me that his life was in danger—that nothing could save him but a trip to the South. Do you think I didn't try diplomacy first? I told him how I longed to have a trip abroad, like other young wives; I wept and prayed; I said he ought to think of my condition, and indulge me; and then I hinted that he could borrow the money. But then, Christina, he almost got angry. He said I was frivolous, and that it was his duty as a husband not to yield to my whims and fancies—so he called them. Very well, I thought, but saved you must be; and then I found the way to do it.

MRS. LINDEN.   And did your husband never learn from your father that the money was not from him?

NORA.   No, never. Father died at that very time. I meant to have told him all about it, and begged him to say nothing. But he was so ill—sadly, it was not necessary.

MRS. LINDEN.   And you have never confessed to your husband?

NORA.   Good heavens! What can you be thinking? Tell him, when he has such a loathing of debt? And besides—how painful and humiliating it would be for Torvald, with his manly self-reliance, to know that he owed anything to me! It would utterly upset the relation between us; our beautiful, happy home would never again be what it is.

MRS. LINDEN.   Will you never tell him?

NORA.   (*Thoughtfully, half-smiling.*) Yes, sometime perhaps—after many years, when I'm—not so pretty. You mustn't laugh at me. Of course I mean when Torvald is not so much in love with me as he is now; when it doesn't amuse him any longer to see me skipping about, and dressing up and acting. Then it might be good to have something in reserve. (*Breaking off.*) Nonsense! Nonsense! That time will never come. Now, what do you say to my grand secret, Christina? Am I fit for nothing now? You may believe it has cost me a lot of anxiety. It has not been easy to meet my commitments on time. You must know, Christina, that in business there are things called installments, and quarterly interest, that are terribly hard to meet. So I had to pinch a little here and there, wherever I could. I could not save anything out of the housekeeping, for of course Torvald had to live well. And I couldn't let the children go about badly dressed; all I got for them, I spent on them, the darlings.

MRS. LINDEN.   Poor Nora! So it had to come out of your own necessities.

NORA.   Yes, of course. After all, the whole thing was my doing. When Torvald gave me money for clothes, and so on, I never spent more than half of it; I always bought the simplest things. It's a mercy everything suits me so well; Torvald never noticed anything. But it was often very hard, Christina dear. For it's nice to be beautifully dressed. Now, isn't it?

MRS. LINDEN.   Indeed it is.

395   NORA. Well, and besides that, I made money in other ways. Last winter I was so lucky—I got a heap of copying to do. I shut myself up every evening and wrote far on into the night. Oh, sometimes I was so tired, so tired. And yet it was splendid to work like that and earn money. I almost felt as if I was a man.

400   MRS. LINDEN. Then how much have you been able to pay off?

NORA. Well, I can't precisely say. It's difficult to keep that sort of business clear. I only know that I paid everything I could scrape together. Sometimes I really didn't know where to turn. (*Smiles.*) Then I used to imagine that a rich old gentleman was in love with me—

405   MRS. LINDEN. What! What gentleman?

NORA. Oh! Nobody—that he was now dead, and that when his will was opened, there stood in large letters: Pay over at once everything I possess to that charming person, Mrs. Nora Helmer.

MRS. LINDEN. But, dear Nora, what gentleman do you mean?

410   NORA. Dear, dear, can't you understand? There wasn't any old gentleman: it was only what I used to dream and dream when I was at my wits' end for money. But it's all over now—the tiresome old creature may stay where he is for me; I care nothing for him or his will; for now my troubles are over. (*Springing up.*) Oh, Christina, how glorious it is to think of! Free from all
415   cares! Free, quite free. To be able to play and romp about with the children; to have things tasteful and pretty in the house, exactly as Torvald likes it! And then the spring is coming, with the great blue sky. Perhaps then we shall have a short holiday. Perhaps I shall see the sea again. Oh, what a wonderful thing it is to live and to be happy! (*The hall doorbell*
420   *rings.*)

MRS. LINDEN. (*Rising.*) There's a ring. Perhaps I had better go.

NORA. No, do stay. No one will come here. It's sure to be someone for Torvald.

ELLEN. (*In the doorway.*) If you please, ma'am, there's a gentleman to speak to Mr. Helmer.

425   NORA. Who is the gentleman?

KROGSTAD. (*In the doorway.*) It is I, Mrs. Helmer. (*Ellen goes. Mrs. Linden starts and turns away to the window.*)

NORA. (*Goes a step towards him, anxiously, half aloud.*) You? What is it? What do you want with my husband?

KROGSTAD. Bank business—in a way. I hold a small post in the Joint Stock
430   Bank, and your husband is to be our new chief, I hear.

NORA. Then it is—?

KROGSTAD. Only tiresome business, Mrs. Helmer; nothing more.

NORA. Then will you please go to his study. (*Krogstad goes. She bows indifferently while she closes the door into the hall. Then she goes to the stove and looks to the fire.*)

MRS. LINDEN. Nora—who was that man?                                          435

NORA. A Mr. Krogstad. Do you know him?

MRS. LINDEN. I used to know him—many years ago. He was in a lawyer's office in our town.

NORA. Yes, so he was.

MRS. LINDEN. How he has changed!                                            440

NORA. I believe his marriage was unhappy.

MRS. LINDEN. And he is a widower now?

NORA. With a lot of children. There! Now it'll burn up. (*She closes the stove, and pushes the rocking chair a little aside.*)

MRS. LINDEN. His business is not of the most creditable, they say?

NORA. Isn't it? I daresay not. I don't know—But don't let us think of busi-  445
ness—it's so tiresome.

> (*Dr. Rank comes out of Helmer's room.*)

RANK. (*Still in the doorway.*) No, no, I won't keep you. I'll just go and have a chat with your wife. (*Shuts the door and sees Mrs. Linden.*) Oh, I beg your pardon. I am in the way here too.

NORA. No, not in the least. (*Introduces them.*) Doctor Rank—Mrs. Linden.  450

RANK. Oh, indeed; I've often heard Mrs. Linden's name; I think I passed you on the stairs as we came up.

MRS. LINDEN. Yes, I go so very slowly. Stairs try me so much.

RANK. You're not very strong?

MRS. LINDEN. Only overworked.                                               455

RANK. Ah! Then you have come to town to find rest in recreation.

MRS. LINDEN. I have come to look for employment.

RANK. Is that an approved remedy for overwork?

MRS. LINDEN. One must live, Doctor Rank.

RANK. Yes, that seems to be the general opinion.                            460

NORA. Come, Doctor Rank, you know you want to live yourself.

RANK. To be sure I do. However wretched I may be, I want to drag on as long as possible. And my patients all have the same mania. And it's the same with people whose complaint is moral. At this very moment Helmer is talking to such a wreck as I mean.                                           465

MRS. LINDEN. (*Softly.*) Ah!

NORA. Whom do you mean?

RANK. Oh, a fellow named Krogstad, a man you know nothing about—corrupt to the very core of his character. But even he began by announcing solemnly that he must live.                                                    470

NORA. Indeed? And what did he want with Torvald?

RANK. I have no idea; I only gathered that it was some bank business.

NORA. I didn't know that Krog—that this Mr. Krogstad had anything to do with the bank?

475 RANK. He has some sort of place there. (*To Mrs. Linden.*) I don't know whether, in your part of the country, you have people who go wriggling and snuffing around in search of moral rottenness—whose policy it is to fill good places with men of tainted character whom they can keep under their eye and in their power? The honest men they leave out in the cold.

480 MRS. LINDEN. Well, I suppose the—delicate characters require most care.

RANK. (*Shrugs his shoulders.*) There we have it! It's that notion that makes society a hospital. (*Nora, deep in her own thoughts, breaks into half-stifled laughter and claps her hands.*) What are you laughing at? Have you any idea what society is?

485 NORA. What do I care for your tiresome society. I was laughing at something else—something awfully amusing. Tell me, Doctor Rank, are all the employees at the bank dependent on Torvald now?

RANK. Is that what strikes you as awfully amusing?

NORA. (*Smiles and hums.*) Never mind, never mind! (*Walks about the room.*)

490 Yes, it *is* amusing to think that we—that Torvald has such power over so many people. (*Takes the bag from her pocket.*) Doctor Rank, will you have a macaroon?

RANK. Oh dear, dear—macaroons! I thought they were contraband here.

NORA. Yes, but Christina brought me these.

495 MRS. LINDEN. What! I?

NORA. Oh, well! Don't be frightened. You couldn't possibly know that Torvald had forbidden them. The fact is, he is afraid of me spoiling my teeth. But, oh bother, just for once! That's for you, Doctor Rank! (*Puts a macaroon into his mouth.*) And you, too, Christina. And I will have one at the

500 same time—only a tiny one, or at most two. (*Walks about again.*) Oh dear, I *am* happy! There is only one thing in the world I really want.

RANK. Well; what's that?

NORA. There's something I should so like to say—in Torvald's hearing.

RANK. Then why don't you say it?

505 NORA. Because I daren't, it's so ugly.

MRS. LINDEN. Ugly?

RANK. In that case you'd better not. But to us you might. What is it you would so like to say in Helmer's hearing?

NORA. I should so love to say—"Damn!"[1]

---

1    [Archer's note] "Död og pine," literally "death and torture"; but by usage a comparatively mild oath.

RANK. Are you out of your mind?                                    510
MRS. LINDEN. Good gracious, Nora!
RANK. Say it. There he is!
NORA. (*Hides the macaroons.*) Hush, hush, hush!

(*Helmer comes out of his room, hat in hand, with his overcoat on his arm.*)

NORA. (*Going toward him.*) Well, Torvald, dear, have you got rid of him?    515
HELMER. Yes, he's just gone.
NORA. May I introduce you? This is Christina, who has come to town—
HELMER. Christina? Pardon me, but I don't know—
NORA. Mrs. Linden, Torvald dear—Christina Linden.
HELMER. (*To Mrs. Linden.*) A school-friend of my wife's, no doubt?    520
MRS. LINDEN. Yes, we knew each other as girls.
NORA. And only think! She has taken this long journey to speak to you.
HELMER. To speak to me!
MRS. LINDEN. Well, not quite—
NORA. You see Christina is tremendously clever at accounts, and she is so    525
anxious to work under a first-rate man of business in order to learn still
more—
HELMER. (*To Mrs. Linden.*) Very sensible indeed.
NORA. And when she heard you were appointed manager—it was tele-
graphed, you know—she started off at once, and—Torvald dear, for my    530
sake, you must do something for Christina. Now can't you?
HELMER. It's not impossible. I presume Mrs. Linden is a widow?
MRS. LINDEN. Yes.
HELMER. And you have already had some experience in office work?
MRS. LINDEN. A good deal.                                          535
HELMER. Well then, it is very likely I may be able to find a place for you.
NORA. (*Clapping her hands.*) There now! There now!
HELMER. You have come at a lucky moment, Mrs. Linden.
MRS. LINDEN. Oh! How can I thank you—?
HELMER. (*Smiling.*) There's no need. (*Puts his overcoat on.*) But for the present    540
you must excuse me.
RANK. Wait; I'll go with you. (*Fetches his fur coat from the hall and warms it
at the fire.*)
NORA. Don't be long, dear Torvald.
HELMER. Only an hour; not more.
NORA. Are you going too, Christina?                                545
MRS. LINDEN. (*Putting on her cloak and hat.*) Yes, I must start looking for
lodgings.
HELMER. Then perhaps we can go together?

NORA. (*Helping her.*) What a pity we haven't a spare room for you, but I'm
550   afraid—

MRS. LINDEN. I shouldn't think of troubling you. Goodbye, dear Nora, and
thank you for all your kindness.

NORA. Goodbye for a little while. Of course you'll come back this evening.
And you, too, Doctor Rank. What! If you're well enough? Of course you'll
555   be well enough. Only wrap up warmly. (*They go out into the hall, talking.
Outside on the stairs are heard children's voices.*) There they are! There they
are! (*She runs to the door and opens it. The nurse Anna enters with the children.*) Come in! Come in! (*Bends down and kisses the children.*) Oh! my
sweet darlings! Do you see them, Christina? Aren't they lovely?

560   RANK. Don't let's stand here chattering in the draught.

HELMER. Come, Mrs. Linden; only mothers can stand such a temperature.
(*Dr. Rank, Helmer, and Mrs. Linden go down the stairs; Anna enters the room
with the children; Nora also, shutting the door.*)

NORA. How fresh and bright you look! And what red cheeks you have! Like
apples and roses. (*The children talk low to her during the following.*) Have
you had great fun? That's splendid! Oh, really! You've been giving Emmy
565   and Bob a ride on your sledge! Both at once, only think! Why you're quite
a man, Ivar. Oh, give her to me a little, Anna. My sweet little dolly! (*Takes
the smallest from the nurse and dances with her.*) Yes, yes, mother will dance
with Bob too. What! Did you have a game of snowballs? Oh! I wish I'd
been there. No, leave them, Anna; I'll take their things off. Oh, yes, let me
570   do it; it's such fun. Go to the nursery; you look frozen. You'll find some hot
coffee on the stove. (*The nurse goes into the room on the left. Nora takes off
the children's things, and throws them down anywhere, while the children talk
to each other and to her.*) Really! A big dog ran after you all the way home?
But he didn't bite you? No, dogs don't bite dear little dolly children. Don't
575   peep into those parcels, Ivar. What is it? Wouldn't you like to know? Take
care—it'll bite! What! Shall we have a game? What shall we play at? Hide-
and-seek? Yes, let's play hide-and-seek. Bob shall hide first. Should I? Yes,
let me hide first. (*She and the children play, with laughter and shouting, in
the room and the adjacent one to the right. At last Nora hides under the table;
the children come rushing in, look for her, but cannot find her, hear her half-
choked laughter, rush to the table, lift up the cover and see her. Loud shouts.
She creeps out, as though to frighten them. Fresh shouts. Meanwhile there has
been a knock at the door leading into the hall. No one has heard it. Now the
door is half opened and Krogstad is seen. He waits a little; the game is renewed.*)

KROGSTAD. I beg your pardon, Mrs. Helmer—

580   NORA. (*With a suppressed cry, turns round and half jumps up.*) Ah! What do
you want?

KROGSTAD.  Excuse me; the outer door was ajar—somebody must have forgotten to shut it—

NORA.  (*Standing up.*) My husband is not at home, Mr. Krogstad.

KROGSTAD.  I know it.    585

NORA.  Then—what do you want here?

KROGSTAD.  To say a few words to you.

NORA.  To me? (*To the children, softly.*) Go in to Anna. What? No, the strange man won't hurt mamma. When he's gone we'll go on playing. (*She leads the children into the left-hand room, and shuts the door behind them. Uneasy,*    590 *with suspense.*) It's with me you wish to speak?

KROGSTAD.  Yes.

NORA.  Today? But it's not the first yet—

KROGSTAD.  No, today is Christmas Eve. It will depend upon yourself whether you have a merry Christmas.    595

NORA.  What do you want? I certainly can't today—

KROGSTAD.  Never mind that just now. It's about another matter. You have a minute to spare?

NORA.  Oh, yes, I suppose so, although—

KROGSTAD.  Good. I was sitting in the restaurant opposite, and I saw your    600 husband go down the street.

NORA.  Well!

KROGSTAD.  With a lady.

NORA.  What then?

KROGSTAD.  May I ask if the lady was a Mrs. Linden?    605

NORA.  Yes.

KROGSTAD.  Who has just come to town?

NORA.  Yes. Today.

KROGSTAD.  I believe she's an intimate friend of yours?

NORA.  Certainly. But I don't understand—    610

KROGSTAD.  I used to know her too.

NORA.  I know you did.

KROGSTAD.  Ah! You know all about it. I thought as much. Now, frankly, is Mrs. Linden to have a place at the bank?

NORA.  How dare you interrogate me in this way, Mr. Krogstad, you, a sub-    615 ordinate of my husband's? But since you ask you shall know. Yes, Mrs. Linden is to be employed. And it's I who recommended her, Mr. Krogstad. Now you know.

KROGSTAD.  Then my guess was right.

NORA.  (*Walking up and down.*) You see one has a little wee bit of influence. It    620 doesn't follow because one's only a woman that—When one is in a subordinate position, Mr. Krogstad, one ought really to take care not to offend anybody who—h'm—

KROGSTAD. Who has influence?

625 NORA. Exactly!

KROGSTAD. (*Taking another tone.*) Mrs. Helmer, will you have the kindness to employ your influence on my behalf?

NORA. What? How do you mean?

KROGSTAD. Will you be so good as to see that I retain my subordinate posi-
630   tion at the bank?

NORA. What do you mean? Who wants to take it from you?

KROGSTAD. Oh, you needn't pretend ignorance. I can very well understand that it cannot be pleasant for your friend to meet me; and I can also un-derstand now for whose sake I am to be hounded out.

635 NORA. But I assure you—

KROGSTAD. Come now, once for all: there is time yet, and I advise you to use your influence to prevent it.

NORA. But, Mr. Krogstad, I have absolutely no influence.

KROGSTAD. None? I thought you just said—

640 NORA. Of course not in that sense! I! How should I have such influence over my husband?

KROGSTAD. Oh! I know your husband from our college days. I don't think he's firmer than other husbands.

NORA. If you talk disrespectfully of my husband, I must ask you to go.

645 KROGSTAD. You are bold, madam.

NORA. I am afraid of you no longer. When New Year's Day is over, I shall soon be out of the whole business.

KROGSTAD. (*Controlling himself.*) Listen to me, Mrs. Helmer. If need be, I shall fight as though for my life to keep my little place at the bank.

650 NORA. Yes, so it seems.

KROGSTAD. It's not only for the money; that matters least to me. It's some-thing else. Well, I'd better make a clean breast of it. Of course you know, like everyone else, that some years ago I—got into trouble.

NORA. I think I've heard something of the sort.

655 KROGSTAD. The matter never came into court, but from that moment all paths were barred to me. Then I took up the business you know about. I was obliged to grasp at something, and I don't think I've been one of the worst. But now I must clear out of it all. My sons are growing up; for their sake I must try to win back as much respectability as I can. This place in
660   the bank was the first step, and now your husband wants to kick me off the ladder, back into the mire.

NORA. But I assure you, Mr. Krogstad, I haven't the power to help you.

KROGSTAD. You have not the will; but I can compel you.

NORA. You won't tell my husband that I owe you money!

KROGSTAD.  H'm; suppose I were to?                                                665

NORA.  It would be shameful of you! (*With tears in her voice.*) This secret which is my joy and my pride—that he should learn it in such an ugly, coarse way—and from you! It would involve me in all sorts of unpleasant-ness.

KROGSTAD.  Only unpleasantness?                                                  670

NORA.  (*Hotly.*) But just do it. It will be worst for you, for then my husband will see what a bad man you are, and then you certainly won't keep your place.

KROGSTAD.  I asked if it was only domestic unpleasantness you feared?

NORA.  If my husband gets to know about it, he will of course pay you off at 675 once, and then we'll have nothing more to do with you.

KROGSTAD.  (*Stepping a pace nearer.*) Listen, Mrs. Helmer. Either you have a weak memory, or you don't know much about business. I must make your position clearer to you.

NORA.  How so?                                                                   680

KROGSTAD.  When your husband was ill, you came to me to borrow twelve hundred dollars.

NORA.  I knew nobody else.

KROGSTAD.  I promised to find you the money—

NORA.  And you did find it.                                                      685

KROGSTAD.  I promised to find you the money under certain conditions. You were then so much taken up with your husband's illness, and so eager to have the money for your journey, that you probably did not give much thought to the details. Let me to remind you of them. I promised to find you the amount in exchange for a promissory note which I drew up.        690

NORA. Yes, and I signed it.

KROGSTAD.  Quite right. But then I added a few lines, making your father a security for the debt. Your father was to sign this.

NORA.  Was to? He did sign it!

KROGSTAD.  I had left the date blank. That is to say, your father was himself 695 to date his signature. Do you recollect that?

NORA.  Yes, I believe—

KROGSTAD.  Then I gave you the paper to send to your father. Is not that so?

NORA.  Yes.

KROGSTAD.  And of course you did so at once? For within five or six days 700 you brought me back the paper, signed by your father, and I gave you the money.

NORA.  Well! Haven't I made my payments punctually?

KROGSTAD.  Fairly—yes. But to return to the point. You were in great trouble at the time, Mrs. Helmer.                                                        705

NORA. I was indeed!

KROGSTAD. Your father was very ill, I believe?

NORA. He was on his deathbed.

KROGSTAD. And died soon after?

710 NORA. Yes.

KROGSTAD. Tell me, Mrs. Helmer, do you happen to recollect the day of his death? The day of the month, I mean?

NORA. Father died on the 29th of September.

KROGSTAD. Quite correct. I have made inquiries, and here comes in the re-
715 markable point—(*produces a paper*) which I cannot explain.

NORA. What remarkable point? I don't know—

KROGSTAD. The remarkable point, madam, that your father signed this paper three days after his death!

NORA. What! I don't understand—

720 KROGSTAD. Your father died on the 29th of September. But look here, he has dated his signature October 2nd! Isn't that remarkable, Mrs. Helmer? (*Nora is silent.*) Can you explain it? (*Nora continues to be silent.*) It is note-worthy too that the words "October 2nd" and the year are not in your father's handwriting, but in one which I believe I know. Well, this may be
725 explained; your father may have forgotten to date his signature, and some-body may have added the date at random before the fact of your father's death was known. There is nothing wrong in that. Everything depends on the signature. Of course it is genuine, Mrs. Helmer? It was really your father who with his own hand wrote his name here?

730 NORA. (*After a short silence throws her head back and looks defiantly at him.*) No. I wrote father's name there.

KROGSTAD. Ah! Are you aware, madam, that that is a dangerous admission?

NORA. Why? You'll soon get your money.

KROGSTAD. May I ask you one more question? Why did you not send the
735 paper to your father?

NORA. It was impossible. Father was ill. If I had asked him for his signature, I should have had to tell him why I wanted the money; but he was so ill I really could not tell him that my husband's life was in danger. It was impossible.

740 KROGSTAD. Then it would have been better to have given up your tour.

NORA. No, I couldn't do that; my husband's life depended on that journey. I couldn't give it up.

KROGSTAD. And did you not consider that you were playing me false?

NORA. That was nothing to me. I didn't care in the least about you. I couldn't
745 endure you for all the cruel difficulties you made, although you knew how ill my husband was.

KROGSTAD.  Mrs. Helmer, you have evidently no clear idea what you have really done. But I can assure you it was nothing more and nothing worse that made me an outcast from society.

NORA.  You! You want me to believe that you did a brave thing to save your 750 wife's life?

KROGSTAD.  The law takes no account of motives.

NORA.  Then it must be a very bad law.

KROGSTAD.  Bad or not, if I lay this document before a court of law you will be condemned according to law.                                               755

NORA.  I don't believe that. Do you mean to tell me that a daughter has no right to spare her dying father anxiety? That a wife has no right to save her husband's life? I don't know much about the law, but I'm sure that, somewhere or another, *that* is allowed. And you don't know that—you, a lawyer! You must be a bad one, Mr. Krogstad.                                          760

KROGSTAD.  Possibly. But business—such business as ours—I do understand. You believe that? Very well; now do as you please. But this I can tell you, that if I am flung into the gutter a second time, you shall keep me company. (*Bows and goes out through hall.*)

NORA.  (*Stands a while thinking, then throws her head back.*) Never! He wants 765 to frighten me. I'm not so foolish as that. (*Begins folding the children's clothes. Pauses.*) But—? No, it's impossible. I did it for love!

CHILDREN.  (*At the door, left.*) Mamma, the strange man is gone now.

NORA.  Yes, yes, I know. But don't tell anyone about the strange man. Do you hear? Not even papa!                                                       770

CHILDREN.  No, mamma; and now will you play with us again?

NORA.  No, no, not now.

CHILDREN.  Oh, do, mamma; you know you promised.

NORA.  Yes, but I can't just now. Run to the nursery; I've so much to do. Run along, run along, and be good, my darlings! (*She pushes them gently into the* 775 *inner room, and closes the door behind them. Sits on the sofa, embroiders a few stitches, but soon pauses.*) No! (*Throws down the work, rises, goes to the hall door and calls out.*) Ellen, bring in the Christmas tree! (*Goes to table, left, and opens the drawer; again pauses.*) No, it's quite impossible!

ELLEN.  (*With Christmas tree.*) Where shall I stand it, ma'am?                780

NORA.  There, in the middle of the room.

ELLEN.  Shall I bring in anything else?

NORA.  No, thank you, I have all I want.

(*Ellen, having put down the tree, goes out.*)

NORA.  (*Busy dressing the tree.*) There must be a candle here, and flowers there.—The horrid man! Nonsense, nonsense! There's nothing in it. The 785

Christmas tree shall be beautiful. I will do everything to please you, Torvald; I'll sing and dance, and—

(*Enter Helmer by the hall door, with bundle of documents.*)

NORA. Oh! You're back already?

HELMER. Yes. Has anybody been here?

790 NORA. Here? No.

HELMER. Curious! I saw Krogstad come out of the house.

NORA. Did you? Oh, yes, by the bye, he was here for a minute.

HELMER. Nora, I can see by your manner that he has been asking you to put in a good word for him.

795 NORA. Yes.

HELMER. And you were to do it as if of your own accord? You were to say nothing to me of his having been here! Didn't he suggest that too?

NORA. Yes, Torvald, but—

HELMER. Nora, Nora! And you could condescend to that! To speak to such
800    a man, to make him a promise! And then to tell me an untruth about it!

NORA. An untruth!

HELMER. Didn't you say nobody had been here? (*Threatens with his finger.*) My little bird must never do that again. A songbird must never sing false notes. (*Puts his arm round her.*) That's so, isn't it? Yes, I was sure of it. (*Lets
805    her go.*) And now we'll say no more about it. (*Sits down before the fire.*) Oh, how cosy and quiet it is here. (*Glances into his documents.*)

NORA. (*Busy with the tree, after a short silence.*) Torvald.

HELMER. Yes.

NORA. I'm looking forward so much to the Stenborgs' fancy ball the day after
810    tomorrow.

HELMER. And I'm incredibly curious to see what surprise you have in store for me.

NORA. Oh, it's too tiresome!

HELMER. What is?

815 NORA. I can't think of anything good. Everything seems so foolish and meaningless.

HELMER. Has little Nora made that discovery?

NORA. (*Behind his chair, with her arms on the back.*) Are you very busy, Torvald?

820 HELMER. Well—

NORA. What papers are those?

HELMER. Bank business.

NORA. Already?

HELMER. I got the retiring manager to let me make some necessary changes

in the staff, and so forth. This will occupy Christmas week. Everything will    825
be straight by the New Year.

NORA. Then that's why that poor Krogstad—

HELMER. H'm.

NORA. (*Still leaning over the chair back, and slowly stroking his hair.*) If you
hadn't been so very busy I should have asked you a great, great favour,    830
Torvald.

HELMER. What can it be? Let's hear it.

NORA. Nobody has such exquisite taste as you. Now, I should so love to look
nice at the fancy ball. Torvald dear, couldn't you take me in hand, and
settle what I'm to be, and arrange my costume for me?    835

HELMER. Aha! So my wilful little woman's at a loss, and making signals of
distress.

NORA. Yes *please*, Torvald. I can't get on without you.

HELMER. Well, well, I'll think it over, and we'll soon hit upon something.

NORA. Oh, how good that is of you! (*Goes to the tree again; pause.*) How well    840
the red flowers show. Tell me, was it anything so very dreadful this Krogstad got into trouble about?

HELMER. Forgery, that's all. Don't you know what that means?

NORA. Mayn't he have been driven to it by need?

HELMER. Yes, or like so many others, done it out of heedlessness. I'm not so    845
hard-hearted as to condemn a man absolutely for a single fault.

NORA. No, surely not, Torvald!

HELMER. Many a man can retrieve his character if he owns his crime and
takes the punishment.

NORA. Crime?    850

HELMER. But Krogstad didn't do that; he resorted to tricks and dodges; and
it's that that has corrupted him.

NORA. Do you think that—?

HELMER. Just think how a man with that on his conscience must be always
lying and shamming. Think of the mask he must wear even toward his own    855
wife and children. It's worst for the children, Nora!

NORA. Why?

HELMER. Because such a dust cloud of lies poisons and contaminates the whole
air of a home. Every breath the children draw contains some germ of evil.

NORA. (*Closer behind him.*) Are you sure of that!    860

HELMER. As a lawyer, my dear, I've seen it often enough. Nearly all cases of
early corruption may be traced to lying mothers.

NORA. Why—mothers?

HELMER. It generally comes from the mother's side, but of course the father's
influence may act in the same way. And this Krogstad has been poison-    865

ing his own children for years with his life of lies and hypocrisy—that's why I say he is morally ruined. (*Stretches out his hands toward her.*) So my sweet little Nora must promise not to plead his cause. Shake hands upon it. Come, come, what's this? Give me your hand. That's right. Then it's a
870    bargain. I assure you it would have been impossible for me to work with him. It gives me a positive sense of physical discomfort to come in contact with such people. (*Nora snatches her hand away, and moves to the other side of the Christmas tree.*)

NORA.  How warm it is here; and I have so much to do.

HELMER.  Yes, and I must try to get some of these papers looked through be-
875    fore dinner; and I'll think over your costume, too. And perhaps I may even find something to hang in gilt paper on the Christmas tree! (*Lays his hand on her head.*) My precious little songbird. (*He goes into his room and shuts the door behind him.*)

NORA.  (*Softly, after a pause.*) It can't be—It's impossible. It must be impossible!

880    ANNA.  (*At the door, left.*) The little ones are begging so prettily to come to mamma.

NORA.  No, no, don't let them come to me! Keep them with you, Anna.

ANNA.  Very well, ma'am. (*Shuts the door.*)

NORA.  (*Pale with terror.*) Corrupt my children! Poison my home! (*Short
885    pause. She raises her head.*) It's not true. It can never, never be true.

## ACT 2

*The same room. In the corner, beside the piano, stands the Christmas tree, stripped, and the candles burnt out. Nora's cloak and hat lie on the sofa. Nora discovered walking about restlessly. She stops by the sofa, and takes up cloak, then lays it down again.*

NORA.  There's somebody coming. (*Goes to hall door; listens.*) Nobody; nobody is likely to come today, Christmas day; nor tomorrow either. But perhaps—(*Opens the door and looks out.*) No, nothing in the letter box; quite empty. (*Comes forward.*) Stuff and nonsense! Of course he only meant to
5    frighten me. There's no fear of any such thing. It's impossible! Why, I have three little children.

(*Enter Anna, from the left with a large cardboard box.*)

ANNA.  At last I've found the box with the fancy dress.

NORA.  Thanks; put it down on the table.

ANNA.  (*Does so.*) But I'm afraid it's in terrible disarray.

10    NORA.  Oh, I wish I could tear it into a hundred thousand pieces.

ANNA.  Oh, no. It can easily be put to rights—just a little patience.

NORA.  I'll go and get Mrs. Linden to help me.

ANNA.  Going out again! In such weather as this! You'll catch cold, ma'am, and be ill.

NORA.  Worse things might happen—What are the children doing?                    15

ANNA.  They're playing with their Christmas presents, poor little dears; but—

NORA.  Do they often ask for me?

ANNA.  You see they've been so used to having their mamma with them.

NORA.  Yes, but, Anna, in future I can't have them so much with me.

ANNA.  Well, little children get used to anything.                    20

NORA.  Do you think they do? Do you believe they would forget their mother if she went quite away?

ANNA.  Gracious me! Quite away?

NORA.  Tell me, Anna—I've so often wondered about it—how could you bring yourself to give your child up to strangers?                    25

ANNA.  I had to when I came as nurse to my little Miss Nora.

NORA.  But how could you make up your mind to it?

ANNA.  When I had the chance of such a good place? A poor girl who's been in trouble must take what comes. That wicked man did nothing for me.

NORA.  But your daughter must have forgotten you.                    30

ANNA.  Oh, no, ma'am, that she hasn't. She wrote to me both when she was confirmed[1] and when she was married.

NORA.  (*Embracing her.*) Dear old Anna—you were a good mother to me when I was little.

ANNA.  My poor little Nora had no mother but me.                    35

NORA.  And if my little ones had nobody else, I'm sure you would—nonsense, nonsense! (*Opens the box.*) Go in to the children. Now I must—Tomorrow you shall see how beautiful I'll be.

ANNA.  I'm sure there will be no one at the ball so beautiful as my Miss Nora. (*She goes into the room on the left.*)                    40

NORA.  (*Takes the costume out of the box, but soon throws it down again.*) Oh, if I dared go out. If only nobody would come. If only nothing would happen here in the meantime. Rubbish; nobody will come. Only not to think. What a delicious muff! Beautiful gloves, beautiful gloves! Away with it all—away with it all! One, two, three, four, five, six—(*With a scream.*) Ah,    45 there they come—(*Goes toward the door, then stands undecidedly.*)

(*Mrs. Linden enters from hall where she has taken off her things.*)

---

1    *confirmed* Fully admitted into the Christian church after affirming religious faith; confirmation ceremonies are most often held for older children or teenagers.

NORA. Oh, it's you, Christina. There's nobody else there? How delightful of you to come.

MRS. LINDEN. I hear you called at my lodgings.

50 NORA. Yes, I was just passing. I do so want you to help me. Let us sit here on the sofa—like so. Tomorrow evening there's to be a fancy ball at Consul Stenborg's, who lives upstairs, and Torvald wants me to appear as a Neapolitan fisher girl, and dance the tarantella; I learnt it at Capri.[1]

MRS. LINDEN. I see—quite a performance!

55 NORA. Yes, Torvald wishes me to. Look, this is the costume; Torvald had it made for me in Italy. But now it is all so torn, I don't know—

MRS. LINDEN. Oh! We'll soon set that to rights. It's only the trimming that's got loose here and there. Have you a needle and thread? Ah! Here's the very thing.

60 NORA. Oh, how kind of you.

MRS. LINDEN. So you're to be in costume tomorrow, Nora? I'll tell you what—I shall come in for a moment to see you in all your glory. But I've quite forgotten to thank you for the pleasant evening yesterday.

NORA. (*Rises and walks across the room.*) Oh! Yesterday, it didn't seem so

65 pleasant as usual. You should have come a little sooner, Christina. Torvald certainly has the art of making a home bright and beautiful.

MRS. LINDEN. You, too, I should think, or you wouldn't be your father's daughter. But tell me—is Doctor Rank always as depressed as he was yesterday?

70 NORA. No, yesterday it was particularly striking. You see he has a terrible illness. He has spinal consumption,[2] poor fellow. They say his father led a terrible life—kept mistresses and all sorts of things—so the son has been sickly from his childhood, you understand.

MRS. LINDEN. (*Lets her sewing fall into her lap.*) Why, my darling Nora, how

75 do you learn such things?

NORA. (*Walking.*) Oh! When one has three children one has visits from women who know something about medicine—and they talk of this and that.

MRS. LINDEN. (*Goes on sewing—a short pause.*) Does Doctor Rank come here every day?

80 NORA. Every day. He's been Torvald's friend from boyhood, and he's a good friend of mine too. Doctor Rank is quite one of the family.

---

1 *tarantella* Italian folkdance. It was thought that the bite of a tarantula caused "tarantism," an irrepressible urge to dance, which an afflicted person could supposedly cure by dancing the tarantella until he or she was too tired to continue; *Capri* Italian island near Naples.

2 *spinal consumption* Pott's disease, a form of tuberculosis that can cause severe curvature of the spine and other health problems.

MRS. LINDEN.  But tell me—is he quite sincere? I mean, doesn't he like to say flattering things to people?

NORA.  On the contrary. Why should you think so?

MRS. LINDEN.  When you introduced us yesterday he declared he had often    85
heard my name, but I noticed your husband had no notion who I was. How could Doctor Rank—?

NORA.  Yes, he was quite right, Christina. You see, Torvald loves me so indescribably, he wants to have me all to himself, as he says. When we were first married he was almost jealous if I even mentioned one of the people    90
at home, so naturally I let it alone. But I often talk to Doctor Rank about the old times, for he likes to hear about them.

MRS. LINDEN.  Listen to me, Nora! You're still a child in many ways. I am older than you, and have had more experience. I'll tell you something: you ought to get clear of all the whole affair with Dr. Rank.
                                                                            95

NORA.  What affair?

MRS. LINDEN.  You were talking yesterday of a rich admirer who was to find you money—

NORA.  Yes, one who never existed, worse luck. What then?

MRS. LINDEN.  Has Doctor Rank money?
                                                                            100

NORA.  Yes, he has.

MRS. LINDEN.  And nobody to provide for?

NORA.  Nobody. But—?

MRS. LINDEN.  And he comes here every day?

NORA.  Yes, every day.

MRS. LINDEN.  I should have thought he'd have acted in better taste.
                                                                            105

NORA.  I don't understand you.

MRS. LINDEN.  Don't pretend, Nora. Do you suppose I don't guess who lent you the twelve hundred dollars?

NORA.  Are you out of your senses? You think *that*! A friend who comes here every day! How painful that would be!
                                                                            110

MRS. LINDEN.  Then it really is not him?

NORA.  No, I assure you. It never for a moment occurred to me. Besides, at that time he had nothing to lend; he came into his property afterward.

MRS. LINDEN.  Well, I believe that was lucky for you, Nora dear.

NORA.  No, really, it would never have struck me to ask Dr. Rank. But I'm    115
certain that if I did—

MRS. LINDEN.  But of course you never would?

NORA.  Of course not. It's inconceivable that it should ever be necessary. But I'm quite sure that if I spoke to Doctor Rank—

MRS. LINDEN.  Behind your husband's back?
                                                                            120

NORA.  I must get out of the other thing; that's behind his back too. I must get out of that.

MRS. LINDEN. Yes, yes, I told you so yesterday; but—

NORA. (*Walking up and down.*) A man can manage these things much better
125    than a woman.

MRS. LINDEN. One's own husband, yes.

NORA. Nonsense. (*Stands still.*) When everything is paid, one gets back the
       paper?

MRS. LINDEN. Of course.

130 NORA. And can tear it into a hundred thousand pieces, and burn it, the nasty,
       filthy thing!

MRS. LINDEN. (*Looks at her fixedly, lays down her work, and rises slowly.*) Nora,
       you're hiding something from me.

NORA. Can you see that in my face?

135 MRS. LINDEN. Something has happened since yesterday morning. Nora,
       what is it?

NORA. (*Going toward her.*) Christina (*listens*)—Hush! There's Torvald coming
       home. Here, go into the nursery. Torvald cannot bear to see dressmaking.
       Let Anna help you.

140 MRS. LINDEN. (*Gathers some of the things together.*) Very well, but I shan't go
       away until you've told me all about it. (*She goes out to the left as Helmer
       enters from the hall.*)

NORA. (*Runs to meet him.*) Oh! How I've been longing for you to come,
       Torvald dear.

HELMER. Was the dressmaker here?

145 NORA. No, Christina. She is helping me with my costume. You'll see how
       nice I shall look.

HELMER. Yes, wasn't that a lucky thought of mine?

NORA. Splendid. But isn't it good of me, too, to have given in to you?

HELMER. (*Takes her under the chin.*) Good of you! To give in to your own
150    husband? Well, well, you little madcap, I know you don't mean it. But I
       won't disturb you. I daresay you want to try on your dress.

NORA. And you are going to work, I suppose?

HELMER. Yes. (*Shows her bundle of papers.*) Look here. (*Goes toward his room.*)
       I've just come from the bank.

155 NORA. Torvald.

HELMER. (*Stopping.*) Yes?

NORA. If your little squirrel were to beg you for something so prettily—

HELMER. Well?

NORA. Would you do it?

160 HELMER. I must know first what it is.

NORA. The squirrel would jump about and play all sorts of tricks if you
       would only be nice and kind.

HELMER. Come, then, out with it.

NORA. Your lark would twitter from morning till night—

HELMER. Oh, that she does in any case.    165

NORA. I'll be an elf and dance in the moonlight for you, Torvald.

HELMER. Nora—you can't mean what you were hinting at this morning?

NORA. (*Coming nearer.*) Yes, Torvald, I beg and implore you.

HELMER. Have you really the courage to begin that again?

NORA. Yes, yes, for my sake, you must let Krogstad keep his place at the bank.    170

HELMER. My dear Nora, it's his place I intend for Mrs. Linden.

NORA. Yes, that's so good of you. But instead of Krogstad, you could dismiss some other clerk.

HELMER. Why, this is incredible obstinacy! Because you thoughtlessly promised to put in a word for him, I am to—    175

NORA. It's not that, Torvald. It's for your own sake. This man writes for the most slanderous newspapers; you said so yourself. He can do you such a lot of harm. I'm terribly afraid of him.

HELMER. Oh, I understand; it's old recollections that are frightening you.

NORA. What do you mean?    180

HELMER. Of course you're thinking of your father.

NORA. Yes, of course. Only think of the shameful things wicked people used to write about father. I believe they'd have got him dismissed if you hadn't been sent to look into the thing and been kind to him and helped him.

HELMER. My dear Nora, between your father and me there is all the differ-    185
ence in the world. Your father was not altogether unimpeachable. I am; and I hope to remain so.

NORA. Oh, no one knows what wicked men can hit upon. We could live so happily now, in our cosy, quiet home, you and I and the children, Torvald! That's why I beg and implore you—    190

HELMER. And it's just by pleading his cause that you make it impossible for me to keep him. It's already known at the bank that I intend to dismiss Krogstad. If it were now reported that the new manager let himself be turned round his wife's little finger—

NORA. What then?    195

HELMER. Oh, nothing! So long as a wilful woman can have her way I am to make myself the laughingstock of everyone, and make people think I depend on all kinds of outside influence? Take my word for it, I should soon feel the consequences. And besides, there's one thing that makes Krogstad impossible for me to work with.    200

NORA. What thing?

HELMER. I could perhaps have overlooked his shady character in a pinch—

NORA. Yes, couldn't you, Torvald?

HELMER. And I hear he is good at his work. But the fact is, he was a college
205    chum of mine—there was one of those rash friendships between us that
one so often repents of later. I don't mind confessing it—he calls me by
my first name, and he insists on doing it even when others are present. He
delights in putting on airs of familiarity—Torvald here, Torvald there! I assure you it's most painful to me. He would make my position at the bank
210    perfectly unendurable.

NORA. Torvald, you're not serious?

HELMER. No? Why not?

NORA. That's such a petty reason.

HELMER. What! Petty! Do you consider me petty?

215    NORA. No, on the contrary, Torvald dear and that's just why—

HELMER. Never mind; you call my motives petty; then I must be petty too.
Petty! Very well. Now we'll put an end to this once for all. (*Goes to the door
into the hall and calls.*) Ellen!

NORA. What do you want?

220    HELMER. (*Searching among his papers.*) To settle the thing. (*Ellen enters.*)
There, take this letter, give it to a messenger. See that he takes it at once.
The address is on it. Here is the money.

ELLEN. Very well. (*Goes with the letter.*)

HELMER. (*Arranging papers.*) There, Madam Obstinacy!

225    NORA. (*Breathless.*) Torvald—what was in that letter?

HELMER. Krogstad's dismissal.

NORA. Call it back again, Torvald! There is still time. Oh, Torvald, get it back
again! For my sake, for your own, for the children's sake! Do you hear,
Torvald? Do it. You don't know what that letter may bring upon us all.

230    HELMER. Too late.

NORA. Yes, too late.

HELMER. My dear Nora, I forgive your anxiety, though it's anything but
flattering to me. Why should I be afraid of a lowlife scribbler's spite? But
I forgive you all the same, for it's a proof of your great love for me. (*Takes
235    her in his arms.*) That's how it should be, my own dear Nora. Let what
will happen—when the time comes, I shall have strength and courage
enough. You shall see, my shoulders are broad enough to bear the whole
burden.

NORA. (*Terror-struck.*) What do you mean by that?

240    HELMER. The whole burden, I say.

NORA. (*With decision.*) That you shall never, never do.

HELMER. Very well, then we'll share it, Nora, as man and wife. (*Petting her.*)
Are you satisfied now? Come, come, come, don't look like a scared dove. It
is all nothing—just fancy. Now you must play the tarantella through, and

practise the tambourine. I shall sit in my inner room and shut both doors,    245
so that I shall hear nothing. You can make as much noise as you please.
(*Turns round in doorway.*) And when Rank comes, just tell him where I'm
to be found. (*He nods to her, and goes with his papers into his room, closing
the door.*)

NORA. (*Bewildered with terror, stands as though rooted to the ground, and whispers.*) He would do it. Yes, he would do it. He would do it, in spite of all    250
the world. No, never that, never, never! Anything rather than that! Oh, for
some way of escape! What to do! (*Hall bell rings.*) Anything rather than
that—anything, anything! (*Nora draws her hands over her face, pulls herself
together, goes to the door and opens it. Rank stands outside hanging up his
overcoat. During the following, it grows dark.*)

NORA.  Good afternoon, Doctor Rank, I knew you by your ring. But you
mustn't go to Torvald now. I believe he's busy.    255

RANK.  And you?

NORA.  Oh, you know very well I've always time for you.

RANK.  Thank you. I shall avail myself of your kindness as long as I can!

NORA.  What do you mean? As long as you can?

RANK.  Yes. Does that frighten you?    260

NORA.  I think it's an odd expression. Do you expect anything to happen?

RANK.  Something I've long been prepared for, but I didn't think it would
come so soon.

NORA. (*Seizing his arm.*) What is it, Doctor Rank? You must tell me.

RANK. (*Sitting down by the stove.*) I am running downhill. There's no help    265
for it.

NORA. (*Draws a long breath of relief.*) It's *you*?

RANK.  Who else should it be? Why lie to oneself? I'm the most wretched
of all my patients, Mrs. Helmer. I have been auditing my life-account—
bankrupt! Before a month is over I shall lie rotting in the churchyard.    270

NORA.  Oh! What an ugly way to talk.

RANK.  The thing itself is so confoundedly ugly, you see. But the worst of it is,
so many other ugly things have to be gone through first. There is only one
last investigation to be made, and when that is over I shall know exactly
when the breakdown will begin. There's one thing I want to say to you:    275
Helmer's delicate nature shrinks with such disgust from all that is horrible;
I will not have him in my sickroom.

NORA.  But, Doctor Rank—

RANK.  I won't have him, I say—not on any account! I shall lock my door
against him. As soon as I have ascertained the worst, I shall send you my    280
visiting card with a black cross on it, and then you will know that the final
horror has begun.

NORA.  Why, you're perfectly unreasonable today. And I did so want you to be in a really good humour.

285 RANK.  With death staring me in the face? And to suffer thus for another's sin! Where's the justice of it? And in every family you can see some such inexorable retribution—

NORA.  (*Stopping her ears.*) Nonsense, nonsense; now cheer up.

RANK.  Well, after all, the whole thing's only worth laughing at. My poor in-
290    nocent spine must do penance for my father's wild oats.

NORA.  (*At table, left.*) I suppose he was too fond of asparagus and Strasbourg paté, wasn't he?

RANK.  Yes; and truffles.

NORA.  Yes, truffles, to be sure. And oysters,[1] I believe?

295 RANK.  Yes, oysters; oysters, of course.

NORA.  And then all the port and champagne. It's sad that all these good things should attack the spine.

RANK.  Especially when the luckless spine attacked never had the good of them.

300 NORA.  Yes, that's the worst of it.

RANK.  (*Looks at her searchingly.*) H'm—

NORA.  (*A moment later.*) Why did you smile?

RANK.  No; it was you that laughed.

NORA.  No; it was you that smiled, Doctor Rank.

305 RANK.  (*Standing up.*) You're more of a rogue than I thought.

NORA.  I'm in such a crazy mood today.

RANK.  So it seems.

NORA.  (*With her hands on his shoulders.*) Dear, dear Doctor Rank, death shall not take you away from Torvald and me.

310 RANK.  Oh, you'll easily get over the loss. The absent are soon forgotten.

NORA.  (*Looks at him anxiously.*) Do you think so?

RANK.  People make fresh ties, and then—

NORA.  Who make fresh ties?

RANK.  You and Helmer will, when I'm gone. You yourself are already on your
315    way to it, it seems to me. What was that Mrs. Linden doing here yesterday?

NORA.  Oh! You're surely not jealous of Christina?

RANK.  Yes, I am. She will be my successor in this house. When I'm gone, this woman will perhaps—

NORA.  Hush! Not so loud; she is in there.

320 RANK.  Today as well? You see!

---

1    *I suppose ... oysters* Asparagus, Strasbourg paté, truffles, and oysters are all foods commonly thought to be aphrodisiacs.

NORA. Only to put my costume in order—how unreasonable you are! (*Sits on sofa.*) Now do be good, Doctor Rank. Tomorrow you shall see how beautifully I dance; and then you may fancy that I am doing it all to please you—and of course Torvald as well. (*Takes various things out of box.*) Doctor Rank, sit here, and I'll show you something. 325

RANK. (*Sitting.*) What is it?

NORA. Look here. Look!

RANK. Silk stockings.

NORA. Flesh-coloured. Aren't they lovely? Oh, it's so dark here now, but tomorrow—No, no, no, you must only look at the feet. Oh, well, I suppose 330 you may look at the rest too.

RANK. H'm—

NORA. What are you looking so critical about? Do you think they won't fit me?

RANK. I can't possibly have any valid opinion on that point.

NORA. (*Looking at him a moment.*) For shame! (*Hits him lightly on the ear* 335 *with the stockings.*) Take that. (*Rolls them up again.*)

RANK. And what other wonders am I to see?

NORA. You shan't see any more, for you don't behave nicely. (*She hums a little and searches among the things.*)

RANK. (*After a short silence.*) When I sit here gossiping with you, I simply can't imagine what would have become of me if I had never entered this 340 house.

NORA. (*Smiling.*) Yes, I think you do feel at home with us.

RANK. (*More softly—looking straight before him.*) And now to have to leave it all—

NORA. Nonsense. You shan't leave us. 345

RANK. (*In the same tone.*) And not to be able to leave behind the slightest token of gratitude; scarcely even a passing regret—nothing but an empty place, that can be filled by the first comer.

NORA. And if I were to ask for—? No—

RANK. For what? 350

NORA. For a great proof of your friendship.

RANK. Yes? Yes?

NORA. No, I mean—for a very, very great service.

RANK. Would you really for once make me so happy?

NORA. Oh! You don't know what it is. 355

RANK. Then tell me.

NORA. No, I really can't; it's far, far too much—not only a service, but help and advice besides—

RANK. So much the better. I can't think what you can mean. But go on. Don't you trust me? 360

NORA. As I trust no one else. I know you are my best and truest friend. So I will tell you. Well then, Doctor Rank, you must help me to prevent something. You know how deeply, how wonderfully Torvald loves me; he would not hesitate a moment to give his very life for my sake.

365 RANK. (*Bending towards her.*) Nora, do you think he is the only one who—

NORA. (*With a slight start.*) Who—?

RANK. Who would gladly give his life for you?

NORA. (*Sadly.*) Oh!

RANK. I have sworn that you shall know it before I—go. I should never find a
370 better opportunity—Yes, Nora, now you know it; and now you know too that you can trust me as you can no one else.

NORA. (*Standing up, simply and calmly.*) Let me pass, please.

RANK. (*Makes way for her, but remains sitting.*) Nora—

NORA. (*In the doorway.*) Ellen, bring the lamp. (*Crosses to the stove.*) Oh, dear,
375 Doctor Rank, that was too bad of you.

RANK. (*Rising.*) That I have loved you as deeply as—anyone else? Was that too bad of me?

NORA. No, but that you should tell me so. It was so unnecessary—

RANK. What do you mean? Did you know—?

(*Ellen enters with the lamp; sets it on the table and goes out again.*)

380 RANK. Nora—Mrs. Helmer—I ask you, did you know?

NORA. Oh, how can I tell what I knew or didn't know. I really can't say— How could you be so clumsy, Doctor Rank? It was all so nice!

RANK. Well, at any rate, you know now that I am at your service, soul and body. And now, go on.

385 NORA. (*Looking at him.*) Go on—now?

RANK. I beg you to tell me what you want.

NORA. I can tell you nothing now.

RANK. Yes, yes! You mustn't punish me in that way. Let me do for you whatever a man can.

390 NORA. You can really do nothing for me now. Besides, I really want no help. You'll see it was only my fancy. Yes, it must be so. Of course! (*Sits in the rocking chair smiling at him.*) You're a nice person, Doctor Rank. Aren't you ashamed of yourself now that the lamp's on the table?

RANK. No, not exactly. But perhaps I ought to go—forever.

395 NORA. No, indeed you mustn't. Of course you must come and go as you've always done. You know very well that Torvald can't do without you.

RANK. Yes, but you?

NORA. Oh, you know I always like to have you here.

RANK. That's just what led me astray. You're a riddle to me. It has often

seemed to me as if you liked being with me almost as much as being with   400
Helmer.

NORA. Yes, don't you see? There are people one loves, and others one likes
to talk to.

RANK. Yes—there's something in that.

NORA. When I was a girl I naturally loved papa best. But it always delighted   405
me to steal into the servants' room. In the first place they never lectured
me, and in the second it was such fun to hear them talk.

RANK. Oh, I see; then it's their place I have taken?

NORA. (*Jumps up and hurries towards him.*) Oh, my dear Doctor Rank, I don't
mean that. But you understand, with Torvald it's the same as with papa—   410

(*Ellen enters from the hall.*)

ELLEN. Please, ma'am—(*Whispers to Nora, and gives her a card.*)

NORA. (*Glances at the card.*) Ah! (*Puts it in her pocket.*)

RANK. Anything wrong?

NORA. No, not in the least. It's only—it's my new costume—

RANK. Why, it's there.   415

NORA. Oh, that one, yes. But it's another that—I ordered it—Torvald
mustn't know—

RANK. Aha! So that's the great secret.

NORA. Yes, of course. Do just go to him; he's in the inner room; do keep him
as long as you can.   420

RANK. Make yourself easy; he shan't escape. (*Goes into Helmer's room.*)

NORA. (*To Ellen.*) Is he waiting in the kitchen?

ELLEN. Yes, he came up the back stair—

NORA. Didn't you tell him I was engaged?

ELLEN. Yes, but it was no use.   425

NORA. He won't go away?

ELLEN. No, ma'am, not until he has spoken to you.

NORA. Then let him come in, but quietly. And, Ellen—say nothing about it;
it's a surprise for my husband.

ELLEN. Oh, yes, ma'am, I understand—(*She goes out.*)   430

NORA. It's coming! It's coming after all. No, no, no, it can never be; it shall
not! (*She goes to Helmer's door and slips the bolt. Ellen opens the hall door for
Krogstad, and shuts it after him. He wears a travelling coat, high boots, and
a fur cap.*)

NORA. Speak quietly; my husband is at home.

KROGSTAD. All right. I don't care.

NORA. What do you want.   435

KROGSTAD. A little information.

NORA. Be quick, then. What is it?

KROGSTAD. You know I've got my dismissal.

NORA. I could not prevent it, Mr. Krogstad. I fought for you to the last, but
440   it was no good.

KROGSTAD. Does your husband care for you so little? He knows what I can
  bring upon you, and yet he dares—

NORA. How can you think I would tell him?

KROGSTAD. I knew very well you hadn't. It wasn't like my friend Torvald
445   Helmer to show so much courage—

NORA. Mr. Krogstad, be good enough to speak respectfully of my husband.

KROGSTAD. Certainly, with all due respect. But since you're so anxious to
  keep the matter secret, I suppose you're a little clearer than yesterday as to
  what you have done.

450 NORA. Clearer than you could ever make me.

KROGSTAD. Yes, such a bad lawyer as I—

NORA. What is it you want?

KROGSTAD. Only to see how you're getting on, Mrs. Helmer. I've been thinking about you all day. Even a mere moneylender, a newspaper hack, a—in
455   short, a creature like me—has a little bit of what people call "heart."

NORA. Then show it; think of my little children.

KROGSTAD. Did you and your husband think of mine? But enough of that.
  I only wanted to tell you that you needn't take this matter too seriously. I
  shall not prosecute you for the present.

460 NORA. No, surely not. I knew you would not.

KROGSTAD. The whole thing can be settled quite quietly. Nobody need know.
  It can remain among us three.

NORA. My husband must never know.

KROGSTAD. How can you prevent it? Can you pay off the debt?

465 NORA. No, not at once.

KROGSTAD. Or have you any means of raising the money in the next few
  days?

NORA. None that I will make use of.

KROGSTAD. And if you had it would be no good to you now. If you offered
470   me ever so much ready money, you should not get back your IOU.

NORA. Tell me what you want to do with it.

KROGSTAD. I only want to keep it, to have it in my possession. No outsider
  shall hear anything of it. So, if you've got any desperate scheme in your
  head—

475 NORA. What if I have?

KROGSTAD. If you should think of leaving your husband and children—

NORA. What if I do?

KROGSTAD. Or if you should think of—something worse—

NORA. How do you know that?

KROGSTAD. Put all that out of your head.  480

NORA. How did you know what I had in my mind?

KROGSTAD. Most of us think of *that* at first. I thought of it, too; but I had not the courage—

NORA. (*Voicelessly.*) Nor I.

KROGSTAD. (*Relieved.*) No, you don't, you haven't the courage either, have  485
you?

NORA. I haven't, I haven't.

KROGSTAD. Besides, it would be very silly—once the first storm is over—I have a letter in my pocket for your husband—

NORA. Telling him everything?  490

KROGSTAD. Sparing you as much as possible.

NORA. (*Quickly.*) He must never have that letter. Tear it up. I will get the money somehow.

KROGSTAD. Pardon me, Mrs. Helmer, but I believe I told you—

NORA. Oh, I'm not talking about the money I owe you. Tell me how much  495
you demand from my husband—I'll get it.

KROGSTAD. I demand no money from your husband.

NORA. What *do* you demand then?

KROGSTAD. I'll tell you. I want to regain my footing in the world. I want to rise, and your husband shall help me to do it. For the last eighteen months  500
my record has been spotless; I've been in bitter need all the time, but I was content to fight my way up, step by step. Now, I've been thrust down, and I won't be satisfied with merely being allowed to sneak back again. I want to rise, I tell you. I must get into the bank again, in a higher position than before. Your husband shall create a place for me—  505

NORA. He will never do that!

KROGSTAD. He will do it; I know him—he won't dare to refuse! And when I'm in, you'll soon see! I shall be the manager's right hand. It won't be Torvald Helmer, but Nils Krogstad, that manages the Joint Stock Bank.

NORA. That will never be.  510

KROGSTAD. Perhaps you'll—?

NORA. *Now* I have the courage for it.

KROGSTAD. Oh, you don't frighten me! A sensitive, petted creature like you—

NORA. You shall see, you shall see!

KROGSTAD. Under the ice, perhaps? Down in the cold, black water? And next  515
spring to come up again, ugly, hairless, unrecognizable—

NORA. You can't frighten me.

KROGSTAD.  Nor you me. People don't do that sort of thing, Mrs. Helmer. And, after all, what good would it be? I have your husband in my pocket all the same.

NORA.  Afterward? When I am no longer—

KROGSTAD.  You forget, your reputation remains in my hands! (*Nora stands speechless and looks at him.*) Well, now you are prepared. Do nothing foolish. As soon as Helmer has received my letter I shall expect to hear from him. And remember that it is your husband himself who has forced me back again onto such paths. That I will never forgive him. Goodbye, Mrs. Helmer. (*Goes through hall. Nora hurries to the door, opens it a little, and listens.*)

NORA.  He's going. He is not putting the letter into the box. No, no, it would be impossible. (*Opens the door farther and farther.*) What's that? He's standing still, not going downstairs. Is he changing his mind? Is he—? (*A letter falls into the box. Krogstad's footsteps are heard gradually receding down the stair. Nora utters a suppressed shriek; pause.*) In the letterbox! (*Slips shrinkingly up to the hall door.*) There it lies—Torvald, Torvald—now we are lost!

(*Mrs. Linden enters from the left with the costume.*)

MRS. LINDEN.  There, I think it's all right now. Shall we just try it on?

NORA.  (*Hoarsely and softly.*) Christina, come here.

MRS. LINDEN.  (*Throws dress on sofa.*) What's the matter? You look quite aghast.

NORA.  Come here. Do you see that letter? There, see—through the glass of the letterbox.

MRS. LINDEN.  Yes, yes, I see it.

NORA.  That letter is from Krogstad—

MRS. LINDEN.  Nora—it was Krogstad who lent you the money!

NORA.  Yes, and now Torvald will know everything.

MRS. LINDEN.  Believe me, Nora, it's the best thing for both of you.

NORA.  You don't know all yet. I have forged a name—

MRS. LINDEN.  Good heavens!

NORA.  Now, listen to me, Christina; you shall bear me witness.

MRS. LINDEN.  What do you mean? Witness? What am I to—?

NORA.  If I should go out of my mind—it might easily happen—

MRS. LINDEN.  Nora!

NORA.  Or if anything else should happen to me—so that I couldn't be here myself—!

MRS. LINDEN.  Now, Nora, you're quite beside yourself!

NORA.  In case anyone wanted to take it all upon himself—the whole blame— you understand—

Mrs. Linden.  Yes, but how can you think—

Nora.  You shall bear witness that it's not true, Christina. I'm not out of my mind at all; I know quite well what I'm saying; and I tell you nobody else knew anything about it; I did the whole thing, I myself. Don't forget that.

Mrs. Linden.  I won't forget. But I don't understand what you mean—    560

Nora.  Oh, how should you? It's the miracle coming to pass.

Mrs. Linden.  The miracle?

Nora.  Yes, the miracle. But it's so terrible, Christina; it mustn't happen for anything in the world.

Mrs. Linden.  I will go straight to Krogstad and talk to him.    565

Nora.  Don't; he will do you some harm.

Mrs. Linden.  Once he would have done anything for me.

Nora.  He?

Mrs. Linden.  Where does he live?

Nora.  Oh, how should I know—? Yes; (*feels in her pocket*) here's his card. But    570
the letter, the letter!

Helmer.  (*Knocking outside.*) Nora!

Nora.  (*Shrieks in terror.*) What is it? What do you want?

Helmer.  Don't be frightened, we're not coming in; you've bolted the door. Are you trying on your dress?    575

Nora.  Yes, yes, I'm trying it on. It suits me so well, Torvald.

Mrs. Linden.  (*Who has read the card.*) Then he lives close by here?

Nora.  Yes, but it's no use now. The letter is actually in the box.

Mrs. Linden.  And your husband has the key?

Nora.  Always.    580

Mrs. Linden.  Krogstad must demand his letter back, unread. He must make some excuse—

Nora.  But this is the very time when Torvald generally—

Mrs. Linden.  Prevent him. Keep him occupied. I'll come back as quickly as I can. (*She goes out quickly through the hall door.*)    585

Nora.  (*Opens Helmer's door and peeps in.*) Torvald!

Helmer.  Well, now may one come back into one's own room? Come, Rank, we'll have a look—(*In the doorway.*) But how's this?

Nora.  What, Torvald dear?

Helmer.  Rank led me to expect a grand dressing-up.    590

Rank.  (*In the doorway.*) So I understood. I suppose I was mistaken.

Nora.  No, no one shall see me in my glory till tomorrow evening.

Helmer.  Why, Nora dear, you look so tired. Have you been practising too hard?

Nora.  No, I haven't practised at all yet.    595

Helmer.  But you'll have to—

NORA. Yes, it's absolutely necessary. But, Torvald, I can't get on without your help. I've forgotten everything.

HELMER. Oh, we shall soon freshen it up again.

600 NORA. Yes, do help me, Torvald. You must promise me—Oh, I'm so nervous about it. Before so many people—this evening you must give yourself up entirely to me. You mustn't do a stroke of work! Now promise, Torvald dear!

HELMER. I promise. All this evening I will be your slave. Little helpless thing!

605 But, by the bye, I must first—(*Going to hall door.*)

NORA. What do you want there?

HELMER. Only to see if there are any letters.

NORA. No, no, don't do that, Torvald.

HELMER. Why not?

610 NORA. Torvald, I beg you not to. There are none there.

HELMER. Let me just see. (*Is going. Nora, at the piano, plays the first bars of the tarantella.*)

HELMER. (*At the door, stops.*) Aha!

NORA. I can't dance tomorrow if I don't rehearse with you first.

HELMER. (*Going to her.*) Are you really so nervous, dear Nora?

615 NORA. Yes, dreadfully! Let me rehearse at once. We have time before dinner. Oh! Do sit down and accompany me, Torvald dear; direct me, as you usually do.

HELMER. With all the pleasure in life, if you wish it. (*Sits at piano. Nora snatches the tambourine out of the box, and hurriedly drapes herself in a long multi-coloured shawl; then, with a bound, stands in the middle of the floor.*)

NORA. Now play for me! Now I'll dance! (*Helmer plays and Nora dances. Rank stands at the piano behind Helmer and looks on.*)

620 HELMER. (*Playing.*) Slower! Slower!

NORA. Can't do it slower.

HELMER. Not so violently, Nora.

NORA. I must! I must!

HELMER. (*Stops.*) Nora—that'll never do.

625 NORA. (*Laughs and swings her tambourine.*) Didn't I tell you so?

RANK. Let me accompany her.

HELMER. (*Rising.*) Yes, do—then I can direct her better. (*Rank sits down to the piano and plays. Nora dances more and more wildly. Helmer stands by the stove and addresses frequent corrections to her. She seems not to hear. Her hair breaks loose, and falls over her shoulders. She does not notice it, but goes on dancing. Mrs. Linden enters and stands spellbound in the doorway.*)

MRS. LINDEN. Ah!

NORA. (*Dancing.*) We're having such fun here, Christina!

HELMER. Why, Nora dear, you're dancing as if it were a matter of life and 630
death.

NORA. So it is.

HELMER. Rank, stop! This is absolute madness. Stop, I say! (*Rank stops playing, and Nora comes to a sudden standstill. Helmer going toward her.*) I couldn't have believed it. You've positively forgotten all I taught you. 635

NORA. (*Throws tambourine away.*) You see for yourself.

HELMER. You really do need teaching.

NORA. Yes, you see how much I need it. You must practise with me up to the last moment. Will you promise me, Torvald?

HELMER. Certainly, certainly. 640

NORA. Neither today nor tomorrow must you think of anything but me. You mustn't open a single letter—mustn't look at the letterbox!

HELMER. Ah, you're still afraid of that man—

NORA. Oh yes, yes, I am.

HELMER. Nora, I can see it in your face—there's a letter from him in the box. 645

NORA. I don't know, I believe so. But you're not to read anything now; nothing ugly must come between us until it's all over.

RANK. (*Softly to Helmer.*) You mustn't contradict her.

HELMER. (*Putting his arm around her.*) The child shall have her own way. But tomorrow night, when the dance is over— 650

NORA. Then you will be free.

(*Ellen appears in doorway, right.*)

ELLEN. Dinner is ready, ma'am.

NORA. We'll have some champagne, Ellen!

ELLEN. Yes, ma'am. (*Goes out.*)

HELMER. Dear me! Quite a feast. 655

NORA. Yes, and we'll keep it up till morning. (*Calling out.*) And macaroons, Ellen—plenty—just this once.

HELMER. (*Seizing her hands.*) Come, come, don't let us have this wild excitement! Be my own little lark again.

NORA. Oh, yes I will. But now go into the dining room; and you too, Doctor 660
Rank. Christina, you must help me to do up my hair.

RANK. (*Softly, as they go.*) There is nothing going on? Nothing—I mean—

HELMER. Oh no, nothing of the kind. It's merely this babyish anxiety I was telling you about. (*They go out to the right.*)

NORA. Well? 665

MRS. LINDEN. He's gone out of town.

NORA. I saw it in your face.

MRS. LINDEN. He comes back tomorrow evening. I left a note for him.

NORA. You shouldn't have done that. Things must take their course. After all,
670    there's something glorious in waiting for the miracle.

MRS. LINDEN. What are you waiting for?

NORA. Oh, you can't understand. Go to them in the dining room; I'll come
in a moment. (*Mrs. Linden goes into the dining room; Nora stands for a moment as though collecting her thoughts; then looks at her watch.*) Five. Seven
675    hours till midnight. Then twenty-four hours till the next midnight. Then
the tarantella will be over. Twenty-four and seven? Thirty-one hours to
live.

(*Helmer appears at the door, right.*)

HELMER. What's become of my little lark?

NORA. (*Runs to him with open arms.*) Here she is!

## ACT 3

*The same room. The table with the chairs around it is in the middle. A
lamp lit on the table. The door to the hall stands open. Dance music is heard
from the floor above. Mrs. Linden sits by the table, and turns the pages of
a book absently. She tries to read, but seems unable to fix her attention; she
frequently listens and looks anxiously toward the hall door.*

MRS. LINDEN. (*Looks at her watch.*) Still not here; and the time's nearly up. If
only he hasn't—(*Listens again.*) Ah, there he is—(*She goes into the hall and
opens the outer door; soft footsteps are heard on the stairs; she whispers:*) Come
in; there's no one here.

5 KROGSTAD. (*In the doorway.*) I found a note from you at my house. What
does it mean?

MRS. LINDEN. I must speak with you.

KROGSTAD. Indeed? And in this house?

MRS. LINDEN. I could not see you at my rooms. They have no separate en-
10    trance. Come in; we are quite alone. The servants are asleep and the Helmers are at the ball upstairs.

KROGSTAD. (*Coming into room.*) Ah! So the Helmers are dancing this evening? Really?

MRS. LINDEN. Yes. Why not?

15 KROGSTAD. Quite right. Why not?

MRS. LINDEN. And now let us talk a little.

KROGSTAD. Have we anything to say to each other?

MRS. LINDEN. A great deal.

KROGSTAD. I should not have thought so.

20 MRS. LINDEN. Because you have never really understood me.

KROGSTAD.  What was there to understand? The most natural thing in the world—a heartless woman throws a man over when a better match offers itself.

MRS. LINDEN.  Do you really think me so heartless? Do you think I broke with you lightly?

KROGSTAD.  Did you not?

MRS. LINDEN.  Do you really think so?

KROGSTAD.  If not, why did you write me that letter?

MRS. LINDEN.  Was it not best? Since I had to break with you, was it not right that I should try to put an end to your love for me?

KROGSTAD.  (*Pressing his hands together.*) So that was it? And all this—for the sake of money!

MRS. LINDEN.  You ought not to forget that I had a helpless mother and two little brothers. We could not wait for you, Nils, as your prospects then stood.

KROGSTAD.  Did that give you the right to discard me for another?

MRS. LINDEN.  I don't know. I've often asked myself whether I did right.

KROGSTAD.  (*More softly.*) When I had lost you the very ground seemed to sink from under my feet. Look at me now. I am a shipwrecked man clinging to a wreck.

MRS. LINDEN.  Rescue may be at hand.

KROGSTAD.  It was at hand, but then you stood in the way.

MRS. LINDEN.  Without my knowledge, Nils. I did not know till today that it was you I was to replace at the bank.

KROGSTAD.  Well, I take your word for it. But now you do know, do you mean to give way?

MRS. LINDEN.  No, for that would not help you.

KROGSTAD.  Oh, help, help! I should do it whether it helped or not.

MRS. LINDEN.  I have learnt prudence. Life and bitter necessity have schooled me.

KROGSTAD.  And life has taught me not to trust fine speeches.

MRS. LINDEN.  Then life has taught you a very sensible thing. But deeds you will trust?

KROGSTAD.  What do you mean?

MRS. LINDEN.  You said you were a shipwrecked man, clinging to a wreck.

KROGSTAD.  I have good reason to say so.

MRS. LINDEN.  I am a shipwrecked woman clinging to a wreck. I have no one to care for.

KROGSTAD.  You made your own choice.

MRS. LINDEN.  I had no choice.

KROGSTAD.  Well, what then?

MRS. LINDEN. Nils, what if we two shipwrecked people could join hands?

KROGSTAD. What!

MRS. LINDEN. Suppose we lashed the wrecks together?

65 KROGSTAD. Christina!

MRS. LINDEN. What do you think brought me to town?

KROGSTAD. Had you any thought of me?

MRS. LINDEN. I must have work, or I can't live. All my life, as long as I can remember, I have worked; work has been my one great joy. Now I stand

70 quite alone in the world, so terribly aimless and forsaken. There is no happiness in working for oneself. Nils, give me somebody and something to work for.

KROGSTAD. No, no, that can never be. It's simply a woman's romantic notion of self-sacrifice.

75 MRS. LINDEN. Have you ever found me romantic?

KROGSTAD. Would you really—? Tell me, do you know my past?

MRS. LINDEN. Yes.

KROGSTAD. And do you know what people say of me?

MRS. LINDEN. Did you not say just now that with me you would have been

80 another man?

KROGSTAD. I am sure of it.

MRS. LINDEN. Is it too late?

KROGSTAD. Christina, do you know what you are doing? Yes, you do; I see it in your face. Have you the courage?

85 MRS. LINDEN. I need someone to tend, and your children need a mother. You need me, and I—I need you. Nils, I believe in your better self. With you I fear nothing.

KROGSTAD. (*Seizing her hands.*) Thank you—thank you, Christina. Now I shall make others see me as you do. Ah, I forgot—

90 MRS. LINDEN. (*Listening.*) Hush! The tarantella! Go, go!

KROGSTAD. Why? What is it?

MRS. LINDEN. Don't you hear the dancing overhead? As soon as that is over they will be here.

KROGSTAD. Oh yes, I'll go. But it's too late now. Of course you don't know

95 the step I have taken against the Helmers?

MRS. LINDEN. Yes, Nils, I do know.

KROGSTAD. And yet you have the courage to—

MRS. LINDEN. I know what lengths despair can drive a man to.

KROGSTAD. Oh, if I could only undo it!

100 MRS. LINDEN. You can. Your letter is still in the box.

KROGSTAD. Are you sure?

MRS. LINDEN. Yes, but—

KROGSTAD. (*Looking to her searchingly.*) Ah, now I understand. You want to save your friend at any price. Say it outright—is that your idea?

MRS. LINDEN. Nils, a woman who has once sold herself for the sake of others    105
does not do so again.

KROGSTAD. I will demand my letter back again.

MRS. LINDEN. No, no.

KROGSTAD. Yes, of course. I'll wait till Helmer comes; I'll tell him to give it back to me—that it's only about my dismissal—that I don't want it read.    110

MRS. LINDEN. No, Nils, you must not recall the letter.

KROGSTAD. But tell me, wasn't that just why you got me to come here?

MRS. LINDEN. Yes, in my first terror. But a day has passed since then, and in that day I have seen incredible things in this house. Helmer must know everything; there must be an end to this unhappy secret. These two must    115
come to a full understanding. They can't possibly go on with all these shifts and concealments.

KROGSTAD. Very well, if you want to risk it. But one thing I can do, and at once—

MRS. LINDEN. (*Listening.*) Make haste! Go, go! The dance is over; we are not    120
safe another moment.

KROGSTAD. I'll wait for you in the street.

MRS. LINDEN. Yes, do; you must see me home.

KROGSTAD. I never was so happy in all my life! (*Krogstad goes, by the outer door. The door between the room and the hall remains open.*)

MRS. LINDEN. (*Setting furniture straight and getting her outdoor things to-*    125
*gether.*) What a change! What a change! To have someone to work for; a home to make happy. I shall have to set to work in earnest. I wish they would come. (*Listens.*) Ah, here they are! I must get my things on. (*Takes bonnet and cloak. Helmer's and Nora's voices are heard outside; a key is turned in the lock, and Helmer drags Nora almost by force into the hall. She wears the Italian costume with a large black shawl over it. He is in evening dress and wears a black domino.[1]*)

NORA. (*Still struggling with him in the doorway.*) No, no, no; I won't go in! I want to go upstairs again; I don't want to leave so early!    130

HELMER. But, my dearest girl—

NORA. Oh, please, please, Torvald, only one hour more.

HELMER. Not one minute more, Nora dear; you know what we agreed! Come, come in; you are catching cold here. (*He leads her gently into the room in spite of her resistance.*)

MRS. LINDEN. Good evening.    135

---

1    *domino* Hooded cloak worn with a mask during masquerades.

NORA. Christina!

HELMER. What, Mrs. Linden, you here so late!

MRS. LINDEN. Yes, pardon me! I did so want to see Nora in her costume!

NORA. Have you been sitting here waiting for me?

140 MRS. LINDEN. Yes; unfortunately I came too late. You had already gone up-stairs, and I couldn't go away without seeing you.

HELMER. (*Taking Nora's shawl off.*) Well then, just look at her! I think she's worth looking at. Isn't she lovely, Mrs. Linden?

MRS. LINDEN. Yes, I must say—

145 HELMER. Isn't she exquisite? Everyone said so. But she is dreadfully obstinate, dear little creature. What's to be done with her? Just think, I almost had to force her away.

NORA. Oh, Torvald, you'll be sorry someday you didn't let me stay, if only for one half hour.

150 HELMER. There! You hear her, Mrs. Linden? She dances her tarantella with wild applause, and well she deserved it, I must say—though there was, perhaps, a little too much nature in her rendering of the idea—more than was, strictly speaking, artistic. But never mind—she was a great success, and that's the main thing. Ought I to let her stay after that—to weaken the

155 impression? Not in the least. I took my sweet little Capri girl—my capricious little Capri girl, I might say—under my arm; a rapid turn round the room, a curtsey to all sides, and—as they say in novels—the lovely apparition vanished! An exit should always be effective, Mrs. Linden, but I can't get Nora to see it. By Jove, it's warm here. (*Throws his domino on a chair*

160 *and opens the door to his room.*) What! No light here? Oh, of course. Excuse me—(*Goes in and lights candles.*)

NORA. (*Whispers breathlessly.*) Well?

MRS. LINDEN. (*Softly.*) I have spoken to him.

NORA. And—?

165 MRS. LINDEN. Nora—you must tell your husband everything—

NORA. (*Almost voiceless.*) I knew it!

MRS. LINDEN. You have nothing to fear from Krogstad, but you must speak out.

NORA. I shall not speak!

170 MRS. LINDEN. Then the letter will.

NORA. Thank you, Christina. Now I know what I have to do. Hush!

HELMER. (*Coming back.*) Well, Mrs. Linden, have you admired her?

MRS. LINDEN. Yes, and now I'll say goodnight.

HELMER. What, already? Does this knitting belong to you?

175 MRS. LINDEN. (*Takes it.*) Yes, thanks; I was nearly forgetting it.

HELMER. Then you do knit?

MRS. LINDEN.  Yes.

HELMER.  Do you know, you ought to embroider instead?

MRS. LINDEN.  Indeed! Why?

HELMER.  Because it's so much prettier. Look now! You hold the embroidery 180
in the left hand so, and then work the needle with the right hand, in a
long, easy curve, don't you?

MRS. LINDEN.  Yes, I suppose so.

HELMER.  But knitting is always ugly. Look now, your arms close to your
sides, and the needles going up and down—there's something Chinese 185
about it—They really gave us splendid champagne tonight.

MRS. LINDEN.  Well, goodnight, Nora, and don't be obstinate any more.

HELMER.  Well said, Mrs. Linden!

MRS. LINDEN.  Goodnight, Mr. Helmer.

HELMER.  (*Going with her to the door.*) Goodnight, goodnight; I hope you'll 190
get safely home. I should be glad to—but really you haven't far to go.
Goodnight, goodnight! (*She goes; Helmer shuts the door after her and comes
down again.*) At last we've got rid of her: she's an awful bore.

NORA.  Aren't you very tired, Torvald?

HELMER.  No, not in the least. 195

NORA.  Nor sleepy?

HELMER.  Not a bit. I feel particularly lively. But you? You do look tired and
sleepy.

NORA.  Yes, very tired. I shall soon sleep now.

HELMER.  There, you see. I was right after all not to let you stay longer. 200

NORA.  Oh, everything you do is right.

HELMER.  (*Kissing her forehead.*) Now my lark is speaking like a reasonable
being. Did you notice how jolly Rank was this evening?

NORA.  Was he? I had no chance to speak to him.

HELMER.  Nor I, much; but, I haven't seen him in such good spirits for a long 205
time. (*Looks at Nora a little, then comes nearer to her.*) It's splendid to be
back in our own home, to be quite alone together! Oh, you enchanting
creature!

NORA.  Don't look at me that way, Torvald.

HELMER.  I am not to look at my dearest treasure? At the loveliness that is 210
mine, mine only, wholly and entirely mine?

NORA.  (*Goes to the other side of the table.*) You mustn't say these things to me
this evening.

HELMER.  (*Following.*) I see you have the tarantella still in your blood—and
that makes you all the more enticing. Listen! the other people are going 215
now. (*More softly.*) Nora—soon the whole house will be still.

NORA.  I hope so.

HELMER. Yes, don't you, Nora darling? When we're among strangers do you
know why I speak so little to you, and keep so far away, and only steal a
220    glance at you now and then—do you know why I do it? Because I am fancying that we love each other in secret, that I am secretly betrothed to you,
and that no one dreams there is anything between us.

NORA. Yes, yes, yes. I know all your thoughts are with me.

HELMER. And then, when we have to go, and I put the shawl about your
225    smooth, soft shoulders, and this glorious neck of yours, I imagine you are
my bride, that our wedding is just over, that I am bringing you for the first
time to my home, and that I am alone with you for the first time, quite
alone with you, in your quivering loveliness! All this evening I was longing
for you, and you only. When I watched you swaying and whirling in the
230    tarantella—my blood boiled—I could endure it no longer, and that's why
I made you come home with me so early.

NORA. Go now, Torvald. Go away from me. I won't have all this.

HELMER. What do you mean? Ah! I see you're teasing me! "Won't! Won't!"
Am I not your husband? (*A knock at the outer door.*)

235    NORA. (*Starts.*) Did you hear?

HELMER. (*Going toward the hall.*) Who's there?

RANK. (*Outside.*) It's I; may I come in for a moment?

HELMER. (*In a low tone, annoyed.*) Oh! What can he want? (*Aloud.*) Wait a
moment. (*Opens door.*) Come, it's nice of you to give us a look in.

240    RANK. I thought I heard your voice, and that put it into my head. (*Looks
round.*) Ah! This dear old place! How cosy you two are here!

HELMER. You seemed to find it pleasant enough upstairs, too.

RANK. Exceedingly. Why not? Why shouldn't one get all one can out of the
world? All one can for as long as one can. The wine was splendid—

245    HELMER. Especially the champagne.

RANK. Did you notice it? It's incredible the quantity I managed to get down.

NORA. Torvald drank plenty of champagne too.

RANK. Did he?

NORA. Yes, and it always puts him in such spirits.

250    RANK. Well, why shouldn't one have a jolly evening after a well-spent day?

HELMER. Well-spent! Well, I haven't much to boast of.

RANK. (*Slapping him on the shoulder.*) But I have, don't you see?

NORA. I suppose you have been engaged in a scientific investigation, Doctor
Rank?

255    RANK. Quite right.

HELMER. Bless me! Little Nora talking about scientific investigations!

NORA. Am I to congratulate you on the result?

RANK. By all means.

NORA. It was good then?

RANK. The best possible, both for doctor and patient—certainty.    260

NORA. (*Quickly and searchingly.*) Certainty?

RANK. Absolute certainty. Wasn't I right to enjoy myself after it?

NORA. Yes, quite right, Doctor Rank.

HELMER. And so say I, provided you don't have to pay for it tomorrow.

RANK. Well, in this life nothing's to be had for nothing.    265

NORA. Doctor Rank, aren't you very fond of masquerades?

RANK. Yes, when there are plenty of comical disguises.

NORA. Tell me, what shall we two be at our next masquerade?

HELMER. Little insatiable! Thinking of your next already!

RANK. We two? I'll tell you. You must go as a good fairy.    270

HELMER. Oh, but what costume would indicate that?

RANK. She has simply to wear her everyday dress.

HELMER. Splendid! But don't you know what you yourself will be?

RANK. Yes, my dear friend, I am perfectly clear upon that point.

HELMER. Well?    275

RANK. At the next masquerade I shall be invisible.

HELMER. What a comical idea!

RANK. There's a big black hat—haven't you heard of the invisible hat? It comes down all over you, and then no one can see you.

HELMER. (*With a suppressed smile.*) No, you're right there.    280

RANK. But I'm quite forgetting what I came for. Helmer, give me a cigar, one of the dark Havanas.

HELMER. With the greatest pleasure. (*Hands case.*)

RANK. (*Takes one and cuts the end off.*) Thanks.

NORA. (*Striking a wax match.*) Let me give you a light.    285

RANK. A thousand thanks. (*She holds match. He lights his cigar at it.*) And now, goodbye.

HELMER. Goodbye, goodbye, my dear fellow.

NORA. Sleep well, Doctor Rank.

RANK. Thanks for the wish.    290

NORA. Wish me the same.

RANK. You? Very well, since you ask me—Sleep well. And thanks for the light. (*He nods to them both and goes out.*)

HELMER. (*In an undertone.*) He's been drinking a good deal.

NORA. (*Absently.*) I daresay. (*Helmer takes his bunch of keys from his pocket and*    295 *goes into the hall.*) Torvald, what are you doing there?

HELMER. I must empty the letterbox, it's quite full; there will be no room for the newspapers tomorrow morning.

NORA. Are you going to work tonight?

300 HELMER. Not very likely! Why, what's this? Someone has been at the lock.

NORA. The lock—?

HELMER. I'm sure of it. What does it mean? I can't think that the servants—? Here's a broken hairpin. Nora, it's one of yours.

NORA. (*Quickly.*) It must have been the children.

305 HELMER. Then you must break them of such tricks. H'm, h'm! There! At last I've got it open. (*Takes contents out and calls into the kitchen.*) Ellen! Ellen, just put the hall door lamp out. (*He returns with letters in his hand, and shuts the inner door.*) Just see how they've accumulated. (*Turning them over.*) Why, what's this?

310 NORA. (*At the window.*) The letter! Oh, no, no, Torvald!

HELMER. Two visiting cards—from Rank.

NORA. From Doctor Rank?

HELMER. (*Looking at them.*) Doctor Rank. They were on the top. He must just have put them in.

315 NORA. Is there anything on them?

HELMER. There's a black cross over the name. Look at it. What a horrid idea! It looks just as if he were announcing his own death.

NORA. So he is.

HELMER. What! Do you know anything? Has he told you anything?

320 NORA. Yes. These cards mean that he has taken his last leave of us. He intends to shut himself up and die.

HELMER. Poor fellow! Of course I knew we couldn't hope to keep him long. But so soon—and to go and creep into his lair like a wounded animal—

NORA. What must be, must be, and the fewer words the better. Don't you

325 think so, Torvald?

HELMER. (*Walking up and down.*) He had so grown into our lives, I can't realize that he's gone. He and his sufferings and his loneliness formed a sort of cloudy background to the sunshine of our happiness. Well, perhaps it's best so—at any rate for him. (*Stands still.*) And perhaps for us, too, Nora.

330 Now we two are thrown entirely upon each other. (*Puts his arm round her.*) My darling wife! I feel as if I could never hold you close enough. Do you know, Nora, I often wish some danger might threaten you, that I might risk body and soul, and everything, everything, for your dear sake.

NORA. (*Tears herself from him and says firmly.*) Now you shall read your let-

335 ters, Torvald.

HELMER. No, no, not tonight. I want to be with you, sweet wife.

NORA. With the thought of your dying friend?

HELMER. You are right. This has shaken us both. Unloveliness has come between us—thoughts of death and decay. We must seek to cast them off.

340 Till then we will remain apart.

NORA. (*Her arms round his neck.*) Torvald! Goodnight, goodnight.

HELMER. (*Kissing her forehead.*) Goodnight, my little songbird. Sleep well, Nora. Now I'll go and read my letters. (*He goes into his room and shuts the door.*)

NORA. (*With wild eyes, gropes about her, seizes Helmer's domino, throws it round her, and whispers quickly, hoarsely, and brokenly.*) Never to see him    345 again. Never, never, never. (*Throws her shawl over her head.*) Never to see the children again. Never, never. Oh that black, icy water! Oh that bottomless—If it were only over! Now he has it; he's reading it. Oh, no, no, no, not yet. Torvald, goodbye. Goodbye, my little ones! (*She is rushing out by the hall; at the same moment Helmer tears his door open, and stands with an open letter in his hand.*)

HELMER. Nora!    350

NORA. (*Shrieking.*) Ah—!

HELMER. What is this? Do you know what is in this letter?

NORA. Yes, I know. Let me go! Let me pass!

HELMER. (*Holds her back.*) Where do you want to go?

NORA. (*Tries to get free.*) You shan't save me, Torvald.    355

HELMER. (*Falling back.*) True! Is it true what he writes? No, no, it cannot be.

NORA. It is true. I have loved you beyond all else in the world.

HELMER. Pshaw—no silly evasions.

NORA. (*A step nearer him.*) Torvald—

HELMER. Wretched woman! What have you done?    360

NORA. Let me go—you shall not save me. You shall not take my guilt upon yourself.

HELMER. I don't want any melodramatic games. (*Locks the door.*) Here you shall stay and give an account of yourself. Do you understand what you have done? Answer. Do you understand it?    365

NORA. (*Looks at him fixedly, and says with a stiffening expression.*) Yes, now I begin fully to understand it.

HELMER. (*Walking up and down.*) Oh, what an awful awakening! During all these eight years—she who was my pride and my joy—a hypocrite, a liar—worse, worse—a criminal. Oh! The hideousness of it! Ugh! Ugh!    370 (*Nora is silent, and continues to look fixedly at him.*) I ought to have foreseen something of the kind. All your father's dishonesty—be silent! I say all your father's dishonesty you have inherited—no religion, no morality, no sense of duty. How I am punished for shielding him! I did it for your sake, and you reward me like this.    375

NORA. Yes—like this!

HELMER. You have destroyed my whole happiness. You have ruined my future. Oh! It's frightful to think of! I am in the power of a scoundrel; he

can do whatever he pleases with me, demand whatever he chooses, and I
380   must submit. And all this disaster is brought upon me by an unprincipled
woman!

NORA.   When I am gone, you will be free.

HELMER.   Oh, no fine phrases. Your father, too, was always ready with them.
What good would it do to me, if you were "gone," as you say? No good in
385   the world! He can publish the story all the same; I might even be suspected
of collusion. People will think I was at the bottom of it all and egged you
on. And for all this I have you to thank—you whom I have done nothing
but pet and spoil during our whole married life. Do you understand now
what you have done to me?

390   NORA.   (*With cold calmness.*) Yes.

HELMER.   It's incredible. I can't grasp it. But we must come to an understanding. Take that shawl off. Take it off, I say. I must try to pacify him
in one way or another—the secret must be kept, cost what it may. As
for ourselves, we must live as we have always done, but of course only in
395   the eyes of the world. Of course you will continue to live here. But the
children cannot be left in your care. I dare not trust them to you—Oh,
to have to say this to one I have loved so tenderly—whom I still—but
that must be a thing of the past. Henceforward there can be no question
of happiness, but merely of saving the ruins, the shreds, the show of it (*A
400   ring; Helmer starts.*) What's that? So late! Can it be the worst? Can he—?
Hide yourself, Nora; say you are ill. (*Nora stands motionless. Helmer goes to
the door and opens it.*)

ELLEN.   (*Half dressed, in the hall.*) Here is a letter for you, ma'am.

HELMER.   Give it to me. (*Seizes the letter and shuts the door.*) Yes, from him.
You shall not have it. I shall read it.

405   NORA.   Read it!

HELMER.   (*By the lamp.*) I have hardly the courage to. We may be lost, both
you and I. Ah! I must know. (*Tears the letter hastily open; reads a few lines,
looks at an enclosure; a cry of joy.*) Nora! (*Nora looks interrogatively at him.*)
Nora! Oh! I must read it again. Yes, yes, it is so. I am saved! Nora, I am
410   saved!

NORA.   And I?

HELMER.   You too, of course; we are both saved, both of us. Look here, he
sends you back your promissory note. He writes that he regrets and apolo-
gizes—that a happy turn in his life—Oh, what matter what he writes. We
415   are saved, Nora! No one can harm you. Oh! Nora, Nora—No, first to get
rid of this hateful thing. I'll just see—(*Glances at the IOU*) No, I won't
look at it; the whole thing shall be nothing but a dream to me. (*Tears
the IOU and both letters in pieces. Throws them into the fire and watches*

*them burn.*) There, it's gone. He wrote that ever since Christmas Eve—Oh, Nora, they must have been three awful days for you!    420

NORA.  I have fought a hard fight for the last three days.

HELMER.  And in your agony you saw no other outlet but—no; we won't think of that horror. We will only rejoice and repeat—it's over, all over. Don't you hear, Nora? You don't seem able to grasp it. Yes, it's over. What is this set look on your face? Oh, my poor Nora, I understand; you can't be-    425 lieve that I have forgiven you. But I have, Nora; I swear it. I have forgiven everything. I know that what you did was all for love of me.

NORA.  That's true.

HELMER.  You loved me as a wife should love her husband. It was only the means you misjudged. But do you think I love you the less for your help-    430 lessness? No, no. Only lean on me. I will counsel and guide you. I should be no true man if this very womanly helplessness did not make you doubly dear in my eyes. You mustn't think of the hard things I said in my first moment of terror, when the world seemed to be tumbling about my ears. I have forgiven you, Nora—I swear I have forgiven you.    435

NORA.  I thank you for your forgiveness. (*Goes out, right.*)

HELMER.  No, stay. (*Looks in.*) What are you going to do?

NORA.  (*Inside.*) To take off my doll's dress.

HELMER.  (*In doorway.*) Yes, do, dear. Try to calm down, and recover your balance, my scared little songbird. You may rest secure. I have broad wings    440 to shield you. (*Walking up and down near the door.*) Oh, how lovely—how cosy our home is, Nora. Here you are safe; here I can shelter you like a hunted dove, whom I have saved from the claws of the hawk. I shall soon bring your poor beating heart to rest; believe me, Nora, I will. Tomorrow all this will seem quite different—everything will be as before. I shall not    445 need to tell you again that I forgive you; you will feel for yourself that it is true. How could you think I could find it in my heart to drive you away, or even so much as to reproach you? Oh, you don't know a true man's heart, Nora. There is something indescribably sweet and soothing to a man in having forgiven his wife—honestly forgiven her from the bottom of his    450 heart. She becomes his property in a double sense. She is as though born again; she has become, so to speak, at once his wife and his child. That is what you shall henceforth be to me, my bewildered, helpless darling. Don't be troubled about anything, Nora; only open your heart to me, and I will be both will and conscience to you. (*Nora enters, crossing to table in*    455 *everyday dress.*) Why, what's this? Not gone to bed? You have changed your dress.

NORA.  Yes, Torvald; now I have changed my dress.

HELMER.  But why now so late?

460 NORA. I shall not sleep tonight.

HELMER. But, Nora dear—

NORA. (*Looking at her watch.*) It's not so late yet. Sit down, Torvald; you and I have much to say to each other. (*She sits on one side of the table.*)

HELMER. Nora, what does this mean? Your cold, set face—

465 NORA. Sit down. It will take some time; I have much to talk over with you. (*Helmer sits at the other side of the table.*)

HELMER. You alarm me; I don't understand you.

NORA. No, that's just it. You don't understand me; and I have never understood you—till tonight. No, don't interrupt. Only listen to what I say. We
470 must come to a final settlement, Torvald!

HELMER. How do you mean?

NORA. (*After a short silence.*) Does not one thing strike you as we sit here?

HELMER. What should strike me?

NORA. We have been married eight years. Does it not strike you that this is
475 the first time we two, you and I, man and wife, have talked together seriously?

HELMER. Seriously! Well, what do you call seriously?

NORA. During eight whole years, and more—ever since the day we first met—we have never exchanged one serious word about serious things.

480 HELMER. Was I always to trouble you with the cares you could not help me to bear?

NORA. I am not talking of cares. I say that we have never yet set ourselves seriously to get to the bottom of anything.

HELMER. Why, my dear Nora, what have you to do with serious things?

485 NORA. There we have it! You have never understood me. I have had great injustice done me, Torvald; first by my father and then by you.

HELMER. What! By your father and me? By us who have loved you more than all the world?

NORA. (*Shaking her head.*) You have never loved me. You only thought it
490 amusing to be in love with me.

HELMER. Why, Nora, what a thing to say!

NORA. Yes, it is so, Torvald. While I was at home with father, he used to tell me all his opinions, and I held the same opinions. If I had others I concealed them, because he would not have liked it. He used to call me his
495 doll child, and play with me as I played with my dolls. Then I came to live in your house—

HELMER. What an expression to use about our marriage!

NORA. (*Undisturbed.*) I mean I passed from father's hands into yours. You settled everything according to your taste; and I got the same tastes as you;
500 or I pretended to—I don't know which—both ways, perhaps. When I look

back on it now, I seem to have been living here like a beggar, from hand to mouth. I lived by performing tricks for you, Torvald. But you would have it so. You and father have done me a great wrong. It's your fault that my life has been wasted.

HELMER. Why, Nora, how unreasonable and ungrateful you are. Haven't you been happy here? 505

NORA. No, never; I thought I was, but I never was.

HELMER. Not—not happy?

NORA. No; only merry. And you have always been so kind to me. But our house has been nothing but a playroom. Here I have been your doll-wife, 510 just as at home I used to be papa's doll-child. And the children in their turn have been my dolls. I thought it fun when you played with me, just as the children did when I played with them. That has been our marriage, Torvald.

HELMER. There is some truth in what you say, exaggerated and overstrained 515 though it is. But henceforth it shall be different. Playtime is over; now comes the time for education.

NORA. Whose education? Mine, or the children's?

HELMER. Both, my dear Nora.

NORA. Oh, Torvald, you are not the man to teach me to be a fit wife for you. 520

HELMER. And you say that?

NORA. And I—am I fit to educate the children?

HELMER. Nora!

NORA. Did you not say yourself a few minutes ago you dared not trust them to me? 525

HELMER. In the excitement of the moment! Why should you dwell upon that?

NORA. No—you are perfectly right. That problem is beyond me. There's another to be solved first—I must try to educate myself. You are not the man to help me in that. I must set about it alone. And that is why I am 530 leaving you!

HELMER. (*Jumping up.*) What—do you mean to say—?

NORA. I must stand quite alone to know myself and my surroundings; so I cannot stay with you.

HELMER. Nora! Nora! 535

NORA. I am going at once. Christina will take me in for tonight—

HELMER. You are mad. I shall not allow it. I forbid it.

NORA. It's no use your forbidding me anything now. I shall take with me what belongs to me. From you I will accept nothing, either now or afterward. 540

HELMER. What madness!

NORA. Tomorrow I shall go home.

HELMER. Home!

NORA. I mean to what was my home. It will be easier for me to find some
545   opening there.

HELMER. Oh, in your blind inexperience—

NORA. I must try to gain experience, Torvald.

HELMER. To forsake your home, your husband, and your children! You don't
consider what the world will say.

550   NORA. I can pay no heed to that! I only know that I must do it.

HELMER. It's exasperating! Can you forsake your holiest duties in this way?

NORA. What do you call my holiest duties?

HELMER. Do you ask me that? Your duties to your husband and your children.

555   NORA. I have other duties equally sacred.

HELMER. Impossible! What duties do you mean?

NORA. My duties toward myself.

HELMER. Before all else you are a wife and a mother.

NORA. That I no longer believe. I believe that before all else I am a human
560   being, just as much as you are—or at least that I will try to become one.
I know that most people agree with you, Torvald, and that they say so in
books. But henceforth I can't be satisfied with what most people say, and
what is in books. I must think things out for myself, and try to get clear
about them.

565   HELMER. Are you not clear about your place in your own home? Have you
not an infallible guide in questions like these? Have you not religion?

NORA. Oh, Torvald, I don't know properly what religion is.

HELMER. What do you mean?

NORA. I know nothing but what our clergyman told me when I was con-
570   firmed. He explained that religion was this and that. When I get away from
here and stand alone I will look into that matter too. I will see whether
what he taught me is true, or, at any rate, whether it is true for me.

HELMER. Oh, this is unheard of! But if religion cannot keep you right, let me
appeal to your conscience—I suppose you have some moral feeling? Or,
575   answer me, perhaps you have none?

NORA. Well, Torvald, it's not easy to say. I really don't know—I am all at sea
about these things. I only know that I think quite differently from you
about them. I hear, too, that the laws are different from what I thought;
but I can't believe that they are right. It appears that a woman has no right
580   to spare her dying father, or to save her husband's life. I don't believe that.

HELMER. You talk like a child. You don't understand the society in which
you live.

NORA.  No, I don't. But now I shall try to. I must make up my mind which is right—society or I.

HELMER.  Nora, you are ill, you are feverish. I almost think you are out of 585 your senses.

NORA.  I have never felt so much clearness and certainty as tonight.

HELMER.  You are clear and certain enough to forsake husband and children?

NORA.  Yes, I am.

HELMER.  Then there is only one explanation possible.    590

NORA.  What is that?

HELMER.  You no longer love me.

NORA.  No, that is just it.

HELMER.  Nora! Can you say so!

NORA.  Oh, I'm so sorry, Torvald, for you've always been so kind to me. But 595 I can't help it. I do not love you any longer.

HELMER.  (*Keeping his composure with difficulty.*) Are you clear and certain on this point too?

NORA.  Yes, quite. That is why I won't stay here any longer.

HELMER.  And can you also make clear to me, how I have forfeited your love? 600

NORA.  Yes, I can. It was this evening, when the miracle did not happen. For then I saw you were not the man I had taken you for.

HELMER.  Explain yourself more clearly; I don't understand

NORA.  I have waited so patiently all these eight years, for, of course, I saw clearly enough that miracles do not happen every day. When this crushing 605 blow threatened me, I said to myself, confidently, "Now comes the miracle!" When Krogstad's letter lay in the box, it never for a moment occurred to me that you would think of submitting to that man's conditions. I was convinced that you would say to him, "Make it known to all the world," and that then—    610

HELMER.  Well? When I had given my own wife's name up to disgrace and shame?

NORA.  Then I firmly believed that you would come forward, take everything upon yourself, and say, "I am the guilty one."

HELMER.  Nora!    615

NORA.  You mean I would never have accepted such a sacrifice? No, certainly not. But what would my assertions have been worth in opposition to yours? That was the miracle that I hoped for and dreaded. And it was to hinder that that I wanted to die.

HELMER.  I would gladly work for you day and night, Nora—bear sorrow 620 and want for your sake—but no man sacrifices his honour, even for one he loves.

NORA.  Millions of women have done so.

HELMER.  Oh, you think and talk like a silly child.

625   NORA.  Very likely. But you neither think nor talk like the man I can share my
life with. When your terror was over—not for me, but for yourself—when
there was nothing more to fear—then it was to you as though nothing had
happened. I was your lark again, your doll—whom you would take twice
as much care of in future, because she was so weak and fragile. (*Stands up.*)

630   Torvald, in that moment it burst upon me that I had been living here these
eight years with a strange man, and had borne him three children—Oh, I
can't bear to think of it—I could tear myself to pieces!

HELMER.  (*Sadly.*) I see it, I see it; an abyss has opened between us—But,
Nora, can it never be filled up?

635   NORA.  As I now am, I am no wife for you.

HELMER.  I have strength to become another man.

NORA.  Perhaps—when your doll is taken away from you.

HELMER.  To part—to part from you! No, Nora, no; I can't grasp the thought.

NORA.  (*Going into room, right.*) The more reason for the thing to happen.
(*She comes back with a cloak, hat, and small travelling bag, which she puts
on a chair.*)

640   HELMER.  Nora, Nora, not now! Wait till tomorrow.

NORA.  (*Putting on cloak.*) I can't spend the night in a strange man's house.

HELMER.  But can't we live here as brother and sister?

NORA.  (*Fastening her hat.*) You know very well that would not last long.
Goodbye, Torvald. No, I won't go to the children. I know they are in better

645   hands than mine. As I now am, I can be nothing to them.

HELMER.  But some time, Nora—some time—

NORA.  How can I tell? I have no idea what will become of me.

HELMER.  But you are my wife, now and always!

NORA.  Listen, Torvald—when a wife leaves her husband's house, as I am do-

650   ing, I have heard that in the eyes of the law he is free from all duties toward
her. At any rate I release you from all duties. You must not feel yourself
bound any more than I shall. There must be perfect freedom on both sides.
There, there is your ring back. Give me mine.

HELMER.  That too?

655   NORA.  That too.

HELMER.  Here it is.

NORA.  Very well. Now it is all over. Here are the keys. The servants know
about everything in the house, better than I do. Tomorrow, when I have
started, Christina will come to pack up my things. I will have them sent

660   after me.

HELMER.  All over! All over! Nora, will you never think of me again?

NORA.  Oh, I shall often think of you, and the children—and this house.

HELMER.  May I write to you, Nora?

NORA.  No, never. You must not.

HELMER.  But I must send you—                                               665

NORA.  Nothing, nothing.

HELMER.  I must help you if you need it.

NORA.  No, I say. I take nothing from strangers.

HELMER.  Nora, can I never be more than a stranger to you?

NORA.  (*Taking her travelling bag.*) Oh, Torvald, then the miracle of miracles  670
would have to happen.

HELMER.  What is the miracle of miracles?

NORA.  Both of us would have to change so that—Oh, Torvald, I no longer
believe in miracles.

HELMER.  But I will believe. We must so change that—?                        675

NORA.  That our lives together could be a marriage. Goodbye. (*She goes out.*)

HELMER.  (*Sinks in a chair by the door with his face in his hands.*) Nora! Nora!
(*He looks around and stands up.*) Empty. She's gone! (*A hope inspires him.*)
Ah! The miracle of miracles—?! (*From below is heard the reverberation of a
heavy door closing.*)

—1879[1]

---

1    *1879* Shortly after the play's first performance, Ibsen wrote an alternative ending to *A
Doll's House* in an attempt to prevent unauthorized, less controversial adaptations from
appearing in Germany. In the alternative ending, after Nora says goodbye, Helmer takes
her by the arm and leads her to the room where their children are sleeping. Unable to
leave her children, Nora is overcome and falls to the floor. Ibsen made the change in an
attempt to maintain control of his play, but publicly stated his dislike of the altered ending, and said that whoever performed it did so against his wishes.

*Betty Hennings in the role of Nora, 1880.* A Doll's House *was first performed at the Royal Danish Theatre in Copenhagen, Denmark; Hennings originated the role in this production.*

# Samuel Beckett

## 1906–1989

Samuel Beckett was a prolific writer of poetry, fiction, and criticism, but he remains best known for plays such as *Waiting for Godot* (1952) and *End-game* (1957). Fragmented, filled with absences and silences, and sparing of plot, characterization, and setting, Beckett's drama attempts to dispense with elements previously thought to be essential to dramatic productions. His plays were defined by Martin Esslin as exemplars of the "Theatre of the Absurd"—they present the absurdity and futility of the human condition as a given. In such plays, Esslin suggests, "everything that happens seems to be beyond rational motivation, happening at random or through the demented caprice of an unaccountable idiot fate."

Beckett was born in Ireland and attended Trinity College in Dublin. Upon attaining his Bachelor of Arts he left to teach in France, where he became close friends with the writer James Joyce; this friendship strongly influenced Beckett's early work. He spent much of World War II as an active member of the French Resistance. In the four years following the war he was extraordinarily productive, composing four novellas, two plays, and four novels. During this period, which he referred to as "the siege in the room," he decided to write entirely in French, translating his work back into English once it was completed. This process enhanced the distinctive sparseness of his writing style.

Disregarding convention, Beckett experimented with new ideas, new media, and even new technology—such as the reel-to-reel tape recorder, which soon after its invention played a central role in his groundbreaking short play *Krapp's Last Tape* (1958). The importance of his work was acknowledged in 1969, when Beckett was awarded the Nobel Prize for Literature. He continued to direct many of his plays and to assist in their production for television, retiring only a few years before his death in 1989.

## Krapp's Last Tape

*A late evening in the future.*

*Krapp's den.*

*Front centre a small table, the two drawers of which open towards audience.*

*Sitting at the table, facing front, i.e. across from the drawers, a wearish old man: Krapp.*

*Rusty black narrow trousers too short for him. Rusty black sleeveless waistcoat, four capacious pockets. Heavy silver watch and chain. Grimy white shirt open at neck, no collar. Surprising pair of dirty white boots, size ten at least, very narrow and pointed.*

*White face. Purple nose. Disordered grey hair. Unshaven.*

*Very near-sighted (but unspectacled). Hard of hearing.*

*Cracked voice. Distinctive intonation.*

*Laborious walk.*

*On the table a tape-recorder with microphone and a number of cardboard boxes containing reels of recorded tapes.*

*Table and immediately adjacent area in strong white light. Rest of stage in darkness.*

*Krapp remains a moment motionless, heaves a great sigh, looks at his watch, fumbles in his pockets, takes out an envelope, puts it back, fumbles, takes out a small bunch of keys, raises it to his eyes, chooses a key, gets up and moves to front of table. He stoops, unlocks first drawer, peers into it, feels about inside it, takes out a reel of tape, peers at it, puts it back, locks drawer, unlocks second drawer, peers into it, feels about inside it, takes out a large banana, peers at it, locks drawer, puts keys back in his pocket. He turns, advances to edge of stage, halts, strokes banana, peels it, drops skin at his feet, puts end of banana in his mouth and remains motionless, staring vacuously before him. Finally he bites off the end, turns aside and begins pacing to and fro at edge of stage, in the light, i.e. not more than four or five paces either way, meditatively eating banana. He treads on skin, slips, nearly falls, recovers himself, stoops and peers at skin and finally pushes it, still stooping, with his foot over the edge of stage into pit. He resumes his pacing, finishes banana, returns to table, sits down, remains a moment motionless, heaves a great sigh, takes keys from his pockets, raises them to his eyes, chooses key, gets up and moves to front of table, unlocks second drawer, takes out a second large banana, peers at it, locks drawer, puts back keys in his pocket, turns, advances to edge of stage, halts, strokes banana, peels it, tosses skin into pit, puts end of banana in his mouth and remains motionless, staring vacuously before him. Finally he has an idea, puts banana in his waistcoat pocket, the end emerging, and goes with all the speed he can muster backstage into darkness. Ten seconds. Loud pop of cork. Fifteen seconds. He comes back into light carrying an old ledger and sits down at table. He lays ledger on table, wipes his mouth, wipes his hands on the front of his waistcoat, brings them smartly together and rubs them.*

KRAPP. (*Briskly.*) Ah! (*He bends over ledger, turns the pages, finds the entry he wants, reads.*) Box ... three ... spool ... five. (*He raises his head and stares front. With relish.*) Spool! (*Pause.*) Spoooool! (*Happy smile. Pause. He bends over table, starts peering and poking at the boxes.*) Box ... thrree ... thrree ...

four … two … (*with surprise*) nine! good God! … seven … ah! the little
rascal! (*He takes up box, peers at it.*) Box thrree. (*He lays it on table, opens it
and peers at spools inside.*) Spool … (*he peers at ledger*) … five … (*he peers
at spools*) … five … five … ah! the little scoundrel! (*He takes out a spool,
peers at it.*) Spool five. (*He lays it on table, closes box three, puts it back with
the others, takes up the spool.*) Box thrree, spool five. (*He bends over the machine, looks up. With relish.*) Spooool! (*Happy smile. He bends, loads spool on
machine, rubs his hands.*) Ah! (*He peers at ledger, reads entry at foot of page.*)
Mother at rest at last … Hm … The black ball … (*He raises his head, stares
blankly front. Puzzled.*) Black ball? … (*He peers again at ledger, reads.*) The
dark nurse … (*He raises his head, broods, peers again at ledger, reads.*) Slight
improvement in bowel condition … Hm … Memorable … what? (*He
peers closer.*) Equinox, memorable equinox. (*He raises his head, stares blankly
front. Puzzled.*) Memorable equinox? … (*Pause. He shrugs his shoulders,
peers again at ledger, reads.*) Farewell to—(*he turns the page*)—love.

(*He raises his head, broods, bends over machine, switches on and assumes
listening posture, i.e., leaning forward, elbows on table, hand cupping ear
towards machine, face front.*)

TAPE. (*Strong voice, rather pompous, clearly Krapp's at a much earlier time.*)
Thirty-nine today, sound as a—(*Settling himself more comfortably he knocks
one of the boxes off the table, curses, switches off, sweeps boxes and ledger
violently to the ground, winds tape back to beginning, switches on, resumes
posture.*) Thirty-nine today, sound as a bell, apart from my old weakness,
and intellectually I have now every reason to suspect at the … (*hesitates*)
… crest of the wave—or thereabouts. Celebrated the awful occasion, as
in recent years, quietly at the Winehouse. Not a soul. Sat before the fire
with closed eyes, separating the grain from the husks. Jotted down a few
notes, on the back of an envelope. Good to be back in my den, in my
old rags. Have just eaten I regret to say three bananas and only with difficulty refrained from a fourth. Fatal things for a man with my condition.
(*Vehemently.*) Cut 'em out! (*Pause.*) The new light above my table is a great
improvement. With all this darkness round me I feel less alone. (*Pause.*) In
a way. (*Pause.*) I love to get up and move about in it, then back here to …
(*hesitates*) … me. (*Pause.*) Krapp.

(*Pause.*)

The grain, now what I wonder do I mean by that, I mean … (*hesitates*) …
I suppose I mean those things worth having when all the dust has—when
all *my* dust has settled. I close my eyes and try and imagine them.

(*Pause. Krapp closes his eyes briefly.*)

40 Extraordinary silence this evening, I strain my ears and do not hear a
sound. Old Miss McGlome always sings at this hour. But not tonight.
Songs of her girlhood, she says. Hard to think of her as a girl. Wonderful
woman though. Connaught,[1] I fancy. (*Pause.*) Shall I sing when I am her
age, if I ever am? No. (*Pause.*) Did I sing as a boy? No. (*Pause.*) Did I ever
sing? No.

(*Pause.*)

45 Just been listening to an old year, passages at random. I did not check in
the book, but it must be at least ten or twelve years ago. At that time I
think I was still living on and off with Bianca in Kedar Street. Well out
of that, Jesus yes! Hopeless business. (*Pause.*) Not much about her, apart
from a tribute to her eyes. Very warm. I suddenly saw them again. (*Pause.*)
50 Incomparable! (*Pause.*) Ah well ... (*Pause.*) These old P.M.s are gruesome,
but I often find them—(*Krapp switches off, broods, switches on.*)—a help
before embarking on a new ... (*hesitates*) ... retrospect. Hard to believe
I was ever that young whelp. The voice! Jesus! And the aspirations! (*Brief
laugh in which Krapp joins.*) And the resolutions! (*Brief laugh in which
55 Krapp joins.*) To drink less, in particular. (*Brief laugh of Krapp alone.*) Sta-
tistics. Seventeen hundred hours, out of the preceding eight thousand odd,
consumed on licensed premises alone. More than 20%, say 40% of his
waking life. (*Pause.*) Plans for a less ... (*hesitates*) ... engrossing sexual
life. Last illness of his father. Flagging pursuit of happiness. Unattainable
60 laxation.[2] Sneers at what he calls his youth and thanks to God that it's over.
(*Pause.*) False ring there. (*Pause.*) Shadows of the opus ... magnum. Closing with a—(*brief laugh*)—yelp to Providence. (*Prolonged laugh in which
Krapp joins.*) What remains of all that misery? A girl in a shabby green coat,
on a railway-station platform? No?

(*Pause.*)

65 When I look—

(*Krapp switches off, broods, looks at his watch, gets up, goes backstage into
darkness. Ten seconds. Pop of cork. Ten seconds. Second cork. Ten seconds.
Third cork. Ten seconds. Brief burst of quavering song.*)

KRAPP. (*Sings.*)   Now the day is over,
Night is drawing nigh-igh,
Shadows—[3]

---

1   *Connaught* Western province of Ireland.
2   *laxation* Relaxed state; also defecation.
3   *Now ... Shadows* From an old hymn, words by Sabine Baring-Gould (1865).

(*Fit of coughing. He comes back into light, sits down, wipes his mouth, switches on, resumes his listening posture.*)

TAPE.   —back on the year that is gone, with what I hope is perhaps a glint of   70
the old eye to come, there is of course the house on the canal where mother
lay a-dying, in the late autumn, after her long viduity (*Krapp gives a start*),
and the—(*Krapp switches off, winds back tape a little, bends his ear closer to
machine, switches on*)—a-dying, after her long viduity, and the—

(*Krapp switches off, raises his head, stares blankly before him. His lips
move in the syllables of "viduity." No sound. He gets up, goes backstage into
darkness, comes back with an enormous dictionary, lays it on table, sits
down and looks up the word.*)

KRAPP.   (*Reading from dictionary.*) State—or condition of being—or remain-   75
ing—a widow—or widower. (*Looks up. Puzzled.*) Being—or remaining?
… (*Pause. He peers again at dictionary. Reading.*) "Deep weeds of viduity"
… Also of an animal, especially a bird … the vidua or weaver-bird … Black
plumage of male … (*He looks up. With relish.*) The vidua-bird!

(*Pause. He closes dictionary, switches on, resumes listening posture.*)

TAPE.   —bench by the weir from where I could see her window. There I sat,   80
in the biting wind, wishing she were gone. (*Pause.*) Hardly a soul, just
a few regulars, nursemaids, infants, old men, dogs. I got to know them
quite well—oh by appearance of course I mean! One dark young beauty
I recollect particularly, all white and starch, incomparable bosom, with a
big black hooded perambulator, most funereal thing. Whenever I looked   85
in her direction she had her eyes on me. And yet when I was bold enough
to speak to her—not having been introduced—she threatened to call a po-
liceman. As if I had designs on her virtue! (*Laugh. Pause.*) The face she had!
The eyes! Like … (*hesitates*) … chrysolite![1] (*Pause.*) Ah well … (*Pause.*) I
was there when—(*Krapp switches off, broods, switches on again*)—the blind   90
went down, one of those dirty brown roller affairs, throwing a ball for a
little white dog, as chance would have it. I happened to look up and there
it was. All over and done with, at last. I sat on for a few moments with
the ball in my hand and the dog yelping and pawing at me. (*Pause.*) Moments. Her moments, my moments. (*Pause.*) The dog's moments. (*Pause.*)   95
In the end I held it out to him and he took it in his mouth, gently, gently.
A small, old, black, hard, solid rubber ball. (*Pause.*) I shall feel it, in my
hand, until my dying day. (*Pause.*) I might have kept it. (*Pause.*) But I gave
it to the dog.

---

1   *chrysolite* Green gem.

(*Pause.*)

100 Ah well ...

(*Pause.*)

Spiritually a year of profound gloom and indigence until that memorable
night in March, at the end of the jetty, in the howling wind, never to be
forgotten, when suddenly I saw the whole thing. The vision, at last. This
I fancy is what I have chiefly to record this evening, against the day when
105 my work will be done and perhaps no place left in my memory, warm or
cold, for the miracle that ... (*hesitates*) ... for the fire that set it alight.
What I suddenly saw then was this, that the belief I had been going on
all my life, namely—(*Krapp switches off impatiently, winds tape forward,
switches on again*)—great granite rocks the foam flying up in the light of
110 the lighthouse and the wind-gauge spinning like a propeller, clear to me
at last that the dark I have always struggled to keep under is in reality my
most—(*Krapp curses, switches off, winds tape forward, switches on again*)—
unshatterable association until my dissolution of storm and night with
the light of the understanding and the fire—(*Krapp curses louder, switches
115 off, winds tape forward, switches on again*)—my face in her breasts and my
hand on her. We lay there without moving. But under us all moved, and
moved us, gently, up and down, and from side to side.

(*Pause.*)

Past midnight. Never knew such silence. The earth might be uninhabited.

(*Pause.*)

Here I end—

(*Krapp switches off, winds tape back, switches on again.*)

120 —upper lake, with the punt,[1] bathed off the bank, then pushed out into
the stream and drifted. She lay stretched out on the floorboards with her
hands under her head and her eyes closed. Sun blazing down, bit of a
breeze, water nice and lively. I noticed a scratch on her thigh and asked her
how she came by it. Picking gooseberries, she said. I said again I thought
125 it was hopeless and no good going on, and she agreed, without opening
her eyes. (*Pause.*) I asked her to look at me and after a few moments—
(*Pause.*)—after a few moments she did, but the eyes just slits, because of
the glare. I bent over her to get them in the shadow and they opened.

---

1   *punt* Shallow, flat-bottomed boat.

(*Pause. Low.*) Let me in. (*Pause.*) We drifted in among the flags[1] and stuck. The way they went down, sighing, before the stem! (*Pause.*) I lay down 130 across her with my face in her breasts and my hand on her. We lay there without moving. But under us all moved, and moved us, gently, up and down, and from side to side.

(*Pause.*)

Past midnight. Never knew—

(*Krapp switches off, broods. Finally he fumbles in his pockets, encounters the banana, takes it out, peers at it, puts it back, fumbles, brings out the envelope, fumbles, puts back envelope, looks at his watch, gets up and goes backstage into darkness. Ten seconds. Sound of bottle against glass, then brief siphon. Ten seconds. Bottle against glass alone. Ten seconds. He comes back a little unsteadily into light, goes to front of table, takes out keys, raises them to his eyes, chooses key, unlocks first drawer, peers into it, feels about inside, takes out reel, peers at it, locks drawer, puts keys back in his pocket, goes and sits down, takes reel off machine, lays it on dictionary, loads virgin reel on machine, takes envelope from his pocket, consults back of it, lays it on table, switches on, clears his throat and begins to record.*)

KRAPP.  Just been listening to that stupid bastard I took myself for thirty 135 years ago, hard to believe I was ever as bad as that. Thank God that's all done with anyway. (*Pause.*) The eyes she had! (*Broods, realizes he is recording silence, switches off, broods. Finally.*) Everything there, everything, all the—(*Realizes this is not being recorded, switches on.*) Everything there, everything on this old muckball, all the light and dark and famine and feast- 140 ing of ... (*hesitates*) ... the ages! (*In a shout.*) Yes! (*Pause.*) Let that go! Jesus! Take his mind off his homework! Jesus! (*Pause. Weary.*) Ah well, maybe he was right. (*Pause.*) Maybe he was right. (*Broods. Realizes. Switches off. Consults envelope.*) Pah! (*Crumples it and throws it away. Broods. Switches on.*) Nothing to say, not a squeak. What's a year now? The sour cud and 145 the iron stool. (*Pause.*) Revelled in the word spool. (*With relish.*) Spooool! Happiest moment of the past half million. (*Pause.*) Seventeen copies sold, of which eleven at trade price to free circulating libraries beyond the seas. Getting known. (*Pause.*) One pound six and something, eight I have little doubt. (*Pause.*) Crawled out once or twice, before the summer was cold. 150 Sat shivering in the park, drowned in dreams and burning to be gone. Not a soul. (*Pause.*) Last fancies. (*Vehemently.*) Keep 'em under! (*Pause.*) Scalded

---

1    *flags* Irises.

the eyes out of me reading *Effie*[1] again, a page a day, with tears again. Effie ... (*Pause.*) Could have been happy with her, up there on the Baltic,
155  and the pines, and the dunes. (*Pause.*) Could I? (*Pause.*) And she? (*Pause.*)
Pah! (*Pause.*) Fanny came in a couple of times. Bony old ghost of a whore.
Couldn't do much, but I suppose better than a kick in the crutch. The last
time wasn't so bad. How do you manage it, she said, at your age? I told her
I'd been saving up for her all my life. (*Pause.*) Went to Vespers[2] once, like
160  when I was in short trousers. (*Pause. Sings.*)

> Now the day is over,
> Night is drawing nigh-igh,
> Shadows—(*coughing, then almost inaudible*)—of the evening
> Steal across the sky.

165  (*Gasping.*) Went to sleep and fell off the pew. (*Pause.*) Sometimes wondered in the night if a last effort mightn't—(*Pause.*) Ah finish your booze
now and get to your bed. Go on with this drivel in the morning. Or leave
it at that. (*Pause.*) Leave it at that. (*Pause.*) Lie propped up in the dark—
and wander. Be again in the dingle[3] on a Christmas Eve, gathering holly,
170  the red-berried. (*Pause.*) Be again on Croghan[4] on a Sunday morning, in
the haze, with the bitch, stop and listen to the bells. (*Pause.*) And so on.
(*Pause.*) Be again, be again. (*Pause.*) All that old misery. (*Pause.*) Once
wasn't enough for you. (*Pause.*) Lie down across her.

(*Long pause. He suddenly bends over machine, switches off, wrenches off
tape, throws it away, puts on the other, winds it forward to the passage he
wants, switches on, listens staring front.*)

TAPE.  —gooseberries, she said. I said again I thought it was hopeless and no
175  good going on, and she agreed, without opening her eyes. (*Pause.*) I asked
her to look at me and after a few moments—(*Pause.*)—after a few moments she did, but the eyes just slits, because of the glare. I bent over her to
get them in the shadow and they opened. (*Pause. Low.*) Let me in. (*Pause.*)
We drifted in among the flags and stuck. The way they went down, sigh-
180  ing, before the stem! (*Pause.*) I lay down across her with my face in her
breasts and my hand on her. We lay there without moving. But under us
all moved, and moved us, gently, up and down, and from side to side.

(*Pause. Krapp's lips move. No sound.*)

---

1  *Effie* The novel *Effi Briest* (1895), a sentimental work by Theodor Fontane about a
   failed love affair.
2  *Vespers* Evening prayer service.
3  *dingle* Valley.
4  *Croghan* Croghan Hill in County Wicklow, Ireland.

Past midnight. Never knew such silence. The earth might be uninhabited.

(*Pause.*)

Here I end this reel. Box—(*Pause.*)—three, spool—(*Pause.*)—five. (*Pause.*)
Perhaps my best years are gone. When there was a chance of happiness. But    185
I wouldn't want them back. Not with the fire in me now. No, I wouldn't
want them back.

(*Krapp motionless staring before him. The tape runs on in silence.*)

**CURTAIN**

—1958

# Tennessee Williams
## 1911–1983

Tennessee Williams helped define American postwar theatre, bringing 18 plays to Broadway and winning the Pulitzer Prize twice—for *A Streetcar Named Desire* (1947) and *Cat on a Hot Tin Roof* (1955). He is best known for memorable characters who, in his words, are often "trapped by circumstance"; for dialogue that combines realism with poetic sensitivity; and for his explicit treatment of sexuality and violence. In response to audiences that were shocked by the content of his plays, he said, "I don't think that anything that occurs in life should be omitted from art, though the artist should present it in a fashion that is artistic and not ugly."

Williams was born Thomas Lanier Williams III in Columbus, Mississippi; his father was a travelling salesman and his mother was the daughter of an Episcopal minister. He had a troubled family life and would find inspiration for his plays in his parents' unstable marriage, as well as in the mental illness of his beloved sister Rose, who was lobotomized in 1943.

Williams had already produced some plays as a student at the University of Iowa when *The Glass Menagerie* (1944), a veiled autobiographical drama, propelled him out of obscurity into sudden fame. His reputation grew with *A Streetcar Named Desire*, the 1951 film version of which won four Academy Awards. Williams's next major success, *Cat on a Hot Tin Roof*, was also transformed into a successful film (1958).

After his partner Frank Merlo died of cancer in 1963, Williams's use of drugs and alcohol became a serious problem, and his work from the last two decades of his life was not as popular or critically acclaimed as his previous work. It is primarily on the strength of his earlier plays that he is considered one of the most important writers in the history of American theatre.

# Cat on a Hot Tin Roof

### CHARACTERS

| | |
|---|---|
| Margaret | Reverend Tooker |
| Brick | Gooper, *sometimes called* |
| Mae, *sometimes called* | Brother Man |
| Sister Woman | Doctor Baugh, *pronounced "Baw"* |
| Big Mama | Lacey, *a Negro servant* |
| Dixie, *a little girl* | Sookey, *another* |
| Big Daddy | Children |

## NOTES FOR THE DESIGNER

The set is the bed-sitting-room of a plantation home in the Mississippi Delta.[1] It is along an upstairs gallery which probably runs around the entire house; it has two pairs of very wide doors opening onto the gallery, showing white balustrades against a fair summer sky that fades into dusk and night during the course of the play, which occupies precisely the time of its performance, excepting, of course, the fifteen minutes of intermission.

Perhaps the style of the room is not what you would expect in the home of the Delta's biggest cotton-planter. It is Victorian with a touch of the Far East. It hasn't changed much since it was occupied by the original owners of the place, Jack Straw and Peter Ochello, a pair of old bachelors who shared this room all their lives together. In other words, the room must evoke some ghosts; it is gently and poetically haunted by a relationship that must have involved a tenderness which was uncommon. This may be irrelevant or unnecessary, but I once saw a reproduction of a faded photograph of the verandah of Robert Louis Stevenson's home on that Samoan Island[2] where he spent his last years, and there was a quality of tender light on weathered wood, such as porch furniture made of bamboo and wicker, exposed to tropical suns and tropical rains, which came to mind when I thought about the set for this play, bringing also to mind the grace and comfort of light, the reassurance it gives, on a late and fair afternoon in summer, the way that no matter what, even dread of death, is gently touched and soothed by it. For the set is the background for a play that deals with human extremities of emotion, and it needs that softness behind it.

The bathroom door, showing only pale-blue tile and silver towel racks, is in one side wall; the hall door in the opposite wall. Two articles of furniture need mention: a big double bed which staging should make a functional part of the set as often as suitable, the surface of which should be slightly raked to make figures on it seen more easily; and against the wall space between the two huge double doors upstage: a monumental monstrosity peculiar to our times, a huge console combination of radio-phonograph (hi-fi with three speakers) TV set and liquor cabinet, bearing and containing many glasses and bottles, all in one piece, which is a composition of muted silver tones, and the opalescent tones of reflecting glass, a chromatic link, this thing, between the sepia (tawny gold) tones of the interior and the cool (white and blue) tones of the gallery and sky. This piece of furniture (?!), this monument, is a very complete and

---

1   *Mississippi Delta*   Area in the state of Mississippi between the Mississippi and Yazoo rivers.
2   *Robert ... Island*   Scottish novelist and poet Robert Louis Stevenson (1850–94) lived on the Samoan island Upolu during the final years of his life.

compact little shrine to virtually all the comforts and illusions behind which we hide from such things as the characters in the play are faced with ...

The set should be far less realistic than I have so far implied in this description of it. I think the walls below the ceiling should dissolve mysteriously into air; the set should be roofed by the sky; stars and moon suggested by traces of milky pallor, as if they were observed through a telescope lens out of focus. Anything else I can think of? Oh, yes, fanlights (transoms shaped like an open glass fan) above all the doors in the set, with panes of blue and amber, and above all, the designer should take as many pains to give the actors room to move about freely (to show their restlessness, their passion for breaking out) as if it were a set for a ballet.

*An evening in summer. The action is continuous, with two intermissions.*

## ACT 1

*At the rise of the curtain someone is taking a shower in the bathroom, the door of which is half open. A pretty young woman, with anxious lines in her face, enters the bedroom and crosses to the bathroom door.*

MARGARET. (*shouting above roar of water*) One of those no-neck monsters hit me with a hot buttered biscuit so I have t' change!

(*Margaret's voice is both rapid and drawling. In her long speeches she has the vocal tricks of a priest delivering a liturgical chant,[1] the lines are almost sung, always continuing a little beyond her breath so she has to gasp for another. Sometimes she intersperses the lines with a little wordless singing, such as "Da-da-daaaa!"*
*Water turns off and Brick calls out to her, but is still unseen. A tone of politely feigned interest, masking indifference, or worse, is characteristic of his speech with Margaret.*)

BRICK. Wha'd you say, Maggie? Water was on s' loud I couldn't hearya....
MARGARET.  Well, I!—just remarked that!—one of th' no-neck monsters
5      messed up m' lovely lace dress so I got t'—cha-a-ange....

(*She opens and kicks shut drawers of the dresser.*)

BRICK.  Why d'ya call Gooper's kiddies no-neck monsters?
MARGARET.  Because they've got no necks! Isn't that a good enough reason?
BRICK.  Don't they have any necks?

---

1      *liturgical chant* Song or spoken passage recited during religious ceremonies.

MARGARET.  None visible. Their fat little heads are set on their fat little bodies without a bit of connection.                                                                                10

BRICK.  That's too bad.

MARGARET.  Yes, it's too bad because you can't wring their necks if they've got no necks to wring! Isn't that right, honey?

(*She steps out of her dress, stands in a slip of ivory satin and lace.*)

Yep, they're no-neck monsters, all no-neck people are monsters ...

(*Children shriek downstairs.*)

Hear them? Hear them screaming? I don't know where their voice boxes   15
are located since they don't have necks. I tell you I got so nervous at that table tonight I thought I would throw back my head and utter a scream you could hear across the Arkansas border an' parts of Louisiana an' Tennessee. I said to your charming sister-in-law, Mae, honey, couldn't you feed those precious little things at a separate table with an oilcloth[1] cover? They   20
make such a mess an' the lace cloth looks so pretty! She made enormous eyes at me and said, "Ohhh, noooooo! On Big Daddy's birthday? Why, he would never forgive me!" Well, I want you to know, Big Daddy hadn't been at the table two minutes with those five no-neck monsters slobbering and drooling over their food before he threw down his fork an' shouted,   25
"Fo' God's sake, Gooper, why don't you put them pigs at a trough in th' kitchen?"—Well, I swear, I simply could have di-ieed!

Think of it, Brick, they've got five of them and number six is coming. They've brought the whole bunch down here like animals to display at a county fair. Why, they have those children doin' tricks all the time! "Junior,   30
show Big Daddy how you do this, show Big Daddy how you do that, say your little piece fo' Big Daddy, Sister. Show your dimples, Sugar. Brother, show Big Daddy how you stand on your head!"—It goes on all the time, along with constant little remarks and innuendos about the fact that you and I have not produced any children, are totally childless and therefore   35
totally useless!—Of course it's comical but it's also disgusting since it's so obvious what they're up to!

BRICK.  (*without interest*) What are they up to, Maggie?

MARGARET.  Why, you know what they're up to!

BRICK.  (*appearing*) No, I don't know what they're up to.                                   40

(*He stands there in the bathroom doorway drying his hair with a towel and hanging onto the towel rack because one ankle is broken, plastered and bound. He is still slim and firm as a boy. His liquor hasn't started*

---

1    *oilcloth*  Fabric treated with oil to increase water resistance.

*tearing him down outside. He has the additional charm of that cool air of detachment that people have who have given up the struggle. But now and then, when disturbed, something flashes behind it, like lightning in a fair sky, which shows that at some deeper level he is far from peaceful. Perhaps in a stronger light he would show some signs of deliquescence, but the fading, still warm, light from the gallery treats him gently.)*

MARGARET. I'll tell you what they're up to, boy of mine!—They're up to cutting you out of your father's estate, and—

*(She freezes momentarily before her next remark. Her voice drops as if it were somehow a personally embarrassing admission.)*

—Now we know that Big Daddy's dyin' of—cancer....

*(There are voices on the lawn below: long-drawn calls across distance. Margaret raises her lovely bare arms and powders her armpits with a light sigh. She adjusts the angle of a magnifying mirror to straighten an eyelash, then rises fretfully saying:)*

There's so much light in the room it—

45  BRICK. *(softly but sharply)* Do we?

MARGARET. Do we what?

BRICK. Know Big Daddy's dyin' of cancer?

MARGARET. Got the report today.

BRICK. Oh ...

50  MARGARET. *(letting down bamboo blinds which cast long, gold-fretted shadows over the room)* Yep, got th' report just now ... it didn't surprise me, Baby....

*(Her voice has range, and music; sometimes it drops low as a boy's and you have a sudden image of her playing boy's games as a child.)*

I recognized the symptoms soon's we got here last spring and I'm willin' to bet you that Brother Man and his wife were pretty sure of it, too. That more than likely explains why their usual summer migration to the cool-
55  ness of the Great Smokies[1] was passed up this summer in favour of—hustlin' down here ev'ry whipstitch[2] with their whole screamin' tribe! And why so many allusions have been made to Rainbow Hill lately. You know what Rainbow Hill is? Place that's famous for treatin' alcoholics an dope fiends in the movies!

60  BRICK. I'm not in the movies.

---

1   *Great Smokies* Mountain range in the southeastern United States.
2   *ev'ry whipstitch* I.e., every moment.

MARGARET.  No, and you don't take dope. Otherwise you're a perfect candidate for Rainbow Hill, Baby, and that's where they aim to ship you—over
my dead body! Yep, over my dead body they'll ship you there, but nothing
would please them better. Then Brother Man could get a-hold of the purse
strings and dole out remittances[1] to us, maybe get power of attorney and
sign checks for us and cut off our credit wherever, whenever he wanted!
Son-of-a-bitch!—How'd you like that, Baby?—Well, you've been doin'
just about ev'rything in your power to bring it about, you've just been doin'
ev'rything you can think of to aid and abet them in this scheme of theirs!
Quittin' work, devoting yourself to the occupation of drinkin'!—Breakin'
your ankle last night on the high school athletic field: doin' what? Jumpin'
hurdles? At two or three in the morning? Just fantastic! Got in the paper.
Clarksdale Register carried a nice little item about it, human interest story
about a well-known former athlete stagin' a one-man track meet on the
Glorious Hill High School athletic field last night, but was slightly out of
condition and didn't clear the first hurdle! Brother Man Gooper claims he
exercised his influence t' keep it from goin' out over AP or UP[2] or every
goddam "P."

  But, Brick? You still have one big advantage!

*(During the above swift flood of words, Brick has reclined with contrapuntal[3]
leisure on the snowy surface of the bed and has rolled over carefully on his
side or belly.)*

BRICK.  (*wryly*) Did you say something, Maggie?
MARGARET.  Big Daddy dotes on you, honey. And he can't stand Brother
Man and Brother Man's wife, that monster of fertility, Mae. Know how I
know? By little expressions that flicker over his face when that woman is
holding fo'th on one of her choice topics such as—how she refused twilight
sleep![4]—when the twins were delivered! Because she feels motherhood's
an experience that a woman ought to experience fully!—in order to fully
appreciate the wonder and beauty of it! HAH!—and how she made Brother
Man come in an' stand beside her in the delivery room so he would not
miss out on the "wonder and beauty" of it either!—producin' those no-
neck monsters....

---

1    *remittances* Monetary allowances.
2    *AP or UP* Associated Press or United Press International, large American news agencies.
3    *contrapuntal* I.e., in contrast or counterpoint to her energy.
4    *twilight sleep* Semi-anaesthetized state induced with the injection of scopolamine and
     morphine. These drugs were administered to women to prevent pain during childbirth.

*(A speech of this kind would be antipathetic from almost anybody but Margaret; she makes it oddly funny, because her eyes constantly twinkle and her voice shakes with laughter which is basically indulgent.)*

—Big Daddy shares my attitude toward those two! As for me, well—I give him a laugh now and then and he tolerates me. In fact!—I sometimes suspect that Big Daddy harbours a little unconscious "lech" fo' me....

BRICK.  What makes you think that Big Daddy has a lech for you, Maggie?

95   MARGARET.  Way he always drops his eyes down my body when I'm talkin' to him, drops his eyes to my boobs an' licks his old chops! Ha ha!

BRICK.  That kind of talk is disgusting.

MARGARET.  Did anyone ever tell you that you're an ass-aching Puritan,[1] Brick?

100     I think it's mighty fine that that ole fellow, on the doorstep of death, still takes in my shape with what I think is deserved appreciation!

And you wanta know something else? Big Daddy didn't know how many little Maes and Goopers had been produced! "How many kids have you got?" he asked at the table, just like Brother Man and his wife were

105   new acquaintances to him! Big Mama said he was jokin', but that ole boy wasn't jokin', Lord, no!

And when they infawmed him that they had five already and were turning out number six!—the news seemed to come as a sort of unpleasant surprise ...

*(Children yell below.)*

110   Scream, monsters!

*(Turns to Brick with a sudden, gay, charming smile which fades as she notices that he is not looking at her but into fading gold space with a troubled expression. It is constant rejection that makes her humour "bitchy.")*

Yes, you should of been at that supper-table, Baby.

*(Whenever she calls him "baby" the word is a soft caress.)*

Y'know, Big Daddy, bless his ole sweet soul, he's the dearest ole thing in the world, but he does hunch over his food as if he preferred not to notice anything else. Well, Mae an' Gooper were side by side at the table, direckly

115   across from Big Daddy, watchin' his face like hawks while they jawed an' jabbered about the cuteness an' brilliance of th' no-neck monsters!

---

1   *Puritan* I.e., morally uptight person. Puritanism was a sixteenth- and seventeenth-century branch of Christianity known for its severe beliefs surrounding morality, luxury, and self-indulgence.

(*She giggles with a hand fluttering at her throat and her breast and her long throat arched. She comes downstage and recreates the scene with voice and gesture.*)

And the no-neck monsters were ranged around the table, some in high chairs and some on th' Books of Knowledge,[1] all in fancy little paper caps in honor of Big Daddy's birthday, and all through dinner, well, I want you to know that Brother Man an' his partner never once, for one moment, stopped exchanging pokes an' pinches an' kicks an' signs an' signals!— 120 Why, they were like a couple of cardsharps[2] fleecing a sucker.—Even Big Mama, bless her ole sweet soul, she isn't th' quickest an' brightest thing in the world, she finally noticed, at last, an' said to Gooper, "Gooper, what are you an' Mae makin' all these signs at each other about?"—I swear t' goodness, I nearly choked on my chicken! 125

(*Margaret, back at the dressing table, still doesn't see Brick. He is watching her with a look that is not quite definable—Amused? shocked? contemptuous?—part of those and part of something else.*)

Y'know—your brother Gooper still cherishes the illusion he took a giant step up on the social ladder when he married Miss Mae Flynn of the Memphis Flynns.

But I have a piece of Spanish news[3] for Gooper. The Flynns never had a thing in this world but money and they lost that, they were nothing at 130 all but fairly successful climbers. Of course, Mae Flynn came out in Memphis eight years before I made my debut in Nashville, but I had friends at Ward-Belmont[4] who came from Memphis and they used to come to see me and I used to go to see them for Christmas and spring vacations, and so I know who rates an' who doesn't rate in Memphis society. Why, y'know 135 ole Papa Flynn, he barely escaped doing time in the Federal pen for shady manipulations on th' stock market when his chain stores crashed, and as for Mae having been a cotton carnival queen,[5] as they remind us so often, lest we forget, well, that's one honour that I don't envy her for!—Sit on a brass throne on a tacky float an' ride down Main Street, smilin', bowin', 140 and blowin' kisses to all the trash on the street—

---

1   *Books of Knowledge* Volumes of *The Book of Knowledge*, a well-known general knowledge encyclopedia.

2   *cardsharps* Players who cheat or hide their superior skill to win at card games.

3   *Spanish news* I.e., bad news.

4   *debut* Extravagant dance held to mark an upper-class girl's coming-of-age; *Ward-Belmont* Ward-Belmont College, a former woman's college in Nashville, Tennessee.

5   *cotton carnival queen* College girl chosen as "queen" for the annual Carnival Memphis, formerly known as the Memphis Cotton Carnival.

*(She picks out a pair of jewelled sandals and rushes to the dressing table.)*

Why, year before last, when Susan McPheeters was singled out fo' that honour, y' know what happened to her? Y'know what happened to poor little Susie McPheeters?

BRICK. *(absently)* No. What happened to little Susie McPheeters?

145 MARGARET. Somebody spit tobacco juice in her face.

BRICK. *(dreamily)* Somebody spit tobacco juice in her face?

MARGARET. That's right, some old drunk leaned out of a window in the Hotel Gayoso[1] and yelled, "Hey, Queen, hey, hey, there, Queenie!" Poor Susie looked up and flashed him a radiant smile and he shot out a squirt of
150 tobacco juice right in poor Susie's face.

BRICK. Well, what d'you know about that.

MARGARET. *(gaily)* What do I know about it? I was there, I saw it!

BRICK. *(absently)* Must have been kind of funny.

MARGARET. Susie didn't think so. Had hysterics. Screamed like a banshee.
155 They had to stop th' parade an' remove her from her throne an' go on with—

*(She catches sight of him in the mirror, gasps slightly, wheels about to face him. Count ten.)*

—Why are you looking at me like that?

BRICK. *(whistling softly, now)* Like what, Maggie?

MARGARET. *(intensely, fearfully)* The way y' were lookin' at me just now, befo'
160 I caught your eye in the mirror and you started t' whistle! I don't know how t' describe it but it froze my blood!—I've caught you lookin' at me like that so often lately. What are you thinkin' of when you look at me like that?

BRICK. I wasn't conscious of lookin' at you, Maggie.

165 MARGARET. Well, I was conscious of it! What were you thinkin'?

BRICK. I don't remember thinking of anything, Maggie.

MARGARET. Don't you think I know that—? Don't you—?—Think I know that—?

BRICK. *(coolly)* Know what, Maggie?

170 MARGARET. *(struggling for expression)* That I've gone through this—hideous!—transformation, become—hard! Frantic!

*(Then she adds, almost tenderly:)*

—cruel!!

---

1   *Hotel Gayoso* Historic hotel in Memphis, Tennessee.

That's what you've been observing in me lately. How could y' help but observe it? That's all right. I'm not—thin-skinned any more, can't afford t' be thin-skinned any more.    175

(*She is now recovering her power.*)

—But Brick? Brick?

BRICK.  Did you say something?

MARGARET.  I was *goin'* t' say something: that I get—lonely. Very!

BRICK.  Ev'rybody gets that ...

MARGARET.  Living with someone you love can be lonelier—than living en-  180
tirely alone!—if the one that y'love doesn't love you ....

(*There is a pause. Brick hobbles downstage and asks, without looking at her:*)

BRICK.  Would you like to live alone, Maggie?

(*Another pause: then—after she has caught a quick, hurt breath:*)

MARGARET.  *No!—God!—God!—I wouldn't!*

(*Another gasping breath. She forcibly controls what must have been an impulse to cry out. We see her deliberately, very forcibly, going all the way back to the world in which you can talk about ordinary matters.*)

Did you have a nice shower?

BRICK.  Uh-huh.    185

MARGARET.  Was the water cool?

BRICK.  No.

MARGARET.  But it made y' feel fresh, huh?

BRICK.  Fresher ...

MARGARET.  I know something would make y' feel *much* fresher!    190

BRICK.  What?

MARGARET.  An alcohol rub. Or cologne, a rub with cologne!

BRICK.  That's good after a workout but I haven't been workin' out, Maggie.

MARGARET.  You've kept in good shape, though.

BRICK.  (*indifferently*) You think so, Maggie?    195

MARGARET.  I always thought drinkin' men lost their looks, but I was plainly mistaken.

BRICK.  (*wryly*) Why, thanks, Maggie.

MARGARET.  You're the only drinkin' man I know that it never seems t' put fat on.    200

BRICK.  I'm gettin' softer, Maggie.

MARGARET.  Well, sooner or later it's bound to soften you up. It was just beginning to soften up Skipper when—

(*She stops short.*)

I'm sorry. I never could keep my fingers off a sore—I wish you *would* lose
205    your looks. If you did it would make the martyrdom of Saint Maggie a
little more bearable. But no such goddam luck. I actually believe you've
gotten better looking since you've gone on the bottle. Yeah, a person who
didn't know you would think you'd never had a tense nerve in your body
or a strained muscle.

    (*There are sounds of croquet*[1] *on the lawn below: the click of mallets, light
voices, near and distant.*)

210    Of course, you always had that detached quality as if you were playing a
game without much concern over whether you won or lost, and now that
you've lost the game, not lost but just quit playing, you have that rare sort
of charm that usually only happens in very old or hopelessly sick people,
the charm of the defeated.—You look so cool, so cool, so enviably cool.
215 REVEREND TOOKER. (*off stage right*) Now looka here, boy, lemme show you
how to get outa that!
MARGARET. They're playing croquet. The moon has appeared and it's white,
just beginning to turn a little bit yellow....
    You were a wonderful lover....
220    Such a wonderful person to go to bed with, and I think mostly because
you were really indifferent to it. Isn't that right? Never had any anxiety
about it, did it naturally, easily, slowly, with absolute confidence and perfect calm, more like opening a door for a lady or seating her at a table
than giving expression to any longing for her. Your indifference made you
225    wonderful at lovemaking—*strange?*—but true....
REVEREND TOOKER. Oh! That's a beauty.
DOCTOR BAUGH. Yeah. I got you boxed.[2]
MARGARET. You know, if I thought you would never, never, *never*, make
love to me again—I would go downstairs to the kitchen and pick out the
230    longest and sharpest knife I could find and stick it straight into my heart,
I swear that I would!
REVEREND TOOKER. Watch out, you're gonna miss it.
DOCTOR BAUGH. You just don't know me, boy!
MARGARET. But one thing I don't have is the charm of the defeated, my hat
235    is still in the ring, and I am determined to win!

---

1   *croquet* Lawn game in which wooden mallets are used to knock wooden balls through a
    series of wickets.
2   *boxed* I.e., trapped.

*(There is the sound of croquet mallets hitting croquet balls.)*

REVEREND TOOKER.  Mmm—You're too slippery for me.

MARGARET.  —What is the victory of a cat on a hot tin roof?—I wish I knew....

Just staying on it, I guess, as long as she can....

DOCTOR BAUGH.  Jus' like an eel, boy, jus' like an eel!                    240

*(More croquet sounds.)*

MARGARET.  Later tonight I'm going to tell you I love you an' maybe by that time you'll be drunk enough to believe me. Yes, they're playing croquet....
Big Daddy is dying of cancer....                                          245

What were you thinking of when I caught you looking at me like that? Were you thinking of Skipper?

*(Brick takes up his crutch, rises.)*

Oh, excuse me, forgive me, but laws of silence don't work! No, laws of silence don't work....

*(Brick crosses to the bar, takes a quick drink, and rubs his head with a towel.)*

Laws of silence don't work....                                            250

When something is festering in your memory or your imagination, laws of silence don't work, it's just like shutting a door and locking it on a house on fire in hope of forgetting that the house is burning. But not facing a fire doesn't put it out. Silence about a thing just magnifies it. It grows and festers in silence, becomes malignant....                                    255

*(He drops his crutch.)*

BRICK.  Give me my crutch.

*(He has stopped rubbing his hair dry but still stands hanging onto the towel rack in a white towel-cloth robe.)*

MARGARET.  Lean on me.

BRICK.  No, just give me my crutch.

MARGARET.  Lean on my shoulder.

BRICK.  *I don't want to lean on your shoulder, I want my crutch!*         260

*(This is spoken like sudden lightning.)*

Are you going to give me my crutch or do I have to get down on my knees on the floor and—

MARGARET. *Here, here, take it, take it!*

(*She has thrust the crutch at him.*)

BRICK. (*hobbling out*) Thanks ...

265  MARGARET. We mustn't scream at each other, the walls in this house have ears....

(*He hobbles directly to liquor cabinet to get a new drink.*)

—but that's the first time I've heard you raise your voice in a long time,
270    Brick. A crack in the wall?—Of composure?
—I think that's a good sign....
A sign of nerves in a player on the defensive!

(*Brick turns and smiles at her coolly over his fresh drink.*)

BRICK. It just hasn't happened yet, Maggie.

MARGARET. What?

275  BRICK. The click I get in my head when I've had enough of this stuff to make me peaceful....
Will you do me a favour?

MARGARET. Maybe I will. What favour?

BRICK. Just, just keep your voice down!

280  MARGARET. (*in a hoarse whisper*) I'll do you that favour, I'll speak in a whisper, if not shut up completely, if *you* will do *me* a favour and make that drink your last one till after the party.

BRICK. What party?

MARGARET. Big Daddy's birthday party.

285  BRICK. Is this Big Daddy's birthday?

MARGARET. You know this is Big Daddy's birthday!

BRICK. No, I don't, I forgot it.

MARGARET. Well, I remembered it for you....

(*They are both speaking as breathlessly as a pair of kids after a fight, drawing deep exhausted breaths and looking at each other with faraway eyes, shaking and panting together as if they had broken apart from a violent struggle.*)

BRICK. Good for you, Maggie.

290  MARGARET. You just have to scribble a few lines on this card.

BRICK. You scribble something, Maggie.

MARGARET. It's got to be your handwriting; it's your present, I've given him my present; it's got to be your handwriting!

(*The tension between them is building again, the voices becoming shrill once more.*)

BRICK. I didn't get him a present.

MARGARET. I got one for you.                                                    295

BRICK. All right. You write the card, then.

MARGARET. And have him know you didn't remember his birthday?

BRICK. I didn't remember his birthday.

MARGARET. You don't have to prove you didn't!

BRICK. I don't want to fool him about it.                                       300

MARGARET. Just write "Love, Brick!" for God's—

BRICK. No.

MARGARET. You've *got* to!

BRICK. I don't have to do anything I don't want to do. You keep forgetting
the conditions on which I agreed to stay on living with you.                    305

MARGARET. (*out before she knows it*) I'm not living with you. We occupy the
same cage.

BRICK. You've got to remember the conditions agreed on.

SONNY. (*off stage*) Mommy, give it to me. I had it first.

MAE. Hush.                                                                      310

MARGARET. They're impossible conditions!

BRICK. Then why don't you—?

SONNY. I want it, I want it!

MAE. Get away!

MARGARET. HUSH! Who is out there? Is somebody at the door?                      315

(*There are footsteps in hall.*)

MAE. (*outside*) May I enter a moment?

MARGARET. Oh, *you!* Sure. Come in, Mae.

(*Mae enters bearing aloft the bow of a young lady's archery set.*)

MAE. Brick, is this thing yours?

MARGARET. Why, Sister Woman—that's my Diana[1] Trophy. Won it at the
intercollegiate archery contest on the Ole Miss campus.[2]                      320

MAE. It's a mighty dangerous thing to leave exposed round a house full of
nawmal rid-blooded children attracted t'weapons.

MARGARET. "Nawmal rid-blooded children attracted t'weapons" ought t'be
taught to keep their hands off things that don't belong to them.

MAE. Maggie, honey, if you had children of your own you'd know how funny  325
that is. Will you please lock this up and put the key out of reach?

---

1    *Diana* In Roman mythology, the goddess of the hunt who is often depicted with a bow
and arrows.

2    *Ole Miss* University of Mississippi.

MARGARET. Sister Woman, nobody is plotting the destruction of your kiddies.—Brick and I still have our special archers' licence. We're goin' deer-
huntin' on Moon Lake as soon as the season starts. I love to run with dogs
330    through chilly woods, run, run leap over obstructions—

(*She goes into the closet carrying the bow.*)

MAE. How's the injured ankle, Brick?

BRICK. Doesn't hurt. Just itches.

MAE. Oh, my! Brick—Brick, you should've been downstairs after supper!
Kiddies put on a show. Polly played the piano, Buster an' Sonny drums, an'
335    then they turned out the lights an' Dixie an' Trixie puhfawmed a toe dance
in fairy costume with *spahkluhs!* Big Daddy just beamed! He just beamed!

MARGARET. (*from the closet with a sharp laugh*) Oh, I bet. It breaks my heart
that we missed it!

(*She reenters.*)

But Mae? Why did y'give dawgs' names to all your kiddies?

340    MAE. *Dogs'* names?

MARGARET. (*sweetly*) Dixie, Trixie, Buster, Sonny, Polly!—Sounds like four
dogs and a parrot ...

MAE. Maggie?

(*Margaret turns with a smile.*)

Why are you so catty?

345    MARGARET. Cause I'm a cat! But why can't *you* take a joke, Sister Woman?

MAE. Nothin' pleases me more than a joke that's funny. You know the real
names of our kiddies. Buster's real name is Robert. Sonny's real name is
Saunders. Trixie's real name is Marlene and Dixie's—

(*Gooper downstairs calls for her.* "Hey, Mae! Sister Woman, intermission
is over!"—*She rushes to door, saying:*)

Intermission is over! See ya later!

350    MARGARET. I wonder what Dixie's real name is?

BRICK. Maggie, being catty doesn't help things any ...

MARGARET. I know! *WHY!*—Am I so catty?—Cause I'm consumed with envy
an' eaten up with longing?—Brick, I'm going to lay out your beautiful
Shantung silk[1] suit from Rome and one of your monogrammed silk shirts.
355    I'll put your cuff links in it, those lovely star sapphires I get you to wear
so rarely....

---

1    *Shantung silk* Silk originally from the province of Shandong in eastern China.

BRICK.  I can't get trousers on over this plaster cast.

MARGARET.  Yes, you can, I'll help you.

BRICK.  I'm not going to get dressed, Maggie.

MARGARET.  Will you just put on a pair of white silk pajamas?    360

BRICK.  Yes, I'll do that, Maggie.

MARGARET.  *Thank* you, thank you so *much!*

BRICK.  Don't mention it.

MARGARET.  *Oh, Brick!* How long does it have t' go on? This punishment? Haven't I done time enough, haven't I served my term, can't I apply for    365 a—pardon?

BRICK.  Maggie, you're spoiling my liquor. Lately your voice always sounds like you'd been running upstairs to warn somebody that the house was on fire!

MARGARET.  Well, no wonder, no wonder. Y'know what I feel like, Brick?    370

(*Children's and grown-ups' voices are blended, below, in a loud but uncertain rendition of "My Wild Irish Rose."*[1])

*I feel all the time like a cat on a hot tin roof!*

BRICK.  Then jump off the roof, jump off it, cats can jump off roofs and land on their four feet uninjured.

MARGARET.  Oh, yes!

BRICK.  Do it!—fo' God's sake, do it ...    375

MARGARET.  Do what?

BRICK.  Take a lover!

MARGARET.  I can't see a man but you! Even with my eyes closed, I just see you! Why don't you get ugly, Brick, why don't you please get fat or ugly or something so I could stand it?    380

(*She rushes to hall door, opens it, listens.*)

The concert is still going on. Bravo, no-necks, bravo!

(*She slams and locks door fiercely.*)

BRICK.  What did you lock the door for?

MARGARET.  To give us a little privacy for a while.

BRICK.  You know better, Maggie.

MARGARET.  No, I don't know better....    385

(*She rushes to gallery doors, draws the rose-silk drapes across them.*)

BRICK.  Don't make a fool of yourself.

---

1    *My Wild Irish Rose* Popular 1899 song by Chancellor Olcott.

MARGARET.  I don't mind makin' a fool of myself over you!

BRICK.  I mind, Maggie. I feel embarrassed for you.

MARGARET.  Feel embarrassed! But don't continue my torture. I can't live on
390    and on under these circumstances.

BRICK.  You agreed to—

MARGARET.  I know but—

BRICK.  —Accept that condition!

MARGARET.  I CAN'T! CAN'T! CAN'T

(*She seizes his shoulder.*)

395    BRICK.  Let go!

(*He breaks away from her and seizes the small boudoir chair and raises
it like a lion-tamer facing a big circus cat. Count five. She stares at him
with her fist pressed to her mouth, then bursts into shrill, almost hysterical
laughter. He remains grave for a moment, then grins and puts the chair
down.*)

(*Big Mama calls through closed door.*)

400    BIG MAMA.  Son? Son? Son?

BRICK.  What is it, Big Mama?

BIG MAMA.  (*outside*) Oh, son! We got the most wonderful news about Big
Daddy. I just had t'run up an' tell you right this—

(*She rattles the knob.*)

—What's this door doin', locked, faw? You all think there's robbers in the
405    house?

MARGARET.  Big Mama, Brick is dressin', he's not dressed yet.

BIG MAMA.  That's all right, it won't be the first time I've seen Brick not
dressed. Come on, open this door!

(*Margaret, with a grimace, goes to unlock and open the hall door, as Brick
hobbles rapidly to the bathroom and kicks the door shut. Big Mama has
disappeared from the hall.*)

MARGARET.  Big Mama?

(*Big Mama appears through the opposite gallery doors behind Margaret,
huffing and puffing like an old bulldog. She is a short, stout woman; her
sixty years and 170 pounds have left her somewhat breathless most of the
time; she's always tensed like a boxer, or rather, a Japanese wrestler. Her
"family" was maybe a little superior to Big Daddy's, but not much. She
wears a black or silver lace dress and at least half a million in flashy gems.
She is very sincere.*)

BIG MAMA. (*loudly, startling Margaret*) Here—I come through Gooper's and  410
Mae's gall'ry door. Where's Brick? *Brick*—Hurry on out of there, son, I just
have a second and want to give you the news about Big Daddy.—I hate
locked doors in a house....

MARGARET. (*with affected lightness*) I've noticed you do, Big Mama, but people have got to have *some* moments of privacy, don't they?  415

BIG MAMA. No, ma'am, not in *my* house. (*without pause*) Whacha took off
you' dress faw? I thought that little lace dress was so sweet on yuh, honey.

MARGARET. I thought it looked sweet on me, too, but one of m' cute little
table-partners used it for a napkin so—!

BIG MAMA. (*picking up stockings on floor*) What?  420

MARGARET. You know, Big Mama, Mae and Gooper's so touchy about those
children—thanks, Big Mama ...

(*Big Mama has thrust the picked-up stockings in Margaret's hand with a
grunt.*)

—that you just don't dare to suggest there's any room for improvement in
their—

BIG MAMA. Brick, hurry out!—Shoot, Maggie, you just don't like children.  425

MARGARET. I do so like children! Adore them!—well brought up!

BIG MAMA. (*gentle—loving*) Well, why don't you have some and bring them
up well, then, instead of all the time pickin' on Gooper's an' Mae's?

GOOPER. (*shouting up the stairs*) Hey, hey, Big Mama, Betsy an' Hugh got to
go, waitin' t' tell yuh g'by!  430

BIG MAMA. Tell 'em to hold their hawses, I'll be right down in a jiffy!

GOOPER. Yes ma'am!

(*She turns to the bathroom door and calls out.*)

BIG MAMA. Son? Can you hear me in there?

(*There is a muffled answer.*)

We just got the full report from the laboratory at the Ochsner Clinic,[1]
completely negative, son, ev'rything negative, right on down the line!  435
Nothin' a-tall's wrong with him but some little functional thing called a
spastic colon.[2] Can you hear me, son?

MARGARET. He can hear you, Big Mama.

---

1    *Ochsner Clinic* Ochsner Medical Center, renowned clinic founded in 1942 and especially
     known for its cancer facilities.

2    *spastic colon* Irritable bowel syndrome.

BIG MAMA.   Then why don't he say something? God Almighty, a piece of
440   news like that should make him shout. It made *me* shout, I can tell you. I
shouted and sobbed and fell right down on my knees!—Look!

(*She pulls up her skirt.*)

See the bruises where I hit my kneecaps? Took both doctors to haul me
back on my feet!

(*She laughs—she always laughs like hell at herself.*)

Big Daddy was furious with me! But ain't that wonderful news?

(*Facing bathroom again, she continues:*)

445   After all the anxiety we been through to git a report like that on Big Daddy's birthday? Big Daddy tried to hide how much of a load that news took
off his mind, but didn't fool *me*. He was mighty close to crying about it
*himself!*

(*Goodbyes are shouted downstairs, and she rushes to door.*)

GOOPER.   Big Mama!
450   BIG MAMA.   *Hold those people down there, don't let them go!*—Now, git dressed,
we're all comin' up to this room fo' Big Daddy's birthday party because of
your ankle.—How's his ankle, Maggie?
MARGARET.   Well, he broke it, Big Mama.
BIG MAMA.   I know he broke it.

(*A phone is ringing in hall. A Negro voice answers: "Mistuh Polly's
res'dence."*)

455   I mean does it hurt him much still.
MARGARET.   I'm afraid I can't give you that information, Big Mama. You'll
have to ask Brick if it hurts much still or not.
SOOKEY.   (*in the hall*) It's Memphis, Mizz Polly, it's Miss Sally in Memphis.
BIG MAMA.   Awright, Sookey.

(*Big Mama rushes into the hall and is heard shouting on the phone:*)

460   Hello, Miss Sally. How are you, Miss Sally?—Yes, well, I was just gonna
call you about it. *Shoot!*—
MARGARET.   Brick, don't!

(*Big Mama raises her voice to a bellow.*)

BIG MAMA.   *Miss Sally? Don't ever call me from the Gayoso Lobby, too much talk*
465   *goes on in that hotel lobby, no wonder you can't hear me!* Now listen, Miss Sally.

They's nothin' serious wrong with Big Daddy. We got the report just now, they's nothin' wrong but a thing called a—spastic! *SPASTIC!*—colon ...

(*She appears at the hall door and calls to Margaret.*)

—Maggie, come out here and talk to that fool on the phone. I'm shouted breathless!

MARGARET. (*goes out and is heard sweetly at phone*) Miss Sally? This is Brick's 470 wife, Maggie. So nice to hear your voice. Can you hear *mine?* Well, *good!*— Big Mama just wanted you to know that they've got the report from the Ochsner Clinic and what Big Daddy has is a spastic colon. Yes. Spastic colon, Miss Sally. That's right, spastic colon. *G'bye, Miss Sally, hope I'll see you real soon!* 475

(*Hangs up a little before Miss Sally was probably ready to terminate the talk. She returns through the hall door.*)

She heard me perfectly. I've discovered with deaf people the thing to do is not shout at them but just enunciate clearly. My rich old Aunt Cornelia was deaf as the dead but I could make her hear me just by sayin' each word slowly, distinctly, close to her ear. I read her the *Commercial Appeal*[1] ev'ry night, read her the classified ads in it, even, she never missed a word of it. 480 But was she a mean ole thing! Know what I got when she died? Her un-expired subscriptions to five magazines and the Book-of-the-Month Club and a LIBRARY full of ev'ry dull book ever written! All else went to her hellcat of a sister ... meaner than she was, even!

(*Big Mama has been straightening things up in the room during this speech.*)

BIG MAMA. (*closing closet door on discarded clothes*) Miss Sally sure is a case! Big 485 Daddy says she's always got her hand out fo' something. He's not mistaken. That poor ole thing always has her hand out fo' somethin'. I don't think Big Daddy gives her as much as he should.

GOOPER. Big Mama! Come on now! Betsy and Hugh can't wait no longer!

BIG MAMA. (*shouting*) I'm comin'! 490

(*She starts out. At the hall door, turns and jerks a forefinger, first toward the bathroom door, then toward the liquor cabinet, meaning: "Has Brick been drinking?" Margaret pretends not to understand, cocks her head and raises her brows as if the pantomimic performance was completely mystifying to her. Big Mama rushes back to Margaret:*)

*Shoot! Stop playin' so dumb!*—I mean has he been drinkin' that stuff much yet?

---

1    *Commercial Appeal* Popular Memphis daily newspaper.

MARGARET. (*with a little laugh*) Oh! I think he had a highball[1] after supper.

BIG MAMA. Don't laugh about it!—Some single men stop drinkin' when they git married and others start! Brick never touched liquor before he—!

495 MARGARET. (*crying out*) THAT'S NOT FAIR!

BIG MAMA. Fair or not fair I want to ask you a question, one question: D'you make Brick happy in bed?

MARGARET. Why don't you ask if he makes *me* happy in bed?

BIG MAMA. Because I know that—

500 MARGARET. *It works both ways!*

BIG MAMA. Something's not right! You're childless and my son drinks!

GOOPER. Come on, Big Mama!

(*Gooper has called her downstairs and she has rushed to the door on the line above. She turns at the door and points at the bed.*)

BIG MAMA. —When a marriage goes on the rocks, the rocks are *there*, right there!

505 MARGARET. *That's*—

(*Big Mama has swept out of the room and slammed the door.*)

—not—*fair* ...

(*Margaret is alone, completely alone, and she feels it. She draws in, hunches her shoulders, raises her arms with fists clenched, shuts her eyes tight as a child about to be stabbed with a vaccination needle. When she opens her eyes again, what she sees is the long oval mirror and she rushes straight to it, stares into it with a grimace and says:* "Who are you?"—*Then she crouches a little and answers herself in a different voice which is high, thin, mocking:* "I am Maggie the Cat!"—*Straightens quickly as bathroom door opens a little and Brick calls out to her.*)

BRICK. Has Big Mama gone?

MARGARET. She's gone.

(*He opens the bathroom door and hobbles out, with his liquor glass now empty, straight to the liquor cabinet. He is whistling softly. Margaret's head pivots on her long, slender throat to watch him. She raises a hand uncertainly to the base of her throat, as if it was difficult for her to swallow, before she speaks:*)

You know, our sex life didn't just peter out in the usual way, it was cut off
510 short, long before the natural time for it to, and it's going to revive again,

---

1 *highball* Type of drink that combines liquor with a non-alcoholic beverage.

just as sudden as that. I'm confident of it. That's what I'm keeping myself attractive for. For the time when you'll see me again like other men see me. Yes, like other men see me. They still see me, Brick, and they like what they see. Uh-huh. Some of them would give their—Look, Brick!

(*She stands before the long oval mirror, touches her breast and then her hips with her two hands.*)

How high my body stays on me!—Nothing has fallen on me—not a frac-  515
tion....

(*Her voice is soft and trembling: a pleading child's. At this moment as he turns to glance at her—a look which is like a player passing a ball to another player, third down and goal to go—she has to capture the audience in a grip so tight that she can hold it till the first intermission without any lapse of attention.*)

Other men still want me. My face looks strained, sometimes, but I've kept my figure as well as you've kept yours, and men admire it. I still turn heads on the street. Why, last week in Memphis everywhere that I went men's eyes burned holes in my clothes, at the country club and in restaurants and  520
department stores, there wasn't a man I met or walked by that didn't just eat me up with his eyes and turn around when I passed him and look back at me. Why, at Alice's party for her New York cousins, the best-lookin' man in the crowd—followed me upstairs and tried to force his way in the powder room[1] with me, followed me to the door and tried to force his way  525
in!

BRICK.  Why didn't you let him, Maggie?

MARGARET.  Because I'm not that common, for one thing. Not that I wasn't almost tempted to. You like to know who it was? It was Sonny Boy Max- well, that's who!  530

BRICK.  Oh, yeah, Sonny Boy Maxwell, he was a good end-runner but had a little injury to his back and had to quit.

MARGARET.  He has no injury now and has no wife and still has a lech for me!

BRICK.  I see no reason to lock him out of a powder room in that case.

MARGARET.  And have someone catch me at it? I'm not that stupid. Oh, I  535
might sometime cheat on you with someone, since you're so insultingly eager to have me do it!—But if I do, you can be damned sure it will be in a place and a time where no one but me and the man could possibly know. Because I'm not going to give you any excuse to divorce me for being un- faithful or anything else....  540

---

1    *powder room* Bathroom.

BRICK. Maggie, I wouldn't divorce you for being unfaithful or anything else. Don't you know that? Hell. I'd be relieved to know that you'd found yourself a lover.

MARGARET. Well, I'm taking no chances. No, I'd rather stay on this hot tin

545  roof.

BRICK. A hot tin roof's 'n uncomfo'table place t' stay on....

(*He starts to whistle softly.*)

MARGARET. (*through his whistle*) Yeah, but I can stay on it just as long as I have to.

BRICK. You could leave me, Maggie.

(*He resumes his whistle. She wheels about to glare at him.*)

550  MARGARET. *Don't want to and will not!* Besides if I did, you don't have a cent to pay for it but what you get from Big Daddy and he's dying of cancer!

(*For the first time a realization of Big Daddy's doom seems to penetrate to Brick's consciousness, visibly, and he looks at Margaret.*)

BRICK. Big Mama just said he *wasn't*, that the report was okay.

MARGARET. That's what she thinks because she got the same story that they gave Big Daddy. And was just as taken in by it as he was, poor ole things....

555  But tonight they're going to tell her the truth about it. When Big Daddy goes to bed, they're going to tell her that he is dying of cancer.

(*She slams the dresser drawer.*)

—It's malignant and it's terminal.

BRICK. Does Big Daddy know it?

MARGARET. Hell, do they *ever* know it? Nobody says, "You're dying." You

560  have to fool them. They have to fool *themselves*.

BRICK. Why?

MARGARET. *Why?* Because human beings dream of life everlasting, that's the reason! But most of them want it on earth and not in heaven.

(*He gives a short, hard laugh at her touch of humour.*)

Well.... (*She touches up her mascara.*) That's how it is, anyhow.... (*She looks

565  about.*) Where did I put down my cigarette? Don't want to burn up the home-place, at least not with Mae and Gooper and their five monsters in it!

(*She has found it and sucks at it greedily. Blows out smoke and continues:*)

So this is Big Daddy's last birthday. And Mae and Gooper, they know it, oh, *they* know it, all right. They got the first information from the Ochsner

Clinic. That's why they rushed down here with their no-neck monsters. 570
Because. Do you know something? Big Daddy's made no will? Big Daddy's
never made out any will in his life, and so this campaign's afoot to impress
him, forcibly as possible, with the fact that you drink and I've borne no
children!

(*He continues to stare at her a moment, then mutters something sharp but
not audible and hobbles rather rapidly out onto the long gallery in the
fading, much faded, gold light.*)

MARGARET. (*continuing her liturgical chant*) Y'know, I'm *fond* of Big Daddy, 575
I am genuinely fond of that old man, I really *am*, you know....
BRICK. (*faintly, vaguely*) Yes, I know you are....
MARGARET. I've always sort of admired him in spite of his coarseness, his
four-letter words and so forth. Because Big Daddy *is* what he *is*, and he
makes no bones about it. He hasn't turned gentleman farmer, he's still a 580
Mississippi redneck, as much of a redneck as he must have been when he
was just overseer here on the old Jack Straw and Peter Ochello place. But
he got hold of it an' built it into th' biggest an' finest plantation in the
Delta.—I've always *liked* Big Daddy....

(*She crosses to the proscenium.*[1])

Well, this is Big Daddy's last birthday. I'm sorry about it. But I'm facing 585
the facts. It takes money to take care of a drinker and that's the office that
I've been elected to lately.
BRICK. You don't have to take care of me.
MARGARET. Yes, I do. Two people in the same boat have got to take care of
each other. At least you want money to buy more Echo Spring[2] when this 590
supply is exhausted, or will you be satisfied with a ten-cent beer?
   Mae an' Gooper are plannin' to freeze us out of Big Daddy's estate because you drink and I'm childless. But we can defeat that plan. We're *going*
to defeat that plan!
   *Brick, y'know, I've been so God damn disgustingly poor all my life!*—That's 595
the *truth*, Brick!
BRICK. I'm not sayin' it isn't.
MARGARET. Always had to suck up to people I couldn't stand because they
had money and I was poor as Job's turkey.[3] You don't know what that's

---

1   *proscenium*  In this context, the arched doorway to the gallery.
2   *Echo Spring*  Brand of bourbon whiskey.
3   *poor ... turkey*  Reference to the biblical Job, who lost all his wealth while his loyalty was
    being tested by God.

600   like. Well, I'll tell you, it's like you would feel a thousand miles away from Echo Spring!—And had to get back to it on that broken ankle ... without a crutch!

That's how it feels to be as poor as Job's turkey and have to suck up to relatives that you hated because they had money and all you had was a
605   bunch of hand-me-down clothes and a few old mouldy three-per-cent government bonds. My daddy loved his liquor, he fell in love with his liquor the way you've fallen in love with Echo Spring!—And my poor Mama, having to maintain some semblance of social position, to keep appearances up, on an income of one hundred and fifty dollars a month on those old
610   government bonds!

When I came out, the year that I made my debut, I had just two evening dresses! One Mother made me from a pattern in *Vogue*, the other a hand-me-down from a snotty rich cousin I hated!

—The dress that I married you in was my grandmother's weddin'
615   gown....

So that's why I'm like a cat on a hot tin roof!

(*Brick is still on the gallery. Someone below calls up to him in a warm Negro voice, "Hiya, Mistuh Brick, how yuh feelin'?" Brick raises his liquor glass as if that answered the question.*)

MARGARET. You can be young without money, but you can't be old without it. You've got to be old *with* money because to be old without it is just too awful, you've got to be one or the other, either *young* or *with money*, you
620   can't be old and *without* it.—That's the *truth*, Brick....

(*Brick whistles softly, vaguely.*)

Well, now I'm dressed, I'm all dressed, there's nothing else for me to do.

(*Forlornly, almost fearfully.*)

I'm dressed, all dressed, nothing else for me to do....

(*She moves about restlessly, aimlessly, and speaks, as if to herself.*)

What am I—? Oh!—my bracelets....

(*She starts working a collection of bracelets over her hands onto her wrists, about six on each, as she talks.*)

I've thought a whole lot about it and now I know when I made my mis-
625   take. Yes, I made my mistake when I told you the truth about that thing with Skipper. Never should have confessed it, a fatal error, tellin' you about that thing with Skipper.

BRICK.  Maggie, shut up about Skipper. I mean it, Maggie; you got to shut up about Skipper.

MARGARET.  You ought to understand that Skipper and I—   630

BRICK.  You don't think I'm serious, Maggie? You're fooled by the fact that I am saying this quiet? Look, Maggie. What you're doing is a dangerous thing to do. You're—you're—you're—foolin' with something that—nobody ought to fool with.

MARGARET.  This time I'm going to finish what I have to say to you. Skipper   635
and I made love, if love you could call it, because it made both of us feel a little bit closer to you. You see, you son of a bitch, you asked too much of people, of me, of him, of all the unlucky poor damned sons of bitches that happen to love you, and there was a whole pack of them, yes, there was a pack of them besides me and Skipper, you asked too goddam much of   640
people that loved you, you—superior creature!—you godlike being!—And so we made love to each other to dream it was you, both of us! Yes, yes, yes! Truth, truth! What's so awful about it? I like it, I think the truth is—yeah! I shouldn't have told you....

BRICK.  (*holding his head unnaturally still and uptilted a bit*) It was Skipper   645
that told me about it. Not you, Maggie.

MARGARET.  I told you!

BRICK.  After he told me!

MARGARET.  What does it matter who—?

DIXIE.  I got your mallet, I got your mallet.   650

TRIXIE.  Give it to me, give it to me. It's mine.

(*Brick turns suddenly out upon the gallery and calls:*)

BRICK.  Little girl! Hey, little girl!

LITTLE GIRL.  (*at a distance*) What, Uncle Brick?

BRICK.  Tell the folks to come up!—Bring everybody upstairs!

TRIXIE.  It's mine, it's mine.   655

MARGARET.  I can't stop myself! I'd go on telling you this in front of them all, if I had to!

BRICK.  Little girl! Go on, go on, will you? Do what I told you, call them!

DIXIE.  Okay.

MARGARET.  Because it's got to be told and you, you!—you never let me!   660

(*She sobs, then controls herself, and continues almost calmly.*)

It was one of those beautiful, ideal things they tell about in the Greek legends, it couldn't be anything else, you being you, and that's what made it so sad, that's what made it so awful, because it was love that never could be carried through to anything satisfying or even talked about plainly.

665   BRICK. Maggie, you gotta stop this.

MARGARET. Brick, I tell you, you got to believe me, Brick, I *do* understand all about it! I—I think it was—*noble!* Can't you tell I'm sincere when I say I respect it? My only point, the only point that I'm making, is life has got to be allowed to continue even after the *dream* of life is—all—over....

> (*Brick is without his crutch. Leaning on furniture, he crosses to pick it up as she continues as if possessed by a will outside herself.*)

670   Why, I remember when we double-dated at college, Gladys Fitzgerald and I and you and Skipper, it was more like a date between you and Skipper. Gladys and I were just sort of tagging along as if it was necessary to chaperone you!—to make a good public impression—

BRICK. (*turns to face her, half lifting his crutch*) Maggie, you want me to hit
675   you with this crutch? Don't you know I could kill you with this crutch?

MARGARET. Good Lord, man, d'you think I'd care if you did?

BRICK. One man has one great good true thing in his life. One great good thing which is true!—I had friendship with Skipper.—You are naming it dirty!

680   MARGARET. I'm not naming it dirty! I am naming it clean.

BRICK. Not love with you, Maggie, but friendship with Skipper was that one great true thing, and you are naming it dirty!

MARGARET. Then you haven't been listenin', not understood what I'm saying! I'm naming it so damn clean that it killed poor Skipper!—You two had
685   something that had to be kept on ice, yes, incorruptible, yes!—and death was the only icebox where you could keep it....

BRICK. I married you, Maggie. Why would I marry you, Maggie, if I was—?

MARGARET. Brick, let me finish!—I know, believe me I know, that it was only Skipper that harboured even any *unconscious* desire for anything not
690   perfectly pure between you two!—Now let me skip a little. You married me early that summer we graduated out of Ole Miss, and we were happy, weren't we, we were blissful, yes, hit heaven together ev'ry time that we loved! But that fall you an' Skipper turned down wonderful offers of jobs in order to keep on bein' football heroes—pro-football heroes. You or-
695   ganized the Dixie Stars that fall, so you could keep on bein' teammates forever! But somethin' was not right with it!—*Me included!*—between you. Skipper began hittin' the bottle ... you got a spinal injury—couldn't play the Thanksgivin' game in Chicago, watched it on TV from a traction bed in Toledo. I joined Skipper. The Dixie Stars lost because poor Skipper was
700   drunk. We drank together that night all night in the bar of the Blackstone[1]

---

1   *Blackstone* Historic hotel in Chicago, Illinois.

and when cold day was comin' up over the Lake an' we were comin' out drunk to take a dizzy look at it, I said, *"SKIPPER! STOP LOVIN' MY HUSBAND OR TELL HIM HE'S GOT TO LET YOU ADMIT IT TO HIM!"*—one way or another!

*HE SLAPPED ME HARD ON THE MOUTH!* —then turned and ran without 705 stopping once, I am sure, all the way back into his room at the Blackstone....

—When I came to his room that night, with a little scratch like a shy little mouse at his door, he made that pitiful, ineffectual little attempt to prove that what I had said wasn't true....    710

(*Brick strikes at her with crutch, a blow that shatters the gem-like lamp on the table.*)

—In this way, I destroyed him, by telling him truth that he and his world which he was born and raised in, yours and his world, had told him could not be told?

—From then on Skipper was nothing at all but a receptacle for liquor and drugs....    715

—*Who shot cock robin? I with my*—

(*She throws back her head with tight shut eyes.*)

—*merciful arrow!* [1]

(*Brick strikes at her; misses.*)

Missed me!—Sorry,—I'm not tryin' to whitewash my behaviour, Christ, no! Brick, I'm not good. I don't know why people have to pretend to be good, nobody's good. The rich or the well-to-do can afford to respect mor- 720 al patterns, conventional moral patterns, but I could never afford to, yeah, but—I'm honest! Give me credit for just that, will you *please?*—Born poor, raised poor, expect to die poor unless I manage to get us something out of what Big Daddy leaves when he dies of cancer! But Brick?!—*Skipper is dead! I'm alive!* Maggie the cat is—    725

(*Brick hops awkwardly forward and strikes at her again with his crutch.*)

—*alive! I am alive, alive! I am ...*

(*He hurls the crutch at her, across the bed she took refuge behind, and pitches forward on the floor as she completes her speech.*)

—*alive!*

---

1    *Who ... arrow* Reference to the popular children's rhyme "Who Killed Cock Robin?"

*(A little girl, Dixie, bursts into the room, wearing an Indian war bonnet and firing a cap pistol at Margaret and shouting: "Bang, bang, bang!" Laughter downstairs floats through the open hall door. Margaret had crouched gasping to bed at child's entrance. She now rises and says with cool fury:)*

730 Little girl, your mother or someone should teach you—*(gasping)*—to knock at a door before you come into a room. Otherwise people might think that you—lack—good breeding....

DIXIE. Yanh, yanh, yanh, what is Uncle Brick doin' on th' floor?

BRICK. I tried to kill your Aunt Maggie, but I failed—and I fell. Little girl, give me my crutch so I can get up off th' floor.

MARGARET. Yes, give your uncle his crutch, he's a cripple, honey, he broke his
735 ankle last night jumping hurdles on the high school athletic field!

DIXIE. What were you jumping hurdles for, Uncle Brick?

BRICK. Because I used to jump them, and people like to do what they used to do, even after they've stopped being able to do it....

MARGARET. That's right, that's your answer, now go away, little girl.

*(Dixie fires cap pistol at Margaret three times.)*

740 *Stop, you stop that, monster! You little no-neck monster!*

*(She seizes the cap pistol and hurls it through gallery doors.)*

DIXIE. *(with a precocious instinct for the cruelest thing)* You're *jealous!*—You're just jealous because you can't have babies!

*(She sticks out her tongue at Margaret as she sashays past her with her stomach stuck out, to the gallery. Margaret slams the gallery doors and leans panting against them. There is a pause. Brick has replaced his spilt drink and sits, faraway, on the great four-poster bed.)*

MARGARET. You see?—they gloat over us being childless, even in front of their five little no-neck monsters!

*(Pause. Voices approach on the stairs.)*

745 Brick?—I've been to a doctor in Memphis, a—a gynecologist....

I've been completely examined, and there is no reason why we can't have a child whenever we want one. And this is my time by the calendar to conceive. Are you listening to me? Are you? Are you LISTENING TO ME!

BRICK. Yes. I hear you, Maggie.

750 *(His attention returns to her inflamed face.)*

—But how in hell on earth do you imagine—that you're going to have a child by a man that can't stand you?

MARGARET. That's a problem that I will have to work out.

(*She wheels about to face the hall door.*)

MAE. (*off stage left*) Come on, Big Daddy. We're all goin' up to Brick's room.

(*From off stage left, voices: Reverend Tooker, Doctor Baugh, Mae.*)

MARGARET. *Here they come!*                                                    755

(*The lights dim.*)

## ACT 2

*There is no lapse of time. Margaret and Brick are in the same positions they held at the end of Act 1.*

MARGARET. (*at door*) *Here they come!*

(*Big Daddy appears first, a tall man with a fierce, anxious look, moving carefully not to betray his weakness even, or especially, to himself.*)

GOOPER. I read in the *Register* that you're getting a new memorial window.

(*Some of the people are approaching through the hall, others along the gallery: voices from both directions. Gooper and Reverend Tooker become visible outside gallery doors, and their voices come in clearly. They pause outside as Gooper lights a cigar.*)

REVEREND TOOKER. (*vivaciously*) Oh, but St. Paul's in Grenada has three memorial windows, and the latest one is a Tiffany[1] stained-glass window that cost twenty-five hundred dollars, a picture of Christ the Good Shepherd    5 with a Lamb in His arms.

MARGARET. Big Daddy.

BIG DADDY. Well, Brick.

BRICK. Hello Big Daddy.—Congratulations!

BIG DADDY. —Crap....                                                          10

GOOPER. Who give that window, Preach?

REVEREND TOOKER. Clyde Fletcher's widow. Also presented St. Paul's with a baptismal font.[2]

---

1    *Tiffany* Louis Comfort Tiffany (1848–1933), American artist and founder of Tiffany Studios, a design company known for its innovative and highly sought-after stained-glass windows, mosaics, and lamps.

2    *baptismal font* Basin or tank found in church sanctuaries and used to hold the holy water in baptism ceremonies.

GOOPER. Y'know what somebody ought t' give your church is a *coolin'* sys-
15  tem, Preach.

REVEREND TOOKER. Yes, siree, Bob! And y'know what Gus Hamma's family
gave in his memory to the church at Two Rivers? A complete new stone
parish-house with a basketball court in the basement and a—

BIG DADDY. (*uttering a loud barking laugh which is far from truly mirthful*)
20  Hey, Preach! What's all this talk about memorials, Preach? Y' think somebody's about t' kick off around here? 'S that it?

> (*Startled by this interjection, Reverend Tooker decides to laugh at the
> question almost as loud as he can. How he would answer the question we'll
> never know, as he's spared that embarrassment by the voice of Gooper's wife,
> Mae, rising high and clear as she appears with "Doc" Baugh, the family
> doctor, through the hall door.*)

MAE. (*almost religiously*)—Let's see now, they've had their tyyy-phoid shots,
and their tetanus shots, their diphtheria shots and their hepatitis shots
and their polio shots, they got *those* shots every month from May through
25  September, and—Gooper? Hey! Gooper!—What all have the kiddies been
shot faw?

MARGARET. (*overlapping a bit*) Turn on the hi-fi,[1] Brick! Let's have some music t' start off th' party with!

BRICK. You turn it on, Maggie.

> (*The talk becomes so general that the room sounds like a great aviary of
> chattering birds. Only Brick remains unengaged, leaning upon the liquor
> cabinet with his faraway smile, an ice cube in a paper napkin with which he
> now and then rubs his forehead. He doesn't respond to Margaret's command.
> She bounds forward and stoops over the instrument panel of the console.*)

30  GOOPER. We gave 'em that thing for a third anniversary present, got three
speakers in it.

> (*The room is suddenly blasted by the climax of a Wagnerian opera or a
> Beethoven symphony.[2]*)

BIG DADDY. *Turn that dam thing off!*

> (*Almost instant silence, almost instantly broken by the shouting charge of
> Big Mama, entering through hall door like a charging rhino.*)

BIG MAMA. *Wha's my Brick, wha's mah precious baby!!*

---

1  *hi-fi* "High fidelity" sound system.
2  *Wagnerian* Intense and theatrical; characteristic of the German composer Richard Wag-
ner (1813–83); *Beethoven* German composer Ludwig van Beethoven (1770–1827).

BIG DADDY. *Sorry! Turn it back on!*

(*Everyone laughs very loud. Big Daddy is famous for his jokes at Big Mama's expense, and nobody laughs louder at these jokes than Big Mama herself, though sometimes they're pretty cruel and Big Mama has to pick up or fuss with something to cover the hurt that the loud laugh doesn't quite cover. On this occasion, a happy occasion because the dread in her heart has also been lifted by the false report on Big Daddy's condition, she giggles, grotesquely, coyly, in Big Daddy's direction and bears down upon Brick, all very quick and alive.*)

BIG MAMA.    Here he is, here's my precious baby! What's that you've got in    35
your hand? You put that liquor down, son, your hand was made fo' holdin'
somethin' better than that!

GOOPER.    Look at Brick put it down!

(*Brick has obeyed Big Mama by draining the glass and handing it to her. Again everyone laughs, some high, some low.*)

BIG MAMA.    Oh, you bad boy, you, you're my bad little boy. Give Big Mama
a kiss, you bad boy, you!—Look at him shy away, will you? Brick never    40
liked bein' kissed or made a fuss over, I guess because he's always had too
much of it!

Son, you turn that thing off!

(*Brick has switched on the TV set.*)

I can't stand TV, radio was bad enough but TV has gone it one better, I
mean—(*plops wheezing in chair*) —one worse, ha, ha! Now what'm I sittin'    45
down here faw? I want t' sit next to my sweetheart on the sofa, hold hands
with him and love him up a little!

(*Big Mama has on a black and white figured chiffon. The large irregular patterns, like the markings of some massive animal, the lustre of her great diamonds and many pearls, the brilliants set in the silver frames of her glasses, her riotous voice, booming laugh, have dominated the room since she entered. Big Daddy has been regarding her with a steady grimace of chronic annoyance.*)

BIG MAMA.    (*still louder*) Preacher, Preacher, hey, Preach! Give me you' hand
an' help me up from this chair!

REVEREND TOOKER.    None of your tricks, Big Mama!    50

BIG MAMA.    What tricks? You give me you' hand so I can get up an'—

(*Reverend Tooker extends her his hand. She grabs it and pulls him into her lap with a shrill laugh that spans an octave in two notes.*)

Ever seen a preacher in a fat lady's lap? Hey, hey, folks! Ever seen a preacher in a fat lady's lap?

(*Big Mama is notorious throughout the Delta for this sort of inelegant horseplay. Margaret looks on with indulgent humour, sipping Dubonnet[1] "on the rocks" and watching Brick, but Mae and Gooper exchange signs of humourless anxiety over these antics, the sort of behaviour which Mae thinks may account for their failure to quite get in with the smartest young married set in Memphis, despite all.*

*One of the Negroes, Lacy or Sookey, peeks in, cackling. They are waiting for a sign to bring in the cake and champagne. But Big Daddy's not amused. He doesn't understand why, in spite of the infinite mental relief he's received from the doctor's report, he still has these same old fox teeth in his guts. "This spastic condition is something else," he says to himself, but aloud he roars at Big Mama:*)

55 BIG DADDY. *BIG MAMA, WILL YOU QUIT HORSIN'?*—You're too old an' too fat fo' that sort of crazy kid stuff an' besides a woman with your blood pressure—she had two hundred last spring!—is riskin' a stroke when you mess around like that....

(*Mae blows on a pitch pipe.*)

60 BIG MAMA. *Here comes Big Daddy's birthday!*

(*Negroes in white jackets enter with an enormous birthday cake ablaze with candles and carrying buckets of champagne with satin ribbons about the bottle necks. Mae and Gooper strike up song, and everybody, including the Negroes and Children, joins in. Only Brick remains aloof.*)

EVERYONE.
*Happy birthday to you.*
*Happy birthday to you.*
*Happy birthday, Big Daddy—*

(*Some sing:* "Dear, Big Daddy!")

*Happy birthday to you.*

(*Some sing:* "How old are you?"

*Mae has come down centre and is organizing her children like a chorus. She gives them a barely audible:* "One, two, three!" *and they are off in the new tune.*)

---

1   *Dubonnet* Sweet alcoholic drink traditionally consumed before a meal.

CHILDREN.

*Skinamarinka—dinka—dink*                                                           65
*Skinamarinka—do*
*We love you.*
*Skinamarinka—dinka—dink*
*Skinamarinka—do.*

(*All together, they turn to Big Daddy.*)

*Big Daddy, you!*                                                                      70

(*They turn back front, like a musical comedy chorus.*)

*We love you in the morning;*
*We love you in the night.*
*We love you when we're with you,*
*And we love you out of sight.*
*Skinamarinka—dinka—dink*                                                           75
*Skinamarinka—do.*

(*Mae turns to Big Mama.*)

*Big Mama, too!*

(*Big Mama bursts into tears. The Negroes leave.*)

BIG DADDY.  Now Ida, what the hell is the matter with you?
MAE.  She's just so happy.
BIG MAMA.  I'm just so happy, Big Daddy, I have to cry or something.          80

(*Sudden and loud in the hush:*)

Brick, do you know the wonderful news that Doc Baugh got from the
clinic about Big Daddy? Big Daddy's one hundred per cent!
MARGARET.  Isn't that wonderful?
BIG MAMA.  He's just one hundred per cent. Passed the examination with flying colours. Now that we know there's nothing wrong with Big Daddy but      85
a spastic colon, I can tell you something. I was worried sick, half out of my
mind, for fear that Big Daddy might have a thing like—

(*Margaret cuts through this speech, jumping up and exclaiming shrilly:*)

MARGARET.  Brick, honey, aren't you going to give Big Daddy his birthday
present?

(*Passing by him, she snatches his liquor glass from him. She picks up a
fancily wrapped package.*)

*Here it is, Big Daddy, this is from Brick!*                                           90

BIG MAMA.  This is the biggest birthday Big Daddy's ever had, a hundred presents and bushels of telegrams from—

MAE.  (*at the same time*) What is it, Brick?

GOOPER.  I bet 500 to 50 that Brick don't *know* what it is.

95  BIG MAMA.  The fun of presents is not knowing what they are till you open the package. Open your present, Big Daddy.

BIG DADDY.  Open it you'self. I want to ask Brick somethin! Come here, Brick.

MARGARET.  Big Daddy's callin' you, Brick.

(*She is opening the package.*)

100  BRICK.  Tell Big Daddy I'm crippled.

BIG DADDY.  I see you're crippled. I want to know how you got crippled.

MARGARET.  (*making diversionary tactics*) *Oh, look, oh, look, why, it's a cashmere robe!*

(*She holds the robe up for all to see.*)

MAE.  You sound surprised, Maggie.

105  MARGARET.  I never saw one before.

MAE.  That's funny.—*Hah!*

MARGARET.  (*turning on her fiercely, with a brilliant smile*) Why is it funny? All my family ever had was family—and luxuries such as cashmere robes still surprise me!

110  BIG DADDY.  (*ominously*) Quiet!

MAE.  (*heedless in her fury*) I don't see how you could be so surprised when you bought it yourself at Loewenstein's[1] in Memphis last Saturday. You know how I know?

BIG DADDY.  I said, Quiet!

115  MAE.  —I know because the salesgirl that sold it to you waited on me and said, Oh, Mrs. Pollitt, your sister-in-law just bought a cashmere robe for your husband's father!

MARGARET.  Sister Woman! Your talents are wasted as a housewife and mother, you really ought to be with the FBI or—

120  BIG DADDY.  QUIET!

(*Reverend Tooker's reflexes are slower than the others'. He finishes a sentence after the bellow.*)

REVEREND TOOKER.  (*to Doc Baugh*)—the Stork and the Reaper are running neck and neck!

---

1   *Loewenstein's* Lowenstein and Bros., a Memphis-based department store that operated until the 1980s.

(*He starts to laugh gaily when he notices the silence and Big Daddy's glare. His laugh dies falsely.*)

BIG DADDY. Preacher, I hope I'm not butting in on more talk about memorial stained-glass windows, am I, Preacher?

(*Reverend Tooker laughs feebly, then coughs dryly in the embarrassed silence.*)

Preacher?    125

BIG MAMA. Now, Big Daddy, don't you pick on Preacher!

BIG DADDY. (*raising his voice*) You ever hear that expression all hawk and no spit? You bring that expression to mind with that little dry cough of yours, all hawk an' no spit....

(*The pause is broken only by a short startled laugh from Margaret, the only one there who is conscious of and amused by the grotesque.*)

MAE. (*raising her arms and jangling her bracelets*) I wonder if the mosquitoes   130 are active tonight?

BIG DADDY. What's that, Little Mama? Did you make some remark?

MAE. Yes, I said I wondered if the mosquitoes would eat us alive if we went out on the gallery for a while.

BIG DADDY. Well, if they do, I'll have your bones pulverized for fertilizer!   135

BIG MAMA. (*quickly*) Last week we had an airplane spraying the place and I think it done some good, at least I haven't had a —

BIG DADDY. (*cutting her speech*) Brick, they tell me, if what they tell me is true, that you done some jumping last night on the high school athletic field?    140

BIG MAMA. Brick, Big Daddy is talking to you, son.

BRICK. (*smiling vaguely over his drink*) What was that, Big Daddy?

BIG DADDY. They said you done some jumping on the high school track field last night.

BRICK. That's what they told me, too.    145

BIG DADDY. Was it jumping or humping that you were doing out there? What were you doing out there at three A.M., layin' a woman on that cinder track?

BIG MAMA. Big Daddy, you are off the sick-list, now, and I'm not going to excuse you for talkin' so—    150

BIG DADDY. Quiet!

BIG MAMA. —*nasty* in front of Preacher and—

BIG DADDY. *QUIET!*—I ast you, Brick, if you was cuttin' you'self a piece o' poon-tang last night on that cinder track? I thought maybe you were chasin' poon-tang on that track an' tripped over something in the heat of the   155 chase—'sthat it?

(*Gooper laughs, loud and false, others nervously following suit. Big Mama stamps her foot, and purses her lips, crossing to Mae and whispering something to her as Brick meets his father's hard, intent, grinning stare with a slow, vague smile that he offers all situations from behind the screen of his liquor.*)

BRICK.  No, sir, I don't think so....

MAE.  (*at the same time, sweetly*) Reverend Tooker, let's you and I take a stroll on the widow's walk.[1]

(*She and the preacher go out on the gallery as Big Daddy says:*)

160  BIG DADDY.  Then what the hell were you doing out there at three o'clock in the morning?

BRICK.  Jumping the hurdles, Big Daddy, runnin' and jumpin' the hurdles, but those high hurdles have gotten too high for me, now.

BIG DADDY.  Cause you was drunk?

165  BRICK.  (*his vague smile fading a little*) Sober I wouldn't have tried to jump the *low* ones....

BIG MAMA.  (*quickly*) Big Daddy, blow out the candles on your birthday cake!

MARGARET.  (*at the same time*) I want to propose a toast to Big Daddy Pollitt on his sixty-fifth birthday, the biggest cotton planter in—

170  BIG DADDY.  (*bellowing with fury and disgust*) I told you to stop it, now stop it, quit this—!

BIG MAMA.  (*coming in front of Big Daddy with the cake*) Big Daddy, I will not allow you to talk that way, not even on your birthday, I—

BIG DADDY.  I'll talk like I want to on my birthday, Ida, or any other goddam

175  day of the year and anybody here that don't like it knows what they can do!

BIG MAMA.  You don't mean that!

BIG DADDY.  What makes you think I don't mean it?

(*Meanwhile various discreet signals have been exchanged and Gooper has also gone out on the gallery.*)

BIG MAMA.  I just know you don't mean it.

BIG DADDY.  You don't know a goddam thing and you never did!

180  BIG MAMA.  Big Daddy, you don't mean that.

BIG DADDY.  Oh, yes, I do, oh, yes, I do, I mean it! I put up with a whole lot of crap around here because I thought I was dying. And you thought I was dying and you started taking over, well, you can stop taking over now, Ida, because I'm not gonna die, you can just stop now this business of taking

185  over because you're not taking over because I'm not dying, I went through

---

1  *widow's walk* Walkway or lookout on a rooftop.

the laboratory and the goddam exploratory operation and there's nothing wrong with me but a spastic colon. And I'm not dying of cancer which you thought I was dying of. Ain't that so? Didn't you think that I was dying of cancer, Ida?

(*Almost everybody is out on the gallery but the two old people glaring at each other across the blazing cake. Big Mama's chest heaves and she presses a fat fist to her mouth. Big Daddy continues, hoarsely:*)

Ain't that so, Ida? Didn't you have an idea I was dying of cancer and now you could take control of this place and everything on it? I got that impression, I seemed to get that impression. Your loud voice everywhere, your fat old body butting in here and there!

BIG MAMA.  Hush! The Preacher!

BIG DADDY.  Fuck the goddam preacher!

(*Big Mama gasps loudly and sits down on the sofa which is almost too small for her.*)

Did you hear what I said? I said fuck the goddam preacher!

(*Somebody closes the gallery doors from outside just as there is a burst of fireworks and excited cries from the children.*)

BIG MAMA.  I never seen you act like this before and I can't think what's got in you!

BIG DADDY.  I went through all that laboratory and operation and all just so I would know if you or me was the boss here! Well, now it turns out that I am and you ain't—and that's my birthday present—and my cake and champagne!—because for three years now you been gradually taking over. Bossing. Talking. Sashaying your fat old body around the place I made! I made this place! I was overseer on it! I was the overseer on the old Straw and Ochello plantation. I quit school at ten! I quit school at ten years old and went to work like a nigger in the fields. And I rose to be overseer of the Straw and Ochello plantation. And old Straw died and I was Ochello's partner and the place got bigger and bigger and bigger and bigger and bigger! I did all that myself with no goddam help from you, and now you think you're just about to take over. Well, I am just about to tell you that you are not just about to take over, you are not just about to take over a God damn thing. Is that clear to you, Ida? Is that very plain to you, now? Is that understood completely? I been through the laboratory from A to Z. I've had the goddam exploratory operation, and nothing is wrong with me but a spastic colon—made spastic, I guess, by *disgust*! By all the goddam lies and liars that I have had to put up with, and all the goddam hypocrisy that I lived with all these forty years that we been livin' together!

Hey! Ida!! Blow out the candles on the birthday cake! Purse up your lips and draw a deep breath and blow out the goddam candles on the

220    cake!

BIG MAMA.   Oh, Big Daddy, oh, oh, oh, Big Daddy!

BIG DADDY.   What's the matter with you?

BIG MAMA.   *In all these years you never believed that I loved you??*

BIG DADDY.   Huh?

225    BIG MAMA.   *And I did, I did so much, I did love you!*—I even loved your hate and your hardness, Big Daddy!

(*She sobs and rushes awkwardly out onto the gallery.*)

BIG DADDY.   (*to himself*) *Wouldn't it be funny if that was true....*

(*A pause is followed by a burst of light in the sky from the fireworks.*)

*BRICK! HEY, BRICK!*

(*He stands over his blazing birthday cake. After some moments, Brick hobbles in on his crutch, holding his glass. Margaret follows him with a bright, anxious smile.*)

MARGARET.   I'm just delivering him to you.

(*She kisses Brick on the mouth which he immediately wipes with the back of his hand. She flies girlishly back out. Brick and his father are alone.*)

230    BIG DADDY.   Why did you do that?

BRICK.   Do what, Big Daddy?

BIG DADDY.   Wipe her kiss off your mouth like she'd spit on you.

BRICK.   I don't know. I wasn't conscious of it.

BIG DADDY.   That woman of yours has a better shape on her than Gooper's

235    but somehow or other they got the same look about them.

BRICK.   What sort of look is that, Big Daddy?

BIG DADDY.   I don't know how to describe it but it's the same look.

BRICK.   They don't look peaceful, do they?

BIG DADDY.   No, they sure in hell don't.

240    BRICK.   They look nervous as cats?

BIG DADDY.   That's right, they look nervous as cats.

BRICK.   Nervous as a couple of cats on a hot tin roof?

BIG DADDY.   That's right, boy, they look like a couple of cats on a hot tin roof.
       It's funny that you and Gooper being so different would pick out the same

245    type of woman.

BRICK.   Both of us married into society, Big Daddy.

BIG DADDY. Crap ... I wonder what gives them both that look?

BRICK. Well. They're sittin' in the middle of a big piece of land, Big Daddy, twenty-eight thousand acres is a pretty big piece of land and so they're squaring off on it, each determined to knock off a bigger piece of it than the other whenever you let it go.    250

BIG DADDY. I got a surprise for those women. I'm not gonna let it go for a long time yet if that's what they're waiting for.

BRICK. That's right, Big Daddy. You just sit tight and let them scratch each other's eyes out....    255

BIG DADDY. You bet your life I'm going to sit tight on it and let those sons of bitches scratch their eyes out, ha ha ha....

But Gooper's wife's a good breeder, you got to admit she's fertile. Hell, at supper tonight she had them all at the table and they had to put a couple of extra leafs in the table to make room for them, she's got five head of them, now, and another one's comin'.    260

BRICK. Yep, number six is comin'....

BIG DADDY. Six hell, she'll probably drop a litter next time. Brick, you know, I swear to God, I don't know the way it happens?

BRICK. The way what happens, Big Daddy?    265

BIG DADDY. You git you a piece of land, by hook or crook, an' things start growin' on it, things accumulate on it, and the first thing you know it's completely out of hand, completely out of hand!

BRICK. Well, they say nature hates a vacuum, Big Daddy.

BIG DADDY. That's what they say, but sometimes I think that a vacuum is a hell of a lot better than some of the stuff that nature replaces it with.    270

Is someone out there by that door?

GOOPER. Hey Mae.

BRICK. Yep.

BIG DADDY. Who?    275

(*He has lowered his voice.*)

BRICK. Someone int'rested in what we say to each other.

BIG DADDY. Gooper?—*GOOPER!*

(*After a discreet pause, Mae appears in the gallery door.*)

MAE. Did you call Gooper, Big Daddy?

BIG DADDY. Aw, it was you.

MAE. Do you want Gooper, Big Daddy?    280

BIG DADDY. No, and I don't want you. I want some privacy here, while I'm having a confidential talk with my son Brick. Now it's too hot in here to close them doors, but if I have to close those fuckin' doors in order to

have a private talk with my son Brick, just let me know and I'll close 'em.
285 Because I hate eavesdroppers, I don't like any kind of sneakin' an' spyin'.

MAE. Why, Big Daddy—

BIG DADDY. You stood on the wrong side of the moon, it threw your shadow!

MAE. I was just—

BIG DADDY. You was just nothing but *spyin'* an' you *know* it!

290 MAE. (*begins to sniff and sob*) Oh, Big Daddy, you're so unkind for some reason to those that really love you!

BIG DADDY. Shut up, shut up, shut up! I'm going to move you and Gooper out of that room next to this! It's none of your goddam business what goes on in here at night between Brick an' Maggie. You listen at night like a
295 couple of rutten peekhole spies and go and give a report on what you hear to Big Mama an' she comes to me and says they say such and such and so and so about what they heard goin' on between Brick an' Maggie, and Jesus, it makes me sick. I'm goin' to move you an' Gooper out of that room, I can't stand sneakin' an' spyin', it makes me puke....

(*Mae throws back her head and rolls her eyes heavenward and extends her arms as if invoking God's pity for this unjust martyrdom; then she presses a handkerchief to her nose and flies from the room with a loud swish of skirts.*)

300 BRICK. (*now at the liquor cabinet*) They listen, do they?

BIG DADDY. Yeah. They listen and give reports to Big Mama on what goes on in here between you and Maggie. They say that—

(*He stops as if embarrassed.*)

—You won't sleep with her, that you sleep on the sofa. Is that true or not true? If you don't like Maggie, get rid of Maggie!—What are you doin'
305 there now?

BRICK. Fresh'nin' up my drink.

BIG DADDY. Son, you know you got a real liquor problem?

BRICK. Yes, sir, yes, I know.

BIG DADDY. Is that why you quit sports-announcing, because of this liquor
310 problem?

BRICK. Yes, sir, yes, sir, I guess so.

(*He smiles vaguely and amiably at his father across his replenished drink.*)

BIG DADDY. Son, don't guess about it, it's too important.

BRICK. (*vaguely*) Yes, sir.

BIG DADDY. And listen to me, don't look at the damn chandelier....

(*Pause. Big Daddy's voice is husky.*)

—Somethin' else we picked up at th' big fire sale[1] in Europe. 315

(*Another pause.*)

Life is important. There's nothing else to hold onto. A man that drinks is throwing his life away. Don't do it, hold onto your life. There's nothing else to hold onto....

Sit down over here so we don't have to raise our voices, the walls have ears in this place. 320

BRICK. (*hobbling over to sit on the sofa beside him*) All right, Big Daddy.

BIG DADDY. Quit!—how'd that come about? Some disappointment?

BRICK. I don't know. Do you?

BIG DADDY. I'm askin' you, God damn it! How in hell would I know if you don't? 325

BRICK. I just got out there and found that I had a mouth full of cotton. I was always two or three beats behind what was goin' on on the field and so I—

BIG DADDY. Quit!

BRICK. (*amiably*) Yes, quit.

BIG DADDY. Son? 330

BRICK. Huh?

BIG DADDY. (*inhales loudly and deeply from his cigar; then bends suddenly a little forward, exhaling loudly and raising his forehead*) —Whew!—ha ha!— I took in too much smoke, it made me a little lightheaded....

(*The mantel clock chimes.*)

*Why is it so damn hard for people to talk?* 335

BRICK. Yeah....

(*The clock goes on sweetly chiming till it has completed the stroke of ten.*)

—Nice peaceful-soundin' clock, I like to hear it all night....

(*He slides low and comfortable on the sofa; Big Daddy sits up straight and rigid with some unspoken anxiety. All his gestures are tense and jerky as he talks. He wheezes and pants and sniffs through his nervous speech, glancing quickly, shyly, from time to time, at his son.*)

BIG DADDY. We got that clock the summer we wint to Europe, me an' Big Mama on that damn Cook's Tour, never had such an awful time in my life, I'm tellin' you, son, those gooks[2] over there, they gouge your eyeballs 340

---

1   *fire sale*  Sale with extremely discounted prices; the term implies that the goods are damaged or the seller is near bankruptcy.

2   *Cook's Tour*  Tour offered by the travel company Thomas Cook and Son; *gooks*  Offensive slang: foreigners.

out in their grand hotels. And Big Mama bought more stuff than you could haul in a couple of boxcars, that's no crap. Everywhere she wint on this whirlwind tour, she bought, bought, bought. Why, half that stuff she bought is still crated up in the cellar, under water last spring!

345    That Europe is nothin' on earth but a great big auction, that's all it is, that bunch of old wornout places, it's just a big fire sale, the whole fuckin' thing, an' Big Mama wint wild in it, why, you couldn't hold that woman with a mule's harness! Bought, bought, bought!—lucky I'm a rich man, yes siree, Bob, an' half that stuff is mildewin' in th' basement. It's lucky I'm

350    a rich man, it sure is lucky, well, I'm a rich man, Brick, yep, I'm a mighty rich man.

*(His eyes light up for a moment.)*

Y'know how much I'm worth? Guess, Brick! Guess how much I'm worth!

*(Brick smiles vaguely over his drink.)*

Close on ten million in cash an' blue-chip stocks,[1] outside, mind you, of twenty-eight thousand acres of the richest land this side of the valley Nile.

355    But a man can't buy his life with it, he can't buy back his life with it when his life has been spent, that's one thing not offered in the Europe fire-sale or in the American markets or any markets on earth, a man can't buy his life with it, he can't buy back his life when his life is finished....

    That's a sobering thought, a very sobering thought, and that's a thought
360    that I was turning over in my head, over and over and over—until today....

    I'm wiser and sadder, Brick, for this experience which I just gone through. They's one thing else that I remember in Europe.

Brick.  What is that, Big Daddy?

Big Daddy.  The hills around Barcelona in the country of Spain and the chil-
365    dren running over those bare hills in their bare skins beggin' like starvin' dogs with howls and screeches, and how fat the priests are on the streets of Barcelona, so many of them and so fat and so pleasant, ha ha!—Y'know I could feed that country? I got money enough to feed that goddam country, but the human animal is a selfish beast and I don't reckon the money
370    I passed out there to those howling children in the hills around Barcelona would more than upholster the chairs in this room, I mean pay to put a new cover on this chair!

    Hell, I threw them money like you'd scatter feed corn for chickens, I threw money at them just to get rid of them long enough to climb back
375    into th' car and—drive away....

---

1   *blue-chip stocks*  High-priced stocks that pay reliable dividends.

And then in Morocco, them Arabs, why, I remember one day in Marrakech,[1] that old walled Arab city, I set on a broken-down wall to have a cigar, it was fearful hot there and this Arab woman stood in the road and looked at me till I was embarrassed, she stood stock still in the dusty hot road and looked at me till I was embarrassed. But listen to this. She had a naked child with her, a little naked girl with her, barely able to toddle, and after a while she set this child on the ground and give her a push and whispered something to her.

The child come toward me, barely able t' walk, come toddling up to me and—

Jesus, it makes you sick t' remember a thing like this!

It stuck out its hand and tried to unbutton my trousers!

That child was not yet five! Can you believe me? Or do you think that I am making this up? I wint back to the hotel and said to Big Mama, Git packed! We're clearing out of this country....

BRICK. Big Daddy, you're on a talkin' jag tonight.

BIG DADDY. (*ignoring this remark*) Yes, sir, that's how it is, the human animal is a beast that dies but the fact that he's dying don't give him pity for others, no, sir, it—

—Did you say something?

BRICK. Yes.

BIG DADDY. What?

BRICK. Hand me over that crutch so I can get up.

BIG DADDY. Where you goin'?

BRICK. I'm takin' a little short trip to Echo Spring.

BIG DADDY. To where?

BRICK. Liquor cabinet....

BIG DADDY. Yes, sir, boy—

(*He hands Brick the crutch.*)

—the human animal is a beast that dies and if he's got money he buys and buys and buys and I think the reason he buys everything he can buy is that in the back of his mind he has the crazy hope that one of his purchases will be life everlasting!—Which it never can be.... The human animal is a beast that—

BRICK. (*at the liquor cabinet*) Big Daddy, you sure are shootin' th' breeze here tonight.

(*There is a pause and voices are heard outside.*)

---

1   *Marrakech* City in western Morocco.

BIG DADDY.  I been quiet here lately, spoke not a word, just sat and stared into space. I had something heavy weighing on my mind but tonight that load was took off me. That's why I'm talking.—The sky looks diff'rent to me....

BRICK.  You know what I like to hear most?

415 BIG DADDY.  What?

BRICK.  Solid quiet. Perfect unbroken quiet.

BIG DADDY.  Why?

BRICK.  Because it's more peaceful.

BIG DADDY.  Man, you'll hear a lot of that in the grave.

(*He chuckles agreeably.*)

420 BRICK.  Are you through talkin' to me?

BIG DADDY.  Why are you so anxious to shut me up?

BRICK.  Well, sir, ever so often you say to me, Brick, I want to have a talk with you, but when we talk, it never materializes. Nothing is said. You sit in a chair and gas about this and that and I look like I listen. I try to look like

425 I listen, but I don't listen, not much. Communication is—awful hard between people an'—somehow between you and me, it just don't—happen.

BIG DADDY.  Have you ever been scared? I mean have you ever felt downright terror of something?

(*He gets up.*)

Just one moment.

(*He looks off as if he were going to tell an important secret.*)

430 BIG DADDY.  Brick?

BRICK.  What?

BIG DADDY.  Son, I thought I had it!

BRICK.  Had what? Had what, Big Daddy?

BIG DADDY.  Cancer!

435 BRICK.  Oh ...

BIG DADDY.  I thought the old man made out of bones had laid his cold and heavy hand on my shoulder!

BRICK.  Well, Big Daddy, you kept a tight mouth about it.

BIG DADDY.  A pig squeals. A man keeps a tight mouth about it, in spite of a

440 man not having a pig's advantage.

BRICK.  What advantage is that?

BIG DADDY.  Ignorance—of mortality—is a comfort. A man don't have that comfort, he's the only living thing that conceives of death, that knows what it is. The others go without knowing which is the way that anything

445 living should go, go without knowing, without any knowledge of it, and

yet a pig squeals, but a man sometimes, he can keep a tight mouth about it..Sometimes he—

(*There is a deep, smouldering ferocity in the old man.*)

—can keep a tight mouth about it. I wonder if—
BRICK. What, Big Daddy?
BIG DADDY. A whiskey highball would injure this spastic condition?          450
BRICK. No, sir, it might do it good.
BIG DADDY. (*grins suddenly, wolfishly*) Jesus, I can't tell you! *The sky is open!
Christ, it's open again! It's open, boy, it's open!*

(*Brick looks down at his drink.*)

BRICK. You feel better, Big Daddy?
BIG DADDY. Better? Hell! I can breathe!—All of my life I been like a doubled   455
up fist....

(*He pours a drink.*)

—Poundin', smashin', drivin'!—now I'm going to loosen these doubled-
up hands and touch things *easy* with them....

(*He spreads his hands as if caressing the air.*)

You know what I'm contemplating?
BRICK. (*vaguely*) No, sir. What are you contemplating?          460
BIG DADDY. Ha ha!—*Pleasure!*—pleasure with *women!*

(*Brick's smile fades a little but lingers.*)

—Yes, boy. I'll tell you something that you might not guess. I still have
desire for women and this is my sixty-fifth birthday.
BRICK. I think that's mighty remarkable, Big Daddy.
BIG DADDY. Remarkable?          465
BRICK. *Admirable*, Big Daddy.
BIG DADDY. You're damn right it is, remarkable and admirable both. I realize
now that I never had me enough. I let many chances slip by because of
scruples about it, scruples, convention—crap.... All that stuff is bull, bull,
bull!—It took the shadow of death to make me see it. Now that shadow's   470
lifted, I'm going to cut loose and have, what is it they call it, have me a—
ball!
BRICK. A ball, huh?
BIG DADDY. That's right, a ball, a ball! Hell!—I slept with Big Mama till, let's
see, five years ago, till I was sixty and she was fifty-eight, and never even   475
liked her, never did!

(*The phone has been ringing down the hall. Big Mama enters, exclaiming:*)

BIG MAMA. Don't you men hear that phone ring? I heard it way out on the gall'ry.

BIG DADDY. There's five rooms off this front gall'ry that you could go through. Why do you go through this one?

(*Big Mama makes a playful face as she bustles out the hall door.*)

480  Hunh!—Why, when Big Mama goes out of a room, I can't remember what that woman looks like—

BIG MAMA. Hello.

BIG DADDY. —But when Big Mama comes back into the room, boy, then I see what she looks like, and I wish I didn't!

(*Bends over laughing at this joke till it hurts his guts and he straightens with a grimace. The laugh subsides to a chuckle as he puts the liquor glass a little distrustfully down on the table.*)

485  BIG MAMA. Hello, Miss Sally.

(*Brick has risen and hobbled to the gallery doors.*)

BIG DADDY. Hey! Where you goin'?

BRICK. Out for a breather.

BIG DADDY. Not yet you ain't. Stay here till this talk is finished, young fellow.

BRICK. I thought it was finished, Big Daddy.

490  BIG DADDY. It ain't even begun.

BRICK. My mistake. Excuse me. I just wanted to feel that river breeze.

BIG DADDY. Set back down in that chair.

(*Big Mama's voice rises, carrying down the hall.*)

BIG MAMA. Miss Sally, you're a case! You're a caution, Miss Sally.

BIG DADDY. Jesus, she's talking to my old maid sister again.

495  BIG MAMA. Why didn't you give me a chance to explain it to you?

BIG DADDY. Brick, this stuff burns me.

BIG MAMA. Well, goodbye, now, Miss Sally. You come down real soon. Big Daddy's dying to see you.

BIG DADDY. Crap!

500  BIG MAMA. Yaiss, goodbye, Miss Sally....

(*She hangs up and bellows with mirth. Big Daddy groans and covers his ears as she approaches. Bursting in:*)

Big Daddy, that was Miss Sally callin' from Memphis again! You know what she done, Big Daddy? She called her doctor in Memphis to git him

to tell her what that spastic thing is! Ha-*HAAAA*!—! And called back to
tell me how relieved she was that—Hey! Let me in!

(*Big Daddy has been holding the door half closed against her.*)

BIG DADDY.  Naw I ain't. I told you not to come and go through this room.    505
You just back out and go through those five other rooms.

BIG MAMA.  Big Daddy? Big Daddy? Oh, Big Daddy!—You didn't mean
those things you said to me, did you? (*He shuts door firmly against her but
she still calls.*) Sweetheart? Sweetheart? Big Daddy? You didn't mean those
awful things you said to me?—I know you didn't. I know you didn't mean    510
those things in your heart....

(*The childlike voice fades with a sob and her heavy footsteps retreat down
the hall. Brick has risen once more on his crutches and starts for the gallery
again.*)

BIG DADDY.  All I ask of that woman is that she leave me alone. But she can't
admit to herself that she makes me sick. That comes of having slept with
her too many years. Should of quit much sooner but that old woman she
never got enough of it—and I was good in bed ... I never should of wasted    515
so much of it on her.... They say you got just so many and each one is
numbered. Well, I got a few left in me, a few, and I'm going to pick me a
good one to spend 'em on! I'm going to pick me a choice one, I don't care
how much she costs, I'll smother her in—minks! Ha ha! I'll strip her naked
and smother her in minks and choke her with diamonds! Ha ha! I'll strip    520
her naked and choke her with diamonds and smother her with minks and
hump her from hell to breakfast. *Ha aha ha ha ha!*
MAE.  (*gaily at door*) Who's that laughin' in there?
GOOPER.  Is Big Daddy laughin' in there?
BIG DADDY.  Crap!—them two—*drips*....    525

(*He goes over and touches Brick's shoulder.*)

Yes, son, Brick, boy.—I'm—*happy!* I'm happy, son, I'm happy!

(*He chokes a little and bites his under lip, pressing his head quickly,
shyly against his son's head and then, coughing with embarrassment, goes
uncertainly back to the table where he set down the glass. He drinks and
makes a grimace as it burns his guts. Brick sighs and rises with effort.*)

What makes you so restless? Have you got ants in your britches?
BRICK.  Yes, sir ...
BIG DADDY.  Why?
BRICK.  —Something—hasn't—happened....    530

BIG DADDY. Yeah? What is that!

BRICK. (*sadly*) —the click....

BIG DADDY. Did you say click?

BRICK. Yes, click.

535 BIG DADDY. What click?

BRICK. A click that I get in my head that makes me peaceful.

BIG DADDY. I sure in hell don't know what you're talking about, but it disturbs me.

BRICK. It's just a mechanical thing.

540 BIG DADDY. What is a mechanical thing?

BRICK. This click that I get in my head that makes me peaceful. I got to drink till I get it. It's just a mechanical thing, something like a—like a—like a—

BIG DADDY. Like a—

BRICK. Switch clicking off in my head, turning the hot light off and the cool

545 night on and—

(*He looks up, smiling sadly.*)

—all of a sudden there's—peace!

BIG DADDY. (*whistles long and soft with astonishment; he goes back to Brick and clasps his son's two shoulders*) Jesus! I didn't know it had gotten that bad with you. Why, boy, you're—*alcoholic!*

550 BRICK. That's the truth, Big Daddy. I'm alcoholic.

BIG DADDY. This shows how I—let things go!

BRICK. I have to hear that little click in my head that makes me peaceful. Usually I hear it sooner than this, sometimes as early as—noon, but—
—Today it's—dilatory....

555 —I just haven't got the right level of alcohol in my bloodstream yet!

(*This last statement is made with energy as he freshens his drink.*)

BIG DADDY. Uh—huh. Expecting death made me blind. I didn't have no idea that a son of mine was turning into a drunkard under my nose.

BRICK. (*gently*) Well, now you do, Big Daddy, the news has penetrated.

BIG DADDY. UH-huh, yes, now I do, the news has—penetrated....

560 BRICK. And so if you'll excuse me—

BIG DADDY. No, I won't excuse you.

BRICK. —I'd better sit by myself till I hear that click in my head, it's just a mechanical thing but it don't happen except when I'm alone or talking to no one....

565 BIG DADDY. You got a long, long time to sit still, boy, and talk to no one, but now you're talkin' to me. At least I'm talking to you. And you set there and listen until I tell you the conversation is over!

BRICK.  But this talk is like all the others we've ever had together in our lives! It's nowhere, nowhere!—it's—it's *painful*, Big Daddy....

BIG DADDY.  All right, then let it be painful, but don't you move from that    570 chair!—I'm going to remove that crutch....

(*He seizes the crutch and tosses it across the room.*)

BRICK.  I can hop on one foot, and if I fall, I can crawl!

BIG DADDY.  If you ain't careful you're gonna crawl off this plantation and then, by Jesus, you'll have to hustle your drinks along Skid Row!

BRICK.  That'll come, Big Daddy.    575

BIG DADDY.  Naw, it won't. You're my son and I'm going to straighten you out; now that *I'm* straightened out, I'm going to straighten out you!

BRICK.  Yeah?

BIG DADDY.  Today the report came in from Ochsner Clinic. Y'know what they told me?    580

(*His face glows with triumph.*)

The only thing that they could detect with all the instruments of science in that great hospital is a little spastic condition of the colon! And nerves torn to pieces by all that worry about it.

(*A little girl bursts into room with a sparkler clutched in each fist, hops and shrieks like a monkey gone mad and rushes back out again as Big Daddy strikes at her. Silence. The two men stare at each other. A woman laughs gaily outside.*)

I want you to know I breathed a sigh of relief almost as powerful as the Vicksburg tornado![1]    585

(*There is laughter outside, running footsteps, the soft, plushy sound and light of exploding rockets. Brick stares at him soberly for a long moment; then makes a sort of startled sound in his nostrils and springs up on one foot and hops across the room to grab his crutch, swinging on the furniture for support. He gets the crutch and flees as if in horror for the gallery. His father seizes him by the sleeve of his white silk pajamas.*)

Stay here, you son of a bitch!—till I say go!

BRICK.  I can't.

BIG DADDY.  You sure in hell will, God damn it.

---

1    *Vicksburg tornado*  1953 tornado that passed through the city of Vicksburg, Mississippi; it was one of the worst tornadoes in the history of the state.

BRICK. No, I can't. We talk, you talk, in—circles! We get no where, no where!
590 It's always the same, you say you want to talk to me and don't have a
fuckin' thing to say to me!

BIG DADDY. Nothin' to say when I'm tellin' you I'm going to live when I
thought I was dying?!

BRICK. Oh—*that!*—Is that what you have to say to me?

595 BIG DADDY. Why, you son of a bitch! Ain't that, ain't that—*important?!*

BRICK. Well, you said that, that's said, and now I—

BIG DADDY. Now you set back down.

BRICK. You're all balled up, you—

BIG DADDY. I ain't balled up!

600 BRICK. You are, you're all balled up!

BIG DADDY. Don't tell me what I am, you drunken whelp! I'm going to tear
this coat sleeve off if you don't set down!

BRICK. Big Daddy—

BIG DADDY. Do what I tell you! I'm the boss here, now! I want you to know
605 I'm back in the driver's seat now!

(*Big Mama rushes in, clutching her great heaving bosom.*)

BIG MAMA. Big Daddy!

BIG DADDY. What in hell do you want in here, Big Mama?

BIG MAMA. Oh, Big Daddy! Why are you shouting like that? I just cain't
stainnnnnnnd—it....

610 BIG DADDY. (*raising the back of his hand above his head*) GIT!—outa here.

(*She rushes back out, sobbing.*)

BRICK. (*softly, sadly*) Christ....

BIG DADDY. (*fiercely*) Yeah! Christ!—is right ...

(*Brick breaks loose and hobbles toward the gallery. Big Daddy jerks his
crutch from under Brick so he steps with the injured ankle. He utters a
hissing cry of anguish, clutches a chair and pulls it over on top of him on
the floor.*)

Son of a—tub of—hog fat....

BRICK. Big Daddy! Give me my crutch.

(*Big Daddy throws the crutch out of reach.*)

615 Give me that crutch, Big Daddy.

BIG DADDY. Why do you drink?

BRICK. Don't know, give me my crutch!

BIG DADDY. You better think why you drink or give up drinking!

BRICK.  Will you please give me my crutch so I can get up off this floor?

BIG DADDY.  First you answer my question. Why do you drink? Why are you    620
throwing your life away, boy, like somethin' disgusting you picked up on
the street?

BRICK.  (*getting onto his knees*) Big Daddy, I'm in pain, I stepped on that foot.

BIG DADDY.  Good! I'm glad you're not too numb with the liquor in you to
feel some pain!    625

BRICK.  You—spilled my—drink ...

BIG DADDY.  I'll make a bargain with you. You tell me why you drink and I'll
hand you one. I'll pour you the liquor myself and hand it to you.

BRICK.  Why do I drink?

BIG DADDY.  Yea! Why?    630

BRICK.  Give me a drink and I'll tell you.

BIG DADDY.  Tell me first!

BRICK.  I'll tell you in one word.

BIG DADDY.  What word?

BRICK.  DISGUST!    635

(*The clock chimes softly, sweetly. Big Daddy gives it a short, outraged glance.*)

Now how about that drink?

BIG DADDY.  What are you disgusted with? You got to tell me that, first. Otherwise being disgusted don't make no sense!

BRICK.  Give me my crutch.

BIG DADDY.  You heard me, you got to tell me what I asked you first.    640

BRICK.  I told you, I said to kill my disgust.

BIG DADDY.  DISGUST WITH WHAT!

BRICK.  You strike a hard bargain.

BIG DADDY.  What are you disgusted with?—an' I'll pass you the liquor.

BRICK.  I can hop on one foot, and if I fall, I can crawl.    645

BIG DADDY.  You want liquor that bad?

BRICK.  (*dragging himself up, clinging to bedstead*) Yeah, I want it that bad.

BIG DADDY.  If I give you a drink, will you tell me what it is you're disgusted
with, Brick?

BRICK.  Yes, sir, I will try to.    650

(*The old man pours him a drink and solemnly passes it to him. There is
silence as Brick drinks.*)

Have you ever heard the word "mendacity?"

BIG DADDY.  Sure. Mendacity is one of them five dollar words that cheap
politicians throw back and forth at each other.

BRICK.  You know what it means?

655 BIG DADDY. Don't it mean lying and liars?

BRICK. Yes, sir, lying and liars.

BIG DADDY. Has someone been lying to you?

CHILDREN. (*chanting in chorus offstage*)

We want Big Dad-dee!

660 We want Big Dad-dee!

(*Gooper appears in the gallery door.*)

GOOPER. Big Daddy, the kiddies are shouting for you out there.

BIG DADDY. (*fiercely*) Keep out, Gooper!

GOOPER. 'Scuse *me!*

(*Big Daddy slams the doors after Gooper.*)

BIG DADDY. Who's been lying to you, has Margaret been lying to you, has

665 your wife been lying to you about something, Brick?

BRICK. Not her. That wouldn't matter.

BIG DADDY. Then who's been lying to you, and what about?

BRICK. No one single person, and no one lie....

BIG DADDY. Then what, what then, for Christ's sake?

670 BRICK. —The whole, the whole—thing....

BIG DADDY. Why are you rubbing your head? You got a headache?

BRICK. No, I'm tryin' to—

BIG DADDY. —Concentrate, but you can't because your brain's all soaked

with liquor, is that the trouble? Wet brain!

(*He snatches the glass from Brick's hand.*)

675 What do you know about this mendacity thing? Hell! I could write a book

on it! Don't you know that? I could write a book on it and still not cover

the subject? Well, I could, I could write a goddam book on it and still not

cover the subject anywhere near enough!!—Think of all the lies I got to

put up with!—Pretenses! Ain't that mendacity? Having to pretend stuff

680 you don't think or feel or have any idea of? Having for instance to act like I

care for Big Mama!—I haven't been able to stand the sight, sound, or smell

of that woman for forty years now!—even when I *laid* her!—regular as a

piston....

Pretend to love that son of a bitch of a Gooper and his wife Mae and

685 those five same screechers out there like parrots in a jungle? Jesus! Can't

stand to look at 'em!

Church!—it bores the bejesus out of me but I go!—I go an' sit there and

listen to the fool preacher! Clubs!—Elks! Masons! Rotary!—*crap!*

*(A spasm of pain makes him clutch his belly. He sinks into a chair and his voice is softer and hoarser.)*

*You* I *do* like for some reason, did always have some kind of real feeling for—affection—respect—yes, always....                                                    690

You and being a success as a planter is all I ever had any devotion to in my whole life!—and that's the truth....

I don't know why, but it is!

*I've* lived with mendacity!—Why can't *you* live with it? Hell, you *got* to live with it, there's nothing *else* to *live* with except mendacity, is there?     695

BRICK. Yes, sir. Yes, sir there is something else that you can live with!

BIG DADDY. What?

BRICK. *(lifting his glass)* This!—Liquor....

BIG DADDY. That's not living, that's dodging away from life.

BRICK. I want to dodge away from it.                                              700

BIG DADDY. Then why don't you kill yourself, man?

BRICK. I like to drink....

BIG DADDY. Oh, God, I can't talk to you....

BRICK. I'm sorry, Big Daddy.

BIG DADDY. Not as sorry as I am. I'll tell you something. A little while back   705
when I thought my number was up—

*(This speech should have torrential pace and fury.)*

—before I found out it was just this—spastic—colon. I thought about you. Should I or should I not, if the jig was up, give you this place when I go— since I hate Gooper an' Mae an' know that they hate me, and since all five same monkeys are little Maes an' Goopers.—And I thought, No!—Then I   710 thought, Yes!—I couldn't make up my mind. I hate Gooper and his five same monkeys and that bitch Mae! Why should I turn over twenty-eight thou- sand acres of the richest land this side of the valley Nile to not my kind?— But why in hell, on the other hand, Brick—should I subsidize a goddam fool on the bottle?—Liked or not liked, well, maybe even—*loved!*—Why   715 should I do that?—Subsidize worthless behaviour? Rot? Corruption?

BRICK. *(smiling)* I understand.

BIG DADDY. Well, if you do, you're smarter than I am, God damn it, because I don't understand. And this I will tell you frankly. I didn't make up my mind at all on that question and still to this day I ain't made out no will!—   720 Well, now I don't *have* to. The pressure is gone. I can just wait and see if you pull yourself together or if you don't.

BRICK. That's right, Big Daddy.

BIG DADDY. You sound like you thought I was kidding.

725 BRICK. (*rising*) No, sir, I know you're not kidding.
BIG DADDY. But you don't care—?
BRICK. (*hobbling toward the gallery door*) No, sir, I don't care....

> (*He stands in the gallery doorway as the night sky turns pink and green and gold with successive flashes of light.*)

BIG DADDY. *WAIT!*—Brick....

> (*His voice drops. Suddenly there is something shy, almost tender, in his restraining gesture.*)

730 Don't let's—leave it like this, like them other talks we've had, we've always—talked around things, we've—just talked around things for some fuckin' reason, I don't know what, it's always like something was left not spoken, something avoided because neither of us was honest enough with the—other....
735 BRICK. I never lied to you, Big Daddy.
BIG DADDY. Did I ever to *you?*
BRICK. No, sir....
BIG DADDY. Then there is at least two people that never lied to each other.
BRICK. But we've never *talked* to each other.
740 BIG DADDY. We can *now.*
BRICK. Big Daddy, there don't seem to be anything much to say.
BIG DADDY. You say that you drink to kill your disgust with lying.
BRICK. You said to give you a reason.
BIG DADDY. Is liquor the only thing that'll kill this disgust?
745 BRICK. Now. Yes.
BIG DADDY. But not once, huh?
BRICK. Not when I was still young an' believing. A drinking man's someone who wants to forget he isn't still young an' believing.
BIG DADDY. Believing what?
750 BRICK. Believing....
BIG DADDY. Believing *what?*
BRICK. (*stubbornly evasive*) Believing....
BIG DADDY. I don't know what the hell you mean by believing and I don't think you know what you mean by believing, but if you still got sports in
755 your blood, go back to sports announcing and—
BRICK. Sit in a glass box watching games I can't play? Describing what I can't do while players do it? Sweating out their disgust and confusion in contests I'm not fit for? Drinkin' a coke, half bourbon, so I can stand it? That's no goddam good any more, no help—time just outran me, Big Daddy—got
760 there first ...

BIG DADDY.  I think you're passing the buck.

BRICK.  You know many drinkin' men?

BIG DADDY.  (*with a slight, charming smile*) I have known a fair number of that species.

BRICK.  Could any of them tell you why he drank?    765

BIG DADDY.  Yep, you're passin' the buck to things like time and disgust with "mendacity" and—crap!—if you got to use that kind of language about a thing, it's ninety-proof[1] bull, and I'm not buying any.

BRICK.  I had to give you a reason to get a drink!

BIG DADDY.  You started drinkin' when your friend Skipper died.    770

(*Silence for five beats. Then Brick makes a startled movement, reaching for his crutch.*)

BRICK.  What are you suggesting?

BIG DADDY.  I'm suggesting nothing.

(*The shuffle and clop of Brick's rapid hobble away from his father's steady, grave attention.*)

—But Gooper an' Mae suggested that there was something not right exactly in your—

BRICK.  (*stopping short downstage as if backed to a wall*) "Not right"?    775

BIG DADDY.  Not, well, exactly *normal* in your friendship with—

BRICK.  They suggested that, too? I thought that was Maggie's suggestion.

(*Brick's detachment is at last broken through. His heart is accelerated; his forehead sweat-beaded; his breath becomes more rapid and his voice hoarse. The thing they're discussing, timidly and painfully on the side of Big Daddy, fiercely, violently on Brick's side, is the inadmissible thing that Skipper died to disavow between them. The fact that if it existed it had to be disavowed to "keep face" in the world they lived in, may be at the heart of the "mendacity" that Brick drinks to kill his disgust with. It may be the root of his collapse. Or maybe it is only a single manifestation of it, not even the most important. The bird that I hope to catch in the net of this play is not the solution of one man's psychological problem. I'm trying to catch the true quality of experience in a group of people, that cloudy, flickering, evanescent—fiercely charged!—interplay of live human beings in the thundercloud of a common crisis. Some mystery should be left in the revelation of character in a play, just as a great deal of mystery is always left in the revelation of character in life, even in one's own character to*)

---

1    *ninety-proof* I.e., concentrated; a ninety-proof alcoholic drink contains forty-five per cent pure alcohol.

*himself. This does not absolve the playwright of his duty to observe and probe as clearly and deeply as he legitimately can: but it should steer him away from "pat" conclusions, facile definitions which make a play just a play, not a snare for the truth of human experience. The following scene should be played with great concentration, with most of the power leashed but palpable in what is left unspoken.)*

Who else's suggestion is it, is it *yours?* How many others thought that Skipper and I were—

780 BIG DADDY. (*gently*) Now, hold on, hold on a minute, son.—I knocked around in my time.

BRICK. What's that got to do with—

BIG DADDY. I said "Hold on!"—I bummed, I bummed this country till I was—

785 BRICK. Whose suggestion, who else's suggestion is it?

BIG DADDY. Slept in hobo jungles and railroad Y's[1] and flophouses in all cities before I—

BRICK. Oh, *you* think so, too, you call me your son and a queer. Oh! Maybe that's why you put Maggie and me in this room that was Jack Straw's and

790 Peter Ochello's, in which that pair of old sisters slept in a double bed where both of 'em died!

BIG DADDY. *Now just don't go throwing rocks at—*

(*Suddenly Reverend Tooker appears in the gallery doors, his head slightly, playfully, fatuously cocked, with a practised clergyman's smile, sincere as a bird call blown on a hunter's whistle, the living embodiment of the pious, conventional lie. Big Daddy gasps a little at this perfectly timed, but incongruous, apparition.*)

—What're you lookin' for, Preacher?

REVEREND TOOKER. The gentleman's lavoratory, ha ha!—heh, heh …

795 BIG DADDY. (*with strained courtesy*)—Go back out and walk down to the other end of the gallery, Reverend Tooker, and use the bathroom connected with my bedroom, and if you can't find it, ask them where it is!

REVEREND TOOKER. Ah, thanks.

(*He goes out with a deprecatory chuckle.*)

BIG DADDY. It's hard to talk in this place …

---

1   *hobo jungles* Camps or communities created near railroads by jobless people who travelled as stowaways on freight trains; *Y's* YMCA (Young Men's Christian Association) facilities, which offered cheap accommodation for young men. They were sometimes built near railway stations for the benefit of rail workers.

BRICK. Son of a—!                                                        800

BIG DADDY. (*leaving a lot unspoken*)—I seen all things and understood a lot
   of them, till 1910. Christ, the year that—I had worn my shoes through,
   hocked my—I hopped off a yellow dog freight car half a mile down the
   road, slept in a wagon of cotton outside the gin—Jack Straw an' Peter
   Ochello took me in. Hired me to manage this place which grew into this   805
   one.—When Jack Straw died—why, old Peter Ochello quit eatin' like a
   dog does when its master's dead, and died, too!

BRICK. Christ!

BIG DADDY. I'm just saying I understand such—

BRICK. (*violently*) Skipper is dead. I have not quit eating!               810

BIG DADDY. No, but you started drinking.

   (*Brick wheels on his crutch and hurls his glass across the room shouting.*)

BRICK. YOU THINK SO, TOO?

   (*Footsteps run on the gallery. There are women's calls. Big Daddy goes
   toward the door. Brick is transformed, as if a quiet mountain blew suddenly
   up in volcanic flame.*)

BRICK. You think so, too? You think so, too? You think me an' Skipper did,
   did, did!—*sodomy!* —together?

BIG DADDY. Hold—!                                                          815

BRICK. That what you—

BIG DADDY. —ON—a minute!

BRICK. You think we did dirty things between us, Skipper an'—

BIG DADDY. Why are you shouting like that? Why are you—

BRICK. —Me, is that what you think of Skipper, is that—                    820

BIG DADDY. —so excited? I don't think nothing. I don't know nothing. I'm
   simply telling you what—

BRICK. You think that Skipper and me were a pair of dirty old men?

BIG DADDY. Now that's—

BRICK. Straw? Ochello? A couple of—                                        825

BIG DADDY. Now just—

BRICK. —fucking sissies? Queers? Is that what you—

BIG DADDY. Shhh.

BRICK. —think?

   (*He loses his balance and pitches to his knees without noticing the pain. He
   grabs the bed and drags himself up.*)

BIG DADDY. Jesus!—Whew.... Grab my hand!                                   830

BRICK. Naw, I don't want your hand....

BIG DADDY. Well, I want yours. Git up! (*He draws him up, keeps an arm about him with concern and affection.*) You broken out in sweat! You're panting like you'd run a race with—

835 BRICK. (*freeing himself from his father's hold*) Big Daddy, you shock me, Big Daddy, you, you—*shock* me! Talkin' so—

(*He turns away from his father.*)

—casually!—about a—thing like that ...

—Don't you know how people *feel* about things like that? How, how *disgusted* they are by things like that? Why, at Ole Miss when it was discov-

840 ered a pledge to our fraternity, Skipper's and mine, did a, *attempted* to do a, unnatural thing with—

We not only dropped him like a hot rock!—We told him to git off the campus, and he did, he got!—All the way to—

(*He halts, breathless.*)

BIG DADDY. —Where?

845 BRICK. —North Africa, last I heard!

BIG DADDY. Well, I have come back from further away than that, I have just now returned from the other side of the moon, death's country, son, and I'm not easy to shock by anything here.

(*He comes downstage and faces out.*)

Always, anyhow, lived with too much space around me to be infected by

850 ideas of other people. One thing you can grow on a big place more important than cotton!—is *tolerance!*—I grown it. (*He returns toward Brick.*)

BRICK. Why can't exceptional friendship, *real, real, deep, deep friendship!* between two men be respected as something clean and decent without being thought of as—

855 BIG DADDY. It can, it is, for God's sake.

BRICK. —*Fairies....*

(*In his utterance of this word, we gauge the wide and profound reach of the conventional mores he got from the world that crowned him with early laurel.[1]*)

BIG DADDY. I told Mae an' Gooper—

BRICK. Frig Mae and Gooper, frig all dirty lies and liars!—Skipper and me had a clean, true thing between us!—had a clean friendship, practically all

860 our lives, till Maggie got the idea you're talking about. Normal? No!—It

---

1    *crowned ... laurel* In classical times a crown of laurels was worn to denote victory.

was too rare to be normal, any true thing between two people is too rare to be normal. Oh, once in a while he put his hand on my shoulder or I'd put mine on his, oh, maybe even, when we were touring the country in pro-football an' shared hotel-rooms we'd reach across the space between the two beds and shake hands to say goodnight, yeah, one or two times we—    865

BIG DADDY.  Brick, nobody thinks that that's not normal!

BRICK.  Well, they're mistaken, it was! It was a pure an' true thing an' that's not normal.

MAE.  (*off stage*) Big Daddy, they're startin' the fireworks.

(*They both stare straight at each other for a long moment. The tension breaks and both turn away as if tired.*)

BIG DADDY.  Yeah, it's—hard t'—talk....    870

BRICK.  All right, then, let's—let it go....

BIG DADDY.  Why did Skipper crack up? Why have you?

(*Brick looks back at his father again. He has already decided, without knowing that he has made this decision, that he is going to tell his father that he is dying of cancer. Only this could even the score between them: one inadmissible thing in return for another.*)

BRICK.  (*ominously*) All right. You're asking for it, Big Daddy. We're finally going to have that real true talk you wanted. It's too late to stop it, now, we got to carry it through and cover every subject.    875

(*He hobbles back to the liquor cabinet.*)

Uh-huh.

(*He opens the ice bucket and picks up the silver tongs with slow admiration of their frosty brightness.*)

Maggie declares that Skipper and I went into pro-football after we left "Ole Miss" because we were scared to grow up ...

(*He moves downstage with the shuffle and clop of a cripple on a crutch. As Margaret did when her speech became "recitative," he looks out into the house, commanding its attention by his direct, concentrated gaze—a broken, "tragically elegant" figure telling simply as much as he knows of "the Truth":*)

—Wanted to—keep on tossing—those long, long!—high, high!—passes that—couldn't be intercepted except by time, the aerial attack that made    880 us famous! And so we did, we did, we kept it up for one season, that aerial attack, we held it high!—Yeah, but—

—that summer, Maggie, she laid the law down to me, said, Now or never, and so I married Maggie....

885   BIG DADDY.  How was Maggie in bed?

BRICK.  (*wryly*) Great! the greatest!

(*Big Daddy nods as if he thought so.*)

She went on the road that fall with the Dixie Stars. Oh, she made a great show of being the world's best sport. She wore a—wore a—tall bearskin cap! A shako, they call it, a dyed moleskin coat, a moleskin coat dyed
890   red!—Cut up crazy! Rented hotel ballrooms for victory celebrations, wouldn't cancel them when it—turned out—defeat....

MAGGIE THE CAT!  Ha ha!

(*Big Daddy nods.*)

—But Skipper, he had some fever which came back on him which doctors couldn't explain and I got that injury—turned out to be just a shadow on
895   the X-ray plate—and a touch of bursitis.[1]...

I lay in a hospital bed, watched our games on TV, saw Maggie on the bench next to Skipper when he was hauled out of a game for stumbles, fumbles!—Burned me up the way she hung on his arm!—Y'know, I think that Maggie had always felt sort of left out because she and me never got
900   any closer together than two people just get in bed, which is not much closer than two cats on a—fence humping....

So! She took this time to work on poor dumb Skipper. He was a less than average student at Ole Miss, you know that, don't you?!—Poured in his mind the dirty, false idea that what we were, him and me, was a frus-
905   trated case of that ole pair of sisters that lived in this room, Jack Straw and Peter Ochello!—He, poor Skipper, went to bed with Maggie to prove it wasn't true, and when it didn't work out, he thought it *was* true!—Skipper broke in two like a rotten stick—nobody ever turned so fast to a lush—or died of it so quick....

910   —Now are you satisfied?

(*Big Daddy has listened to this story, dividing the grain from the chaff. Now he looks at his son.*)

BIG DADDY.  Are *you* satisfied?

BRICK.  With what?

BIG DADDY.  That half-ass story!

BRICK.  What's half-ass about it?

---

1    *bursitis* Inflammation of the joints.

BIG DADDY. Something's left out of that story. What did you leave out?    915

(*The phone has started ringing in the hall.*)

GOOPER. (*off stage*) Hello.

(*As if it reminded him of something, Brick glances suddenly toward the sound and says:*)

BRICK. Yes!—I left out a long-distance call which I had from Skipper—
GOOPER. Speaking, go ahead.
BRICK. —In which he made a drunken confession to me and on which I hung up!    920
GOOPER. No.
BRICK. —Last time we spoke to each other in our lives ...
GOOPER. No, sir.
BIG DADDY. You musta said something to him before you hung up.
BRICK. What could I say to him?    925
BIG DADDY. Anything. Something.
BRICK. Nothing.
BIG DADDY. Just hung up?
BRICK. Just hung up.
BIG DADDY. Uh-huh. Anyhow now!—we have tracked down the lie with    930
which you're disgusted and which you are drinking to kill your disgust with, Brick. You been passing the buck. This disgust with mendacity is disgust with yourself.

*You!*—dug the grave of your friend and kicked him in it!—before you'd face truth with him!    935
BRICK. *His* truth, not *mine!*
BIG DADDY. His truth, okay! But you wouldn't face it with him!
BRICK. Who *can* face truth? Can *you?*
BIG DADDY. Now don't start passin' the rotten buck again, boy!
BRICK. How about these birthday congratulations, these many, many happy    940
returns of the day, when ev'rybody knows there won't be any except you!

(*Gooper, who has answered the hall phone, lets out a high, shrill laugh; the voice becomes audible saying:* "No, no, you got it all wrong! Upside down! Are you crazy?"

*Brick suddenly catches his breath as he realizes that he has made a shocking disclosure. He hobbles a few paces, then freezes, and without looking at this father's shocked face, says:*)

Let's, let's—go out, now, and—watch the fireworks. Come on, Big Daddy.

*(Big Daddy moves suddenly forward and grabs hold of the boy's crutch like it was a weapon for which they were fighting for possession.)*

945 BIG DADDY. Oh, no, no! No one's going out! What did you start to say?

BRICK. I don't remember.

BIG DADDY. "Many happy returns when they know there won't be any"?

BRICK. Aw, hell, Big Daddy, forget it. Come on out on the gallery and look at the fireworks they're shooting off for your birthday....

950 BIG DADDY. First you finish that remark you were makin' before you cut off. "Many happy returns when they know there won't be any"?—Ain't that what you just said?

BRICK. Look, now. I can get around without that crutch if I have to but it would be a lot easier on the furniture an' glassware if I didn' have to go

955 swinging along like Tarzan of th'—

BIG DADDY. *FINISH! WHAT YOU WAS SAYIN'!*

*(An eerie green glow shows in sky behind him.)*

BRICK. *(sucking the ice in his glass, speech becoming thick).* Leave th' place to Gooper and Mae an' their five little same little monkeys. All I want is—

BIG DADDY. "LEAVE TH' PLACE," did you say?

960 BRICK. *(vaguely)* All twenty-eight thousand acres of the richest land this side of the valley Nile.

BIG DADDY. Who said I was "leaving the place" to Gooper or anybody? This is my sixty-fifth birthday! I got fifteen years or twenty years left in me! I'll outlive *you!* I'll bury you an' have to pay for your coffin!

965 BRICK. Sure. Many happy returns. Now let's go watch the fireworks, come on, let's—

BIG DADDY. Lying, have they been lying? About the report from th'—clinic? Did they, did they—find something?—*Cancer.* Maybe?

BRICK. Mendacity is a system that we live in. Liquor is the one way out an'

970 death's the other....

*(He takes the crutch from Big Daddy's loose grip and swings out on the gallery leaving the doors open. A song, "Pick a Bale of Cotton,"[1] is heard.)*

MAE. *(appearing in door)* Oh, Big Daddy, the field hands are singin' fo' you!

BRICK. I'm sorry, Big Daddy. My head don't work any more and it's hard for me to understand how anybody could care if he lived or died or was dying or cared about anything but whether or not there was liquor left in the bot-

975 tle and so I said what I said without thinking. In some ways I'm no better than the others, in some ways worse because I'm less alive. Maybe it's be-

1   *"Pick a Bale of Cotton"* Traditional Southern folk song.

ing alive that makes them lie, and being almost *not* alive makes me sort of accidentally truthful—I don't know but—anyway—we've been friends ...
—And being friends is telling each other the truth....

(*There is a pause.*)

You told *me!* I told *you!*                                                         980
BIG DADDY. (*slowly and passionately*) CHRIST—DAMN—
GOOPER. (*off stage*) Let her go!

(*Fireworks off stage right.*)

BIG DADDY. —ALL—LYING SONS OF—LYING BITCHES!

(*He straightens at last and crosses to the inside door. At the door he turns and looks back as if he had some desperate question he couldn't put into words. Then he nods reflectively and says in a hoarse voice:*)

Yes, all liars, all liars, all lying dying liars!

(*This is said slowly, slowly, with a fierce revulsion. He goes on out.*)

—Lying! Dying! Liars!                                                            985

(*Brick remains motionless as the lights dim out and the curtain falls.*)

**CURTAIN**

—

## ACT 3

*There is no lapse of time. Big Daddy is seen leaving as at the end of Act II.*

BIG DADDY. ALL LYIN'—DYIN'!—LIARS! LIARS!—LIARS!

(*Margaret enters.*)

MARGARET. Brick, what in the name of God was goin' on in this room?

(*Dixie and Trixie enter through the doors and circle around Margaret shouting. Mae enters from the lower gallery window.*)

MAE. Dixie, Trixie, you quit that!

(*Gooper enters through the doors.*)

Gooper, will y' please get these kiddies to bed right now!
GOOPER. Mae, you seen Big Mama?                                                  5
MAE. Not yet.

(*Gooper and kids exit through the doors. Reverend Tooker enters through the windows.*)

REVEREND TOOKER. Those kiddies are so full of vitality. I think I'll have to be starting back to town.

MAE. Not yet, Preacher. You know we regard you as a member of this family, one of our closest an' dearest, so you just got t' be with us when Doc Baugh gives Big Mama th'actual truth about th' report from the clinic.

MARGARET. Where do you think you're going?

BRICK. Out for some air.

MARGARET. Why'd Big Daddy shout "Liars?"

MAE. Has Big Daddy gone to bed, Brick?

GOOPER. (*entering*) Now where is that old lady?

REVEREND TOOKER. I'll look for her.

(*He exits to the gallery.*)

MAE. Cain'tcha find her, Gooper?

GOOPER. She's avoidin' this talk.

MAE. I think she senses somethin'.

MARGARET. (*going out on the gallery to Brick*) Brick, they're goin' to tell Big Mama the truth about Big Daddy and she's goin' to need you.

DOCTOR BAUGH. This is going to be painful.

MAE. Painful things caint always be avoided.

REVEREND TOOKER. I see Big Mama.

GOOPER. Hey, Big Mama, come here.

MAE. Hush, Gooper, don't holler.

BIG MAMA. (*entering*) Too much smell of burnt fireworks makes me feel a little bit sick at my stomach.—Where is Big Daddy?

MAE. That's what I want to know, where has Big Daddy gone?

BIG MAMA. He must have turned in, I reckon he went to baid ...

GOOPER. Well, then, now we can talk.

BIG MAMA. What *is* this talk, *what* talk?

(*Margaret appears on the gallery, talking to Doctor Baugh.*)

MARGARET. (*musically*) My family freed their slaves ten years before abolition.[1] My great-great-grandfather gave his slaves their freedom five years before the War between the States[2] started!

MAE. Oh, for God's sake! Maggie's climbed back up in her family tree!

MARGARET. (*sweetly*) What, Mae?

---

1    *abolition* In the United States, slavery was officially abolished in 1865.

2    *War between the States* I.e., the American Civil War (1861–65).

(*The pace must be very quick: great Southern animation.*)

BIG MAMA. (*addressing them all*) I think Big Daddy was just worn out. He
loves his family, he loves to have them around him, but it's a strain on his
nerves. He wasn't himself tonight, Big Daddy wasn't himself, I could tell
he was all worked up.

REVEREND TOOKER. I think he's remarkable.

BIG MAMA. Yaisss! Just remarkable. Did you all notice the food he ate at that
table? Did you all notice the supper he put away? Why he ate like a hawss!

GOOPER. I hope he doesn't regret it.

BIG MAMA. What? Why that man—ate a huge piece of cawn bread with
molasses on it! Helped himself twice to hoppin' John.[1]

MARGARET. Big Daddy loves hoppin' John.—We had a real country dinner.

BIG MAMA. (*overlapping Margaret*) Yaiss, he simply adores it! an' candied
yams? Son? That man put away enough food at that table to stuff a *field*
hand!

GOOPER. (*with grim relish*) I hope he don't have to pay for it later on ...

BIG MAMA. (*fiercely*) What's *that*, Gooper?

MAE. Gooper says he hopes Big Daddy doesn't suffer tonight.

BIG MAMA. Oh, shoot, Gooper says, Gooper says! Why should Big Daddy
suffer for satisfying a normal appetite? There's nothin' wrong with that
man but nerves, he's sound as a dollar! And now he knows he is an' that's
why he ate such a supper. He had a big load off his mind, knowin' he
wasn't doomed t'—what he thought he was doomed to ...

MARGARET. (*sadly and sweetly*) Bless his old sweet soul ...

BIG MAMA. (*vaguely*) Yais, bless his heart, where's Brick?

MAE. Outside.

GOOPER. —Drinkin' ...

BIG MAMA. I know he's drinkin'. Cain't I see he's drinkin' without you continually tellin' me that boy's drinkin'?

MARGARET. Good for you, Big Mama!

(*She applauds.*)

BIG MAMA. Other people *drink* and *have* drunk an' will *drink*, as long as they
make that stuff an' put it in bottles.

MARGARET. That's the truth. I never trusted a man that didn't drink.

BIG MAMA. *Brick? Brick!*

MARGARET. He's still on the gall'ry. I'll go bring him in so we can talk.

BIG MAMA. (*worriedly*) I don't know what this mysterious family conference
is about.

---

1    *hoppin' John* Southern dish made with black-eyed peas, rice, bacon, and onions.

*(Awkward silence. Big Mama looks from face to face, then belches slightly and mutters, "Excuse me ..." She opens an ornamental fan suspended about her throat. A black lace fan to go with her black lace gown, and fans her wilting corsage, sniffing nervously and looking from face to face in the uncomfortable silence as Margaret calls "Brick?" and Brick sings to the moon on the gallery.)*

75  MARGARET. Brick, they're gonna tell Big Mama the truth an' she's gonna need you.

BIG MAMA. I don't know what's wrong here, you all have such long faces! Open that door on the hall and let some air circulate through here, will you please, Gooper?

80  MAE. I think we'd better leave that door closed, Big Mama, till after the talk.

MARGARET. Brick!

BIG MAMA. Reveren' Tooker, will *you* please open that door?

REVEREND TOOKER. I sure will, Big Mama.

MAE. I just didn't think we ought t' take any chance of Big Daddy hearin' a

85  word of this discussion.

BIG MAMA. *I swan!*[1] Nothing's going to be said in Big Daddy's house that he caint hear if he wants to!

GOOPER. Well, Big Mama, it's—

*(Mae gives him a quick, hard poke to shut him up. He glares at her fiercely as she circles before him like a burlesque[2] ballerina, raising her skinny bare arms over her head, jangling her bracelets, exclaiming:)*

MAE. A breeze! A breeze!

90  REVEREND TOOKER. I think this house is the coolest house in the Delta.— Did you all know that Halsey Banks's widow put air-conditioning units in the church and rectory at Friar's Point in memory of Halsey?

*(General conversation has resumed; everybody is chatting so that the stage sounds like a bird cage.)*

GOOPER. Too bad nobody cools your church off for you. I bet you sweat in that pulpit these hot Sundays, Reverend Tooker.

95  REVEREND TOOKER. Yes, my vestments[3] are drenched. Last Sunday the gold in my chasuble[4] faded into the purple.

GOOPER. Reveren', you musta been preachin' hell's fire last Sunday.

---

1   *I swan* I.e., I swear.

2   *burlesque* Exaggerated for comedic effect.

3   *vestments* Garments worn by religious officials during public ceremonies.

4   *chasuble* Outer vestment worn by Catholic and Anglican priests during Mass.

MAE. (*at the same time to Doctor Baugh*) You reckon those vitamin B12 injections are what they're cracked up t' be, Doc Baugh?

DOCTOR BAUGH.  Well, if you want to be stuck with something I guess they're    100
as good to be stuck with as anything else.

BIG MAMA. (*at the gallery door*) Maggie, Maggie, aren't you comin' with Brick?

MAE. (*suddenly and loudly, creating a silence*) I have a strange feeling, I have a
peculiar feeling!

BIG MAMA. (*turning from the gallery*) What feeling?    105

MAE.  That Brick said somethin' he shouldn't of said t' Big Daddy.

BIG MAMA.  Now what on earth could Brick of said t' Big Daddy that he
shouldn't say?

GOOPER.  Big Mama, there's somethin'—

MAE.  NOW, WAIT!    110

(*She rushes up to Big Mama and gives her a quick hug and kiss. Big Mama
pushes her impatiently off.*)

DOCTOR BAUGH.  In my day they had what they call the Keeley cure[1] for
heavy drinkers.

BIG MAMA.  Shoot!

DOCTOR BAUGH.  But now I understand they just take some kind of tablets.

GOOPER.  They call them "Annie Bust" tablets.[2]    115

BIG MAMA.  *Brick* don't need to take *nothin'*.

(*Brick and Margaret appear in gallery doors, Big Mama unaware of his
presence behind her.*)

That boy is just broken up over Skipper's death. You know how poor Skipper died. They gave him a big, big dose of that sodium amytal[3] stuff at his home and then they called the ambulance and give him another big, big dose of it at the hospital and that and all of the alcohol in his system fo'    120
months an' months just proved too much for his heart ... I'm scared of needles! I'm more scared of a needle than the knife ... I think more people have been needled out of this world than—

(*She stops short and wheels about.*)

Oh—here's Brick! My precious baby—

---

1    *Keeley cure* Treatment for alcoholism from the Keeley Institute. Especially popular in the
1890s, the Keeley cure utilized ineffective secret tonics and injections of "gold chloride."

2    *"Annie Bust" tablets* Tablets of Antabuse, the trade name of the drug disulfiram, which
causes unpleasant reactions after the consumption of alcohol.

3    *sodium amytal* Sedative not recommended for people with histories of alcoholism or impaired liver function.

(*She turns upon Brick with short, fat arms extended, at the same time uttering a loud, short sob, which is both comic and touching. Brick smiles and bows slightly, making a burlesque gesture of gallantry for Margaret to pass before him into the room. Then he hobbles on his crutch directly to the liquor cabinet and there is absolute silence, with everybody looking at Brick as everybody has always looked at Brick when he spoke or moved or appeared. One by one he drops ice cubes in his glass, then suddenly, but not quickly, looks back over his shoulder with a wry, charming smile, and says:*)

125 BRICK. I'm sorry! Anyone else?

BIG MAMA. (*sadly*) No, son, I *wish* you wouldn't!

BRICK. I wish I didn't have to, Big Mama, but I'm still waiting for that click in my head which makes it all smooth out!

BIG MAMA. Ow, Brick, you—BREAK MY HEART!

130 MARGARET. (*at the same time*) Brick, go sit with Big Mama!

BIG MAMA. I just cain't staiiiiii-nnnnnnnd-it ...

(*She sobs.*)

MAE. Now that we're all assembled—

GOOPER. We kin talk ...

BIG MAMA. Breaks my heart ...

135 MARGARET. Sit with Big Mama, Brick, and hold her hand.

(*Big Mama sniffs very loudly three times, almost like three drumbeats in the pocket of silence.*)

BRICK. You do that, Maggie. I'm a restless cripple. I got to stay on my crutch.

(*Brick hobbles to the gallery door; leans there as if waiting. Mae sits beside Big Mama, while Gooper moves in front and sits on the end of the couch, facing her. Reverend Tooker moves nervously into the space between them; on the other side, Doctor Baugh stands looking at nothing in particular and lights a cigar. Margaret turns away.*)

BIG MAMA. Why're you all *surroundin'* me—like this? Why're you all starin' at me like this an' makin' signs at each other?

(*Reverend Tooker steps back startled.*)

MAE. Calm yourself, Big Mama.

140 BIG MAMA. Calm you'self, *you'self*, Sister Woman. How could I calm myself with everyone starin' at me as if big drops of blood had broken out on m'face? What's this all about, annh! What?

(*Gooper coughs and takes a centre position.*)

GOOPER. Now, Doc Baugh.

MAE. Doc Baugh?

GOOPER. Big Mama wants to know the complete truth about the report we   145
got from the Ochsner Clinic.

MAE. (*eagerly*)—on Big Daddy's condition!

GOOPER. Yais, on Big Daddy's condition, we got to face it.

DOCTOR BAUGH. Well ...

BIG MAMA. (*terrified, rising*) Is there? Something? Something that I? Don't—   150
know?

> (*In these few words, this startled, very soft, question, Big Mama reviews the history of her forty-five years with Big Daddy, her great, almost embarrassingly true-hearted and simple-minded devotion to Big Daddy, who must have had something Brick has, who made himself loved so much by the "simple expedient" of not loving enough to disturb his charming detachment, also once coupled, like Brick, with virile beauty. Big Mama has a dignity at this moment; she almost stops being fat.*)

DOCTOR BAUGH. (*after a pause, uncomfortably*) Yes?—Well—

BIG MAMA. I!!!—want to—*knowwwwww* ...

> (*Immediately she thrusts her fist to her mouth as if to deny that statement. Then for some curious reason, she snatches the withered corsage from her breast and hurls it on the floor and steps on it with her short, fat feet.*)

*Somebody must be lyin'!—I want to know!*

MAE. Sit down, Big Mama, sit down on this sofa.   155

MARGARET. Brick, go sit with Big Mama.

BIG MAMA. *What is it, what is it?*

DOCTOR BAUGH. I never have seen a more thorough examination than Big
Daddy Pollitt was given in all my experience with the Ochsner Clinic.

GOOPER. It's one of the best in the country.   160

MAE. It's THE best in the country—bar *none!*

> (*For some reason she gives Gooper a violent poke as she goes past him. He slaps at her hand without removing his eyes from his mother's face.*)

DOCTOR BAUGH. Of course they were ninety-nine and nine-tenths per cent
sure before they even started.

BIG MAMA. Sure of what, sure of what, sure of—*what?*—*what?*

> (*She catches her breath in a startled sob. Mae kisses her quickly. She thrusts Mae fiercely away from her, staring at the Doctor.*)

MAE. Mommy, be a brave girl!   165

BRICK. (*in the doorway, singing softly*) "By the light, by the light, Of the sil-
ve-ry mo-oo-n ..."[1]
GOOPER. Shut up!—Brick.
BRICK. Sorry ...

(*He wanders out on the gallery.*)

170 DOCTOR BAUGH. But now, you see, Big Mama, they cut a piece off this
growth, a specimen of the tissue and—
BIG MAMA. Growth? You told Big Daddy—
DOCTOR BAUGH. Now wait.
BIG MAMA. (*fiercely*) You told me and Big Daddy there wasn't a thing wrong
175 with him but—
MAE. Big Mama, they always—
GOOPER. Let Doc Baugh talk, will yuh?
BIG MAMA. —little spastic condition of—

(*Her breath gives out in a sob.*)

DOCTOR BAUGH. Yes, that's what we told Big Daddy. But we had this bit of
180 tissue run through the laboratory and I'm sorry to say the test was positive
on it. It's—well—malignant ...

(*Pause*)

BIG MAMA. —Cancer?! Cancer?!

(*Doctor Baugh nods gravely. Big Mama gives a long gasping cry.*)

MAE AND GOOPER. Now, now, now, Big Mama, you had to know ...
BIG MAMA. WHY DIDN'T THEY CUT IT OUT OF HIM? HANH? HANH?
185 DOCTOR BAUGH. Involved too much, Big Mama, too many organs affected.
MAE. Big Mama, the liver's affected and so's the kidneys, both! It's gone way
past what they call a—
GOOPER. A surgical risk.
MAE. —Uh-huh ...
190
(*Big Mama draws a breath like a dying gasp.*)

REVEREND TOOKER. Tch, tch, tch, tch, tch!
DOCTOR BAUGH. Yes it's gone past the knife.
MAE. *That's why he's turned yellow, Mommy!*

---

1    *By the light ... mo-oo-on* Line from "By the Light of the Silvery Moon" (1909), a popular
song by Gus Edwards and Edward Madden.

BIG MAMA. *Git away from me, git away from me, Mae!*

(*She rises abruptly.*)

*I want Brick! Where's Brick? Where is my only son?*    195

MAE. Mama! Did she say "*only* son"?

GOOPER. What does that make *me*?

MAE. A sober responsible man with five precious children!—*Six!*

BIG MAMA. I want Brick to tell me! Brick! Brick!

MARGARET. (*rising from her reflections in a corner*) Brick was so upset he went    200
back out.

BIG MAMA. *Brick!*

MARGARET. Mama, let *me* tell you!

BIG MAMA. No, no, leave me alone, you're not my blood!

GOOPER. *Mama, I'm your son!* Listen to *me!*    205

MAE. Gooper's your son, he's your first-born!

BIG MAMA. Gooper never liked Daddy.

MAE. (*as if terribly shocked*) That's not TRUE!

(*There is a pause. The minister coughs and rises.*)

REVEREND TOOKER. (*to Mae*) I think I'd better slip away at this point.

(*Discreetly*)

Good night, good night, everybody, and God bless you all ... on this    210
place ...

(*He slips out. Mae coughs and points at Big Mama.*)

GOOPER. Well, Big Mama ...

(*He sighs.*)

BIG MAMA. It's all a mistake, I know it's just a bad dream.

DOCTOR BAUGH. We're gonna keep Big Daddy as comfortable as we can.

BIG MAMA. Yes, it's just a bad dream, that's all it is, it's just an awful dream.    215

GOOPER. In my opinion Big Daddy is having some pain but won't admit
that he has it.

BIG MAMA. Just a dream, a bad dream.

DOCTOR BAUGH. That's what lots of them do, they think if they don't admit
they're having the pain they can sort of escape the fact of it.    220

GOOPER. (*with relish*) Yes, they get sly about it, they get real sly about it.

MAE. Gooper and I think—

GOOPER. Shut up, Mae! Big Mama, I think—Big Daddy ought to be started
on morphine.

225  BIG MAMA.  Nobody's going to give Big Daddy morphine.

DOCTOR BAUGH.  Now, Big Mama, when that pain strikes it's going to strike mighty hard and Big Daddy's going to need the needle to bear it.

BIG MAMA.  I tell you, nobody's going to give him morphine.

MAE.  Big Mama, you don't want to see Big Daddy suffer, you know you—

(*Gooper, standing beside her, gives her a savage poke.*)

230  DOCTOR BAUGH.  (*placing a package on the table*) I'm leaving this stuff here, so if there's a sudden attack you all won't have to send out for it.

MAE.  I know how to give a hypo.

BIG MAMA.  Nobody's gonna give Big Daddy morphine.

GOOPER.  Mae took a course in nursing during the war.

235  MARGARET.  Somehow I don't think Big Daddy would want Mae to give him a hypo.

MAE.  You think he'd want *you* to do it?

DOCTOR BAUGH.  Well ...

(*Doctor Baugh rises.*)

GOOPER.  Doctor Baugh is goin'.

240  DOCTOR BAUGH.  Yes, I got to be goin'. Well, keep you chin up, Big Mama.

GOOPER.  (*with jocularity*) She's gonna keep *both* chins up, aren't you, Big Mama?

(*Big Mama sobs.*)

Now stop that, Big Mama.

GOOPER.  (*at the door with Doctor Baugh*) Well, Doc, we sure do appreciate all you done. I'm telling you, we're surely obligated to you for—

245

(*Doctor Baugh has gone out without a glance at him.*)

—I guess that doctor has got a lot on his mind but it wouldn't hurt him to act a little more human ... (*Big Mama sobs.*)

Now be a brave girl, Mommy.

BIG MAMA.  It's not true, I know that it's just not true!

250  GOOPER.  Mama, those tests are infallible!

BIG MAMA.  Why are you so determined to see your father daid?

MAE.  Big Mama!

MARGARET.  (*gently*) I know what Big Mama means.

MAE.  (*fiercely*) Oh, do you?

255  MARGARET.  (*quietly and very sadly*) Yes, I think I do.

MAE.  For a newcomer in the family you sure do show a lot of understanding.

MARGARET.  Understanding is needed on this place.

MAE. I guess you must have needed a lot of it in your family, Maggie, with your father's liquor problem and now you've got Brick with his!

MARGARET. Brick does not have a liquor problem at all. Brick is devoted to Big Daddy. This thing is a terrible strain on him.

BIG MAMA. Brick is Big Daddy's boy, but he drinks too much and it worries me and Big Daddy, and, Margaret, you've got to co-operate with us, you've got to co-operate with Big Daddy and me in getting Brick straightened out. Because it will break Big Daddy's heart if Brick don't pull himself together and take hold of things.

MAE. Take hold of *what* things, Big Mama?

BIG MAMA. The place.

(*There is a quick and violent look between Mae and Gooper.*)

GOOPER. Big Mama, you've had a shock.

MAE. Yais, we've all had a shock, but ...

GOOPER. Let's be realistic—

MAE. —Big Daddy would never, would *never*, be foolish enough to—

GOOPER. —put this place in irresponsible hands!

BIG MAMA. Big Daddy ain't going to leave the place in anybody's hands; Big Daddy is *not* going to die. I want you to get that in your heads, all of you!

MAE. Mommy, Mommy, Big Mama, we're just as hopeful an' optimistic as you are about Big Daddy's prospects, we have faith in *prayer*—but nevertheless there are certain matters that have to be discussed an' dealt with, because otherwise—

GOOPER. Eventualities have to be considered and now's the time ... Mae, will you please get my brief case out of our room?

MAE. Yes, honey.

(*She rises and goes out through the hall door.*)

GOOPER. (*standing over Big Mama*) Now, Big Mom. What you said just now was not at all true and you know it. I've always loved Big Daddy in my own quiet way. I never made a show of it, and I know that Big Daddy has always been fond of me in a quiet way, too, and he never made a show of it neither.

(*Mae returns with Gooper's brief case.*)

MAE. Here's your brief case, Gooper, honey.

GOOPER. (*handing the brief case back to her*) Thank you ... Of cou'se, my relationship with Big Daddy is different from Brick's.

MAE. You're eight years older'n Brick an' always had t' carry a bigger load of th' responsibilities than Brick ever had t' carry. He never carried a thing in his life but a football or a highball.

GOOPER. Mae, will y' let me talk, please?

295 MAE. Yes, honey.

GOOPER. Now, a twenty-eight-thousand-acre plantation's a mighty big thing t' run.

MAE. Almost singlehanded.

> (*Margaret has gone out onto the gallery and can be heard calling softly to Brick.*)

BIG MAMA. You never had to run this place! What are you talking about? As
300 if Big Daddy was dead and in his grave, you had to run it? Why, you just helped him out with a few business details and had your law practice at the same time in Memphis!

MAE. Oh, Mommy, Mommy, Big Mommy! Let's be fair!

MARGARET. Brick!

305 MAE. Why, Gooper has given himself body and soul to keeping this place up for the past five years since Big Daddy's health started failing.

MARGARET. Brick!

MAE. Gooper won't say it, Gooper never thought of it as a duty, he just did it. And what did Brick do? Brick kept living in his past glory at college! Still
310 a football player at twenty-seven!

MARGARET. (*returning alone*) Who are you talking about now? Brick? A football player? He isn't a football player and you know it. Brick is a sports announcer on T.V. and one of the best-known ones in the country!

MAE. I'm talking about what he was.

315 MARGARET. Well, I wish you would just stop talking about my husband.

GOOPER. I've got a right to discuss my brother with other members of MY OWN family, which don't include *you*. Why don't you go out there and drink with Brick?

MARGARET. I've never seen such malice toward a brother.

320 GOOPER. How about his for me? Why, he can't stand to be in the same room with me!

MARGARET. This is a deliberate campaign of vilification for the most disgusting and sordid reason on earth, and I know what it is! It's *avarice, avarice, greed, greed!*

325 BIG MAMA. *Oh, I'll scream! I will scream in a moment unless this stops!*

> (*Gooper has stalked up to Margaret with clenched fists at his sides as if he would strike her. Mae distorts her face again into a hideous grimace behind Margaret's back.*)

BIG MAMA. (*sobs*) Margaret. Child. Come here. Sit next to Big Mama.

MARGARET. Precious Mommy. I'm sorry, I'm sorry, I—!

*(She bends her long graceful neck to press her forehead to Big Mama's bulging shoulder under its black chiffon.)*

MAE. How beautiful, how touching, this display of devotion! Do you know why she's childless? She's childless because that big, beautiful athlete husband of hers won't go to bed with her!                                                      330

GOOPER. You jest won't let me do this in a nice way, will yah? Aw right—I don't give a goddam if Big Daddy likes me or don't like me or did or never did or will or will never! I'm just appealing to a sense of common decency and fair play. I'll tell you the truth. I've resented Big Daddy's partiality to Brick ever since Brick was born, and the way I've been treated like I was 335 just barely good enough to spit on and sometimes not even good enough for that. Big Daddy is dying of cancer, and it's spread all through him and it's attacked all his vital organs including the kidneys and right now he is sinking into uremia, and you all know what uremia is, it's poisoning of the whole system due to the failure of the body to eliminate its poisons.          340

MARGARET. *(to herself, downstage, hissingly)* Poisons, poisons! Venomous thoughts and words! In hearts and minds!—That's poisons!

GOOPER. *(overlapping her)* I am asking for a square deal, and, by God, I expect to get one. But if I don't get one, if there's any peculiar shenanigans going on around here behind my back, well, I'm not a corporation lawyer 345 for nothing, I know how to protect my own interests.

*(Brick enters from the gallery with a tranquil, blurred smile, carrying an empty glass with him.)*

BRICK. Storm coming up.

GOOPER. Oh! A late arrival!

MAE. Behold the conquering hero comes!

GOOPER. The fabulous Brick Pollitt! Remember him?—Who could forget 350 him!

MAE. He looks like he's been injured in a game!

GOOPER. Yep, I'm afraid you'll have to warm the bench at the Sugar Bowl[1] this year, Brick!

*(Mae laughs shrilly.)*

Or was it the Rose Bowl[2] that he made that famous run in?—                         355

*(Thunder)*

---

1    *Sugar Bowl* Popular American college football game played annually in New Orleans, Louisiana.

2    *Rose Bowl* Popular American college football game played annually in Pasadena, California.

MAE. The punch bowl, honey. It was in the punch bowl, the cut-glass punch bowl!

GOOPER. Oh, that's right, I'm getting the bowls mixed up!

MARGARET. Why don't you stop venting your malice and envy on a sick boy?

360 BIG MAMA. *Now you two hush, I mean it, hush, all of you, hush!*

DAISY, SOOKEY. Storm! Storm comin'! Storm! Storm!

LACEY. Brightie, close them shutters.

GOOPER. Lacey, put the top up on my Cadillac, will yuh?

LACEY. Yes, suh, Mistah Pollitt!

365 GOOPER. (*at the same time*) Big Mama, you know it's necessary for me t' go back to Memphis in th' mornin' t' represent the Parker estate in a lawsuit.

(*Mae sits on the bed and arranges papers she has taken from the brief case.*)

BIG MAMA. Is it, Gooper?

MAE. Yaiss.

GOOPER. That's why I'm forced to—to bring up a problem that—

370 MAE. Somethin' that's too important t' be put off!

GOOPER. If Brick was sober, he ought to be in on this.

MARGARET. Brick is present; we're present.

GOOPER. Well, good. I will now give you this outline my partner, Tom Bullitt, an' me have drawn up—a sort of dummy—trusteeship.

375 MARGARET. Oh, that's it! You'll be in charge an' dole out remittances, will you?

GOOPER. This we did as soon as we got the report on Big Daddy from th' Ochsner Laboratories. We did this thing, I mean we drew up this dummy outline with the advice and assistance of the Chairman of the Boa'd of

380 Directors of th' Southern Plantahs Bank and Trust Company in Memphis, C.C. Bellowes, a man who handles estates for all th' prominent fam'lies in West Tennessee and th' Delta.

BIG MAMA. Gooper?

GOOPER. (*crouching in front of Big Mama*) Now this is not—not final, or

385 anything like it. This is just a preliminary outline. But it does provide a basis—a design—a—possible, feasible—*plan!*

MARGARET. Yes, I'll bet it's a plan.

(*Thunder*)

MAE. It's a plan to protect the biggest estate in the Delta from irresponsibility an'—

390 BIG MAMA. Now you listen to me, all of you, you listen here! They's not goin' to be any more catty talk in my house! And Gooper, you put that away before I grab it out of your hand and tear it right up! I don't know what the

hell's in it, and I don't want to know what the hell's in it. I'm talkin' in Big
Daddy's language now; I'm his *wife*, not his *widow*, I'm still his *wife!* And
I'm talkin' to you in his language an'—                                    395
GOOPER. Big Mama, what I have here is—
MAE. (*at the same time*) Gooper explained that it's just a plan ...
BIG MAMA. I don't care what you got there. Just put it back where it came
    from, an' don't let me see it again, not even the outside of the envelope of
    it! Is that understood? Basis! Plan! Preliminary! Design! I say—what is it  400
    Big Daddy always says when he's disgusted?
BRICK. (*from the bar*) Big Daddy says "crap" when he's disgusted.
BIG MAMA. (*rising*) That's right—CRAP! I say CRAP too, like Big Daddy!

> (*Thunder rolls.*)

MAE. Coarse language doesn't seem called for in this—
GOOPER. Somethin' in me is *deeply outraged* by hearin' you talk like this.     405
BIG MAMA. *Nobody's goin' to take nothin'!*—till Big Daddy lets go of it—may-
    be, just possibly, not—not even then! No, not even then!

> (*Thunder.*)

MAE. Sookey, hurry up an' git that po'ch furniture covahed; want th' paint
    to come off?
GOOPER. Lacey, put mah car away!                                               410
LACEY. Caint, Mistah Pollitt, you got the keys!
GOOPER. Naw, you got 'em, man. (*Calls to Mae.*) *Where* th' keys to th' car,
    honey?
MAE. You got 'em in your pocket!

> (*Gooper exits R.*)

BRICK. (*singing*) "You can always hear me singin' this song, Show me the way  415
    to go home."[1]

> (*Thunder distantly*)

BIG MAMA. Brick! Come here, Brick, I need you. Tonight Brick looks like he
    used to look when he was a little boy, just like he did when he played wild
    games and used to come home when I hollered myself hoarse for him, all
    sweaty and pink cheeked and sleepy, with his—red curls shining ...        420

> (*She comes over to him and runs her fat, shaky hand through his hair. Brick
> draws aside as he does from all physical contact and continues the song in*

---

1    *You can ... go home*  From "Show Me the Way to Go Home" (1925), a popular song writ-
     ten by Irvine King (pseudonym of Jimmy Campbell and Reg Connelly).

*a whisper, opening the ice bucket and dropping in the ice cubes one by one as if he were mixing some important chemical formula. Distant thunder.)*

Time goes by so fast. Nothin' can outrun it. Death commences too early— almost before you're half acquainted with life—you meet the other ... Oh, you know we just got to love each other an' stay together, all of us, just as close as we can, especially now that such a *black* thing has come and moved 425    into this place without invitation.

*(Awkwardly embracing Brick, she presses her head to his shoulder. A dog howls off stage.)*

Oh, Brick, son of Big Daddy, Big Daddy does so love you. Y'know what would be his fondest dream come true? If before he passed on, if Big Daddy has to pass on ...

*(A dog howls.)*

... you give him a child of yours, a grandson as much like his son as his son 430    is like Big Daddy.
MARGARET.  I know that's Big Daddy's dream.
BIG MAMA.  That's his dream.
MAE.  Such a pity that Maggie and Brick can't oblige.
BIG DADDY.  *(off down stage right on the gallery)* Looks like the wind was takin' 435    liberties with this place.
SERVANT.  *(off stage)* Yes, sir, Mr. Pollitt.
MARGARET.  *(crossing to the right door)* Big Daddy's on the gall'ry.

*(Big Mama has turned toward the hall door at the sound of Big Daddy's voice on the gallery.)*

BIG MAMA.  I can't stay here. He'll see somethin' in my eyes.

*(Big Daddy enters the room from up stage right.)*

BIG DADDY.  Can I come in?

*(He puts his cigar in an ash tray.)*

440    MARGARET.  Did the storm wake you up, Big Daddy?
BIG DADDY.  Which stawm are you talkin' about—th' one outside or th' hullaballoo in here?

*(Gooper squeezes past Big Daddy.)*

GOOPER.  'Scuse me:

*(Mae tries to squeeze past Big Daddy to join Gooper, but Big Daddy puts his arm firmly around her.)*

BIG DADDY.  I heard some mighty loud talk. Sounded like somethin' important was bein' discussed. What was the powwow about?    445
MAE.  (*flustered*) Why—nothin', Big Daddy ...
BIG DADDY.  (*crossing to extreme left centre, taking Mae with him*) What is that
    pregnant-lookin' envelope you're puttin' back in your brief case, Gooper?
GOOPER.  (*at the foot of the bed, caught, as he stuffs papers into envelope*) That?
    Nothin', suh—nothin' much of anythin' at all ...    450
BIG DADDY.  Nothin'? It looks like a whole lot of nothin'!

> (*He turns up stage to the group.*)

You all know th' story about th' young married couple—
GOOPER.  Yes, sir!
BIG DADDY.  Hello, Brick—
BRICK.  Hello, Big Daddy.    455

> (*The group is arranged in a semicircle above Big Daddy, Margaret at the
> extreme right, then Mae and Gooper, then Big Mama, with Brick at the
> left.*)

BIG DADDY.  Young married couple took Junior out to th' zoo one Sunday,
    inspected all of God's creatures in their cages, with satisfaction.
GOOPER.  Satisfaction.
BIG DADDY.  (*crossing to up stage centre, facing front*) This afternoon was a
    warm afternoon in spring an' that ole elephant had somethin' else on his    460
    mind which was bigger'n peanuts. You know this story, Brick?

> (*Gooper nods.*)

BRICK.  No, sir, I don't know it.
BIG DADDY.  Y'see, in th' cage adjoinin' they was a young female elephant in
    heat!
BIG MAMA.  (*at Big Daddy's shoulder*) Oh, Big Daddy!    465
BIG DADDY.  What's the matter, preacher's gone, ain't he? All right. That female elephant in the next cage was permeatin' the atmosphere about her
    with a powerful and excitin' odour of female fertility! Huh! Ain't that a nice
    way to put it, Brick?
BRICK.  Yes, sir, nothin' wrong with it.    470
BIG DADDY.  Brick says th's nothin' wrong with it!
BIG MAMA.  Oh, Big Daddy!
BIG DADDY.  (*crossing to down stage centre*) So this ole bull elephant still had a
    couple of fornications left in him. He reared back his trunk an' got a whiff
    of that elephant lady next door!—began to paw at the dirt in his cage an'    475
    butt his head against the separatin' partition and, first thing y'know, there

was a conspicuous change in his *profile*—very *conspicuous!* Ain't I tellin' this story in decent language, Brick?

BRICK.  Yes, sir, too fuckin' decent!

480  BIG DADDY.  So, the little boy pointed at it and said, "What's that?" His mama said, "Oh, that's—nothin'!"—His papa said, "She's spoiled!"

(*Big Daddy crosses to Brick at left.*)

You didn't laugh at that story, Brick.

(*Big Mama crosses to down stage right crying. Margaret goes to her. Mae and Gooper hold up stage right centre.*)

BRICK.  No, sir, I didn't laugh at that story.

BIG DADDY.  What is the smell in this room? Don't you notice it, Brick? Don't
485  you notice a powerful and obnoxious odour of mendacity in this room?

BRICK.  Yes, sir, I think I do, sir.

GOOPER.  Mae, Mae ...

BIG DADDY.  There is nothing more powerful. Is there, Brick?

BRICK.  No, sir. No, sir, there isn't, an' nothin' more obnoxious.

490  BIG DADDY.  Brick agrees with me. The odour of mendacity is a powerful and obnoxious odour an' the stawm hasn't blown it away from this room yet. You notice it, Gooper?

GOOPER.  What, sir?

BIG DADDY.  How about you, Sister Woman? You notice the unpleasant
495  odour of mendacity in this room?

MAE.  Why, Big Daddy, I don't even know what that is.

BIG DADDY.  You can smell it. Hell it smells like death!

(*Big Mama sobs. Big Daddy looks toward her.*)

What is wrong with that fat woman over there, loaded with diamonds? Hey, what's-you-name, what's the matter with you?

500  MARGARET.  (*crossing toward Big Daddy*) She had a slight dizzy spell, Big Daddy.

BIG DADDY.  You better watch that, Big Mama. A stroke is a bad way to go.

MARGARET.  (*crossing to Big Daddy at centre*) Oh, Brick, Big Daddy has on your birthday present to him, Brick, he has on your cashmere robe, the
505  softest material I have ever felt.

BIG DADDY.  Yeah, this is my soft birthday, Maggie ... Not my gold or my silver birthday, but my soft birthday, everything's got to be soft for Big Daddy on this soft birthday.

(*Maggie kneels before Big Daddy at centre.*)

MARGARET.  Big Daddy's got on his Chinese slippers that I gave him, Brick. Big Daddy, I haven't given you my big present yet, but now I will, now's the time for me to present it to you! I have an announcement to make! 510

MAE.  What? What kind of announcement?

GOOPER.  A sports announcement, Maggie?

MARGARET.  Announcement of life beginning! A child is coming, sired by Brick, and out of Maggie the Cat! I have Brick's child in my body, an' that's my birthday present to Big Daddy on this birthday! 515

(*Big Daddy looks at Brick who crosses behind Big Daddy to down stage portal, left.*)

BIG DADDY.  Get up, girl, get up off your knees, girl.

(*Big Daddy helps Margaret to rise. He crosses above her, to her right, bites off the end of a fresh cigar, taken from his bathrobe pocket, as he studies Margaret.*)

*Uh-huh, this girl has life in her body, that's no lie!*

BIG MAMA.  BIG DADDY'S DREAM COME TRUE!

BRICK.  JESUS! 520

BIG DADDY.  (*crossing right below wicker stand*) Gooper, I want my lawyer in the morning'.

BRICK.  Where are you goin', Big Daddy?

BIG DADDY.  Son, I'm goin' up on the roof, to the belvedere[1] on th' roof to look over my kingdom before I give up my kingdom—twenty-eight thou- sand acres of th' richest land this side of the valley Nile! 525

(*He exits through right doors, and down right on the gallery.*)

BIG MAMA.  (*following*) Sweetheart, sweetheart, sweetheart—can I come with you?

(*She exits down stage right. Margaret is down stage centre in the mirror area. Mae has joined Gooper and she gives him a fierce poke, making a low hissing sound and a grimace of fury.*)

GOOPER.  (*pushing her aside*) Brick, could you possibly spare me one small shot of that liquor? 530

BRICK.  Why, help yourself, Gooper boy.

GOOPER.  I will.

MAE.  (*shrilly*) Of course we know that this is—a lie.

GOOPER.  *Be still, Mae.*

---

1    *belvedere* Gallery with a view.

535 MAE.  I won't be still! I know she's made this up!

GOOPER.  Goddam it, I said shut up!

MARGARET.  Gracious! I didn't know that my little announcement was going to provoke such a storm!

MAE.  *That* woman isn't *pregnant!*

540 GOOPER.  Who said she was?

MAE.  *She* did.

GOOPER.  The doctor didn't. Doc Baugh didn't.

MARGARET.  I haven't gone to Doc Baugh.

GOOPER.  Then who'd you go to, Maggie?

545 MARGARET.  One of the best gynecologists in the South.

GOOPER.  Uh huh, uh huh!—I see ...

(*He takes out a pencil and notebook.*)

—May we have his name, please?

MARGARET.  No, you may not, Mister Prosecuting Attorney!

MAE.  He doesn't have any name, he doesn't exist!

550 MARGARET.  Oh, he exists all right, and so does my child, Brick's baby!

MAE.  You can't conceive a child by a man that won't sleep with you unless you think you're—

(*Brick has turned on the phonograph. A scat[1] song cuts Mae's speech.*)

GOOPER.  *Turn that off!*

MAE.  We know it's a lie because we hear you in here; he won't sleep with you,
555 we hear you! So don't imagine you're going to put a trick over on us, to fool a dying man with a—

(*A long drawn cry of agony and rage fills the house. Margaret turns the phonograph down to a whisper. The cry is repeated.*)

MAE.  Did you hear that, Gooper, did you hear that?

GOOPER.  Sounds like the pain has struck.

Come along and leave these lovebirds together in their nest!

(*He goes out first. Mae follows but turns at the door, contorting her face and hissing at Margaret.*)

560 MAE.  *Liar!*

(*She slams the door. Margaret exhales with relief and moves a little unsteadily to catch hold of Brick's arm.*)

---

1    *scat* Type of jazz music in which singers improvise long vocal runs using nonsense words.

MARGARET.  Thank you for—keeping still ...
BRICK.  O.K., Maggie.
MARGARET.  It was gallant of you to save my face!

(*He now pours down three shots in quick succession and stands waiting,
silent. All at once he turns with a smile and says:*)

BRICK.  *There!*
MARGARET.  What?                                                                  565
BRICK.  The *click* ...

(*His gratitude seems almost infinite as he hobbles out on the gallery with a
drink. We hear his crutch as he swings out of sight. Then, at some distance,
he begins singing to himself a peaceful song. Margaret holds the big pillow
forlornly as if it were her only companion, for a few moments, then throws
it on the bed. She rushes to the liquor cabinet, gathers all the bottles in
her arms, turns about undecidedly, then runs out of the room with them,
leaving the door ajar on the dim yellow hall. Brick is heard hobbling back
along the gallery, singing his peaceful song. He comes back in, sees the pillow
on the bed, laughs lightly, sadly, picks it up. He has it under his arm as
Margaret returns to the room. Margaret softly shuts the door and leans
against it, smiling softly at Brick.*)

MARGARET.  Brick, I used to think that you were stronger than me and I
didn't want to be overpowered by you. But now, since you've taken to
liquor—you know what?—I guess it's bad, but now I'm stronger than you
and I can love you more truly! Don't move that pillow. I'll move it right   570
back if you do!—Brick?

(*She turns out all the lamps but a single rose-silk-shaded one by the bed.*)

I really have been to a doctor and I know what to do and—Brick?—this is
my time by the calendar to conceive?
BRICK.  Yes, I understand, Maggie. But how are you going to conceive a child
by a man in love with his liquor?                                              575
MARGARET.  By locking his liquor up and making him satisfy my desire before
I unlock it!
BRICK.  Is that what you've done, Maggie?
MARGARET.  Look and see. The cabinet's mighty empty compared to before!
BRICK.  Well, I'll be a son of a—                                              580

(*He reaches for his crutch but she beats him to it and rushes out on the
gallery, hurls the crutch over the rail and comes back in, panting.*)

MARGARET. And so tonight we're going to make the lie true, and when that's done, I'll bring the liquor back here and we'll get drunk together, here, tonight, in this place that death has come into ...—What do you say?

BRICK. I don't say anything. I guess there's nothing to say.

585   MARGARET. Oh, you weak people, you weak, beautiful people!—who give up with such grace. What you want is someone to—

(*She turns out the rose-silk lamp.*)

—take hold of you.—Gently, gently with love hand your life back to you, like somethin' gold you let go of. I do love you, Brick, I do!

BRICK. (*smiling with charming sadness*) Wouldn't it be funny if that was

590   true?

**THE END**

—1954, 1974[1]

---

1   *1954, 1974* Tennessee Williams wrote three different versions of *Cat on a Hot Tin Roof*'s third act. Initially the final act of the play (published for the first time in 1955) did not include Big Daddy at all and was much bleaker than the version that ultimately debuted on Broadway in 1954. For the Broadway debut, stage director Elia Kazan requested three major changes: a final appearance by Big Daddy; a visible change in Brick's demeanour as a result of the conversation in Act 2; and a more likeable version of Maggie. Williams approved of making Maggie more sympathetic but was not satisfied with the other changes, especially Brick's transformation. In 1974, Williams's final rewrite of the play was performed. This rewrite—the text presented here—combines elements from both earlier versions.

# Sharon Pollock
b. 1936

Sharon Pollock is known for stage and radio plays with politically charged ideas at their centre. Her daring choice of subject matter is matched by an experimental approach to playwriting; as critic Anne Nothof observes, in Pollock's work "scenes intersect or blend, time inhabits a simultaneous present and past, [and] characters are divided into multiple selves who interact with and observe each other."

Pollock was born in New Brunswick in 1936. Her young adult life was marked by a series of personal hardships, including her mother's suicide and an abusive marriage. Pollock moved to Calgary in 1966, and a few years later she won the Alberta Culture playwriting competition with her first work, *A Compulsory Option* (1972).

Especially in her early plays, Pollock often incorporates events from Canadian history; *Walsh* (1973), for example, addresses the relationship between a Mounted Police superintendent and the Sioux chief Sitting Bull, while *The Komagata Maru Incident* (1976) is based on a 1914 confrontation that resulted from Canada's racist immigration policies. Such plays use the past to comment on present-day issues while also correcting, Pollock says, Canadians' false "view of themselves as nice civilized people who have never participated in historical crimes and atrocities."

With works such as *Generations* (1981) and the semi-autobiographical *Doc* (1986), Pollock shifted her focus from major events to the ways in which family dynamics and individual psychology are shaped by political or historical circumstances. Her sources range from the Lizzie Borden murder trial in 1890s Massachusetts—the subject of *Blood Relations* (1980)—to the treatment of suspected terrorists held by the American military in *Man Out of Joint* (2007).

As well as a prolific playwright, Pollock is an award-winning actor and has been artistic director at several theatres. She received Governor General's Awards for *Doc* and for *Blood Relations*, and in 2012 she was awarded the Order of Canada.

# Blood Relations

## CHARACTERS

Miss Lizzie, *who will play* Bridget, *the Irish maid*
The Actress, *who will play* Lizzie Borden[1]
Harry, *Mrs. Borden's brother*
Emma, *Lizzie's older sister*
Andrew, *Lizzie's father*
Abigail, *Lizzie's step-mother*
Dr. Patrick, *the Irish doctor; sometimes* The Defence

## SETTING

*The time proper is late Sunday afternoon and evening, late fall, in Fall River, 1902; the year of the "dream thesis," if one might call it that, is 1892.*

*The playing areas include (a) within the Borden house: the dining room from which there is an exit to the kitchen; the parlour; a flight of stairs leading to the second floor; and (b) in the Borden yard: the walk outside the house; the area in which the birds are kept.*

## PRODUCTION NOTE

*Action must be free-flowing. There can be no division of the script into scenes by blackout, movement of furniture, or sets. There may be freezes of some characters while other scenes are being played. There is no necessity to "get people off" and "on" again for, with the exception of The Actress and Miss Lizzie (and Emma in the final scene), all characters are imaginary, and all action in reality would be taking place between Miss Lizzie and The Actress in the dining room and parlour of her home.*

*The defence may actually be seen, may be a shadow, or a figure behind a scrim.[2]*

*While Miss Lizzie exits and enters with her Bridget business, she is a presence, often observing unobtrusively when as Bridget she takes no part in the action.*

---

1   *Lizzie Borden* American murder suspect (1860–1927) who in 1892 allegedly killed her father and stepmother with a hatchet. She was tried for the crime but acquitted, and she continued to live in her hometown of Fall River, Massachussetts, until her death. The case was never solved, and many remained convinced that she was guilty.

2   *scrim* Screen that is opaque when lit from the front and translucent when lit from behind.

# ACT 1

*Lights up on the figure of a woman standing centre stage. It is a somewhat formal pose. A pause. She speaks:*

"Since what I am about to say must be but that
Which contradicts my accusation, and
The testimony on my part no other
But what comes from myself, it shall scarce boot me
To say 'Not Guilty.'                                                                    5
But, if Powers Divine
Behold our human action as they do,
I doubt not then but innocence shall make
False accusation blush and tyranny
Tremble at ... at ..."[1]                                                              10

*(She wriggles the fingers of an outstretched hand searching for the word.)*

"Aaaat" ... Bollocks!!

*(She raises her script, takes a bite of chocolate.)*

"Tremble at Patience," patience patience! ...

*(Miss Lizzie enters from the kitchen with tea service. The actress's attention drifts to Miss Lizzie. The actress watches Miss Lizzie sit in the parlour and proceed to pour two cups of tea. The actress sucks her teeth a bit to clear the chocolate as she speaks:)*

THE ACTRESS. Which ... is proper, Lizzie?
MISS LIZZIE. Proper?
THE ACTRESS. To pour first the cream, and add the tea—or first tea and add    15
cream. One is proper. Is the way you do the proper way, the way it's done in circles where it counts?
MISS LIZZIE. Sugar?
THE ACTRESS. Well, is it?
MISS LIZZIE. I don't know, sugar?                                                   20
THE ACTRESS. Mmmn. *(Miss Lizzie adds sugar.)* I suppose if we had Mrs. Beeton's *Book of Etiquette*,[2] we could look it up.
MISS LIZZIE. I do have it, shall I get it?

---

1   *Since what ... at ...* See Shakespeare's *The Winter's Tale* 3.2.22–32; the actress is rehearsing Hermione's speech, delivered when the character is falsely accused of adultery and attempted poisoning; *boot* Benefit.
2   *Mrs. Beeton's ... Etiquette* First published in 1861, *Mrs. Beeton's Book of Household Management*, a wide-ranging book of recipes and domestic advice, remained popular until well into the twentieth century.

THE ACTRESS.  No.... You could ask your sister, she might know.

25 MISS LIZZIE.  Do you want this tea or not?

THE ACTRESS.  I hate tea.

MISS LIZZIE.  You drink it every Sunday.

THE ACTRESS.  I drink it because you like to serve it.

MISS LIZZIE.  Pppu.

30 THE ACTRESS.  It's true. You've no idea how I suffer from this toast and tea ritual. I really do. The tea upsets my stomach and the toast makes me fat because I eat so much of it.

MISS LIZZIE.  Practice some restraint then.

THE ACTRESS.  Mmmm ... Why don't we ask your sister which is proper?

35 MISS LIZZIE.  You ask her.

THE ACTRESS.  How can I? She doesn't speak to me. I don't think she even sees me. She gives no indication of it. (*She looks up the stairs.*) What do you suppose she does up there every Sunday afternoon?

MISS LIZZIE.  She sulks.

40 THE ACTRESS.  And reads the Bible I suppose, and Mrs. Beeton's *Book of Etiquette.* Oh Lizzie.... What a long day. The absolutely longest day.... When does that come anyway, the longest day?

MISS LIZZIE.  June.

THE ACTRESS.  Ah yes, June. (*She looks at Miss Lizzie.*) June?

45 MISS LIZZIE.  June.

THE ACTRESS.  Mmmmmm....

MISS LIZZIE.  I know what you're thinking.

THE ACTRESS.  Of course you do.... I'm thinking ... shall I pour the sherry— or will you.

50 MISS LIZZIE.  No.

THE ACTRESS.  I'm thinking ... June ... in Fall River.

MISS LIZZIE.  No.

THE ACTRESS.  August in Fall River? (*She smiles. Pause.*)

MISS LIZZIE.  We could have met in Boston.

55 THE ACTRESS.  I prefer it here.

MISS LIZZIE.  You don't find it ... a trifle boring?

THE ACTRESS.  Au contraire.

(*Miss Lizzie gives a small laugh at the affectation.*)

THE ACTRESS.  What?

MISS LIZZIE.  I find it a trifle boring ... I know what you're doing. You're soak-
60 ing up the ambience.

THE ACTRESS.  Nonsense, Lizzie. I come to see you.

MISS LIZZIE.  Why?

THE ACTRESS. Because ... of us. (*Pause.*)

MISS LIZZIE. You were a late arrival last night. Later than usual.

THE ACTRESS. Don't be silly.  65

MISS LIZZIE. I wonder why.

THE ACTRESS. The show was late, late starting, late coming down.

MISS LIZZIE. And?

THE ACTRESS. And—then we all went out for drinks.

MISS LIZZIE. We?  70

THE ACTRESS. The other members of the cast.

MISS LIZZIE. Oh yes.

THE ACTRESS. And then I caught a cab ... all the way from Boston.... Do you know what it cost?

MISS LIZZIE. I should. I paid the bill, remember?  75

THE ACTRESS. (*Laughs.*) Of course. What a jumble all my thoughts are. There're too many words running round inside my head today. It's terrible.

MISS LIZZIE. It sounds it.

(*Pause.*)

THE ACTRESS. ... You know ... you do this thing ... you stare at me ... You look directly at my eyes. I think ... you think ... that if I'm lying ... it will come  80 up, like lemons on a slot machine. (*She makes a gesture at her eyes.*) Tick. Tick ... (*Pause.*) In the alley, behind the theatre the other day, there were some kids. You know what they were doing?

MISS LIZZIE. How could I?

THE ACTRESS. They were playing skip rope, and you know what they were  85 singing? (*She sings, and claps her hands arhythmically to:*)
>"Lizzie Borden took an ax,
>Gave her Mother forty whacks,
>When the job was nicely done,
>She gave her father forty-one."  90

MISS LIZZIE. Did you stop them?

THE ACTRESS. No.

MISS LIZZIE. Did you tell them I was acquitted?

THE ACTRESS. No.

MISS LIZZIE. What did you do?  95

THE ACTRESS. I shut the window.

MISS LIZZIE. A noble gesture on my behalf.

THE ACTRESS. We were doing lines—the noise they make is dreadful. Sometimes they play ball, ka-thunk, ka-thunk, ka-thunk against the wall. Once I saw them with a cat and—  100

MISS LIZZIE. And you didn't stop them?

THE ACTRESS. That time I stopped them.

(*The actress crosses to table where there is a gramophone. She prepares to play a record. She stops.*)

THE ACTRESS. Should I?
MISS LIZZIE. Why not?
105 THE ACTRESS. Your sister, the noise upsets her.
MISS LIZZIE. And she upsets me. On numerous occasions.
THE ACTRESS. You're incorrigible, Lizzie.

(*The actress holds out her arms to Miss Lizzie. They dance the latest "in" dance, a Scott Joplin[1] composition. It requires some concentration, but they chat while dancing rather formally in contrast to the music.*)

THE ACTRESS. ... Do you think your jawline's heavy?
MISS LIZZIE. Why do you ask?
110 THE ACTRESS. They said you had jowls.
MISS LIZZIE. Did they.
THE ACTRESS. The reports of the day said you were definitely jowly.
MISS LIZZIE. That was ten years ago.
THE ACTRESS. Imagine. You were only thirty-four.
115 MISS LIZZIE. Yes.
THE ACTRESS. It happened here, this house.
MISS LIZZIE. You're leading.
THE ACTRESS. I know.
MISS LIZZIE. ... I don't think I'm jowly. Then or now. Do you?
120 THE ACTRESS. Lizzie? Lizzie.
MISS LIZZIE. What?
THE ACTRESS. ... did you?
MISS LIZZIE. Did I what?

(*Pause.*)

THE ACTRESS. You never tell *me* anything. (*She turns off the music.*)
125 MISS LIZZIE. I tell you everything.
THE ACTRESS. No you don't!
MISS LIZZIE. Oh yes, I tell you the most personal things about myself, my thoughts, my dreams, my—
THE ACTRESS. But never that one thing.... (*She lights a cigarette.*)
130 MISS LIZZIE. And don't smoke those—they stink.

(*The actress ignores her, inhales, exhales a volume of smoke in Miss Lizzie's direction.*)

---

1    *Scott Joplin* Ragtime composer and pianist (1868–1917).

MISS LIZZIE. Do you suppose ... people buy you drinks ... or cast you even ... because you have a "liaison" with Lizzie Borden? Do you suppose they do that?

THE ACTRESS. They cast me because I'm good at what I do.

MISS LIZZIE. They never pry? They never ask? What's she really like? Is she really jowly? Did she? Didn't she? 135

THE ACTRESS. What could I tell them? You never tell me anything.

MISS LIZZIE. I tell you everything.

THE ACTRESS. But that! (*Pause.*) You think everybody talks about you—they don't. 140

MISS LIZZIE. Here they do.

THE ACTRESS. You think they talk about you.

MISS LIZZIE. But never to me.

THE ACTRESS. Well ... you give them lots to talk about.

MISS LIZZIE. You know you're right, your mind is a jumble. 145

THE ACTRESS. I told you so.

(*Pause.*)

MISS LIZZIE. You remind me of my sister.

THE ACTRESS. Oh God, in what way?

MISS LIZZIE. Day in, day out, ten years now, sometimes at breakfast as she rolls little crumbs of bread in little balls, sometimes at noon, or late at night ... "Did you, Lizzie?" "Lizzie, did you?" 150

THE ACTRESS. Ten years, day in, day out?

MISS LIZZIE. Oh yes. She sits there where Papa used to sit and I sit there, where I have always sat. She looks at me and at her plate, then at me, and at her plate, then at me and then she says "Did you Lizzie?" "Lizzie, did you?" 155

THE ACTRESS. (*A nasal imitation of Emma's voice.*) "Did-you-Lizzie—Lizzie-did-you." (*Laughs.*)

MISS LIZZIE. Did I what? 160

THE ACTRESS. (*Continues her imitation of Emma.*) "You know."

MISS LIZZIE. Well, what do you think?

THE ACTRESS. "Oh, I believe you didn't, in fact I know you didn't, what a thought! After all, you were acquitted."

MISS LIZZIE. Yes, I was. 165

THE ACTRESS. "But sometimes when I'm on the street ... or shopping ... or at the church even, I catch somebody's eye, they look away ... and I think to myself 'Did-you-Lizzie—Lizzie-did-you.'"

MISS LIZZIE. (*Laughs.*) Ah, poor Emma.

THE ACTRESS. (*Dropping her Emma imitation.*) Well, did you? 170

MISS LIZZIE. Is it important?

THE ACTRESS. Yes.

MISS LIZZIE. Why?

THE ACTRESS. I have ... a compulsion to know the truth.

175 MISS LIZZIE. The truth?

THE ACTRESS. Yes.

MISS LIZZIE. ... Sometimes I think you look like me, and you're not jowly.

THE ACTRESS. No.

MISS LIZZIE. You look like me, or how I think I look, or how I ought to look

180     ... sometimes you think like me ... do you feel that?

THE ACTRESS. Sometimes.

MISS LIZZIE. (*Triumphant.*) You shouldn't have to ask then. You should know. "Did I, didn't I." You tell me.

THE ACTRESS. I'll tell you what I think.... I think ... that you're aware there is

185     a certain fascination in the ambiguity.... You always paint the background but leave the rest to my imagination. Did Lizzie Borden take an axe? ... If you didn't I should be disappointed ... and if you did I should be horrified.

MISS LIZZIE. And which is worse?

THE ACTRESS. To have murdered one's parents, or to be a pretentious small-

190     town spinster? I don't know.

MISS LIZZIE. Why're you so cruel to me?

THE ACTRESS. I'm teasing, Lizzie, I'm only teasing. Come on, paint the background again.

MISS LIZZIE. Why?

195 THE ACTRESS. Perhaps you'll give something away.

MISS LIZZIE. Which you'll dine out on.

THE ACTRESS. Of course. (*Laughs.*) Come on, Lizzie. Come on.

MISS LIZZIE. A game.

THE ACTRESS. What?

200 MISS LIZZIE. A game? ... And you'll play me.

THE ACTRESS. Oh—

MISS LIZZIE. It's your stock in trade, my love.

THE ACTRESS. Alright.... A game!

MISS LIZZIE. Let me think ... Bridget ... Brrridget. We had a maid then. And

205     her name was Bridget. Oh, she was a great one for stories, stood like this, very straight back, and her hair ... and there she was in the courtroom in her new dress on the stand. "Do you swear to tell the truth, the whole truth, and nothing but the truth, so help you God?" (*Imitates Irish accent.*) "I do sir," she said.

210     "Would you give the court your name."

    "Bridget O'Sullivan, sir."

(*Very faint echo of the voice of the defence under Miss Lizzie's next line.*)

"And occupation."

"I'm like what you'd call a maid, sir. I do a bit of everything, cleanin' and cookin'."

(*The actual voice of the defence is heard alone; he may also be seen.*)

THE DEFENCE. You've been in Fall River how long?    215

MISS LIZZIE. (*Who continues as Bridget, while the actress [who will play Lizzie] observes.*) Well now, about five years sir, ever since I came over. I worked up on the hill for a while but it didn't—well, you could say, suit me, too lah-de-dah—so I—

THE DEFENCE. Your employer in June of 1892 was?    220

BRIDGET. Yes sir. Mr. Borden, sir. Well, more rightly, Mrs. Borden for she was the one who—

THE DEFENCE. Your impression of the household?

BRIDGET. Well ... the man of the house, Mr. Borden, was a bit of a ... tight-wad, and Mrs. B. could nag you into the grave, still she helped with the    225 dishes and things which not everyone does when they hire a maid. (*Harry appears on the stairs; approaches Bridget stealthily. She is unaware of him.*) Then there was the daughters, Miss Emma and Lizzie, and that day, Mr. Wingate, Mrs. B.'s brother who'd stayed for the night and was—(*He grabs her ass with both hands. She screams.*)    230

BRIDGET. Get off with you!

HARRY. Come on, Bridget, give me a kiss!

BRIDGET. I'll give you a good poke in the nose if you don't keep your hands to yourself.

HARRY. Ohhh-hh-hh Bridget!    235

BRIDGET. Get away you old sod!

HARRY. Haven't you missed me?

BRIDGET. I have not! I was pinched black and blue last time—and I'll be suf-ferin' the same before I see the end of you this time.

HARRY. (*Tilts his ass at her.*) You want to see my end?    240

BRIDGET. You're a dirty old man.

HARRY. If Mr. Borden hears that, you'll be out on the street. (*Grabs her.*) Where's my kiss!

BRIDGET. (*Dumps glass of water on his head.*) There! (*Harry splutters.*) Would you like another? You silly thing you—and leave me towels alone!    245

HARRY. You've soaked my shirt.

BRIDGET. Shut up and pour yourself a cup of coffee.

HARRY. You got no sense of fun, Bridget.

BRIDGET. Well now, if you tried actin' like the gentleman farmer you're sup-
250  posed to be, Mr. Wingate—

HARRY. I'm tellin' you you can't take a joke.

BRIDGET. If Mr. Borden sees you jokin', it's not his maid he'll be throwin' out
on the street, but his brother-in-law, and that's the truth.

HARRY. What's between you and me's between you and me, eh?

255  BRIDGET. There ain't nothin' between you and me.

HARRY. ... Finest cup of coffee in Fall River.

BRIDGET. There's no gettin' on the good side of me now, it's too late for
that.

HARRY. ... Bridget? ... You know what tickles my fancy?

260  BRIDGET. No and I don't want to hear.

HARRY. It's your Irish temper.

BRIDGET. It is, is it? ... Can I ask you something?

HARRY. Ooohhh—anything.

BRIDGET. (*Innocently.*) Does Miss Lizzie know you're here? ... I say does Miss
265  Lizzie—

HARRY. Why do you bring her up?

BRIDGET. She don't then, eh? (*Teasing.*) It's a surprise visit?

HARRY. No surprise to her father.

BRIDGET. Oh?

270  HARRY. We got business.

BRIDGET. I'd of thought the last bit of business was enough.

HARRY. It's not for—[*you to say*]

BRIDGET. You don't learn a thing, from me or Lizzie, do you?

HARRY. Listen here—

275  BRIDGET. You mean you've forgotten how mad she was when you got her
father to sign the rent from the mill house over to your sister? Oh my.

HARRY. She's his wife, isn't she?

BRIDGET. (*Lightly.*) Second wife.

HARRY. She's still got her rights.

280  BRIDGET. Who am I to say who's got a right? But I can tell you this—Miss
Lizzie don't see it that way.

HARRY. It don't matter how Miss Lizzie sees it.

BRIDGET. Oh it matters enough—she had you thrown out last time, didn't
she? By jasus that was a laugh!

285  HARRY. You mind your tongue.

BRIDGET. And after you left, you know what happened?

HARRY. Get away.

BRIDGET. She and sister Emma got her father's rent money from the other
mill house to make it all even-steven—and now, here you are back again?

What kind of business you up to this time? (*Whispers in his ear.*) Mind  290
Lizzie doesn't catch you.

HARRY.  Get away!

BRIDGET.  (*Laughs.*) Ohhhh—would you like some more coffee, sir? It's the
finest coffee in all Fall River! (*She pours it.*) Thank you sir. You're welcome,
sir. (*She exits to the kitchen.*)  295

HARRY.  There'll be no trouble this time!! Do you hear me!

BRIDGET.  (*Off.*) Yes sir.

HARRY.  There'll be no trouble. (*Sees a basket of crusts.*) What the hell's this? I
said is this for breakfast!

BRIDGET.  (*Entering.*) Is what for—oh no—Mr. Borden's not economizin' to  300
that degree yet, it's the crusts for Miss Lizzie's birds.

HARRY.  What birds?

BRIDGET.  Some kind of pet pigeons she's raisin' out in the shed. Miss Lizzie
loves her pigeons.

HARRY.  Miss Lizzie loves kittens and cats and horses and dogs. What Miss  305
Lizzie doesn't love is people.

BRIDGET.  Some people. (*She looks past Harry to the actress/Lizzie. Harry turns
to follow Bridget's gaze. Bridget speaks, encouraging an invitation for the actress to join her.*) Good mornin' Lizzie.

THE ACTRESS.  (*She is a trifle tentative in the role of Lizzie.*) Is the coffee on?  310

BRIDGET.  Yes ma'am.

LIZZIE.  I'll have some then.

BRIDGET.  Yes ma'am. (*She makes no move to get it, but watches as Lizzie stares
at Harry.*)

HARRY.  Well ... I think ... maybe I'll ... just split a bit of that kindling out  315
back. (*He exits. Lizzie turns to Bridget.*)

LIZZIE.  Silly ass.

BRIDGET.  Oh Lizzie. (*She laughs. She enjoys the actress/Lizzie's comments as she
guides her into her role by "painting the background."*)

LIZZIE.  Well, he is. He's a silly ass.  320

BRIDGET.  Can you remember him last time with your Papa? Oh, I can still
hear him: "Now Andrew, I've spent my life raisin' horses and I'm gonna tell
you somethin'—a *woman* is just like a *horse*! You keep her on a tight rein,
or she'll take the bit in her teeth and next thing you know, road, destination, and purpose is all behind you, and you'll be damn lucky if she don't  325
pitch you right in a sewer ditch!"

LIZZIE.  Stupid bugger.

BRIDGET.  Oh Lizzie, what language! What would your father say if he heard
you?

LIZZIE.  Well ... I've never used a word I didn't hear from him first.  330

BRIDGET. Do you think he'd be congratulatin' you?

LIZZIE. Possibly. (*Bridget gives a subtle shake of her head.*) Not.

BRIDGET. Possibly not is right.... And what if *Mrs.* B. should hear you?

LIZZIE. I hope and pray that she does.... Do you know what I think, Bridget?
335     I think there's nothing wrong with Mrs. B.... that losing 80 pounds and
        tripling her intellect wouldn't cure.

BRIDGET. (*Loving it.*) You ought to be ashamed.

LIZZIE. It's the truth, isn't it?

BRIDGET. Still, what a way to talk of your Mother.

340 LIZZIE. Step-mother.

BRIDGET. Still you don't mean it, do you?

LIZZIE. Don't I? (*Louder.*) She's a *silly ass* too!

BRIDGET. Shhhh.

LIZZIE. It's alright, she's deaf as a picket fence when she wants to be.... What's
345     he here for?

BRIDGET. Never said.

LIZZIE. He's come to worm more money out of Papa I bet.

BRIDGET. Lizzie.

LIZZIE. What.

350 BRIDGET. Your sister, Lizzie. (*Bridget indicates Emma, Lizzie turns to see her
        on the stairs.*)

EMMA. You want to be quiet, Lizzie, a body can't sleep for the racket upstairs.

LIZZIE. Oh?

EMMA. You've been makin' too much noise.

355 LIZZIE. It must have been Bridget, she dropped a pot, didn't you, Bridget.

EMMA. A number of pots from the sound of it.

BRIDGET. I'm all thumbs this mornin', ma'am.

EMMA. You know it didn't sound like pots.

LIZZIE. Oh.

360 EMMA. Sounded more like voices.

LIZZIE. Oh?

EMMA. Sounded like your voice, Lizzie.

LIZZIE. Maybe you dreamt it.

EMMA. I wish I had, for someone was using words no lady would use.

365 LIZZIE. When Bridget dropped the pot, she did say "pshaw!" didn't you,
        Bridget.

BRIDGET. Pshaw! That's what I said.

EMMA. That's not what I heard.

        (*Bridget will withdraw.*)

LIZZIE. Pshaw?

EMMA. If Mother heard you, you know what she'd say. 370
LIZZIE. She's not my mother or yours.
EMMA. Well she married our father twenty-seven years ago, if that doesn't make her our mother—
LIZZIE. It doesn't.
EMMA. Don't talk like that. 375
LIZZIE. I'll talk as I like.
EMMA. We're not going to fight, Lizzie. We're going to be quiet and have our breakfast!
LIZZIE. Is that what we're going to do?
EMMA. Yes. 380
LIZZIE. Oh.
EMMA. At least—that's what I'm going to do.
LIZZIE. Bridget, Emma wants her breakfast!
EMMA. I could have yelled myself.
LIZZIE. You could, but you never do. 385

*(Bridget serves Emma, Emma is reluctant to argue in front of Bridget.)*

EMMA. Thank you, Bridget.
LIZZIE. Did you know Harry Wingate's back for a visit? ... He must have snuck in late last night so I wouldn't hear him. Did you?

*(Emma shakes her head. Lizzie studies her.)*

LIZZIE. Did you know he was coming?
EMMA. No. 390
LIZZIE. No?
EMMA. But I do know he wouldn't be here unless Papa asked him.
LIZZIE. That's not the point. You know what happened last time he was here. Papa was signing property over to her.
EMMA. Oh Lizzie. 395
LIZZIE. Oh Lizzie nothing. It's bad enough Papa's worth thousands of dollars, and here we are, stuck in this tiny bit of a house on Second Street, when we should be up on the hill—and that's her doing. Or hers and Harry's.
EMMA. Shush.
LIZZIE. I won't shush. They cater to Papa's worst instincts. 400
EMMA. They'll hear you.
LIZZIE. I don't care if they do. It's true, isn't it? Papa tends to be miserly, he probably has the first penny he ever earned—or more likely *she* has it.
EMMA. You talk rubbish.
LIZZIE. Papa *can* be very warm-hearted and generous *but he needs encourage-* 405
*ment.*

EMMA. If Papa didn't save his money, Papa wouldn't have any money.

LIZZIE. And neither will we if he keeps signing things over to her.

EMMA. I'm not going to listen.

410 LIZZIE. Well try thinking.

EMMA. Stop it.

LIZZIE. (*Not a threat, a simple statement of fact.*) Someday Papa will die—

EMMA. Don't say that.

LIZZIE. Someday Papa will die. And I don't intend to spend the rest of my life
415   licking Harry Wingate's boots, or toadying to his sister.

MRS. BORDEN. (*From the stairs.*) What's that?

LIZZIE. Nothing.

MRS. BORDEN. (*Making her way downstairs.*) Eh?

LIZZIE. I said, nothing!

420 BRIDGET. (*Holds out basket of crusts. Lizzie looks at it.*) For your birds, Miss
   Lizzie.

LIZZIE. (*She takes the basket.*) You want to know what I think? I think she's a
   fat cow and I hate her. (*She exits.*)

EMMA. ... Morning, Mother.

425 MRS. BORDEN. Morning Emma.

EMMA. ... Did you have a good sleep?

(*Bridget will serve breakfast.*)

MRS. BORDEN. So so.... It's the heat you know. It never cools off proper at
   night. It's too hot for a good sleep.

EMMA. ... Is Papa up?

430 MRS. BORDEN. He'll be down in a minute ... sooo.... What's wrong with
   Lizzie this morning?

EMMA. Nothing.

MRS. BORDEN. ... Has Harry come down?

EMMA. I'm not sure.

435 MRS. BORDEN. Bridget. Has Harry come down?

BRIDGET. Yes ma'am.

MRS. BORDEN. And?

BRIDGET. And he's gone out back for a bit.

MRS. BORDEN. Lizzie see him?

440 BRIDGET. Yes ma'am. (*Beats it back to the kitchen.*)

(*Emma concentrates on her plate.*)

MRS. BORDEN. ... You should have said so.... She have words with him?

EMMA. Lizzie has more manners than that.

MRS. BORDEN. She's incapable of disciplining herself like a lady and we all know it.

EMMA. Well she doesn't make a habit of picking fights with people. 445

MRS. BORDEN. That's just it. She does.

EMMA. Well—she may—

MRS. BORDEN. And you can't deny that.

EMMA. (*Louder.*) Well this morning she may have been a bit upset because no one told her he was coming and when she came down he was here. But 450 that's all there was to it.

MRS. BORDEN. If your father wants my brother in for a stay, he's to ask Lizzie's permission I suppose.

EMMA. No.

MRS. BORDEN. You know, Emma— 455

EMMA. She didn't argue with him or anything like that.

MRS. BORDEN. You spoiled her. You may have had the best of intentions, but you spoiled her.

(*Miss Lizzie/Bridget is speaking to Actress/Lizzie.*)

MISS LIZZIE/BRIDGET. I was thirty-four years old, and I still daydreamed.... I did ... I daydreamed ... I dreamt that my name was Lisbeth ... and I lived 460 up on the hill in a corner house ... and my hair wasn't red. I hate red hair. When I was little, everyone teased me.... When I was little, we never stayed in this house for the summer, we'd go to the farm.... I remember ... my knees were always covered with scabs, god knows how I got them, but you know what I'd do? I'd sit in the field, and haul up my skirts, and my pet- 465 ticoat and my bloomers and roll down my stockings and I'd *pick* the scabs on my knees! And Emma would catch me! You know what she'd say? "Nice little girls don't have scabs on their knees!"

(*They laugh.*)

LIZZIE. Poor Emma.

MISS LIZZIE/BRIDGET. I dreamt ... someday I'm going to live ... in a corner 470 house on the hill.... I'll have parties, grand parties. I'll be ... witty, not bit- ing, but witty. Everyone will be witty. Everyone who is *any*one will want to come to my parties ... and if ... I can't ... live in a corner house on the hill ... I'll live on the farm, all by myself on the farm! There was a barn there, with barn cats and barn kittens and two horses and barn swallows that lived in 475 the eaves.... The birds I kept here were pigeons, not swallows.... They were grey, a dull grey ... but ... when the sun struck their feathers, I'd see blue, a steel blue with a sheen, and when they'd move in the sun they were bright blue and maroon and over it all, an odd sparkle as if you'd ... grated a new

480   silver dollar and the gratings caught in their feathers.... Most of the time
      they were dull ... and stupid perhaps ... but they weren't really. They were
      ... hiding I think.... They knew me.... They liked me.... The truth ... is ...
      ACTRESS/LIZZIE. The truth is ... thirty-four is too old to daydream....
      MRS. BORDEN. The truth is she's spoilt rotten. (*Mr. Borden will come down*
485   *stairs and take his place at the table. Mrs. Borden continues for his benefit.*
      *Mr. Borden ignores her. He has learned the fine art of tuning her out. He is not*
      *intimidated or henpecked.*) And we're paying the piper for that. In most of
      the places I've been the people who pay the piper call the tune. Of course I
      haven't had the advantage of a trip to Europe with a bunch of lady friends
490   like our Lizzie had three years ago, all expenses paid by her father.
      EMMA. Morning Papa.
      MR. BORDEN. Mornin'.
      MRS. BORDEN. I haven't had the benefit of that experience.... Did you know
      Lizzie's seen Harry?
495   MR. BORDEN. Has she.
      MRS. BORDEN. You should have met him down town. You should never have
      asked him to stay over.
      MR. BORDEN. Why not?
      MRS. BORDEN. You know as well as I do why not. I don't want a repeat of last
500   time. She didn't speak civil for months.
      MR. BORDEN. There's no reason for Harry to pay for a room when we've got
      a spare one.... Where's Lizzie?
      EMMA. Out back feeding the birds.
      MR. BORDEN. She's always out at those birds.
505   EMMA. Yes Papa.
      MR. BORDEN. And tell her to get a new lock for the shed. There's been some-
      one in it again.
      EMMA. Alright.
      MR. BORDEN. It's those little hellions from next door. We had no trouble with
510   them playin' in that shed before, they always played in their own yard before.
      EMMA. ... Papa?
      MR. BORDEN. It's those damn birds, that's what brings them into the yard.
      EMMA. ... About Harry ...
      MR. BORDEN. What about Harry?
515   EMMA. Well ... I was just wondering why ... [*he's here*]
      MR. BORDEN. You never mind Harry—did you speak to Lizzie about Johnny
      MacLeod?
      EMMA. I ah—
      MR. BORDEN. Eh?
520   EMMA. I said I tried to—

MR. BORDEN.  What do you mean, you tried to.

EMMA.  Well, I was working my way round to it but—

MR. BORDEN.  What's so difficult about telling Lizzie Johnny MacLeod wants to call?

EMMA.  Then why don't you tell her? I'm always the one that has to go running to Lizzie telling her this and telling her that, and taking the abuse for it!    525

MRS. BORDEN.  We all know why that is, she can wrap her father round her little finger, always has, always could. If everything else fails, she throws a tantrum and her father buys her off, trip to Europe, rent to the mill house, it's all the same.    530

EMMA.  Papa, what's Harry here for?

MR. BORDEN.  None of your business.

MRS. BORDEN.  And don't you go runnin' to Lizzie stirring things up.

EMMA.  You know I've never done that!    535

MR. BORDEN.  What she means—

EMMA.  (*With anger but little fatigue.*) I'm tired, do you hear? Tired! (*She gets up from the table and leaves for upstairs.*)

MR. BORDEN.  Emma!

EMMA.  You ask Harry here, you know there'll be trouble, and when I try to find out what's going on, so once again good old Emma can stand between you and Lizzie, all you've got to say is "none of your business"! Well then, it's *your* business, you look after it, because I'm not! (*She exits.*)    540

MRS. BORDEN.  ... She's right.

MR. BORDEN.  That's enough. I've had enough. I don't want to hear from you too.    545

MRS. BORDEN.  I'm only saying she's right. You have to talk straight and plain to Lizzie and tell her things she don't want to hear.

MR. BORDEN.  About the farm?

MRS. BORDEN.  About Johnny MacLeod! Keep your mouth shut about the farm and she won't know the difference.    550

MR. BORDEN.  Alright.

MRS. BORDEN.  Speak to her about Johnny MacLeod.

MR. BORDEN.  Alright!

MRS. BORDEN.  You know what they're sayin' in town. About her and that doctor.    555

(*Miss Lizzie/Bridget is speaking to the actress/Lizzie.*)

MISS LIZZIE/BRIDGET.  They're saying if you live on Second Street and you need a house call, and you don't mind the Irish, call Dr. Patrick. Dr. Patrick is very prompt with his Second Street house calls.

560 ACTRESS/LIZZIE. Do they really say that?

MISS LIZZIE/BRIDGET. No they don't. I'm telling a lie. But he is very prompt with a Second Street call, do you know why that is?

ACTRESS/LIZZIE. Why?

MISS LIZZIE/BRIDGET. Well—he's hoping to see someone who lives on Sec-
565    ond Street—someone who's yanking up her skirt and showing her ankle— so she can take a decent-sized step—and forgetting everything she was ever taught in Miss Cornelia's School for Girls, and talking to the Irish as if she never heard of the Pope! Oh yes, he's very prompt getting to Second Street ... getting away is something else....

570 DR. PATRICK. Good morning, Miss Borden!

LIZZIE. I haven't decided ... if it is ... or it isn't ...

DR. PATRICK. No, you've got it all wrong. The proper phrase is "good morn- ing, Dr. Patrick," and then you smile, discreetly of course, and lower the eyes just a titch, twirl the parasol—

575 LIZZIE. The parasol?

DR. PATRICK. The parasol, but not too fast; and then you murmur in a voice that was ever sweet and low, "And how are you doin' this morning, Dr. Patrick?" Your education's been sadly neglected, Miss Borden.

LIZZIE. You're forgetting something. You're married—and Irish besides—I'm
580    supposed to ignore you.

DR. PATRICK. No.

LIZZIE. Yes. Don't you realize Papa and Emma have fits every time we engage in "illicit conversation." They're having fits right now.

DR. PATRICK. Well, does Mrs. Borden approve?

585 LIZZIE. Ahhh. She's the real reason I keep stopping and talking. Mrs. Borden is easily shocked. I'm hoping she dies from the shock.

DR. PATRICK. (Laughs.) Why don't you ... run away from home, Lizzie?

LIZZIE. Why don't you "run away" with me?

DR. PATRICK. Where'll we go?

590 LIZZIE. Boston.

DR. PATRICK. Boston?

LIZZIE. For a start.

DR. PATRICK. And when will we go?

LIZZIE. Tonight.

595 DR. PATRICK. But you don't really mean it, you're havin' me on.

LIZZIE. I do mean it.

DR. PATRICK. How can you joke—and look so serious?

LIZZIE. It's a gift.

DR. PATRICK. (Laughs.) Oh Lizzie—

600 LIZZIE. Look!

DR. PATRICK. What is it?

LIZZIE. It's those little beggars next door. Hey! Hey get away! Get away there! ... They break into the shed to get at my birds and Papa gets angry.

DR. PATRICK. It's a natural thing.

LIZZIE. Well, Papa doesn't like it.                                              605

DR. PATRICK. They just want to look at them.

LIZZIE. Papa says what's his is his own—you need a formal invitation to get into our yard.... (*Pause.*) How's your wife?

DR. PATRICK. My wife.

LIZZIE. Shouldn't I ask that? I thought nice polite ladies always inquired after   610
the wives of their friends or acquaintances or ... whatever.

(*Harry observes them.*)

DR. PATRICK. You've met my wife, my wife is always the same.

LIZZIE. How boring for you.

DR. PATRICK. Uh-huh.

LIZZIE. And for her—                                                             615

DR. PATRICK. Yes indeed.

LIZZIE. And for me.

DR. PATRICK. Do you know what they say, Lizzie? They say if you live on Second Street, and you need a house call, and you don't mind the Irish, call Dr. Patrick. Dr. Patrick is very prompt with his Second Street house calls.   620

LIZZIE. I'll tell you what I've heard them say—Second Street is a nice place to visit, but you wouldn't want to live there. I certainly don't.

HARRY. Lizzie.

LIZZIE. Well, look who's here. Have you had the pleasure of meeting my uncle, Mr. Wingate.                                                           625

DR. PATRICK. No, Miss Borden, that pleasure has never been mine.

LIZZIE. That's exactly how I feel.

DR. PATRICK. Mr. Wingate, sir.

HARRY. Dr.... Patrick is it?

DR. PATRICK. Yes it is, sir.                                                     630

HARRY. Who's sick? (*In other words, "What the hell are you doing here?"*)

LIZZIE. No one. He just dropped by for a visit; you see Dr. Patrick and I are very old, very dear friends, isn't that so?

(*Harry stares at Dr. Patrick.*)

DR. PATRICK. Well ... (*Lizzie jabs him in the ribs.*) Ouch! ... It's her sense of humour, sir ... a rare trait in a woman....                                 635

HARRY. You best get in, Lizzie, it's gettin' on for lunch.

LIZZIE. Don't be silly, we just had breakfast.

HARRY.  You best get in!

LIZZIE.  ... Would you give me your arm, Dr. Patrick? (*She moves away with Dr. Patrick, ignoring Harry.*)

640  DR. PATRICK.  Now see what you've done?

LIZZIE.  What?

DR. PATRICK.  You've broken two of my ribs and ruined my reputation all in one blow.

LIZZIE.  It's impossible to ruin an Irishman's reputation.

645  DR. PATRICK.  (*Smiles.*) ... I'll be seeing you, Lizzie....

MISS LIZZIE/BRIDGET.  They're sayin' it's time you were married.

LIZZIE.  What time is that?

MISS LIZZIE/BRIDGET.  You need a place of your own.

LIZZIE.  How would getting married get me that?

650  MISS LIZZIE/BRIDGET.  Though I don't know what man would put up with your moods!

LIZZIE.  What about me putting up with his!

MISS LIZZIE/BRIDGET.  Oh Lizzie!

LIZZIE.  What's the matter, don't men have moods?

655  HARRY.  I'm tellin' you, as God is my witness, she's out in the walk talkin' to that Irish doctor, and he's fallin' all over her.

MRS. BORDEN.  What's the matter with you? For her own sake you should speak to her.

MR. BORDEN.  I will.

660  HARRY.  The talk around town can't be doin' you any good.

MRS. BORDEN.  Harry's right.

HARRY.  Yes sir.

MRS. BORDEN.  He's tellin' you what you should know.

HARRY.  If a man can't manage his own daughter, how the hell can he manage

665  a business—that's what people say, and it don't matter a damn whether there's any sense in it or not.

MR. BORDEN.  I know that.

MRS. BORDEN.  Knowin' is one thing, doin' something about it is another. What're you goin' to do about it?

670  MR. BORDEN.  God damn it! I said I was goin' to speak to her and I am!

MRS. BORDEN.  Well speak good and plain this time!

MR. BORDEN.  Jesus christ woman!

MRS. BORDEN.  Your "speakin' to Lizzie" is a ritual around here.

MR. BORDEN.  Abbie—

675  MRS. BORDEN.  She talks, you listen, and nothin' changes!

MR. BORDEN.  That's enough!

MRS. BORDEN.  Emma isn't the only one that's fed to the teeth!

MR. BORDEN.   Shut up!

MRS. BORDEN.   You're gettin' old, Andrew! You're gettin' old! (*She exits.*)

(*An air of embarrassment from Mr. Borden at having words in front of Harry. Mr. Borden fumbles with his pipe.*)

HARRY.   (*Offers his pouch of tobacco.*) Here ... have some of mine.   680

MR. BORDEN.   Don't mind if I do.... Nice mix.

HARRY.   It is.

MR. BORDEN.   ... I used to think ... by my seventies ... I'd be bouncin' a grandson on my knee....

HARRY.   Not too late for that.   685

MR. BORDEN.   Nope ... never had any boys ... and girls ... don't seem to have the same sense of family.... You know it's all well and good to talk about speakin' plain to Lizzie, but the truth of the matter is, if Lizzie puts her mind to a thing, she does it, and if she don't, she don't.

HARRY.   It's up to you to see she does.   690

MR. BORDEN.   It's like Abigail says, knowin' is one thing, doin' is another.... You're lucky you never brought any children into the world, Harry, you don't have to deal with them.

HARRY.   Now that's no way to be talkin'.

MR. BORDEN.   There's Emma ... Emma's a good girl ... when Abbie and I get   695
on, there'll always be Emma.... Well! You're not sittin' here to listen to me and my girls, are you, you didn't come here for that. Business, eh, Harry?

(*Harry whips out a sheet of figures.*)

MISS LIZZIE/BRIDGET.   I can remember distinctly ... that moment I was undressing for bed, and I looked at my knees—and there were no scabs! At last! I thought I'm the nice little girl Emma wants me to be! ... But it wasn't   700
that at all. I was just growing up. I didn't fall down so often.... (*She smiles.*) Do you suppose ... do you suppose there's a formula, a magic formula for being "a woman"? Do you suppose every girl baby receives it at birth, it's the last thing that happens just before birth, the magic formula is stamped indelibly on the brain—Ka Thud!! (*Her mood of amusement changes.*) ...   705
and ... through some terrible oversight ... perhaps the death of my Mother ... I didn't get that Ka Thud!! I was born ... defective.... (*She looks at the actress.*)

LIZZIE.   (*Low.*) No.

MISS LIZZIE/BRIDGET.   Not defective?

LIZZIE.   Just ... born.   710

THE DEFENCE.   Gentlemen of the Jury!! I ask you to look at the defendant, Miss Lizzie Borden. I ask you to recall the nature of the crime of which she is accused. I ask you—do you believe Miss Lizzie Borden, the youngest daughter of a scion of our community, a recipient of the fullest amenities our society can bestow upon its most fortunate members, do you believe Miss Lizzie Borden capable of wielding the murder weapon—thirty-two blows, gentlemen, thirty-two blows—fracturing Abigail Borden's skull, leaving her bloody and broken body in an upstairs bedroom, then, Miss Borden, with no hint of frenzy, hysteria, or trace of blood upon her person, engages in casual conversation with the maid, Bridget O'Sullivan, while awaiting her father's return home, upon which, after sending Bridget to her attic room, Miss Borden deals thirteen blows to the head of her father, and minutes later—in a state utterly compatible with that of a loving daughter upon discovery of murder most foul—Miss Borden calls for aid! Is this the aid we give her? Accusation of the most heinous and infamous of crimes? Do you believe Miss Lizzie Borden capable of these acts? I can tell you I do not!! I can tell you these acts of violence are acts of madness!! Gentlemen! If this gentlewoman is capable of such an act—I say to you—look to your daughters—if this gentlewoman is capable of such an act, which of us can lie abed at night, hear a step upon the stairs, a rustle in the hall, a creak outside the door.... Which of you can plump your pillow, nudge your wife, close your eyes, and sleep? Gentlemen, Lizzie Borden is not mad. Gentlemen, Lizzie Borden is not guilty.

MR. BORDEN. Lizzie?

LIZZIE. Papa ... have you and Harry got business?

HARRY. 'lo Lizzie. I'll ah ... finish up later. (*He exits with the figures. Lizzie watches him go.*)

MR. BORDEN. Lizzie?

LIZZIE. What?

MR. BORDEN. Could you sit down a minute?

LIZZIE. If it's about Dr. Patrick again, I—

MR. BORDEN. It isn't.

LIZZIE. Good.

MR. BORDEN. But we could start there.

LIZZIE. Oh Papa.

MR. BORDEN. Sit down Lizzie.

LIZZIE. But I've heard it all before, another chat for a wayward girl.

MR. BORDEN. (*Gently.*) Bite your tongue, Lizzie.

(*She smiles at him, there is affection between them. She has the qualities he would like in a son but deplores in a daughter.*)

MR. BORDEN. Now ... first off ... I want you to know that I ... understand about you and the doctor.

LIZZIE.  What do you understand?

MR. BORDEN.  I understand ... that it's a natural thing.

LIZZIE.  What is?

MR. BORDEN.  I'm saying there's nothing unnatural about an attraction between a man and a woman. That's a natural thing.                         755

LIZZIE.  I find Dr. Patrick ... amusing and entertaining ... if that's what you
mean ... is that what you mean?

MR. BORDEN.  This attraction ... points something up—you're a woman of
thirty-four years—

LIZZIE.  I know that.                                                    760

MR. BORDEN.  Just listen to me, Lizzie.... I'm choosing my words, and I want
you to listen. Now ... in most circumstances ... a woman of your age would
be married, eh? have children, be running her own house, that's the natural
thing, eh? (*Pause.*) Eh, Lizzie?

LIZZIE.  I don't know.                                                   765

MR. BORDEN.  Of course you know.

LIZZIE.  You're saying I'm unnatural ... am I supposed to agree, is that what
you want?

MR. BORDEN.  No, I'm not saying that! I'm saying the opposite to that! ... I'm
saying the feelings you have towards Dr. Patrick—                        770

LIZZIE.  What feelings?

MR. BORDEN.  What's ... what's happening there, I can understand, but what
you have to understand is that he's a married man, and there's nothing for
you there.

LIZZIE.  If he weren't married, Papa, I wouldn't be bothered talking to him!   775
It's just a game, Papa, it's a game.

MR. BORDEN.  A game.

LIZZIE.  You have no idea how boring it is looking eligible, interested, and
alluring, when I feel none of the three. So I play games. And it's a blessed
relief to talk to a married man.                                        780

MR. BORDEN.  What're his feelings for you?

LIZZIE.  I don't know, I don't care. Can I go now?

MR. BORDEN.  I'm not finished yet! ... You know Mr. MacLeod, Johnny Mac-
Leod?

LIZZIE.  I know his three little monsters.                               785

MR. BORDEN.  He's trying to raise three boys with no mother!

LIZZIE.  That's not my problem! I'm going.

MR. BORDEN.  Lizzie!

LIZZIE.  What!

MR. BORDEN.  Mr. MacLeod's asked to come over next Tuesday.              790

LIZZIE.  I'll be out that night.

MR. BORDEN. No you won't!

LIZZIE. Yes I will! ... Whose idea was this?

MR. BORDEN. No one's.

795 LIZZIE. That's a lie. She wants to get rid of me.

MR. BORDEN. I want what's best for you!

LIZZIE. No you don't! 'Cause you don't care what I want!

MR. BORDEN. You don't know what you want!

LIZZIE. But I know what you want! You want me living my life by the Farm-
800 ers' Almanac; having everyone over for Christmas dinner; waiting up for
my husband; and *serving at socials!*

MR. BORDEN. It's good enough for your mother!

LIZZIE. She is *not* my *mother!*

MR. BORDEN. ... John MacLeod is looking for a wife.

805 LIZZIE. No, god damn it, he isn't!

MR. BORDEN. Lizzie!

LIZZIE. He's looking for a housekeeper and it isn't going to be me!

MR. BORDEN. You've a filthy mouth!

LIZZIE. Is that why you hate me?

810 MR. BORDEN. You don't make sense.

LIZZIE. Why is it when I pretend things I don't feel, that's when you like me?

MR. BORDEN. You talk foolish.

LIZZIE. I'm supposed to be a mirror. I'm supposed to reflect what you want to
see, but everyone wants something different. If no one looks in the mirror,
815 I'm not even there, I don't exist!

MR. BORDEN. Lizzie, you talk foolish!

LIZZIE. No, I don't, that isn't true.

MR. BORDEN. About Mr. MacLeod—

LIZZIE. You can't make me get married!

820 MR. BORDEN. Lizzie, do you want to spend the rest of your life in this house?

LIZZIE. No ... No ... I want out of it, but I won't get married to do it.

MRS. BORDEN. (*On her way through to the kitchen.*) You've never been asked.

LIZZIE. Oh listen to her! I must be some sort of failure, then, eh? You had no
son and a daughter that failed! What does that make you, Papa!

825 MR. BORDEN. I want you to think about Johnny MacLeod!

LIZZIE. To hell with him!!!

(*Mr. Borden appears defeated. After a moment, Lizzie goes to him, she holds
his hand, strokes his hair.*)

LIZZIE. Papa? ... Papa, I love you, I try to be what you want, really I do try, I
try ... but ... I don't want to get married. I wouldn't be a good mother, I—

MR. BORDEN. How do you know—

LIZZIE. I know it! ... I want out of all this ... I hate this house, I hate ... I want   830
out. Try to understand how I feel ... Why can't I do something? ... Eh? I
mean ... I could ... I could go into your office ... I could ... learn how to
keep books?

MR. BORDEN. Lizzie.

LIZZIE. Why can't I do something like that?   835

MR. BORDEN. For god's sake, talk sensible.

LIZZIE. Alright then! Why can't we move up on the hill to a house where we
aren't in each other's laps!

MRS. BORDEN. (*Returning from kitchen.*) Why don't you move out!

LIZZIE. Give me the money and I'll go!   840

MRS. BORDEN. Money.

LIZZIE. And give me enough that I won't ever have to come back!

MRS. BORDEN. She always gets round to money!

LIZZIE. You drive me to it!

MRS. BORDEN. She's crazy!   845

LIZZIE. You drive me to it!

MRS. BORDEN. She should be locked up!

LIZZIE. (*Begins to smash the plates in the dining room.*) There!! There!!

MR. BORDEN. Lizzie!

MRS. BORDEN. Stop her!   850

LIZZIE. There!

(*Mr. Borden attempts to restrain her.*)

MRS. BORDEN. For god's sake, Andrew!

LIZZIE. Lock me up! Lock me up!

MR. BORDEN. Stop it! Lizzie!

(*She collapses against him, crying.*)

LIZZIE. Oh, Papa, I can't stand it.   855

MR. BORDEN. There, there, come on now, it's alright, listen to me, Lizzie, it's
alright.

MRS. BORDEN. You may as well get down on your knees.

LIZZIE. Look at her. She's jealous of me. She can't stand it whenever you're
nice to me.   860

MR. BORDEN. There now.

MRS. BORDEN. Ask her about Dr. Patrick.

MR. BORDEN. I'll handle this my way.

LIZZIE. He's an entertaining person, there're very few around!

MRS. BORDEN. Fall River ain't Paris and ain't that a shame for our Lizzie!   865

LIZZIE. One trip three years ago and you're still harping on it; it's true, Papa, an elephant never forgets!

MR. BORDEN. Show some respect!

LIZZIE. She's a fat cow and I hate her!

(*Mr. Borden slaps Lizzie. There is a pause as he regains control of himself.*)

870 MR. BORDEN. Now ... now ... you'll see Mr. MacLeod Tuesday night.

LIZZIE. No.

MR. BORDEN. God damn it!! I said you'll see Johnny MacLeod Tuesday night!!

LIZZIE. No.

875 MR. BORDEN. Get the hell upstairs to your room!

LIZZIE. No.

MR. BORDEN. I'm telling you to go upstairs to your room!!

LIZZIE. I'll go when I'm ready.

MR. BORDEN. I said, Go!

(*He grabs her arm to move her forcibly, she hits his arm away.*)

880 LIZZIE. No! ... There's something you don't understand, Papa. You can't make me do one thing that I don't want to do. I'm going to keep on doing just what I want just when I want—like always!

MR. BORDEN. (*Shoves her to the floor to gain a clear exit from the room. He stops on the stairs, looks back to her on the floor.*) ... I'm ... (*He continues off.*)

885 MRS. BORDEN. (*Without animosity.*) You know, Lizzie, your father keeps you. You know you got nothing but what he gives you. And that's a fact of life. You got to come to deal with facts. I did.

LIZZIE. And married Papa.

MRS. BORDEN. And married your father. You never made it easy for me. I

890 took on a man with two little ones, and Emma was your mother.

LIZZIE. You got stuck so I should too, is that it?

MRS. BORDEN. What?

LIZZIE. The reason I should marry Johnny MacLeod.

MRS. BORDEN. I just know, this time, in the end, you'll do what your Papa

895 says, you'll see.

LIZZIE. No, I won't. I have a right. A right that frees me from all that.

MRS. BORDEN. No, Lizzie, you got no rights.

LIZZIE. I've a legal right to one-third because I am his flesh and blood.

MRS. BORDEN. What you don't understand is your father's not dead yet, your

900 father's got many good years ahead of him, and when his time comes, well, we'll see what his will says then.... Your father's no fool, Lizzie.... Only a fool would leave money to you. (*She exits.*)

*(After a moment, Bridget enters from the kitchen.)*

BRIDGET. Ah Lizzie ... you outdid yourself that time. *(She is comforting Lizzie.)* ... Yes you did ... an elephant never forgets!

LIZZIE. Oh Bridget. 905

BRIDGET. Come on now.

LIZZIE. I can't help it.

BRIDGET. Sure you can ... sure you can ... stop your cryin' and come and sit down ... you want me to tell you a story?

LIZZIE. No. 910

BRIDGET. Sure, a story. I'll tell you a story. Come on now ... now ... before I worked here I worked up on the hill and the lady of the house ... are you listenin'? Well, she swore by her cook, finest cook in creation, yes, always bowin' and scrapin' and smilin' and givin' up her day off if company arrived. Oh the lady of the house she loved that cook—and I'll tell you 915 her name! It was Mary! Now listen! Do you know what Mary was doin'? *(Lizzie shakes her head.)* Before eatin' the master'd serve drinks in the parlour—and out in the kitchen, Mary'd be spittin' in the soup!

LIZZIE. What?

BRIDGET. She'd spit in the soup! And she'd smile when they served it! 920

LIZZIE. No.

BRIDGET. Yes. I've seen her cut up hair for an omelette.

LIZZIE. You're lying.

BRIDGET. Cross me heart.... They thought it was pepper!

LIZZIE. Oh, Bridget! 925

BRIDGET. These two eyes have seen her season up mutton stew when it's off and gone bad.

LIZZIE. Gone bad?

BRIDGET. Oh and they et it, every bit, and the next day they was hit with ... *stomach flu!* So cook called it. By jasus Lizzie, I daren't tell you what she 930 served up in their food, for fear you'd be sick!

LIZZIE. That's funny.... *(A fact—Lizzie does not appear amused.)*

BRIDGET. *(Starts to clear up the dishes.)* Yes, well, I'm tellin' you I kept on the good side of cook.

*(Lizzie watches her for a moment.)*

LIZZIE. ... Do you ... like me? 935

BRIDGET. Sure I do ... You should try bein' more like cook, Lizzie. Smile and get round them. You can do it.

LIZZIE. It's not ... *fair* that I have to.

BRIDGET. There ain't nothin' fair in this world.

940 LIZZIE. Well then ... well then, I don't want to!

BRIDGET. You dream, Lizzie ... you dream dreams ... Work. Be sensible. What could you do?

LIZZIE. I could ...

MISS LIZZIE/BRIDGET. No.

945 LIZZIE. I could ...

MISS LIZZIE/BRIDGET. No.

LIZZIE. I could ...

MISS LIZZIE/BRIDGET. No!

LIZZIE. I ... dream.

950 MISS LIZZIE/BRIDGET. You dream ... of a carousel ... you see a carousel ... you see lights that go on and go off ... you see yourself on a carousel horse, a red-painted horse with its head in the air, and green staring eyes, and a white flowing mane, it looks wild! ... It goes up and comes down, and the carousel whirls round with the music and lights, on and off ... and you

955 watch ... watch yourself on the horse. You're wearing a mask, a white mask like the mane of the horse, it looks like your face except that it's rigid and white ... and it changes! With each flick of the lights, the expression, it changes, but always so rigid and hard, like the flesh of the horse that is red that you ride. You ride with no hands! No hands on this petrified horse,

960 its head flung in the air, its wide staring eyes like those of a doe run down by the dogs! ... And each time you go round, your hands rise a fraction nearer the mask ... and the music and the carousel and the horse ... they all three slow down, and they stop.... You can reach out and touch ... you ... you on the horse ... with your hands so at the eyes.... You look into the

965 eyes! (*A sound from Lizzie, she is horrified and frightened. She covers her eyes.*) There are none! None! Just black holes in a white mask.... (*Pause.*) Only a dream.... The eyes of your birds ... are round ... and bright ... a light shines from inside ... they ... can see into your heart ... they're pretty ... they love you....

970 MR. BORDEN. I want this settled, Harry, I want it settled while Lizzie's out back.

(*Miss Lizzie/Bridget draws Lizzie's attention to the Mr. Borden/Harry scene. Lizzie listens, will move closer.*)

HARRY. You know I'm for that.

MR. BORDEN. I want it all done but the signin' of the papers tomorrow, that's if I decide to—

975 HARRY. You can't lose, Andrew. That farm's just lyin' fallow.

MR. BORDEN. Well, let's see what you got.

HARRY. (*Gets out his papers.*) Look at this ... I'll run horse auctions and a buggy rental—now I'll pay no rent for the house or pasturage but you get twenty percent, eh? That figure there—

MR. BORDEN. Mmmn.                                                                    980

HARRY. From my horse auctions last year, it'll go up on the farm and you'll get twenty percent off the top.... My buggy rental won't do so well ... that's that figure there, approximate ... but it all adds up, eh? Adds up for you.

MR. BORDEN. It's a good deal, Harry, but ...

HARRY. Now I know why you're worried—but the farm will still be in the 985 family, 'cause aren't I family? and whenever you or the girls want to come over for a visit, why I'll send a buggy from the rental, no need for you to have the expense of a horse, eh?

MR. BORDEN. It looks good on paper.

HARRY. There's ... ah ... something else, it's a bit awkward but I got to men- 990 tion it; I'll be severin' a lot of my present connections, and what I figure I've a right to, is some kind of guarantee....

MR. BORDEN. You mean a renewable lease for the farm?

HARRY. Well—what I'm wondering is ... No offence, but you're an older man, Andrew ... now if something should happen to you, where would the 995 farm stand in regards to your will? That's what I'm wondering.

MR. BORDEN. I've not made a will.

HARRY. You know best—but I wouldn't want to be in a position where Lizzie would be havin' anything to do with that farm. The less she knows now the better, but she's bound to find out—I don't feel I'm steppin' out of line 1000 by bringin' this up.

(*Lizzie is within earshot. She is staring at Harry and Mr. Borden. They do not see her.*)

MR. BORDEN. No.

HARRY. If you mind you come right out and say so.

MR. BORDEN. That's alright.

HARRY. Now ... if you ... put the farm—in Abbie's name, what do you think? 1005

MR. BORDEN. I don't know, Harry.

HARRY. I don't want to push.

MR. BORDEN. ... I should make a will ... I want the girls looked after, it don't seem like they'll marry ... and Abbie, she's younger than me, I know Emma will see to her, still ... money-wise I got to consider these things ... it makes 1010 a difference no men in the family.

HARRY. You know you can count on me for whatever.

MR. BORDEN. If ... *If* I changed title to the farm, Abbie'd have to come down to the bank, I wouldn't want Lizzie to know.

1015 HARRY. You can send a note for her when you get to the bank; she can say it's a note from a friend, and come down and meet you. Simple as that.

MR. BORDEN. I'll give it some thought.

HARRY. You see, Abbie owns the farm, it's no difference to you, but it gives me protection.

1020 MR. BORDEN. Who's there?

HARRY. It's Lizzie.

MR. BORDEN. What do you want? ... Did you lock the shed? ... Is the shed locked? (*Lizzie makes a slow motion which Mr. Borden takes for assent.*) Well you make sure it stays locked! I don't want any more of those god
1025 damned.... I ... ah ... I think we about covered everything, Harry, we'll ... ah ... we'll let it go till tomorrow.

HARRY. Good enough ... well ... I'll just finish choppin' that kindlin', give a shout when it's lunchtime. (*He exits.*)

(*Lizzie and Mr. Borden stare at each other for a moment.*)

LIZZIE. (*Very low.*) What are you doing with the farm?

(*Mr. Borden slowly picks up the papers, places them in his pocket.*)

1030 LIZZIE. Papa! ... Papa. I want you to show me what you put in your pocket.

MR. BORDEN. It's none of your business.

LIZZIE. The farm is my business.

MR. BORDEN. It's nothing.

LIZZIE. Show me!

1035 MR. BORDEN. I said it's nothing!

(*Lizzie makes a quick move towards her father to seize the paper from his pocket. Even more quickly and smartly he slaps her face. It is all very quick and clean. A pause as they stand frozen.*)

HARRY. (*Off.*) Andrew, there's a bunch of kids broken into the shed!

MR. BORDEN. Jesus christ.

LIZZIE. (*Whispers.*) What about the farm.

MR. BORDEN. You! You and those god damn birds! I've told you! I've told
1040 you time and again!

LIZZIE. What about the farm!

MR. BORDEN. Jesus christ ... You never listen! Never!

HARRY. (*Enters carrying the hand hatchet.*) Andrew!!

MR. BORDEN. (*Grabs the hand hatchet from Harry, turns to Lizzie.*) There'll be
1045 no more of your god damn birds in this yard!!

LIZZIE. No!

(*Mr. Borden raises the hatchet and smashes it into the table as Lizzie screams.*)

LIZZIE.  No Papa!! Nooo!!

(*The hatchet is embedded in the table. Mr. Borden and Harry assume a soft freeze as the actress/Lizzie whirls to see Miss Lizzie/Bridget observing the scene.*)

LIZZIE.  Nooo!

MISS LIZZIE.  I loved them.

(*Blackout.*)

## ACT 2

*Lights come up on the actress/Lizzie sitting at the dining-room table. She is very still, her hands clasped in her lap. Miss Lizzie/Bridget is near her. She too is very still. A pause.*

ACTRESS/LIZZIE.  (*Very low.*) Talk to me.

MISS LIZZIE/BRIDGET.  I remember ...

ACTRESS/LIZZIE.  (*Very low.*) No.

MISS LIZZIE/BRIDGET.  On the farm, Papa's farm, Harry's farm, when I was little and thought it was my farm and I loved it, we had some puppies, 5 the farm dog had puppies, brown soft little puppies with brown ey ... (*She does not complete the word "eyes."*) And one of the puppies got sick. I didn't know it was sick, it seemed like the others, but the mother, she knew. It would lie at the back of the box, she would lie in front of it while she nursed all the others. They ignored it, that puppy didn't exist for the oth- 10 ers.... I think inside it was different, and the mother thought the difference she sensed was a sickness ... and after a while ... anyone could tell it was sick. It had nothing to eat! ... And Papa took it and drowned it. That's what you do on a farm with things that are different.

ACTRESS/LIZZIE.  Am I different? 15

MISS LIZZIE/BRIDGET.  You kill them.

(*Actress/Lizzie looks at Miss Lizzie/Bridget. Miss Lizzie/Bridget looks towards the top of the stairs. Bridget gets up and exits to the kitchen. Emma appears at the top of the stairs. She is dressed for travel and carries a small suitcase and her gloves. She stares down at Lizzie still sitting at the table. After several moments Lizzie becomes aware of that gaze and turns to look at Emma. Emma then descends the stairs. She puts down her suitcase. She is not overjoyed at seeing Lizzie, having hoped to get away before Lizzie arose, nevertheless she begins with an excess of enthusiasm to cover the implications of her departure.*)

EMMA.  Well! You're up early ... Bridget down? ... did you put the coffee on? (*She puts her gloves on the table.*) My goodness, Lizzie, cat got your tongue? (*She exits to the kitchen. Lizzie picks up the gloves. Emma returns.*)

20    Bridget's down, she's in the kitchen.... Well ... looks like a real scorcher today, doesn't it? ...

LIZZIE.  What's the bag for?

EMMA.  I ... decided I might go for a little trip, a day or two, get away from the heat.... The girls've rented a place out beach way and I thought ... with

25    the weather and all ...

LIZZIE.  How can you do that?

EMMA.  Do what? ... Anyway, I thought I might stay with them a few days.... Why don't you come with me?

LIZZIE.  No.

30  EMMA.  Just for a few days, come with me.

LIZZIE.  No.

EMMA.  You know you like the water.

LIZZIE.  I said no!

EMMA.  Oh, Lizzie.

(*Pause.*)

35  LIZZIE.  I don't see how you can leave me like this.

EMMA.  I asked you to come with me.

LIZZIE.  You know I can't do that.

EMMA.  Why not?

LIZZIE.  Someone has to *do* something, you just run away from things.

(*Pause.*)

40  EMMA.  ... Lizzie ... I'm sorry about the—[*birds*]

LIZZIE.  No!

EMMA.  Papa was angry.

LIZZIE.  I don't want to talk about it.

EMMA.  He's sorry now.

45  LIZZIE.  Nobody *listens* to me, can't you hear me? I said *don't* talk about it. I don't want to talk about it. Stop talking about it!!

(*Bridget enters with the coffee.*)

EMMA.  Thank you, Bridget.

(*Bridget withdraws.*)

EMMA.  Well! ... I certainly can use this this morning.... Your coffee's there.

LIZZIE.  I don't want it.

EMMA.  You're going to ruin those gloves.                                    50

LIZZIE.  I don't care.

EMMA.  Since they're not yours.

(*Lizzie bangs the gloves down on the table. A pause. Then Emma picks them up and smooths them out.*)

LIZZIE.  Why are you leaving me?

EMMA.  I feel like a visit with the girls. Is there something wrong with that?

LIZZIE.  How can you go now?                                                  50

EMMA.  I don't know what you're getting at.

LIZZIE.  I heard them. I heard them talking yesterday. Do you know what they're saying?

EMMA.  How could I?

LIZZIE.  "How could I?" What do you mean "How could I?" Did you know?   55

EMMA.  No, Lizzie, I did not.

LIZZIE.  *Did-not-what.*

EMMA.  Know.

LIZZIE.  But you know now. How do you know now?

EMMA.  I've put two and two together and I'm going over to the girls for a   60
   visit!

LIZZIE.  Please Emma!

EMMA.  It's too hot.

LIZZIE.  I need you, don't go.

EMMA.  I've been talking about this trip.                                     65

LIZZIE.  That's a lie.

EMMA.  They're expecting me.

LIZZIE.  You're lying to me!

EMMA.  I'm going to the girls' place. You can come if you want, you can stay
   if you want. I planned this trip and I'm taking it!                       70

LIZZIE.  Stop lying!

EMMA.  If I want to tell a little white lie to avoid an altercation in this house,
   I'll do so. Other people have been doing it for years!

LIZZIE.  You don't understand, you don't understand anything.

EMMA.  Oh, I understand enough.                                               75

LIZZIE.  You don't! Let me explain it to you. You listen carefully, you listen....
   Harry's getting the farm, can you understand that? Harry is here and he's
   moving on the farm and he's going to be there, on the farm, living on the
   farm. *Our farm.* Do you understand that? ... Do you understand that!

EMMA.  Yes.                                                                   80

LIZZIE.  Harry's going to be on the farm. That's the first thing.... No ... no it
   isn't.... The first thing ... was the mill house, that was the first thing! And
   *now* the farm. You see there's a pattern, Emma, you can see that, can't you?

EMMA. I don't—

85 LIZZIE. You can see it! The mill house, then the farm, and the next thing is the papers for the farm—do you know what he's doing, Papa's doing? He's signing the farm over to her. It will never be ours, we will never have it, not ever. It's ours by rights, don't you feel that?

EMMA. The farm—has always meant a great deal to me, yes.

90 LIZZIE. Then what are you doing about it! You can't leave me now ... but that's not all. Papa's going to make a will, and you can see the pattern, can't you, and if the pattern keeps on, what do you suppose his will will say. What do you suppose, answer me!

EMMA. I don't know.

95 LIZZIE. Say it!

EMMA. He'll see we're looked after.

LIZZIE. I don't want to be looked after! What's the matter with you? Do you really want to spend the rest of your life with that cow, listening to her drone on and on for years! That's just what they think you'll do. Papa'll

100 leave you a monthly allowance, just like he'll leave me, just enough to keep us all living together. We'll be worth millions on paper, and be stuck in this house and by and by Papa will die and Harry will move in and you will wait on that cow while she gets fatter and fatter and I—will—sit in my room.

105 EMMA. Lizzie.

LIZZIE. We have to do something, you can see that. We have to do something!

EMMA. There's nothing we can do.

LIZZIE. Don't say that!

110 EMMA. Alright, then, what can we do?

LIZZIE. I ... I ... don't know. But we have to do something, you have to help me, you can't go away and leave me alone, you can't do that.

EMMA. Then—

LIZZIE. You know what I thought? I thought you could talk to him, really

115 talk to him, make him understand that we're people. *Individual people*, and we have to live separate lives, and his will should make it possible for us to do that. And the farm can't go to Harry.

EMMA. You know it's no use.

LIZZIE. I can't talk to him anymore. Every time I talk to him I make every-

120 thing worse. I hate him, no. No I don't. I hate her.

(*Emma looks at her brooch watch.*)

LIZZIE. Don't look at the time.

EMMA. I'll miss my connections.

LIZZIE.  No!

EMMA.  (*Puts on her gloves.*) Lizzie. There's certain things we have to face. One of them is, we can't change a thing.    125

LIZZIE.  I won't let you go!

EMMA.  I'll be back on the weekend.

LIZZIE.  He killed my birds! He took the axe and he killed them! Emma, I ran out and held them in my hands, I felt their hearts throbbing and pumping and the blood gushed out of their necks, it was all over my hands, don't    130 you care about that?

EMMA.  I ... I ... have a train to catch.

LIZZIE.  He didn't care how much he hurt me and you don't care either. Nobody cares.

EMMA.  I ... have to go now.    135

LIZZIE.  That's right. Go away. I don't even like you, Emma. Go away! (*Emma leaves, Lizzie runs after her calling.*) I'm sorry for all the things I told you! Things I really felt! You pretended to me, and I don't like you!! Go away!! (*Lizzie runs to the window and looks out after Emma's departing figure. After a moment she slowly turns back into the room. Miss Lizzie/Bridget is there.*)    140

LIZZIE.  I want to die ... I want to die, but something inside won't let me ... inside something says *no*. (*She shuts her eyes.*) I can do anything.

DEFENCE. Miss Borden.

(*Both Lizzies turn.*)

DEFENCE. Could you describe the sequence of events upon your father's arrival home?    145

LIZZIE.  (*With no animation.*) Papa came in ... we exchanged a few words ... Bridget and I spoke of the yard goods sale downtown, whether she would buy some. She went up to her room....

DEFENCE. And then?

LIZZIE.  I went out back ... through the yard ... I picked up several pears from    150 the ground beneath the trees ... I went into the shed ... I stood looking out the window and ate the pears ...

DEFENCE. How many?

LIZZIE.  Four.

DEFENCE. It wasn't warm, stifling in the shed?    155

LIZZIE.  No, it was cool.

DEFENCE. What were you doing, apart from eating the pears?

LIZZIE.  I suppose I was thinking. I just stood there, looking out the window, thinking, and eating the pears I'd picked up.

DEFENCE. You're fond of pears?    160

LIZZIE.  Otherwise, I wouldn't eat them.

DEFENCE. Go on.

LIZZIE. I returned to the house. I found—Papa. I called for Bridget.

(*Mrs. Borden descends the stairs. Lizzie and Bridget turn to look at her. Mrs. Borden is only aware of Lizzie's stare. Pause.*)

MRS. BORDEN. ... What're you staring at? ... I said what're you staring at?

165 LIZZIE. (*Continuing to stare at Mrs. Borden.*) Bridget.

BRIDGET. Yes ma'am.

(*Pause.*)

MRS. BORDEN. Just coffee and a biscuit this morning, Bridget, it's too hot for a decent breakfast.

BRIDGET. Yes ma'am.

(*She exits for the biscuit and coffee. Lizzie continues to stare at Mrs. Borden.*)

170 MRS. BORDEN. ... Tell Bridget I'll have it in the parlour.

(*Lizzie is making an effort to be pleasant, to be "good." Mrs. Borden is more aware of this as unusual behaviour from Lizzie than were she to be rude, biting, or threatening. Lizzie, at the same time, feels caught in a dimension other than the one in which the people around her are operating. For Lizzie, a bell-jar[1] effect. Simple acts seem filled with significance. Lizzie is trying to fulfill other people's expectations of "normal."*)

LIZZIE. It's not me, is it?

MRS. BORDEN. What?

LIZZIE. You're not moving into the parlour because of me, are you?

MRS. BORDEN. What?

175 LIZZIE. I'd hate to think I'd driven you out of your own dining room.

MRS. BORDEN. No.

LIZZIE. Oh good, because I'd hate to think that was so.

MRS. BORDEN. It's cooler in the parlour.

LIZZIE. You know, you're right.

180 MRS. BORDEN. Eh?

LIZZIE. It is cooler....

(*Bridget enters with the coffee and biscuit.*)

LIZZIE. I will, Bridget.

---

1   *bell-jar* Bell-shaped glass lid placed over objects to isolate, protect, or contain them.

(*She takes the coffee and biscuit, gives it to Mrs. Borden. Lizzie watches her eat and drink. Mrs. Borden eats the biscuit delicately. Lizzie's attention is caught by it.*)

LIZZIE.  Do you like that biscuit?

MRS. BORDEN.  It could be lighter.

LIZZIE.  You're right.                                                              185

(*Mr. Borden enters, makes his way into the kitchen, Lizzie watches him pass.*)

LIZZIE.  You know, Papa doesn't look well, Papa doesn't look well at all. Papa looks sick.

MRS. BORDEN.  He had a bad night.

LIZZIE.  Oh?

MRS. BORDEN.  Too hot.                                                              190

LIZZIE.  But it's cooler in here, isn't it ... (*Not trusting her own evaluation of the degree of heat.*) Isn't it?

MRS. BORDEN.  Yes, yes, it's cooler in here.

(*Mr. Borden enters with his coffee. Lizzie goes to him.*)

LIZZIE.  Papa? You should go in the parlour. It's much cooler in there, really it is.                                                              195

(*He goes into the parlour. Lizzie remains in the dining room. She sits at the table, folds her hands in her lap. Mr. Borden begins to read the paper.*)

MRS. BORDEN.  ... I think I'll have Bridget do the windows today ... they need doing ... get them out of the way first thing.... Anything in the paper, Andrew?

MR. BORDEN.  (*As he continues to read.*) Nope.

MRS. BORDEN.  There never is ... I don't know why we buy it.                         200

MR. BORDEN.  (*Reading.*) Yup.

MRS. BORDEN.  You going out this morning?

MR. BORDEN.  Business.

MRS. BORDEN.  ... Harry must be having a bit of a sleep-in.

MR. BORDEN.  Yup.                                                                   205

MRS. BORDEN.  He's always up by—(*Harry starts down the stairs.*) Well, speak of the devil—coffee and biscuits?

HARRY.  Sounds good to me.

(*Mrs. Borden starts off to get it. Lizzie looks at her, catching her eye. Mrs. Borden stops abruptly.*)

LIZZIE. (*Her voice seems too loud.*) Emma's gone over to visit at the girls' place.
210   (*Mr. Borden lowers his paper to look at her. Harry looks at her. Suddenly aware of the loudness of her voice, she continues softly, too softly.*) ... Till the weekend.
MR. BORDEN. She didn't say she was going, when'd she decide that?

(*Lizzie looks down at her hands, doesn't answer. A pause. Then Mrs. Borden continues out to the kitchen.*)

HARRY. Will you be ah ... going down town today?
MR. BORDEN. This mornin'. I got ... business at the bank.

(*A look between them. They are very aware of Lizzie's presence in the dining room.*)

215   HARRY. This mornin' eh? Well now ... that works out just fine for me. I can ... I got a bill to settle in town myself.

(*Lizzie turns her head to look at them.*)

HARRY. I'll be on my way after that.
MR. BORDEN. Abbie'll be disappointed you're not stayin' for lunch.
HARRY. 'Nother time.
220   MR. BORDEN. (*Aware of Lizzie's gaze.*) I ... I don't know where she is with that coffee. I'll—
HARRY. Never you mind, you sit right there, I'll get it. (*He exits.*)

(*Lizzie and Mr. Borden look at each other. The bell-jar effect is lessened.*)

LIZZIE. (*Softly.*) Good mornin' Papa.
MR. BORDEN. Mornin' Lizzie.
225   LIZZIE. Did you have a good sleep?
MR. BORDEN. Not bad.
LIZZIE. Papa?
MR. BORDEN. Yes Lizzie.
LIZZIE. You're a very strong-minded person, Papa, do you think I'm like you?
230   MR. BORDEN. In some ways ... perhaps.
LIZZIE. I must be like someone.
MR. BORDEN. You resemble your mother.
LIZZIE. I look like my mother?
MR. BORDEN. A bit like your mother.
235   LIZZIE. But my mother's dead.
MR. BORDEN. Lizzie—
LIZZIE. I remember you told me she died because she was sick ... I was born and she died.... Did you love her?
MR. BORDEN. I married her.

LIZZIE.  Can't you say if you loved her?                                          240

MR. BORDEN.  Of course I did, Lizzie.

LIZZIE.  Did you hate me for killing her?

MR. BORDEN.  You don't think of it that way, it was just something that happened.

LIZZIE.  Perhaps she just got tired and died. She didn't want to go on, and the   245
chance came up and she took it. I could understand that.... Perhaps she
was like a bird, she could see all the blue sky and she wanted to fly away
but she couldn't. She was caught, Papa, she was caught in a horrible snare,
and she saw a way out and she took it.... Perhaps it was a very brave thing
to do, Papa, perhaps it was the only way, and she hated to leave us because   250
she loved us so much, but she couldn't breathe all caught in the snare....
(*Long pause.*) Some people have very small wrists, have you noticed? Mine
aren't ...

> (*There is a murmur from the kitchen, then muted laughter. Mr. Borden
> looks towards it.*)

LIZZIE.  Papa! ... I'm a very strong person.

MRS. BORDEN.  (*Off, laughing.*) You're tellin' tales out of school, Harry!        255

HARRY.  (*Off.*) God's truth. You should have seen the buggy when they
brought it back.

MRS. BORDEN.  (*Off.*) You've got to tell Andrew. (*Pokes her head in.*) Andrew,
come on out here, Harry's got a story. (*Off.*) Now you'll have to start at the
beginning again. Oh my goodness.                                                  260

> (*Mr. Borden starts for the kitchen. He stops, and looks back at Lizzie.*)

LIZZIE.  Is there anything you want to tell me, Papa?

MRS. BORDEN.  (*Off.*) Andrew!

LIZZIE.  (*Softly, an echo.*) Andrew.

MR. BORDEN.  What is it, Lizzie?

LIZZIE.  If I promised to be a good girl forever and ever, would anything          265
change?

MR. BORDEN.  I don't know what you're talking about.

LIZZIE.  I would be lying ... Papa! ... Don't do any business today. Don't go
out. Stay home.

MR. BORDEN.  What for?                                                             270

LIZZIE.  Everyone's leaving. Going away. Everyone's left.

MRS. BORDEN.  (*Off.*) Andrew!

LIZZIE.  (*Softly, an echo.*) Andrew.

MR. BORDEN.  What is it?

LIZZIE.  I'm calling you.                                                          275

(*Mr. Borden looks at her for a moment, then leaves for the kitchen. Dr. Patrick is heard whistling very softly. Lizzie listens.*)

LIZZIE. Listen ... can you hear it ... can you?
MISS LIZZIE/BRIDGET. I can hear it.... It's stopped.

(*Dr. Patrick can't be seen. Only his voice is heard.*)

DR. PATRICK. (*Very low.*) Lizzie?
LIZZIE. (*Realization.*) I could hear it before [*you*]. (*Pause.*) It sounded so sad
280  I wanted to cry.
MISS LIZZIE/BRIDGET. You mustn't cry.
LIZZIE. I mustn't cry.
DR. PATRICK. I bet you know this one. (*He whistles an Irish jig.*)
LIZZIE. I know that! (*She begins to dance. Dr. Patrick enters. He claps in time to the dance. Lizzie finishes the jig.*)

(*Dr. Patrick applauds.*)

285  DR. PATRICK. Bravo! Bravo!!
LIZZIE. You didn't know I could do that, did you?
DR. PATRICK. You're a woman of many talents, Miss Borden.
LIZZIE. You're not making fun of me?
DR. PATRICK. I would never do that.
290  LIZZIE. I can do anything I want.
DR. PATRICK. I'm sure you can.
LIZZIE. If I wanted to die—I could even do that, couldn't I?
DR. PATRICK. Well now, I don't think so.
LIZZIE. Yes, I could!
295  DR. PATRICK. Lizzie—
LIZZIE. You wouldn't know—you can't see into my heart.
DR. PATRICK. I think I can.
LIZZIE. Well you can't.
DR. PATRICK. ... It's only a game.
300  LIZZIE. I never play games.
DR. PATRICK. Sure you do.
LIZZIE. I hate games.
DR. PATRICK. You're playin' one now.
LIZZIE. You don't even know me!
305  DR. PATRICK. Come on Lizzie, we don't want to fight. I know what we'll do ... we'll start all over.... Shut your eyes, Lizzie. (*She does so.*) Good mornin' Miss Borden.... Good mornin' Miss Borden....
LIZZIE. ... I haven't decided.... (*She slowly opens her eyes.*) ... if it is or it isn't.

DR. PATRICK. Much better ... and now ... would you take my arm, Miss Borden? How about a wee promenade?    310

LIZZIE. There's nowhere to go.

DR. PATRICK. That isn't so.... What about Boston? ... Do you think it's too far for a stroll? ... I know what we'll do, we'll walk 'round to the side and you'll show me your birds. (*They walk.*) ... I waited last night but you never showed up ... there I was, travellin' bag and all, and you never appeared.... I   315  know what went wrong! We forgot to agree on an hour! Next time, Lizzie, you must set the hour.... Is this where they're kept?

(*Lizzie nods, she opens the cage and looks in it.*)

DR. PATRICK. It's empty. (*He laughs.*) And you say you never play games?

LIZZIE. They're gone.

DR. PATRICK. You've been havin' me on again, yes you have.    320

LIZZIE. They've run away.

DR. PATRICK. Did they really exist?

LIZZIE. I had blood on my hands.

DR. PATRICK. What do you say?

LIZZIE. You can't see it now, I washed it off, see?    325

DR. PATRICK. (*Takes her hands.*) Ah Lizzie....

LIZZIE. Would you ... help someone die?

DR. PATRICK. Why do you ask that?

LIZZIE. Some people are better off dead. I might be better off dead.

DR. PATRICK. You're a precious and unique person, Lizzie, and you shouldn't   330  think things like that.

LIZZIE. Precious and unique?

DR. PATRICK. All life is precious and unique.

LIZZIE. I am precious and unique? ... I *am* precious and unique. You said that.    335

DR. PATRICK. Oh, I believe it.

LIZZIE. And I am. I know it. People mix things up on you, you have to be careful. I am a person of worth.

DR. PATRICK. Sure you are.

LIZZIE. Not like that fat cow in there.    340

DR. PATRICK. Her life too is—

LIZZIE. No!

DR. PATRICK. Liz—

LIZZIE. Do you know her!

DR. PATRICK. That doesn't matter.    345

LIZZIE. Yes it does, it does matter.

DR. PATRICK. You can't be—

LIZZIE.  You're a doctor, isn't that right?

DR. PATRICK.  Right enough there.

350  LIZZIE.  So, tell me, tell me, if a dreadful accident occurred ... and two people were dying ... but you could only save one.... Which would you save?

DR. PATRICK.  You can't ask questions like that.

LIZZIE.  Yes I can, come on, it's a game. How does a doctor determine? If one were old and the other were young—would you save the younger one first?

355  DR. PATRICK.  Lizzie.

LIZZIE.  You said you liked games! If one were a bad person and the other was good, was trying to be good, would you save the one who was good and let the bad person die?

DR. PATRICK.  I don't know.

360  LIZZIE.  Listen! If you could go back in time ... what would you do if you met a person who was evil and wicked?

DR. PATRICK.  Who?

LIZZIE.  I don't know, Attila the Hun!

DR. PATRICK.  (*Laughs.*) Oh my.

365  LIZZIE.  Listen, if you met Attila the Hun, and you were in a position to kill him, would you do it?

DR. PATRICK.  I don't know.

LIZZIE.  Think of the suffering he caused, the unhappiness.

DR. PATRICK.  Yes, but I'm a doctor, not an assassin.

370  LIZZIE.  I think you're a coward.

(*Pause.*)

DR. PATRICK.  What I do is try to save lives ...

LIZZIE.  But you put poison out for the slugs in your garden.

DR. PATRICK.  You got something mixed up.

LIZZIE.  I've never been clearer. Everything's clear. I've lived all of my life for

375  this one moment of absolute clarity! If war were declared, would you serve?

DR. PATRICK.  I would fight in a war.

LIZZIE.  You wouldn't fight, you would kill—you'd take a gun and shoot people, people who'd done nothing to you, people who were trying to be good, you'd kill them! And you say you wouldn't kill Attila the Hun, or

380  that that stupid cow's life is precious—*My life is precious!!*

DR. PATRICK.  To you.

LIZZIE.  Yes to me, are you stupid!?

DR. PATRICK.  And hers is to her.

LIZZIE.  I don't care about her! (*Pause.*) I'm glad you're not my doctor, you

385  can't make decisions, can you? You are a coward.

(*Dr. Patrick starts off.*)

LIZZIE.  You're afraid of your wife ... you can *only* play games.... If I really wanted to go to Boston, you wouldn't come with me because you're a coward! *I'm not a coward!!*

(*Lizzie turns to watch Mrs. Borden sit with needlework. After a moment Mrs. Borden looks at Lizzie, aware of her scrutiny.*)

LIZZIE.  ... Where's Papa?

MRS. BORDEN.  Out.                                                                    390

LIZZIE.  And Mr. Wingate?

MRS. BORDEN.  He's out too.

LIZZIE.  So what are you going to do ... Mrs. Borden?

MRS. BORDEN.  I'm going to finish this up.

LIZZIE.  You do that.... (*Pause.*) Where's Bridget?                                   395

MRS. BORDEN.  Out back washing windows.... You got clean clothes to go upstairs, they're in the kitchen.

(*Pause.*)

LIZZIE.  Did you know Papa killed my birds with the axe? He chopped off their heads. (*Mrs. Borden is uneasy.*) ... It's alright. At first I felt bad, but I feel better now. I feel much better now.... I am a woman of decision, Mrs.   400
Borden. When I decide to do things, I do them, yes, I do. (*Smiles.*) How many times has Papa said—when Lizzie puts her mind to a thing, she does it—and I do.... It's always me who puts the slug poison out because they eat all the flowers and you don't like that, do you? They're bad things, they must die. You see, not all life is precious, is it?                                        405

(*After a moment Mrs. Borden makes an attempt casually to gather together her things, to go upstairs. She does not want to be in the room with Lizzie.*)

LIZZIE.  Where're you going?

MRS. BORDEN.  Upstairs.... (*An excuse.*) The spare room needs changing.

(*A knock at the back door.... A second knock.*)

LIZZIE.  Someone's at the door.... (*A third knock.*) I'll get it.

(*She exits to the kitchen. Mrs. Borden waits. Lizzie returns. She's a bit out of breath. She carries a pile of clean clothes which she puts on the table. She looks at Mrs. Borden.*)

LIZZIE.  Did you want something?

MRS. BORDEN.  Who was it?—the door?                                                    410

LIZZIE.  Oh yes. I forgot. I had to step out back for a moment and—it's a note. A message for you.

MRS. BORDEN. Oh.

LIZZIE. Shall I open it?

415  MRS. BORDEN. That's alright. (*She holds out her hand.*)

LIZZIE. Looks like Papa's handwriting.... (*She passes over the note.*) Aren't you going to open it?

MRS. BORDEN. I'll read it upstairs.

LIZZIE. Mrs. Borden! ... Would you mind ... putting my clothes in my room?

420  (*She gets some clothes from the table, Mrs. Borden takes them, something she would never normally do. Before she can move away, Lizzie grabs her arm.*) Just a minute ... I would like you to look into my eyes. What's the matter? Nothing's wrong. It's an experiment.... Look right into them. Tell me ... what do you see ... can you see anything?

425  MRS. BORDEN. ... Myself.

LIZZIE. Yes. When a person dies, retained on her eye is the image of the last thing she saw. Isn't that interesting? (*Pause.*)

(*Mrs. Borden slowly starts upstairs. Lizzie picks up remaining clothes on table. The hand hatchet is concealed beneath them. She follows Mrs. Borden up the stairs.*)

LIZZIE. Do you know something? If I were to kill someone, I would come up behind them very slowly and quietly. They would never even hear me, they

430  would never turn around. (*Mrs. Borden stops on the stairs. She turns around to look at Lizzie who is behind her.*) They would be too frightened to turn around even if they heard me. They would be so afraid they'd see what they feared. (*Mrs. Borden makes a move which might be an effort to go past Lizzie back down the stairs. Lizzie stops her.*) Careful. Don't fall. (*Mrs. Borden turns*

435  *and slowly continues up the stairs with Lizzie behind her.*) And then, I would strike them down. With them not turning around, they would retain no image of me on their eye. It would be better that way.

(*Lizzie and Mrs. Borden disappear at the top of the stairs. The stage is empty for a moment. Bridget enters. She carries the pail for washing the windows. She sets the pail down, wipes her forehead. She stands for a moment looking towards the stairs as if she might have heard a sound. She picks up the pail and exits to the kitchen. Lizzie appears on the stairs. She is carrying the pile of clothes she carried upstairs. The hand hatchet is concealed under the clothes. Lizzie descends the stairs, she seems calm, self-possessed. She places the clothes on the table. She pauses, then she slowly turns to look at Mrs. Borden's chair at the table. After a moment she moves to it, pauses a moment, then sits down in it. She sits there at ease, relaxed, thinking. Bridget enters from the kitchen, she sees Lizzie, she stops, she takes in Lizzie*) *sitting in Mrs. Borden's chair. Bridget glances towards the stairs, back to Lizzie. Lizzie looks, for the first time, at Bridget.*)

LIZZIE. We must hurry before Papa gets home.

BRIDGET. Lizzie?

LIZZIE. I have it all figured out, but you have to help me, Bridget, you have to help me.    440

BRIDGET. What have you done?

LIZZIE. He would never leave me the farm, not with her on his back, but now (*She gets up from the chair*) I will have the farm, and I will have the money, yes, to do what I please! And you too Bridget, I'll give you some of    445
my money but you've got to help me. (*She moves towards Bridget who backs away a step.*) Don't be afraid, it's me, it's Lizzie, you like me!

BRIDGET. What have you done! (*Pause. Bridget moves towards the stairs.*)

LIZZIE. Don't go up there!

BRIDGET. You killed her!    450

LIZZIE. Someone broke in and they killed her.

BRIDGET. They'll know!

LIZZIE. Not if you help me.

BRIDGET. I can't Miss Lizzie, I can't!

LIZZIE. (*Grabs Bridget's arm.*) Do you want them to hang me! Is that what    455
you want! Oh Bridget, look! Look! (*She falls to her knees.*) I'm begging for my life, I'm begging. Deny me, and they will kill me. Help me, Bridget, please help me.

BRIDGET. But ... what ... could we do?

LIZZIE. (*Up off her knees.*) Oh I have it all figured out. I'll go down town as    460
quick as I can and you leave the doors open and go back outside and work on the windows.

BRIDGET. I've finished them, Lizzie.

LIZZIE. Then do them again! Remember last year when the burglar broke in?
Today someone broke in and she caught them.    465

BRIDGET. They'll never believe us.

LIZZIE. Have coffee with Lucy next door, stay with her till Papa gets home and he'll find her, and then each of us swears she was fine when we left, she was alright when we left!—it's going to work, Bridget, I know it!

BRIDGET. Your papa will guess.    470

LIZZIE. (*Getting ready to leave for down town.*) If he found me here he might guess, but he won't.

BRIDGET. Your papa will know!

LIZZIE. Papa loves me, if he has another story to believe, he'll believe it. He'd want to believe it, he'd have to believe it.    475

BRIDGET. Your papa will know.

LIZZIE. Why aren't you happy? I'm happy. We both should be happy! (*Lizzie embraces Bridget. Lizzie steps back a pace.*) Now—how do I look?

(*Mr. Borden enters. Bridget sees him. Lizzie slowly turns to see what Bridget is looking at.*)

LIZZIE. Papa?

480 MR. BORDEN. What is it? Where's Mrs. Borden?

BRIDGET. I ... don't know ... sir ... I ... just came in, sir.

MR. BORDEN. Did she leave the house?

BRIDGET. Well, sir ...

LIZZIE. She went out. Someone delivered a message and she left.

(*Lizzie takes off her hat and looks at her father.*)

485 LIZZIE. ... You're home early, Papa.

MR. BORDEN. I wanted to see Abbie. She's gone out, has she? Which way did she go? (*Lizzie shrugs, he continues, more thinking aloud.*) Well ... I ... I ... best wait for her here. I don't want to miss her again.

LIZZIE. Help Papa off with his coat, Bridget.... I hear there's a sale of dress

490 goods on down-town. Why don't you go buy yourself a yard?

BRIDGET. Oh ... I don't know, ma'am.

LIZZIE. You don't want any?

BRIDGET. I don't know.

LIZZIE. Then ... why don't you go upstairs and lie down. Have a rest before

495 lunch.

BRIDGET. I don't think I should.

LIZZIE. Nonsense.

BRIDGET. Lizzie, I—

LIZZIE. You go up and lie down. I'll look after things here.

(*Lizzie smiles at Bridget. Bridget starts up the stairs, suddenly stops. She looks back at Lizzie.*)

500 LIZZIE. It's alright ... go on ... it's alright. (*Bridget continues up the stairs. For the last bit of interchange, Mr. Borden has lowered the paper he's reading. Lizzie looks at him.*) Hello Papa. You look so tired.... I make you unhappy.... I don't like to make you unhappy. I love you.

MR. BORDEN. (*Smiles and takes her hand.*) I'm just getting old, Lizzie.

505 LIZZIE. You've got on my ring.... Do you remember when I gave you that? ... When I left Miss Cornelia's—it was in a little blue velvet box, you hid it behind your back, and you said, "guess which hand, Lizzie!" And I guessed. And you gave it to me and you said, "it's real gold, Lizzie, it's for

you because you are very precious to me." Do you remember, Papa? (*Mr. Borden nods.*) And I took it out of the little blue velvet box, and I took your hand, and I put my ring on your finger and I said "thank you, Papa, I love you." ... You've never taken it off ... see how it bites into the flesh of your finger. (*She presses his hand to her face.*) I forgive you, Papa, I forgive you for killing my birds.... You look so tired, why don't you lie down and rest, put your feet up, I'll undo your shoes for you. (*She kneels and undoes his shoes.*)

MR. BORDEN. You're a good girl.

LIZZIE. I could never stand to have you hate me, Papa. Never. I would do anything rather than have you hate me.

MR. BORDEN. I don't hate you, Lizzie.

LIZZIE. I would not want you to find out anything that would make you hate me. Because I love you.

MR. BORDEN. And I love you, Lizzie, you'll always be precious to me.

LIZZIE. (*Looks at him, and then smiles.*) Was I—when I had scabs on my knees?

MR. BORDEN. (*Laughs.*) Oh yes. Even then.

LIZZIE. (*Laughs.*) Oh Papa! ... Kiss me! (*He kisses her on the forehead.*) Thank you, Papa.

MR. BORDEN. Why're you crying?

LIZZIE. Because I'm so happy. Now ... put your feet up and get to sleep ... that's right ... shut your eyes ... go to sleep ... go to sleep....

(*She starts to hum, continues humming as Mr. Borden falls asleep. Miss Lizzie/Bridget appears on the stairs unobtrusively. Lizzie still humming, moves to the table, slips her hand under the clothes, withdraws the hatchet. She approaches her father with the hatchet behind her back. She stops humming. A pause, then she slowly raises the hatchet very high to strike him. Just as the hatchet is about to start its descent, there is a blackout. Children's voices are heard singing:*)

"Lizzie Borden took an axe,
Gave her Mother forty whacks,
When the job was nicely done,
She gave her father forty-one!
Forty-one!
Forty-one!"

(*The singing increases in volume and in distortion as it nears the end of the verse till the last words are very loud but discernible, just. Silence. Then the sound of slow measured heavy breathing which is growing into a wordless sound of hysteria. Light returns to the stage, dim light from late in the day.*)

*The actress stands with the hatchet raised in the same position in which we saw her before the blackout, but the couch is empty. Her eyes are shut. The sound comes from her. Miss Lizzie is at the foot of the stairs. She moves to the actress, reaches up to take the hatchet from her. When Miss Lizzie's hand touches the actress's, the actress releases the hatchet and whirls around to face Miss Lizzie who is left holding the hatchet. The actress backs away from Miss Lizzie. There is a flickering of light at the top of the stairs.)*

EMMA. (*From upstairs.*) Lizzie! Lizzie! You're making too much noise!

*(Emma descends the stairs carrying an oil lamp. The actress backs away from Lizzie, turns and runs into the kitchen. Miss Lizzie turns to see Emma. The hand hatchet is behind Miss Lizzie's back concealed from Emma. Emma pauses for a moment.)*

EMMA. Where is she?

MISS LIZZIE. Who?

540 EMMA. (*A pause then Emma moves to the window and glances out.*) It's raining.

MISS LIZZIE. I know.

EMMA. (*Puts the lamp down, sits, lowers her voice.*) Lizzie.

MISS LIZZIE. Yes?

EMMA. I want to speak to you, Lizzie.

545 MISS LIZZIE. Yes Emma.

EMMA. That ... actress who's come up from Boston.

MISS LIZZIE. What about her?

EMMA. People talk.

MISS LIZZIE. You needn't listen.

550 EMMA. In your position you should do nothing to *inspire talk*.

MISS LIZZIE. People need so little in the way of inspiration. And Miss Cornelia's classes didn't cover "Etiquette for Acquitted Persons."

EMMA. Common sense should tell you what you ought or ought not do.

MISS LIZZIE. Common sense is repugnant to me. I prefer uncommon sense.

555 EMMA. I forbid her in this house, Lizzie!

(*Pause.*)

MISS LIZZIE. Do you?

EMMA. (*Backing down, softly.*) It's ... disgraceful.

MISS LIZZIE. I see.

*(Miss Lizzie turns away from Emma a few steps.)*

EMMA. I simply cannot—

560 MISS LIZZIE. You could always leave.

EMMA. Leave?

MISS LIZZIE. Move. Away. Why don't you?

EMMA. I—

MISS LIZZIE. You could never, could you?

EMMA. If I only—                                                                565

MISS LIZZIE. Knew.

EMMA. Lizzie, did you?

MISS LIZZIE. Oh Emma, do you intend asking me that question from now till death us do part?

EMMA. It's just—                                                                570

MISS LIZZIE. For if you do, I may well take something sharp to you.

EMMA. Why do you joke like that!

MISS LIZZIE. (*Turning back to Emma who sees the hatchet for the first time. Emma's reaction is not any verbal or untoward movement. She freezes as Miss Lizzie advances on her.*) Did you never stop and think that if I did, then   575 you were guilty too?

EMMA. What?

(*The actress will enter unobtrusively on the periphery. We are virtually unaware of her entrance until she speaks and moves forward.*)

MISS LIZZIE. It was you who brought me up, like a mother to me. Almost like a mother. Did you ever stop and think that I was like a puppet, your puppet. My head your hand, yes, your hand working my mouth, me say-   580 ing all the things you felt like saying, me doing all the things you felt like doing, me spewing forth, me hitting out, and you, you—!

THE ACTRESS. (*Quietly.*) Lizzie.

(*Miss Lizzie is immediately in control of herself.*)

EMMA. (*Whispers.*) I wasn't even here that day.

MISS LIZZIE. I can swear to that.                                               585

EMMA. Do you want to drive me mad?

MISS LIZZIE. Oh yes.

EMMA. You didn't ... did you?

MISS LIZZIE. Poor ... Emma.

THE ACTRESS. Lizzie. (*She takes the hatchet from Miss Lizzie.*) Lizzie you did.   590

MISS LIZZIE. I didn't. (*The actress looks to the hatchet—then to the audience.*) You did.

(*Blackout.*)

—1980

# Tom Stoppard
b. 1937

Tom Stoppard is a British dramatist who writes prolifically for radio, stage, and screen. His plays have been as distinctive as they have been popular. Typically they bring together improbable story elements in ways that open up possibilities for both sophisticated wordplay and farcical humour; typically too they touch on genuinely serious philosophical themes.

Stoppard's early years were tumultuous. In 1939 his family was displaced from Zlín, Czechoslovakia (Stoppard's birthplace), to Singapore by the invasion of the Nazis. World War II eventually forced them to Australia, then to India. Stoppard's father died during the war, and after his mother was re-married to a British army officer, the family moved to England.

Stoppard dropped out of grammar school to work as a newspaper reporter, and then spent a year as a drama critic while building his career as a playwright. He made his name with clever, absurdist dramas in which theatricality itself becomes a central thematic concern. His first major success was the Tony Award-winning *Rosencrantz and Guildenstern Are Dead* (1966), in which two minor characters from Shakespeare's *Hamlet* are controlled by narrative forces beyond their understanding. In the late 1970s Stoppard's Czech roots led him toward issues of censorship and brutality in the Soviet Union, addressed in plays such as *Every Good Boy Deserves Favour* (1977). Intellectual inquiry remains an important engine for his writing; *Arcadia* (1993), for example, incorporates concepts from mathematics, science, and history, juxtaposing events taking place in 1809 with their interpretation by academics in 1989. Stoppard's 2002 trilogy of plays *The Coast of Utopia* concerns a series of philosophical debates between literary and political characters in pre-revolutionary Russia.

Stoppard has found an even wider audience with his original screenplays and screen adaptations. In 1990, he adapted and directed a successful film version of *Rosencrantz and Guildenstern Are Dead*. He also wrote the screenplay for Terry Gilliam's influential film *Brazil* (1985), and in 1998 he won an Academy Award as co-author of the screenplay for *Shakespeare in Love*.

# Arcadia[1]

## CHARACTERS

(*In order of appearance*)
Thomasina Coverly, *aged thirteen, later sixteen*
Septimus Hodge, *her tutor, aged twenty-two, later twenty-five*
Jellaby, *a butler, middle-aged*
Ezra Chater, *a poet, aged thirty-one*
Richard Noakes, *a landscape architect, middle-aged*
Lady Croom, *middle thirties*
Capt. Brice, RN,[2] *middle thirties*
Hannah Jarvis, *an author, late thirties*
Chloë Coverly, *aged eighteen*
Bernard Nightingale, *a don,*[3] *late thirties*
Valentine Coverly, *aged twenty-five to thirty*
Gus Coverly, *aged fifteen*
Augustus Coverly, *aged fifteen*

## ACT 1, SCENE 1

*A room on the garden front of a very large country house in Derbyshire*[4] *in April 1809. Nowadays, the house would be called a stately home. The upstage wall is mainly tall, shapely, uncurtained windows, one or more of which work as doors. Nothing much need be said or seen of the exterior beyond. We come to learn that the house stands in the typical English park of the time. Perhaps we see an indication of this, perhaps only light and air and sky.*

*The room looks bare despite the large table which occupies the centre of it. The table, the straight-backed chairs and, the only other item of furniture, the architect's stand or reading stand, would all be collectable pieces now but here, on an uncarpeted wood floor, they have no more pretension than a schoolroom, which is indeed the main use of this room at this time. What elegance there is, is architectural, and nothing is impressive but the scale. There is a door in each of the side walls. These are closed, but one of the french windows*[5] *is open to a bright but sunless morning.*

---

1   *Arcadia* Figuratively, an ideal pastoral paradise; literally, a real region of Greece that was often depicted as a paradise in classical literature.
2   *RN* Royal Navy.
3   *don* University instructor.
4   *Derbyshire* County in the East Midlands of England.
5   *french windows* Windows that also function as doors.

*There are two people, each busy with books and paper and pen and ink, separately occupied. The pupil is Thomasina Coverly, aged 13. The tutor is Septimus Hodge, aged 22. Each has an open book. Hers is a slim mathematics primer. His is a handsome thick quarto,[1] brand new, a vanity production, with little tapes to tie when the book is closed. His loose papers, etc, are kept in a stiff-backed portfolio which also ties up with tapes.*

*Septimus has a tortoise which is sleepy enough to serve as a paperweight.*

*Elsewhere on the table there is an old-fashioned theodolite[2] and also some other books stacked up.*

THOMASINA.   Septimus, what is carnal embrace?

SEPTIMUS.   Carnal embrace is the practice of throwing one's arms around a side of beef.

THOMASINA.   Is that all?

SEPTIMUS.   No ... a shoulder of mutton, a haunch of venison well hugged, an
5   embrace of grouse ... *caro, carnis*;[3] feminine; flesh.

THOMASINA.   Is it a sin?

SEPTIMUS.   Not necessarily, my lady, but when carnal embrace is sinful it is a sin of the flesh, QED. We had *caro* in our Gallic Wars—"The Britons live on milk and meat"—"*lacte et carne vivunt.*" I am sorry that the seed fell
10   on stony ground.[4]

THOMASINA.   That was the sin of Onan,[5] wasn't it, Septimus?

SEPTIMUS.   Yes. He was giving his brother's wife a Latin lesson and she was hardly the wiser after it than before. I thought you were finding a proof for Fermat's last theorem.[6]
15

---

1    *quarto* Large book composed of quarto pages, which are created when a printer folds a large sheet of paper twice to make four leaves.

2    *theodolite* Surveying tool used to measure angles.

3    *caro, carnis* Latin: flesh or meat.

4    *QED* Abbreviation of the Latin term *quod erat demonstrandum*—meaning "which was to be shown"—used to indicate the end of a logical argument or mathematical proof; *Gallic Wars* Roman campaigns led by Julius Ceasar in 58–51 BCE, during which Britain was invaded twice; *lacte ... vivunt* From Julius Caesar, *Commentarii de Bello Gallico* (*Commentaries on the Gallic War*). Septimus provides a translation; *seed ... stony ground* See Mark 4.5.

5    *Onan* Biblical figure who was struck down by God. When his brother died, Onan was instructed by God to give his childless sister-in-law Tamar an heir. Onan slept with Tamar but ejaculated onto the floor instead of impregnating her. See Genesis 38.8–10.

6    *Fermat's last theorem* 1637 conjecture made by French mathematician Pierre de Fermat and recorded without an accompanying proof. It states that, when $n$ has a value higher than 2 in the equation $x^n + y^n = z^n$, there are no three positive integers that can be successfully substituted for $x$, $y$, and $z$. The theorem remained unverified until the first successful proof was published in the 1990s.

THOMASINA.  It is very difficult, Septimus. You will have to show me how.

SEPTIMUS.  If I knew how, there would be no need to ask *you*. Fermat's last theorem has kept people busy for a hundred and fifty years, and I hoped it would keep *you* busy long enough for me to read Mr. Chater's poem in praise of love with only the distraction of its own absurdities.                    20

THOMASINA.  Our Mr. Chater has written a poem?

SEPTIMUS.  He believes he has written a poem, yes. I can see that there might be more carnality in your algebra than in Mr. Chater's "Couch of Eros."[1]

THOMASINA.  Oh, it was not my algebra. I heard Jellaby telling cook that Mrs. Chater was discovered in carnal embrace in the gazebo.                    25

SEPTIMUS.  (*Pause*) Really? With whom, did Jellaby happen to say?

(*Thomasina considers this with a puzzled frown.*)

THOMASINA.  What do you mean, with whom?

SEPTIMUS.  With what? Exactly so. The idea is absurd. Where did this story come from?

THOMASINA.  Mr. Noakes.                    30

SEPTIMUS.  Mr. Noakes!

THOMASINA.  Papa's landskip[2] gardener. He was taking bearings in the garden when he saw—through his spyglass—Mrs. Chater in the gazebo in carnal embrace.

SEPTIMUS.  And do you mean to tell me that Mr. Noakes told the butler?                    35

THOMASINA.  No. Mr. Noakes told Mr. Chater. *Jellaby* was told by the groom, who overheard Mr. Noakes telling Mr. Chater, in the stable yard.

SEPTIMUS.  Mr. Chater being engaged in closing the stable door.

THOMASINA.  What do you mean, Septimus?

SEPTIMUS.  So, thus far, the only people who know about this are Mr. Noakes    40
the landskip gardener, the groom, the butler, the cook and, of course, Mrs. Chater's husband, the poet.

THOMASINA.  And Arthur who was cleaning the silver, and the bootboy. And now you.

SEPTIMUS.  Of course. What else did he say?                    45

THOMASINA.  Mr. Noakes?

SEPTIMUS.  No, not Mr. Noakes. Jellaby. You heard Jellaby telling the cook.

THOMASINA.  Cook hushed him almost as soon as he started. Jellaby did not see that I was being allowed to finish yesterday's upstairs' rabbit pie[3] before

---

1    *Eros* Greek god of love.

2    *landskip* Landscape.

3    *upstairs' rabbit pie* I.e., the rabbit pie made for the upper-class inhabitants of the house (as opposed to the servants).

50      I came to my lesson. I think you have not been candid with me, Septimus.
        A gazebo is not, after all, a meat larder.[1]
SEPTIMUS.  I never said my definition was complete.
THOMASINA.  Is carnal embrace kissing?
SEPTIMUS.  Yes.
55  THOMASINA.  And throwing one's arms around Mrs. Chater?
SEPTIMUS.  Yes. Now, Fermat's last theorem—
THOMASINA.  I thought as much. I hope you are ashamed.
SEPTIMUS.  I, my lady?
THOMASINA.  If *you* do not teach me the true meaning of things, who will?
60  SEPTIMUS.  Ah. Yes, I am ashamed. Carnal embrace is sexual congress, which
        is the insertion of the male genital organ into the female genital organ for
        purposes of procreation and pleasure. Fermat's last theorem, by contrast,
        asserts that when $x$, $y$ and $z$ are whole numbers each raised to power of $n$,
        the sum of the first two can never equal the third when $n$ is greater than 2.

        (*Pause.*)

65  THOMASINA.  Eurghhh!
SEPTIMUS.  Nevertheless, that is the theorem.
THOMASINA.  It is disgusting and incomprehensible. Now when I am grown
        to practise it myself I shall never do so without thinking of you.
SEPTIMUS.  Thank you very much, my lady. Was Mrs. Chater down this
70      morning?
THOMASINA.  No. Tell me more about sexual congress.
SEPTIMUS.  There is nothing more to be said about sexual congress.
THOMASINA.  Is it the same as love?
SEPTIMUS.  Oh no, it is much nicer than that.

        (*One of the side doors leads to the music room. It is the other side door which
        now opens to admit Jellaby, the butler.*)

75      I am teaching, Jellaby.
JELLABY.  Beg your pardon, Mr. Hodge, Mr. Chater said it was urgent you
        receive his letter.
SEPTIMUS.  Oh, very well. (*Septimus takes the letter.*) Thank you. (*And to dis-
        miss Jellaby.*) Thank you.
80  JELLABY.  (*Holding his ground*) Mr. Chater asked me to bring him your an-
        swer.
SEPTIMUS.  My answer?

        (*He opens the letter. There is no envelope as such, but there is a "cover"
        which, folded and sealed, does the same service. Septimus tosses the cover
        negligently aside and reads.*)

---

1   *larder* Cool room used to store perishable foods.

Well, my answer is that as is my custom and my duty to his lordship I am engaged until a quarter to twelve in the education of his daughter. When I am done, and if Mr. Chater is still there, I will be happy to wait upon him in—(*he checks the letter*)—in the gunroom. 85

JELLABY. I will tell him so, thank you, sir.

(*Septimus folds the letter and places it between the pages of "The Couch of Eros."*)

THOMASINA. What is for dinner, Jellaby?

JELLABY. Boiled ham and cabbages, my lady, and a rice pudding.

THOMASINA. Oh, goody. 90

(*Jellaby leaves.*)

SEPTIMUS. Well, so much for Mr. Noakes. He puts himself forward as a gentleman, a philosopher of the picturesque, a visionary who can move mountains and cause lakes, but in the scheme of the garden he is as the serpent.[1]

THOMASINA. When you stir your rice pudding, Septimus, the spoonful of 95 jam spreads itself round making red trails like the picture of a meteor in my astronomical atlas. But if you stir backward, the jam will not come together again. Indeed, the pudding does not notice and continues to turn pink just as before. Do you think this is odd?

SEPTIMUS. No. 100

THOMASINA. Well, I do. You cannot stir things apart.

SEPTIMUS. No more you can, time must needs run backward, and since it will not, we must stir our way onward mixing as we go, disorder out of disorder into disorder until pink is complete, unchanging and unchangeable, and we are done with it for ever. This is known as free will or self- 105 determination.

(*He picks up the tortoise and moves it a few inches as though it had strayed, on top of some loose papers, and admonishes it.*)

Sit!

---

1   *picturesque* Aesthetic principle bridging the gap between the awe-inspiring qualities of untamed nature and the beauty of harmonious, deliberate composition; picturesque gardens look much rougher and less manicured than the gardens of the preceding period. The concept of the picturesque is also applied to art and literature, and is associated with Romanticism, a major social and cultural movement that began in the late eighteenth century and valued individualism, humans' relationship to nature, and emotion over reason; *serpent* Reference to Genesis 3.1–20, in which a serpent persuades Adam and Eve to eat the fruit forbidden them by God in the Garden of Eden.

THOMASINA.  Septimus, do you think God is a Newtonian?[1]

SEPTIMUS.   An Etonian?[2] Almost certainly, I'm afraid. We must ask your
brother to make it his first enquiry.

THOMASINA.  No, Septimus, a Newtonian. Septimus! Am I the first person to
have thought of this?

SEPTIMUS.  No.

THOMASINA.  I have not said yet.

SEPTIMUS.  "If everything from the furthest planet to the smallest atom of
our brain acts according to Newton's law of motion, what becomes of free
will?"

THOMASINA.  No.

SEPTIMUS.  God's will.

THOMASINA.  No.

SEPTIMUS.  Sin.

THOMASINA.  (*Derisively*) No!

SEPTIMUS.  Very well.

THOMASINA.  If you could stop every atom in its position and direction, and
if your mind could comprehend all the actions thus suspended, then if you
were really, *really* good at algebra you could write the formula for all the
future; and although nobody can be so clever as to do it, the formula must
exist just as if one could.

SEPTIMUS.  (*Pause*) Yes. (*Pause*) Yes, as far as I know, you are the first person
to have thought of this. (*Pause. With an effort.*) In the margin of his copy
of *Arithmetica*,[3] Fermat wrote that he had discovered a wonderful proof
of his theorem but, the margin being too narrow for his purpose, did not
have room to write it down. The note was found after his death, and from
that day to this—

THOMASINA.  Oh! I see now! The answer is perfectly obvious.

SEPTIMUS.  This time you may have overreached yourself.

(*The door is opened, somewhat violently. Chater enters.*)

Mr. Chater! Perhaps my message miscarried. I will be at liberty at a quarter
to twelve, if that is convenient.

---

1   *Newtonian* Follower of the English mathematician and physicist Isaac Newton (1642–
    1727); more specifically, a follower of Newtonian mechanics, a subfield of physics based
    on Newton's laws describing the motion of objects. Until the late nineteenth century, it
    was thought that Newtonian mechanics could be extended to explain all physical phe-
    nomena in the universe.

2   *Etonian* Student or alumnus of Eton, a prestigious British boarding school founded in
    1440.

3   *Arithmetica* Algebra text of the third century CE composed by the ancient Greek math-
    ematician Diophantus.

CHATER.  It is not convenient, sir. My business will not wait.

SEPTIMUS.  Then I suppose you have Lord Croom's opinion that your busi-    140
ness is more important than his daughter's lesson.

CHATER.  I do not, but, if you like, I will ask his lordship to settle the point.

SEPTIMUS.  (*Pause*) My lady, take Fermat into the music room. There will be
an extra spoonful of jam if you find his proof.

THOMASINA.  There is no proof, Septimus. The thing that is perfectly obvious    145
is that the note in the margin was a joke to make you all mad.

(*Thomasina leaves.*)

SEPTIMUS.  Now, sir, what is this business that cannot wait?

CHATER.  I think you know it, sir. You have insulted my wife.

SEPTIMUS.  Insulted her? That would deny my nature, my conduct, and the
admiration in which I hold Mrs. Chater.    150

CHATER.  I have heard of your admiration, sir! You insulted my wife in the
gazebo yesterday evening!

SEPTIMUS.  You are mistaken. I made love to your wife in the gazebo. She
asked me to meet her there, I have her note somewhere, I dare say I could
find it for you, and if someone is putting it about that I did not turn up,    155
by God, sir, it is a slander.

CHATER.  You damned lecher! You would drag down a lady's reputation to
make a refuge for your cowardice. It will not do! I am calling you out!

SEPTIMUS.  Chater! Chater, Chater, Chater! My dear friend!

CHATER.  You dare to call me that. I demand satisfaction!    160

SEPTIMUS.  Mrs. Chater demanded satisfaction and now you are demanding
satisfaction. I cannot spend my time day and night satisfying the demands
of the Chater family. As for your wife's reputation, it stands where it ever
stood.

CHATER.  You blackguard![1]    165

SEPTIMUS.  I assure you. Mrs. Chater is charming and spirited, with a pleasing voice and a dainty step, she is the epitome of all the qualities society
applauds in her sex—and yet her chief renown is for a readiness that keeps
her in a state of tropical humidity as would grow orchids in her drawers
in January.    170

CHATER.  Damn you, Hodge, I will not listen to this! Will you fight or not?

SEPTIMUS.  (*Definitively*) Not! There are no more than two or three poets of
the first rank now living, and I will not shoot one of them dead over a per-
pendicular poke in a gazebo with a woman whose reputation could not be
adequately defended with a platoon of musketry deployed by rota.[2]    175

---

1    *blackguard* Dishonourable person.

2    *rota* Schedule.

CHATER.  Ha! You say so! Who are the others? In your opinion?—no—
no—!—this goes very ill, Hodge. I will not be flattered out of my course.
You say so, do you?

SEPTIMUS.  I do. And I would say the same to Milton[1] were he not already
dead. Not the part about his wife, of course—

CHATER.  But among the living? Mr. Southey?[2]

SEPTIMUS.  Southey I would have shot on sight.

CHATER.  (*Shaking his head sadly*) Yes, he has fallen off. I admired "Thalaba" *quite*, but "Madoc,"[3] (*he chuckles*) oh dear me!—but we are straying
from the business here—you took advantage of Mrs. Chater, and if that
were not bad enough, it appears every stableboy and scullery maid on the
strength—

SEPTIMUS.  Damn me! Have you not listened to a word I said?

CHATER.  I have heard you, sir, and I will not deny I welcome your regard,
God knows one is little appreciated if one stands outside the coterie of
hacks and placemen who surround Jeffrey and the *Edinburgh*[4]—

SEPTIMUS.  My dear Chater, they judge a poet by the seating plan of Lord
Holland's[5] table!

CHATER.  By heaven, you are right! And I would very much like to know the
name of the scoundrel who slandered my verse drama "The Maid of Turkey" in the *Piccadilly Recreation*, too!

SEPTIMUS.  "The Maid of Turkey!" I have it by my bedside! When I cannot
sleep I take up "The Maid of Turkey" like an old friend!

CHATER.  (*Gratified*) There you are! And the scoundrel wrote he would not
give it to his dog for dinner were it covered in bread sauce and stuffed with
chestnuts. When Mrs. Chater read that, she wept, sir, and would not give
herself to me for a fortnight—which recalls me to my purpose—

SEPTIMUS.  The new poem, however, will make your name perpetual—

CHATER.  Whether it do or not—

SEPTIMUS.  It is not a question, sir. No coterie can oppose the acclamation of
the reading public. "The Couch of Eros" will take the town.

CHATER.  Is that your estimation?

SEPTIMUS.  It is my intent.

---

1    *Milton* English poet John Milton (1608–74).

2    *Southey* English poet Robert Southey (1774–1843).

3    *"Thalaba" quite, but "Madoc"* "Thalaba the Destroyer" (1801) and "Madoc" (1805) are
two epic poems by Southey.

4    *coterie* Exclusive group of people with shared tastes; *Jeffrey and the Edinburgh* Scottish
literary critic Francis Jeffrey (1773–1850) was the editor of the *Edinburgh Review* (1802–
1929).

5    *Lord Holland* Henry Richard Vassall-Fox (1773–1840), English politician.

CHATER. Is it, is it? Well, well! I do not understand you.

SEPTIMUS. You see I have an early copy—sent to me for review. I say review, but I speak of an extensive appreciation of your gifts and your rightful place in English literature.

CHATER. Well, I must say. That is certainly ... You have written it?

SEPTIMUS. (*Crisply*) Not yet.

CHATER. Ah. And how long does ...?

SEPTIMUS. To be done right, it first requires a careful re-reading of your book, of both your books, several readings, together with outlying works for an exhibition of deference or disdain as the case merits. I make notes, of course, I order my thoughts, and finally, when all is ready and I am *calm in my mind* ...

CHATER. (*Shrewdly*) Did Mrs. Chater know of this before she—before you—

SEPTIMUS. I think she very likely did.

CHATER. (*Triumphantly*) There is nothing that woman would not do for me! Now you have an insight to her character. Yes, by God, she is a wife to me, sir!

SEPTIMUS. For that alone, I would not make her a widow.

CHATER. Captain Brice once made the same observation!

SEPTIMUS. Captain Brice did?

CHATER. Mr. Hodge, allow me to inscribe your copy in happy anticipation. Lady Thomasina's pen will serve us.

SEPTIMUS. Your connection with Lord and Lady Croom you owe to your fighting her ladyship's brother?

CHATER. No! It was all nonsense, sir—a canard![1] But a fortunate mistake, sir. It brought me the patronage of a captain of His Majesty's Navy and the brother of a countess. I do not think Mr. Walter Scott[2] can say as much, and here I am, a respected guest at Sidley Park.

SEPTIMUS. Well, sir, you can say you have received satisfaction.

(*Chater is already inscribing the book, using the pen and ink-pot on the table. Noakes enters through the door used by Chater. He carries rolled-up plans. Chater, inscribing, ignores Noakes. Noakes on seeing the occupants, panics.*)

NOAKES. Oh!

SEPTIMUS. Ah, Mr. Noakes!—my muddy-mettled rascal! Where's your spyglass?

NOAKES. I beg your leave—I thought her ladyship—excuse me—

---

1    *canard* Misleading report.

2    *Walter Scott* Sir Walter Scott (1771–1832), Scottish poet and novelist.

(*He is beating an embarrassed retreat when he becomes rooted by Chater's voice. Chater reads his inscription in ringing tones.*)

CHATER. "To my friend Septimus Hodge, who stood up and gave his best on behalf of the Author—Ezra Chater, at Sidley Park, Derbyshire, April 10th, 1809." (*Giving the book to Septimus.*) There, sir—something to show your
245　grandchildren!
SEPTIMUS. This is more than I deserve, this is handsome, what do you say, Noakes?

(*They are interrupted by the appearance, outside the windows, of Lady Croom and Captain Edward Brice, RN. Her first words arrive through the open door.*)

LADY CROOM. Oh, no! Not the gazebo!

(*She enters, followed by Brice who carries a leatherbound sketch book.*)

Mr. Noakes! What is this I hear?
250　BRICE. Not only the gazebo, but the boat-house, the Chinese bridge, the shrubbery—
CHATER. By God, sir! Not possible!
BRICE. Mr. Noakes will have it so.
SEPTIMUS. Mr. Noakes, this is monstrous!
255　LADY CROOM. I am glad to hear it from *you*, Mr. Hodge.
THOMASINA. (*Opening the door from the music room*) May I return now?
SEPTIMUS. (*Attempting to close the door*) Not just yet—
LADY CROOM. Yes, let her stay. A lesson in folly is worth two in wisdom.

(*Brice takes the sketch book to the reading stand, where he lays it open. The sketch book is the work of Mr. Noakes, who is obviously an admirer of Humphry Repton's "Red Books."*[1] *The pages, drawn in watercolours, show "before" and "after" views of the landscape, and the pages are cunningly cut to allow the latter to be superimposed over portions of the former, though Repton did it the other way round.*)

BRICE. Is Sidley Park to be an Englishman's garden or the haunt of Corsican
260　brigands?[2]
SEPTIMUS. Let us not hyperbolize, sir.

---

1　*Humphry Repton's "Red Books"* English landscape designer Humphry Repton (1752–1818) kept a series of watercolours in bound books in order to be able to show before-and-after pictures of his projects.
2　*Corsican brigands* Highway robbers from Corsica, a French island in the Mediterranean Sea. Corsicans were often stereotyped as highwaymen and bandits.

BRICE. It is rape, sir!

NOAKES. (*Defending himself.*) It is the modern style.

CHATER. (*Under the same misapprehension as Septimus*) Regrettable, of course, but so it is.    265

(*Thomasina has gone to examine the sketch book.*)

LADY CROOM. Mr. Chater, you show too much submission. Mr. Hodge, I appeal to you.

SEPTIMUS. Madam, I regret the gazebo, I sincerely regret the gazebo—and the boat-house up to a point—but the Chinese bridge, fantasy!—and the shrubbery I reject with contempt! Mr. Chater!—would you take the word    270 of a jumped-up jobbing[1] gardener who sees carnal embrace in every nook and cranny of the landskip!

THOMASINA. Septimus, they are not speaking of carnal embrace, are you, Mama?

LADY CROOM. Certainly not. What do you know of carnal embrace?    275

THOMASINA. Everything, thanks to Septimus. In my opinion, Mr. Noakes's scheme for the garden is perfect. It is a Salvator!

LADY CROOM. What does she mean?

NOAKES. (*Answering the wrong question*) Salvator Rosa,[2] your ladyship, the painter. He is indeed the very exemplar of the picturesque style.    280

BRICE. Hodge, what is this?

SEPTIMUS. She speaks from innocence not from experience.

BRICE. You call it innocence? Has he ruined you, child?

(*Pause.*)

SEPTIMUS. Answer your uncle!

THOMASINA. (*To Septimus.*) How is a ruined child different from a ruined    285 castle?

SEPTIMUS. On such questions I defer to Mr. Noakes.

NOAKES. (*Out of his depth*) A ruined castle is picturesque, certainly.

SEPTIMUS. That is the main difference. (*To Brice*) I teach the classical authors. If I do not elucidate their meaning, who will?    290

BRICE. As her tutor you have a duty to keep her in ignorance.

LADY CROOM. Do not dabble in paradox, Edward, it puts you in danger of fortuitous wit. Thomasina, wait in your bedroom.

THOMASINA. (*Retiring*) Yes, mama. I did not intend to get you into trouble, Septimus. I am very sorry for it. It is plain that there are some things a girl    295

---

1    *jobbing* Working odd jobs.

2    *Salvator Rosa* Italian poet and painter (1615–73) known for his landscape paintings, which frequently feature ruins and bandits.

is allowed to understand, and these include the whole of algebra, but there are others, such as embracing a side of beef, that must be kept from her until she is old enough to have a carcass of her own.

LADY CROOM.  One moment.

300  BRICE.  What is she talking about?

LADY CROOM.  Meat.

BRICE.  Meat?

LADY CROOM.  Thomasina, you had better remain. Your knowledge of the picturesque obviously exceeds anything the rest of us can offer. Mr. Hodge,

305  ignorance should be like an empty vessel waiting to be filled at the well of truth—not a cabinet of vulgar curios. Mr. Noakes—now at last it is your turn.

NOAKES.  Thank you, your ladyship—

LADY CROOM.  Your drawing is a very wonderful transformation. I would

310  not have recognized my own garden but for your ingenious book—is it not?—look! Here is the Park as it appears to us now, and here as it might be when Mr. Noakes has done with it. Where there is the familiar pastoral refinement of an Englishman's garden, here is an eruption of gloomy forest and towering crag, of ruins where there was never a house, of water dash-

315  ing against rocks where there was neither spring nor a stone I could not throw the length of a cricket pitch. My hyacinth dell is become a haunt for hobgoblins, my Chinese bridge, which I am assured is superior to the one at Kew, and for all I know at Peking, is usurped by a fallen obelisk[1] overgrown with briars—

320  NOAKES.  (*Bleating*) Lord Little has one very similar—

LADY CROOM.  I cannot relieve Lord Little's misfortunes by adding to my own. Pray, what is this rustic hovel that presumes to superpose itself on my gazebo?

NOAKES.  That is the hermitage,[2] madam.

325  LADY CROOM.  The hermitage? I am bewildered.

BRICE.  It is all irregular, Mr. Noakes.

NOAKES.  It is, sir. Irregularity is one of the chiefest principles of the pictur-esque style—

LADY CROOM.  But Sidley Park is already a picture, and a most amiable pic-

330  ture too. The slopes are green and gentle. The trees are companionably

---

1   *crag* Steep cliff; *cricket pitch* In the sport of cricket, a 20-metre strip at the centre of the field; *hobgoblins* Pesky or bothersome sprites from folklore; *Kew* I.e., London's Royal Botanic Gardens, also known as Kew Gardens; *Peking* Beijing, capital city of China; *obelisk* Large tapering stone pillar. Picturesque gardens often incorporated artificial ruins.

2   *hermitage* Sanctuary and retreat of a hermit, usually quite small and isolated.

grouped at intervals that show them to advantage. The rill is a serpentine ribbon unwound from the lake peaceably contained by meadows on which the right amount of sheep are tastefully arranged—in short, it is nature as God intended, and I can say with the painter, "*Et in Arcadia ego!*"[1] "Here I am in Arcadia," Thomasina.   335

THOMASINA.  Yes, mama, if you would have it so.

LADY CROOM.  Is she correcting my taste or my translation?

THOMASINA.  Neither are beyond correction, mama, but it was your geography caused the doubt.

LADY CROOM.  Something has occurred with the girl since I saw her last, and   340 surely that was yesterday. How old are you this morning?

THOMASINA.  Thirteen years and ten months, mama.

LADY CROOM.  Thirteen years and ten months. She is not due to be pert for six months at the earliest, or to have notions of taste for much longer. Mr. Hodge, I hold you accountable. Mr. Noakes, back to you—   345

NOAKES.  Thank you, my—

LADY CROOM.  You have been reading too many novels by Mrs. Radcliffe, that is my opinion. This is a garden for *The Castle of Otranto*[2] or *The Mysteries of Udolpho*—

CHATER.  *The Castle of Otranto*, my lady, is by Horace Walpole.   350

NOAKES.  (*Thrilled*) Mr. Walpole the gardener?![3]

LADY CROOM.  Mr. Chater, you are a welcome guest at Sidley Park but while you are one, *The Castle of Otranto* was written by whomsoever I say it was, otherwise what is the point of being a guest or having one?

(*The distant popping of guns heard.*)

Well, the guns have reached the brow—I will speak to his lordship on the   355 subject, and we will see by and by—(*She stands looking out.*) Ah!—your friend has got down a pigeon, Mr. Hodge. (*Calls out.*) Bravo, sir!

SEPTIMUS.  The pigeon, I am sure, fell to your husband or to your son, your ladyship—my schoolfriend was never a sportsman.

---

1   *rill* Stream; *Et in Arcadia ego* Title given to two paintings by the French artist Nicolas Poussin (1594–1665), both of which depict classical shepherds gathered around a tomb inscribed with the title phrase. Lady Croom mistranslates the Latin; a more accurate translation would be "Even in Arcadia, I (am)." The "I" in the expression is understood to be death.

2   *Mrs. Radcliffe* Anne Radcliffe (1764–1823), English Gothic novelist and the author of *The Mysteries of Udolpho*; *The Castle of Otranto* Written in 1765 by Horace Walpole and generally considered the first English-language Gothic novel.

3   *Mr. Walpole the gardener* Although he was better known as a writer and politician, Walpole also designed his personal home, a tourist attraction noted for its Gothic architecture and landscape. His "Essay on Modern Gardening" (1780) was influential.

360 BRICE. (*Looking out*) Yes, to Augustus!—bravo, lad!

LADY CROOM. (*Outside*) Well, come along! Where are my troops?

(*Brice, Noakes and Chater obediently follow her, Chater making a detour to shake Septimus's hand fervently.*)

CHATER. My dear Mr. Hodge!

(*Chater leaves also. The guns are heard again, a little closer.*)

THOMASINA. Pop, pop, pop ... I have grown up in the sound of guns like the
365 child of a siege. Pigeons and rooks in the close season, grouse on the heights from August, and the pheasants to follow—partridge, snipe, woodcock, and teal—pop—pop—pop, and the culling of the herd. Papa has no need of the recording angel, his life is written in the game book.[1]

SEPTIMUS. A calendar of slaughter. "Even in Arcadia, there am I!"

370 THOMASINA. Oh, phooey to Death!

(*She dips a pen and takes it to the reading stand.*)

I will put in a hermit, for what is a hermitage without a hermit? Are you in love with my mother, Septimus?

SEPTIMUS. You must not be cleverer than your elders. It is not polite.

THOMASINA. Am I cleverer?

375 SEPTIMUS. Yes. Much.

THOMASINA. Well, I am sorry, Septimus. (*She pauses in her drawing and produces a small envelope from her pocket.*) Mrs. Chater came to the music room with a note for you. She said it was of scant importance, and that therefore I should carry it to you with the utmost safety, urgency and dis-
380 cretion. Does carnal embrace addle the brain?

SEPTIMUS. (*Taking the letter*) Invariably. Thank you. That is enough education for today.

THOMASINA. There. I have made him like the Baptist in the wilderness.[2]

SEPTIMUS. How picturesque.

(*Lady Croom is heard calling distantly for Thomasina who runs off into the garden, cheerfully, an uncomplicated girl. Septimus opens Mrs. Chater's note. He crumples the envelope and throws it away. He reads the note, folds it and inserts it into the pages of "The Couch of Eros."*)

---

1   *recording angel* Angel who writes down all the events and deeds of a person's life; *game book* Record of the gaming (i.e., hunting) occurring on an estate.

2   *the Baptist in the wilderness* Biblical prophet John the Baptist, who preached in the wilderness. See Matthew 3.

# ACT 1, SCENE 2

*The lights come up on the same room, on the same sort of morning, in the present day, as is instantly clear from the appearance of Hannah Jarvis; and from nothing else.*

*Something needs to be said about this. The action of the play shuttles back and forth between the early nineteenth century and the present day, always in this same room. Both periods must share the state of the room, without the additions and subtractions which would normally be expected. The general appearance of the room should offend neither period. In the case of props—books, paper, flowers, etc., there is no absolute need to remove the evidence of one period to make way for another. However, books, etc., used in both periods should exist in both old and new versions. The landscape outside, we are told, has undergone changes. Again, what we see should neither change nor contradict.*

*On the above principle, the ink and pens etc., of the first scene can remain. Books and papers associated with Hannah's research, in Scene Two, can have been on the table from the beginning of the play. And so on. During the course of the play the table collects this and that, and where an object from one scene would be an anachronism in another (say a coffee mug) it is simply deemed to have become invisible. By the end of the play the table has collected an inventory of objects.*

*Hannah is leafing through the pages of Mr. Noakes's sketch book. Also to hand, opened and closed, are a number of small volumes like diaries (these turn out to be Lady Croom's "garden books"). After a few moments, Hannah takes the sketch book to the windows, comparing the view with what has been drawn, and then she replaces the sketch book on the reading stand.*

*She wears nothing frivolous. Her shoes are suitable for the garden, which is where she goes now after picking up the theodolite from the table. The room is empty for a few moments.*

*One of the other doors opens to admit Chloë and Bernard. She is the daughter of the house and is dressed casually. Bernard, the visitor, wears a suit and a tie. His tendency is to dress flamboyantly, but he has damped it down for the occasion, slightly. A peacock-coloured display handkerchief boils over in his breast pocket. He carries a capacious leather bag which serves as a briefcase.*

CHLOË.  Oh! Well, she *was* here ...
BERNARD.  Ah ... the french window ...
CHLOË.  Yes. Hang on.

(*Chloë steps out through the garden door and disappears from view. Bernard hangs on. The second door opens and Valentine looks in.*)

VALENTINE.  Sod.[1]

(*Valentine goes out again, closing the door. Chloë returns, carrying a pair of rubber boots. She comes in and sits down and starts exchanging her shoes for the boots, while she talks.*)

5   CHLOË.  The best thing is, you wait here, save you tramping around. She spends a good deal of time in the garden, as you may imagine.

BERNARD.  Yes. Why?

CHLOË.  Well, she's writing a history of the garden, didn't you know?

BERNARD.  No, I knew she was working on the Croom papers but ...

10   CHLOË.  Well, it's not exactly a history of the garden either. I'll let Hannah explain it. The trench you nearly drove into is all to do with it. I was going to say make yourself comfortable but that's hardly possible, everything's been cleared out, it's en route to the nearest lavatory.[2]

BERNARD.  Everything is?

15   CHLOË.  No, this room is. They drew the line at chemical "Ladies'."[3]

BERNARD.  Yes, I see. Did you say Hannah?

CHLOË.  Hannah, yes. Will you be all right?

(*She stands up wearing the boots.*)

I won't be ... (*But she has lost him.*) Mr. Nightingale?

BERNARD.  (*Waking up*) Yes. Thank you. Miss Jarvis is Hannah Jarvis the
20   author?

CHLOË.  Yes. Have you read her book?

BERNARD.  Oh, yes. Yes.

CHLOË.  I bet she's in the hermitage, can't see from here with the marquee[4] ...

BERNARD.  Are you having a garden party?

25   CHLOË.  A dance for the district, our annual dressing up and general drunkenness. The wrinklies[5] won't have it in the house, there was a teapot we once had to bag back from Christie's in the nick of time, so anything that can be destroyed, stolen or vomited on has been tactfully removed; tactlessly, I should say—

---

1   *Sod* Mild British swear word.
2   *lavatory* Bathroom.
3   *chemical "Ladies'"* Ladies' portable toilets.
4   *marquee* Tent used for outdoor events.
5   *wrinklies* Older members of the household.

(*She is about to leave.*)

BERNARD. Um—look—would you tell her—would you mind not mention-    30
ing my name just yet?

CHLOË. Oh. All right.

BERNARD. (*Smiling*) More fun to surprise her. Would you mind?

CHLOË. No. But she's bound to ask ... Should I give you another name, just
for the moment?    35

BERNARD. Yes, why not?

CHLOË. Perhaps another bird, you're not really a Nightingale.

(*She leaves again. Bernard glances over the books on the table. He puts his
briefcase down. There is the distant pop-pop of a shotgun. It takes Bernard
vaguely to the window. He looks out. The door he entered by now opens and
Gus looks into the room. Bernard turns and sees him.*)

BERNARD. Hello.

(*Gus doesn't speak. He never speaks. Perhaps he cannot speak. He has no
composure, and faced with a stranger, he caves in and leaves again. A
moment later the other door opens again and Valentine crosses the room,
not exactly ignoring Bernard and yet ignoring him.*)

VALENTINE. Sod, sod, sod, sod, sod, sod ... (*As many times as it takes him to
leave by the opposite door, which he closes behind him. Beyond it, he can be
heard shouting. "Chlo! Chlo!" Bernard's discomfort increases. The same door
opens and Valentine returns. He looks at Bernard.*)

BERNARD. She's in the garden looking for Miss Jarvis.    40

VALENTINE. Where is everything?

BERNARD. It's been removed for the, er ...

VALENTINE. The dance is all in the tent, isn't it?

BERNARD. Yes, but this is the way to the nearest toilet.

VALENTINE. I need the commode.    45

BERNARD. Oh. Can't you use the toilet?[1]

VALENTINE. It's got all the game books in it.

BERNARD. Ah. The toilet has or the commode has?

VALENTINE. Is anyone looking after you?

BERNARD. Yes. Thank you. I'm Bernard Nigh—I've come to see Miss Jarvis.    50
I wrote to Lord Croom but unfortunately I never received a reply, so I—

VALENTINE. Did you type it?

BERNARD. Type it?

---

1    *commode ... toilet* Play on the word "commode," which can mean either a chest of drawers, a toilet, or, more traditionally, a piece of furniture that disguises a chamber pot.

VALENTINE. Was your letter typewritten?

55 BERNARD. Yes.

VALENTINE. My father never replies to typewritten letters.

(*He spots a tortoise which has been half-hidden on the table.*)

Oh! Where have you been hiding, Lightning? (*He picks up the tortoise.*)

BERNARD. So I telephoned yesterday and I think I spoke to you—

VALENTINE. To me? Ah! Yes! Sorry! You're doing a talk about—someone—

60 and you wanted to ask Hannah—something—

BERNARD. Yes. As it turns out. I'm hoping Miss Jarvis will look kindly on me.

VALENTINE. I doubt it.

BERNARD. Ah, you know about research?

VALENTINE. I know Hannah.

65 BERNARD. Has she been here long?

VALENTINE. Well in possession, I'm afraid. My mother had read her book, you see. Have you?

BERNARD. No. Yes. Her book. Indeed.

VALENTINE. She's terrifically pleased with herself.

70 BERNARD. Well, I dare say if I wrote a bestseller—

VALENTINE. No, for reading it. My mother basically reads gardening books.

BERNARD. She must be delighted to have Hannah Jarvis writing a book about her garden.

VALENTINE. Actually it's about hermits.

(*Gus returns through the same door, and turns to leave again.*)

75 It's all right, Gus—what do you want?—

(*But Gus has gone again.*)

Well ... I'll take Lightning for his run.

BERNARD. Actually, we've met before. At Sussex, a couple of years ago, a seminar ...

VALENTINE. Oh. Was I there?

80 BERNARD. Yes. One of my colleagues believed he had found an unattributed short story by D.H. Lawrence,[1] and he analyzed it on his home computer, most interesting, perhaps you remember the paper?

VALENTINE. Not really. But I often sit with my eyes closed and it doesn't necessarily mean I'm awake.

85 BERNARD. Well, by comparing sentence structures and so forth, this chap showed that there was a ninety per cent chance that the story had indeed

---

1 *D.H. Lawrence* English writer (1885–1930).

been written by the same person as *Women in Love*. To my inexpressible joy, one of your maths mob was able to show that on the same statistical basis there was a ninety per cent chance that Lawrence also wrote the *Just William* books and much of the previous day's *Brighton and Hove Argus*.[1]   90

VALENTINE. (*Pause*) Oh, Brighton. Yes. I was there. (*And looking out.*) Oh— here she comes, I'll leave you to talk. By the way, is yours the red Mazda?

BERNARD. Yes.

VALENTINE. If you want a tip I'd put it out of sight through the stable arch before my father comes in. He won't have anyone in the house with a Japa-   95 nese car. Are you queer?

BERNARD. No, actually.

VALENTINE. Well, even so.

(*Valentine leaves, closing the door. Bernard keeps staring at the closed door. Behind him, Hannah comes to the garden door.*)

HANNAH. Mr. Peacock?

(*Bernard looks round vaguely then checks over his shoulder for the missing Peacock, then recovers himself and turns on the Nightingale bonhomie.*)

BERNARD. Oh ... hello! Hello. Miss Jarvis, of course. Such a pleasure. I was   100 thrown for a moment—the photograph doesn't do you justice.

HANNAH. Photograph?

(*Her shoes have got muddy and she is taking them off.*)

BERNARD. On the book. I'm sorry to have brought you indoors, but Lady Chloë kindly insisted she—

HANNAH. No matter—you would have muddied your shoes.   105

BERNARD. How thoughtful. And how kind of you to spare me a little of your time.

(*He is overdoing it. She shoots him a glance.*)

HANNAH. Are you a journalist?

BERNARD. (*Shocked*) No!

HANNAH. (*Resuming*) I've been in the ha-ha,[2] very squelchy.   110

BERNARD. (*Unexpectedly*) Ha-*hah*!

1   *Women in Love* 1921 novel by D.H. Lawrence; *Just William books* Children's book se- ries by English writer Richmal Crompton (1890–1969); *Brighton and Hove Argus* Local newspaper out of Brighton and Hove, East Sussex.

2   *ha-ha* Ditch with one sloped side and one straight side. A ha-ha cannot be seen from a distance and is used to create a boundary, especially for livestock, without altering the view.

HANNAH.  What?

BERNARD.  A theory of mine. Ha-hah, not ha-ha. If you were strolling down the garden and all of a sudden the ground gave way at your feet, you're not

115 going to go "ha-ha," you're going to jump back and go "ha-hah!," or more probably, "Bloody 'ell!" ... though personally I think old Murray was up the pole[1] on that one—in France, you know, "ha-ha" is used to denote a strikingly ugly woman, a much more likely bet for something that keeps the cows off the lawn.

(*This is not going well for Bernard but he seems blithely unaware. Hannah stares at him for a moment.*)

120 HANNAH.  Mr. Peacock, what can I do for you?

BERNARD.  Well, to begin with, you can call me Bernard, which is my name.

HANNAH.  Thank you.

(*She goes to the garden door to bang her shoes together and scrape off the worst of the mud.*)

BERNARD.  The book!—the book is a revelation! To see Caroline Lamb[2] through your eyes is really like seeing her for the first time. I'm ashamed

125 to say I never read her fiction, and how right you are, it's extraordinary stuff—Early Nineteenth is my period as much as anything is.

HANNAH.  You teach?

BERNARD.  Yes. And write, like you, like we all, though I've never done anything which has sold like *Caro*.[3]

130 HANNAH.  I don't teach.

BERNARD.  No. All the more credit to you. To rehabilitate a forgotten writer, I suppose you could say that's the main reason for an English don.

HANNAH.  Not to teach?

BERNARD.  Good God, no, let the brats sort it out for themselves. Anyway,

135 many congratulations. I expect someone will be bringing out Caroline Lamb's oeuvre[4] now?

HANNAH.  Yes, I expect so.

BERNARD.  How wonderful! Bravo! Simply as a document shedding reflected light on the character of Lord Byron,[5] it's bound to be—

---

1   *old Murray* Sir James Murray (1837–1915), Scottish lexicographer and main editor of the *Oxford English Dictionary*; *up the pole* I.e., crazy, incorrect, off the mark.

2   *Caroline Lamb* Lady Caroline Lamb (1725–1828), English writer.

3   *Caro* Diminutive form of Caroline, adopted as a nickname by Lady Lamb.

4   *oeuvre* Body of work.

5   *Lord Byron* George Gordon Byron (1788–1824), English poet and satirist. One of the most influential figures of the British Romantic movement, Byron was notorious for his frequent love affairs, including one with Lady Caroline Lamb.

HANNAH. Bernard. You did say Bernard, didn't you?                    140
BERNARD. I did.
HANNAH. I'm putting my shoes on again.
BERNARD. Oh. You're not going to go out?
HANNAH. No, I'm going to kick you in the balls.
BERNARD. Right. Point taken. Ezra Chater.                           145
HANNAH. Ezra Chater.
BERNARD. Born Twickenham, Middlesex,[1] 1778, author of two verse narra-
    tives, "The Maid of Turkey," 1808, and "The Couch of Eros," 1809. Noth-
    ing known after 1809, disappears from view.
HANNAH. I see. And?                                                 150
BERNARD. (*Reaching for his bag*) There is a Sidley Park connection.

(*He produces "The Couch of Eros" from the bag. He reads the inscription.*)

To my friend Septimus Hodge, who stood up and gave his best on behalf of the Author—Ezra Chater, at Sidley Park, Derbyshire, April 10th,
1809."

(*He gives her the book.*)

I am in your hands.                                                 155
HANNAH. "The Couch of Eros." Is it any good?
BERNARD. Quite surprising.
HANNAH. You think there's a book in him?
BERNARD. No, no—a monograph[2] perhaps for the *Journal of English Studies*.
    There's almost nothing on Chater, not a word in the *DNB*,[3] of course—by    160
    that time he'd been completely forgotten.
HANNAH. Family?
BERNARD. Zilch. There's only one other Chater in the British Library data-
    base.
HANNAH. Same period?                                                165
BERNARD. Yes, but he wasn't a poet like our Ezra, he was a botanist who
    described a dwarf dahlia in Martinique[4] and died there after being bitten
    by a monkey.
HANNAH. And Ezra Chater?
BERNARD. He gets two references in the Periodical index, one for each book,    170

---

1    *Twickenham, Middlesex* English town that became a part of Greater London in the twen-
     tieth century.
2    *monograph* Academic essay or book on a single subject, intended for a specialist audience.
3    *DNB* Abbreviated title of the *Dictionary of National Biography*, originally published in
     1885. It provides a regularly updated listing of notable British historical figures.
4    *Martinique* French island in the Caribbean Sea.

in both cases a substantial review in the *Piccadilly Recreation*, a thrice week-
ly folio sheet,[1] but giving no personal details.

HANNAH.   And where was this (*the book*)?

BERNARD.   Private collection. I've got a talk to give next week, in London, and
175   I think Chater is interesting, so anything on him, or this Septimus Hodge,
Sidley Park, any leads at all ... I'd be most grateful.

(*Pause.*)

HANNAH.   Well! This is a new experience for me. A grovelling academic.

BERNARD.   Oh, I say.

HANNAH.   Oh, but it is. All the academics who reviewed my book patronized
180   it.

BERNARD.   Surely not.

HANNAH.   Surely yes. The Byron gang unzipped their flies and patronized all
over it. Where is it you don't bother to teach, by the way?

BERNARD.   Oh, well, Sussex, actually.

185   HANNAH.   Sussex. (*She thinks a moment.*) Nightingale. Yes; a thousand words
in the *Observer*[2] to see me off the premises with a pat on the bottom. You
must know him.

BERNARD.   As I say, I'm in your hands.

HANNAH.   Quite. Say please, then.

190   BERNARD.   Please.

HANNAH.   Sit down, do.

BERNARD.   Thank you.

(*He takes a chair. She remains standing. Possibly she smokes; if so, perhaps
now. A short cigarette-holder sounds right, too. Or brown-paper cigarillos.*[3])

HANNAH.   How did you know I was here?

BERNARD.   Oh, I didn't. I spoke to the son on the phone but he didn't men-
195   tion you by name ... and then he forgot to mention me.

HANNAH.   Valentine. He's at Oxford, technically.

BERNARD.   Yes, I met him. Brideshead Regurgitated.[4]

HANNAH.   My fiancé.

(*She holds his look.*)

BERNARD.   (*Pause*) I'll take a chance. You're lying.

---

1   *folio sheet* Single large page.

2   *Observer* Major British newspaper.

3   *cigarillos* Small, thin cigars.

4   *Brideshead Regurgitated* Reference to *Brideshead Revisited* (1945), a novel by English
writer Evelyn Waugh in which the primary characters meet as students at Oxford University.

HANNAH. (*Pause*) Well done, Bernard.                                       200

BERNARD. Christ.

HANNAH. He calls me his fiancée.

BERNARD. Why?

HANNAH. It's a joke.

BERNARD. You turned him down?                                               205

HANNAH. Don't be silly, do I look like the next Countess of—

BERNARD. No, no—a freebie. The joke that consoles. My tortoise Lightning, my fiancée Hannah.

HANNAH. Oh. Yes. You have a way with you, Bernard. I'm not sure I like it.

BERNARD. What's he doing, Valentine?                                        210

HANNAH. He's a postgrad. Biology.

BERNARD. No, he's a mathematician.

HANNAH. Well, he's doing grouse.

BERNARD. Grouse?

HANNAH. Not actual grouse. Computer grouse.                                 215

BERNARD. Who's the one who doesn't speak?

HANNAH. Gus.

BERNARD. What's the matter with him?

HANNAH. I didn't ask.

BERNARD. And the father sounds like a lot of fun.                           220

HANNAH. Ah yes.

BERNARD. And the mother is the gardener. What's going on here?

HANNAH. What do you mean?

BERNARD. I nearly took her head off—she was standing in a trench at the time.                                                                        225

HANNAH. Archaeology. The house had a formal Italian garden until about 1740. Lady Croom is interested in garden history. I sent her my book—it contains, as you know if you've read it—which I'm not assuming, by the way—a rather good description of Caroline's garden at Brocket Hall.[1] I'm here now helping Hermione.                                            230

BERNARD. (*Impressed*) Hermione.

HANNAH. The records are unusually complete and they have never been worked on.

BERNARD. I'm beginning to admire you.

HANNAH. Before was bullshit?                                                235

BERNARD. Completely. Your photograph does you justice, I'm not sure the book does.

   (*She considers him. He waits, confident.*)

---

1    *Brocket Hall* Country house in Hertfordshire, England, owned by the Lamb family.

HANNAH. Septimus Hodge was the tutor.

BERNARD. (*Quietly*) Attagirl.

240 HANNAH. His pupil was the Croom daughter. There was a son at Eton. Septimus lived in the house: the pay book specifies allowances for wine and candles. So, not quite a guest but rather more than a steward.[1] His letter of self-recommendation is preserved among the papers. I'll dig it out for you. As far as I remember he studied mathematics and natural philosophy

245 at Cambridge. A scientist, therefore, as much as anything.

BERNARD. I'm impressed. Thank you. And Chater?

HANNAH. Nothing.

BERNARD. Oh. Nothing at all?

HANNAH. I'm afraid not.

250 BERNARD. How about the library?

HANNAH. The catalogue was done in the 1880s. I've been through the lot.

BERNARD. Books or catalogue?

HANNAH. Catalogue.

BERNARD. Ah. Pity.

255 HANNAH. I'm sorry.

BERNARD. What about the letters? No mention?

HANNAH. I'm afraid not. I've been very thorough in your period because, of course, it's my period too.

BERNARD. Is it? Actually, I don't quite know what it is you're ...

260 HANNAH. The Sidley hermit.

BERNARD. Ah. Who's he?

HANNAH. He's my peg for the nervous breakdown of the Romantic Imagination. I'm doing landscape and literature 1750 to 1834.

BERNARD. What happened in 1834?

265 HANNAH. My hermit died.

BERNARD. Of course.

HANNAH. What do you mean, of course?

BERNARD. Nothing.

HANNAH. Yes, you do.

270 BERNARD. No, no ... However, Coleridge[2] also died in 1834.

HANNAH. So he did. What a stroke of luck. (*Softening.*) Thank you, Bernard.

(*She goes to the reading stand and opens Noakes's sketch book.*)

Look—there he is.

---

1    *steward* Primary servant in charge of fellow servants and household affairs.

2    *Coleridge* English poet Samuel Taylor Coleridge (1772–1834); he was a central figure of the Romantic movement.

(*Bernard goes to look.*)

BERNARD.  Mmm.

HANNAH.  The only known likeness of the Sidley hermit.

BERNARD.  Very biblical.                                                    275

HANNAH.  Drawn in by a later hand, of course. The hermitage didn't yet exist
  when Noakes did the drawings.

BERNARD.  Noakes ... the painter?

HANNAH.  Landscape gardener. He'd do these books for his clients, as a sort
  of prospectus. (*She demonstrates.*) Before and after, you see. This is how it  280
  all looked until, say, 1810—smooth, undulating, serpentine—open water,
  clumps of trees, classical boat-house—

BERNARD.  Lovely. The real England.

HANNAH.  You can stop being silly now, Bernard. English landscape was invented by gardeners imitating foreign painters who were evoking classical  285
  authors. The whole thing was brought home in the luggage from the grand
  tour. Here, look—Capability Brown doing Claude, who was doing Virgil.[1]
  Arcadia! And here, superimposed by Richard Noakes, untamed nature in
  the style of Salvator Rosa. It's the Gothic novel expressed in landscape.
  Everything but vampires. There's an account of my hermit in a letter by  290
  your illustrious namesake.

BERNARD.  Florence?

HANNAH.  What?

BERNARD.  No. You go on.

HANNAH.  Thomas Love Peacock.[2]                                            295

BERNARD.  Ah yes.

HANNAH.  I found it in an essay on hermits and anchorites published in the
  *Cornhill Magazine*[3] in the 1860s ... (*She fishes for the magazine itself among
  the books on the table, and finds it.*) ... 1862 ... Peacock calls him (*She quotes
  from memory.*) "Not one of your village simpletons to frighten the ladies,  300
  but a savant among idiots, a sage of lunacy."

BERNARD.  An oxy-moron, so to speak.

HANNAH.  (*Busy*) Yes. What?

BERNARD.  Nothing.

---

1    *Capability Brown* Lancelot Brown (1716–83), English landscaper who popularized Eng-
     lish gardens that were designed to look undomesticated and wild; *Claude* Claude Lor-
     rain (1600–82), French painter known for his landscape paintings; *Virgil* Roman poet
     (70–19 BCE); some of his works depict country life.

2    *Thomas Love Peacock* English novelist and satirist (1785–1866).

3    *anchorites* Religious recluses; *Cornhill Magazine* Literary journal (1859–1975) once ed-
     ited by English novelist and satirist William Makepeace Thackeray (1811–63).

305 HANNAH. (*Having found the place*) Here we are. "A letter we have seen, written by the author of *Headlong Hall*[1] nearly thirty years ago, tells of a visit to the Earl of Croom's estate, Sidley Park—"

BERNARD. Was the letter to Thackeray?

HANNAH. (*Brought up short*) I don't know. Does it matter?

310 BERNARD. No. Sorry.

> (*But the gaps he leaves for her are false promises—and she is not quick enough. That's how it goes.*)

Only, Thackeray edited the *Cornhill* until '63 when, as you know, he died. His father had been with the East India Company[2] where Peacock, of course, had held the position of Examiner, so it's quite possible that if the essay were by Thackeray, the *letter* ... Sorry. Go on. Of course, the East
315 India Library in Blackfriars[3] has most of Peacock's letters, so it would be quite easy to ... Sorry. Can I look?

> (*Silently she hands him the Cornhill.*)

Yes, it's been topped and tailed,[4] of course. It might be worth ... Go on. I'm listening ...
(*Leafing through the essay, he suddenly chuckles.*) Oh yes, it's Thackeray all
320 right ...
(*He slaps the book shut.*) Unbearable ...
(*He hands it back to her.*) What were you saying?

HANNAH. Are you always like this?

BERNARD. Like what?

325 HANNAH. The point is, the Crooms, of course, had the hermit under their noses for twenty years so hardly thought him worth remarking. As I'm finding out. The Peacock letter is still the main source, unfortunately. When I read this (*the magazine in her hand*) well, it was one of those moments that tell you what your next book is going to be. The hermit of
330 Sidley Park was my ...

BERNARD. Peg.

HANNAH. Epiphany.

BERNARD. Epiphany, that's it.

HANNAH. The hermit was *placed* in the landscape exactly as one might place
335 a pottery gnome. And there he lived out his life as a garden ornament.

---

1   *the author of Headlong Hall* Peacock.
2   *East India Company* Powerful British trading company (1600–1873) that dominated the government of India during the late eighteenth and early nineteenth centuries.
3   *Blackfriars* Area of central London.
4   *topped and tailed* I.e., with the beginning and end removed (and therefore with the name of the recipient omitted).

BERNARD.  Did he do anything?

HANNAH.  Oh, he was very busy. When he died, the cottage was stacked solid with paper. Hundreds of pages. Thousands. Peacock says he was suspected of genius. It turned out, of course, he was off his head. He'd covered every sheet with cabalistic[1] proofs that the world was coming to an end. It's per- 340 fect, isn't it? A perfect symbol, I mean.

BERNARD.  Oh, yes. Of what?

HANNAH.  The whole Romantic sham, Bernard! It's what happened to the Enlightenment,[2] isn't it? A century of intellectual rigour turned in on itself. A mind in chaos suspected of genius. In a setting of cheap thrills and 345 false emotion. The history of the garden says it all, beautifully. There's an engraving of Sidley Park in 1730 that makes you want to weep. Paradise in the age of reason. By 1760 everything had gone—the topiary, pools and terraces, fountains, an avenue of limes—the whole sublime geometry was ploughed under by Capability Brown. The grass went from the doorstep to 350 the horizon and the best box hedge in Derbyshire was dug up for the ha-ha so that the fools could pretend they were living in God's countryside. And then Richard Noakes came in to bring God up to date. By the time he'd finished it looked like this (*the sketch book*). The decline from thinking to feeling, you see. 355

BERNARD.  (*A judgement*) That's awfully good.

(*Hannah looks at him in case of irony but he is professional.*)

No, that'll stand up.

HANNAH.  Thank you.

BERNARD.  Personally I like the ha-ha. Do you like hedges?

HANNAH.  I don't like sentimentality. 360

BERNARD.  Yes, I see. Are you sure? You seem quite sentimental over geometry. But the hermit is very very good. The genius of the place.

HANNAH.  (*Pleased*) That's my title!

BERNARD.  Of course.

HANNAH.  (*Less pleased*) Of course? 365

BERNARD.  Of course. Who was he when he wasn't being a symbol?

HANNAH.  I don't know.

BERNARD.  Ah.

HANNAH.  I mean, yet.

BERNARD.  Absolutely. What did they do with all the paper? Does Peacock say? 370

---

1    *cabalistic* Mystical, esoteric.

2    *Enlightenment* Movement of the seventeenth and eighteenth centuries that placed importance on reason and scientific thought. The Romantic period followed the Enlightenment and is often seen as a reaction to it.

HANNAH. Made a bonfire.

BERNARD. Ah, well.

HANNAH. I've still got Lady Croom's garden books to go through.

BERNARD. Account books or journals?

375 HANNAH. A bit of both. They're gappy but they span the period.

BERNARD. Really? Have you come across Byron at all? As a matter of interest.

HANNAH. A first edition of "Childe Harold" in the library, and *English Bards*,[1] I think.

BERNARD. Inscribed?

380 HANNAH. No.

BERNARD. And he doesn't pop up in the letters at all?

HANNAH. Why should he? The Crooms don't pop up in his.

BERNARD. (*Casually*) That's true, of course. But Newstead[2] isn't so far away. Would you mind terribly if I poked about a bit? Only in the papers you've
385     done with, of course.

(*Hannah twigs[3] something.*)

HANNAH. Are you looking into Byron or Chater?

(*Chloë enters in stockinged feet through one of the side doors, laden with an armful of generally similar leather-covered ledgers. She detours to collect her shoes.*)

CHLOË. Sorry—just cutting through—there's tea in the pantry if you don't mind mugs—

BERNARD. How kind.

390 CHLOË. Hannah will show you.

BERNARD. Let me help you.

CHLOË. No, it's all right—

(*Bernard opens the opposite door for her.*)

Thank you—I've been saving Val's game books. Thanks.

(*Bernard closes the door.*)

BERNARD. Sweet girl.

395 HANNAH. Mmm.

BERNARD. Oh, really?

---

1   "*Childe Harold*"... *English Bards*   Hannah mentions two long poems by Byron: the semi-autobiographical *Childe Harold's Pilgrimage* (1812–16) and *English Bards and Scotch Reviewers* (1809), a satire.

2   *Newstead*   Newstead Abbey, Lord Byron's home.

3   *twigs*   I.e., realizes.

HANNAH.  Oh really what?

(*Chloë's door opens again and she puts her head round it.*)

CHLOË.  Meant to say, don't worry if father makes remarks about your car, Mr. Nightingale, he's got a thing about—(*and the Nightingale now being out of the bag*) ooh—ah, how was the surprise?—not yet, eh? Oh, well— 400 sorry—tea, anyway—so sorry if I—(*Embarrassed, she leaves again, closing the door. Pause.*)

HANNAH.  You absolute shit.

(*She heads off to leave.*)

BERNARD.  The thing is, there's a Byron connection too.

(*Hannah stops and faces him.*)

HANNAH.  I don't care.                                                        405

BERNARD.  You should. The Byron gang are going to get their dicks caught in their zip.

HANNAH.  (*Pause*) Oh really?

BERNARD.  If we collaborate.

HANNAH.  On what?                                                             410

BERNARD.  Sit down, I'll tell you.

HANNAH.  I'll stand for the moment.

BERNARD.  This copy of "The Couch of Eros" belonged to Lord Byron.

HANNAH.  It belonged to Septimus Hodge.

BERNARD.  Originally, yes. But it was in Byron's library which was sold to pay 415 his debts when he left England for good in 1816. The sales catalogue is in the British Library. "Eros" was lot 74A and was bought by the bookseller and publisher John Nightingale of Opera Court, Pall Mall[1] ... whose name survives in the firm of Nightingale and Matlock, the present Nightingale being my cousin.                                                                 420

(*He pauses. Hannah hesitates and then sits down at the table.*)

I'll just give you the headlines. 1939, stock removed to Nightingale country house in Kent.[2] 1945, stock returned to bookshop. Meanwhile, overlooked box of early nineteenth-century books languish in country house cellar until house sold to make way for the Channel Tunnel[3] rail-link. "Eros" discovered with sales slip from 1816 attached—photocopy avail- 425 able for inspection.

---

1    *Pall Mall* Famous street in London.

2    *Kent* County in Southeast England.

3    *Channel Tunnel* Tunnel that runs under the English Channel to connect Folkestone, Kent, to Coquelles, Pas-de-Calais, in France. It was completed in 1994.

(*He brings this from his bag and gives it to Hannah who inspects it.*)

HANNAH. All right. It was in Byron's library.

BERNARD. A number of passages have been underlined.

(*Hannah picks up the book and leafs through it.*)

All of them, and only them—no, no, look at me, not at the book—all the
430 underlined passages, word for word, were used as quotations in the review
of "The Couch of Eros" in the *Piccadilly Recreation* of April 30th 1809. The
reviewer begins by drawing attention to his previous notice in the same
periodical of "The Maid of Turkey."

HANNAH. The reviewer is obviously Hodge. "My friend Septimus Hodge
435 who stood up and gave his best on behalf of the Author."

BERNARD. That's the point. The *Piccadilly* ridiculed both books.

HANNAH. (*Pause.*) Do the reviews read like Byron?

BERNARD. (*Producing two photocopies from his case*) They read a damn sight
more like Byron than Byron's review of Wordsworth[1] the previous year.

(*Hannah glances over the photocopies.*)

440 HANNAH. I see. Well, congratulations. Possibly. Two previously unknown
book reviews by the young Byron. Is that it?

BERNARD. No. Because of the tapes, three documents survived undisturbed
in the book.

(*He has been carefully opening a package produced from his bag. He has the
originals. He holds them carefully one by one.*)

"Sir—we have a matter to settle. I wait on you in the gun room. E. Chater,
445 Esq."

"My husband has sent to town for pistols. Deny what cannot be proven—
for Charity's sake—I keep my room this day." Unsigned.

"Sidley Park, April 11th 1809. Sir—I call you a liar, a lecher, a slanderer
in the press and a thief of my honour. I wait upon your arrangements for
450 giving me satisfaction as a man and a poet. E. Chater, Esq."

(*Pause.*)

HANNAH. Superb. But inconclusive. The book had seven years to find its
way into Byron's possession. It doesn't connect Byron with Chater, or with
Sidley Park. Or with Hodge for that matter. Furthermore, there isn't a hint
in Byron's letters and this kind of scrape is the last thing he would have
455 kept quiet about.

---

1    *Wordsworth* William Wordsworth (1770–1850), English poet.

BERNARD. *Scrape?*

HANNAH. He would have made a comic turn out of it.

BERNARD. Comic turn, fiddlesticks! (*He pauses for effect.*) He killed Chater!

HANNAH. (*A raspberry*) Oh, really!

BERNARD. Chater was thirty-one years old. The author of two books. Noth-   460
ing more is heard from him after "Eros." He disappears completely after
April 1809. And Byron—Byron had just published his satire, *English Bards
and Scotch Reviewers*, in March. He was just getting a name. Yet he sailed
for Lisbon as soon as he could find a ship, and stayed abroad for two
years. Hannah, *this is fame.* Somewhere in the Croom papers there will be   465
*something—*

HANNAH. There isn't, I've looked.

BERNARD. But you were looking for something else! It's not going to jump
out at you like "Lord Byron remarked wittily at breakfast!"

HANNAH. Nevertheless his presence would be unlikely to have gone unre-   470
marked. But there is nothing to suggest that Byron was here, and I don't
believe he ever was.

BERNARD. All right, but let me have a look.

HANNAH. You'll queer my pitch.[1]

BERNARD. Dear girl, I know how to handle myself—   475

HANNAH. And don't call me dear girl. If I find anything on Byron, or Chater,
or Hodge, I'll pass it on. Nightingale, Sussex.

(*Pause. She stands up.*)

BERNARD. Thank you. I'm sorry about that business with my name.

HANNAH. Don't mention it ...

BERNARD. What was Hodge's college, by the way?   480

HANNAH. Trinity.[2]

BERNARD. Trinity?

HANNAH. Yes. (*She hesitates.*) Yes. Byron's old college.

BERNARD. How old was Hodge?

HANNAH. I'd have to look it up but a year or two older than Byron. Twenty-   485
two ...

BERNARD. Contemporaries at Trinity?

HANNAH. (*Wearily*) Yes, Bernard, and no doubt they were both in the cricket
eleven when Harrow played Eton at Lords![3]

---

1    *queer my pitch* I.e., spoil my work.

2    *Trinity* Trinity College, a college of Cambridge University.

3    *cricket eleven* Cricket teams are made up of eleven players; *Harrow* Harrow School,
English school for boys; *Lords* Lord's Cricket Ground in London, which has held the
Eton vs. Harrow cricket match annually since the early 1800s.

(*Bernard approaches her and stands close to her.*)

490 BERNARD. (*Evenly*) Do you mean that Septimus Hodge was at school with Byron?

HANNAH. (*Falters slightly*) Yes ... he must have been ... as a matter of fact.

BERNARD. Well, you silly cow.

(*With a large gesture of pure happiness, Bernard throws his arms around Hannah and gives her a great smacking kiss on the cheek. Chloë enters to witness the end of this.*)

CHLOË. Oh—erm ... I thought I'd bring it to you.

(*She is carrying a small tray with two mugs on it.*)

495 BERNARD. I have to go and see about my car.

HANNAH. Going to hide it?

BERNARD. Hide it? I'm going to sell it! Is there a pub I can put up at in the village?

(*He turns back to them as he is about to leave through the garden.*)

Aren't you glad I'm here?

(*He leaves.*)

500 CHLOË. He said he knew you.

HANNAH. He couldn't have.

CHLOË. No, perhaps not. He said he wanted to be a surprise, but I suppose that's different. I thought there was a lot of sexual energy there, didn't you?

HANNAH. What?

505 CHLOË. Bouncy on his feet, you see, a sure sign. Should I invite him for you?

HANNAH. To what? No.

CHLOË. You can invite him—that's better. He can come as your partner.

HANNAH. Stop it. Thank you for the tea.

CHLOË. If you don't want him, I'll have him. Is he married?

510 HANNAH. I haven't the slightest idea. Aren't you supposed to have a pony?

CHLOË. I'm just trying to fix you up, Hannah.

HANNAH. Believe me, it gets less important.

CHLOË. I mean for the dancing. He can come as Beau Brummell.[1]

HANNAH. I don't want to dress up and I don't want a dancing partner, least

515 of all Mr. Nightingale. I don't dance.

CHLOË. Don't be such a prune. You were kissing him, anyway.

HANNAH. He was kissing me, and only out of general enthusiasm.

---

1  *Beau Brummell* George Bryan "Beau" Brummell (1778–1840), a trendsetter in men's fashion often credited with popularizing the British dandy look.

CHLOË.  Well, don't say I didn't give you first chance. My genius brother will be much relieved. He's in love with you, I suppose you know.
HANNAH.  (*Angry*) That's a joke!                                                  520
CHLOË.  It's not a joke to him.
HANNAH.  Of course it is—not even a joke—how can you be so ridiculous?

(*Gus enters from the garden, in his customary silent awkwardness.*)

CHLOË.  Hello, Gus, what have you got?

(*Gus has an apple, just picked, with a leaf or two still attached. He offers the apple to Hannah.*)

HANNAH.  (*Surprised*) Oh! ... Thank you!
CHLOË.  (*Leaving*) Told you.                                                      525

(*Chloë closes the door on herself.*)

HANNAH.  Thank you. Oh dear.

(*Hannah puts the apple on the table.*)


## ACT 1, SCENE 3

*The schoolroom. The next morning. Present are: Thomasina, Septimus, Jellaby. We have seen this composition before: Thomasina at her place at the table; Septimus reading a letter which has just arrived; Jellaby waiting, having just delivered the letter.*
*"The Couch of Eros" is in front of Septimus, open, together with sheets of paper on which he has been writing. His portfolio is on the table. Plautus[1] (the tortoise) is the paperweight. There is also an apple on the table now.*

SEPTIMUS.  (*With his eyes on the letter*) Why have you stopped?

(*Thomasina is studying a sheet of paper, a "Latin unseen" lesson.[2] She is having some difficulty.*)

THOMASINA.  *Solio insessa ... in igne ...* seated on a throne ... in the fire ... and also on a ship ... *sedebat regina ...* sat the queen ...
SEPTIMUS.  There is no reply, Jellaby. Thank you.

(*He folds the letter up and places it between the leaves of "The Couch of Eros."*)

---

1   *Plautus* After Roman comic playwright Titus Maccius Plautus (c. 254–184 BCE).
2   *"Latin unseen" lesson* Unfamiliar passage given to a student as a translation test.

5 JELLABY. I will say so, sir.

THOMASINA.  ... the wind smelling sweetly ... *purpureis velis* ... by, with or from purple sails—

SEPTIMUS. (*To Jellaby*) I will have something for the post, if you would be so kind.

10 JELLABY. (*Leaving*) Yes, sir.

THOMASINA.  ... was like as to—something—by, with or from lovers—oh, Septimus!—*musica tibiarum imperabat* ... music of pipes commanded ...

SEPTIMUS. "Ruled" is better.

THOMASINA.  ... the silver oars—exciting the ocean—as if—as if—amorous—

15 SEPTIMUS. That is very good.

> (*He picks up the apple. He picks off the twig and leaves, placing these on the table. With a pocket knife he cuts a slice of apple, and while he eats it, cuts another slice which he offers to Plautus.*)

THOMASINA. *Regina reclinabat* ... the queen—was reclining—*praeter descriptionem*—indescribably—in a golden tent ... like Venus and yet more—

SEPTIMUS. Try to put some poetry into it.

THOMASINA. How can I if there is none in the Latin?

20 SEPTIMUS. Oh, a critic!

THOMASINA. Is it Queen Dido?[1]

SEPTIMUS. No.

THOMASINA. Who is the poet?

SEPTIMUS. Known to you.

25 THOMASINA. Known to me?

SEPTIMUS. Not a Roman.

THOMASINA. Mr. Chater?

SEPTIMUS. Your translation is quite like Chater.

> (*Septimus picks up his pen and continues with his own writing.*)

THOMASINA. I know who it is, it is your friend Byron.

30 SEPTIMUS. Lord Byron, if you please.

THOMASINA. Mama is in love with Lord Byron.

SEPTIMUS. (*Absorbed*) Yes. Nonsense.

THOMASINA. It is not nonsense. I saw them together in the gazebo.

> (*Septimus's pen stops moving, he raises his eyes to her at last.*)

Lord Byron was reading to her from his satire, and mama was laughing,
35 with her head in her best position.

---

1    *Queen Dido* Legendary founder and first queen of Carthage; she appears in Virgil's *Aeneid*.

SEPTIMUS.  She did not understand the satire, and was showing politeness to a guest.

THOMASINA.  She is vexed with papa for his determination to alter the park, but that alone cannot account for her politeness to a guest. She came downstairs hours before her custom. Lord Byron was amusing at breakfast. 40 He paid you a tribute, Septimus.

SEPTIMUS.  Did he?

THOMASINA.  He said you were a witty fellow, and he had almost by heart an article you wrote about—well, I forget what, but it concerned a book called "The Maid of Turkey" and how you would not give it to your dog 45 for dinner.

SEPTIMUS.  Ah. Mr. Chater was at breakfast, of course.

THOMASINA.  He was, not like certain lazybones.

SEPTIMUS.  He does not have Latin to set and mathematics to correct.

(*He takes Thomasina's lesson book from underneath Plautus and tosses it down the table to her.*)

THOMASINA.  Correct? What was incorrect in it? (*She looks into the book.*) 50 Alpha minus? Pooh! What is the minus for?

SEPTIMUS.  For doing more than was asked.

THOMASINA.  You did not like my discovery?

SEPTIMUS.  A fancy is not a discovery.

THOMASINA.  A gibe is not a rebuttal. 55

(*Septimus finishes what he is writing. He folds the pages into a letter. He has sealing wax and the means to melt it. He seals the letter and writes on the cover. Meanwhile—*)

You are churlish with me because mama is paying attention to your friend. Well, let them elope, they cannot turn back the advancement of knowledge. I think it is an excellent discovery. Each week I plot your equations dot for dot, *x*s against *y*s in all manner of algebraical relation, and every week they draw themselves as commonplace geometry, as if the world of 60 forms were nothing but arcs and angles. God's truth, Septimus, if there is an equation for a curve like a bell, there must be an equation for one like a bluebell, and if a bluebell, why not a rose? Do we believe nature is written in numbers?

SEPTIMUS.  We do. 65

THOMASINA.  Then why do your equations only describe the shapes of manufacture?

SEPTIMUS.  I do not know.

THOMASINA.  Armed thus, God could only make a cabinet.

70 SEPTIMUS.  He has mastery of equations which lead into infinities where we
cannot follow.

THOMASINA.  What a faint-heart! We must work outward from the middle of
the maze. We will start with something simple. (*She picks up the apple leaf.*)
I will plot this leaf and deduce its equation. You will be famous for being
75 my tutor when Lord Byron is dead and forgotten.

(*Septimus completes the business with his letter. He puts the letter in his
pocket.*)

SEPTIMUS.  (*Firmly*) Back to Cleopatra.[1]

THOMASINA.  Is it Cleopatra?—I hate Cleopatra!

SEPTIMUS.  You hate her? Why?

THOMASINA.  Everything is turned to love with her. New love, absent love,
80 lost love—I never knew a heroine that makes such noodles of our sex. It
only needs a Roman general to drop anchor outside the window and away
goes the empire like a christening mug into a pawn shop. If Queen Elizabeth had been a Ptolemy[2] history would have been quite different—we
would be admiring the pyramids of Rome and the great Sphinx of Verona.

85 SEPTIMUS.  God save us.

THOMASINA.  But instead, the Egyptian noodle made carnal embrace with the
enemy who burned the great library of Alexandria[3] without so much as a
fine for all that is overdue. Oh, Septimus!—can you bear it? All the lost
plays of the Athenians! Two hundred at least by Aeschylus, Sophocles, Eu-
90 ripides—thousands of poems—Aristotle's[4] own library brought to Egypt
by the noodle's ancestors! How can we sleep for grief?

---

1   *Cleopatra*  Cleopatra VII Philopator (c. 69–30 BCE), Egyptian pharaoh often remembered
for her political alliances and romantic relationships with Julius Caesar and later Marc
Antony. When it became clear that Egypt would fall to Roman rule, Cleopatra committed suicide.

2   *Queen Elizabeth*  Elizabeth I (1533–1603), queen of England, a very successful ruler. She
never married and was known as "The Virgin Queen"; *Ptolemy* Member of the Ptolemaic dynasty, which ruled Egypt from 323 BCE until the death of Cleopatra, who was
the last Ptolemaic pharaoh.

3   *great library of Alexandria*  One of the most important libraries of the ancient world until
its destruction by fire.  It is not known exactly when the fire occurred, but a popular story
is that Julius Caesar caused it accidentally as he was destroying a fleet of his own ships in
48 BCE. The last existing copies of many ancient works are thought to have been lost in
the fire.

4   *Aeschylus, Sophocles, Euripides*  Considered to be the three greatest tragedians of ancient
Greece. Only a fraction of their work survives in complete form; *Aristotle* Greek phi-
losopher (384–322 BCE) considered one of the most important figures in the history of
Western thought.

SEPTIMUS.  By counting our stock. Seven plays from Aeschylus, seven from
Sophocles, *nineteen* from Euripides, my lady! You should no more grieve
for the rest than for a buckle lost from your first shoe, or for your lesson
book which will be lost when you are old. We shed as we pick up, like      95
travellers who must carry everything in their arms, and what we let fall
will be picked up by those behind. The procession is very long and life is
very short. We die on the march. But there is nothing outside the march
so nothing can be lost to it. The missing plays of Sophocles will turn up
piece by piece, or be written again in another language. Ancient cures      100
for diseases will reveal themselves once more. Mathematical discoveries
glimpsed and lost to view will have their time again. You do not suppose,
my lady, that if all of Archimedes[1] had been hiding in the great library of
Alexandria, we would be at a loss for a corkscrew? I have no doubt that the
improved steam-driven heat-engine which puts Mr. Noakes into an ecstasy      105
that he and it and the modern age should all coincide, was described on
papyrus.[2] Steam and brass were not invented in Glasgow. Now, where are
we? Let me see if I can attempt a free translation for you. At Harrow I was
better at this than Lord Byron.

> (*He takes the piece of paper from her and scrutinizes it, testing one or two
> Latin phrases speculatively before committing himself.*)

Yes—"The barge she sat in, like a burnished throne ... burned on the water      110
... the—something—the poop was beaten gold, purple the sails, and—
what's this?—oh yes,—so perfumed that[3]—"
THOMASINA.  (*Catching on and furious*) Cheat!
SEPTIMUS.  (*Imperturbably*) "—the winds were lovesick with them ..."
THOMASINA.  Cheat!      115
SEPTIMUS.  "... the oars were silver which to the tune of flutes kept stroke ..."
THOMASINA.  (*Jumping to her feet*) Cheat! Cheat! Cheat!
SEPTIMUS.  (*As though it were too easy to make the effort worthwhile*) "... and
made the water which they beat to follow faster, as *amorous* of their strokes.
For her own person, it beggared all description—she did lie in her pavil-      120
ion—"

> (*Thomasina, in tears of rage, is hurrying out through the garden.*)

---

1   *Archimedes* Ancient Greek mathematician and physicist (287–212 BCE); one of his surviving works is titled *On Spirals.*
2   *papyrus* Material similar to paper; it was used for writing by the ancient Egyptians.
3   *The barge ...perfumed that* From Shakespeare's *Antony and Cleopatra* 2.2.902–11. Septimus has translated the passage into Latin and given it to Thomasina to translate back into
English; his supposed "free translation" is actually a memorized quotation.

THOMASINA. I hope you die!

(*She nearly bumps into Brice who is entering. She runs out of sight. Brice enters.*)

BRICE. Good God, man, what have you told her?
SEPTIMUS. Told her? Told her what?
125 BRICE. Hodge!

(*Septimus looks outside the door, slightly contrite about Thomasina, and sees that Chater is skulking out of view.*)

SEPTIMUS. Chater! My dear fellow! Don't hang back—come in, sir!

(*Chater allows himself to be drawn sheepishly into the room, where Brice stands on his dignity.*)

CHATER. Captain Brice does me the honour—I mean to say, sir, whatever you have to say to me, sir, address yourself to Captain Brice.
SEPTIMUS. How unusual. (*To Brice*) Your wife did not appear yesterday, sir. I
130 trust she is not sick?
BRICE. My wife? I have no wife. What the devil do you mean, sir?

(*Septimus makes to reply, but hesitates, puzzled. He turns back to Chater.*)

SEPTIMUS. I do not understand the scheme, Chater. Whom do I address when I want to speak to Captain Brice?
BRICE. Oh, slippery, Hodge—slippery!
135 SEPTIMUS. (*To Chater*) By the way, Chater—(*he interrupts himself and turns back to Brice, and continues as before*) by the way, Chater, I have amazing news to tell you. Someone has taken to writing wild and whirling letters in your name. I received one not half an hour ago.
BRICE. (*Angrily*) Mr. Hodge! Look to your honour, sir! If you cannot attend
140 to me without this foolery, nominate your second[1] who might settle the business as between gentlemen. No doubt your friend Byron would do you the service.

(*Septimus gives up the game.*)

SEPTIMUS. Oh yes, he would do me the service. (*His mood changes, he turns to Chater.*) Sir—I repent your injury. You are an honest fellow with no more
145 malice in you than poetry.
CHATER. (*Happily*) Ah well!—that is more like the thing! (*Overtaken by doubt.*) Is he apologizing?

---

1    *second* Person who assists the primary fighter in a duel.

BRICE.  There is still the injury to his conjugal property, Mrs. Chater's—

CHATER.  Tush,[1] sir!

BRICE.  As you will—her tush. Nevertheless—    150

(*But they are interrupted by Lady Croom, also entering from the garden.*)

LADY CROOM.  Oh—excellently found! Mr. Chater, this will please you very much. Lord Byron begs a copy of your new book. He dies to read it and intends to include your name in the second edition of his *English Bards and Scotch Reviewers*.

CHATER.  *English Bards and Scotch Reviewers*, your ladyship, is a doggerel[2]   155 aimed at Lord Byron's seniors and betters. If he intends to include me, he intends to insult me.

LADY CROOM.  Well, of course he does, Mr. Chater. Would you rather be thought not worth insulting? You should be proud to be in the company of Rogers and Moore[3] and Wordsworth—ah! "The Couch of Eros!" (*For*   160 *she has spotted Septimus's copy of the book on the table.*)

SEPTIMUS.  That is my copy, madam.

LADY CROOM.  So much the better—what are a friend's books for if not to be borrowed?

(*Note: "The Couch of Eros" now contains the three letters, and it must do so without advertising the fact. This is why the volume has been described as a substantial quarto.*)

Mr. Hodge, you must speak to your friend and put him out of his affecta-   165 tion of pretending to quit us. I will not have it. He says he is determined on the Malta packet sailing out of Falmouth! His head is full of Lisbon and Lesbos, and his portmanteau[4] of pistols, and I have told him it is not to be thought of. The whole of Europe is in a Napoleonic[5] fit, all the best ruins will be closed, the roads entirely occupied with the movement of armies,   170 the lodgings turned to billets and the fashion for godless republicanism not

---

1   *Tush* Slang expression of disapproval; its alternative meaning of "rear end" is punningly suggested in the next line.

2   *doggerel* Poorly written verse.

3   *Rogers* English poet Samuel Rogers (1763–1855); *Moore* Thomas Moore (1779–1852), Irish poet and musician.

4   *Malta* European island country located in the Mediterranean Sea; *packet* Ship that runs a pre-determined route with scheduled stops; *Falmouth* Falmouth harbour in Cornwall, England; *Lisbon* Capital city of Portugal; *Lesbos* Greek island; *portmanteau* Luggage bag.

5   *Napoleonic* Reference to the Napoleonic Wars (1803–15) in which the French Empire, under the leadership of Napoleon Bonaparte, conquered much of Europe and then lost it.

yet arrived at its natural reversion. He says his aim is poetry. One does not aim at poetry with pistols. At poets, perhaps. I charge you to take command of his pistols, Mr. Hodge! He is not safe with them. His lameness,[1] he confessed to me, is entirely the result of his habit from boyhood of shooting himself in the foot. What is that *noise*?

> (*The noise is a badly played piano in the next room. It has been going on for some time since Thomasina left.*)

SEPTIMUS.   The new Broadwood pianoforte,[2] madam. Our music lessons are at an early stage.

LADY CROOM.   Well, restrict your lessons to the *piano* side of the instrument and let her loose on the *forte*[3] when she has learned something.

> (*Lady Croom, holding the book, sails out back into the garden.*)

BRICE.   Now! If that was not God speaking through Lady Croom, he never spoke through anyone!

CHATER.   (*Awed*) Take command of Lord Byron's pistols!

BRICE.   You hear Mr. Chater, sir—how will you answer him?

> (*Septimus has been watching Lady Croom's progress up the garden. He turns back.*)

SEPTIMUS.   By killing him. I am tired of him.

CHATER.   (*Startled*) Eh?

BRICE.   (*Pleased*) Ah!

SEPTIMUS.   Oh, damn your soul, Chater! Ovid would have stayed a lawyer and Virgil a farmer if they had known the bathos to which love would descend in your sportive satyrs and noodle nymphs![4] I am at your service with a half-ounce ball[5] in your brain. May it satisfy you—behind the boathouse at daybreak—shall we say five o'clock? My compliments to Mrs. Chater—have no fear for her, she will not want for protection while Captain Brice has a guinea[6] in his pocket, he told her so himself.

BRICE.   You lie, sir!

---

1   *His lameness* Byron suffered from a club foot.

2   *Broadwood pianoforte* Piano made by well-known manufacturer Broadwood and Sons.

3   *piano ... forte* The word "pianoforte" comes from the musical terms "piano" and "forte," directives to play softly and loudly, respectively.

4   *Ovid* Roman poet (43 BCE–c. 17 CE) famous for *Metamorphoses*. He studied law before becoming a writer; *bathos* Ridiculousness caused by a writer's unintentional descent from an elevated subject or tone to a trivial one; *satyrs* Greek mythological goat-men. In classical art and literature, they are often depicted in the lustful pursuit of nymphs; *nymphs* In Greek mythology, beautiful female nature spirits.

5   *half-ounce ball* Musket ball used as ammunition in duelling pistols.

6   *guinea* Gold coin worth about 21 shillings.

SEPTIMUS.  No, sir. Mrs. Chater, perhaps.

BRICE.  You lie, or you will answer to me!

SEPTIMUS.  (*Wearily*) Oh, very well—I can fit you in at five minutes after five. And then it's off to the Malta packet out of Falmouth. You two will be dead, my penurious[1] schoolfriend will remain to tutor Lady Thomasina, and I trust everybody including Lady Croom will be satisfied! 200

(*Septimus slams the door behind him.*)

BRICE.  He is all bluster and bladder. Rest assured, Chater, I will let the air out of him.

(*Brice leaves by the other door. Chater's assurance lasts only a moment. When he spots the flaw ...*)

CHATER.  Oh! But ... Captain Brice ...!

(*He hurries out after Brice.*)

## ACT 1, SCENE 4

*Hannah and Valentine. She is reading aloud. He is listening. Lightning, the tortoise, is on the table and is not readily distinguishable from Plautus. In front of Valentine is Septimus's portfolio, recognizably so but naturally somewhat faded. It is open. Principally associated with the portfolio (although it may contain sheets of blank paper also) are three items: a slim maths primer; a sheet of drawing paper on which there is a scrawled diagram and some mathematical notations, arrow marks, etc.; and Thomasina's mathematics lesson book, i.e., the one she writes in, which Valentine is leafing through as he listens to Hannah reading from the primer.*

HANNAH.  "I, Thomasina Coverly, have found a truly wonderful method whereby all the forms of nature must give up their numerical secrets and draw themselves through number alone. This margin being too mean for my purpose, the reader must look elsewhere for the New Geometry of Irregular Forms discovered by Thomasina Coverly." 5

(*Pause. She hands Valentine the text book. Valentine looks at what she has been reading.*
   *From the next room, a piano is heard, beginning to play quietly, unintrusively, improvisationally.*)

Does it mean anything?

---

1    *penurious* Very poor.

VALENTINE. I don't know. I don't know what it means, except mathematically.

HANNAH. I meant mathematically.

VALENTINE. (*Now with the lesson book again*) It's an iterated algorithm.

10   HANNAH. What's that?

VALENTINE. Well, it's ... Jesus ... it's an algorithm that's been ... iterated. How'm I supposed to ...? (*He makes an effort.*) The left-hand pages are graphs of what the numbers are doing on the right-hand pages. But all on different scales. Each graph is a small section of the previous one, blown

15   up. Like you'd blow up a detail of a photograph, and then a detail of the detail, and soon, forever. Or in her case, till she ran out of pages.

HANNAH. Is it difficult?

VALENTINE. The maths isn't difficult. It's what you did at school. You have some $x$-and-$y$ equation. Any value for $x$ gives you a value for $y$. So you

20   put a dot where it's right for both $x$ and $y$. Then you take the next value for $x$ which gives you another value for $y$, and when you've done that a few times you join up the dots and that's your graph of whatever the equation is.

HANNAH. And is that what she's doing?

25   VALENTINE. No. Not exactly. Not at all. What she's doing is, every time she works out a value for $y$, she's using *that* as her next value for $x$. And so on. Like a feedback. She's feeding the solution back into the equation, and then solving it again. Iteration, you see.

HANNAH. And that's surprising, is it?

30   VALENTINE. Well, it is a bit. It's the technique I'm using on my grouse numbers, and it hasn't been around for much longer than, well, call it twenty years.

(*Pause.*)

HANNAH. Why would she be doing it?

VALENTINE. I have no idea.

(*Pause.*)

35   I thought you were doing the hermit.

HANNAH. I am. I still am. But Bernard, damn him ... Thomasina's tutor turns out to have interesting connections. Bernard is going through the library like a bloodhound. The portfolio was in a cupboard.

VALENTINE. There's a lot of stuff around. Gus loves going through it. No old

40   masters or anything ...

HANNAH. The maths primer she was using belonged to him—the tutor; he wrote his name in it.

VALENTINE. (*Reading*) "Septimus Hodge."

HANNAH.  Why were these things saved, do you think?

VALENTINE.  Why should there be a reason?                                45

HANNAH.  And the diagram, what's it of?

VALENTINE.  How would I know?

HANNAH.  Why are you cross?

VALENTINE.  I'm not cross. (*Pause.*) When your Thomasina was doing maths
    it had been the same maths for a couple of thousand years. Classical. And    50
    for a century after Thomasina. Then maths left the real world behind, just
    like modern art, really. Nature was classical, maths was suddenly Picassos.[1]
    But now nature is having the last laugh. The freaky stuff is turning out to
    be the mathematics of the natural world.

HANNAH.  This feedback thing?                                            55

VALENTINE.  For example.

HANNAH.  Well, could Thomasina have—

VALENTINE.  (*Snaps*) No, of course she bloody couldn't!

HANNAH.  All right, you're not cross. What did you mean you were doing the
    same thing she was doing? (*Pause.*) What *are* you doing?             60

VALENTINE.  Actually I'm doing it from the other end. She started with an
    equation and turned it into a graph. I've got a graph—real data—and I'm
    trying to find the equation which would give you the graph if you used it
    the way she's used hers. Iterated it.

HANNAH.  What for?                                                       65

VALENTINE.  It's how you look at population changes in biology. Goldfish in
    a pond, say. This year there are $x$ goldfish. Next year there'll be $y$ goldfish.
    Some get born, some get eaten by herons, whatever. Nature manipulates
    the $x$ and turns it into $y$. Then $y$ goldfish is your starting population for the
    following year. Just like Thomasina. Your value for $y$ becomes your next    70
    value for $x$. The question is: what is being done to $x$? What is the manipu-
    lation? Whatever it is, it can be written down as mathematics. It's called
    an algorithm.

HANNAH.  It can't be the same every year.

VALENTINE.  The details change, you can't keep tabs on everything, it's not    75
    nature in a box. But it isn't necessary to know the details. When they are
    all put together, it turns out the population is obeying a mathematical rule.

HANNAH.  The goldfish are?

VALENTINE.  Yes. No. The numbers. It's not about the behaviour of fish. It's
    about the behaviour of numbers. This thing works for any phenomenon    80

---

1    *Picassos* Reference to the Spanish painter Pablo Picasso (1881–1973), best known for his
     work in Cubism, a movement in which artists attempted to portray objects as though
     seen from multiple perspectives at once.

which eats its own numbers—measles, epidemics, rainfall averages, cotton prices, it's a natural phenomenon in itself. Spooky.

HANNAH. Does it work for grouse?

VALENTINE. I don't know yet. I mean, it does undoubtedly, but it's hard to
85  show. There's more noise with grouse.

HANNAH. Noise?

VALENTINE. Distortions. Interference. Real data is messy. There's a thousand acres of moorland that had grouse on it, always did till about 1930. But nobody counted the grouse. They shot them. So you count the grouse they
90  shot. But burning the heather interferes, it improves the food supply. A good year for foxes interferes the other way, they eat the chicks. And then there's the weather. It's all very, very noisy out there. Very hard to spot the tune. Like a piano in the next room, it's playing your song, but unfortunately it's out of whack, some of the strings are missing, and the pianist is
95  tone deaf and drunk—I mean, the *noise*! Impossible!

HANNAH. What do you do?

VALENTINE. You start guessing what the tune might be. You try to pick it out of the noise. You try this, you try that, you start to get something—it's half-baked but you start putting in notes which are missing or not quite
100  the right notes ... and bit by bit ... (*He starts to dumdi-da to the tune of "Happy Birthday."*) Dumdi-dum-dum, dear Val-en-tine, dumdi-dum-dum to you—the lost algorithm!

HANNAH. (*Soberly*) Yes, I see. And then what?

VALENTINE. I publish.

105  HANNAH. Of course. Sorry. Jolly good.

VALENTINE. That's the theory. Grouse are bastards compared to goldfish.

HANNAH. Why did you choose them?

VALENTINE. The game books. My true inheritance. Two hundred years of real data on a plate.

110  HANNAH. Somebody wrote down everything that's shot?

VALENTINE. Well, that's what a game book is. I'm only using from 1870, when butts and beaters[1] came in.

HANNAH. You mean the game books go back to Thomasina's time?

VALENTINE. Oh yes. Further. (*And then getting ahead of her thought.*) No—
115  really. I promise you. I *promise* you. Not a schoolgirl living in a country house in Derbyshire in eighteen-something!

HANNAH. Well, what was she doing?

---

1  *butts* Camouflaged bird blinds used in grouse hunting; *beaters* Workers who drive game out of sheltered areas toward a blind by making noise by or swinging sticks.

VALENTINE.  She was just playing with the numbers. The truth is, she wasn't doing anything.

HANNAH.  She must have been doing something.    120

VALENTINE.  Doodling. Nothing she understood.

HANNAH.  A monkey at a typewriter?[1]

VALENTINE.  Yes. Well, a piano.

(*Hannah picks up the algebra book and reads from it.*)

HANNAH.  "... a method whereby all the forms of nature must give up their numerical secrets and draw themselves through number alone." This feed-    125 back, is it a way of making pictures of forms in nature? Just tell me if it is or it isn't.

VALENTINE.  (*Irritated*) To *me* it is. Pictures of turbulence—growth— change—creation—it's not a way of drawing an elephant, for God's sake!

HANNAH.  I'm sorry.    130

(*She picks up an apple leaf from the table. She is timid about pushing the point.*)

So you couldn't make a picture of this leaf by iterating a whatsit?

VALENTINE.  (*Off-hand*) Oh yes, you could do that.

HANNAH.  (*Furiously*) Well, tell me! Honestly, I could kill you!

VALENTINE.  If you knew the algorithm and fed it back say ten thousand times, each time there'd be a dot somewhere on the screen. You'd never    135 know where to expect the next dot. But gradually you'd start to see this shape, because every dot will be inside the shape of this leaf. It wouldn't *be* a leaf, it would be a mathematical object. But yes. The unpredictable and the predetermined unfold together to make everything the way it is. It's how nature creates itself, on every scale, the snowflake and the snowstorm.    140 It makes me so happy. To be at the beginning again, knowing almost noth- ing. People were talking about the end of physics. Relativity and quan- tum[2] looked as if they were going to clean out the whole problem between them. A theory of everything. But they only explained the very big and the very small. The universe, the elementary particles. The ordinary-sized    145 stuff which is our lives, the things people write poetry about—clouds—

---

1    *monkey ... typewriter* Refers to the popular idea that, given infinite time, a monkey ran- domly hitting keys on a typewriter would eventually hit the right combinations to repro- duce the works of Shakespeare.

2    *Relativity and quantum* Twentieth-century advances in physics that address phenomena Newtonian physics does not. The theory of relativity describes the motion of objects at extreme speeds and levels of gravity, while quantum mechanics applies to the behaviour of particles at the atomic level.

daffodils—waterfalls—and what happens in a cup of coffee when the cream goes in—these things are full of mystery, as mysterious to us as the heavens were to the Greeks. We're better at predicting events at the edge
150   of the galaxy or inside the nucleus of an atom than whether it'll rain on auntie's garden party three Sundays from now. Because the problem turns out to be different. We can't even predict the next drip from a dripping tap when it gets irregular. Each drip sets up the conditions for the next, the smallest variation blows prediction apart, and the weather is unpredictable
155   the same way, will always be unpredictable. When you push the numbers through the computer you can see it on the screen. The future is disorder. A door like this has cracked open five or six times since we got up on our hind legs. It's the best possible time to be alive, when almost everything you thought you knew is wrong.

(*Pause.*)

160   HANNAH.  The weather is fairly predictable in the Sahara.[1]
VALENTINE.  The scale is different but the graph goes up and down the same way. Six thousand years in the Sahara looks like six months in Manchester, I bet you.
HANNAH.  How much?
165   VALENTINE.  Everything you have to lose.
HANNAH.  (*Pause*) No.
VALENTINE.  Quite right. That's why there was corn in Egypt.[2]

(*Hiatus. The piano is heard again.*)

HANNAH.  What is he playing?
VALENTINE.  I don't know. He makes it up.
170   HANNAH.  Chloë called him "genius."
VALENTINE.  It's what my mother calls him—only *she* means it. Last year some expert had her digging in the wrong place for months to find something or other—the foundations of Capability Brown's boat-house—and Gus put her right first go.
175   HANNAH.  Did he ever speak?
VALENTINE.  Oh yes. Until he was five. You've never asked about him. You get high marks here for good breeding.
HANNAH.  Yes, I know. I've always been given credit for my unconcern.

(*Bernard enters in high excitement and triumph.*)

---

1    *Sahara* Largest desert in the world, located in Northern Africa.
2    *corn in Egypt* See Genesis 42.1. In Genesis 41, Joseph predicts seven years of abundance followed by seven years of famine.

BERNARD.  *English Bards and Scotch Reviewers.* A pencilled superscription. Listen and kiss my cycle-clips!                                                    180

(*He is carrying the book. He reads from it.*)

"O harbinger of Sleep, who missed the press
And hoped his drone might thus escape redress!
The wretched Chater, bard of Eros' Couch,
For his narcotic let my pencil vouch!"

You see, *you have to turn over every page.*                                      185

HANNAH.  Is it his handwriting?

BERNARD.  Oh, come *on*.

HANNAH.  Obviously not.

BERNARD.  Christ, what do you want?

HANNAH.  Proof.                                                                    190

VALENTINE.  Quite right. Who are you talking about?

BERNARD.  Proof? *Proof?* You'd have to be there, you silly bitch!

VALENTINE.  (*Mildly*) I say, you're speaking of my fiancée.

HANNAH.  Especially when I have a present for you. Guess what I found. (*Producing the present for Bernard.*) Lady Croom writing from London to  195 her husband. Her brother, Captain Brice, married a Mrs. Chater. In other words, one might assume, a widow.

(*Bernard looks at the letter.*)

BERNARD.  I *said* he was dead. What year? 1810! Oh my God, 1810! Well *done*, Hannah! Are you going to tell me it's a different Mrs. Chater?

HANNAH.  Oh no. It's her all right. Note her Christian name.                       200

BERNARD.  Charity. Charity ... "Deny what cannot be proven for Charity's sake!"

HANNAH.  Don't kiss me!

VALENTINE.  She won't let anyone kiss her.

BERNARD.  You see! They wrote—they scribbled—they put it on paper. It was their employment. Their diversion. Paper is what they had. And there'll be  205 more. There is always more. We can find it!

HANNAH.  Such passion. First Valentine, now you. It's moving.

BERNARD.  The aristocratic friend of the tutor—under the same roof as the poor sod whose book he savaged—the first thing he does is seduce Chater's wife. All is discovered. There is a duel. Chater dead, Byron fled! P.S. guess  210 what?, the widow married her ladyship's brother! Do you honestly think no one wrote a word? How could they not! It dropped from sight but we will write it again!

HANNAH.  You can, Bernard. I'm not going to take any credit, I haven't done anything.                                                                          215

(*The same thought has clearly occurred to Bernard. He becomes instantly po-faced.*[1])

BERNARD.  Well, that's—very fair—generous—

HANNAH.  Prudent. Chater could have died of anything, anywhere.

(*The po-face is forgotten.*)

BERNARD.  But he fought a duel with Byron!

HANNAH.  You haven't established it was fought. You haven't established it
220    was Byron. For God's sake, Bernard, you haven't established Byron was
even here!

BERNARD.  I'll tell you your problem. No guts.

HANNAH.  Really?

BERNARD.  By which I mean a visceral belief in yourself. Gut instinct. The
225    part of you which doesn't reason. The certainty for which there is no back-
reference. Because time is reversed. Tock, tick goes the universe and then
recovers itself, but it was enough, you were in there and you bloody *know*.

VALENTINE.  Are you talking about Lord Byron, the poet?

BERNARD.  No, you fucking idiot, we're talking about Lord Byron the char-
230    tered accountant.

VALENTINE.  (*Unoffended*) Oh well, *he* was here all right, the poet.

(*Silence.*)

HANNAH.  How do you know?

VALENTINE.  He's in the game book. I think he shot a hare. I read through
the whole lot once when I had mumps—some quite interesting people—

235  HANNAH.  Where's the book?

VALENTINE.  It's not one I'm using—too early, of course—

HANNAH.  1809.

VALENTINE.  They've always been in the commode. Ask Chloë.

(*Hannah looks to Bernard. Bernard has been silent because he has been
incapable of speech. He seems to have gone into a trance, in which only his
mouth tries to work. Hannah steps over to him and gives him a demure
kiss on the cheek. It works. Bernard lurches out into the garden and can be
heard croaking for "Chloë ... Chloë!"*)

VALENTINE.  My mother's lent him her bicycle. Lending one's bicycle is a form
240    of safe sex, possibly the safest there is. My mother is in a flutter about Bernard, and he's no fool. He gave her a first edition of Horace Walpole, and
now she's lent him her bicycle.

---

1    *po-faced* I.e., with a disapproving expression.

(*He gathers up the three items [the primer, the lesson book and the diagram] and puts them into the portfolio.*)

Can I keep these for a while?

HANNAH. Yes, of course.

(*The piano stops. Gus enters hesitantly from the music room.*)

VALENTINE. (*To Gus*) Yes, finished ... coming now. (*To Hannah*) I'm trying to work out the diagram.   245

(*Gus nods and smiles, at Hannah too, but she is preoccupied.*)

HANNAH. What I don't understand is ... why nobody did this feedback thing before—it's not like relativity, you don't have to be Einstein.[1]

VALENTINE. You couldn't see to look before. The electronic calculator was what the telescope was for Galileo.[2]   250

HANNAH. Calculator?

VALENTINE. There wasn't enough time before. There weren't enough *pencils*! (*He flourishes Thomasina's lesson book.*) This took her I don't know how many days and she hasn't scratched the paintwork. Now she'd only have to press a button, the same button over and over. Iteration. A few minutes.   255 And what I've done in a couple of months, with only a *pencil* the calculations would take me the rest of my life to do again—thousands of pages— tens of thousands! And so boring!

HANNAH. Do you mean—?

(*She stops because Gus is plucking Valentine's sleeve.*)

Do you mean—?   260

VALENTINE. All right, Gus, I'm coming.

HANNAH. Do you mean that was the only problem? Enough time? And paper? And the boredom?

VALENTINE. We're going to get out the dressing-up box.

HANNAH. (*Driven to raising her voice*) Val! Is that what you're saying?   265

VALENTINE. (*Surprised by her. Mildly*) No, I'm saying you'd have to have a reason for doing it.

(*Gus runs out of the room, upset.*)

(*Apologetically*) He hates people shouting.

---

1   *Einstein* Albert Einstein (1876–1955), German-born physicist responsible for the theory of relativity.

2   *Galileo* Galileo Galilei (1564–1642), Italian physicist and astronomer; the discoveries he made using early telescopes transformed the study of astronomy.

HANNAH. I'm sorry.

(*Valentine starts to follow Gus.*)

270 But anything else?

VALENTINE. Well, the other thing is, you'd have to be insane.

(*Valentine leaves.*

*Hannah stays, thoughtful. After a moment, she turns to the table and picks up the Cornhill Magazine. She looks into it briefly, then closes it, and, after going to look at the open page showing Noake's hermitage on the reading stand, she leaves the room, taking the magazine with her.*

*The empty room.*

*The light changes to early morning. From a long way off, there is a pistol shot. A moment later there is the cry of dozens of crows disturbed from the unseen trees.*)

## ACT 2, SCENE 5[1]

*Bernard is pacing around, reading aloud from a handful of typed sheets. Valentine, Chloë and Gus are his audience. Gus sits somewhat apart, perhaps less attentive. Valentine has his tortoise and is eating a sandwich from which he extracts shreds of lettuce to offer the tortoise.*

BERNARD. "Did it happen? Could it happen?

"Undoubtedly it could. Only three years earlier the Irish poet Tom Moore appeared on the field of combat to avenge a review by Jeffrey of the *Edinburgh*. These affairs were seldom fatal and sometimes farcical but,

5 potentially, the duellist stood in respect to the law no differently from a murderer. As for the murderee, a minor poet like Ezra Chater could go to his death in a Derbyshire glade as unmissed and unremembered as his contemporary and namesake, the minor botanist who died in the forests of the West Indies, lost to history like the monkey that bit him. On April

10 16th 1809, a few days after he left Sidley Park, Byron wrote to his solicitor John Hanson: 'If the consequences of my leaving England were ten times as ruinous as you describe, I have no alternative; there are circumstances which render it absolutely indispensable, and quit the country I must immediately.' To which, the editor's note in the Collected Letters reads as

15 follows: 'What Byron's urgent reasons for leaving England were at this time has never been revealed.' The letter was written from the family seat, Newstead Abbey, Nottinghamshire. A long day's ride to the north-west

---

1   ACT 2, Scene 5 As in the 1993 published version of *Arcadia*, scene numbers for this play
    do not restart at the beginning of the second act.

lay Sidley Park, the estate of the Coverlys—a far grander family, raised by Charles II[1] to the Earldom of Croom ..."

(*Hannah enters briskly, a piece of paper in her hand.*)

HANNAH.  Bernard ...! Val ...                                                  20
BERNARD.  Do you mind?

(*Hannah puts her piece of paper down in front of Valentine.*)

CHLOË.  (*Angrily*) *Hannah!*
HANNAH.  What?
CHLOË.  She's so *rude!*
HANNAH.  (*Taken aback*) What? Am I?                                           25
VALENTINE.  Bernard's reading us his lecture.
HANNAH.  Yes, I know. (*Then recollecting herself.*) Yes—yes—that *was* rude. I'm sorry, Bernard.
VALENTINE.  (*With the piece of paper*) What is this?
HANNAH.  (*To Bernard*) Spot on—the India Office Library. (*To Valentine*)     30
    Peacock's letter in holograph, I got a copy sent—
CHLOË.  *Hannah!* Shut up!
HANNAH.  (*Sitting down*) Yes, sorry.
BERNARD.  It's all right, I'll read it to myself.
CHLOË.  *No.*                                                                  35

(*Hannah reaches for the Peacock letter and takes it back.*)

HANNAH.  Go on, Bernard. Have I missed anything? Sorry.

(*Bernard stares at her balefully but then continues to read.*)

BERNARD.  "The Byrons of Newstead in 1809 comprised an eccentric widow and her undistinguished son, the 'lame brat,' who until the age of ten when he came into the title, had been carted about the country from lodging to lodging by his vulgar hectoring monster of a mother—" (*Hannah's*    40
    *hand has gone up*)—overruled—"and who four months past his twenty-first birthday was master of nothing but his debts and his genius. Between the Byrons and the Coverlys there was no social equality and none to be expected. The connection, undisclosed to posterity until now, was with Septimus Hodge, Byron's friend at Harrow and Trinity College—" (*Han-*    45
    *nah's hand goes up again*)—sustained—(*He makes an instant correction with a silver pencil.*) "Byron's contemporary at Harrow and Trinity College, and now tutor in residence to the Croom daughter, Thomasina Coverly.

---

1    *Charles II* King of England, Scotland, and Ireland from 1660–85.

Byron's letters tell us where he was on April 8th and on April 12th. He
50   was at Newstead. But on the 10th he was at Sidley Park, as attested by the
game book preserved there: 'April 10th 1809—forenoon. High cloud, dry,
and sun between times, wind southeasterly. Self—Augustus—Lord Byron.
Fourteen pigeon, one hare (Lord B.).' But, as we know now, the drama
of life and death at Sidley Park was not about pigeons but about sex and
55   literature."

VALENTINE. Unless you were the pigeon.

BERNARD. I don't have to do this. I'm paying you a compliment.

CHLOË. Ignore him, Bernard—go on, get to the duel.

BERNARD. Hannah's not even paying attention.

60 HANNAH. Yes I am, it's all going in. I often work with the radio on.

BERNARD. Oh thanks!

HANNAH. Is there much more?

CHLOË. *Hannah!*

HANNAH. No, it's fascinating. I just wondered how much more there was. I
65   need to ask Valentine about this (*letter*)—sorry, Bernard, go on, this will
keep.

VALENTINE. Yes—sorry, Bernard.

CHLOË. Please, Bernard!

BERNARD. Where was I?

70 VALENTINE. Pigeons.

CHLOË. Sex.

HANNAH. Literature.

BERNARD. Life and death. Right. "Nothing could be more eloquent of that
than the three documents I have quoted: the terse demand to settle a mat-
75   ter in private; the desperate scribble of 'my husband has sent for pistols';
and on April 11th, the gauntlet thrown down by the aggrieved and cuck-
olded author Ezra Chater. The covers have not survived. What is certain is
that all three letters were in Byron's possession when his books were sold
in 1816—preserved in the pages of 'The Couch of Eros' which seven years
80   earlier at Sidley Park Byron had borrowed from Septimus Hodge."

HANNAH. Borrowed?

BERNARD. I will be taking questions at the end. Constructive comments will
be welcome. Which is indeed my reason for trying out in the provinces
before my London opening under the auspices of the Byron Society prior
85   to publication. By the way, Valentine, do you want a credit?—"the game
book recently discovered by"?

VALENTINE. It was never lost, Bernard.

BERNARD. "As recently pointed out by." I don't normally like giving credit
where it's due, but with scholarly articles as with divorce, there is a certain

cachet in citing a member of the aristocracy. I'll pop it in ad lib for the ⁹⁰ lecture, and give you a mention in the press release. How's that?

VALENTINE. Very kind.

HANNAH. Press release? What happened to the *Journal of English Studies*?

BERNARD. That comes later with the apparatus, and in the recognized tone— very dry, very modest, absolutely gloat-free, and yet unmistakably "Eat ⁹⁵ your heart out, you dozy bastards." But first, it's "Media Don, book early to avoid disappointment." Where was I?

VALENTINE. Game book.

CHLOË. Eros.

HANNAH. Borrowed. ¹⁰⁰

BERNARD. Right. "—borrowed from Septimus Hodge. Is it conceivable that the letters were already in the book when Byron borrowed it?"

VALENTINE. Yes.

CHLOË. Shut up, Val.

VALENTINE. Well, it's conceivable. ¹⁰⁵

BERNARD. "Is it *likely* that Hodge would have lent Byron the book without first removing the three private letters?"

VALENTINE. Look, sorry—I only meant, Byron could have borrowed the book without asking.

HANNAH. That's true. ¹¹⁰

BERNARD. Then why wouldn't Hodge get them back?

HANNAH. I don't know, I wasn't there.

BERNARD. That's right, you bloody weren't.

CHLOË. Go on, Bernard.

BERNARD. "It is the third document, the challenge itself, that convinces. ¹¹⁵ Chater 'as a man and a poet,' points the finger at his 'slanderer in the press.' Neither as a man nor a poet did Ezra Chater cut such a figure as to be habitually slandered or even mentioned in the press. It is surely indisputable that the slander was the review of 'The Maid of Turkey' in the *Piccadilly Recreation*. Did Septimus Hodge have any connection with the London ¹²⁰ periodicals? No. Did Byron? Yes! He had reviewed Wordsworth two years earlier, he was to review Spencer[1] two years later. And do we have any clue as to Byron's opinion of Chater the poet? Yes! Who but Byron could have written the four lines pencilled into Lady Croom's copy of *English Bards and Scotch Reviewers*—" ¹²⁵

HANNAH. Almost anybody.

BERNARD. Darling—

HANNAH. Don't call me darling.

---

1    *Spencer* English poet William Spencer (1770–1834).

BERNARD. Dickhead, then, is it likely that the man Chater calls his friend
130  Septimus Hodge is the same man who screwed his wife and kicked the shit
out of his last book?

HANNAH. Put it like that, almost certain.

CHLOË. (*Earnestly*) You've been deeply wounded in the past, haven't you,
Hannah?

135  HANNAH. Nothing compared to listening to this. Why is there nothing in
Byron's letters about the *Piccadilly* reviews?

BERNARD. Exactly. Because he killed the author.

HANNAH. But the first one, "The Maid of Turkey," was the year before. Was
he clairvoyant?

140  CHLOË. Letters get lost.

BERNARD. Thank you! Exactly! There is a platonic letter which confirms everything—lost but ineradicable, like radio voices rippling through the universe for all eternity. "My dear Hodge—here I am in Albania and you're the
only person in the whole world who knows why. Poor C! I never wished
145  him any harm—except in the *Piccadilly*, of course—it was the woman who
bade me eat, dear Hodge!—what a tragic business, but thank God it ended
well for poetry. Yours ever, B.—PS. Burn this."

VALENTINE. How did Chater find out the reviewer was Byron?

BERNARD. (*Irritated*) I don't know, I wasn't there, was I? (*Pause. To Hannah*)
150  You wish to say something?

HANNAH. Moi?

CHLOË. I know. Byron told Mrs. Chater in bed. Next day he dumped her so
she grassed[1] on him, and pleaded date rape.

BERNARD. (*Fastidiously*) Date rape? What do you mean, date rape?

155  HANNAH. April the tenth.

(*Bernard cracks. Everything becomes loud and overlapped as Bernard
threatens to walk out and is cajoled into continuing.*)

BERNARD. Right!—forget it!

HANNAH. Sorry—

BERNARD. No—I've had nothing but sarcasm and childish interruptions—

VALENTINE. What did I do?

160  BERNARD. No credit for probably the most sensational literary discovery of
the century—

CHLOË. I think you're jolly unfair—they're jealous, Bernard—

HANNAH. I won't say another word—

---

1   *grassed* Told.

VALENTINE.  Yes, go on, Bernard—we promise.

BERNARD.  (*Finally*) Well, only if you stop *feeding tortoises*!   165

VALENTINE.  Well, it's his lunch time.

BERNARD.  And on condition that I am afforded the common courtesy of a scholar among scholars—

HANNAH.  Absolutely mum till you're finished—

BERNARD.  After which, any comments are to be couched in terms of accepted   170 academic—

HANNAH.  Dignity—you're right, Bernard.

BERNARD.  —respect.

HANNAH.  Respect. Absolutely. The language of scholars. Count on it.

(*Having made a great show of putting his pages away, Bernard reassembles them and finds his place, glancing suspiciously at the other three for signs of levity.*)

BERNARD.  Last paragraph. "Without question, Ezra Chater issued a chal-   175 lenge to *somebody*. If a duel was fought in the dawn mist of Sidley Park in April 1809, his opponent, on the evidence, was a critic with a gift for ridicule and a taste for seduction. Do we need to look far? Without question, Mrs. Chater was a widow by 1810. If we seek the occasion of Ezra Chater's early and unrecorded death, do we need to look far? Without question,   180 Lord Byron, in the very season of his emergence as a literary figure, quit the country in a cloud of panic and mystery, and stayed abroad for two years at a time when Continental travel was unusual and dangerous. If we seek his reason, *do we need to look far?*"

(*No mean performer, he is pleased with the effect of his peroration. There is a significant silence.*)

HANNAH.  Bollocks.   185

CHLOË.  Well, I think it's true.

HANNAH.  You've left out everything which doesn't fit. Byron had been banging on for months about leaving England—there's a letter in *February*—

BERNARD.  But he didn't go, did he?

HANNAH.  And then he didn't sail until the beginning of July!   190

BERNARD.  Everything moved more slowly then. Time was different. He was two weeks in Falmouth waiting for wind or something—

HANNAH.  Bernard, I don't know why I'm bothering—you're arrogant, greedy and reckless. You've gone from a glint in your eye to a sure thing in a hop, skip and a jump. You deserve what you get and I think you're mad. But I   195 can't help myself, you're like some exasperating child pedalling its tricycle towards the edge of a cliff, and I have to do something. So listen to me. If Byron killed Chater in a duel I'm Marie of Romania.[1] You'll end up with so much *fame* you won't leave the house without a paper bag over your head.

200 VALENTINE. Actually, Bernard, as a scientist, your theory is incomplete.

BERNARD. But I'm not a scientist.

VALENTINE. (*Patiently*) No, *as a scientist*—

BERNARD. (*Beginning to shout*) I have yet to hear a proper argument.

HANNAH. Nobody would kill a man and then pan his book. I mean, not in

205   that order. So he must have borrowed the book, written the review, *posted it*, seduced Mrs. Chater, fought a duel and departed, all in the space of two or three days. Who would do that?

BERNARD. Byron.

HANNAH. It's hopeless.

210 BERNARD. You've never understood him, as you've shown in your novelette.

HANNAH. In my what?

BERNARD. Oh, sorry—did you think it was a work of historical revisionism? Byron the spoilt child promoted beyond his gifts by the spirit of the age! And Caroline the closet intellectual shafted by a male society!

215 VALENTINE. I read that somewhere—

HANNAH. It's his review.

BERNARD. And bloody well said, too!

(*Things are turning a little ugly and Bernard seems in a mood to push them that way.*)

You got them backwards, darling. Caroline was Romantic waffle on wheels with no talent, and Byron was an eighteenth-century Rationalist[2] touched

220   by genius. And he killed Chater.

HANNAH. (*Pause*) If it's not too late to change my mind, I'd like you to go ahead.

BERNARD. I intend to. Look to the mote in your own eye![3]—you even had the wrong bloke on the dust-jacket!

225 HANNAH. Dust-jacket?

VALENTINE. What about my computer model? Aren't you going to mention it?

BERNARD. It's inconclusive.

VALENTINE. (*To Hannah*) The *Piccadilly* reviews aren't a very good fit with

230   Byron's other reviews, you see.

---

1   *Marie of Romania* Queen of Romania from 1914–27.
2   *Rationalist* Someone who believes that reason is the basis for all knowledge.
3   *mote … eye* See Matthew 7.5: "Thou hypocrite, first cast out the beam out of thine own eye; and then shalt thou see clearly to cast out the mote out of thy brother's eye."

HANNAH. (*To Bernard*) What do you mean, the wrong bloke?

BERNARD. (*Ignoring her*) The other reviews aren't a very good fit for each other, are they?

VALENTINE. No, but differently. The parameters—

BERNARD. (*Jeering*) Parameters! You can't stick Byron's head in your laptop! Genius isn't like your average grouse.

VALENTINE. (*Casually*) Well, it's all trivial anyway.

BERNARD. What is?

VALENTINE. Who wrote what when ...

BERNARD. Trivial?

VALENTINE. Personalities.

BERNARD. I'm sorry—did you say trivial?

VALENTINE. It's a technical term.

BERNARD. Not where I come from, it isn't.

VALENTINE. The questions you're asking don't matter, you see. It's like arguing who got there first with the calculus. The English say Newton, the Germans say Leibniz.[1] But it doesn't *matter*. Personalities. What matters is the calculus. Scientific progress. Knowledge.

BERNARD. Really? Why?

VALENTINE. Why what?

BERNARD. Why does scientific progress matter more than personalities?

VALENTINE. Is he serious?

HANNAH. No, he's trivial. Bernard—

VALENTINE. (*Interrupting, to Bernard*) Do yourself a favour, you're on a loser.

BERNARD. Oh, you're going to zap me with penicillin and pesticides. Spare me that and I'll spare you the bomb and aerosols. But don't confuse progress with perfectibility. A great poet is always timely. A great philosopher is an urgent need. There's no rush for Isaac Newton. We were quite happy with Aristotle's cosmos.[2] Personally, I preferred it. Fifty-five crystal spheres geared to God's crankshaft is my idea of a satisfying universe. I can't think of anything more trivial than the speed of light. Quarks, quasars[3]—big bangs, black holes—who gives a shit? How did you people con

---

1    *Leibniz* Gottfried Wilhelm Leibniz (1646–1716), German philosopher and mathematician. Leibniz and Newton were contemporaries and each invented calculus independently.

2    *Aristotle's cosmos* Aristotle proposed that the universe was composed of nested, rotating spheres with planets and stars fixed inside them.

3    *Quarks* In quantum physics, fundamental particles that join to form composite particles, such as protons and neutrons; *quasars* Distant, extremely bright celestial objects that resemble stars but are thought to be the result of a black hole in the centre of a galaxy.

us out of all that status? All that money? And why are you so pleased with yourselves?

265 CHLOË. Are you against penicillin, Bernard?

BERNARD. Don't feed the animals. (*Back to Valentine*) I'd push the lot of you over a cliff myself. Except the one in the wheelchair,[1] I think I'd lose the sympathy vote before people had time to think it through.

HANNAH. (*Loudly*) What the hell do you mean, the dust-jacket?

270 BERNARD. (*Ignoring her*) If knowledge isn't self-knowledge it isn't doing much, mate. Is the universe expanding? Is it contracting? Is it standing on one leg and singing "When Father Painted the Parlour"?[2] Leave me out. I can expand my universe without you. "She walks in beauty, like the night of cloudless climes and starry skies, and all that's best of dark and bright

275 meet in her aspect and her eyes."[3] There you are, he wrote it after coming home from a party. (*With offensive politeness.*) What is it that you're doing with grouse, Valentine, I'd love to know?

(*Valentine stands up and it is suddenly apparent that he is shaking and close to tears.*)

VALENTINE. (*To Chloë*) He's not against penicillin, and he knows I'm not against poetry. (*To Bernard*) I've given up on the grouse.

280 HANNAH. You haven't, Valentine!

VALENTINE. (*Leaving*) I can't do it.

HANNAH. *Why?*

VALENTINE. Too much noise. There's just too much *bloody noise!*

(*On which, Valentine leaves the room. Chloë, upset and in tears, jumps up and briefly pummels Bernard ineffectually with her fists.*)

CHLOË. You bastard, Bernard!

(*She follows Valentine out and is followed at a run by Gus. Pause.*)

285 HANNAH. Well, I think that's everybody. You can leave now, give Lightning a kick on your way out.

BERNARD. Yes, I'm sorry about that. It's no fun when it's not among pros, is it?

HANNAH. No.

---

1   *the one on the wheelchair* I.e., Stephen Hawking (b. 1942), an important theoretical physicist who has a severe physical disability.

2   *When Father Painted the Parlour* Reference to the 1910 comic song "When Father Papered the Parlour."

3   *She walks ... her eyes* Opening lines of Byron's poem "She Walks in Beauty" (1815).

BERNARD. Oh, well ... (*he begins to put his lecture sheets away in his briefcase,* 290
*and is thus reminded ...*) do you want to know about your book jacket?
"Lord Byron and Caroline Lamb at the Royal Academy?" Ink study by
Henry Fuseli?[1]

HANNAH. What about it?

BERNARD. It's not them.                                                                       295

HANNAH. (*She explodes*) Who says!?

(*Bernard brings the* Byron Society Journal *from his briefcase.*)

BERNARD. This Fuseli expert in the *Byron Society Journal.* They sent me the
latest ... as a distinguished guest speaker.

HANNAH. But of course it's them! Everyone knows—

BERNARD. Popular tradition only. (*He is finding the place in the journal.*) Here 300
we are. "No earlier than 1820." He's analyzed it. (*Offers it to her.*) Read at
your leisure.

HANNAH. (*She sounds like Bernard jeering*) Analyzed it?

BERNARD. Charming sketch, of course, but Byron was in Italy ...

HANNAH. But, Bernard—I *know* it's them.                                                      305

BERNARD. How?

HANNAH. How? It just *is*. "Analyzed it," my big toe!

BERNARD. Language!

HANNAH. He's wrong.

BERNARD. Oh, gut instinct, you mean?                                                          310

HANNAH. (*Flatly*) He's wrong.

(*Bernard snaps shut his briefcase.*)

BERNARD. Well, it's all trivial, isn't it? Why don't you come?

HANNAH. Where?

BERNARD. With me.

HANNAH. To London? What for?                                                                  315

BERNARD. What for.

HANNAH. Oh, your lecture.

BERNARD. No, no, bugger that. Sex.

HANNAH. Oh ... No. Thanks ... (*then, protesting*) Bernard!

BERNARD. You should try it. It's very underrated.                                            320

HANNAH. Nothing against it.

BERNARD. Yes, you have. You should let yourself go a bit. You might have
written a better book. Or at any rate the right book.

---

1    *Henry Fuseli* Swiss painter (1741–1825), a notable figure in the Romantic movement.

HANNAH. Sex and literature. Literature and sex. Your conversation, left to
325    itself, doesn't have many places to go. Like two marbles rolling around a
       pudding basin. One of them is always sex.
BERNARD. Ah well, yes. Men all over.
HANNAH. No doubt. Einstein—relativity and sex. Chippendale[1]—sex and
       furniture. Galileo—"Did the earth move?" What the hell is it with you
330    people? Chaps sometimes wanted to marry me, and I don't know a worse
       bargain. Available sex against not being allowed to fart in bed. What do
       you mean the right book?
BERNARD. It takes a romantic to make a heroine of Caroline Lamb. You were
       cut out for Byron.

       (*Pause.*)

335 HANNAH. So, cheerio.
BERNARD. Oh, I'm coming back for the dance, you know. Chloë asked me.
HANNAH. She meant well, but I don't dance.
BERNARD. No, no—I'm going with her.
HANNAH. Oh, I see. I don't, actually.
340 BERNARD. I'm her date. Sub rosa.[2] Don't tell Mother.
HANNAH. She doesn't want her mother to know?
BERNARD. No—*I* don't want her mother to know. This is my first experience
       of the landed aristocracy. I tell you, I'm boggle-eyed.
HANNAH. Bernard!—you haven't seduced that girl?
345 BERNARD. Seduced her? Every time I turned round she was up a library lad-
       der. In the end I gave in. That reminds me—I spotted something between
       her legs that made me think of you.

       (*He instantly receives a sharp stinging slap on the face but manages to
       remain completely unperturbed by it. He is already producing from his
       pocket a small book. His voice has hardly hesitated.*)

       *The Peaks Traveller and Gazetteer*—James Godolphin 1832—unillustrated,
       I'm afraid. (*He has opened the book to a marked place.*) "Sidley Park in Der-
350    byshire, property of the Earl of Croom ..."
HANNAH. (*Numbly*) The world is going to hell in a handcart.
BERNARD. "Five hundred acres including forty of lake—the Park by Brown
       and Noakes has pleasing features in the horrid style—viaduct, grotto,[3]

---

1    *Chippendale* Thomas Chippendale (1718–79), influential English furniture-maker; also
     refers to Chippendales, a well-known dance troupe of male strippers.
2    *Sub rosa* Latin: under the rose; i.e., secretly.
3    *viaduct* Bridge supported by a series of small arches; *grotto* Small cave, often built arti-
     ficially as a garden feature.

etc—a hermitage occupied by a lunatic since twenty years without discourse or companion save for a pet tortoise, Plautus by name, which he suffers children to touch on request." (*He holds out the book for her.*) A tortoise. They must be a feature. 355

(*After a moment Hannah takes the book.*)

HANNAH. Thank you.

(*Valentine comes to the door.*)

VALENTINE. The station taxi is at the front ...
BERNARD. Yes ... thanks ... Oh—did Peacock come up trumps? 360
HANNAH. For some.
BERNARD. Hermit's name and CV?[1]

(*He picks up and glances at the Peacock letter.*)

"My dear Thackeray ..." God, I'm good.

(*He puts the letter down.*)

Well, wish me luck—(*Vaguely to Valentine*) Sorry about ... you know ...
(*and to Hannah*) and about your ... 365
VALENTINE. Piss off, Bernard.
BERNARD. Right.

(*Bernard goes.*)

HANNAH. Don't let Bernard get to you. It's only performance art, you know. Rhetoric. They used to teach it in ancient times, like PT.[2] It's not about being right, they had philosophy for that. Rhetoric was their talk show. 370 Bernard's indignation is a sort of aerobics for when he gets on television.
VALENTINE. I don't care to be rubbished by the dustbin man. (*He has been looking at the letter.*) The what of the lunatic?

(*Hannah reclaims the letter and reads it for him.*)

HANNAH. "The testament of the lunatic serves as a caution against French fashion ... for it was Frenchified mathematick that brought him to the 375 melancholy certitude of a world without light or life ... as a wooden stove that must consume itself until ash and stove are as one, and heat is gone from the earth."
VALENTINE. (*Amused, surprised*) Huh!

---

1    *CV* Curriculum vitae; a résumé.
2    *PT* Physical training, also called "physical education" or "gym class."

380    HANNAH. "He died aged two score years and seven, hoary as Job[1] and meagre as a cabbage-stalk, the proof of his prediction even yet unyielding to his labours for the restitution of hope through good English algebra."

VALENTINE. That's it?

HANNAH. (*Nods*) Is there anything in it?

385    VALENTINE. In what? We are all doomed? (*Casually.*) Oh yes, sure—it's called the second law of thermodynamics.[2]

HANNAH. Was it known about?

VALENTINE. By poets and lunatics from time immemorial.

HANNAH. Seriously.

390    VALENTINE. No.

HANNAH. Is it anything to do with ... you know, Thomasina's discovery?

VALENTINE. She didn't discover anything.

HANNAH. Her lesson book.

VALENTINE. No.

395    HANNAH. A coincidence, then?

VALENTINE. What is?

HANNAH. (*Reading*) "He died aged two score years and seven." That was in 1834. So he was born in 1787. So was the tutor. He says so in his letter to Lord Croom when he recommended himself for the job: "Date of

400    birth—1787." The hermit was born in the same year as Septimus Hodge.

VALENTINE. (*Pause*) Did Bernard bite you in the leg?

HANNAH. Don't you see? I thought my hermit was a perfect symbol. An idiot in the landscape. But this is better. The Age of Enlightenment banished into the Romantic wilderness! The genius of Sidley Park living on in a

405    hermit's hut!

VALENTINE. You don't *know* that.

HANNAH. Oh, but I do. I do. Somewhere there will be *something* ... if only I can find it.

---

1    *hoary* Grey-haired, old; *Job* Biblical figure who lived a long and blessed life after being tested by God.

2    *second law of thermodynamics* Physical law formulated in 1850. According to this law, heat can only move from warmer objects to colder ones—never from colder objects to warmer ones—so the amount of available energy in a closed system can never increase. A possible implication of this law is that eventually all matter in the universe will be of equal temperature, no energy will be available, and nothing will ever change again. The effect of the second law of thermodynamics on the universe is sometimes also interpreted as an irreversible increase in disorder, meaning that all matter in the universe will eventually blend together until everything is completely uniform.

# ACT 2, SCENE 6

*The room is empty.*

*A reprise: early morning—a distant pistol shot—the sound of the crows.*

*Jellaby enters the dawn-dark room with a lamp. He goes to the windows and looks out. He sees something. He returns to put the lamp on the table, and then opens one of the french windows and steps outside.*

JELLABY. (*Outside*) Mr. Hodge!

(*Septimus comes in, followed by Jellaby, who closes the garden door. Septimus is wearing a greatcoat.*)

SEPTIMUS. Thank you, Jellaby. I was expecting to be locked out. What time is it?

JELLABY. Half past five.

SEPTIMUS. That is what I have. Well!—what a bracing experience!                      5

(*He produces two pistols from inside his coat and places them on the table.*)

The dawn, you know. Unexpectedly lively. Fishes, birds, frogs ... rabbits ... (*he produces a dead rabbit from inside his coat*) and very beautiful. If only it did not occur so early in the day. I have brought Lady Thomasina a rabbit. Will you take it?

JELLABY. It's dead.                                                                  10

SEPTIMUS. Yes. Lady Thomasina loves a rabbit pie.

(*Jellaby takes the rabbit without enthusiasm. There is a little blood on it.*)

JELLABY. You were missed, Mr. Hodge.

SEPTIMUS. I decided to sleep last night in the boat-house. Did I see a carriage leaving the Park?

JELLABY. Captain Brice's carriage, with Mr. and Mrs. Chater also.                    15

SEPTIMUS. Gone?!

JELLABY. Yes, sir. And Lord Byron's horse was brought round at four o'clock.

SEPTIMUS. Lord Byron too!

JELLABY. Yes, sir. The house has been up and hopping.

SEPTIMUS. But I have his rabbit pistols! What am I to do with his rabbit            20
pistols?

JELLABY. You were looked for in your room.

SEPTIMUS. By whom?

JELLABY. By her ladyship.

SEPTIMUS. In my room?                                                               25

JELLABY. I will tell her ladyship you are returned.

(*He starts to leave.*)

SEPTIMUS. Jellaby! Did Lord Byron leave a book for me?
JELLABY. A book?
SEPTIMUS. He had the loan of a book from me.
30 JELLABY. His lordship left nothing in his room, sir, not a coin.
SEPTIMUS. Oh. Well, I'm sure he would have left a coin if he'd had one. Jellaby—here is a half-guinea for you.
JELLABY. Thank you very much, sir.
SEPTIMUS. What has occurred?
35 JELLABY. The servants are told nothing, sir.
SEPTIMUS. Come, come, does a half-guinea buy nothing any more?
JELLABY. (*Sighs*) Her ladyship encountered Mrs. Chater during the night.
SEPTIMUS. Where?
JELLABY. On the threshold of Lord Byron's room.
40 SEPTIMUS. Ah. Which one was leaving and which entering?
JELLABY. Mrs. Chater was leaving Lord Byron's room.
SEPTIMUS. And where was Mr. Chater?
JELLABY. Mr. Chater and Captain Brice were drinking cherry brandy. They had the footman to keep the fire up until three o'clock. There was a loud
45 altercation upstairs, and—

(*Lady Croom enters the room.*)

LADY CROOM. Well, Mr. Hodge.
SEPTIMUS. My lady.
LADY CROOM. All this to shoot a hare?
SEPTIMUS. A rabbit. (*She gives him one of her looks.*) No, indeed, a hare, though very rabbit-like—
50

(*Jellaby is about to leave.*)

LADY CROOM. My infusion.[1]
JELLABY. Yes, my lady.

(*He leaves. Lady Croom is carrying two letters. We have not seen them before. Each has an envelope which has been opened. She flings them on the table.*)

LADY CROOM. How dare you!
SEPTIMUS. I cannot be called to account for what was written in private and
55 read without regard to propriety.
LADY CROOM. Addressed to me!

---

1   *infusion* Steeped tea.

SEPTIMUS. Left in my room, in the event of my death—

LADY CROOM. Pah!—what earthly use is a love letter from beyond the grave?

SEPTIMUS. As much, surely, as from this side of it. The second letter, however, was not addressed to your ladyship.    60

LADY CROOM. I have a mother's right to open a letter addressed by you to my daughter, whether in the event of your life, your death, or your imbecility. What do you mean by writing to her of rice pudding when she has just suffered the shock of violent death in our midst?

SEPTIMUS. Whose death?    65

LADY CROOM. Yours, you wretch!

SEPTIMUS. Yes, I see.

LADY CROOM. I do not know which is the madder of your ravings. One envelope full of rice pudding, the other of the most insolent familiarities regarding several parts of my body, but have no doubt which is the more    70 intolerable to me.

SEPTIMUS. Which?

LADY CROOM. Oh, aren't we saucy when our bags are packed! Your friend has gone before you, and I have despatched the harlot Chater and her husband—and also my brother for bringing them here. Such is the sentence,    75 you see, for choosing unwisely in your acquaintance. Banishment. Lord Byron is a rake and a hypocrite, and the sooner he sails for the Levant[1] the sooner he will find society congenial to his character.

SEPTIMUS. It has been a night of reckoning.

LADY CROOM. Indeed I wish it had passed uneventfully with you and Mr.    80 Chater shooting each other with the decorum due to a civilized house. You have no secrets left, Mr. Hodge. They spilled out between shrieks and oaths and tears. It is fortunate that a lifetime's devotion to the sporting gun has halved my husband's hearing to the ear he sleeps on.

SEPTIMUS. I'm afraid I have no knowledge of what has occurred.    85

LADY CROOM. Your trollop was discovered in Lord Byron's room.

SEPTIMUS. Ah. Discovered by Mr. Chater?

LADY CROOM. Who else?

SEPTIMUS. I am very sorry, madam, for having used your kindness to bring my unworthy friend to your notice. He will have to give an account of    90 himself to me, you may be sure.

*(Before Lady Croom can respond to this threat, Jellaby enters the room with her "infusion." This is quite an elaborate affair: a pewter tray on small feet on which there is a kettle suspended over a spirit lamp.[2] There*

---

1    *Levant*  Land bordering the eastern side of the Mediterranean Sea.

2    *spirit lamp*  Lamp that burns spirits or another solution.

*is a cup and saucer and the silver "basket" containing the dry leaves for the tea. Jellaby places the tray on the table and is about to offer further assistance with it.)*

LADY CROOM.  I will do it.

JELLABY.  Yes, my lady. (*To Septimus*) Lord Byron left a letter for you with the valet, sir.

95  SEPTIMUS.  Thank you.

*(Septimus takes the letter off the tray. Jellaby prepares to leave. Lady Croom eyes the letter.)*

LADY CROOM.  When did he do so?

JELLABY.  As he was leaving, your ladyship.

*(Jellaby leaves. Septimus puts the letter into his pocket.)*

SEPTIMUS.  Allow me.

*(Since she does not object, he pours a cup of tea for her. She accepts it.)*

LADY CROOM.  I do not know if it is proper for you to receive a letter written
100    in my house from someone not welcome in it.

SEPTIMUS.  Very improper, I agree. Lord Byron's want of delicacy is a grief to his friends, among whom I no longer count myself. I will not read his letter until I have followed him through the gates.

*(She considers that for a moment.)*

LADY CROOM.  That may excuse the reading but not the writing.

105  SEPTIMUS.  Your ladyship should have lived in the Athens of Pericles![1] The philosophers would have fought the sculptors for your idle hour!

LADY CROOM.  (*Protesting*) Oh, really! ... (*Protesting less.*) Oh really ...

*(Septimus has taken Byron's letter from his pocket and is now setting fire to a corner of it using the little flame from the spirit lamp.)*

Oh ... really ...

*(The paper blazes in Septimus's hand and he drops it and lets it burn out on the metal tray.)*

SEPTIMUS.  Now there's a thing—a letter from Lord Byron never to be read by
110    a living soul. I will take my leave, madam, at the time of your desiring it.

LADY CROOM.  To the Indies?

---

1    *Pericles* Greek general and statesman (c. 495–429 BCE) known for fostering Athenian cultural and political prominence.

SEPTIMUS.  The Indies! Why?

LADY CROOM.  To follow the Chater, of course. She did not tell you?

SEPTIMUS.  She did not exchange half-a-dozen words with me.

LADY CROOM.  I expect she did not like to waste the time. The Chater sails    115
with Captain Brice.

SEPTIMUS.  Ah. As a member of the crew?

LADY CROOM.  No, as wife to Mr. Chater, plant-gatherer to my brother's
expedition.

SEPTIMUS.  I knew he was no poet. I did not know it was botany under the    120
false colours.

LADY CROOM.  He is no more a botanist. My brother paid fifty pounds to
have him published, and he will pay a hundred and fifty to have Mr. Chater picking flowers in the Indies for a year while the wife plays mistress of
the Captain's quarters. Captain Brice has fixed his passion on Mrs. Chater,    125
and to take her on voyage he has not scrupled to deceive the Admiralty, the
Linnean Society and Sir Joseph Banks,[1] botanist to His Majesty at Kew.

SEPTIMUS.  Her passion is not as fixed as his.

LADY CROOM.  It is a defect of God's humour that he directs our hearts everywhere but to those who have a right to them.    130

SEPTIMUS.  Indeed, madam. (*Pause.*) But is Mr. Chater deceived?

LADY CROOM.  He insists on it, and finds the proof of his wife's virtue in his
eagerness to defend it. Captain Brice is *not* deceived but cannot help himself. He would die for her.

SEPTIMUS.  I think, my lady, he would have Mr. Chater die for her.    135

LADY CROOM.  Indeed, I never knew a woman worth the duel, or the other
way about. Your letter to me goes very ill with your conduct to Mrs. Chater, Mr. Hodge. I have had experience of being betrayed before the ink is
dry, but to be betrayed before the pen is even dipped, and with the village
noticeboard, what am I to think of such a performance?    140

SEPTIMUS.  My lady, I was alone with my thoughts in the gazebo, when Mrs.
Chater ran me to ground, and I being in such a passion, in an agony of
unrelieved desire—

LADY CROOM.  Oh ...!

SEPTIMUS.  —I thought in my madness that the Chater with her skirts over    145
her head would give me the momentary illusion of the happiness to which
I dared not put a face.

(*Pause.*)

---

1    *Linnean Society* Long-standing scientific society with a specific focus on natural history; *Sir Joseph Banks* English naturalist and botanist (1743–1820).

LADY CROOM. I do not know when I have received a more unusual compliment, Mr. Hodge. I hope I am more than a match for Mrs. Chater with
150 her head in a bucket. Does she wear drawers?

SEPTIMUS. She does.

LADY CROOM. Yes, I have heard that drawers are being worn now. It is unnatural for women to be got up like jockeys. I cannot approve.

(*She turns with a whirl of skirts and moves to leave.*)

I know nothing of Pericles or the Athenian philosophers. I can spare them
155 an hour, in my sitting room when I have bathed. Seven o'clock. Bring a book.

(*She goes out. Septimus picks up the two letters, the ones he wrote, and starts to burn them in the flame of the spirit lamp.*)

## ACT 2, SCENE 7

*Valentine and Chloë are at the table. Gus is in the room.*

*Chloë is reading from two Saturday newspapers. She is wearing workaday period clothes, a Regency[1] dress, no hat.*

*Valentine is pecking at a portable computer. He is wearing unkempt Regency clothes, too.*

*The clothes have evidently come from a large wicker laundry hamper, from which Gus is producing more clothes to try on himself. He finds a Regency coat and starts putting it on.*

*The objects on the table now include two geometrical solids, pyramid and cone, about twenty inches high, of the type used in a drawing lesson; and a pot of dwarf dahlias (which do not look like modern dahlias).*

CHLOË. "Even in Arcadia—Sex, Literature and Death at Sidley Park." Picture of Byron.

VALENTINE. Not of Bernard?

CHLOË. "Byron Fought Fatal Duel, Says Don" ... Valentine, do you think I'm the first person to think of this?

5 VALENTINE. No.

CHLOË. I haven't said yet. The future is all programmed like a computer—that's a proper theory, isn't it?

VALENTINE. The deterministic universe,[2] yes.

---

1    *Regency* I.e., in the style of early nineteenth-century England.

2    *deterministic universe* Theoretical system in which all events are already determined by the universe's physical laws; the concept precludes free will.

CHLOË.  Right. Because everything including us is just a lot of atoms bounc-
ing off each other like billiard balls.                                    10

VALENTINE.  Yes. There was someone, forget his name, 1820s, who pointed
out that from Newton's laws you could predict everything to come—I
mean, you'd need a computer as big as the universe but the formula would
exist.

CHLOË.  But it doesn't work, does it?                                      15

VALENTINE.  No. It turns out the maths is different.

CHLOË.  No, it's all because of sex.

VALENTINE.  Really?

CHLOË.  That's what I think. The universe is deterministic all right, just like
Newton said, I mean it's trying to be, but the only thing going wrong is   20
people fancying people who aren't supposed to be in that part of the plan.

VALENTINE.  Ah. The attraction that Newton left out. All the way back to
the apple in the garden. Yes. (*Pause.*) Yes, I think you're the first person to
think of this.

(*Hannah enters, carrying a tabloid paper, and a mug of tea.*)

HANNAH.  Have you seen this? "Byron Bangs Wife, Shoots Hubby."       25

CHLOË.  (*Pleased*) Let's see.

(*Hannah gives her the paper, smiles at Gus.*)

VALENTINE.  He's done awfully well, hasn't he? How did they all know?

HANNAH.  Don't be ridiculous. (*To Chloë*) Your father wants it back.

CHLOË.  All right.

HANNAH.  What a fool.                                                      30

CHLOË.  Jealous. I think it's brilliant. (*She gets up to go. To Gus*) Yes, that's perfect, but not with trainers. Come on, I'll lend you a pair of flatties, they'll
look period on you—

HANNAH.  Hello, Gus. You all look so romantic.

(*Gus following Chloë out, hesitates, smiles at her.*)

CHLOË.  (*Pointedly*) Are you coming?                                      35

(*She holds the door for Gus and follows him out, leaving a sense of her
disapproval behind her.*)

HANNAH.  The important thing is not to give two monkeys for what young
people think about you.

(*She goes to look at the other newspapers.*)

VALENTINE.  (*Anxiously*) You don't think she's getting a thing about Bernard,
do you?

40   HANNAH.   I wouldn't worry about Chloë, she's old enough to vote on her back. "Byron Fought Fatal Duel, Says Don." Or rather—(*skeptically*) "Says Don!"

VALENTINE.   It may all prove to be true.

HANNAH.   It can't prove to be true, it can only not prove to be false yet.

45   VALENTINE.   (*Pleased*) Just like science.

HANNAH.   If Bernard can stay ahead of getting the rug pulled till he's dead, he'll be a success.

VALENTINE.   *Just* like science ... The ultimate fear is of posterity ...

HANNAH.   Personally I don't think it'll take that long.

50   VALENTINE.   ... and then there's the afterlife. An afterlife would be a mixed blessing. "Ah—Bernard Nightingale, I don't believe you know Lord Byron." It must be heaven up there.

HANNAH.   You can't believe in an afterlife, Valentine.

VALENTINE.   Oh, you're going to disappoint me at last.

55   HANNAH.   Am I? Why?

VALENTINE.   Science and religion.

HANNAH.   No, no, been there, done that, boring.

VALENTINE.   Oh, Hannah. Fiancée. Have pity. Can't we have a trial marriage and I'll call it off in the morning?

60   HANNAH.   (*Amused*) I don't know when I've received a more unusual proposal.

VALENTINE.   (*Interested*) Have you had many?

HANNAH.   That would be telling.

VALENTINE.   Well, why not? Your classical reserve is only a mannerism; and
65   neurotic.

HANNAH.   Do you want the room?

VALENTINE.   You get nothing if you give nothing.

HANNAH.   I ask nothing.

VALENTINE.   No, stay.

(*Valentine resumes work at his computer. Hannah establishes herself among her references at "her" end of the table. She has a stack of pocket-sized volumes, Lady Croom's "garden books."*)

70   HANNAH.   What are you doing? Valentine?

VALENTINE.   The set of points on a complex plane made by—

HANNAH.   Is it the grouse?

VALENTINE.   Oh, the grouse. The damned grouse.

HANNAH.   You mustn't give up.

75   VALENTINE.   Why? Didn't you agree with Bernard?

HANNAH.   Oh, that. It's *all* trivial—your grouse, my hermit, Bernard's Byron.

Comparing what we're looking for misses the point. It's wanting to know that makes us matter. Otherwise we're going out the way we came in. That's why you can't believe in the afterlife, Valentine. Believe in the after, by all means, but not the life. Believe in God, the soul, the spirit, the infinite, believe in angels if you like, but not in the great celestial get-together for an exchange of views. If the answers are in the back of the book I can wait, but what a drag. Better to struggle on knowing that failure is final. (*She looks over Valentine's shoulder at the computer screen. Reacting*) Oh!, but ... how beautiful!

VALENTINE. The Coverly set.

HANNAH. The Coverly set! My goodness, Valentine!

VALENTINE. Lend me a finger.

(*He takes her finger and presses one of the computer keys several times.*)

See? In an ocean of ashes, islands of order. Patterns making themselves out of nothing. I can't show you how deep it goes. Each picture is a detail of the previous one, blown up. And so on. For ever. Pretty nice, eh?

HANNAH. Is it important?

VALENTINE. Interesting. Publishable.

HANNAH. Well done!

VALENTINE. Not me. It's Thomasina's. I just pushed her equation through the computer a few million times further than she managed to do with her pencil.

(*From the old portfolio he takes Thomasina's lesson book and gives it to Hannah. The piano starts to be heard.*)

You can have it back now.

HANNAH. What does it mean?

VALENTINE. Not what you'd like it to.

HANNAH. Why not?

VALENTINE. Well, for one thing, she'd be famous.

HANNAH. No, she wouldn't. She was dead before she had time to be famous ...

VALENTINE. She died?

HANNAH. ... burned to death.

VALENTINE. (*Realizing*) Oh ... the girl who died in the fire!

HANNAH. The night before her seventeenth birthday. You can see where the dormer[1] doesn't match. That was her bedroom under the roof. There's a memorial in the Park.

---

1    *dormer* Protruding, usually windowed, section of a sloped roof.

VALENTINE. (*Irritated*) I know—it's my house.

(*Valentine turns his attention back to his computer. Hannah goes back to her chair. She looks through the lesson book.*)

HANNAH. Val, Septimus was her tutor—he and Thomasina would have—
VALENTINE. You do yours.

(*Pause. Two researchers.*

*Lord Augustus, fifteen years old, wearing clothes of 1812, bursts in through the non-music room door. He is laughing. He dives under the table. He is chased into the room by Thomasina, aged sixteen and furious. She spots Augustus immediately.*)

THOMASINA. You swore! You crossed your heart!

(*Augustus scampers out from under the table and Thomasina chases him around it.*)

115 AUGUSTUS. I'll tell mama! I'll tell mama!
THOMASINA. You beast!

(*She catches Augustus as Septimus enters from the other door, carrying a book, a decanter and a glass, and his portfolio.*)

SEPTIMUS. Hush! What is this? My lord! Order, order!

(*Thomasina and Augustus separate.*)

I am obliged.

(*Septimus goes to his place at the table. He pours himself a glass of wine.*)

AUGUSTUS. Well, good day to you, Mr. Hodge!

(*He is smirking about something.*
*Thomasina dutifully picks up a drawing book and settles down to draw the geometrical solids.*
*Septimus opens his portfolio.*)

120 SEPTIMUS. Will you join us this morning, Lord Augustus? We have our drawing lesson.
AUGUSTUS. I am a master of it at Eton, Mr. Hodge, but we only draw naked women.
SEPTIMUS. You may work from memory.
125 THOMASINA. Disgusting!
SEPTIMUS. We will have silence now, if you please.

(*From the portfolio Septimus takes Thomasina's lesson book and tosses it to her; returning homework. She snatches it and opens it.*)

THOMASINA.  No marks?! Did you not like my rabbit equation?
SEPTIMUS.  I saw no resemblance to a rabbit.
THOMASINA.  It eats its own progeny.
SEPTIMUS.  (*Pause*) I did not see that.                                              130

(*He extends his hand for the lesson book. She returns it to him.*)

THOMASINA.  I have not room to extend it.

(*Septimus and Hannah turn the pages doubled by time. Augustus indolently starts to draw the models.*)

HANNAH.  Do you mean the world is saved after all?
VALENTINE.  No, it's still doomed. But if this is how it started, perhaps it's how the next one will come.
HANNAH.  From good English algebra?                                          1135
SEPTIMUS.  It will go to infinity or zero, or nonsense.
THOMASINA.  No, if you set apart the minus roots they square back to sense.

(*Septimus turns the pages.
    Thomasina starts drawing the models.*

*Hannah closes the lesson book and turns her attention to her stack of "garden books."*)

VALENTINE.  Listen—you know your tea's getting cold.
HANNAH.  I like it cold.
VALENTINE.  (*Ignoring that*) I'm telling you something. Your tea gets cold by   140
itself, it doesn't get hot by itself. Do you think that's odd?
HANNAH.  No.
VALENTINE.  Well, it is odd. Heat goes to cold. It's a one-way street. Your tea will end up at room temperature. What's happening to your tea is happening to everything everywhere. The sun and the stars. It'll take a while   145
but we're all going to end up at room temperature. When your hermit set up shop nobody understood this. But let's say you're right, in 18-whatever nobody knew more about heat than this scribbling nutter living in a hovel in Derbyshire.
HANNAH.  He was at Cambridge—a scientist.                                      150
VALENTINE.  Say he was. I'm not arguing. And the girl was his pupil, she had a genius for her tutor.
HANNAH.  Or the other way round.

VALENTINE.  Anything you like. But not *this*! Whatever he thought he was
155   doing to save the world with good English algebra it wasn't this!

HANNAH.  Why? Because they didn't have calculators?

VALENTINE.  No. Yes. Because there's an order things can't happen in. You
   can't open a door till there's a house.

HANNAH.  I thought that's what genius was.

160   VALENTINE.  Only for lunatics and poets.

(*Pause.*)

HANNAH.  "I had a dream which was not all a dream.
         The bright sun was extinguished, and the stars
         Did wander darkling in the eternal space,
         Rayless, and pathless, and the icy earth
165         Swung blind and blackening in the moonless air ..."[1]

VALENTINE.  Your own?

HANNAH.  Byron.

(*Pause. Two researchers again.*)

THOMASINA.  Septimus, do you think that I will marry Lord Byron?

AUGUSTUS.  Who is he?

170   THOMASINA.  He is the author of "Childe Harold's Pilgrimage," the most
   poetical and pathetic and bravest hero of any book I ever read before, and
   the most modern and the handsomest, for Harold is Lord Byron himself to
   those who know him, like myself and Septimus. Well, Septimus?

SEPTIMUS.  (*Absorbed*) No.

(*Then he puts her lesson book away into the portfolio and picks up his own
book to read.*)

175   THOMASINA.  Why not?

SEPTIMUS.  For one thing, he is not aware of your existence.

THOMASINA.  We exchanged many significant glances when he was at Sidley
   Park. I do wonder that he has been home almost a year from his adventures
   and has not written to me once.

180   SEPTIMUS.  It is indeed improbable, my lady.

AUGUSTUS.  Lord Byron?!—he claimed my hare, although my shot was the
   earlier! He said I missed by a hare's breadth. His conversation was very
   facetious. But I think Lord Byron will not marry you, Thom, for he was
   only lame and not blind.

---

1   *I had a dream ... air* Opening lines of Bryon's poem "Darkness" (1816).

SEPTIMUS.  Peace! Peace until a quarter to twelve. It is intolerable for a tutor   185
to have his thoughts interrupted by his pupils.

AUGUSTUS.  You are not *my* tutor, sir. I am visiting your lesson by my free will.

SEPTIMUS.  If you are so determined, my lord.

(*Thomasina laughs at that, the joke is for her. Augustus, not included, becomes angry.*)

AUGUSTUS.  Your peace is nothing to me, sir. You do not rule over me.

THOMASINA.  (*Admonishing*) Augustus!   190

SEPTIMUS.  I do not rule here, my lord. I inspire by reverence for learning and the exaltation of knowledge whereby man may approach God. There will be a shilling for the best cone and pyramid drawn in silence by a quarter to twelve *at the earliest*.

AUGUSTUS.  You will not buy my silence for a shilling, sir. What I know to tell   195
is worth much more than that.

(*And throwing down his drawing book and pencil, he leaves the room on his dignity, closing the door sharply. Pause. Septimus looks enquiringly at Thomasina.*)

THOMASINA.  I told him you kissed me. But he will not tell.

SEPTIMUS.  When did I kiss you?

THOMASINA.  What! Yesterday!

SEPTIMUS.  Where?   200

THOMASINA.  On the lips!

SEPTIMUS.  In which county?

THOMASINA.  In the hermitage, Septimus!

SEPTIMUS.  On the lips in the hermitage! That? That was not a shilling kiss! I would not give sixpence to have it back. I had almost forgot it already.   205

THOMASINA.  Oh, cruel! Have you forgotten our compact?

SEPTIMUS.  God save me! Our compact?

THOMASINA.  To teach me to waltz! Sealed with a kiss, and a second kiss due when I can dance like mama!

SEPTIMUS.  Ah yes. Indeed. We were all waltzing like mice in London.   210

THOMASINA.  I must waltz, Septimus! I will be despised if I do not waltz! It is the most fashionable and gayest and boldest invention conceivable— started in Germany!

SEPTIMUS.  Let them have the waltz, they cannot have the calculus.

THOMASINA.  Mama has brought from town a whole book of waltzes for the   215
Broadwood, to play with Count Zelinsky.

SEPTIMUS.  I need not be told what I cannot but suffer. Count Zelinsky banging on the Broadwood without relief has me reading in waltz time.

THOMASINA. Oh, stuff! What is your book?

220 SEPTIMUS. A prize essay of the Scientific Academy in Paris.[1] The author deserves your indulgence, my lady, for you are his prophet.

THOMASINA. I? What does he write about? The waltz?

SEPTIMUS. Yes. He demonstrates the equation of the propagation of heat in a solid body. But in doing so he has discovered heresy—a natural contradic-

225 tion of Sir Isaac Newton.

THOMASINA. Oh!—he contradicts determinism?

SEPTIMUS. No! ... Well, perhaps. He shows that the atoms do not go according to Newton.[2]

> (*Her interest has switched in the mercurial way characteristic of her—she has crossed to take the book.*)

THOMASINA. Let me see—oh! In French?

230 SEPTIMUS. Yes. Paris is the capital of France.

THOMASINA. Show me where to read.

> (*He takes the book back from her and finds the page for her. Meanwhile, the piano music from the next room has doubled its notes and its emotion.*)

THOMASINA. Four-handed now! Mama is in love with the Count.

SEPTIMUS. He is a Count in Poland. In Derbyshire he is a piano tuner.

> (*She has taken the book and is already immersed in it. The piano music becomes rapidly more passionate, and then breaks off suddenly in mid-phrase. There is an expressive silence next door which makes Septimus raise his eyes. It does not register with Thomasina. The silence allows us to hear the distant regular thump of the steam engine which is to be a topic. A few moments later Lady Croom enters from the music room, seeming surprised and slightly flustered to find the schoolroom occupied. She collects herself, closing the door behind her. And remains watching, aimless and discreet, as though not wanting to interrupt the lesson. Septimus has stood, and she nods him back into his chair.*)

> *Chloë, in Regency dress, enters from the door opposite the music room. She takes in Valentine and Hannah but crosses without pausing to the music room door.*)

---

1   *prize essay ... in Paris* Septimus is reading "On the Propagation of Heat in Solid Bodies" (1812), an essay by the French physicist Joseph Fourier.

2   *the atoms ... to Newton* Newton's laws do not distinguish a temporal direction—theoretically, the processes they describe could happen either backwards or forwards in time—but processes involving the transfer of heat cannot be reversed. Fourier did not show this, but his work constituted a step toward the formulation of the second law of thermodynamics, which would.

CHLOË.  Oh!—where's Gus?

VALENTINE.  Dunno.                                                                        235

(*Chloë goes into the music room.*)

LADY CROOM.  (*Annoyed*) Oh!—Mr. Noakes's engine!

(*She goes to the garden door and steps outside.*

*Chloë re-enters.*)

CHLOË.  Damn.

LADY CROOM.  (*Calls out*) Mr. Noakes!

VALENTINE.  He was there not long ago ...

LADY CROOM.  Halo!?                                                                       240

CHLOË.  Well, he has to be in the photograph—is he dressed?

HANNAH.  Is Bernard back?

CHLOË.  No—he's late!

(*The piano is heard again, under the noise of the steam engine.*
*Lady Croom steps back into the room.*

*Chloë steps outside the garden door. Shouts.*)

Gus!

LADY CROOM.  I wonder you can teach against such a disturbance and I am           245
sorry for it, Mr. Hodge.

(*Chloë comes back inside.*)

VALENTINE.  (*Getting up*) Stop ordering everybody about.

LADY CROOM.  It is an unendurable noise.

VALENTINE.  The photographer will wait.

(*But, grumbling, he follows Chloë out of the door she came in by, and closes*
*the door behind them. Hannah remains absorbed.*
   *In the silence, the rhythmic thump can be heard again.*)

LADY CROOM.  The ceaseless dull overbearing monotony of it! It will drive me        250
distracted. I may have to return to town to escape it.

SEPTIMUS.  Your ladyship could remain in the country and let Count Zelinsky return to town where you would not hear him.

LADY CROOM.  I mean Mr. Noakes's engine! (*Semi-aside to Septimus.*) Would
you sulk? I will not have my daughter study sulking.                               255

THOMASINA.  (*Not listening*) What, mama?

(*Thomasina remains lost in her book. Lady Croom returns to close the garden door and the noise of the steam engine subsides.*

*Hannah closes one of the "garden books," and opens the next. She is making occasional notes.*

*The piano ceases.*)

LADY CROOM. (*To Thomasina*) What are we learning today? (*Pause.*) Well, not manners.

SEPTIMUS. We are drawing today.

(*Lady Croom negligently examines what Thomasina had started to draw.*)

260 LADY CROOM. Geometry. I approve of geometry.

SEPTIMUS. Your ladyship's approval is my constant object.

LADY CROOM. Well, do not despair of it. (*Returning to the window impatiently.*) Where is "Culpability" Noakes? (*She looks out and is annoyed.*) Oh!—he has gone for his hat so that he may remove it.

(*She returns to the table and touches the bowl of dahlias.*

*Hannah sits back in her chair, caught by what she is reading.*)

265 For the widow's dowry of dahlias I can almost forgive my brother's marriage. We must be thankful the monkey bit Mr. Chater. If it had bit Mrs. Chater the monkey would be dead and we would not be first in the kingdom to show a dahlia. (*Hannah, still reading the garden book, stands up.*) I sent one potted to Chatsworth. The Duchess was most satisfactorily put
270 out by it when I called at Devonshire House. Your friend was there lording it as a poet.

(*Hannah leaves through the door, following Valentine and Chloë.*

*Meanwhile, Thomasina thumps the book down on the table.*)

THOMASINA. Well! Just as I said! Newton's machine which would knock our atoms from cradle to grave by the laws of motion is incomplete! Determinism leaves the road at every corner, as I knew all along, and the cause is very
275 likely hidden in this gentleman's observation.

LADY CROOM. Of what?

THOMASINA. The action of bodies in heat.

LADY CROOM. Is this geometry?

THOMASINA. This? No, I despise geometry!

280 LADY CROOM. (*Touching the dahlias she adds, almost to herself.*) The Chater would overthrow the Newtonian system in a weekend.

SEPTIMUS.  Geometry, Hobbes[1] assures us in the *Leviathan*, is the only science God has been pleased to bestow on mankind.

LADY CROOM.  And what does he mean by it?

SEPTIMUS.  Mr. Hobbes or God?

LADY CROOM.  I am sure I do not know what either means by it.

THOMASINA.  Oh, pooh to Hobbes! Mountains are not pyramids and trees are not cones. God must love gunnery and architecture if Euclid[2] is his only geometry. There is another geometry which I am engaged in discovering by trial and error, am I not, Septimus?

SEPTIMUS.  Trial and error perfectly describes your enthusiasm, my lady.

LADY CROOM.  How old are you today?

THOMASINA.  Sixteen years and eleven months, mama, and three weeks.

LADY CROOM.  Sixteen years and eleven months. We must have you married before you are educated beyond eligibility.

THOMASINA.  I am going to marry Lord Byron.

LADY CROOM.  Are you? He did not have the manners to mention it.

THOMASINA.  You have spoken to him?!

LADY CROOM.  Certainly not.

THOMASINA.  Where did you see him?

LADY CROOM.  (*With some bitterness*) Everywhere.

THOMASINA.  Did you, Septimus?

SEPTIMUS.  At the Royal Academy where I had the honour to accompany your mother and Count Zelinsky.

THOMASINA.  What was Lord Byron doing?

LADY CROOM.  Posing.

SEPTIMUS.  (*Tactfully*) He was being sketched during his visit ... by the Professor of Painting ... Mr. Fuseli.

LADY CROOM.  There was more posing *at* the pictures than *in* them. His companion likewise reversed the custom of the Academy that the ladies viewing wear more than the ladies viewed—well, enough! Let him be hanged there for a Lamb. I have enough with Mr. Noakes, who is to a garden what a bull is to a china shop.

(*This as Noakes enters.*)

---

1    *Hobbes* Thomas Hobbes, English philosopher best known for his book *Leviathan* (1651), in which he argues that without a powerful government to keep its natural tendencies in check, humankind would revert to lawlessness and violence.

2    *Euclid* Greek mathematician (fl. 300 BCE) whose work provided the foundation for all geometry for the next two millennia; the first work to explicitly contradict Euclid's geometry was published in the 1820s. Euclidean geometry is still used for most practical applications, such as architecture, but more complex forms of geometry also have applications in the physical world.

THOMASINA. The Emperor of Irregularity!

(*She settles down to drawing the diagram which is to be the third item in the surviving portfolio.*)

320  LADY CROOM. Mr. Noakes!

NOAKES. Your ladyship—

LADY CROOM. What have you done to me!

NOAKES. Everything is satisfactory, I assure you. A little behind, to be sure, but my dam will be repaired within the month—

325  LADY CROOM. (*Banging the table*) Hush!

(*In the silence, the steam engine thumps in the distance.*)

Can you hear, Mr. Noakes?

NOAKES. (*Pleased and proud*) The Improved Newcomen steam pump[1]—the only one in England!

LADY CROOM. That is what I object to. If everybody had his own I would

330  bear my portion of the agony without complaint. But to have been singled out by the only Improved Newcomen steam pump in England, this is hard, sir, this is not to be borne.

NOAKES. Your lady—

LADY CROOM. And for what? My lake is drained to a ditch for no purpose

335  I can understand, unless it be that snipe and curlew[2] have deserted three counties so that they may be shot in our swamp. What you painted as forest is a mean plantation, your greenery is mud, your waterfall is wet mud, and your mount is an opencast mine for the mud that was lacking in the dell. (*Pointing through the window.*) What is that cowshed?

340  NOAKES. The hermitage, my lady?

LADY CROOM. It is a cowshed.

NOAKES. Madam, it is, I assure you, a very habitable cottage, properly founded and drained, two rooms and a closet under a slate roof and a stone chimney—

345  LADY CROOM. And who is to live in it?

NOAKES. Why, the hermit.

LADY CROOM. Where is he?

NOAKES. Madam?

LADY CROOM. You surely do not supply a hermitage without a hermit?

350  NOAKES. Indeed, madam—

1  *Newcomen steam pump* The first steam engine to convert steam into practical mechanical energy; it was created in 1712 by the English inventor Thomas Newcomen.

2  *snipe and curlew* Two different types of long-legged birds, found in marshes and wetlands.

LADY CROOM.  Come, come, Mr. Noakes. If I am promised a fountain I expect it to come with water. What hermits do you have?

NOAKES.  I have no hermits, my lady.

LADY CROOM.  Not one? I am speechless.

NOAKES.  I am sure a hermit can be found. One could advertise.    355

LADY CROOM.  Advertise?

NOAKES.  In the newspapers.

LADY CROOM.  But surely a hermit who takes a newspaper is not a hermit in whom one can have complete confidence.

NOAKES.  I do not know what to suggest, my lady.    360

SEPTIMUS.  Is there room for a piano?

NOAKES.  (*Baffled*) A piano?

LADY CROOM.  We are intruding here—this will not do, Mr. Hodge. Evidently, nothing is being learned. (*To Noakes*) Come along, sir!

THOMASINA.  Mr. Noakes—bad news from Paris!    365

NOAKES.  Is it the Emperor Napoleon?

THOMASINA.  No. (*She tears the page off her drawing block, with her "diagram" on it.*) It concerns your heat engine. Improve it as you will, you can never get out of it what you put in. It repays eleven pence in the shilling[1] at most. The penny is for this author's thoughts.    370

(*She gives the diagram to Septimus who looks at it.*)

NOAKES.  (*Baffled again*) Thank you, my lady.

(*Noakes goes out into the garden.*)

LADY CROOM.  (*To Septimus*) Do you understand her?

SEPTIMUS.  No.

LADY CROOM.  Then this business is over. I was married at seventeen. *Ce soir il faut qu'on parle français, je te demande,*[2] Thomasina, as a courtesy to the    375 Count. Wear your green velvet, please, I will send Briggs to do your hair. Sixteen and eleven months ...!

(*She follows Noakes out of view.*)

THOMASINA.  Lord Byron was with a lady?

SEPTIMUS.  Yes.

THOMASINA.  Huh!    380

(*Now Septimus retrieves his book from Thomasina. He turns the pages, and also continues to study Thomasina's diagram. He strokes the tortoise*

---

1    *shilling* Twelve pence.
2    *Ce soir ... demande* French: I ask that tonight we speak French.

468    DRAMA

*absently as he reads. Thomasina takes up pencil and paper and starts to draw Septimus with Plautus.)*

SEPTIMUS.  Why does it mean Mr. Noakes's engine pays eleven pence in the shilling? Where does he say it?

THOMASINA.  Nowhere. I noticed it by the way. I cannot remember now.

SEPTIMUS.  Nor is he interested by determinism—

385 THOMASINA.  Oh ... yes. Newton's equations go forwards and backwards, they do not care which way. But the heat equation cares very much, it goes only one way. That is the reason Mr. Noakes's engine cannot give the power to drive Mr. Noakes's engine.

SEPTIMUS.  Everybody knows that.

390 THOMASINA.  Yes, Septimus, they know it about engines!

SEPTIMUS.  (*Pause. He looks at his watch.*) A quarter to twelve. For your essay this week, explicate your diagram.

THOMASINA.  I cannot. I do not know the mathematics.

SEPTIMUS.  Without mathematics, then.

*(Thomasina has continued to draw. She tears the top page from her drawing pad and gives it to Septimus.)*

395 THOMASINA.  There. I have made a drawing of you and Plautus.

SEPTIMUS.  (*Looking at it*) Excellent likeness. Not so good of me.

*(Thomasina laughs, and leaves the room.*
*Augustus appears at the garden door. His manner cautious and diffident.*
*Septimus does not notice him for a moment.*
*Septimus gathers his papers together.)*

AUGUSTUS.  Sir ...

SEPTIMUS.  My lord ...?

AUGUSTUS.  I gave you offence, sir, and I am sorry for it.

400 SEPTIMUS.  I took none, my lord, but you are kind to mention it.

AUGUSTUS.  I would like to ask you a question, Mr. Hodge. (*Pause.*) You have an elder brother, I dare say, being a Septimus?[1]

SEPTIMUS.  Yes, my lord. He lives in London. He is the editor of a newspaper, the *Piccadilly Recreation*. (*Pause.*) Was that your question?

*(Augustus, evidently embarrassed about something, picks up the drawing of Septimus.)*

405 AUGUSTUS.  No. Oh ... it is you? ... I would like to keep it. (*Septimus inclines his head in assent.*) There are things a fellow cannot ask his friends. Carnal

---

1    *Septimus*  In Latin, "*septimus*" means "seventh."

things. My sister has told me ... my sister believes such things as I cannot, I assure you, bring myself to repeat.

SEPTIMUS.  You must not repeat them, then. The walk between here and dinner will suffice to put us straight, if we stroll by the garden. It is an   410 easy business. And then I must rely on you to correct your sister's state of ignorance.

(*A commotion is heard outside—Bernard's loud voice in a sort of agony.*)

BERNARD.  (*outside the door*) Oh no—no—no—oh, bloody hell!—

AUGUSTUS.  Thank you, Mr. Hodge, I will.

(*Taking the drawing with him, Augustus allows himself to be shown out through the garden door, and Septimus follows him.*

*Bernard enters the room, through the door Hannah left by. Valentine comes in with him, leaving the door open and they are followed by Hannah who is holding the "garden book."*)

BERNARD.  Oh, no—no—   415

HANNAH.  I'm sorry, Bernard.

BERNARD.  Fucked by a dahlia! Do you think? Is it open and shut? Am I fucked? What does it really amount to? When all's said and done? Am I fucked? What do you think, Valentine? Tell me the truth.

VALENTINE.  You're fucked.   420

BERNARD.  Oh God! Does it mean that?

HANNAH.  Yes, Bernard, it does.

BERNARD.  I'm not sure. Show me where it says. I want to see it. No—read it—no, wait ...

(*Bernard sits at the table. He prepares to listen as though listening were an oriental art.*)

Right.   425

HANNAH.  (*Reading*) "October 1st, 1810. Today under the direction of Mr. Noakes, a parterre[1] was dug on the south lawn and will be a handsome show next year, a consolation for the picturesque catastrophe of the second and third distances. The dahlia having propagated under glass with no ill effect from the sea voyage, is named by Captain Brice 'Charity' for his   430 bride, though the honour properly belongs to the husband who exchanged beds with my dahlia, and an English summer for everlasting night in the Indies."

---

1   *parterre* Type of level garden with carefully arranged flowerbeds and pathways.

(*Pause.*)

BERNARD. Well it's so round the houses, isn't it? Who's to say what it means?

435 HANNAH. (*Patiently*) It means that Ezra Chater of the Sidley Park connection is the same Chater who described a dwarf dahlia in Martinique in 1810 and died there, of a monkey bite.

BERNARD. (*Wildly*) Ezra wasn't a botanist! He was a poet!

HANNAH. He was not much of either, but he was both.

440 VALENTINE. It's not a disaster.

BERNARD. Of course it's a disaster! I was on "The Breakfast Hour!"

VALENTINE. It doesn't mean Byron didn't fight a duel, it only means Chater wasn't killed in it.

BERNARD. Oh, pull yourself together!—do you think I'd have been on "The
445 Breakfast Hour" if Byron had *missed*!

HANNAH. Calm down, Bernard. Valentine's right.

BERNARD. (*Grasping at straws*) Do you think so? You mean the *Piccadilly* reviews? Yes, two completely unknown Byron essays—*and* my discovery of the lines he added to 'English Bards'. That counts for something.

450 HANNAH. (*Tactfully*) Very possible—persuasive, indeed.

BERNARD. Oh, bugger persuasive! I've proved Byron was here and as far as I'm concerned he wrote those lines as sure as he shot that hare. If only I hadn't somehow ... made it all about *killing Chater*. Why didn't you stop me?! It's bound to get out, you know—I mean this—this *gloss* on my discovery—I
455 mean how long do you think it'll be before some botanical pedant blows the whistle on me?

HANNAH. The day after tomorrow. A letter in *The Times*.

BERNARD. You wouldn't.

HANNAH. It's a dirty job but somebody—

460 BERNARD. Darling. Sorry. Hannah—

HANNAH. —and, after all, it is my discovery.

BERNARD. Hannah.

HANNAH. Bernard.

BERNARD. Hannah.

465 HANNAH. Oh, shut up. It'll be very short, very dry, absolutely gloat-free. Would you rather it were one of your friends?

BERNARD. (*Fervently*) Oh God, no!

HANNAH. And then in *your* letter to *The Times*—

BERNARD. Mine?

470 HANNAH. Well, of course. Dignified congratulations to a colleague, in the language of scholars, I trust.

BERNARD. Oh, eat shit, you mean?

HANNAH. Think of it as a breakthrough in dahlia studies.

(*Chloë hurries in from the garden.*)

CHLOË. Why aren't you coming?!—Bernard! And you're not dressed! How long have you been back?  475

(*Bernard looks at her and then at Valentine and realizes for the first time that Valentine is unusually dressed.*)

BERNARD. Why are you wearing those clothes?
CHLOË. Do be quick!

(*She is already digging into the basket and producing odd garments for Bernard.*)

Just put anything on. We're all being photographed. Except Hannah.
HANNAH. I'll come and watch.

(*Valentine and Chloë help Bernard into a decorative coat and fix a lace collar round his neck.*)

CHLOË. (*To Hannah*) Mummy says have you got the theodolite?  480
VALENTINE. What are you supposed to be, Chloë? Bo-Peep?
CHLOË. Jane Austen![1]
VALENTINE. Of course.
HANNAH. (*To Chloë*) Oh—it's in the hermitage! Sorry.
BERNARD. I thought it wasn't till this evening. What photograph?  485
CHLOË. The local paper of course—they always come before we start. We want a good crowd of us—Gus looks gorgeous—
BERNARD. (*Aghast*) The newspaper!

(*He grabs something like a bishop's mitre[2] from the basket and pulls it down completely over his face.*)

(*Muffled*) I'm ready!

(*And he staggers out with Valentine and Chloë, followed by Hannah.*
*A light change to evening. The paper lanterns outside begin to glow. Piano music from the next room.*

*Septimus enters with an oil lamp. He carries Thomasina's algebra primer, and also her essay on loose sheets. He settles down to read at the table. It is nearly dark outside, despite the lanterns.*)

---

1  *Jane Austen* English author (1775–1817).
2  *mitre* Tall, pointed hat.

*Thomasina enters, in a nightgown and barefoot, holding a candlestick. Her manner is secretive and excited.*)

490   SEPTIMUS.  My lady! What is it?
THOMASINA.  Septimus! Shush!

(*She closes the door quietly.*)

Now is our chance!
SEPTIMUS.  For what, dear God?

(*She blows out the candle and puts the candlestick on the table.*)

THOMASINA.  Do not act the innocent! Tomorrow I will be seventeen!

(*She kisses Septimus full on the mouth.*)

495   There!
SEPTIMUS.  Dear Christ!
THOMASINA.  Now you must show me, you are paid in advance.
SEPTIMUS.  (*Understanding*) Oh!
THOMASINA.  The Count plays for us, it is God-given! I cannot be seventeen
500   and not waltz.
SEPTIMUS.  But your mother—
THOMASINA.  While she swoons, we can dance. The house is all abed. I heard
the Broadwood. Oh, Septimus, teach me now!
SEPTIMUS.  Hush! I cannot now!
505   THOMASINA.  Indeed you can, and I am come barefoot so mind my toes.
SEPTIMUS.  I cannot because it is not a waltz.
THOMASINA.  It is not?
SEPTIMUS.  No, it is too slow for waltzing.
THOMASINA.  Oh! Then we will wait for him to play quickly.
510   SEPTIMUS.  My lady—
THOMASINA.  Mr. Hodge!

(*She takes a chair next to him and looks at his work.*)

Are you reading my essay? Why do you work here so late?
SEPTIMUS.  To save my candles.
THOMASINA.  You have my old primer.
515   SEPTIMUS.  It is mine again. You should not have written in it.

(*She takes it, looks at the open page.*)

THOMASINA.  It was a joke.
SEPTIMUS.  It will make me mad as you promised. Sit over there. You will have
us in disgrace.

(*Thomasina gets up and goes to the furthest chair.*)

THOMASINA.  If mama comes I will tell her we only met to kiss, not to waltz.
SEPTIMUS.  Silence or bed.                                                      520
THOMASINA.  Silence!

(*Septimus pours himself some more wine. He continues to read her essay.*
   *The music changes to party music from the marquee. And there are fireworks—small against the sky, distant flares of light like exploding meteors.*

*Hannah enters. She has dressed for the party. The difference is not, however, dramatic. She closes the door and crosses to leave by the garden door. But as she gets there, Valentine is entering. He has a glass of wine in his hand.*)

HANNAH.  Oh ...

(*But Valentine merely brushes past her, intent on something, and half-drunk.*)

VALENTINE.  (*To her*) Got it!

(*He goes straight to the table and roots about in what is now a considerable mess of papers, books and objects. Hannah turns back, puzzled by his manner. He finds what he has been looking for—the "diagram."*

*Meanwhile, Septimus reading Thomasina's essay, also studies the diagram. Septimus and Valentine study the diagram doubled by time.*)

VALENTINE.  It's heat.
HANNAH.  Are you tight,[1] Val?                                                 525
VALENTINE.  It's a diagram of heat exchange.
SEPTIMUS.  So, we are all doomed!
THOMASINA.  (*Cheerfully*) Yes.
VALENTINE.  Like a steam engine, you see—

(*Hannah fills Septimus's glass from the same decanter, and sips from it.*)

She didn't have the maths, not remotely. She saw what things meant, way   530
ahead, like seeing a picture.
SEPTIMUS.  This is not science. This is story-telling.
THOMASINA.  Is it a waltz now?
SEPTIMUS.  No.

(*The music is still modern.*)

---

1    *tight* Drunk.

535  VALENTINE.  Like a film.

HANNAH.  What did she see?

VALENTINE.  That you can't run the film backwards. Heat was the first thing which didn't work that way. Not like Newton. A film of a pendulum, or a ball falling through the air—backwards, it looks the same.

540  HANNAH.  The ball would be going the wrong way.

VALENTINE.  You'd have to know that. But with heat—friction—a ball breaking a window—

HANNAH.  Yes.

VALENTINE.  It won't work backwards.

545  HANNAH.  Who thought it did?

VALENTINE.  She saw why. You can put back the bits of glass but you can't collect up the heat of the smash. It's gone.

SEPTIMUS.  So the Improved Newtonian Universe must cease and grow cold. Dear me.

550  VALENTINE.  The heat goes into the mix.

(*He gestures to indicate the air in the room, in the universe.*)

THOMASINA.  Yes, we must hurry if we are going to dance.

VALENTINE.  And everything is mixing the same way, all the time, irreversibly ...

SEPTIMUS.  Oh, we have time, I think.

555  VALENTINE.  ... till there's no time left. That's what time means.

SEPTIMUS.  When we have found all the mysteries and lost all the meaning, we will be alone, on an empty shore.

THOMASINA.  Then we will dance. Is this a waltz?

SEPTIMUS.  It will serve.

(*He stands up.*)

560  THOMASINA.  (*Jumping up*) Goody!

(*Septimus takes her in his arms carefully and the waltz lesson, to the music from the marquee, begins.*

*Bernard, in unconvincing Regency dress, enters carrying a bottle.*)

BERNARD.  Don't mind me, I left my jacket ...

(*He heads for the area of the wicker basket.*)

VALENTINE.  Are you leaving?

(*Bernard is stripping off his period coat. He is wearing his own trousers, tucked into knee socks and his own shirt.*)

BERNARD. Yes, I'm afraid so.

HANNAH. What's up, Bernard?

BERNARD. Nothing I can go into—    565

VALENTINE. Should I go?

BERNARD. No, *I'm* going!

(*Valentine and Hannah watch Bernard struggling into his jacket and adjusting his clothes.*

*Septimus, holding Thomasina, kisses her on the mouth. The waltz lesson pauses. She looks at him. He kisses her again, in earnest. She puts her arms round him.*)

THOMASINA. Septimus ...

(*Septimus hushes her. They start to dance again, with the slight awkwardness of a lesson.*

*Chloë bursts in from the garden.*)

CHLOË. I'll kill her! I'll *kill* her!

BERNARD. Oh dear.    570

VALENTINE. What the hell is it, Chlo?

CHLOË. (*Venomously*) Mummy!

BERNARD. (*To Valentine*) Your mother caught us in that cottage.

CHLOË. She snooped!

BERNARD. I don't think so. She was rescuing a theodolite.    575

CHLOË. I'll come with you, Bernard.

BERNARD. No, you bloody won't.

CHLOË. Don't you want me to?

BERNARD. Of course not. What for? (*To Valentine*) I'm sorry.

CHLOË. (*In furious tears*) What are you saying sorry to *him* for?    580

BERNARD. Sorry to you too. Sorry one and all. Sorry, Hannah—sorry, Hermione—sorry, Byron—sorry, sorry, sorry, now can I go?

(*Chloë stands stiffly, tearfully.*)

CHLOË. Well ...

(*Thomasina and Septimus dance.*)

HANNAH. What a bastard you are, Bernard.

(*Chloë rounds on her.*)

CHLOË. And you mind your own business! What do you know about any-    585
thing?

HANNAH. Nothing.

CHLOË. (*to Bernard*) It *was* worth it, though, wasn't it?

BERNARD. It was wonderful.

(*Chloë goes out, through the garden door, towards the party.*)

590 HANNAH. (*An echo*) Nothing.

VALENTINE. Well, you shit. I'd drive you but I'm a bit sloshed.

(*Valentine follows Chloë out and can be heard outside calling "Chlo! Chlo!"*)

BERNARD. A scrape.

HANNAH. Oh ... (*she gives up*) Bernard!

BERNARD. I look forward to *The Genius of the Place*. I hope you find your
595   hermit. I think out front is the safest.

(*He opens the door cautiously and looks out.*)

HANNAH. Actually, I've got a good idea who he was, but I can't prove it.

BERNARD. (*With a carefree expansive gesture*) Publish!

(*He goes out closing the door.*

*Septimus and Thomasina are now waltzing freely. She is delighted with
herself.*)

THOMASINA. Am I waltzing?

SEPTIMUS. Yes, my lady.

(*He gives her a final twirl, bringing them to the table where he bows to her.
He lights her candlestick.*

*Hannah goes to sit at the table, playing truant from the party. She pours
herself more wine. The table contains the geometrical solids, the computer,
decanter, glasses, tea mug, Hannah's research books, Septimus's books, the
two portfolios, Thomasina's candlestick, the oil lamp, the dahlia, the Sunday
papers ...*

*Gus appears in the doorway. It takes a moment to realize that he is not
Lord Augustus; perhaps not until Hannah sees him.*)

600 SEPTIMUS. Take your essay, I have given it an alpha in blind faith. Be careful
with the flame.

THOMASINA. I will wait for you to come.

SEPTIMUS. I cannot.

THOMASINA. You may.

605 SEPTIMUS. I may not.

THOMASINA. You must.

SEPTIMUS.  I will not.

(*She puts the candlestick and the essay on the table.*)

THOMASINA.  Then I will not go. Once more, for my birthday.

(*Septimus and Thomasina start to waltz together.*

*Gus comes forward, startling Hannah.*)

HANNAH.  Oh!—you made me jump.

(*Gus looks resplendent. He is carrying an old and somewhat tattered stiff-backed folio fastened with a tape tied in a bow. He comes to Hannah and thrusts this present at her.*)

Oh ...                                                                    610

(*She lays the folio down on the table and starts to open it. It consists only of two boards hinged, containing Thomasina's drawing.*)

"Septimus holding Plautus." (*To Gus*) I was looking for that. Thank you.

(*Gus nods several times. Then, rather awkwardly, he bows to her. A Regency bow, an invitation to dance.*)

Oh, dear, I don't really ...

(*After a moment's hesitation, she gets up and they hold each other, keeping a decorous distance between them, and start to dance, rather awkwardly.*

*Septimus and Thomasina continue to dance, fluently, to the piano.*)

**END**

—1993

# *Hannah Moscovitch*
b. 1978

Toronto-based playwright Hannah Moscovitch, called "the wunderkind of Canadian theatre" by CBC radio, achieved national success early in her career. She made her name by addressing difficult subjects—in her words, finding "unusual slants on old topics, complex stories, and unheard voices"—in a style that often blends satire and dark humour with emotional sensitivity. "The darker the story gets, the funnier it gets," she has said; "that's what life seems like to me."

Moscovitch was born in Ottawa and grew up in a left-leaning, academic environment; her father was a professor of social policy and her mother a labour researcher and writer of feminist non-fiction. After graduating from the National Theatre School of Canada in the acting stream, Moscovitch studied literature at the University of Toronto. She worked as a waitress at an upscale Toronto restaurant for several years before her successes enabled her to write full-time.

Moscovitch first gained widespread acclaim with the debut of her short plays *Essay* (2005) and *The Russian Play* (2006) at Toronto's SummerWorks festival; *Essay* won the Contra Guys Award for Best New Play, and *The Russian Play* was awarded Jury Prize for Best New Production. She is still perhaps best known for these works—together with *East of Berlin* (2007), which won the Dora Mavor Moore Award and was nominated for a Governor General's Award in 2009.

The content of Moscovitch's work is often challenging or controversial: *Essay* confronts issues of gender and power in academia, *East of Berlin* addresses the legacy of the Holocaust, and *This Is War* (2013) is based on a true story involving Canadian soldiers in 2008 Afghanistan. Regarding the social and political complexity of her plays, she says, "I want to ask the audience questions. I get excited by the idea of a character being forced to confront a hostile audience. There's something so fascinating about watching those dynamics play out."

# Essay

## CHARACTERS

Jeffrey: thirty
Pixie: eighteen
Professor Galbraith: early sixties

## SCENE 1

*A small office on campus. An open laptop sits on a desk amidst piles of papers, files and books. The greenish hue of fluorescent lighting fills the room. Lights up on Jeffrey, behind the desk, and Pixie, in front of it.*

JEFFREY. Just, uh, please take a seat while I finish this paragraph and then I'll leave off.

PIXIE. Am I early ...? Or ...?

JEFFREY. No, no, just finishing up, just finishing up.

(*Jeffrey closes his laptop.*)

Now. Essay proposal, is that right? Essay due on the eighteenth?    5

PIXIE. Thank you for letting me come and—

JEFFREY. No, please. Just remind me. I rejected your proposal, is that ...?

PIXIE. Uh, yes, you did, but—

JEFFREY. Right. Good. Well, my notes are vague sometimes, and my hand-writing is very bad, so before you raze the field, we might as well take a    10
closer look at it.

PIXIE. (*getting out her essay proposal*) Okay, great, um, well what I wanted to—

JEFFREY. It's usually just a question of coming up with an alteration that will render it—    15

PIXIE. —um, okay—

JEFFREY. —more precise, more scholarly.

PIXIE. Okay. That's what I wanted to talk to you about.

JEFFREY. Good. Yes. Let's talk!

PIXIE. Your objections, because I—I think I can make an argument for this    20
essay proposal.

JEFFREY. This one?

PIXIE. Yeah.

JEFFREY. This essay proposal?

PIXIE. Yes?    25

(*Beat.*)

JEFFREY. Ah. I see. You've come to contest.

PIXIE. Or at least I just wanted to—

JEFFREY. To make your case, is that it?

PIXIE. I—I just think that—that it's possible—that it's possible to argue, I
30    mean if the problem is just sourcing.

JEFFREY. Let me take a look at it, can I?

(*Pixie hands him the essay proposal.*)

Let's just see what we've got here before we ... (*laughs*) ... have it out.

(*Beat.*)

PIXIE. (*waiting, shifting*) If—if you read the notes you made ...

(*Jeffrey holds out his hand to indicate to Pixie that she should give him a
minute to finish reading.*)

(*Beat.*)

JEFFREY. (*scanning*) Elizabeth Farnese.[1] Strategies of, important contributions
35    to. Summary, summary, more summary. Look. What you've got here is
very interesting. A very interesting historical figure—

PIXIE. Yeah, well I thought—

JEFFREY. —who no doubt deserves more.... An argument could be made
that this is an oversight. The historical record has failed to illuminate this
40    neglected but highly engaging corner of European history.

PIXIE. Unhunh, well—

JEFFREY. Hoards of insensitive historians have obscured a very important
character, as it were.

PIXIE. Yeah, well—

45   JEFFREY. And she is worthy, entitled to, a second glance, now, in our modern
era. However, that said—

PIXIE. Unhunh.

JEFFREY. —that said, I'm not sure that for the purposes of this first year
course it's—it's—if there would be enough material to support a ten-page
50    essay on the topic.

PIXIE. Yeah, but—

JEFFREY. Ten pages. You'll need more than a cursory—

PIXIE. Yeah.

---

1    *Elizabeth Farnese* Italian noblewoman (1692–1766) and queen consort of Spain.
Through her influence over her husband Philip V, she orchestrated Spain's foreign policy,
including the country's involvement in several wars. Because Philip already had children
by his first wife, Elizabeth's primary ambition was to secure Italian thrones for her sons.

JEFFREY. —more than a brief mention in a larger—

PIXIE. Yeah, I have. I have plenty of material. And also, there's one listed at    55
the bottom of the supplementary readings, on page twenty-one.

JEFFREY. One what?

PIXIE. An article on her.

(*Beat.*)

JEFFREY. That's very possible, all right.

PIXIE. And I found ample sources in the stacks.    60

JEFFREY. That's very possible.

PIXIE. And the article was on the list—

JEFFREY. Right, right I see the—now we're getting to the bottom of the—

PIXIE. —and so—

JEFFREY. This is progress!    65

PIXIE. And so, I thought—

JEFFREY. You thought it was on the list, it must be—

PIXIE. Yeah.

JEFFREY. And I want to stress that your idea is not invalid, by any means, all
right?    70

PIXIE. Unhunh.

JEFFREY. At least not in general terms, all right?

PIXIE. Unhunh?

(*Beat.*)

JEFFREY. I'm not the—I don't want to be the big bad—

PIXIE. Yeah?    75

JEFFREY. —the big bad—

PIXIE. Yeah?

JEFFREY. Is that ...? Is it Pixie? Is that your ...?

PIXIE. Yeah. Pixie.

JEFFREY. Look, Pixie—    80

PIXIE. Yeah?

JEFFREY. I understand you feel very passionately about this. Here you are in
my office, overflowing with passion ... (*laughs*) ...

(*Pixie shifts away from Jeffrey.*)

No, no, what I mean is you've made the effort to come here, to defend
your proposal to me, the topic you've chosen indicates that you're trying to    85
avoid the banal and revitalize history, as it were, and so—

PIXIE. Yeah?

JEFFREY. I want to stress that I appreciate your passion.

(*Beat.*)

PIXIE. But—

90 JEFFREY. Your topic is frankly.... You see, this is a history course that—

PIXIE. And this is history.

JEFFREY. Yes, yes it's history, but Pixie, this course deals with war and state-craft. In the eighteenth and early nineteenth century.

PIXIE. Yeah?

95 JEFFREY. Eighteenth and early nineteenth century. Now I'm not saying that women haven't, in more recent times, made very valuable contributions to war efforts. But, in the eighteenth century, women didn't yet—

PIXIE. —unhuhn—

JEFFREY. —possess the freedom of movement, the—the wherewithal to—

100 PIXIE. —unhuhn—

JEFFREY. —and so women couldn't as yet be classified as "military leaders," per se.

PIXIE. Okay, but—

JEFFREY. And—just a minute—and that is why I can't allow you to write a

105 paper on a woman who, while she may be very compelling from a social history perspective—

PIXIE. Yeah, but she—

JEFFREY. —is not an appropriate subject given the requirements of this par-ticular writing assignment. Now I commend you for finding source mate-

110 rial. Good work there! But the thing is you're simply not on topic.

(*Jeffrey hands back Pixie's essay proposal.*)

If you need to hear this from a higher source, by all means, take it up with the professor, he is the final word—

PIXIE. No, it's fine, I'm just—I don't know, a little—

JEFFREY. Disappointed, I see that.

115 PIXIE. No, I'm confused.

JEFFREY. Yes. Confused, disappointed, and believe me, I understand. Euro-pean history is a ... bewildering series of men who prance about, waging war, and making a nuisance of themselves. And so, you light on Elizabeth Farnese because you'd like to champion her, establish her worth, she is one

120 of the unacknowledged greats of history, and that's a very understandable response given the material—

PIXIE. Wait.

JEFFREY. —the time period—

PIXIE. You—wait—you think I picked her because she's a girl? You think I

125 picked Elizabeth Farnese because she's a girl.

(*Beat.*)

JEFFREY. Well, what I was suggesting wasn't quite so simplistic—

PIXIE. I didn't. I really—I'm not a feminist. It said war and strategy and she was a great strategist, really, if you read the material I found.

JEFFREY. I—Pixie, I'm sure she was, but—

PIXIE. She was.                                                                    130

JEFFREY. I'm sure she was, but—

PIXIE. She was. She was a great strategist, she played everyone. The French, the Austrians—

JEFFREY. Yes, Pixie, that's the history.

PIXIE. Well, that's why I picked her. 'Cause I thought that was on topic.           135

JEFFREY. I—let's back up here for a moment—

PIXIE. I thought I was on topic.

JEFFREY. Pixie, let's—please, let's back up for a moment—

PIXIE. If I'm not on topic, then—

JEFFREY. Pixie! Please. I want to—we must address a statement you made a   140
moment ago. Did I, or am I mistaken, hear you say you're not a feminist?

PIXIE. No, I'm not, I was just doing the assignment.

JEFFREY. Yes, yes, but—

PIXIE. I thought it was just a question of sources. That's what you wrote on my sheet, that's why I came here.                                                      145

JEFFREY. Yes, but Pixie. Feminism—

PIXIE. I'm not a feminist.

JEFFREY. But you ... (*laughs uncomfortably*) ... I don't think you—

PIXIE. I'm not. I took this course. I wanted to take the history of war, I didn't take a women's studies course—                                                      150

JEFFREY. —but—

PIXIE. —I took this course.

JEFFREY. But, Pixie, women's studies is a very valuable body of knowledge, and you are a feminist.

PIXIE. No I'm not.                                                                  155

JEFFREY. Yes you ...! Perhaps you don't realize—

PIXIE. I'm not a feminist—

JEFFREY. —because the very fact that you're standing here, before me, in this institution—a hundred years ago, fifty, that would not have been possible, and you would not have received adequate education to be able to argue to   160
me that Elizabeth Farnese is a military leader—

PIXIE. No, this is the point. I didn't pick her because she's a girl.

JEFFREY. But Pixie—

PIXIE. I didn't go looking for some girl so I could pick her, so I could make some big point to you to vindicate women or whatever you're thinking—   165

JEFFREY. Why did you pick her, then?

(*Beat.*)

Why pick her?

(*Beat.*)

PIXIE. Okay. Fine. I picked a girl. But the point I was trying to make about not being a feminist was—

170 JEFFREY. You are a feminist.

PIXIE. No I'm not.

JEFFREY. Yes you ...! Pixie, look—

PIXIE. I'm not.

JEFFREY. Look. Take you and I, you and I, Pixie. You believe yourself to be

175 equal to me, don't you?

PIXIE. I'm your student.

JEFFREY. Yes, but, aside from our status as—as—I'm a bad example. Take any of your fellow students, the male members of your classes, you believe yourself to be equal to them, don't you?

(*Beat.*)

180 That's feminism. That is feminism. And so you are, by definition—

PIXIE. Fine. Fine. I'm a feminist.

JEFFREY. Now, all right—

PIXIE. I'm a fucking feminist.

JEFFREY. All right. Let's not—let's please—

185 PIXIE. All I was trying to say was I thought Elizabeth Farnese was really effective and interesting, but I don't care, okay? I'll write on Napoleon.

JEFFREY. Yes, all right.

PIXIE. I'll write on Napoleon like everyone else.

JEFFREY. Pixie. Please, just slow down. Let's not raise our voices please.

(*Beat.*)

190 PIXIE. (*more confused than sorry*) Sorry.

JEFFREY. That's all right.

(*Beat.*)

Napoleon would be a highly appropriate choice, in the context of this ...

(*Pixie has walked out.*)

Pixie, where are you going?

(*Jeffrey walks after her.*)

Can you—can we please finish our ...?

(*Beat.*)

Pixie?                                                                                        195

(*Pixie is gone. Jeffrey shakes his head, and goes back over to his desk. He crosses off his meeting with Pixie in his date book. Lights out.*)


## SCENE 2

*Jeffrey's office, a week and a half later. There is a pile of essays on his desk. Jeffrey is marking. Professor Galbraith enters and looks at the office.*

GALBRAITH.  This is a dismal little office, Jeffrey.

JEFFREY.  (*standing*) Professor Galbraith!

GALBRAITH.  I haven't been down here since, well, the seventies, and I don't think it's changed.

JEFFREY.  Thank you for ... stopping by.                                                      5

GALBRAITH.  Who are you sharing it with, some social science ...?

JEFFREY.  She's, yes, an anthropology Ph.D., but she's on a very different schedule, opposite hours—

GALBRAITH.  Good.

JEFFREY.  It's worked out well. I barely ever see her.                                        10

(*Beat.*)

And I keep meaning to say thank you for finding me this office—

GALBRAITH.  So what's the matter, Jeffrey? Hm? Your email, your phone call? I'm sorry I've been unresponsive, the conference—

JEFFREY.  Yes, I know, the timing—

GALBRAITH.  I agreed to moderate a couple of panels, deliver a keynote, and      15
suddenly when the coffee machine breaks down, they all come to me.

JEFFREY.  Yes, I can see how that would happen.

GALBRAITH.  This is the downside of heading the department. There are up-sides! There are upsides!

JEFFREY.  I'm sure there are.                                                                 20

(*Beat.*)

So, Professor—

GALBRAITH.  So what is it, Jeffrey? Hm? You need to consult? You need to be supervised? Someone to hold your hand?

JEFFREY.  Well—

GALBRAITH.  It's difficult, this juncture in the dissertation-writing process.      25

The tunnel, they call it.

JEFFREY. Uh, no—

GALBRAITH. Which is apt because you're pretty much hunting down your own asshole at this point, excuse the.... Because, once the research is done
30   and you're writing—

JEFFREY. Yes, no, I—

GALBRAITH. —there it is, looming on the horizon, your own anus. That's what a Ph.D. is. An heroic-apocalyptic confrontation with the self.

JEFFREY. Professor, that's very ... funny, and sometimes it does feel as though
35   I'm peering into my own ... but no, it's not my dissertation.

GALBRAITH. Dissertation is going well, is it?

JEFFREY. Yes, it's going, but I've been trying to grade the essays for History 103?

(*Galbraith picks up a pile of essays.*)

GALBRAITH. This them?

40   JEFFREY. Yes, and what I need to ask you is—

GALBRAITH. Lots of little comments. Good point. This is awkward.

JEFFREY. (*laughs*) Yes.

GALBRAITH. Where's your thesis?

JEFFREY. Yes ... (*laughs*) ... and, uh, Professor, what I wanted to ask you is—

45   GALBRAITH. I haven't seen you at the conference, by the way.

(*Beat.*)

JEFFREY. No. I haven't been attending. I've been so intent on getting through these—

GALBRAITH. I chaired what turned out to be a very energetic panel on interpretations of Napoleonic law.

50   JEFFREY. Well, I'm sorry I missed it.

GALBRAITH. Also a lecture on problems of coalition warfare. Quite compelling. A Chicago University professor, Sheila Newbery. Right up your alley, research wise. I hope you weren't grading undergraduate essays rather than attending the conference?

55   JEFFREY. I—well—I—

GALBRAITH. I hope you were at least chasing—or—what's the euphemism these days for female companionship? The conference falls a little short there. One look at the participants and.... (*laughs*) Don't expect to find love in the history department, Jeffrey.

60   JEFFREY. I ... won't hold my breath. (*trying to joke*) Perhaps the English department.

GALBRAITH. There's a good hunting ground. The English department!

(*Professor Galbraith and Jeffrey share a laugh. Beat.*)

JEFFREY.  Professor, I wanted to ask you—
GALBRAITH.  Oh, right, yes, ask me the—
JEFFREY.  A student of mine, an essay—                                    65
GALBRAITH.  Right.

(*Jeffrey begins looking through the pile for Pixie's essay.*)

JEFFREY.  I'm trying to grade this one paper, but it's very difficult. I rejected
this student's essay proposal when she submitted it two weeks ago. We   70
discussed it, I thought she'd resolved to write on a more appropriate topic,
but, as it turns out, she hasn't. She's written on the original.
GALBRAITH.  Ah.
JEFFREY.  And, yes, and now I'm not sure whether to fail her, or what's the
procedure? I told her to come by my office this afternoon, thinking I'd   75
have a chance to confer with you first—

(*Jeffrey finds the essay and hands it to Professor Galbraith.*)

The title should give you a good sense of the type of—
GALBRAITH.  Cock-up?
JEFFREY.  Yes.

(*Beat. Professor Galbraith and Jeffrey look at the title.*)

GALBRAITH.  Hmmm, yes! Quite the—                                         80
JEFFREY.  You see the ...

(*Beat.*)

GALBRAITH.  (*reading*) Elizabeth Farnese and Napoleon Bonaparte: A Critical
Comparison of their Wartime Strategies.
JEFFREY.  You see the difficulty. And, for grading, it reads like an English
paper, all conjecture and—                                                85
GALBRAITH.  Yes.

(*Beat.*)

JEFFREY.  The sources are fine, but—
GALBRAITH.  Yes.

(*Beat.*)

Yes, this certainly isn't what I discussed with her. I didn't approve a comparison. Although, I suppose she was trying to appease you and write on   90
her topic. Servant of two masters.

(*Professor Galbraith looks through the essay.*)

JEFFREY.  I'm ... sorry. I'm sorry, Professor. You—did she—

GALBRAITH.  Didn't I tell you, Jeffrey? This girl came to see me a week, a week and a half ago, asked if she could write on Elizabeth Farnese, Philip the fifth's second wife?

95

JEFFREY.  (*to confirm that he knows who she is*) Yes.

GALBRAITH.  How Elizabeth Farnese is a military leader ... (*laughs*) ... I'm interested to know.

(*Professor Galbraith flips through the essay.*)

JEFFREY.  Yes, but, she's not. I'm sorry, she's not, at least not considered to be—

100

GALBRAITH.  Elizabeth Farnese?

JEFFREY.  She's not generally considered to be a military leader—

GALBRAITH.  No, no, of course not. But, she seemed.... This girl—the girl ...?

JEFFREY.  Pixie Findley?

105 GALBRAITH.  She seemed very—I'm probably looking for attractive, but let's say determined for the sake of decorum. I thought, why not let her have a go, she's likely going to argue something preposterous. Has she?

JEFFREY.  I—I don't know.

GALBRAITH.  I was hoping for something a little risqué, at least euphemisti-

110  cally, as in Elizabeth Farnese's victories were won not on the battlefield but in the bedroom, or Frederick the Great favoured the oblique attack while Elizabeth perfected the horizontal one, something to that effect.

(*Professor Galbraith reads through the essay.*)

JEFFREY.  But the guidelines for this essay were very specific—

GALBRAITH.  I let the leash out a little.

(*Beat.*)

115 JEFFREY.  I—yes—I can see why you might. I hesitated, uh, briefly before I rejected her proposal. It's sensitive, of course, and highly charged, but the reason why I ultimately did turn her down was—

GALBRAITH.  (*referring to Pixie's essay*) This is quite good, this opening.

(*Beat.*)

JEFFREY.  The reason, Professor, why I didn't allow Pixie to write on Elizabeth

120  Farnese is that I felt fairly certain that, given the parameters of the assign-ment that you set, military leader, it would result in her producing a very weak essay.

(*Beat.*)

And she has produced a very weak essay. Professor.

GALBRAITH.  Ah, now, here we have it! (reading from Pixie's essay) "While Napoleon engaged in warfare to resolve international strife," very nice, 125 "Elizabeth relied on her feminine wiles."

JEFFREY.  Professor.

GALBRAITH.  Very nice phrasing. Wiles. Where do you suppose her wiles were located?

JEFFREY.  Look, I— 130

GALBRAITH.  Adjacent to her thighs, presumably.

JEFFREY.  I—Professor—this is a student's essay!

(*Galbraith stops reading Pixie's essay and looks at Jeffrey.*)

I realize some of it's laughable, but ...

(*Beat.*)

I'm sorry, I'm just a little surprised you allowed a student to write on Elizabeth Farnese. 135

GALBRAITH.  What are you concerned about, Jeffrey? Her grade?

JEFFREY.  Well, yes, her grade, but also—

GALBRAITH.  Pass her, write a few comments on it. Good effort. Fails to convince.

JEFFREY.  I suppose I can do that. This essay certainly doesn't deserve a passing 140 grade. I don't feel all that comfortable with—

GALBRAITH.  Jeffrey—

JEFFREY.  —arbitrarily assigning it one.

(*Beat.*)

GALBRAITH.  B minus.

(*Beat.*)

JEFFREY.  No—you—no, the point is, I'm forced to arbitrarily assign her a 145 grade because she was allowed to write on a, I think, inappropriate ... B minus. That's at least a firm hold on the material. Look, I—I really don't like being put in this position at all, I feel very—

GALBRAITH.  Jeffrey.

JEFFREY.  B minus? Based on what criteria? 150

GALBRAITH.  Well, no doubt she learned something while writing it.

JEFFREY.  She learned. She learned something. That's your criterion?

GALBRAITH.  You don't like my criterion?

JEFFREY.  This is a very unconvincing essay!

155 GALBRAITH.  How bad can it be?

JEFFREY.  It's a terrible essay! It's ridiculous.

GALBRAITH.  Jeffrey.

JEFFREY.  A short story would be more convincing. A finger-painting!

GALBRAITH.  Oh, for Christ's sake, Jeffrey, she wrote a bad essay! The girl is

160   seventeen. Eighteen. Let her go skip off and neck in the quad.

(*Beat.*)

JEFFREY.  Neck in the ...!

GALBRAITH.  Or what do they say, make out?

(*Beat.*)

JEFFREY.  Professor, this is the student who argued that Elizabeth Farnese is a
military leader, and now you're trivializing—

165 GALBRAITH.  All right—

JEFFREY.  —and—and ridiculing her very earnest attempt—

GALBRAITH.  All right!

JEFFREY.  —to include women in the history of—

GALBRAITH.  Yes, I know, Jeffrey, because I'm the one who let her. I approved

170   her essay topic. I said yes. Write on Elizabeth Farnese. Prove she's on par
with Nelson,[1] Napoleon. Set us all straight, us men.

(*Beat.*)

(*smiling*) We have to let the girls have their day, Jeffrey.

(*Beat.*)

JEFFREY.  We have to ... let the girls ...?

(*Beat.*)

I'm sorry?

175 GALBRAITH.  In my experience, it's best to just let them, well, have their day.

(*Beat.*)

JEFFREY.  What do you mean?

GALBRAITH.  It may make for weak scholarship, but I think it's best to allow
for it, at the moment, despite its weaknesses.

(*Beat.*)

---

1   *Nelson* Viscount Horatio Nelson (1758–1805), famous English admiral responsible for
British victories in the important naval battles of several wars.

JEFFREY. I—I'm sorry. What—what makes for weak scholarship?

GALBRAITH. There's a great deal of so-called research in circulation these days    180
that's entirely based on resentment.

JEFFREY. What are you talking about?

GALBRAITH. Gendered revisionism,[1] Jeffrey. Biographies of Napoleon's lover,
James Joyce's wife,[2] the unsung women of history, herstory, all very fashionable, but at a certain point ... (*laughs*) ... it fails to convince.    185

(*Beat.*)

JEFFREY. It—it fails to ... are you joking? Professor?

GALBRAITH. You said it yourself. Pixie's essay is a failure. Why? Because Elizabeth Farnese is, at best, a second-rate figure who cannot yield any important historical insight.

JEFFREY. Yes, perhaps in the context of this assignment—    190

GALBRAITH. And the result, an unscholarly, as you said, paper—

JEFFREY. But not as a general—

GALBRAITH. That you deemed weak—

JEFFREY. I—I wouldn't make that kind of a sweeping—

GALBRAITH. That you rejected—    195

JEFFREY. Yes! I—yes—I rejected her essay proposal, not the whole field of
inquiry!

(*Beat.*)

GALBRAITH. All right, Jeffrey, what is history? What is it?

(*Beat.*)

JEFFREY. What is ... history?

GALBRAITH. Too broad? What isn't history?    200

(*Beat.*)

JEFFREY. What is not—

GALBRAITH. What can we say is not history?

(*Beat.*)

Seventeenth, eighteenth century. What are men doing?

---

1    *revisionism* I.e., reinterpretation of history in opposition to conventional approaches; although the term can be value-neutral, it is sometimes used disparagingly to suggest an
intellectually unjustified denial of accepted facts.

2    *Napoleon's lover* Napoleon's several lovers included a countess, a queen, and a famous
actress; *James Joyce's wife* The Irish novelist James Joyce was married to Nora Barnacle
(1884–1951), who inspired the character of Molly Bloom in his novel *Ulysses* (1922).

(*Beat.*)

Revolutionizing warfare. And what are women doing?

205 JEFFREY.  Well, they're—

GALBRAITH.  Curling their hair, boiling potatoes, et cetera, et cetera. They are not central to the major events. They are—it's unfortunate, it's unlikeable—marginal to them. If we want to include women, we have to reorient history to the mundane, and frankly—

210 JEFFREY.  —uh, Professor—

GALBRAITH.  —frankly—

JEFFREY.  —Professor—

GALBRAITH.  —then it's no longer history, is it? It's sociology, anthropology, women's studies-ology.

(*Beat.*)

215 JEFFREY.  Look, Professor, that is all ... very controversial and I—

GALBRAITH.  What?

JEFFREY.  I—I—

GALBRAITH.  What?

JEFFREY.  —disagree. I think we should be privileging a female discourse, given how excluded and sidelined—

220

GALBRAITH.  So Elizabeth Farnese is a military leader.

JEFFREY.  No, that's not—that's a bad example.

GALBRAITH.  Which is it?

JEFFREY.  I don't think it's an either-or—

225 GALBRAITH.  So she is?

JEFFREY.  Well, one could argue, I mean, as it stands, no.

GALBRAITH.  So she isn't.

JEFFREY.  No—she—I just—no, I don't think it's that simple. Because—

GALBRAITH.  Jeffrey.

230 JEFFREY.  No! Because one could argue, one could radically redefine the term military leader—

GALBRAITH.  Yes, and one could write an essay about how Napoleon's horse influenced his decisions. If a horse came to you and asked if it could write that essay, you would probably say, let the horse have its day. Call it horsestory. And it may be true, to a certain extent, that Napoleon's horse did influence his decisions, but who really gives a damn?

235

(*Beat.*)

JEFFREY.  Professor, I'm sorry, are you actually not joking? Because I—I can't believe I'm hearing this.

GALBRAITH.  Jeffrey, relax, all right?

JEFFREY.  I can't believe you just said horsestory.                        240

GALBRAITH.  Jeffrey.

JEFFREY.  Horsestory? Professor? Horsestory? That's a very pejorative, uh, derisive, misogynist—

GALBRAITH.  Misogynist?

JEFFREY.  I, yes, I think, misogynist—                                      245

GALBRAITH.  All right, all right, relax, I'm ... what? Toying with your liberal sensibilities? I'm not rejecting all revisionism, per se. However, one gets tired, worn down. The relentless onslaught of victimology. The history department's awash in it. We're being strangled to death by cultural studies. They've got their own fucking department, why do they want mine?  250 What is wrong with Napoleon? Personally, I love the guy. You love the guy!

(*Beat.*)

JEFFREY.  Well, yes, but—

GALBRAITH.  That's history, Jeffrey. That's history. A love affair with Napoleon.

JEFFREY.  I—no, you see—no—I don't agree.

(*Beat.*)

I disagree!                                                                 255

GALBRAITH.  You're researching Napoleon—

JEFFREY.  Yes, fine, I am, but I don't think Napoleon Bonaparte is the only valid ...! I think this whole argument only highlights the fact that we've constructed a false notion of history as male, as centred on male events, male figures, in which case, we should be trying to update, and redress—  260

GALBRAITH.  —yes, fine—

JEFFREY.  —to try and right the balance.

GALBRAITH.  Yes. You're right.

JEFFREY.  And broaden the scope of ...

(*Beat.*)

I'm right.                                                                  265

GALBRAITH.  Yes, I agree. I agree with you, as in Pixie's case. Pixie got to write her essay. Write on a female figure, have her say—

JEFFREY.  No, but, no—

GALBRAITH.  Right the balance, redress the what-have-you—

JEFFREY.  But, no—that's not—no—you think her say has no merit.            270

(*Beat.*)

You think it's merit-less.

GALBRAITH.  So do you.

JEFFREY.  But, no, look, that's patronizing.

GALBRAITH.  No Jeffrey.

275  JEFFREY.  That's—yes it is. You're humouring her, you're cynically appeasing her—

GALBRAITH.  Pixie is happy.

(*Beat.*)

JEFFREY.  That's ...! You're patronizing her!

GALBRAITH.  I am allowing her to have her say.

280  JEFFREY.  You don't value her say!

GALBRAITH.  She can't tell the difference. If she can't tell the difference, then—

JEFFREY.  What? Then it's not patronizing?

GALBRAITH.  Then, no, it's not patronizing, largely because she doesn't feel patronized.

285  JEFFREY.  Yes, but that's only because—

GALBRAITH.  Or are you claiming to be better qualified to determine what's patronizing for Pixie than Pixie is herself?

JEFFREY.  No, no I'm not. Except, yes, at this moment, yes, I'm the one who's—

GALBRAITH.  What?

290  JEFFREY.  Here! Listening to—privy to—

GALBRAITH.  What?

JEFFREY.  To ... your—

GALBRAITH.  What? Jeffrey?

JEFFREY.  —sexism!

(*Long beat.*)

295  GALBRAITH.  Hm.

(*Beat.*)

Do you think you might be a little worn down?

JEFFREY.  Uh, no, I think I'm fine.

GALBRAITH.  (*considering*) Three, four years into your Ph.D. Middle of your thesis, three tutorials, this little office, working until all hours, you haven't

300  been attending the conference, leaving me a series of phone and email messages about one undergraduate paper.

(*Beat.*)

JEFFREY.  If you're suggesting that—

GALBRAITH.  Because it's inadvisable to throw around words like sexist, all right Jeffrey? Given the current climate in campus politics. And, once you've been in the department a little longer, then you'll start to—    305

JEFFREY.  What? Then I'll what? I'll start referring to my female students as girls and allowing the attractive ones to write personal responses instead of essays. "How do you feel about Napoleon, Pixie?" "Oh, I really like him." B minus!

GALBRAITH.  (*laughs*) No, but, over time, you will come to realize that stu-    310
dents such as Pixie float through here every year on their way to the cultural studies department. Next year she'll switch to commerce, business admin. Why? Because she likes their building better. And then, when you've seen enough Pixies come and go, you'll realize it's best to just let them have their little say.    315

(*A momentary standoff between the men. Pixie enters at the doorway.*)

PIXIE.  Hi! Sorry to interrupt. (*to Galbraith*) Hi Professor. (*to Jeffrey*) I just wanted to let you know I'm here. If you're—uh—in the middle of something, I'll just wait in the hallway until you're—

GALBRAITH.  No, Pixie, please, come in.

PIXIE.  I can just wait in the hallway.    320

GALBRAITH.  No, no, please, come in. Jeffrey and I were just discussing, but please.

JEFFREY.  Uh, yes. Come in Pixie.

(*Pixie enters.*)

PIXIE.  Am I in trouble ... or ...?

JEFFREY.  Uh no, no Pixie, I'm sorry, please sit down—    325

PIXIE.  Okay, just with the two of you standing there ...

JEFFREY.  Yes, I'm sorry, we were just finishing up. (*to Professor Galbraith*) Professor, I asked Pixie here to talk about her essay.

GALBRAITH.  Right, right.

JEFFREY.  And so I think I should, uh—    330

GALBRAITH.  Right. Well, I'm off. I'll leave you to it.

(*Beat.*)

Jeffrey, the conference resumes at ten tomorrow morning, should you choose to grace us. (*to Pixie*) Pixie. Nice to see you again so soon.

PIXIE.  Yeah.

GALBRAITH.  And the assignment we discussed ...? When was it, a week, a    335
week and a half ago?

PIXIE.  Yeah.

GALBRAITH.  How did it go? Hm? Did you enjoy writing it?

PIXIE.  (*with a quick glance at Jeffrey*) I, yes, I really enjoyed—I learned a lot.

340 GALBRAITH. That's good. That's good. That's very good.

> (*Galbraith looks at Jeffrey. So does Pixie, causing Jeffrey to turn away. Beat.*)

There are sources, Pixie, that suggest Elizabeth Farnese may have led the Spanish Army against the French in 1717,[1] not long after her accession.

PIXIE. Yeah, I came across that.

GALBRAITH. (*picturing it*) On horseback, at the head of the Spanish Army, as
345 the formidable Louis XV crossed the Pyrenees.[2]

PIXIE. Yes.

GALBRAITH. Quite the—quite the—

PIXIE. Yeah—

GALBRAITH. —feat! For a young ...!

350 PIXIE. (*with a quick glance at Jeffrey*) Unhunh, yeah, I thought so too.

GALBRAITH. A very ambitious young person. Shared a number of qualities with Napoleon Bonaparte.

PIXIE. Uh, yeah! The comparison is kind of a stretch, of course. Napoleon conquered Europe, and Elizabeth got her sons thrones through her diplo-
355 macy, but, um, I think it holds.

GALBRAITH. (*considering her*) Elizabeth Farnese! It's a shame she wasn't al-lowed to cultivate her talents more fully. But, in the eighteenth century—

PIXIE. Yeah! I, uh—it's weird. There's not a lot of, um, women in this history we're covering—

360 GALBRAITH. No.

PIXIE. No, and the funny thing is, all term I've had this feeling of being left out. Like, it's all been very interesting, but it doesn't feel like it's about me, or for me, if that makes any sense?

> (*Galbraith smiles at her.*)

I thought it might just be because I'm in first year, and everything is a little
365 ...! But I think it's actually the content of the course. (*to Jeffrey*) And I was thinking about, uh, what you asked. Why—why I chose Elizabeth, why I wanted to write on her, and I think that probably, without realizing it, I chose her because—I don't know.

> (*Beat.*)

---

1   *Spanish Army ... in 1717* In 1717, Spain briefly conquered Sardinia, initiating the War of the Quadruple Alliance (1718–20), in which France, Britain, the Netherlands, and the Holy Roman Empire united against Spain.

2   *Louis XV* King Louis XV of France (1710–74) was still a child when the French army invaded Spain as part of the War of the Quadruple Alliance; *Pyrenees* Mountain range separating France and Spain.

(*to Jeffrey*) Because I wanted to be in it, you know?

(*Beat.*)

GALBRAITH. Well, that's very nice, Pixie. That's a very nice sentiment.     370
PIXIE. Uh, yeah.

(*Beat.*)

JEFFREY. And Pixie, now that you've written on Elizabeth Farnese, do you feel
there is a place for women in history? Or, are they just left out?

(*Beat.*)

PIXIE. Uh, um—
GALBRAITH. I'm sorry, Pixie. We're interrogating you. (*to Jeffrey*) Jeffrey, we're     375
interrogating her, I think we should stop.
PIXIE. No, I just didn't, uh, come prepared to—
GALBRAITH. No, of course you didn't—
JEFFREY. I—I'm sorry Pixie, just the one last question, if you don't mind, and
then we'll talk about your essay.     380

(*Beat.*)

PIXIE. What was the question?
GALBRAITH. Jeffrey, this is getting a little heavy-handed—
JEFFREY. The question was, is there a place for women in history?

(*Beat.*)

PIXIE. Well, from the lectures and the textbooks, I would say women don't
have a place in history. But I don't know if I believe that.     385
JEFFREY. What do you believe?

(*Beat.*)

PIXIE. Is this about my essay?
GALBRAITH. All right, we've asked our questions. I think we should stop now
before Pixie begins to feel put upon—
JEFFREY. (*a little too vehement*) She—no—she wants to answer!     390

(*Beat.*)

I—I'm sorry, is there some reason why Pixie shouldn't be allowed to offer
a response?

(*Beat.*)

GALBRAITH. Pixie, would you please wait in the hallway for a moment—

PIXIE. Uh, okay—

395 JEFFREY. (*motioning for Pixie to wait*) Uh, no, Pixie. (*to Galbraith*) Professor, why? Is there some reason why Pixie can't answer?

GALBRAITH. She can answer, Jeffrey, it's not a question of whether or not she can answer—

JEFFREY. Then—

400 GALBRAITH. I have no objections to hearing Pixie's response—

JEFFREY. Then, good! Let's—

GALBRAITH. —but I'm afraid we're overburdening her—

JEFFREY. With one question?

(*Beat.*)

GALBRAITH. (*to Pixie*) Pixie, I'm sorry, if you could please wait in the hallway
405   for one moment—

PIXIE. Uh, okay—

JEFFREY. I don't see why Pixie should wait in the hallway—

GALBRAITH. (*to Pixie*) Jeffrey and I are ... (*laughs*)—

JEFFREY. (*to Galbraith*)—while we—

410 GALBRAITH. (*to Pixie*)—in the midst of a.... Your essay raised a number of questions—

JEFFREY. (*to Pixie*)—about women and their under-representation in the historical record, and, Pixie, your essay interests us in that—

GALBRAITH. (*low, to Jeffrey*) Jeffrey—

415 JEFFREY. (*to Pixie*)—in that it speaks to the deficit of female figures—

GALBRAITH. (*low, to Jeffrey*) I'd really prefer if you didn't—

JEFFREY. (*to Pixie*)—as well as history departments' traditional unwillingness to—

GALBRAITH. (*to Jeffrey*)—extend our argument into student affairs!

420 JEFFREY. (*to Galbraith*) Extend it into ...! It's about her. Her essay is the subject of the argument!

(*Beat.*)

GALBRAITH. (*to Pixie*) Thank you, Pixie, it will just be one minute.

PIXIE. Okay—

JEFFREY. (*to Galbraith*) Just now, Professor, Pixie very clearly expressed feel-
425   ings of exclusion. She's been left out. The subject matter doesn't seem to be addressed to her—

GALBRAITH. Yes, I heard her—

JEFFREY. —the history excludes her.

GALBRAITH. I heard her.

430 JEFFREY. I'd like to—can we hear her out? Because I don't see how she can be included in the discourse if she's sitting in the hallway.

(*Beat.*)

GALBRAITH.  Fine, go ahead.

(*Jeffrey stares at Galbraith.*)

Go ahead.

(*Galbraith indicates that Jeffrey can ask his question.*)

JEFFREY.  Pixie, I'm sorry, the question, should women have a place in history? I would very much like to hear your response.                                    435

(*Beat.*)

PIXIE.  Look, I—I don't know, okay? You're the experts. Why don't you tell me. I came here to learn, to be taught, so I really don't know.

(*Beat.*)

JEFFREY.  Yes—
PIXIE.  You're the experts.
JEFFREY.  Yes, we are, but, we're asking you because you wrote on Elizabeth    440 Farnese, and, arguably, that makes you an expert. An Elizabeth Farnese expert.
PIXIE.  Okay, but that's a pretty limited, um, field, Elizabeth Farnese. And you asked me if women should be in history?
JEFFREY.  Yes.                                                              445
PIXIE.  I think Elizabeth Farnese should be in history, is that what you're asking me?

(*Beat.*)

JEFFREY.  Well, Pixie, yes, okay, that's—yes, Elizabeth Farnese is part of this because you appealed your essay topic to Professor Galbraith, and that was a very strong gesture on your part, and it indicates to me that you are em-    450 bracing feminist—but I'd like to broaden our discussion from—and talk about what you said a moment ago—that while taking this course history seemed closed to, or seemed to leave out, women.

(*Beat.*)

PIXIE.  Yeah?
JEFFREY.  And you said, I don't know if I believe that.                     455

(*Beat.*)

PIXIE.  Yeah?

JEFFREY. And you meant ... what?

(*Beat. Pixie shifts, thinks.*)

All right. Pixie, look, the essay topic, military leader, Elizabeth Farnese is not a military leader.

460 PIXIE. Well—

JEFFREY. Yes! Exactly! You questioned that! And I think this is important, because what you hit upon, Pixie, is that there's a certain amount of exclusivity, a certain sexism built into the terminology, into the wording of the essay questions, which are, of course, formulated by Professor Galbraith.

(*Jeffrey looks at Professor Galbraith, who looks away.*)

465 And I think this relates to what you said a moment ago, about the textbooks, and the lectures—

PIXIE. —okay—

JEFFREY. —about your growing awareness of the emphasis on male figures—

PIXIE. —okay—

470 JEFFREY. (*half to Galbraith*)—and of the almost complete absence of female figures—

PIXIE. Yeah, okay—

JEFFREY. —and of the feelings of exclusion generated by what is a pronounced bias in the course material—

475 PIXIE. —unhunh—

JEFFREY. —as well as your skepticism. Your sense that women are a part of history—

PIXIE. (*soft*)—unhunh—

JEFFREY. —and that—that they would be a part of history if they weren't
480 being under-represented in Professor Galbraith's lectures and on Professor Galbraith's course lists, and that, Pixie, that is what I'd like to hear about!

(*Beat.*)

PIXIE. Why are you yelling at me?

JEFFREY. I'm not ...! (*dropping the intensity level*) I'm not yelling, I'm trying to—

485 PIXIE. I, no, I don't want to answer this anymore.

(*Beat.*)

JEFFREY. No, Pixie, I'm sorry, let's—please, let's—

PIXIE. I feel uncomfortable answering this.

JEFFREY. But, but, Pixie—

GALBRAITH. Jeffrey—

JEFFREY. (*to Galbraith*) No. (*to Pixie*) Pixie—                                    490
PIXIE. No. I don't want to—
JEFFREY. But ...! Listen, let's just—
PIXIE. No.
GALBRAITH. Jeffrey—
JEFFREY. Look Pixie, let's just—                                                     495
PIXIE. No.
JEFFREY. But, but Pixie!
PIXIE. You're yelling at me!
JEFFREY. I'm not—I'm not ...! Pixie, just listen for one—
PIXIE. No.                                                                            500
JEFFREY. Just for one—
PIXIE. No.
JEFFREY. Please! Pixie! Just for one—
PIXIE. No, I—no. I don't care. I don't care about women in history, okay?
    This is my fucking elective. I have no idea!                                      505

    (*Beat.*)

JEFFREY. You don't care.

    (*Beat.*)

    Doesn't it, for one second, occur to you that I am trying to defend you?
GALBRAITH. Jeffrey, I think we should stop now—
JEFFREY. That more is at stake than just your essay, and your grades—
GALBRAITH. Jeffrey, let's stop this right now.                                        510
JEFFREY. But, you know what, Pixie? Why don't you just glaze over—
GALBRAITH. —Jeffrey!—
JEFFREY. —while we determine that women and horses have equal historic
    significance! Or—or apply your fucking lip gloss one more time—
GALBRAITH. All right, Jeffrey!                                                        515
JEFFREY. —while Professor Galbraith eliminates women from the historical
    record!
GALBRAITH. That's enough!
JEFFREY. You are being degraded and—and patronized—
GALBRAITH. That's enough, Jeffrey!                                                    520
JEFFREY. —and you are sitting there like a lobotomized ...! Like a lobotomy
    in a ... skirt!

    (*Long beat. Long enough for Jeffrey to contemplate the possible ramifications
    of his outburst. Very little motion occurs on stage. Pixie begins to cry and
    covers her face.*)

I—shit.

(*Beat.*)

I—Pixie—I didn't—I didn't mean to—fuck.

(*Beat.*)

525   I—I—fuck.

GALBRAITH.   Hm, yes. Jeffrey? Would you please wait in the hallway for a moment?

JEFFREY.   (*half to Galbraith, half to Pixie*) I—no, look, I—I'm sorry—

GALBRAITH.   Yes, I know you are—

530   JEFFREY.   I just got—I got—

GALBRAITH.   Yes, I know. But now I would prefer if you went out into the hallway.

JEFFREY.   But—I—Professor, I—

GALBRAITH.   Because, as you can see, Pixie is crying, and I think it would be

535   best to give her a chance to collect herself.

(*Jeffrey doesn't go.*)

Jeffrey?

JEFFREY.   I—yes, I just—I don't feel all that comfortable leaving her ... with ...

GALBRAITH.   The head of the department?

(*A standoff between the two men. Beat. Pixie's crying is audible.*)

All right, Jeffrey. Can we please offer Pixie some Kleenex?

(*Jeffrey gets a box of tissues off the bookshelf. Galbraith takes the box of tissues from Jeffrey, and goes over to Pixie. She takes a couple of tissues without looking up. Long beat of crying.*)

540   PIXIE.   I'm just trying to ... (*gestures*) ...

GALBRAITH.   Please. I think it would be very strange if you weren't crying. I would cry if the dean yelled at me.

(*Galbraith smiles at Pixie. Pixie tries to pull it together again. Another beat of crying.*)

(*with sympathy*) You're upset.

(*Pixie nods.*)

PIXIE.   (*quiet*) Yeah.

545   GALBRAITH.   (*with sympathy*) Hm.

*(Beat.)*

I'm very sorry about this, Pixie. I shouldn't have let Jeffrey yell at you, I should have ... stepped in. *(for Jeffrey's benefit)* This is not how we encourage our TAs to behave.

*(Beat.)*

Jeffrey hasn't been raising his voice in tutorial, has he?

*(Pixie shakes her head no.)*

PIXIE.  No.                                                                                  550
GALBRAITH.  No. Hm.

*(Beat.)*

You should know that we do have a formal complaints procedure at the university, Pixie. There is a women's coordinator. Or, rather, what is the current ...?

*(Beat.)*

Jeffrey?                                                                                     555
JEFFREY.  Yes?
GALBRAITH.  What's the new title for the women's coordinator?
JEFFREY.  The equity officer?
GALBRAITH.  The equity officer. *(to Pixie)* She's in the Office of the Dean of Students. She's a very approachable person, and I'm sure she would help  560
you make your case.

*(Beat.)*

One of the avenues of appeal, when incidents of this type occur, is to come and talk with me. We've bypassed that step, as I witnessed the incident. And, in my experience, handling these types of incidents in the department, I've found that it's important for the student to hear from the pro-  565
fessor, or, in this case, TA, themselves. What's important for the student is to hear the faculty member acknowledge that their behaviour was not ... appropriate. Then, hopefully, a teaching relationship can be re-established.

*(Beat.)*

I know Jeffrey would like to apologize to you. And I will be here supervising, so if anything makes you feel uncomfortable, then we'll stop, and I'll  570
ask Jeffrey to leave.

*(Beat.)*

Hm? Pixie? Is that ...?

(*Pixie shrugs—sure. Galbraith smiles at her.*)

Jeffrey.

(*Galbraith indicates to Jeffrey that he should speak to Pixie.*)

JEFFREY. (*half to Galbraith*) I—I—yes. I'm very sorry. I lost my—I uh—I
575    shouldn't have used that language to—
GALBRAITH. (*sharp*) Are you apologizing to Pixie, Jeffrey?
JEFFREY. (*confused*) Yes?

(*Galbraith indicates that Pixie is over there.*)

(*to Pixie*) Pixie, I shouldn't have used—I was frustrated, and I chose the
    wrong words to express that—
580  PIXIE. You yelled at me!
JEFFREY. Yes. I—yes. I'm sorry.
PIXIE. I came here to get my essay. I came here to pick up my essay, so can I
    have it please, or are you all on crack?
JEFFREY. Yes, I—I know that this must seem—
585  PIXIE. You wanted to talk to me about my essay, that's what you said, that's
    why I came here, to talk about my essay! And then—
JEFFREY. Yes, I know, I see that—
PIXIE. —and then you YELL AT ME!!!
JEFFREY. I—yes, I appreciate that this isn't what you were expecting. You were
590    expecting a formal discussion of your essay and your grade, but Pixie, we
    were, in fact, talking about your essay—
PIXIE. No we weren't. You were arguing with Professor Galbraith.

(*Beat.*)

JEFFREY. (*quiet*) But ... (*laughs*) ... Pixie, yes, but—
PIXIE. You were arguing.
595  JEFFREY. Yes, but, what you don't understand is, I was trying to—I was advo-
    cating for you, because, you see—
PIXIE. You were in the middle of an argument! You and the Professor were
    arguing!
JEFFREY. But—yes—I—yes, but you see, the argument was ... about you.
600  PIXIE. No it wasn't!
JEFFREY. But you don't ...! (*laughs*) It—it—yes, it was about ... you—
PIXIE. No.

(*Beat.*)

JEFFREY.  But it—yes—
PIXIE.  It wasn't about me!

(*Beat.*)

JEFFREY.  But—but, okay, Pixie—                                                605
PIXIE.  This wasn't about me.
JEFFREY.  But I was—I was advocating for you. I was trying to advocate for
     you. You—what do you want? I was trying to—what do you women fuck-
     ing want!
GALBRAITH.  Jeffrey!                                                           610
JEFFREY.  I was putting my—I was—fuck—I was advocating for women!
PIXIE.  You were arguing with Professor Galbraith! You were arguing with
     him about women in history. I was just ... in the room!

(*Beat.*)

Which is so funny, because in the textbook—the reason—the reason why
I wrote the essay is because in the textbook, at the bottom of one of the   615
pages, there's a footnote. Elizabeth Farnese, second wife of Philip the Fifth
of Spain, secured her sons the thrones of Parma and Tuscany. She got her
sons thrones. How? It doesn't say. There's just the footnote. So I wrote the
essay. And I was sitting here, looking at you, and I could tell you wanted
me to say certain things for the sake of your argument, and I was thinking,   620
my history TA is yelling at me for no reason and I am pissed off because I
am kind of like a footnote here!

(*Beat.*)

"Professor Galbraith and Jeffrey had an argument about whether or not
women should be included in history. And by the way, they were arguing because of Pixie Findley." "Pixie Findley? Who's she?" "Let's check the   625
footnote." And somehow, even though you think it's about me, it's not.
It's about you. And your argument. I'm just the excuse for you to argue
with each other. So I don't care which one of you wins because it's not
about me.

(*Beat.*)

So ... yeah.                                                                  630

(*Long beat.*)

JEFFREY.  I see what you're ... saying, but, Pixie, I didn't mean to.... It's—
     yes—you're talking about—yes, I see what you're pointing out, and I didn't
     mean to—to—I—you're right. I shouldn't have—I didn't, uh—I never,

uh, asked you if you wanted me to—but my intention—my intention
wasn't to appropriate, to—uh … yeah.

(*Beat.*)

I'm—Pixie, I'm sorry.

(*Beat.*)

I'm … sorry.
PIXIE. That's okay.
JEFFREY. I'm sorry. You're right, I—yes. I was—yes.
PIXIE. That's okay.
GALBRAITH. Have we, perhaps, resolved this? Pixie?

(*Pixie shrugs, nods.*)

PIXIE. Yeah.
GALBRAITH. Good, good. Good. Then perhaps we can leave this for now?
PIXIE. Yeah.

(*Pixie picks up her bag and Professor Galbraith ushers her to the doorway over the course of his speech.*)

GALBRAITH. We have a lot to offer here in the history department, Pixie. Perhaps not as much as the business school—that's the large architectural tribute to Fort Knox and the Playboy Mansion up that way—but we have a lot to offer. And Pixie? Please come to me if you feel uncomfortable, or if you would like to discuss this further.
PIXIE. Okay. Thanks.

(*Pixie exits. The men look after her for a moment. Beat.*)

GALBRAITH. Off she goes.

(*Long beat.*)

If you were tenured, Jeffrey, I would say, by all means, go ahead and yell gendered slurs at the female undergraduates. But, at this juncture in your career … (*laughs*).

(*Beat.*)

I appreciate that you wanted to argue your point to me. But we're the— you're a Ph.D. candidate, I'm a professor; distinguished, books published, summa cum laude, et cetera, et cetera. What could Pixie Findley possibly have contributed to our discussion? Hm?

(*Beat.*)

Connect up the dots for me.

JEFFREY. It started off with me trying to defend her—                    660

GALBRAITH. (*sharp*) From?

JEFFREY. Yes, I—I—yes, I'm the one who insulted her, who verbally ... insulted her, in a gendered—in a language that was—I don't know where I—how I—what made me—

GALBRAITH. Oh, for Christ's sake, the girl's name is Pixie! Her name is Pixie!  665
She's asking to be patronized.

(*Beat.*)

If you were to crack her skull open, butterflies would flutter out. Or, what did you say? Lobotomy in a skirt?

(*Galbraith laughs, regards Jeffrey, laughs again. Jeffrey stares at Galbraith.*)

Lucky for you. Let's just pray she doesn't pick up Simone de Beauvoir over the weekend, hm?                                                      670

(*Beat.*)

Let's just pray she sticks to *Cosmopolitan*, or what is it my wife reads? *Vanity Fair.*

(*Beat.*)

And Jeffrey? Give her a B minus.

(*Galbraith hands Jeffrey the essay and exits. Jeffrey holds it for a moment, then he opens it and begins to read. Lights out.*)

—2005

# Glossary

**Absurdist:** characterized by a minimalist style and bleak worldview. The term is most frequently used with reference to certain plays of the post-World-War-II period (notable examples include Samuel Beckett's *Waiting for Godot* and Tom Stoppard's *Rosencrantz and Guildenstern Are Dead*). Such works seem set in a world stripped of faith in god or a rational cosmos, in which idealism has been lost, and human action and communication are futile. Absurdist characters are often portrayed as trapped in a pointless round of trivial, self-defeating acts of comical repetitiveness. For this reason, absurdism can verge on *farce* or *black comedy*. See also *existentialism*.

**Act** [of a play]: the sections into which a play or other theatrical work have been divided, either by the playwright or a later editor. Dividing plays into five acts became popular during the Renaissance in imitation of Roman tragedy; modern works are sometimes divided into three.

**Aesthetes:** members of a late nineteenth-century movement that valued "art for art's sake"—for its purely aesthetic qualities, as opposed to valuing art for the moral content it may convey, for the intellectual stimulation it may provide, or for a range of other qualities.

**Allegory:** a narrative with both a literal meaning and secondary, often symbolic meaning or meanings. Allegory frequently employs personification to give concrete embodiment to abstract concepts or entities, such as feelings or personal qualities. It may also present one set of characters or events in the guise of another, using implied parallels for the purposes of satire or political comment.

**Alliteration:** the grouping of words with the same initial consonant (e.g., "break, blow, burn, and make me new"). See also *assonance* and *consonance*.

**Allusion:** a reference, often indirect or unidentified, to a person, thing, or event. A reference in one literary work to another literary work, whether to its content or its form, also constitutes an allusion.

**Ambiguity:** an "opening" of language created by the writer to allow for multiple meanings or differing interpretations. In literature, ambiguity may be deliberately employed by the writer to enrich meaning; this differs from any unintentional, unwanted ambiguity in non-literary prose.

**Anachronism:** accidentally or intentionally attributing people, things, ideas, and events to historical periods in which they do not and could not possibly belong.

**Analepsis:** see *flashback*.

**Analogy:** a broad term that refers to our processes of noting similarities among things or events. Specific forms of analogy include *simile* and *metaphor*.

**Apostrophe:** a figure of speech (a *trope*; see *figures of speech*) in which a writer directly addresses an object—or a dead or absent person—as if the imagined audience were actually listening.

**Apron:** the part of a stage that extends into the auditorium or audience beyond the *proscenium* arch; sometimes called a *forestage* or a *thrust stage*.

**Archetype:** in literature and mythology, a recurring idea, symbol, motif, character, or place. To some scholars and psychologists, an archetype represents universal human thought-patterns or experiences.

**Arena Theatre:** see *theatre-in-the-round*.

**Asides:** words delivered by actors to the audience, or by characters to themselves, which by *convention* are treated as if they were inaudible to the other characters on stage.

**Assonance:** the repetition of identical or similar vowel sounds in stressed syllables in which the surrounding consonants are different: for example, "shame" and "fate"; "gale" and "cage"; or the long "i" sounds in "Beside the pumice isle...."

**Atmosphere:** see *tone*.

**Baroque:** powerful and heavily ornamented in style. "Baroque" is a term from the history of visual art and of music that is sometimes also used to describe certain literary styles.

**Bathos:** an anticlimactic effect brought about by a writer's descent from an elevated subject or tone to the ordinary or trivial.

**Black Comedy:** humour based on death, horror, or any incongruously macabre subject matter.

**Blank Verse:** unrhymed lines written in iambic pentameter. (A form introduced to English verse by Henry Howard, Earl of Surrey, in his translation of parts of Virgil's *Aeneid* in 1547.)

**Bombast:** inappropriately inflated or grandiose language.

**Burlesque:** satire of a particularly exaggerated sort, particularly that which ridicules its subject by emphasizing its vulgar or ridiculous aspects.

**Canon:** in literature, those works that are commonly accepted as possessing authority or importance. In practice, "canonical" texts or authors are those that are discussed most frequently by scholars and taught most frequently in university courses.

**Caricature:** an exaggerated and simplified depiction of character; the reduction of a personality to one or two telling traits at the expense of all other nuances and contradictions.

**Catharsis:** the arousal through the performance of a dramatic tragedy of "emotions of pity and fear" to a point where "purgation" or "purification" occurs and the feelings are released or transformed. The concept was developed by Aristotle in his *Poetics* from an ancient Greek medical concept, and adapted by him into an aesthetic principle.

**Characterization:** the means by which an author develops and presents a character's personality qualities and distinguishing traits. A character may be established in the story by descriptive commentary or may be developed less directly—for example, through his or her words, actions, thoughts, and interactions with other characters.

**Chiasmus:** a figure of speech (a scheme) that reverses word order in successive parallel clauses. If the word order is A-B-C in the first clause, it becomes C-B-A in the second: for example, Donne's line "She is all states, and all princes, I" ("The Sun Rising") incorporates this reversal.

**Chorus:** originally, the choir of singing, dancing, masked young men who performed in ancient Greek tragedy and comedy. It gradually disappeared from tragedy and comedy, but many attempts have been made to revive some version of it, notably during the Italian and English Renaissance, under Weimar Classicism, and by such twentieth-century playwrights as Jean Anouilh, T.S. Eliot, and Michel Tremblay.

**Chronology:** the way a story is organized in terms of time. Linear narratives run continuously from one point in time to a later point, while non-linear narratives are non-continuous and may jump forward and backward in time. A *flashback*, in which a story jumps to a scene previous in time, is an example of non-linearity.

**Classical:** originating in or relating to ancient Greek or Roman culture. As commonly conceived, *classical* implies a strong sense of formal order. The term *neoclassical* is often used with reference to literature of the Restoration and eighteenth century that was strongly influenced by ancient Greek and Roman models.

**Closet Drama:** a play (typically in verse) written to be read rather than performed. The term came into use in the first half of the nineteenth century.

**Comedy:** as a literary term, used originally to denote that class of ancient Greek drama in which the action ends happily. More broadly the term has been used to describe a wide variety of literary forms of a more or less light-hearted character.

**Comedy of Manners:** a type of comic play that flourished in the late seventeenth century in London, and elsewhere since, which bases its humour on the sexual and marital intrigues of "high society." It is sometimes contrasted with "comedy of character" as its *satire* is directed at the social habits and conventional hypocrisy of the whole leisured class. Also called Restoration comedy; exemplified by the plays of Aphra Behn, William Wycherley, and William Congreve.

**Commedia dell'arte:** largely improvised comic performances conducted by masked performers and involving considerable physical activity. The genre of *commedia dell'arte* originated in Italy in the sixteenth century; it was influential throughout Europe for more than two centuries thereafter.

**Conflict:** struggles between characters and opposing forces. Conflict can be internal (psychological) or external (conflict with another character, for instance, or with society or nature).

**Connotation:** the implied, often unspoken meaning(s) of a given word, as distinct from its *denotation*, or literal meaning. Connotations may have highly emotional undertones and are usually culturally specific.

**Convention:** aesthetic approach, technique, or practice accepted as characteristic and appropriate for a particular form. It is a convention of certain sorts of plays, for example, that the characters speak in blank verse, of other sorts of plays that characters speak in rhymed couplets, and of still other sorts of dramatic performances that characters frequently break into song to express their feelings.

**Denotation:** see *connotation*.

**Dénouement:** that portion of a narrative that follows a dramatic climax, in which conflicts are resolved and the narrative is brought to a close. Traditional accounts of narrative structure often posit a triangle or arc, with rising action followed by a climax and then by a dénouement. (Such accounts bear little relation, however, to the ways in which most actual narratives are structured—particularly most twentieth- and twenty-first-century literary fictions.)

**Dialogue:** words spoken by characters to one another. (When a character is addressing him or her self or the audience directly, the words spoken are referred to as a *soliloquy*.)

**Diction:** word choice. Whether the diction of a literary work (or of a literary character) is colloquial, conversational, formal, or of some other type contributes significantly to the tone of the text as well as to characterization.

**Didacticism:** aesthetic approach emphasizing moral instruction.

**Dramatic Irony:** this form of *irony* occurs when an audience has access to information not available to the character.

**Elision:** omitting or suppressing a letter or an unstressed syllable at the beginning or end of a word, so that a line of verse may conform to a given metrical scheme. For example, the three syllables at the beginning of

Shakespeare's sonnet 129 are reduced to two by the omission of the first vowel: "Th' expense of spirit in a waste of shame."

**Ellipsis:** the omission of a word or words necessary for the complete grammatical construction of a sentence, but not necessary for our understanding of the sentence.

**Enjambment:** the "running-on" of the sense from one line of verse to the next, with no pause created by punctuation or syntax.

**Epic Simile:** an elaborate simile, developed at such length that the vehicle of the comparison momentarily displaces the primary subject with which it is being compared.

**Epigraph:** a quotation placed at the beginning of a work to indicate or foreshadow the theme.

**Epiphany:** a moment at which matters of significance are suddenly illuminated for a literary character (or for the reader), typically triggered by something small and seemingly of little import. The term first came into wide currency in connection with the fiction of James Joyce.

**Episodic Plot:** plot comprising a variety of episodes that are only loosely connected by threads of story material (as opposed to plots that present one or more continually unfolding narratives, in which successive episodes build one on another).

**Ethos:** the perceived character, trustworthiness, or credibility of a writer or narrator.

**Euphemism:** mode of expression through which aspects of reality considered to be vulgar, crudely physical, or unpleasant are referred to indirectly rather than named explicitly. A variety of euphemisms exist for the processes of urination and defecation; *passed away* is often used as a euphemism for *died*.

**Existentialism:** a philosophical approach according to which the meaning of human life is derived from the actual experience of the living individual. The existential worldview, in which life is assumed to have no essential or pre-existing meanings other than those we personally choose to endow it with, can produce an *absurdist* sensibility.

**Exposition:** the setting out of material in an ordered (and usually concise) form, either in speech or in writing. In a play those parts of the action that do not occur on stage but are rather recounted by the characters are frequently described as being presented in exposition. Similarly, when the background narrative is filled in near the beginning of a novel, such material is often described as having been presented in exposition.

**Farce:** sometimes classed as the "lowest" form of *comedy*. Its humour depends not on verbal wit, but on physicality and sight gags.

**Fiction:** imagined or invented narrative. In literature, the term is usually used to refer to prose narratives (such as novels and short stories).

**Figures of Speech:** deliberate, highly concentrated uses of language to achieve particular purposes or effects on an audience. There are two kinds of figures: schemes and *tropes*. Schemes involve changes in word-sound and word-order, such as *alliteration* and *chiasmus*. Tropes play on our understandings of words to extend, alter, or transform meaning, as in *metaphor* and *personification*.

**Flashback:** the inclusion in the primary thread of a story's narrative of a scene (or scenes) from an earlier point in time. Flashbacks may be used to revisit from a different viewpoint events that have already been recounted in the main thread of narrative; to present material that has been left out in the initial recounting; or to present relevant material from a time before the beginning of the main thread of narrative. The use of flashbacks is sometimes referred to as *analepsis*.

**Flashforward:** the inclusion in the primary thread of a story's narrative of a scene (or scenes) from a later point in time. See also *prolepsis*.

**Flat Character:** the opposite of a *round character*, a flat character is defined by a small number of traits and does not possess enough complexity to be psychologically realistic. "Flat character" can be a disparaging term, but need not be; flat characters serve different purposes in a fiction than round characters, and are often better suited to some types of literature, such as allegory or farcical comedy.

**Foil:** in literature, a character whose behaviour and/or qualities set in relief for the reader or audience those of a strongly contrasting character who plays a more central part in the story.

**Foreshadowing:** the inclusion of elements in a story that hint at some later development(s) in the same story. For example, in Flannery O'Connor's "A Good Man Is Hard to Find," the old family burying ground that the family sees on their drive foreshadows the violence that follows.

**Found Space:** a site that is not normally a theatre but is used for the staging of a theatrical production. Often, the choice of found space can reflect the play's setting or thematic content.

**Freytag's Pyramid:** a model of plot structure developed by the German novelist, playwright, and critic Gustav Freytag and introduced in his book *Die Technik des Dramas* (1863). In the pyramid, five stages of plot are identified as occurring in the following order: exposition, rising action, climax, falling action, and *dénouement*. Freytag intended his pyramid to diagram the structure of classical five-act plays, but it is also used as a tool to analyze other forms of fiction (even though many individual plays and stories do not follow the structure outlined in the pyramid).

**Genre:** a class or type of literary work. The concept of genre may be used with different levels of generality. At the most general, poetry, drama, and prose fiction are distinguished as separate genres. At a lower level of generality various sub-genres are frequently distinguished, such as (within the genre of prose fiction) the novel, the novella, and the short story; and, at a still lower level of generality, the mystery novel, the detective novel, the novel of manners, and so on.

**Gothic:** in architecture and the visual arts, a term used to describe styles prevalent from the twelfth to the fourteenth centuries, but in literature a term used to describe work with a sinister or grotesque tone that seeks to evoke a sense of terror on the part of the reader or audience. Gothic literature originated as a genre in the eighteenth century with works such as Horace Walpole's *The Castle of Otranto*. To some extent the notion of the medieval itself then carried with it associations of the dark and the grotesque, but from the beginning an element of intentional exaggeration (sometimes verging on self-parody) attached itself to the genre. The Gothic trend of youth culture that began in the late twentieth century is less clearly associated with the medieval, but shares with the various varieties of Gothic literature (from Walpole in the eighteenth century, to Bram Stoker in the early twentieth, to Stephen King and Anne Rice in the late twentieth) a fondness for the sensational and the grotesque, as well as a propensity to self-parody.

**Grotesque:** literature of the grotesque is characterized by a focus on extreme or distorted aspects of human characteristics. (The term can also refer particularly to a character who is odd or disturbing.) This focus can serve to comment on and challenge societal norms. The story "A Good Man Is Hard to Find" employs elements of the grotesque.

**Hyperbole:** a *figure of speech* (a *trope*) that deliberately exaggerates or inflates meaning to achieve particular effects, such as the irony in A.E. Housman's claim (from "Terence, This Is Stupid Stuff") that "malt does more than Milton can / To justify God's ways to man."

**Iamb:** the most common metrical foot in English verse, containing one unstressed syllable followed by a stressed syllable: x / (e.g., between, achieve).

**Image:** a representation of a sensory experience or of an object that can be known by the senses.

**Imagery:** the range of images in a given work. We can gain much insight into works by looking for patterns of imagery. For example, the imagery of spring (budding trees, rain, singing birds) in Kate Chopin's "The Story of an Hour" reinforces the suggestions of death and rebirth in the plot and theme.

**Improvisation:** the seemingly spontaneous invention of dramatic dialogue and/or a dramatic plot by actors without the assistance of a written text.

**Interlude:** a short and often comical play or other entertainment performed between the *acts* of a longer or more serious work, particularly during the later Middle Ages and early Renaissance.

**Intertextuality:** the relationships between one literary work and other literary works. A literary work may connect with other works through *allusion, parody*, or *satire, or in a variety of other ways.*

**Irony:** the use of irony draws attention to a gap between what is said and what is meant, or what appears to be true and what is true. Types of irony include verbal irony (which includes *hyberbole, litotes*, and *sarcasm*), *dramatic irony*, and structural irony (in which the gap between what is "said" and meant is sustained throughout an entire piece, as when an author makes use of an unreliable narrator or speaker—see Robert Browning's "My Last Duchess").

**Litotes:** a *figure of speech* (a *trope*) in which a writer deliberately uses understatement to highlight the importance of an argument, or to convey an ironic attitude.

**Liturgical Drama:** drama based on and/or incorporating text from the liturgy—the text recited during religious services.

**Melodrama:** originally a term used to describe nineteenth-century plays featuring sensational story lines and a crude separation of characters into moral categories, with the pure and virtuous pitted against evil villains. Early melodramas employed background music throughout the action of the play as a means of heightening the emotional response of the audience. By extension, certain sorts of prose fictions or poems are often described as having melodramatic elements.

**Metafiction:** fiction that calls attention to itself as fiction. Metafiction is a means by which authors render us conscious of our status as readers, often in order to explore the relationships between fiction and reality.

**Metaphor:** a *figure of speech* (in this case, a *trope*) in which a comparison is made or identity is asserted between two unrelated things or actions without the use of "like" or "as."

**Metonymy:** a *figure of speech* (a *trope*), meaning "change of name," in which a writer refers to an object or idea by substituting the name of another object or idea closely associated with it: for example, the substitution of "crown" for monarchy, "the press" for journalism, or "the pen" for writing. *Synecdoche* is a kind of metonymy.

**Metre:** the pattern of stresses, syllables, and pauses that constitutes the regular rhythm of a line of verse. The metre of a poem written in the English accentual-syllabic tradition is determined by identifying the stressed and unstressed syllables in a line of verse, and grouping them into recurring units known as feet.

**Mise en scène:** French expression, literally meaning "the putting on stage," which has been adopted in other languages to describe the sum total of creative choices made in the staging of a play.

**Modernism:** in the history of literature, music, and the visual arts, a movement that began in the early twentieth century, characterized by a thoroughgoing rejection of the then-dominant conventions of literary plotting and characterization, of melody and harmony, and of perspective and other naturalistic forms of visual representation. In literature (as in music and the visual arts), modernists endeavoured to represent the complexity of what seemed to them to be an increasingly fragmented world by adopting techniques of presenting story material, illuminating character, and employing imagery that emphasized (in the words of Virginia Woolf) "the spasmodic, the obscure, the fragmentary."

**Monologue:** an extended speech by a single speaker or character in a poem or play. Unlike a *soliloquy*, a dramatic monologue has an implied listener.

**Mood:** this can describe the writer's attitude, implied or expressed, toward the subject (see *tone*); or it may refer to the atmosphere that a writer creates in a passage of description or narration.

**Motif:** pattern formed by the recurrence of an idea, image, action, or plot element throughout a literary work, creating new levels of meaning and strengthening structural coherence. The term is taken from music, where it describes recurring melodies or themes. See also *theme*.

**Motivation:** the forces that seem to cause characters to act, or reasons why characters do what they do.

**Narration:** the process of disclosing information, whether fictional or nonfictional.

**Narrative Perspective:** the point of view from which a story is narrated. A first-person narrative is recounted using *I* and *me*, whereas a third-person narrative is recounted using *he*, *she*, *they*, and so on. When a narrative is written in the third person and the narrative voice evidently "knows" all that is being done and thought, the story is typically described as being recounted by an "omniscient narrator." Second-person narratives, in which the narrative is recounted using *you*, are very rare.

**Narrator:** the voice (or voices) disclosing information. The narrator is distinguished from both the author (a real, historical person) and the implied author (whom the reader imagines the author to be). Narrators can also be distinguished according to the degree to which they share the reality of the other characters in the story and the extent to which they participate in the action; according to how much information they are privy to (and how much of that information they are willing to share with the reader); and according to whether or not they are perceived by the reader as reliable or unreliable sources of information. See also *narrative perspective*.

**Neoclassical Dramaturgy:** the principles, rules, and *conventions* of writing plays according to the precepts and ideals of *neoclassicism*. Often based on the so-called *unities* of time, place, and action.

**Neoclassicism:** literally the "new classicism," the aesthetic style that dominated high culture in Europe through the seventeenth and eighteenth centuries, and in some places into the nineteenth century. Its subject matter was often taken from Greek and Roman myth and history; in *style*, it valued order, reason, clarity, and moderation.

**Omniscient Narrator:** see *narrative perspective*.

**Orchestra:** literally, "the dancing place." In the ancient world it was the lower, flat, circular surface-area of the outdoor theatre where the *chorus* danced and sang.

**Oxymoron:** a *figure of speech* (a *trope*) in which two words whose meanings seem contradictory are placed together; we see an example in Shakespeare's *Twelfth Night*, when Orsino refers to the "sweet pangs" of love.

**Parody:** a close, usually mocking imitation of a particular literary work, or of the well-known style of a particular author, in order to expose or magnify weaknesses. Parody is a form of *satire*—that is, humour that may ridicule and scorn its object.

**Pastiche:** a discourse that borrows or imitates other writers' characters, forms, style, or ideas, sometimes creating something of a literary patchwork. Unlike a parody, a pastiche can be intended as a compliment to the original writer.

**Pathetic Fallacy:** a form of *personification* in which inanimate objects are given human emotions: for example, rain clouds "weeping." The word "fallacy" in this connection is intended to suggest the distortion of reality or the false emotion that may result from an exaggerated use of personification.

**Pathos:** the emotional quality of a discourse; or the ability of a discourse to appeal to our emotions. It is usually applied to the mood conveyed by images of pain, suffering, or loss that arouse feelings of pity or sorrow in the reader.

**Pentameter:** verse containing five metrical feet in a line.

**Persona:** the assumed identity or "speaking voice" that a writer projects in a discourse. The term "persona" literally means "mask."

**Personification:** a *figure of speech* (a *trope*), also known as "prosopopoeia," in which a writer refers to inanimate objects, ideas, or non-human animals as if they were human, or creates a human figure to represent an abstract entity such as Philosophy or Peace.

**Plot:** the organization of story materials within a literary work. Matters of plotting include the order in which story material is presented; the inclusion of elements that allow or encourage the reader or audience to form expectations as to what is likely to happen; and the decision to present some story material through exposition rather than present it directly to the reader as part of the narrative.

**Point of View:** see *narrative perspective.*

**Postmodernism:** in literature and the visual arts, a movement influential in the late twentieth and early twenty-first centuries. In some ways postmodernism represents a reaction to modernism, in others an extension of it. With roots in the work of French philosophers such as Jacques Derrida and Michel Foucault, it is deeply coloured by theory; indeed, it may be said to have begun·at the "meta" level of theorizing rather than at the level of practice. Like modernism, postmodernism embraces difficulty and distrusts the simple and straightforward. More broadly, postmodernism is characterized by a rejection of absolute truth or value, of closed systems, of grand unified narratives.

Postmodernist fiction is characterized by a frequently ironic or playful tone in dealing with reality and illusion; by a willingness to combine different styles or forms in a single work (just as in architecture the postmodernist spirit embodies a willingness to borrow from seemingly disparate styles in designing a single structure); and by a highly attuned awareness of the problematized state of the writer, artist, or theorist as observer.

**Prolepsis:** originally a rhetorical term used to refer to the anticipation of possible objections by someone advancing an argument, prolepsis is used to refer to elements in a narrative that anticipate the future of the story. The *flashforward* technique of storytelling is often described as a form of prolepsis; the inclusion in a narrative of material that foreshadows future developments is also sometimes treated as a form of prolepsis.

**Proscenium:** a Latin architectural term derived from the Greek *proskenion,* the frontmost section of the theatre building as it developed in the post-Classical, Hellenistic period. Stages on which a pictorial illusion is created with the help of a border or frame are called "proscenium arch" or "picture-frame" theatres; they reached their heyday during the nineteenth century, the age of *realism.*

**Protagonist:** the central character in a literary work.

**Pun:** a play on words, in which a word with two or more distinct meanings, or two words with similar sounds, may create humorous ambiguities. Also known as "paranomasia."

**Realism:** as a literary term, the presentation through literature of material closely resembling real life. As notions both of what constitutes "real life" and of how it may be most faithfully represented in literature have varied widely, "realism" has taken a variety of meanings. The term "naturalistic" has sometimes been used as a synonym for *realistic*; naturalism originated in the nineteenth century as a term denoting a form of realism focusing in particular on grim, unpleasant, or ugly aspects of the real.

**Rhyme:** the repetition of identical or similar sounds, usually in pairs and generally at the ends of metrical lines.

**End-Rhyme:** a rhyming word or syllable at the end of a line.

**Eye Rhyme:** rhyming that pairs words whose spellings are alike but whose pronunciations are different: for example, though/slough.

**Feminine Rhyme:** a two-syllable (also known as "double") rhyme. The first syllable is stressed and the second unstressed: for example, hasty/tasty. See also *triple rhyme*.

**Interlocking Rhyme:** the repetition of rhymes from one stanza to the next, creating links that add to the poem's continuity and coherence. Examples may be found in Shelley's use of *terza rima* in "Ode to the West Wind" and in Dylan Thomas's *villanelle* "Do Not Go Gentle into That Good Night."

**Internal Rhyme:** the placement of rhyming words within lines so that at least two words in a line rhyme with each other.

**Masculine Rhyme:** a correspondence of sound between the final stressed syllables at the end of two or more lines, as in grieve/leave, ar-rive/sur-vive.

**Slant Rhyme:** an imperfect or partial rhyme (also known as "near" or "half" rhyme) in which the consonant sounds of stressed syllables match but the vowel sounds do not. E.g., spoiled/spilled, taint/stint.

**Triple Rhyme:** a three-syllable rhyme in which the first syllable of each rhyme-word is stressed and the other two unstressed (e.g., lottery/coterie).

**True Rhyme:** a rhyme in which everything but the initial consonant matches perfectly in sound and spelling.

**Rhythm:** in speech, the arrangement of stressed and unstressed syllables creates units of sound. In song or verse, these units may be shaped into a regular rhythmic pattern, described in prosody as *metre*.

**Romanticism:** a major social and cultural movement, originating in Europe, that shaped much of Western artistic thought in the late eighteenth and nineteenth centuries. Opposing the ideal of controlled, rational order associated with the Enlightenment, Romanticism emphasizes the importance of spontaneous self-expression, emotion, and personal experience in producing art. In Romanticism, the "natural" is privileged over the conventional or the artificial.

**Round Character:** a complex and psychologically realistic character, often one who changes as a work progresses. The opposite of a round character is a *flat character*.

**Sarcasm:** a form of *irony* (usually spoken) in which the meaning is conveyed largely by the tone of voice adopted; something said sarcastically is meant to imply its opposite.

**Satire:** literary work designed to make fun of or seriously criticize its subject. According to many literary theories of the Renaissance and neoclassical periods, the ridicule through satire of a certain sort of behaviour may function for the reader or audience as a corrective of such behaviour.

**Scheme:** see *figures of speech*.

**Setting:** the time, place, and cultural environment in which a story or work takes place.

**Simile:** a *figure of speech* (a *trope*) which makes an explicit comparison between a particular object and another object or idea that is similar in some (often unexpected) way. A simile always uses "like" or "as" to signal the connection. Compare with *metaphor*.

**Soliloquy:** in drama (or, less often, poetry), a speech in which a character, usually alone, reveals his or her thoughts, emotions, and/or motivations without being heard by other characters. The convention was frequently employed during the Elizabethan era, and many of the best-known examples are from Shakespeare; for example, Hamlet's "To be, or not to be" speech is a soliloquy. Soliloquies differ from *dramatic monologues* in that dramatic monologues address an implied listener, while the speaker of a soliloquy thinks aloud or addresses the audience.

**Stock Character:** a character defined by a set of characteristics that are stereotypical and/or established by literary convention; examples include the "wicked stepmother" and the "absent-minded professor."

**Story:** narrative material, independent of the manner in which it may be presented or the ways in which the narrative material may be organized. Story is thus distinct from *plot*.

**Stream of Consciousness**: a narrative technique that conveys the inner workings of a character's mind, in which a character's thoughts, feelings, memories, and impressions are related in an unbroken flow, without concern for *chronology* or coherence.

**Style:** a distinctive or specific use of language and form.

**Subplot:** a line of story that is subordinate to the main storyline of a narrative. (Note that properly speaking a subplot is a category of story material, not of plot.)

**Subtext:** implied or suggested meaning of a passage of text, or of an entire work.

**Surrealism:** Surrealism incorporates elements of the true appearance of life and nature, combining these elements according to a logic more typical of dreams than waking life. Isolated aspects of surrealist art may create powerful illusions of reality, but the effect of the whole is usually to disturb or question our sense of reality rather than to confirm it.

**Suspension of Disbelief:** a willingness on the part of the audience member or reader to temporarily accept the fictional world presented in a narrative.

**Symbol:** something that represents itself but goes beyond this in suggesting other meanings. Like metaphor, the symbol extends meaning; but while the tenor and vehicle of metaphor are bound in a specific relationship, a symbol may have a range of connotations. For example, the image of a rose may call forth associations of love, passion, transience, fragility, youth, and beauty, among others. Depending upon the context, such an image could be interpreted in a variety of ways, as in Blake's lyric, "The Sick Rose."

**Synecdoche:** a kind of *metonymy* in which a writer substitutes the name of a part of something to signify the whole: for example, "sail" for ship or "hand" for a member of the ship's crew.

**Syntax:** the ordering of words in a sentence.

**Theatre-in-the-Round:** a type of staging in which seating for the audience surrounds the stage on all (or at least most) of its sides. This approach was common in ancient Greek, ancient Roman, and medieval theatre; it was not often used after the seventeenth century, but in the mid-twentieth century its popularity increased, especially in experimental theatre. Also called "arena theatre."

**Theme:** in general, an idea explored in a work through character, action, and/or image. To be fully developed, however, a theme must consist of more than a single concept or idea: it should also include an argument about the idea. Thus if a poem examines the topic of jealousy, we might say the theme is that jealousy undermines love or jealousy is a manifestation of insecurity. Few, if any, literary works have single themes.

**Third-Person Narrative:** see *narrative perspective*.

**Tone:** the writer's attitude toward a given subject or audience, as expressed through an authorial persona or "voice." Tone can be projected through particular choices of wording, imagery, figures of speech, and rhythmic devices. Compare *mood*.

**Tragedy:** in the traditional definition originating in discussions of ancient Greek drama, a serious narrative recounting the downfall of the protagonist, usually a person of high social standing. More loosely, the term has been applied to a wide variety of literary forms in which the tone is predominantly a dark one and the narrative does not end happily.

**Tragicomedy:** a genre of drama in which many elements of *tragedy* are present, but which generally has a happy end, or—more generally—which includes both serious and comic components.

**Trope:** any figure of speech that plays on our understandings of words to extend, alter, or transform "literal" meaning. Common tropes include *metaphor, simile, personification, hyperbole, metonymy, oxymoron, synecdoche*, and *irony*. See also *figures of speech*.

**Unities:** Many literary theorists of the late sixteenth through late eighteenth centuries held that a play should ideally be presented as representing a single place, and confining the action to a single day and a single dominant event. They disapproved of plots involving gaps or long periods of time, shifts in place, or subplots. These concepts, which came to be referred to as the unities of space, time, and action, were based on a misreading of classical authorities (principally of Aristotle).

**Zeugma:** a *figure of speech* (*trope*) in which one word links or "yokes" two others in the same sentence, often to comic or ironic effect. For example, a verb may govern two objects, as in Pope's line "Or stain her honour, or her new brocade."

**Acknowledgement:** The glossary for *The Broadview Introduction to Literature* incorporates some material initially prepared for the following Broadview anthologies: *The Broadview Anthology of Poetry*, edited by Herbert Rosengarten and Amanda Goldrick-Jones; *The Broadview Anthology of Drama*, edited by Jennifer Wise and Craig Walker; *The Broadview Anthology of Short Fiction*, edited by Julia Gaunce et al.; *The Broadview Anthology of British Literature*, edited by Joseph Black et al. The editors gratefully acknowledge the contributions of the editors of these other anthologies. Please note that all material in the glossary, whether initially published in another Broadview anthology or appearing here for the first time, is protected by copyright.

# Permission Acknowledgements

Please note that texts in the public domain do not appear in the list below and that all introductory materials and annotations in this volume are copyright © Broadview Press.

Samuel Beckett. "Krapp's Last Tape," from *The Collected Shorter Plays of Samuel Beckett*, copyright © 1958 by the Estate of Samuel Beckett. Used by permission of Grove/Atlantic, Inc.

Hannah Moscovitch. "Essay," copyright © 2008 by Hannah Moscovitch. Reprinted by permission of Playwrights Canada Press.

Sharon Pollock. *Blood Relations* (1980), from *Blood Relations and Other Plays* (revised edition). NeWest Press, 2002. Reprinted with the permission of Sharon Pollock and NeWest Press.

William Shakespeare. *Twelfth Night*, edited by David Swain, from *The Broadview Anthology of British Literature*. Annotations copyright © 2011 Broadview Press.

Tom Stoppard. *Arcadia*, published by Faber & Faber, London. Reprinted with permission.

Tennessee Williams. *Cat on a Hot Tin Roof*, copyright © 1954, 1955, 1971, 1975 by The University of the South. Reprinted by permission of New Directions Publishing Corp.

The publisher has endeavoured to contact rights holders for all copyrighted material, and would appreciate receiving any information as to errors or omissions.

# Index of Authors and Titles

Arcadia   387
**Beckett, Samuel**   243
Blood Relations   338
Cat on a Hot Tin Roof   252
Doll's House, A   183
Essay   479
**Ibsen, Henrik**   182
Krapp's Last Tape   243

**Moscovitch, Hannah**   478
**Pollock, Sharon**   337
School for Scandal, The   106
**Shakespeare, William**   11
**Sheridan, Richard Brinsley**   105
**Stoppard, Tom**   386
Twelfth Night, or What You Will   12
**Williams, Tennessee**   252